INTRODUCTION TO
Electroacoustics
&
Audio Amplifier Design

Fourth Edition

W. Marshall Leach, Jr.
Georgia Institute of Technology

Kendall Hunt
publishing company

Cover image © Shutterstock, Inc.

www.kendallhunt.com
Send all inquiries to:
4050 Westmark Drive
Dubuque, IA 52004-1840

Printed in the United States of America
10 9 8 7 6 5 4 3 2 1

Contents

Preface

This book is an outgrowth of a senior level elective course in audio engineering that I have taught to electrical engineering students at the Georgia Institute of Technology. The first part of the book covers basic acoustics. The emphasis is on that part of acoustics that pertains to the field of audio engineering. Most of the remainder of the book concerns the application of the tools of electroacoustics to the analysis and synthesis of microphones, loudspeakers, crossover networks, and acoustic horns. The book also concludes with a chapter that covers the basic theory of audio amplifier design.

Electroacoustics is that part of acoustics that pertains to the modeling of acoustical systems with electrical circuits. Because most acoustical devices have a mechanical part, the modeling of mechanical systems with electrical circuits is a basic part of electroacoustics. Separate chapters in the book are devoted to analogous circuits of mechanical systems and to analogous circuits of acoustical systems. The traditional approach in these circuits has been to use transformers to model the coupling between the electrical, the mechanical, and the acoustical parts. A major departure in this book is the use of controlled sources to model the coupling. An advantage of this approach is that it avoids the need for mobility analogs. In addition, I have found that students have much less difficulty with the approach. Perhaps this is because the controlled-source circuits are more intuitive than the transformer circuits. The circuits can be easily analyzed with circuit simulation software such as SPICE.

The SPICE examples in the text are based on the use of LTSpice. This is a full version of SPICE that is distributed by Linear Technologies. It can be downloaded free of charge from the Linear Technologies web page.

Electroacoustic models are developed for the more common microphone types and for the moving-coil loudspeaker driver. Separate chapters cover closed-box and vented-box loudspeaker systems. Although the emphasis is on basic system theory, practical methods of design are also presented. Because crossover networks are such an important part of loudspeaker systems, a chapter is devoted to crossover networks. Acoustic horns are a vital component in public address systems. A chapter is devoted to horn models. A chapter entitled "A Loudspeaker Potpourri" covers topics such as the isobaric loudspeaker connection, band-pass systems, passive-radiator systems, equalized systems, and loudspeaker parameter measurements. In all cases, SPICE simulation examples are presented where appropriate. The version of SPICE used for the examples is LTSpice. It is distributed by Linear Technology and is available free of charge from the Linear Technology web site.

One might ask why a chapter on audio amplifiers is included in a book that is primarily concerned with electroacoustics. Without a power amplifier, a loudspeaker could not make sound. Therefore, one might say that the role of an amplifier in a system is just as important as the role of a loudspeaker. The chapter on amplifiers is not intended to be an in-depth chapter on electronic theory. Instead, it addresses the more important aspects of amplifier design with an emphasis on the basic operation of the circuits. Practical examples are presented that illustrate how some of the pitfalls of amplifier design can be avoided.

In the text, two parallel lines between quantities denote the product divided by the sum, i.e.

$$R_1 \| R_2 = \frac{R_1 R_2}{R_1 + R_2}$$

represents the parallel combination of resistors R_1 and R_2.

W. Marshall Leach, Jr.
October 2009

Chapter 1

Basic Principles of Sound

1.1   Sound

Unlike electromagnetic waves which propagate through free space, sound waves require a medium. The medium can be a gas, a liquid, or a solid. The definition of sound is *an acoustical or a mechanical wave motion in an elastic medium.* The most familiar medium is air because it is the medium through which we communicate with speech. A solid can be a better medium for the propagation of sound than air. For example, many have seen old western movies where "train robbers" put their ears to the tracks to listen for a distant train.

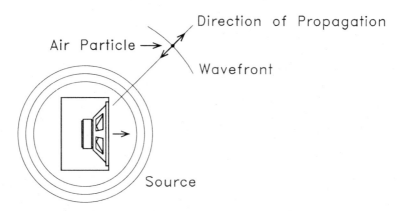

Figure 1.1: Motion of an air particle in an acoustic wave.

When a sound wave propagates in air, the air molecules or particles vibrate in a direction parallel to the direction of wave propagation. This is illustrated in Fig. 1.1. If steady-state sinusoidal time variations are assumed, the position or displacement of an air particle with respect to its rest position can be written

$$x(t) = \operatorname{Re}\left[x_0 e^{j\omega t}\right] = |x_0| \cos(\omega t + \varphi) \tag{1.1}$$

where Re is the real part operator, x_0 is a complex phasor, φ is the phase angle of x_0, and $\omega = 2\pi f$ is the angular frequency. The average displacement of the air particle is zero.

1.2 Sources of Sound

Sources of sound can be divided into six categories. These are (1) vibrating body, (2) throttled air stream, (3) thermal, (4) explosion, (5) arc, and (6) aeolian or vortex. The vibrating body is the most familiar. A loudspeaker is a good example. More common is speech which is produced by a vibrating vocal cord. A whistle produces sound by means of a throttled air stream. A fine wire connected to an alternating current generates sound by the thermal effects. As the current increases, the wire heats the adjacent air causing it to expand. When the instantaneous current goes through zero, the air cools and contracts. A sound wave is generated which has a frequency that is twice that of the current in the wire. The sound of a firecracker is an example of an explosion. Thunder is an example of sound produced by an arc. When wind blows over a fine wire stretched between two supports, an aeolian or vortex sound is generated. The aeolian harp is a very old stringed musical instrument that generates sound by this mechanism. Encased in a furniture box, the harp is set in an open window to generate an ethereal musical sound when wind blows through it.

1.3 Velocity of Sound

The velocity of sound is the velocity with which the wave propagates, not the velocity of the air particles. In free air, an acoustic wave is modeled thermodynamically as an adiabatic process for which the velocity of propagation is given by

$$c = \sqrt{\frac{\gamma P_0}{\rho_0}} \qquad (1.2)$$

where γ is the ratio of the specific heat of air at constant pressure to the specific heat at constant volume, P_0 is the static air pressure, and ρ_0 is the density of air. For air at standard pressure and temperature, these have the accepted values $\gamma = 1.4$, $P_0 = 1.013 \times 10^5 \, \mathrm{Pa} \, (\mathrm{N/m^2})$, and $\rho_0 = 1.18 \, \mathrm{kg/m^3}$. At a temperature of $22°$ C, the velocity of sound in many references on loudspeakers is often taken to be $c = 345 \, \mathrm{m/s}$ or $1131 \, \mathrm{ft/s}$.

1.4 Frequency of Sound

The frequency of a sound wave can be defined only if the wave is periodic in time. Musical notes produced by acoustical instruments do not normally have a frequency because they are not periodic. A sound wave that varies sinusoidally with time is called a pure tone, and it has a definable frequency. The air particles exhibit the motion described by Eq. (1.1). The frequency of the wave in Hz (cycles/s) is the reciprocal of the period, i.e. $f = 1/T$. The radian frequency is given by $\omega = 2\pi f \, \mathrm{rad/s}$.

The audible frequency band is often taken to be from 20 Hz to 20 kHz. However, the range from 30 Hz to 15 kHz is probably more realistic. Most people cannot hear frequencies as high as 20 kHz. Anyone who has ever taken a good tweeter loudspeaker and connected it to a function generator can easily test his or her high-frequency hearing. Even if frequencies above 15 kHz can be heard, anyone who tries this would agree that such high-frequency sounds have little relation to what is heard in music or speech. In analog FM broadcasting, the bandwidth of the signal is intentionally limited to 15 kHz with sharp cutoff low-pass filters. These filters are necessary to prevent aliasing distortion from being produced by the stereo generation process. On the low end, sounds with a frequency below 30 Hz are felt more than heard. Aside from the lowest swell notes of the largest pipe organs, acoustical instruments do not produce sound waves below about 30 Hz.

The infrasonic band is the band below the lowest frequency that can be heard. These sounds are felt and not heard. Organs of the human body can exhibit resonance frequencies in the infrasonic band. An organ can be damaged by intense infrasonic sounds having a frequency equal to the resonance frequency of the organ. A method of crowd control during riots that has been jokingly proposed consists of generating intense infrasonic sounds at the resonance frequency of the colon. Jimi Hendrix, a successful rock guitarist of the late 1960s and early 1970s, was quoted saying that a particular low-frequency note he played affected the bladders of people in his audience. The infrasonic band is often incorrectly called the subsonic band. To call an infrasonic filter a "subsonic filter" implies that the filter is "slower than the velocity of sound."

The ultrasonic band is the band above the highest frequency that can be heard. Not to be confused with the term supersonic, which means faster than the velocity of sound, ultrasonic sounds are used in ultrasonic cleaners, traffic detectors, ultrasonic imaging in medical applications, burglar alarm systems, remote controls, etc. If one has good high-frequency hearing, ultrasonic traffic detectors can often be heard at traffic lights. The flyback transformers in analog television sets with cathode-ray-tube displays often develop mechanical problems which cause them to emit an ultrasonic sound at the 15.75 kHz frequency of the horizontal oscillator.

1.5 Pitch

The term pitch is used to denote the perceived frequency of sound. A common unit of pitch is the mel. By definition, the mel pitch of a 1 kHz tone is 1000. Psychoacoustic tests are used to generate curves which relate pitch to frequency for the average person. These curves are generated by letting auditors first hear a 1 kHz tone which they are told has a mel pitch of 1000. The frequency of the tone is then changed and the auditors are asked for a best estimate of the pitch of the new tone. The data are then averaged over many persons to generate the perceived frequency or pitch of a tone versus its actual frequency. Such a curve is shown in Fig. 1.2. This graph is based on data published by Stevens and Volkman in the *American Journal of Psychology,* vol. 53, pp. 329-353 (1940).

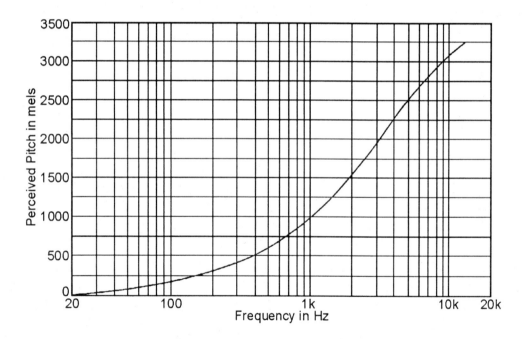

Figure 1.2: Mel pitch versus frequency.

The way that the human ear perceives the pitch of a note produced by a musical instrument is not known. If the voltage output of a microphone is observed on an oscilloscope while picking up a note played by an instrument, the observed waveform would look nothing like the sine wave of a pure tone. Therefore, the curve of mels versus frequency is meaningless for non-sinusoidal sounds. To illustrate these effects, it has been shown that a series of tones having the frequencies 1 kHz, 1.2 kHz, 1.4 kHz, 1.6 kHz, etc., when added together have a pitch of 200 mels. This was established by allowing auditors to alternately listen to the sum of the tones and a pure tone while adjusting the frequency of the pure tone until the two sounds have the same pitch. Early researchers investigated this by generating the sounds with a throttled air stream blowing through equally spaced holes around concentric circles on a rotating disk. The frequency of the individual terms was controlled by the angular velocity of the disk and the number of holes around each circle. Although pure tones are not generated by this method, the component terms are periodic and are in phase synchronism with each other.

Helmholtz conceived his famous distortion hypothesis to explain how the ear determines pitch. He believed that nonlinearities in the ear produce a heterodyne mixing effect to produce sum and difference frequency components between the individual terms of a complex sound. The theory was that the brain responds to the lowest difference frequency term. This explained how the ear interprets a series of tones having the frequencies 1 kHz, 1.2 kHz, 1.4 kHz, 1.6 kHz, etc., as having a pitch of 200 mels. In the 1930s, however, J. F. Shouten in the Netherlands showed that a series of tones having the frequencies 1.04 kHz, 1.24 kHz, 1.44 kHz, 1.64 kHz, etc., has a mel pitch of 205 rather than the 200 predicted by Helmholtz's law. It was not commonly accepted that Shouten's work defeated Helmholtz's law until the 1950s. The way that the ear perceives pitch is still not well known.

The same pitch note on different musical instruments may have very different distributions in the frequency domain. The differences can be investigated by using a Fourier transform to analyze time records of notes produced by instruments. For example, the 7th through the 10th pitch harmonics predominate for the low to mid-pitch notes on a saxophone. For the French horn, less than 0.4% of the power is at the pitch frequency for some notes. Higher pitch notes from different instruments tend to sound more alike than the lower pitch notes because the overtones of the higher pitch notes often fall outside the range of human hearing. It is the audible overtone structure of a note that makes instruments sound different.

1.6   Human Speech

Most of the power in human speech is in the frequency band from 200 Hz to 4 kHz. Speech limited to a range less than this is still intelligible. For example, the frequency response of a telephone is normally taken to be from 300 Hz to 3 kHz. This frequency band is commonly referred to as the "telephone band." Not only is speech limited to this band intelligible, but also the talker can be easily recognized. The labial sounds (formed mainly with the lips, e.g. b, m, and p) and the fricative sounds (pronounced by forcing the breath through a narrow opening between the teeth, e.g. f, s, v, and z) have frequency components as high as 8 kHz to 10 kHz. However, there is relatively little power at these high frequencies.

1.7   Frequency Bands

Audio frequency bands are normally expressed in octaves or fractions of octaves. By definition, an octave, a half octave, and a third octave, respectively, are defined as the frequency band between two frequencies f_1 and f_2 such that

$$\text{Octave: } f_2/f_1 = 2 \qquad \text{Half Octave: } f_2/f_1 = 2^{1/2} \qquad \text{Third Octave: } f_2/f_1 = 2^{1/3} \qquad (1.3)$$

Example 1 *Calculate the number of half-octaves in the band from 20 Hz to 20 kHz.*

Solution. Denote the number by n. It must satisfy $2^{n/2} = 20\,\text{kHz}/20\,\text{Hz} = 1000$. Solution for n yields $n = 19.9$.

The International Standards Organization, commonly referred to as the ISO, has established a standard for specifying frequencies that are commonly used for the center frequencies of band-pass filters and cutoff frequencies of high-pass and low-pass filters used for acoustical measurements. These frequencies are given by

$$f_n = 1000 \times 2^{n/q} \qquad n = 0, \ \pm 1, \ \pm 2, \ \pm 3, \text{ etc.} \qquad (1.4)$$

where $q = 1$ for octave spacings, $q = 2$ for half-octave spacings, $q = 3$ for third-octave spacings, etc. The ISO frequency standards are often used in consumer and professional audio equipment. For example, a ten-band octave graphic equalizer covering the 20 Hz to 20 kHz band might have controls at the ISO frequencies 31.25 Hz, 62.5 Hz, 125 Hz, 250 Hz, 500 Hz, 1 kHz, 2 kHz, 4 kHz, 8 kHz, and 16 kHz.

In professional audio applications, third-octave graphic equalizers are often used to equalize or flatten out the frequency response of loudspeakers. Psychoacoustic research has shown that the human ear can tell little difference if the filter bandwidths are less than one-third an octave. The equalizers are installed preceding the power amplifiers that drive the loudspeakers. They are adjusted by driving the system with a random signal that is called pink noise. The output of the loudspeakers is picked up by a microphone that drives a third-octave real-time spectrum analyzer. This instrument displays the frequency spectrum of the signal in third-octave bands. Because pink noise has equal power for any octave or fraction of an octave, the spectrum displayed shows the frequency response of the loudspeaker. By observing the real-time analyzer, the graphic equalizer can be adjusted for the flattest overall frequency response at the position of the microphone.

Example 2 *Calculate the center frequency and the two* -3 dB *cutoff frequencies of a band-pass filter if the center frequency is the third ISO half-octave frequency below 1 kHz.*

Solution. The center frequency is $f_c = 1000 \times 2^{-3/2} = 353.6$ Hz. The lower and upper cutoff frequencies satisfy $f_u/f_\ell = 2^{1/2}$ and $f_c = \sqrt{f_\ell f_u}$. Solution for the cutoff frequencies yields $f_\ell = f_c/2^{1/4} = 297.3$ Hz and $f_u = f_c \times 2^{1/4} = 420.5$ Hz. Filter cutoff frequencies are normally specified as the frequencies where the response is down by a factor of $\sqrt{2}$, i.e. by 3 dB. This is illustrated in Fig. 1.3(a) for the band-pass filter and in Fig. 1.3(b) for the low-pass and high-pass filters.

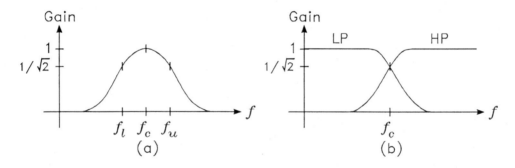

Figure 1.3: Filter gain versus frequency. (a) Band pass. (b) Low pass and high pass.

1.8 Audio Sub Bands

The audio band can be divided into five sub bands which have distinctly different characteristics. The first is between 20 Hz and 30 Hz. Sounds in this range are both felt and heard. In music, only the lowest swell notes of the largest pipe organs have power in this band. The majority of loudspeakers do not reproduce this range. The next band is between 30 Hz and 500 Hz. This band contains the lower and upper bass frequencies of music. The rhythm section of music is in this band. A boost in the band from 60 Hz to 120 Hz causes music to have a "boomy" sound. Such a boost is characteristic of poorly designed or inexpensive loudspeakers. The band from 500 Hz to 3 kHz forms the midrange band. Speech limited to this band has a telephone like sound. If this band is boosted, it can cause listener fatigue. Cheaper radios have loudspeakers that predominantly reproduce this range.

The band from 3 kHz to 8 kHz forms the presence range. The labial and fricative sounds of speech are reproduced in this range. If these sounds are not reproduced, speech is still intelligible, but it is obvious to the listener that the talker is not present. The band from 8 kHz to 16 kHz is called the brilliance range.

In music, the sounds produced by bells, triangles, cymbals, etc., are reproduced in this range. Sibilance in speech also extends into this band.

Prior to the mid 1940s, it was commonly accepted that reproduction of the brilliance range was not preferred by most listeners. Consequently, manufacturers of high quality record players and broadcast receivers intentionally suppressed the reproduction in this range. In a classic experiment with live music at the former RCA Laboratories, Harry F. Olson demonstrated that the majority of listeners preferred response beyond 4 kHz. This was done by letting audiences listen to a live band behind a curtain with an acoustical low-pass filter between the curtain and the band. The filter was alternately opened and closed between musical selections. Although the audiences did not know what was taking place, a majority preference was expressed for the sounds heard with the acoustical filter open. It was concluded from this experiment that the distortion and noise in reproduction systems was the reason that most people did not like reproduction of the brilliance range. This work was reported in the paper by H. F. Olson, "Frequency Range Preference for Speech and Music," *J. Acoust. Soc. Am.*, **19**, 4, 549-555 (1947). As the high-frequency distortion was eliminated with advancements in recording and broadcast technology, reproduction systems were designed to reproduce the brilliance range.

1.9   Sound Pressure Level

The sound pressure level or SPL is a measure of the strength of sound. To define it, we must first define acoustic pressure. When a sound wave propagates past a point, the air pressure fluctuates about the ambient pressure. Let us denote the total pressure by $P(t)$ and the ambient pressure by P_0. The instantaneous acoustic pressure is denoted by $p(t)$ and is defined by

$$p(t) = P(t) - P_0 \qquad (1.5)$$

Although $P(t)$ can be greater than or less than P_0, it must have an average value of P_0. Thus $p(t)$ varies positively and negatively about an average value of zero. In an electronic circuit, an analog of $P(t)$ is the total voltage at a node, i.e. the dc bias voltage plus the ac signal voltage. The corresponding analog of P_0 is the dc voltage while that of $p(t)$ is the small-signal ac voltage.

The SPL is a dB measure of the rms or root-mean-square pressure. It is given by

$$SPL = 20 \log\left(\frac{p_{rms}}{p_{ref}}\right) \text{ dB} \qquad (1.6)$$

where p_{rms} is the rms value of $p(t)$. By definition, the rms value of a variable is obtained by squaring the variable, taking the average value, then taking the square root. This can be written $p_{rms} = \sqrt{\langle p^2(t)\rangle}$, where the symbols $\langle \cdot \rangle$ denote a time average. The rms value of a sine wave is its peak value divided by $\sqrt{2}$. The rms value of a triangle wave is its peak value divided by $\sqrt{3}$. The rms value of a square wave is equal to its peak value. The 0 dB reference pressure for the SPL is $p_{ref} = 2 \times 10^{-5}$ Pa. This is approximately the rms pressure of the lowest level sound that can be heard by a person who has no hearing loss.

The SPLs of independent or uncorrelated sounds can be added to obtain the combined SPL by first converting each SPL back into its corresponding rms pressure. The rms pressures are then added by taking the square root of the sum of the squares. The result is then converted back to an SPL. It is straightforward to show that this combination of operations yields the formula

$$SPL_{total} = 10 \log\left[\sum_i 10^{SPL_i/10}\right] \text{ dB} \qquad (1.7)$$

For example, 58 dB is the combined SPL of two 55 dB sounds. The combined SPL of a 60 dB sound and a 70 dB sound is 70.4 dB. This latter example illustrates how little the lower SPL sound affects the combined SPL when the two differ by 10 dB.

The ear is a very sensitive measuring instrument which has a very wide dynamic range. This is the reason that the logarithmic decibel scale is used to specify the sound pressure level. (The original bel scale is named for Alexander Graham Bell who invented it. There are 10 decibels in a bel.) The total dynamic range of the ear is normally taken to be about 120 dB. This is determined by taking 0 dB as the threshold of hearing and 120 dB as the discomfort threshold. A dynamic range of 120 dB corresponds to an acoustic pressure range from 2×10^{-5} Pa to 20 Pa. Because the power density in a sound wave varies as the square of the pressure, this range represents a power ratio of 10^{12} to 1.

The instrument that is used to measure SPL is called a sound level meter. Such an instrument consists of a calibrated microphone, a microphone preamplifier, a calibrated attenuator, and a mechanical or electronic readout. The most familiar SPL meters are hand held. Laboratory sound level meters with elaborate filtering circuits are not so portable. Some examples of the SPLs of familiar sounds are tabulated in Table 1.1.

Table 1.1: Example SPL Levels

Threshold of Pain	140dB
Jet Aircraft	120dB
Truck	100 dB
Orator	80 dB
Low Conversation	60 dB
Quiet Room	40 dB
Rustling of Leaves	20 dB

Exposure to high SPL sounds can permanently damage one's hearing. Loud impulsive sounds such as those created by a gunshot or by an air hammer are particularly bad. It is often said that 90 dB represents the SPL threshold above which the ear can be damaged. The potential for damage depends on the length of exposure. It is believed that some of the exposure effects are cumulative. For this reason, one should always use hearing protectors when exposed to loud sounds. Some of the simplest and most effective hearing protectors are made of a soft foam material that can be pushed into the outer ear canal. These are commonly sold at drug stores.

A common form of early hearing loss in humans is a decreased sensitivity at about 4 kHz. The hearing response below and above 4 kHz remains close to normal. This loss can be simulated with a graphic equalizer by notching out the gain with the 4 kHz control. As hearing loss progresses, the width of the notch increases until there is little or no high-frequency response left.

1.10   Equal Loudness Contours

The ear does not have a flat frequency response. Its frequency response varies with SPL. Although no two persons hear alike, psychoacoustic data have been collected and averaged over a large number of people to obtain the average frequency response of the human ear as a function of SPL. When displayed graphically, these data are called equal loudness contours. Probably the best known curves were produced by Fletcher and Munson and were published by the ASA in 1942 as the *American Standard for Noise Measurement, Z24.2-1942*. (The American Standard Association or ASA has been replaced by the ISO.) Fig. 1.4 is based on the original Fletcher-Munson contours.

The equal loudness contours give the SPL as a function of frequency for tones that are perceived as having equal loudness. By definition, the loudness level of each curve is equal to its SPL at 1 kHz. This loudness level is called the phon level of the curve. For example, it can be seen from the curves that an SPL of 40 dB at 200 Hz has the same perceived loudness as an SPL of 20 dB at 1 kHz. The loudness level of both tones is 20 phons. The curves show that the frequency at which the ear is the most sensitive is about 4 kHz. Because the low level curves rise much more at low frequencies than at high frequencies, the ear is less sensitive to low frequencies than to high frequencies at low levels. This is why the bass frequencies in music do not seem to reproduce well at low volume levels.

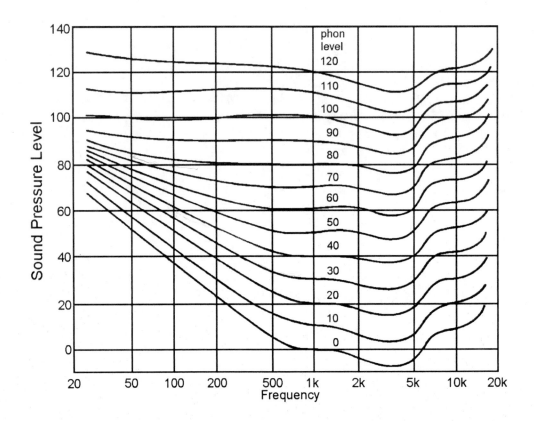

Figure 1.4: Fletcher-Munson equal-loudness contours for pure tones.

Many home audio components have a switch labeled "loudness compensation." When activated, it causes the frequency response of the volume control to approximate one of the equal loudness contours. In theory, the boost at low and high frequencies overcomes the loss of response by the ear at these frequencies. The equal loudness curves vary with level, however, so that the exact amount of loudness compensation required is a function of the loudness. Because this depends on the gain of the amplifier and the efficiency of the loudspeakers, it is doubtful if most loudness compensation circuits are ever calibrated correctly. In effect many of these circuits amount to little more than bass boost circuits. Combined with the bass boost that is built into many loudspeakers, loudness compensation usually results in a "boomy" loudspeaker sounding more "boomy."

Fig. 1.5(a) shows the circuit diagram of a volume control with loudness compensation that is often found in audio preamplifiers and receivers. It is called a loudness control. The circuit consists of a tapped potentiometer, two resistors, two capacitors, and a switch. With the switch in position A, the loudness compensation is off and the frequency response of the control is flat, i.e. the gain does not vary with frequency. In position B, the loudness compensation is activated. Maximum compensation occurs when the potentiometer wiper is at the tap or below. When the wiper is above the tap, the frequency response is flatter, becoming flat when the wiper is at the top of the potentiometer. When the wiper is at the tap, as shown in the figure, the voltage gain transfer function can be written

$$\frac{V_o}{V_i} = \frac{R_2}{R_1 + R_2} \times \frac{1 + \tau_2 s}{1 + \tau_1 s} \times \frac{1 + \tau_3 s}{1 + \tau_4 s} \tag{1.8}$$

If the break frequencies are well separated, the time constants for C_2 can be calculated with C_1 an open and the time constants for C_1 can be calculated with C_2 a short. The time constants are given by $\tau_1 = (R_1 \| R_2 + R_4) C_2$, $\tau_2 = R_4 C_2$, $\tau_3 = (R_1 + R_3) C_1$, and $\tau_4 = (R_1 \| R_2 \| R_4 + R_3) C_1$.

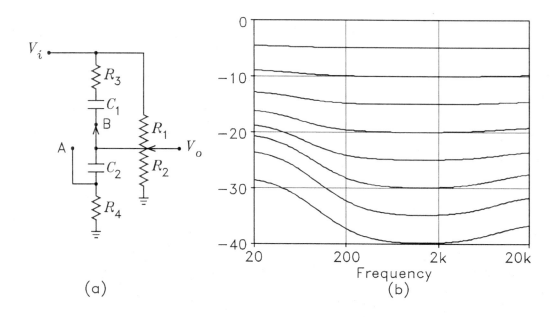

Figure 1.5: (a) Tapped potentiometer connected as a loudness control. (b) Response in dB versus frequency at several wiper settings.

Example 3 *A log taper* $25\,\mathrm{k\Omega}$ *rotary potentiometer is to be used in a loudness control. The potentiometer has a tap that is located at one-half its angular rotation. Specify the elements in the circuit of Fig. 1.5(a) for the following specifications: the total bass boost at low levels is to be* $12\,\mathrm{dB}$*, the total treble boost at low levels is to be* $4\,\mathrm{dB}$*, the frequency below which the bass boost occurs is* $f_1 = 200\,\mathrm{Hz}$*, and the frequency above which the treble boost occurs is* $f_2 = 7\,\mathrm{kHz}$*.*

Solution. We assume that the control sees a source impedance that is zero and a load impedance that is infinite. When a log control is at its mid position (at the center tap in this case), the ratio of the resistances on each side of the wiper is 10 to 1. Thus we have $R_1 = 10R_2$ and $R_1 + R_2 = 25\,\mathrm{k\Omega}$. Solution yields $R_1 = 22.7\,\mathrm{k\Omega}$ and $R_2 = 2.27\,\mathrm{k\Omega}$. The amount of bass boost is $20\log\left(\tau_1/\tau_2\right) = 20\log\left[\left(R_1\|R_2 + R_4\right)/R_4\right] = 12$. Solution for R_4 yields $R_4 = 689\,\Omega$. The amount of treble boost is $20\log\left(\tau_3/\tau_4\right) = 20\log\left[\left(R_1 + R_3\right)/\left(R_1\|R_2\|R_4 + R_3\right)\right] = 4$. Solution for R_3 yields $R_3 = 37.5\,\mathrm{k\Omega}$. The capacitors are given by $C_1 = 1/\left[2\pi f_2\left(R_1 + R_3\right)\right] = 378\,\mathrm{pF}$ and $C_2 = 1/\left(2\pi f_1 R_4\right) = 1.16\,\mu\mathrm{F}$. The frequency response in dB of the control is shown in Fig. 1.5(b) for several settings of the wiper.

1.11   Loudness Levels

Two scales are commonly used to specify the loudness of sound. These are the phon and the sone scales. The phon level of a pure tone is related to the SPL by a set of equal loudness contours such as the Fletcher-Munson curves. The phon level varies logarithmically with loudness. That is, multiplying the loudness by a constant translates into adding a constant to the phon level. It has been experimentally determined by psychoacoustic tests that a doubling of the perceived loudness level corresponds to an increase in the phon level by approximately 10 phons. (This holds only above the 40 phon level and then only approximately.) The logarithmic nature of the phon scale is desirable because the ear tends to have a logarithmic response to loudness.

The sone scale is a linear loudness scale in that a doubling of the loudness results in a doubling of the sone level. To convert the phon level of a pure tone to the sone level, the following formula is used

$$S = 2^{(P-40)/10} \text{ sones} \tag{1.9}$$

where S is the sone level and P is the phon level. The 40 phon level is chosen as the reference level for $S = 1$. Each time the phon level increases by 10, the formula predicts a doubling of the sone level.

Suppose that the loudness level of a combination of pure tones is desired. An approach to determine this might be as follows: (a) Measure the SPL of each tone by itself. (b) Use equal loudness curves to convert the SPL of each tone to a phon level. (c) Calculate the total phon level or, if desired, the total sone level by using the formulas

$$P_{total} = 10 \log \left(\sum_i 10^{P_i/10} \right) \text{ phons} \qquad S_{total} = \frac{1}{16} \left(\sum_i 10^{P_i/10} \right)^{\log 2} \text{ sones} \tag{1.10}$$

The methods discussed above for determining loudness levels are correct for pure tones only. Because audio signals are non-sinusoidal, alternate methods have been devised for determining the loudness level of non-sinusoidal signals. The most commonly used method for measuring the loudness of noise signals is the A-weighted SPL. An electrical filter is used inside the SPL meter which mimics the frequency response of the ear at the 40 phon level. The signal picked up by the microphone passes through the filter before the signal is detected and displayed on the meter. The meter reading is called the A-weighted SPL and its units are designated dBA. The frequency response of the A-weighting filter is obtained by taking the 40 phon equal loudness curve and flipping it over about a horizontal line. Because it is impossible to design an electrical filter that exactly follows the curve, the resulting filter is only approximate. An example circuit for an A-weighting filter and its normalized frequency response in dB are given in Fig. 1.6.

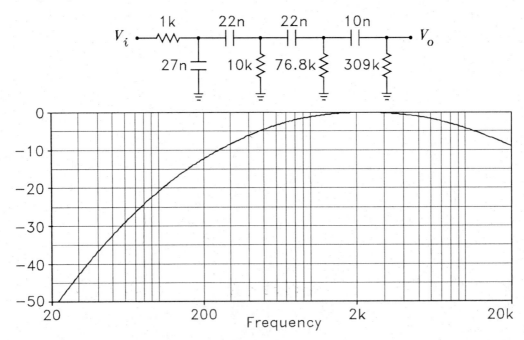

Figure 1.6: A weighting filter and its normalized gain versus frequency in dB.

Four other filter weightings have been devised to measure noise levels. The B-weighting filter mimics the response of the ear at the 60 phon level. The C-weighting filter mimics the response of the ear at the 80 phon level. The D-weighting filter has been proposed to be used for aircraft noise measurement. It has approximately the same response as the B-weighting filter with the exception that it has about a 4 dB peak in its response between 3 and 4 kHz. The use of all of these filters is somewhat questionable because measurements made with them do not exactly correlate with psychoacoustic tests. The A-weighting filter has been used for so long to document so many noise measurements that it is almost considered a standard. For this reason, most noise measurements are specified in dBA.

1.12 Audio Test Signals

The sine wave is the "king of the test signals." It is the only test signal in nature which is preserved in shape by all linear systems. It is used to measure frequency response, distortion, and overload characteristics of electronic circuits, microphones, and loudspeakers. If a pure sine wave is analyzed with a Fourier transform, its spectrum would be found to contain only one frequency component. Analog function generators synthesize sine waves by passing a triangle wave through a nonlinear diode wave shaping circuit to shape the triangle wave into a sine wave. If the signal is analyzed with a spectrum analyzer, it would be found to contain frequency components at harmonic frequencies of the fundamental. These harmonics are called distortion components or harmonic distortion.

The purest sine waves are generated by low distortion analog oscillators. These circuits are feedback amplifiers designed to have positive feedback at the frequency of oscillation. To minimize distortion, the amplifier loop-gain must be exactly unity. This can be achieved with an automatic gain control circuit which detects the amplitude of the oscillations and generates a control voltage to adjust the loop gain. If the amplitude of the oscillations increases, the gain is reduced. If the amplitude decreases, the gain is increased. Low-distortion oscillators are commonly used when it is desired to measure the distortion generated in circuits such as audio power amplifiers. For general purpose testing, the function generator is an acceptable sine wave source.

The square wave is a second periodic type of test signal that is used for audio frequency tests. It is used to measure what is called the "transient response" of amplifier circuits, filters, etc. The square wave is rarely used in loudspeaker testing because the phase and amplitude characteristics of loudspeakers do not preserve the square wave shape well enough to be able to interpret the results. The reason the square wave makes such a good test signal is that it contains a fundamental frequency component and harmonics which must be reproduced precisely with correct amplitude and phase if the signal shape is to be preserved. By observing the square-wave response of an amplifier on an oscilloscope, both the amplitude and the phase response can be judged without changing the frequency of the signal. Some of these effects at low frequencies are illustrated in Fig. 1.7.

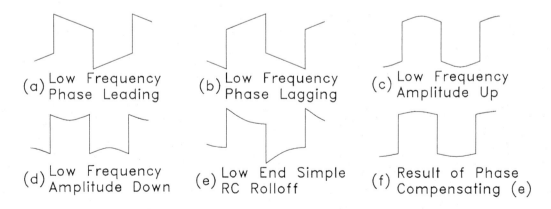

Figure 1.7: Effects of low-frequency gain and phase on square-wave response.

Amplifiers that do not have sufficient stability margin can exhibit a square wave response that exhibits high-frequency ringing, i.e. a damped sinusoidal oscillation is generated each time the square wave switches states. This is a very undesirable condition, for it indicates that the amplifier can break into sustained high-frequency oscillations if some parameter in the circuit is unavoidably changed.

A random signal that is used in testing loudspeakers is called pink noise. Pink noise is generated from white noise which is a random noise that exists to some extent in all electronic circuits. For example, white noise is generated by all resistors, BJTs, JFETs, MOSFETs, vacuum tubes, signal diodes, Zener diodes, etc. The basic mechanism that generates it is the random flow of current carriers in the devices. That is, current flow is not continuous but consists of discrete charges which flow randomly to form the total current. The random component of the current flow normally exhibits the characteristics of white noise.

With white light as an optical analog, white noise by definition has constant power per unit frequency. That is, it has the same power between 100 Hz and 200 Hz as it has between 1 kHz and 1.1 kHz. Another description is that white noise exhibits a flat spectral density. That is, a plot of the power per unit frequency versus frequency has a zero or flat slope. One method that has been used to generate white noise is to amplify the noise voltage produced by a pn junction that is biased in its Zener breakdown region.

Pink noise is generated from white noise by passing it through a pink-noise filter. The gain versus frequency of a pink-noise filter has a slope of -10 dB/dec over the frequency band of interest. The optical analog to pink noise is pink light which has more power at the longer wavelengths, i.e. at the lower frequencies.

The spectral density of a signal is the mean-square voltage per unit bandwidth, where the mean-square voltage is the square of the rms voltage. For pink noise, the spectral density is written

$$S\left(f\right) = \frac{V_0^2}{f}\,\mathrm{V}^2/\,\mathrm{Hz} \tag{1.11}$$

where V_0 is a constant having units of volts. The mean-square voltage in any frequency interval is obtained by integrating this function over the interval and taking the square root. It is given by

$$V_{rms} = V_0\sqrt{\int_{f_1}^{f_2} \frac{df}{f}} = V_0\sqrt{\ln\left(\frac{f_2}{f_1}\right)} \tag{1.12}$$

It follows from this equation that pink noise has equal voltage per octave, per decade, per one-third octave, etc. For example, pink noise has the same voltage between 100 Hz and 200 Hz as it does between 1 kHz and 2 kHz.

In testing loudspeakers, pink noise is commonly used to measure the frequency response with the aid of an instrument called a real-time spectrum analyzer. This device typically contains 24 third-octave band-pass filters which cover the audio frequency band. There is a rectifier at the output of each filter. The voltage outputs of the rectifiers are displayed as a function of frequency on a CRT screen or on an LED matrix. If pure pink noise is applied to the spectrum analyzer, equal voltage outputs from each rectifier are generated. This causes a flat frequency response to be displayed. If the pink noise is applied to a loudspeaker and the output of the loudspeaker is picked up by a microphone which drives the real-time analyzer, the frequency response displayed corresponds to that of the loudspeaker and microphone in combination. If the microphone is assumed to be perfect, the frequency response corresponds to that of the loudspeaker.

The combination of a real-time analyzer, a pink-noise generator, and a calibrated microphone makes a very powerful development tool for loudspeaker system design. In crossover network design, for example, inductors, capacitors, and resistors must be connected to the loudspeaker drivers to properly divide the audio signal between the drivers and to optimize the frequency response of the system. The experimental part of crossover network design is greatly simplified if the frequency response of the loudspeaker system can be observed in real time as the changes are made. Another application of pink noise and a real-time spectrum analyzer is in setting up a graphic equalizer for a loudspeaker system in an auditorium.

1.13   Problems

1. (a) What is the number of 1/3 octaves (whole number and fraction) in a decade? [9.97] (b) How many octaves are in a decade? [3.32]

2. *(a)* Calculate the 5*th* and 6*th* ISO preferred center frequencies above $1\,\text{kHz}$ for a 1/3-octave band-pass measuring filter. [$3.18\,\text{kHz}$, $4\,\text{kHz}$] *(b)* How many 1/6-octave ISO frequencies are in the $20\,\text{Hz}$ to $20\,\text{kHz}$ band? [59.8]

3. *(a)* To the nearest whole number, how many octaves are in the frequency band from $20\,\text{Hz}$ to $20\,\text{kHz}$? [10] *(b)* To the nearest whole number, how many 1/3-octaves are in the frequency band from $20\,\text{Hz}$ to $20\,\text{kHz}$? [30]

4. *(a)* A 1/3-octave band-pass filter has a center frequency of $8\,\text{kHz}$. What are its lower and upper $-3\,\text{dB}$ cutoff frequencies? [$7.13\,\text{kHz}$, $8.98\,\text{kHz}$] *(b)* An octave band-pass filter has a center frequency of $4\,\text{kHz}$. What are its lower and upper $-3\,\text{dB}$ frequencies? [$2.83\,\text{kHz}$, $5.66\,\text{kHz}$]

5. Find the rms value of the following pressure functions: *(a)* $p(t) = p_1\cos\omega_1 t + p_1\sin\omega_1 t$ [p_1], *(b)* $p(t) = p_1\cos\omega_1 t + p_2\cos\omega_2 t$, $\omega_1 \neq \omega_2$ $\left[\left[\left(p_1^2 + p_2^2\right)/2\right]^{1/2}\right]$, *(c)* $p(t) = p_1\cos\omega_1 t + p_2\sin\left(\omega_1 t + \pi/4\right)$ $\left[\left[\left(p_1^2 + \sqrt{2}p_1 p_2 + p_2^2\right)/2\right]^{1/2}\right]$

6. What fraction of the atmospheric pressure is the rms acoustic pressure in a sound wave with an *SPL* of *(a)* $40\,\text{dB}$, *(b)* $90\,\text{dB}$? [1.97×10^{-8}, 6.24×10^{-6}]

7. *(a)* What is the rms acoustic pressure in a sound wave which has an *SPL* of $110\,\text{dB}$? [$6.33\,\text{Pa}$] *(b)* If the acoustic pressure in the wave varies sinusoidally with time, what is the peak acoustic pressure? [$8.94\,\text{Pa}$] *(c)* If the acoustic pressure in the wave varies as a square wave with time, what is the peak acoustic pressure? [$6.33\,\text{Pa}$]

8. *(a)* What rms voltage is required across an $8\,\Omega$ load if $10\,\text{W}$ of average power is to be dissipated? [$8.94\,\text{V rms}$] *(b)* If the voltage is sinusoidal, what are the peak voltage and the peak power? [$12.6\,\text{V}$, $20\,\text{W}$]

9. The rms or root-mean-square value of a function of time is defined as the square root of the average value of the square of the variable. For example, the rms value of a voltage $v(t)$ is given be $v_{rms} = \sqrt{\left\langle v(t)^2 \right\rangle}$, where the symbols $\langle\cdot\rangle$ denote a time average. Let $v(t) = V_1\sin 2\pi f_1 t$ be the voltage across a resistor R. *(a)* Calculate the rms voltage across the resistor. [$V_1/\sqrt{2}$], *(b)* The instantaneous power dissipated in the resistor is given by $P(t) = v(t)^2/R$. Calculate the average value of $P(t)$, i.e. calculate $\langle P(t)\rangle$. [$V_1^2/2R$], *(c)* Using the definition of the rms value of a variable, calculate the rms value of the power $P(t)$, i.e. calculate $\sqrt{\left\langle P(t)^2 \right\rangle}$. [$0.6124 V_1^2/R$], *(d)* If the average sine wave power dissipated in an $8\,\Omega$ resistor is $100\,\text{W}$, what are the peak and rms values of the voltage across the resistor? [$40\,\text{V}$, $28.28\,\text{V}$] What is the rms value of the power? [$122.5\,\text{W}$] Note: Although it is correct to speak of rms voltage, current, pressure, etc., the concept of rms power is meaningless. Despite this, advertisements use the term rms power when they really mean average power.

10. The *SPL* for each of four different sounds is $70\,\text{dB}$, $72\,\text{dB}$, $62\,\text{dB}$, and $75\,\text{dB}$. What is the total *SPL* due to all of these sounds? [$77.7\,\text{dB}$]

11. *(a)* Use the Fletcher Munsen curves to determine the phon level of a $90\,\text{dB}$ sound wave at $10\,\text{kHz}$? [about 80 phons] *(b)* What is the sone level of the sound wave? [16 sones]

12. What is the total phon level of two tones, one with a frequency of $100\,\text{Hz}$ and an unweighted *SPL* of $80\,\text{dB}$ and the other with a frequency of $5\,\text{kHz}$ and an unweighted *SPL* of $70\,\text{dB}$? [75 phons + 70 phons = 76.2 phons]

13. *(a)* Use the Fletcher Munsen curves to determine the unweighted *SPL* of a $100\,\text{Hz}$ sound wave having a sone level of 12.3. [about 80 dB] *(b)* What is the A-weighted *SPL*? [59 dBA]

14. The phon level for each of four different sounds is 68, 73, 60, and 70 phons. What is the total sone level due to all of these sounds? [11.9 sones]

15. *(a)* A 100 Hz sound wave has an *SPL* of 90 dB as measured with a sound level meter having a flat response. Use the A weighting frequency response graph in Fig. 1.6 to determine the *SPL* on an A-weighted sound level meter. [about 69 dBA] *(b)* If a 100 Hz sound wave has an A-weighted *SPL* of 90 dBA, what would be the *SPL* on an unweighted sound level meter? [about 111 dB] *(c)* What is the relative amplitude response of the A-weighting filter at a frequency of 80 Hz? [about −24 dB] *(d)* An A-weighted sound level meter has a reading of 50 dBA for a 400 Hz tone. What is the unweighted *SPL*? [about 56.2 dB]

16. *(a)* What is the total phon level of two sound waves, one with a frequency of 200 Hz and an unweighted *SPL* of 60 dB and the other with a frequency of 2 kHz and an unweighted *SPL* of 50 dB? [50 phons +50 phons = 53 phons] *(b)* What is the total loudness in phons of a 40 dB 200 Hz tone plus a 70 dB 50 Hz tone? [20 phons +35 phons = 35.1 phons] What is the combined *SPL* of the two tones? [40 dB +70 dB = 70 dB]

17. *(a)* A sone level of 24 corresponds to what phon level? [85.85 phons] *(b)* If the frequency is 200 Hz, what unweighted *SPL* would it correspond to? [about the same] *(c)* To what A-weighted *SPL*? [73.85 dBA]

18. A method for measuring the loudness level of an audio signal that involves filtering the signal with 10 band-pass filters is described in Section 1.11. Construct a block diagram for the loudness measuring system and label the function of each block in the diagram.

19. Pink noise has a spectral density of the form $S(f) = V_0^2/f \, \text{V}^2/\text{Hz}$, where V_0 is a constant. The total voltage in a frequency band is obtained by integrating $S(f)$ over that band and taking the square root. *(a)* Obtain the expression for the voltage in pink noise in the band from f_1 to f_2. $[V = V_0\sqrt{\ln(f_2/f_1)}\,\text{V}]$, *(b)* If $f_2 = 2f_1$, show that the voltage is independent of f_1. $[V = V_0\sqrt{\ln 2}\,\text{V}]$

20. The voltage spectrum of a signal is the square root of the spectral density defined in problem 19. It has the units $\text{V}/\sqrt{\text{Hz}}$. On a dB-log plot, sketch the plot of the voltage spectrum for *(a)* White noise which has a constant power per unit bandwidth. [a straight line of zero slope] *(b)* Pink noise which has a constant power per octave (or any fraction of an octave). [a straight line with a slope of −3 dB /octave]

Chapter 2

Fundamentals of Acoustics

2.1 Basic Equations of Acoustics

In the analysis of acoustic waves in a gas, the two basic variables are pressure and particle velocity. Acoustic pressure p is defined as the difference between the instantaneous total pressure in a wave and the ambient or static pressure. Particle velocity $\vec{u}$ is defined as the velocity of the air molecules in the wave. In general, both p and $\vec{u}$ are functions of position and time. This is denoted by writing $p = p(\vec{r}, t)$ and $\vec{u} = \vec{u}(\vec{r}, t)$, where $\vec{r}$ is the position vector from the origin to the point (x, y, z). An acoustic wave is a nonlinear process. If the pressure variations are small, approximations can be used to model the process with linear equations. The two basic small-signal equations that relate p and $\vec{u}$ in a gas are derived in this section.

Let P be the total pressure of a gas contained in a volume V. A general statement of the Charles-Boyle gas law from thermodynamics is

$$PV = nRT \tag{2.1}$$

where n is the number of moles of gas, $R = 8317\,\mathrm{J/\,kg\,K}$, and T is the absolute temperature. When a gas is compressed, its temperature rises. When the gas is expanded, its temperature drops. If the compressions and expansions occur fast enough so that no heat exchange occurs between the gas and its surroundings, the process is said to be adiabatic. An acoustic wave in a gas is an adiabatic process. For an adiabatic process, the temperature varies such that

$$TV^{(\gamma - 1)} = \text{a constant} \tag{2.2}$$

where $\gamma = c_p/c_v$, c_p is the specific heat of the gas at constant pressure, and c_v is the specific heat at constant volume. For air at standard temperature and pressure, $\gamma = 1.4$. When Eqs. (2.1) and (2.2) are combined, we obtain

$$PV^{\gamma} = \text{a constant} \tag{2.3}$$

Consider a small volume of gas for which P and V vary with time. Let $P = P_0 + p$ and $V = V_0 + v$, where P_0 and V_0 are the quiescent values and p and v are small-signal time-varying values. We can write

$$P_0 V_0^{\gamma} = (P_0 + p)(V_0 + v)^{\gamma} = P_0 V_0^{\gamma}\left(1 + \frac{p}{P_0}\right)\left(1 + \frac{v}{V_0}\right)^{\gamma} \simeq P_0 V_0^{\gamma}\left(1 + \frac{p}{P_0} + \gamma\frac{v}{V_0}\right) \tag{2.4}$$

where the approximation $(1 + v/V_0)^{\gamma} \simeq (1 + \gamma v/V_0)$ has been used and the term $p\gamma v/P_0 V_0$ has been neglected. Solution for p yields

$$p = -\frac{\gamma P_0}{V_0} v \tag{2.5}$$

Next, we take the time derivative of p to obtain

$$\frac{\partial p}{\partial t} = -\frac{\gamma P_0}{V_0}\frac{\partial v}{\partial t} = -\frac{\gamma P_0}{V_0}\frac{\partial V}{\partial t} \tag{2.6}$$

15

If V is changing with time, the air particles must be moving. Let $\vec{u}$ be the velocity of the air particles. We can write

$$\frac{\partial V}{\partial t} = \oint_{\Sigma} \vec{u} \cdot \hat{n} dS = \int_{V} \nabla \cdot \vec{u} \, dv \simeq V \nabla \cdot \vec{u} \tag{2.7}$$

where Σ is the surface enclosing V, the divergence theorem has been used to convert the surface integral into a volume integral, and the approximation holds if V is sufficiently small. When this equation is combined with Eq. (2.6), we obtain

$$\frac{\partial p}{\partial t} = -\gamma P_0 \nabla \cdot \vec{u} \tag{2.8}$$

To obtain the second equation, consider a small volume $V = \Delta x \Delta y \Delta z$ of gas with density ρ_0 moving with a velocity u_x in the x-direction. By Newton's second law, the x-component of the force on the gas is $f_x = \rho_0 V \partial u_x / \partial t$. Let Δp_x be the drop in pressure across V in the distance Δx. A second relation for the force can be written $f_x = \Delta p_x \Delta y \Delta z$. When these two equations are combined, we obtain $\Delta p_x / \Delta x = \rho_0 \partial u_x / \partial t$. But $\Delta p_x / \Delta x$ is the negative of the x-component of the gradient of p, i.e. the x-component of $-\nabla p$, where the minus sign is required to make Δp_x positive when p decreases. Similar equations are obtained when the volume moves in the y and z-directions. When the three equations are combined, the following vector equation is obtained:

$$\nabla p = -\rho_0 \frac{\partial \vec{u}}{\partial t} \tag{2.9}$$

Eqs. (2.8) and (2.9) form the basis for almost all acoustic wave calculations in a gas. Together with boundary conditions, these equations can be used to predict radiation, propagation, diffraction, etc. For air at standard temperature and pressure, the following numerical values are used here: $\rho_0 = 1.18 \, \text{kg} / \text{m}^3$, $\gamma = 1.4$, and $P_0 = 1.013 \times 10^5 \, \text{Pa}$.

2.2 The Acoustic Wave Equation

Eqs. (2.8) and (2.9) can be solved simultaneously to obtain a single equation for p. This is done by first taking the divergence of Eq. (2.9) to obtain $\nabla \cdot \nabla p = \nabla^2 p = -\rho_0 \partial \left(\nabla \cdot \vec{u} \right) / \partial t$, where $\nabla^2 p$ is the scalar Laplacian of p. Then Eq. (2.8) is used to eliminate $\nabla \cdot \vec{u}$ to obtain

$$\nabla^2 p - \frac{1}{c^2} \frac{\partial^2 p}{\partial t^2} = 0 \qquad \text{where} \qquad c = \sqrt{\frac{\gamma P_0}{\rho_0}} \tag{2.10}$$

This equation is called the homogeneous wave equation for p, where c is the velocity of sound.

The wave equation for $\vec{u}$ can be solved for by taking the gradient of Eq. (2.8) to obtain

$$\nabla \left(\nabla \cdot \vec{u} \right) = \frac{-1}{\gamma P_0} \frac{\partial}{\partial t} \left(\nabla p \right) = \frac{-1}{\gamma P_0} \frac{\partial}{\partial t} \left(-\rho_0 \frac{\partial \vec{u}}{\partial t} \right) = \frac{1}{c^2} \frac{\partial^2 \vec{u}}{\partial t^2} \tag{2.11}$$

where Eq. (2.9) has been used for ∇p. By an identity of vector calculus, we can write $\nabla \left(\nabla \cdot \vec{u} \right) = \nabla^2 \vec{u} + \nabla \times \nabla \times \vec{u}$, where $\nabla^2 \vec{u}$ is the vector Laplacian of $\vec{u}$. But by Eq. (2.9), $\nabla \times \vec{u} = 0$ because the curl of the gradient of any scalar is identically zero, i.e. $\nabla \times \nabla p \equiv 0$. Therefore, the equation for $\vec{u}$ reduces to

$$\nabla^2 \vec{u} - \frac{1}{c^2} \frac{\partial^2 \vec{u}}{\partial t^2} = 0 \tag{2.12}$$

This is the homogeneous wave equation for $\vec{u}$.

Sinusoidal time variations are often assumed in solving acoustical problems. In this case, p and $\vec{u}$, can be written

$$p \left(\vec{r}, t \right) = \text{Re} \left[p \left(\vec{r} \right) \exp \left(j \omega t \right) \right] \qquad \vec{u} \left(\vec{r}, t \right) = \text{Re} \left[\vec{u} \left(\vec{r} \right) \exp \left(j \omega t \right) \right] \tag{2.13}$$

where $p\left(\overrightarrow{r}\right)$ and $\overrightarrow{u}\left(\overrightarrow{r}\right)$ are phasor functions of position (they have a real and imaginary part) and $\exp\left(j\omega t\right) = \cos\omega t + j\sin\omega t$. The time derivative operator $\partial/\partial t$ can be replaced by $j\omega$ in the equations to obtain the relations which the phasor functions satisfy. The phasor forms of Eqs. (2.8), (2.9), (2.10), and (2.12) are

$$j\omega p = -\gamma P_0\nabla\cdot\overrightarrow{u} \qquad \nabla p = -j\omega\rho_0\overrightarrow{u} \qquad \nabla^2 p + k^2 p = 0 \qquad \nabla^2\overrightarrow{u} + k^2\overrightarrow{u} = 0 \qquad (2.14)$$

where k is called the wavenumber which is given by

$$k = \frac{\omega}{c} = \frac{2\pi f}{c} \qquad (2.15)$$

The latter two equations in Eq. (2.14) are commonly called reduced wave equations or Helmholtz equations. In writing solutions for sinusoidal time variations, phasor solutions are converted to time domain solutions by multiplying by $\exp\left(j\omega t\right)$ and taking the real part.

2.3 The Plane Wave

A plane wave is a wave in which the surfaces of constant instantaneous pressure are planes. It is impossible to generate such a wave in nature because it requires a source of infinite extent. However, sufficiently far away from any source, the radiated sound can be approximated by a local plane wave. To solve the wave equation for the plane wave pressure and particle velocity, we assume sinusoidal time variations and we assume that the pressure is a function of z alone. In this case, the equation for p in Eq. (2.14) reduces to

$$\frac{d^2 p}{dz^2} + k^2 p = 0 \qquad (2.16)$$

The general solution for the wave that propagates in the $+z$ direction is

$$p\left(z\right) = p_0 e^{-jkz} \qquad (2.17)$$

where p_0 is the phasor amplitude of the wave. The solution for a wave which propagates in the $-z$ direction is obtained by changing the sign of the exponent in the exponential.

The particle velocity can be obtained from the second relation in Eq. (2.14). Because the pressure is a function of z alone, the particle velocity has only a z-directed component. It is given by

$$u_z\left(z\right) = \frac{-1}{j\omega\rho_0}\frac{dp}{dz} = \frac{-1}{j\omega\rho_0}\left[-jkp\left(z\right)\right] = \frac{p\left(z\right)}{\rho_0 c} \qquad (2.18)$$

Example 1 *It is given that the peak phasor pressure p_0 at $z = 0$ in Eq. (2.17) is a function of frequency given by*

$$p_0 = \frac{p_1}{1 + j\omega/\omega_1} \qquad (2.19)$$

where p_1 and ω_1 are real constants. What is the time domain expression for the acoustic pressure?

Solution. The time domain pressure is obtained as follows:

$$p\left(z,t\right) = \text{Re}\left(\frac{p_1}{1 + j\omega/\omega_1}e^{-jkz}e^{j\omega t}\right) = \frac{p_1}{\sqrt{1 + \left(\omega/\omega_1\right)^2}}\cos\left[\omega t - kz - \tan^{-1}\left(\frac{\omega}{\omega_1}\right)\right] \qquad (2.20)$$

2.4 Specific Impedance

The specific impedance is defined as the ratio of the phasor pressure to the phasor particle velocity at a point in an acoustic wave, where the particle velocity is treated as a scalar. It is denoted by the symbol Z_s and the units are mks rayls, named in honor of Lord Rayleigh. For the plane wave, it follows from Eqs. (2.17) and (2.18) that the specific impedance for air is

$$Z_s = \frac{p(z)}{u_z(z)} = \rho_0 c = 407 \text{ mks rayls} \tag{2.21}$$

Example 2 *If the density of air is doubled, by what factor does the specific impedance change?*

Solution. By Eq. (2.10), c is inversely proportional to $\sqrt{\rho_0}$. Thus the specific impedance increases by $\sqrt{2}$.

2.5   Acoustic Energy

Consider a small volume of gas V having a mass $m = \rho_0 V$. If the volume is moving with the velocity $\vec{u}$, the kinetic energy stored is $W_{KE} = m|\vec{u}|^2/2 = \rho_0 V|\vec{u}|^2/2$ J. This expression is divided by V to obtain the kinetic energy density D_{KE} given by

$$D_{KE}(\vec{r}, t) = \frac{1}{2}\rho_0 |\vec{u}(\vec{r}, t)|^2 \text{ J/m}^3 \tag{2.22}$$

Suppose V is a function of time. Let the pressure outside V be the ambient pressure P_0. Let the pressure inside V be written $P = P_0 + p$, where p is the small-signal time varying pressure. Let V increase by an amount ΔV. The surface area S enclosing V must expand by a distance δ so that $\Delta V = S\delta$. The force exerted on S is $f = pS$. Thus the work done is $\Delta W = f\delta = pS\delta = p\Delta V$. It follows that the change in potential energy stored in V is given by $\Delta W_{PE} = -p\Delta V$. Thus we can write

$$\frac{\partial W_{PE}}{\partial t} = -p\frac{\partial V}{\partial t} = -pV\nabla \cdot \vec{u} = -pV\left(\frac{-1}{\gamma P_0}\frac{\partial p}{\partial t}\right) = \frac{V}{2\gamma P_0}\frac{\partial}{\partial t}(p^2) \tag{2.23}$$

where Eq. (2.7) has been used for $\partial V/\partial t$ and Eq. (2.8) has been used for $\nabla \cdot \vec{u}$. When both sides of this equation are divided by V, the left side becomes $\partial D_{PE}/\partial t$, where D_{PE} is the potential energy density. If both sides of the resulting equation are integrated in t, the equation yields

$$D_{PE}(\vec{r}, t) = \frac{1}{2}\frac{|p(\vec{r}, t)|^2}{\gamma P_0} \text{ J/m}^3 \tag{2.24}$$

The total energy density is the sum of the kinetic and potential energy densities. It is given by

$$D(\vec{r}, t) = \frac{1}{2}\rho_0 |\vec{u}(\vec{r}, t)|^2 + \frac{1}{2}\frac{|p(\vec{r}, t)|^2}{\gamma P_0} \tag{2.25}$$

2.6   Acoustic Intensity

The acoustic intensity in a sound wave is the power flow per unit area. To obtain an expression for this, we use a theorem of vector calculus to write

$$\begin{aligned}
\nabla \cdot (p\vec{u}) &= \vec{u} \cdot \nabla p + p\nabla \cdot \vec{u} = \vec{u} \cdot \left(-\rho_0 \frac{\partial \vec{u}}{\partial t}\right) + p\left(\frac{-1}{\gamma P_0}\frac{\partial p}{\partial t}\right) \\
&= -\frac{\partial}{\partial t}\left(\frac{\rho_0}{2}|\vec{u}|^2 + \frac{1}{2\gamma P_0}p^2\right) = -\frac{\partial D(\vec{r}, t)}{\partial t}
\end{aligned} \tag{2.26}$$

where Eqs. (2.8), (2.9), and (2.25) have been used. Let the surface Σ enclose the volume V. We can use the divergence theorem and the above result to write

$$\oint_\Sigma p\vec{u} \cdot \hat{n}dS = \int_V \nabla \cdot (p\vec{u})\, dv = -\frac{d}{dt}\int D(\vec{r}, t)\, dv = -\frac{d}{dt}[W_{KE}(\vec{r}, t) + W_{PE}(\vec{r}, t)] \tag{2.27}$$

where $W_{KE}\left(\overrightarrow{r},t\right)$ and $W_{PE}\left(\overrightarrow{r},t\right)$, respectively, are the kinetic and the potential energies stored in V. This equation states the flux of the vector $p\overrightarrow{u}$ through Σ equals the negative time derivative of the total energy stored inside Σ. Thus the vector $p\overrightarrow{u}$ must represent the acoustic power density flowing through Σ.

The acoustic intensity $\overrightarrow{I}$ is defined as the vector power flow per unit area in a wave. It follows from the above that it is given by

$$\overrightarrow{I} = p\overrightarrow{u} \tag{2.28}$$

The units of $\overrightarrow{I}$ are W/m^2. We see that the direction of power flow is in the direction of the particle velocity.

It is common to treat the intensity as a scalar quantity. Its direction is understood to be in the same direction as $\overrightarrow{u}$. For sinusoidal time variations, the time average power flow in a wave is calculated from the phasor pressure and particle velocity as follows:

$$I_{ave} = \frac{1}{2}\,\mathrm{Re}\,(pu^*) = \frac{1}{2}\,|p|^2\,\mathrm{Re}\left[\frac{1}{Z_s^*}\right] = \frac{1}{2}\,|u|^2\,\mathrm{Re}\,(Z_s) \tag{2.29}$$

where p is the phasor pressure, u is the phasor particle velocity treated as a scalar, and Z_s is the specific impedance. The asterisk denotes the complex conjugate. In terms of the rms pressure and particle velocity, the time average intensity is given by

$$I_{ave} = \frac{p_{rms}^2}{\rho_0 c} = u_{rms}^2 \rho_0 c \tag{2.30}$$

Example 3 *What is the power density in* mW/m^2 *in a plane wave having an SPL of* 90 dB*?*

Solution. The rms pressure is $p_{rms} = 2 \times 10^{-5} \times 10^{90/20} = 0.63\,\mathrm{Pa}$. Thus the intensity is $I_{ave} = (0.63)^2/407 = 0.98\,\mathrm{mW/m^2}$.

2.7   Wavelength

Wavelength is defined as the distance a sinusoidal wave travels in one period, where the period is the reciprocal of the frequency, i.e. $T = 1/f$. Let the wavelength be denoted by λ. For the plane wave, λ is given by

$$\lambda = cT = \frac{c}{f} = \frac{2\pi c}{\omega} = \frac{2\pi}{k} \tag{2.31}$$

where $k = \omega/c$ is the wavenumber.

Example 4 *The radiation from a flat circular piston in an infinite baffle is approximately omni-directional for frequencies such that the piston circumference is less than a wavelength. For a piston radius of* 10 cm*, calculate the frequency band for which the radiation is omni-directional.*

Solution. The piston circumference is $C = 2\pi \times 0.10 = 0.628\,\mathrm{m}$. The wavelength of the radiated sound is greater than this if the frequency satisfies $f \leq c/C = 345/0.628 = 549\,\mathrm{Hz}$.

2.8   Particle Displacement

The particle displacement in a wave is defined as the displacement of the air molecules about their rest position. It is a vector quantity. We denote the displacement by $\overrightarrow{\xi}$. It is related to the velocity $\overrightarrow{u}$ by

$$\overrightarrow{u} = \frac{d\overrightarrow{\xi}}{dt} \qquad \text{or} \qquad \overrightarrow{u} = j\omega\overrightarrow{\xi} \tag{2.32}$$

where the second equation is the phasor relation.

The particle displacement is often treated as a scalar quantity. For the plane wave, the phasor displacement is related to the phasor pressure by

$$\xi = \frac{u}{j\omega} = \frac{p}{j\omega\rho_0 c} = \frac{p}{j2\pi f \rho_0 c} \tag{2.33}$$

where Eq. (2.18) for u has been used. For a constant SPL, ξ is inversely proportional to frequency. This is the reason that high SPL sounds can be felt if the frequency is low enough.

Example 5 *What is the peak-to-peak particle displacement in a sinusoidal plane wave having an SPL of 90 dB at 200 Hz and at 20 Hz?*

Solution. The rms pressure is $p_{rms} = \left(2 \times 10^{-5}\right) 10^{90/20} = 0.6325$ Pa. The peak-to-peak displacement is given by $\xi_{p-p} = 2\sqrt{2} p_{rms}/2\pi f \rho_0 c$. At 200 Hz, it is $\xi_{p-p} = 0.0035$ mm. At 20 Hz, it is $\xi_{p-p} = 0.035$ mm.

2.9   The Omni-Directional Spherical Wave

An omni-directional spherical wave is one in which the surfaces of constant instantaneous pressure are concentric spheres. For sinusoidal time variations, a source of sound radiates an omni-directional spherical wave if the source is sufficiently small compared to the wavelength. This condition is often expressed as $R < \lambda/2\pi$, where λ is the wavelength and R is the radius of the smallest sphere completely enclosing the source. The radiation from most loudspeakers at very low frequencies can be modeled by an omni-directional spherical wave.

For a source at the origin, the reduced wave equation in spherical coordinates for an omni-directional spherical wave is obtained by assuming that p is a function of r alone in the third relation in Eq. (2.14). In this case, the wave equation for the phasor pressure simplifies to

$$\frac{1}{r^2} \frac{d}{dr} \left(r^2 \frac{dp}{dr} \right) + k^2 p = 0 \tag{2.34}$$

There are two solutions to this equation, one representing a wave traveling in the $+r$ direction and one representing a wave traveling in the $-r$ direction. The solution for the $+r$ direction is

$$p(r) = K \frac{e^{-jkr}}{r} \tag{2.35}$$

where K is a constant. The pressure is inversely proportional to the distance from the source. Thus the SPL decreases by $20 \log 2 = 6$ dB each time r is doubled.

The phasor particle velocity can be obtained from the second relation in Eq. (2.14). It has only a r-directed component that is given by

$$u_r(r) = \frac{1}{j\omega\rho_0} \left(\frac{1}{r} + jk \right) K \frac{e^{-jkr}}{r} \tag{2.36}$$

Thus the specific impedance is

$$Z_s = \frac{p(r)}{u_r(r)} = \frac{j\omega\rho_0}{1/r + jk} = \frac{\rho_0 c}{1 + c/j\omega r} = \frac{\rho_0 c}{1 + c/j2\pi f r} \tag{2.37}$$

If $c/2\pi f r \leq 0.1$, it follows that $Z_s \simeq \rho_0 c$, which is the specific impedance for a plane wave. For $f = 20$ Hz, this inequality yields $r \geq 90$ ft for the distance from a source at which the wave looks like a local plane wave.

Example 6 *If the pressure in an omni-directional spherical wave is held constant, how does the particle velocity vary with frequency?*

Solution. For $|p(r)|$ constant, $|u_r(r)| \propto 1/|Z_s| = \sqrt{1 + (c/\omega r)^2}$.

For $c/\omega r \gg 1$, the above example predicts that $|u_r(r)|$ varies inversely with frequency. Pressure gradient or velocity microphones have an output that is proportional to the particle velocity. When a talker is close to such a microphone, a pronounced boost in the bass frequencies occurs, which is called the "proximity effect." The dB boost as a function of frequency and distance is given by $10\log\left[1 + \left[c/\left(2\pi f r\right)\right]^2\right]$.

2.10 Volume Velocity

The volume velocity U emitted by a source is the time derivative of the volume of air it displaces. It a source variable as opposed to a wave variable. As an example, consider the loudspeaker mounted in a closed-box shown in Fig. 2.1(a). Denote the diaphragm piston area, displacement, and velocity, respectively, by S_D, x_D, and u_D. The volume of air displaced is $V = S_D x$. The volume velocity emitted is

$$U = \frac{dV}{dt} = S_D \frac{dx}{dt} = S_D u \qquad (2.38)$$

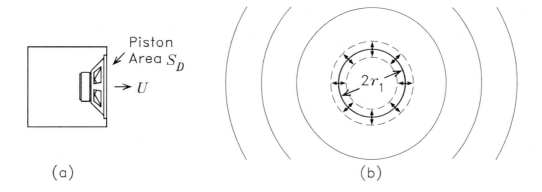

(a)   (b)

Figure 2.1: (a) Volume velocity U emitted by a loudspeaker. (b) Pulsating sphere source.

The equivalent piston area of a diaphragm is defined as the area of a flat piston which emits the same volume velocity. For a circular loudspeaker diaphragm, a convenient rule of thumb is often used to estimate the piston radius. The rule states that the piston radius in centimeters is equal to the advertised diameter in inches. Thus a 12-inch woofer has a piston radius of approximately $12\,\text{cm}$. Although this rule can only be considered to be approximate, it is assumed to hold in the following for most loudspeaker calculations. In practice, the piston radius of a driver is normally measured with a ruler as the distance from the center axis of the diaphragm to a point halfway into the outer suspension.

Fig. 2.1(b) illustrates a pulsating sphere source of sound. Let the nominal radius of the sphere be r_1. At $r = r_1$, the phasor volume velocity emitted is given by

$$U = 4\pi r_1^2 u_r(r_1) = 4\pi r_1^2 \frac{p(r_1)}{Z_s} = \frac{4\pi K}{j\omega\rho_0}\left[1 + j\frac{\omega r_1}{c}\right]e^{-jkr_1} \qquad (2.39)$$

This equation can be solved for the constant K in terms of U. When the resulting expression for K is used in Eq. (2.35), $p(r)$ can be written

$$p(r) = \frac{j\omega\rho_0 U}{1 + j\omega r_1/c}\frac{e^{-jk(r-r_1)}}{4\pi r} \qquad (2.40)$$

2.11   The Simple Spherical Source

The radius r_1 in the exponent of Eq. (2.40) represents a relative phase shift which can usually be neglected. If $\omega r_1/c \ll 1$ and the r_1 in the exponent is omitted, the equation can be written

$$p\left(r\right) \simeq j\omega\rho_0 U \frac{e^{-jkr}}{4\pi r} \tag{2.41}$$

This equation is often referred to as the pressure radiated by a simple spherical source. For sinusoidal variations, a source radiates approximately as a simple source if it can be contained in a sphere of radius $R < \lambda/2\pi$, where λ is the wavelength. The root-mean-square form of Eq. (2.41) is $p_{rms} = \omega\rho_0 U_{rms}/4\pi r$. This is obtained by taking the magnitude of both sides of the equation and adding the subscritps rms to the variables.

Example 7 *A loudspeaker driver with a diaphragm piston radius of $a = 4\,$cm is mounted in a small closed-box. The loudspeaker radiates as a simple source at $f = 150\,$Hz. Calculate the peak-to-peak diaphragm displacement if the SPL at $r = 3\,$m is $80\,$dB.*

Solution. The rms pressure and volume velocity, respectively, are $p_{rms} = \left(2\times 10^{-5}\right)10^{80/20} = 0.2\,$Pa and $U_{rms} = 4\pi r p_{rms}/2\pi f\rho_0 = 0.00678\,$m^3/s. Thus the peak-to-peak diaphragm displacement is given by $x_{p-p} = 2\sqrt{2}U_{rms}/2\pi f\pi a^2 = 4.05\,$mm.

The power radiated by a simple source can be obtained by integrating the normal component of the acoustic intensity over a sphere centered on the source. Because the intensity is constant over the sphere, the total power can be obtained by multiplying the acoustic intensity by the area of the sphere. To do this, we use Eq. (2.29) for the acoustic intensity, Eq. (2.41) for the pressure, and Eq. (2.37) for the specific impedance. The power radiated is given by

$$P_{AR} = 4\pi r^2 \times \frac{1}{2}\left|p\right|^2 \mathrm{Re}\left[\frac{1}{Z_s^*}\right] = \frac{1}{2}\frac{\omega^2\rho_0}{4\pi c}\left|U\right|^2 \tag{2.42}$$

The above equation can be written

$$P_{AR} = \frac{1}{2}\left|U\right|^2 R_{AR} = U_{rms}^2 R_{AR} \tag{2.43}$$

where R_{AR} is defined as the radiation resistance for the wave. It is given by

$$R_{AR} = \frac{\omega^2\rho_0}{4\pi c} \qquad \text{for a } 4\pi \text{ steradian load} \tag{2.44}$$

where the steradian is a measure of solid angle. There are 4π steradians in a sphere. If the simple source is operated against an infinite rigid wall, called an infinite baffle, it radiates into a 2π steradian load. It is shown in the next section that the radiation resistance in this case is doubled to the value

$$R_{AR} = \frac{\omega^2\rho_0}{2\pi c} \qquad \text{for a } 2\pi \text{ steradian load} \tag{2.45}$$

Example 8 *A small closed-box loudspeaker is mounted in an infinite baffle. Solve for the peak displacement of the diaphragm as a function of frequency if the power radiated is to remain constant. Assume that the loudspeaker radiates as a simple source.*

Solution. Denote the piston area of the diaphragm by S_D and the peak diaphragm displacement by x_0. Eqs. (2.43) and (2.45) can be use to solve for the power. It is given by

$$P_{AR} = \frac{1}{2}\left|U\right|^2\frac{\omega^2\rho_0}{2\pi c} = \frac{1}{2}\left|\omega x_0 S_D\right|^2\frac{\omega^2\rho_0}{2\pi c} = \frac{1}{2}\frac{\rho_0 S_D^2}{2\pi c}\left(\omega^2\left|x_0\right|\right)^2 \tag{2.46}$$

It follows from the above example that $\left|x_0\right|$ must be inversely proportional to ω^2 for a constant power output. For example, if the loudspeaker radiates as a simple source below $200\,$Hz, the peak displacement at $20\,$Hz must be 100 times greater than the peak displacement at $200\,$Hz for the same power output.

2.12 Acoustic Images

When a simple source is operated in free air, the acoustic radiation is omni-directional. When the source is placed against an infinite baffle, all of the radiation is forced to occur into one hemisphere. The changes in acoustic pressure and power radiated can be predicted by the theory of acoustic images.

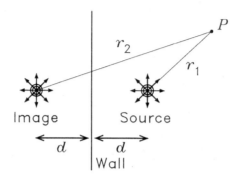

Figure 2.2: Simple source located in front of a rigid flat wall.

Fig. 2.2 shows a simple source in front of a wall. The boundary conditions require the normal component of the particle velocity at the wall to be zero. Let an image source be placed behind the wall as shown in the figure. If both sources emit the same volume velocity U, the wall can be removed and the boundary conditions do not change. That is, the normal component of the particle velocity at the wall remains zero. The acoustic pressure at point P can then be written

$$p = j\omega\rho_0 U \left[\frac{e^{-jkr_1}}{4\pi r_1} + \frac{e^{-jkr_2}}{4\pi r_2} \right] \tag{2.47}$$

If the original source is now brought up against the wall so that $r_1 = r_2 = r$, the two sources merge and the acoustic pressure at P becomes

$$p = j\omega\rho_0 2U \frac{e^{-jkr}}{4\pi r} = j\omega\rho_0 U \frac{e^{-jkr}}{2\pi r} \tag{2.48}$$

Thus the pressure at P is the same as that radiated by a single source which emits a volume velocity $2U$.

We conclude that a simple source operated against an infinite baffle radiates an acoustic pressure that is twice as great as it would in full space. Because the intensity varies as the square of the pressure, the acoustic intensity goes up by a factor of 4. However, the source radiates into half space so that the total power radiated goes up only by a factor of 2. Thus the radiation resistance R_{AR} goes up by a factor of 2. If the source is placed in a corner between two walls, it radiates into one-quarter space. The pressure radiated is equivalent to the original source plus three images. The pressure goes up by a factor of 4, the intensity increases by a factor of 16, the acoustic power radiated increases by a factor of 4, and the radiation resistance goes up by a factor of 4. If the source is placed in a corner between three walls, it radiates into one-eighth space. The pressure radiated is equivalent to the original source plus 7 images. The pressure goes up by a factor of 8, the intensity increases by a factor of 64, the acoustic power radiated increases by a factor of 8, and the radiation resistance goes up by a factor of 8. Fig. 2.3 summarizes the image effects for each case.

Image effects can be used to predict what can happen when the position of a loudspeaker is changed in a room. Only the very low frequencies where the loudspeaker radiates as a simple source are affected. We can conclude that the most bass is obtained from the loudspeaker when it is placed on the floor in the corner of a room. If it sounds "boomy" in this location, it can be pulled away from the corner. If it still sounds "boomy," it can be raised off of the floor.

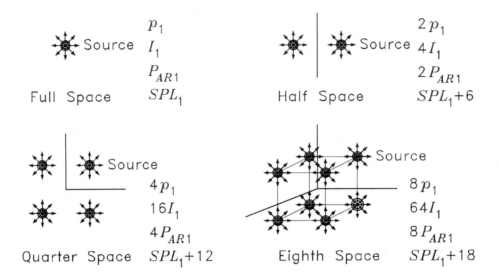

Figure 2.3: Simple source radiating into full space, half space, quarter space, and eighth space.

2.13   The Plane Circular Piston

The vibrating plane circular piston is a source which is often used to model the radiation from a loudspeaker diaphragm. Fig. 2.4 shows the geometry of such a piston in an infinite baffle. We assume that the disk vibrates sinusoidally with a z-directed velocity u. We wish to calculate the pressure radiated at point $P(r,\theta)$ in the yz-plane. By symmetry, the pressure is rotationally symmetric about the z-axis. The point P has the rectangular coordinates $x = 0$, $y = r\sin\theta$, and $z = r\cos\theta$. The point P' on the disk has the rectangular coordinates $x' = r'\cos\varphi'$, $y' = r'\sin\varphi'$, and $z' = 0$. The distance between the points P and P' is given by

$$d = \sqrt{(x-x')^2 + (y-y')^2 + (z-z')^2} = \sqrt{r^2 + r'^2 - 2rr'\sin\theta\sin\varphi} \tag{2.49}$$

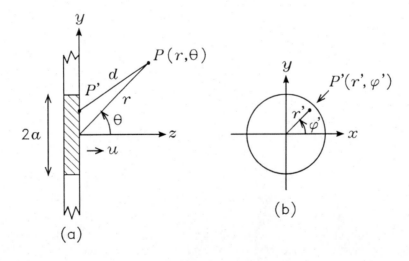

Figure 2.4: Plane circular piston radiator in an infinite baffle.

Let the surface of the disk be divided into differential area elements in polar coordinates. Superposition of the pressure radiated by each element can be used to solve for the total pressure at P. The area element at P' radiates as a simple source into a 2π steradian load. The pressure at P radiated by the area element at P' is obtained by doubling the pressure for a 4π steradian load in Eq. (2.41) and is given by

$$dp = j\omega\rho_0 dU \frac{e^{-jkd}}{2\pi d} = j\omega\rho_0 u \frac{e^{-jkd}}{2\pi d} da \tag{2.50}$$

where $dU = u\,da$ and $da = r'd\varphi'dr'$ is the area element in polar coordinates. If $r \gg r'$, two approximations can be made that are called the far-field approximations. First, the d in the denominator is approximated by r. Second, the binomial theorem is applied to Eq. (2.49) to approximate the d in the exponent by

$$d \simeq r - r'\sin\theta\sin\varphi' \tag{2.51}$$

The total pressure at point P can be solved for by summing the pressures radiated by each area element on the disk. In the limit as the area of each element approaches zero, the sum becomes the superposition integral given by

$$p(r,\theta) = j\omega\rho_0 u \frac{e^{-jkr}}{2\pi r} \int_0^a \int_0^{2\pi} e^{jkr'\sin\theta\sin\varphi'} r'd\varphi'dr' = j\omega\rho_0 U \left[\frac{2J_1(ka\sin\theta)}{ka\sin\theta}\right] \frac{e^{-jkr}}{2\pi r} \tag{2.52}$$

where $J_1(ka\sin\theta)$ is a Bessel function and $U = \pi a^2 u$ is the total volume velocity emitted by the disk.

To obtain the on-axis pressure from the above expression, the small argument expansion for the Bessel function can be used. For $|ka\sin\theta|$ small, this approximation is $J_1(ka\sin\theta) \simeq (ka\sin\theta)/2$. It follows that the pressure for $\theta = 0$, i.e. along the z-axis, is given by

$$p(r,0) = j\omega\rho_0 U \frac{e^{-jkr}}{2\pi r} \tag{2.53}$$

This is an important result for it shows that the far-field on-axis pressure radiated by the circular disk is the same as the pressure radiated by a simple source against a rigid wall into 2π steradians.

When the point P is on the z-axis, a criterion that is commonly used to specify the distance to the far field is that the distance d given by Eq. (2.49) varies by no more than $\lambda/16$ as r' varies over the disk. The minimum value of d occurs when $r' = 0$ and is $d_{min} = r$. The maximum value of d occurs when $r' = a$, so that $d_{max} = \sqrt{r^2 + a^2} \simeq r + a^2/2r$ for $r \gg a$. Thus the far-field distance satisfies the relation $d_{max} - d_{min} = a^2/2r \leq \lambda/16$. Solution for r yields

$$r \geq \frac{8a^2}{\lambda} = \frac{2D^2}{\lambda} \tag{2.54}$$

where $D = 2a$ is the diameter of the disk. When r satisfies this condition, the exponent term kd in Eq. (2.50) can vary by no more than $(2\pi/\lambda) \times (\lambda/16) = \pi/8 = 22.5°$ as r' varies over the surface of the disk. This makes the radiation from each element on the disk arrive at the observation point P in approximately the same phase so that phase cancellation cannot occur along the z-axis.

For r a constant, it follows from Eq. 2.52 that

$$|p| \propto \left|\frac{2J_1(ka\sin\theta)}{ka\sin\theta}\right| \tag{2.55}$$

This equation shows that the dependence of the pressure on the angle θ is determined by the argument $ka\sin\theta = (2\pi a/\lambda)\sin\theta = (C/\lambda)\sin\theta$, where $C = 2\pi a$ is the circumference of the disk. Thus the pressure is a function of the ratio of the disk circumference to the wavelength. This is a function of frequency.

Fig. 2.5 gives plots over the dB range from 0 to $-30\,\text{dB}$ of the normalized SPL for a constant r as a function of θ for $C = \lambda$, 2λ, 3λ, 4λ, 5λ, and 10λ. These plots are called radiation patterns. It can be seen that the case $\lambda = C$ gives a pattern that is almost omni-directional over the hemisphere in front of the

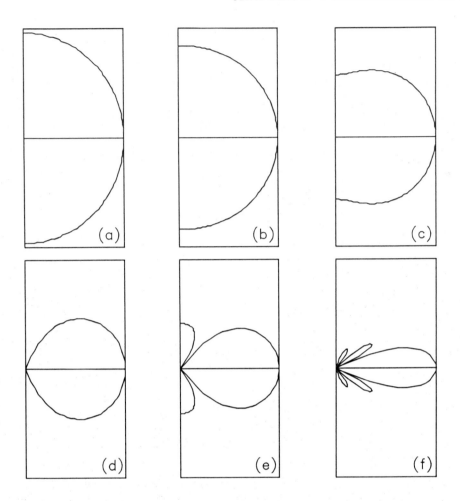

Figure 2.5: Circular piston radiation patterns for $-90° \leq \theta \leq 90°$. (a) $\lambda = C$, (b) $\lambda = C/2$, (c) $\lambda = C/3$, (d) $\lambda = C/4$, (e) $\lambda = C/5$, (f) $\lambda = C/10$.

disk. As λ decreases, the pattern becomes narrower and pressure side lobes begin to form. The shortest wavelength for which no pressure sidelobes exist is $\lambda = C/4$. For $\lambda < C/4$, the radiation becomes highly directional.

If the diaphragm of a loudspeaker is modeled as a flat circular piston, it follows from Fig. 2.5 that the low-frequency radiation is omni-directional while the high-frequency sounds are radiated in a narrow beam in front of the diaphragm. If the circumference of the diaphragm is made smaller, the frequency at which the radiation becomes directional is increased so that the high frequency dispersion is improved. This is one of the reasons why small diaphragm loudspeakers are used for tweeters.

2.14   Fresnel Diffraction Effects

The near-field pressure radiated by a source is referred to as Fresnel diffraction. The near field of a source is the region close to the source where the far-field approximations do not hold. In general, it is impossible to obtain closed form expressions for the near-field pressure radiated by a source. It is possible, however, to solve for the on-axis, near-field pressure radiated by a flat circular piston in an infinite baffle. This pressure is solved for in this section.

Fig. 2.6 illustrates a flat circular piston of radius a in an infinite baffle. The piston vibrates sinusoidally with a z-directed velocity u and emits a volume velocity $U = \pi a^2 u$. The observation point P is on the piston axis a distance z from its center. Let the piston area be divided into concentric rings or zones. The figure illustrates the first two such zones. The radii of the circles dividing the zones are labeled r_1', r_2', etc. The distances from the observation point P to the circles dividing the zones are labeled d_1, d_2, etc. Let the radii of the zones be chosen such that $d_1 = z + \lambda/2$, $d_2 = d_1 + \lambda/2$, $d_3 = d_2 + \lambda/2$, etc. Because of the half-wavelength difference in path lengths, the acoustic radiation from the second zone on the disk arrives at P out of phase from the radiation from the first or central zone. The acoustic radiation from the third zone arrives at P out of phase from the radiation from the second zone. The acoustic radiation from the fourth zone arrives at P out of phase from the radiation from the third zone, etc.

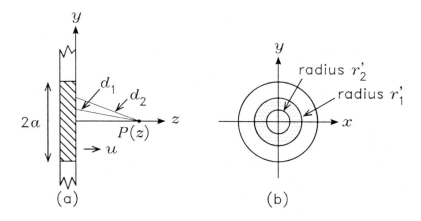

Figure 2.6: Construction of Fresnel zones. (a) Side view. (b) Front view.

The total number N of zones on the disk depends on the disk radius a, the wavelength λ, and the distance z. If the number is even, the acoustic radiation from adjacent zones approximately cancels at P, thus forming a null or a minimum in the radiation. If the number is odd, cancellation occurs between $N-1$ zones, leaving one zone as the effective radiator. This causes a maximum in the radiation. If the frequency is held constant and the distance z is varied, the number of zones varies between an even number and an odd number. Thus the on-axis radiation oscillates between a maximum and a minimum as z is increased until only one zone exists. This occurs when z becomes large enough so that $\sqrt{z^2 + a^2} - z < \lambda/2$. These effects are called Fresnel or near-field diffraction effects.

The superposition integral for the on-axis pressure radiated by the plane circular disk can be written as the integral of Eq. (2.50) over the disk, where $d = \sqrt{z^2 + r'^2}$ and $da = 2\pi r' dr'$. The integral is

$$p(z) = j\omega\rho_0 u \int_0^a \frac{1}{\sqrt{z^2 + r'^2}} e^{-jk\sqrt{z^2+r'^2}} dr' = j\omega\rho_0 u \left[\frac{e^{-jkz} - e^{-jk\sqrt{z^2+a^2}}}{jk} \right] \qquad (2.56)$$

To put Eq. (2.56) into a form that makes the Fresnel diffraction effects more obvious, the equation can be written

$$p(z) = j\omega\rho_0 u \exp\left[-j\frac{k}{2}\left(\sqrt{z^2 + a^2} + z \right) \right] \times \frac{2}{k} \sin\left[\frac{k}{2}\left(\sqrt{z^2 + a^2} - z \right) \right] \qquad (2.57)$$

This expression predicts that a maximum in the pressure occurs when the argument of the sine function is an odd multiple of $\pi/2$ and a minimum when the argument is a multiple of π. Because $k = 2\pi/\lambda$, the condition for a maximum is $\sqrt{z^2 + a^2} - z = \lambda/2$, $3\lambda/2$, $5\lambda/2$, etc. The condition for a minimum is $\sqrt{z^2 + a^2} - z = \lambda$, 2λ, 3λ, etc.

Example 9 *A flat circular piston in an infinite baffle has a radius of* 10 cm. *The piston vibrates with a frequency at which the radius of the disk is* $a = 5\lambda/2$. *Plot the normalized on-axis pressure as a function of the distance from the disk.*

Solution. Because the disk has a radius that is an odd multiple of $\lambda/2$, it follows that a pressure maximum occurs at $z = 0$. Therefore, the pressure at $z = 0$ will be used for the reference pressure in normalizing the on-axis pressure. Eq. (2.57) can be evaluated at $z = 0$ to obtain

$$p_{ref} = j\omega\rho_0 u \exp\left(-j\frac{ka}{2}\right) \times \frac{2}{k}\sin\left(\frac{ka}{2}\right) \tag{2.58}$$

It follows from Eqs. (2.57) and (2.58) that the normalized on-axis pressure magnitude is given by

$$\left|\frac{p}{p_{ref}}\right| = \left|\frac{\sin\left[k\left(\sqrt{z^2 + a^2} - z\right)/2\right]}{\sin(ka/2)}\right| = \left|\frac{\sin\left[\left(\sqrt{(z/\lambda)^2 + 6.25} - (z/\lambda)\right)\pi\right]}{\sin(2.5\pi)}\right| \tag{2.59}$$

A plot of $|p/p_{ref}|$ as a function of z/λ is given in Fig. 2.7. The far-field distance is $r = 8a^2/\lambda = 50\lambda$.

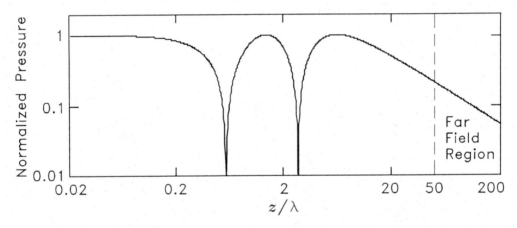

Figure 2.7: Normalized pressure radiated by a circular piston showing Fresnel diffraction effects.

2.15   Acoustic Reflections

As an introduction to the phenomenon of reflections, we first look at the reflection of an acoustic wave from an infinite baffle, i.e. an infinite rigid wall. Let the wall be located in the xy-plane at $z = 0$. Suppose that a plane wave that propagates in the $+z$ direction strikes the wall. In order for the boundary conditions to be satisfied, a reflected wave is generated at the interface which propagates in the $-z$ direction. The total acoustic pressure in the region $z \leq 0$ can be written

$$p_t = p_i e^{-jkz} + p_r e^{+jkz} \tag{2.60}$$

where p_i is the amplitude of the incident wave and p_r is the amplitude of the reflected wave. The boundary conditions at the wall require the z-component of the air particle velocity to be zero, i.e. $u_z = 0$ at $z = 0$. Because $u_z = (-1/j\omega\rho_0)\,\partial p/\partial z$, it follows that p_r must be equal to p_i. Thus the total pressure for $z \leq 0$ is given by

$$p_t = p_i\left(e^{-jkz} + e^{+jkz}\right) = 2p_i\cos kz \tag{2.61}$$

At $z = 0$, the total pressure is $p_t = 2p_i$ which is double the amplitude of the incident pressure. Thus a sound wave which strikes an infinite wall would have an SPL that is 6 dB higher at the baffle compared to the SPL in the absence of the wall. This is a simple example of how the acoustic pressure is modified by the presence of an obstacle in the path of propagation.

The mathematical solution of reflection problems is very difficult when the obstacle has an irregular shape. One problem that can be solved which is of interest in the modeling of microphones is the reflection that occurs when an acoustic wave is incident normally on the end of a long solid cylinder. The geometry of the problem is illustrated in Fig. 2.8(a). The figure shows a propagating plane wave that is incident normally on a long solid cylinder. The acoustic pressure at the center of the end of the cylinder is equal to the incident pressure plus the pressure in the waves that are reflected from the cylinder. At very low frequencies where the diameter of the cylinder is small compared to the wavelength, i.e. $D \ll \lambda$, the incident wave bends around the cylinder so that the amplitude of the reflected wave is very small. In this case, the pressure at the center of the cylinder is approximately equal to the incident pressure, i.e. the pressure increase due to the reflections is 0 dB.

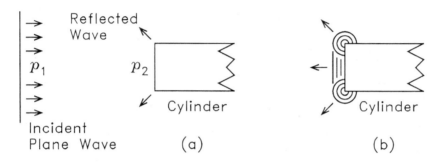

Figure 2.8: (a) Incident plane wave on a cylinder. (b) Reflected wave.

As the frequency is increased so that the cylinder diameter to wavelength ratio increases, the reflected waves begin to look like a local plane wave at the cylinder plus higher order waves at the edge as illustrated in Fig. 2.8(b). In this case a pressure increase occurs at the cylinder similar to the increase in pressure at an infinite plane described above. The first pressure maximum occurs when the wavelength is equal to the cylinder diameter. The magnitude of the pressure increase is slightly less than 10 dB. This is greater than the factor of 2 increase in pressure at the infinite plane because of a focusing effect of the reflected waves from the edge of the cylinder toward its center. Fig. 2.9 gives a plot of the dB pressure increase as a function of the diameter to wavelength ratio $D/\lambda = (D/c) f$. This figure is based on data published in the *Brüel and Kjær Technical Review*, No. 1, Jan. 1959. As frequency is increased, the pressure increase drops back to 0 dB when $D/\lambda = 2$. It then alternates between a maximum when the ratio is odd and a minimum when the ratio is even as frequency is increased further. This is called a comb-filter effect.

Reflection effects play an important role in microphone design. The shape of many microphones is that of a short cylinder where the diaphragm which responds to the incident acoustic pressure is at one end of the cylinder. Reflections at the diaphragm cause the incident pressure to increase as the frequency is increased so that the electrical signal output from the microphone becomes boosted at high frequencies. If the effect is not taken into account in the design of the microphone, it may not have a flat frequency response. A properly designed microphone has a diameter such that the first maximum in the reflection effect occurs at or above the highest frequency of interest so that the comb-filter effects at higher frequencies do not occur in the audio band. Many microphones that are designed for flat free-field response make use of the boost caused by reflections to flatten out a high-frequency response that would otherwise roll off.

Example 10 *Calculate the frequency of the first maximum in the reflection effect for a 3/4-inch microphone. Assume that the microphone can be modeled as a rigid cylinder.*

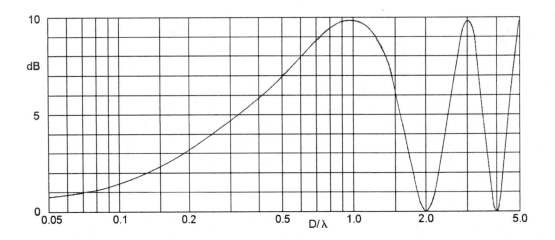

Figure 2.9: dB increase in pressure at the end of a cylinder versus $D/\lambda = Df/c$.

Solution. The maximum occurs when $D/\lambda = 1$. Because $\lambda = c/f$, the frequency is given by $f = c/D = 1131 \times 12/0.75 = 18.1\,\text{kHz}$.

Example 11 *For the microphone of the preceding example, what is the frequency at which the theoretical response would be increased by 7 dB by reflections?*

Solution. From Fig. 2.9, $D/\lambda \simeq 0.5$ at the desired frequency. Thus $f = 0.5c/D = 9.05\,\text{kHz}$.

Example 12 *A cylindrical microphone that is designed for flat frequency response when used in a free-field environment is mounted in a hole in a large wall with its diaphragm flush with the wall. Describe the effect of the wall on the frequency response of the microphone.*

Solution. The reflections at the wall cause the pressure to double at the microphone diaphragm. The pressure doubling is independent of frequency. Because the microphone is no longer in a free field, the high-frequency boost due to reflections no longer occurs. It follows, therefore, that the high-frequency response of the microphone is reduced so that it no longer has a flat frequency response.

2.16 Problems

1. *(a)* Verify that Eq. (2.17) is a solution to Eq. (2.16). *(b)* Show that the particle velocity given by Eq. (2.18) follows from the second relation in Eq. (2.14) and Eq. (2.17).

2. The peak phasor pressure p_0 at $z = 0$ in Eq. (2.17) is given by $p_0 = p_{01}(j\omega/\omega_0)/(1 + j\omega/\omega_0)$. Following Example 1, determine the time domain expression for the acoustic pressure. $[p(t) = p_0 \frac{\omega/\omega_0}{\sqrt{1+(\omega/\omega_0)^2}} \cos\left[\omega t - kz + \pi/2 - \tan^{-1}(\omega/\omega_0)\right]]$

3. What is the rms particle velocity in a plane wave that has an SPL of 90 dB? $[1.554 \times 10^{-3}\,\text{m/s}]$

4. If the density of air is halved, by what factor does the specific impedance change? [changes by a factor of $1/\sqrt{2}$]

5. A source of sound is located at the center of a hypothetical sphere of radius $r = 2\,\text{m}$. The source radiates an SPL of 86 dB over the surface of the sphere. *(a)* Solve for the acoustic intensity on the sphere. $[3.91 \times 10^{-4}\,\text{W/m}^2]$. *(b)* Solve for the total power radiated by the source. [19.7 mW]

6. Calculate the wavelength of a sound wave in meters and in feet at the frequencies 20 Hz, 200 Hz, 2 kHz, and 20 kHz. [at 20 Hz, $\lambda = 17.25\,\text{m} = 56.55\,\text{ft}$]

7. Calculate the frequency of a sinusoidal sound wave in air at $22\,°\text{C}$ which has the wavelength $\lambda = 1\,\text{m}$, $\lambda = 1\,\text{ft}$, and $\lambda = 1\,\text{in}$. [343.32 Hz, 1126.4 Hz, 13517 Hz]

8. The radiation from a loudspeaker driver in an infinite baffle is omnidirectional if the circumference of the diaphragm is less than the wavelength. *(a)* A woofer diaphragm has a piston radius of 12 cm. Calculate the highest frequency that it radiates an omni-directional wave. [458 Hz]. *(b)* Repeat the calculation for a midrange driver with a 4 cm piston radius. [1.37 kHz]

9. What is the rms, peak, and peak-to-peak particle displacement in a 100 dB 20 Hz tone? [0.039 mm, 0.055 mm, 0.11 mm]

10. In the far field of a source, the acoustic pressure varies with time as a square wave with peak values $+p_0$ and $-p_0$. The period of the wave is T_0. *(a)* Sketch the time waveform of the acoustic pressure. [zero-mean square wave with peak value p_0] *(b)* Sketch the time waveform of the particle velocity. [zero-mean square wave with peak value $p_0/\rho_0 c$] *(c)* Sketch the time waveform of the particle displacement. [zero-mean triangle wave with peak value $p_0 T_0/4\rho_0 c$]

11. Solve for the rms values of the waveforms in problem 10. [p_0, $p_0/\rho_0 c$, and $p_0 T_0/(4\sqrt{3}\rho_0 c)$]

12. *(a)* Verify that Eq. (2.35) is a solution of Eq. (2.34). *(b)* Use the second relation in Eq. (2.14) and Eq. (2.35) to verify Eq. (2.36). *(c)* Use Eqs. (2.35) and (2.36) to verify Eq. (2.37).

13. How many wavelengths must one be from a simple source in order for the magnitude of the imaginary part of the specific impedance of the wave to be less than or equal to 1/10 the real part? [1.59]

14. A microphone has an output voltage that is proportional to the particle velocity in a wave. (a) If the incident wave is a simple spherical wave and the source is located 0.5 m from the microphone, use the results of Example 6 to calculate the lower frequency at which the microphone response is boosted by 3 dB compared to its midband response. [110 Hz] (b) Calculate the lower frequency at which the microphone response is boosted by 6 dB compared to its midband response. [63.6 Hz]

15. The external measurements of a loudspeaker cabinet are 19 in by 12 in by 7 in. What is the highest frequency that the loudspeaker radiates as a simple source? [184 Hz]

16. A circular piston of radius 6 cm vibrates sinusoidally in one wall of a sealed enclosure with a peak-to-peak displacement of 8 mm. Calculate the rms volume velocity it emits if the frequency is *(a)* 100 Hz [0.0201 m^3/ s], *(b)* 1000 Hz [0.201 m^3/ s], and *(c)* 10,000 Hz [2.01 m^3/ s].

17. A midrange driver has a circular diaphragm with an effective piston diameter of 3.5 in. Calculate the required peak-to-peak diaphragm displacement if the loudspeaker is required to radiate 80 mW of acoustic power at 250 Hz into a 2π-steradian load. [2.24 mm]

18. A circular piston of radius 6 cm vibrates sinusoidally with a peak-to-peak displacement of 0.8 cm. Calculate the power it radiates into a 2π-steradian load at 100 Hz. [86.8 mW]

19. An 8-inch woofer has an effective diaphragm radius of 8 cm. At a distance $r = 1\,\text{m}$, it is required to radiate an SPL of 100 dB at 100 Hz when operated into a 2π-steradian load. *(a)* What is the total output power? [61.7 mW] *(b)* What is the peak-to-peak diaphragm displacement? [3.80 mm]

20. A circular piston of radius 6 cm vibrates sinusoidally in one wall of a sealed box at a frequency of 100 Hz. The radiated wave is a simple spherical wave. At a distance of 10 m from the source, the unweighted SPL is 80 dB. *(a)* Calculate the power radiated and the peak-to-peak piston displacement for a 4π steradian load. [124 mW, 1.35 cm] *(b)* Calculate the power radiated and the peak-to-peak displacement for a 2π steradian load. [61.8 mW, 0.675 cm]

21. The SPL at 8 m from a 200 Hz source operated against a rigid, flat wall is 110 dB. The source radiates a simple spherical wave. *(a)* Calculate the rms volume velocity emitted by the source. [0.214 m³/s] *(b)* If the source is a piston of radius 12 cm, what must be its peak-to-peak displacement? [1.07 cm] *(c)* What is the total power radiated? [39.52 W]

22. A loudspeaker radiates a simple spherical wave into 4π steradians. The SPL is 70 dB at a distance of 100 ft from the loudspeaker. *(a)* Calculate the total power radiated. [0.1147 W] *(b)* Calculate the sound pressure level at a distance of 200 ft. [64 dB]

23. A loudspeaker that radiates as a simple source is operated in the corner of a room (3 walls). It requires 10 W of electrical input power to radiate an SPL of 100 dB at 10 m from the loudspeaker. What electrical input power is required to produce the same SPL at the same distance if the loudspeaker is operated against a rigid flat wall? Assume that the volume velocity output is proportional to the electrical voltage and that the proportionality constant does not change when the loudspeaker is moved. [160 W]

24. *(a)* Solve for the distance to the far field for a 12 in woofer at 100 Hz if the diaphragm can be modeled as a flat circular piston in an infinite baffle having a radius of 12 cm. [0.033 m] *(b)* Solve for the distance to the far field for a 1-inch tweeter at 10 kHz if the diaphragm can be modeled as a flat circular piston in an infinite baffle having a radius of 1 cm. [0.023 m]

25. A 12 cm radius plane circular piston is mounted in an infinite baffle. What is the highest frequency that can be radiated by the piston if no side lobes in the pressure pattern are to be radiated? [From Fig. 2.5, $C = 4\lambda$, $f = 1.83$ kHz]

26. Solve for the two values of the on-axis distance from the piston in Example 9 at which the pressure exhibits a null. [$r/\lambda = 0.5625$ and $r/\lambda = 2.625$]

27. A flat circular piston in an infinite baffle has a radius of 10 cm. The piston vibrates with a frequency at which the disk radius is $a = 3\lambda$. *(a)* Show that the on-axis pressure exhibits a null at $r = 0$. *(b)* What is the on-axis distance to the first maximum in the pattern? [$d\,|p|\,/dr = 0$ yields $r = 8.75\lambda$]

Chapter 3

Analogous Circuits of Acoustical Systems

The two basic variables in acoustical systems are pressure p and volume velocity U. In the analogous circuits covered here, voltage is taken as the analog of pressure and current as the analog of volume velocity. Circuits of this type are called impedance analogous circuits. Circuits in which voltage is the analog of volume velocity and current is the analog of pressure are called mobility analogous circuits. In general, impedance analogs for acoustical systems are more intuitive than mobility analogs.

It is simple to justify these choices. Inside an acoustical device, e.g. a loudspeaker enclosure or a microphone capsule, the variable that can be measured the easiest is pressure. It can be measured by inserting a small probe microphone into the device. If the microphone is small, the internal pressure is not perturbed. This can be considered to be analogous to measuring the voltage in an electrical circuit. The mass of air which flows into the device must equal the mass of air which flows out. If we assume that the air density does not change, the volume of air which flows in must equal the volume of air which flows out. If electric charge is considered to be analogous to the air volume, electric current is analogous to volume velocity.

3.1 Acoustic Sources

Fig. 3.1 shows the circuit symbols for pressure and volume velocity sources. The circular symbols represent independent sources. The diamond symbols represent dependent sources.

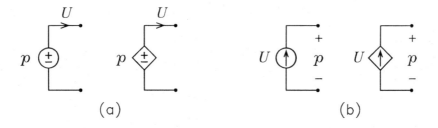

Figure 3.1: (a) Pressure sources. (b) Volume velocity sources.

3.2   Acoustic Impedance

The acoustic impedance seen by a source is defined as the ratio of the average pressure p over its surface to the total volume velocity U that it emits. While specific impedance is a property of a wave, acoustic impedance is a property of a source. The acoustic impedance is denoted by Z_A and is given by

$$Z_A = \frac{p}{U} \, \text{N s/ m}^5 \qquad (3.1)$$

As an example, consider the pulsating sphere source in Fig. 2.1(b). From Eq. (2.40), the pressure radiated by a pulsating sphere of radius r_1 is given by

$$p(r) = \frac{j\omega\rho_0 U}{1 + j\omega r/c} \, \frac{e^{-jk(r-r_1)}}{4\pi r} \qquad (3.2)$$

where U is the volume velocity emitted. The acoustic impedance seen by the sphere is given by

$$Z_A = \frac{p(r_1)}{U} = \frac{j\omega\rho_0}{1 + j\omega r_1/c} \, \frac{1}{4\pi r_1} \qquad (3.3)$$

To form a circuit which has the same impedance, we first take the reciprocal of Z_A to form an admittance Y_A given by

$$Y_A = \frac{1}{Z_A} = \frac{1}{j\omega\rho_0} \left[1 + \frac{j\omega r_1}{c} \right] 4\pi r_1 = \frac{4\pi r_1}{j\omega\rho_0} + \frac{4\pi r_1^2}{\rho_0 c} \qquad (3.4)$$

An acoustic mass has an admittance which varies inversely as $j\omega$. An acoustic resistor has an admittance which is independent of frequency. The circuit consists of a parallel mass M_A and resistor R_A given by

$$M_A = \frac{\rho_0}{4\pi r_1} \, \text{kg/ m}^4 \qquad R_A = \frac{\rho_0 c}{4\pi r_1^2} \, \text{N s/ m}^5 \qquad (3.5)$$

The circuit is shown in Fig. 3.2.

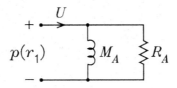

Figure 3.2: Acoustic impedance seen by a pulsating sphere.

Example 1 *Solve for the real and imaginary parts of the acoustic impedance seen by a pulsating sphere. At low frequencies, show that the real part of Z_A varies as the square of the frequency while the imaginary part varies directly with frequency.*

Solution. It follows from Fig. 3.2 and Eq. (3.5) that

$$Z_A = \frac{R_A j\omega M_A}{R_A + j\omega M_A} = \frac{\omega^2 \rho_0/4\pi c}{1 + (\omega r_1/c)^2} + \frac{j\omega\rho_0/4\pi r_1}{1 + (\omega r_1/c)^2} \simeq \frac{\omega^2 \rho_0}{4\pi c} + \frac{j\omega\rho_0}{4\pi r_1} \qquad (3.6)$$

where the approximation is valid for frequencies such that $(\omega r_1/c)^2 \ll 1$. Note that the real part is equal to the radiation resistance for a spherical wave for a 4π steradian load given by Eq. (2.44).

3.3   The Plane Wave Tube

A plane wave tube is a cylindrical tube in which an acoustic plane wave propagates. To solve for the acoustic impedance seen looking into a plane wave tube, we must first solve the wave equation for the pressure and particle velocity in the tube. Fig. 3.3 shows a flat circular piston in one end of a circular tube of cross-section S, length ℓ, and internal volume $V = S\ell$. The end of the tube is shown with an acoustic terminating impedance Z_{AL}. We assume that the piston is driven sinusoidally so that its mechanical velocity can be written $u_p(t) = u_0 \cos \omega t = \mathrm{Re}\left[u_0 e^{j\omega t}\right]$.

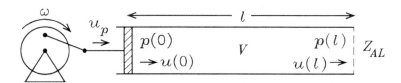

Figure 3.3: Piston radiator in one end of a plane wave tube terminated in an acoustic impedance Z_{AL}.

The pressure in the tube must satisfy the wave equation derived in Section 2.2. From the geometry of the problem, the phasor pressure p must be a function of only the z coordinate so that the wave equation for p reduces to

$$\frac{d^2 p}{dz^2} + k^2 p = 0 \tag{3.7}$$

where $k = \omega/c$ is the wavenumber. The general solution to this equation is

$$p(z) = p_0^+ e^{-jkz} + p_0^- e^{+jkz} \tag{3.8}$$

where p_0^+ is the amplitude of the forward $(+z)$ traveling wave and p_0^- is the amplitude of the backward $(-z)$ traveling wave. The particle velocity is given by $\vec{u} = -\nabla p / j\omega\rho_0$. It has only a z-directed component and is given by

$$u_z(z) = \frac{-1}{j\omega\rho_0}\frac{dp}{dz} = \frac{1}{\rho_0 c}\left(p_0^+ e^{-jkz} - p_0^- e^{+jkz}\right) \tag{3.9}$$

The time varying pressure and particle velocity are obtained by multiplying Eqs. (3.8) and (3.9) by $e^{j\omega t}$ and taking the real parts.

At the load, the ratio of the pressure to the volume velocity must be equal to the acoustic impedance Z_{AL}. Thus we can write

$$Z_{AL} = \frac{p(\ell)}{U(\ell)} = \frac{p(\ell)}{Su_z(\ell)} = \frac{\rho_0 c}{S}\frac{p_0^+ e^{-jk\ell} + p_0^- e^{+jk\ell}}{p_0^+ e^{-jk\ell} - p_0^- e^{+jk\ell}} \tag{3.10}$$

This equation can be solved for p_0^- as a function of p_0^+ to obtain

$$p_0^- = p_0^+ \frac{Z_{AL} - \rho_0 c/S}{Z_{AL} + \rho_0 c/S} e^{-j2k\ell} \tag{3.11}$$

It follows from this equation that $p_0^- = 0$ if $Z_{AL} = \rho_0 c/S$. In this case, there is only a forward propagating wave that is completely absorbed by the load.

The impedance Z_A seen by the source is given by the ratio of the pressure at the source to the volume velocity emitted by the source. With the aid Eqs. (3.8), (3.9), and (3.11), it is straightforward to show that Z_A is given by

$$Z_A = \frac{p(0)}{U(0)} = \frac{p(0)}{Su_z(0)} = \frac{\rho_0 c}{S}\frac{Z_{AL} + j(\rho_0 c/S)\tan(k\ell)}{(\rho_0 c/S) + jZ_{AL}\tan(k\ell)} \tag{3.12}$$

Infinitely Long Tube

The first case of special interest is that of the infinitely long tube for which no backward wave exists, i.e. $p_0^- = 0$. It follows from Eqs. (3.8) and (3.9) that the pressure and particle velocity in the tube can be written

$$p(z) = p_0^+ e^{-jkz} \qquad u_z(z) = \frac{p_0^+}{\rho_0 c} e^{-jkz} \qquad (3.13)$$

These equations are the same as for a plane wave in free air. The acoustic impedance seen by the piston is an acoustic resistance given by

$$R_A = \frac{p(0)}{U(0)} = \frac{p(0)}{S u_z(0)} = \frac{\rho_0 c}{S} \, \mathrm{N\,s/\,m^5} \qquad (3.14)$$

The analogous circuit is given in Fig. 3.4(a).

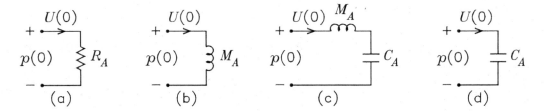

Figure 3.4: (a) Impedance of an infinitely long tube. (b) Impedance of an open-ended tube of length less than $\lambda/10$. (c) Impedance of a closed tube. (d) Impedance of a closed tube of length less than $\lambda/10$.

For a finite length tube, Eq. (3.11) predicts that there is no reflected load if $Z_{AL} = \rho_0 c/S$. In this case, the tube is said to have a matched load and Eq. (3.12) predicts that the impedance looking into the tube is the same as for an infinitely long tube.

Example 2 *Fig. 3.5(a) shows a loudspeaker driver in one end of an infinitely long tube having an internal diameter of 10 cm. The front of the loudspeaker radiates into half space and the back radiates into the tube. At a frequency of 200 Hz, the SPL is 80 dB at 3 m from the loudspeaker on the free-air side. The wave radiated on the free-air side is a simple spherical wave. What is the power radiated on each side of the diaphragm?*

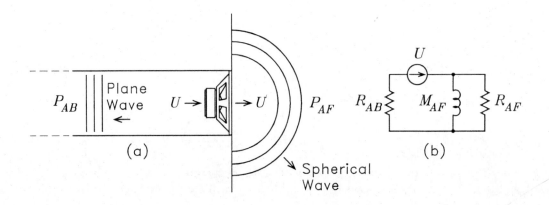

Figure 3.5: (a) Small loudspeaker mounted in one end of infinitely long tube. (b) Analogous circuit.

Solution. Fig. 3.5(b) shows the analogous circuit. An SPL of $80\,\mathrm{dB}$ corresponds to $p_{rms} = 0.2\,\mathrm{Pa}$. Thus $I = 0.2^2/407 = 9.83 \times 10^{-5}\,\mathrm{W/m^2}$. The power radiated to the front is $P_{AF} = I \times 2\pi 3^2 = 5.56\,\mathrm{mW}$. By Eq. (2.45), $P_{AF} = \omega^2 \rho_0 U_{rms}^2/2\pi c$. Solution for U_{rms} yields $U_{rms} = \sqrt{2\pi c P_{AF}/\omega^2 \rho_0} = 2.54 \times 10^{-3}\,\mathrm{m^3/s}$. The power radiated to the back is $P_{AB} = U_{rms}^2 R_{AB} = U_{rms}^2 \rho_0 c/S = 0.335\,\mathrm{W}$. This is 60 times larger than P_{AF}. This example illustrates that a driver is more efficient when radiating into a tube than when radiating into free air. This is the basic reason that a higher efficiency can be obtained from a horn-loaded driver, i.e. one which radiates into a horn, compared to a direct radiator driver.

Open-Ended Tube

If the end of the tube radiates into free air, it can be shown that a very good approximation to the pressure at the end of the tube is $p(\ell) \simeq 0$. In this case, the load impedance is $Z_{AL} \simeq 0$. It follows from Eq. (3.12) that the impedance seen by the source is given by

$$Z_A = \frac{\rho_0 c}{S} \frac{j(\rho_0 c/S)\tan(k\ell)}{(\rho_0 c/S)} = j\frac{\rho_0 c}{S}\tan(k\ell) \qquad (3.15)$$

It is impossible to make an analogous circuit for Z_A from this equation that holds at all frequencies. If the frequency is low enough, $k\ell = \omega\ell/c$ is small, a small argument approximation for $\tan(k\ell)$ can be used which leads to an analogous circuit. This approximation is $\tan(k\ell) \simeq k\ell$. It leads to the relation

$$Z_A = j\omega\frac{\rho_0 \ell}{S} = j\omega M_A \qquad \text{where} \qquad M_A = \frac{\rho_0 \ell}{S}\,\mathrm{kg/m^4} \qquad (3.16)$$

This approximation is valid for $\ell \le \lambda/10$. An acoustic mass has an impedance that is directly proportional to $j\omega$. Thus the analogous circuit for Z_A is a mass. The circuit is shown in Fig. 3.4(b). This is the basic model which we use for the air in a vent or port in a loudspeaker enclosure.

Closed Tube

If the terminating impedance at the end of the tube is a rigid cap, the particle velocity at $z = \ell$ must be zero. Thus $U(\ell) = 0$ so that $Z_{AL} = p(\ell)/U(\ell) = \infty$. To obtain the acoustic impedance seen by the source, we divide the numerator and denominator of Eq. (3.12) by Z_{AL} and take the limit as $Z_{AL} \to \infty$ to obtain

$$Z_A = \frac{\rho_0 c}{S}\frac{1}{j\tan(k\ell)} = -j\frac{\rho_0 c}{S}\cot(k\ell) \qquad (3.17)$$

If the frequency is low enough, $k\ell = \omega\ell/c$ is small and the small argument approximation $\cot(k\ell) \simeq 1/(k\ell) - k\ell/3$ can be used to obtain an analogous circuit. It leads to the relation

$$Z_A \simeq \frac{-j\rho_0 c}{S}\left[\frac{1}{k\ell} - \frac{k\ell}{3}\right] = \frac{-j\rho_0 c}{S}\left[\frac{c}{\omega\ell} - \frac{\omega\ell}{3c}\right] = \frac{\rho_0 c^2}{j\omega V} + \frac{j\omega\rho_0 \ell}{3S} \qquad (3.18)$$

where $V = S\ell$. An acoustic compliance has an impedance that varies inversely as $j\omega$. An acoustic mass has an impedance that is directly proportional to $j\omega$. The analogous circuit for Z_A is a series mass and compliance. The circuit is shown in Fig. 3.4(c), where C_A and M_A are given by

$$C_A = \frac{V}{\rho_0 c^2}\,\mathrm{m^5/N} \qquad M_A = \frac{\rho_0 \ell}{3S}\,\mathrm{kg/m^4} \qquad (3.19)$$

If the frequency is low enough, the reactance of the acoustic mass is negligible compared to that of the compliance and the circuit can be approximated by that given in Fig. 3.4(d). This second circuit gives acceptable results for frequencies such that $\ell \le \lambda/10$.

Because C_A is not a function of geometry, the circuit in Fig. 3.4(d) is valid for any closed volume provided its largest dimension is less than $\lambda/10$. This is the basic model which we use for the air in a microphone capsule and in a loudspeaker enclosure.

3.4 Acoustic Resistance

Acoustic resistance is associated with dissipative losses that occur when there is a viscous flow of air through a fine mesh screen or through a capillary tube. Fig. 3.6(a) illustrates a fine mesh screen with a volume velocity U flowing through it. The pressure difference across the screen is given by $p = p_1 - p_2$, where p_1 is the pressure on the side that U enters and p_2 is the pressure on the side that U exits. The pressure difference is related to the volume velocity through the screen by

$$p = p_1 - p_2 = R_A U \tag{3.20}$$

where R_A (kg/ m^4 s) is the acoustic resistance of the screen. The circuit is shown in Fig. 3.6(b).

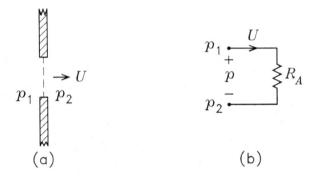

Figure 3.6: (a) An acoustic resistance consisting of a fine mesh screen. (b) Analogous circuit.

Theoretical formulas for acoustic resistances are generally not available. The values are usually determined by experiments. Table 3.1 gives the acoustic resistances of typical screens as a function of the area S of the screen, the number of wires in the screen, and the diameter of the wires. Fibrous materials such as felt and fiberglass also exhibit an acoustic resistance, the value of which can be varied by varying the density of the material. For example, a tube that is filled with fiberglass has an analogous circuit that consists of an inductor that represents the acoustic mass of the air in the tube in series with a resistor that represents the acoustic resistance of the fiberglass.

Table 3.1: Acoustic Resistance of a Screen of Area S

Number of wires per inch	Wire diameter centimeters	Acoustic Resistance N s/ m^5
30	0.033	$5.67/S$
50	0.022	$5.88/S$
100	0.0115	$9.10/S$
120	0.0092	$13.5/S$
200	0.0057	$24.6/S$

Perforated sheets are often used as an acoustic resistance in applications where an acoustic mass in series with the resistance is acceptable. Fig. 3.7(a) illustrates the geometry. If the holes in the sheet have centers that are spaced more than one diameter apart and the radius a of the holes satisfies the inequality $0.01/\sqrt{f} < a < 10/f$, where f is the frequency and a is in m, the acoustic impedance of the sheet is given by

$$Z_A = \frac{\rho_0}{N\pi a^2}\left\{\sqrt{2\omega\mu}\left[\frac{t}{a} + 2\left(1 - \frac{\pi a^2}{b^2}\right)\right] + j\omega\left[t + 1.7a\left(1 - \frac{a}{b}\right)\right]\right\} \tag{3.21}$$

where N is the number of holes. The parameter μ is the kinematic coefficient of viscosity. For air at $20\,^{\circ}\mathrm{C}$ and $0.76\,\mathrm{m}$ Hg, $\mu \simeq 1.56 \times 10^{-5}\,\mathrm{m^2/s}$. This parameter varies approximately as $T^{1.7}/P_0$, where T is the Kelvin temperature and P_0 is the atmospheric pressure.

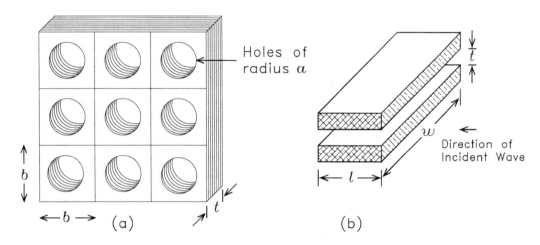

Figure 3.7: (a) Perforated sheet of thickness t having holes of radius a spaced a distance b on centers. (b) Geometry of the narrow slit.

A tube having a very small diameter is another example of an acoustic element which exhibits both a resistance and a mass. If the tube radius a in meters satisfies the inequality $a < 0.002/\sqrt{f}$, the acoustic impedance is given by

$$Z_A = \frac{8\eta\ell}{\pi a^4} + j\omega\frac{4\rho_0\ell'}{3\pi a^2} \tag{3.22}$$

where ℓ is the actual length of the tube and ℓ' is the length including end corrections. The parameter η is the viscosity coefficient. For air, $\eta = 1.86 \times 10^{-5}\,\mathrm{N\,s/m^2}$ at $20\,^{\circ}\mathrm{C}$ and $0.76\,\mathrm{m}$ Hg. This parameter varies with temperature as $T^{0.7}$, where T is the Kelvin temperature. If the radius of the tube satisfies the inequality $0.01/\sqrt{f} < a < 10/f$, the acoustic impedance is given by

$$Z_A = \frac{\rho_0}{\pi a^2}\sqrt{2\omega\mu}\left(\frac{\ell}{a}+2\right) + j\omega\frac{\rho_0\ell'}{\pi a^2} \tag{3.23}$$

For a tube with a radius such that $0.002/\sqrt{f} < a < 0.01/\sqrt{f}$, interpolation must be used between the two equations.

A narrow slit also exhibits both acoustic resistance and mass. Fig. 3.7(b) shows the geometry of such a slit. If the height t of the slit in meters satisfies the inequality $t < 0.003/\sqrt{f}$, the acoustic impedance of the slit, neglecting end corrections for the mass term, is given by

$$Z_A = \frac{12\eta\ell}{t^3 w} + j\omega\frac{6\rho_0\ell}{5wt} \tag{3.24}$$

3.5 Acoustic Compliance

We have seen that a short closed-end tube has an acoustic impedance that is modeled as a compliance. Acoustic compliance is a parameter that is associated with any volume of air that is compressed by an applied force without an acceleration of its center of gravity.

To illustrate an acoustic compliance, consider an enclosed volume of air as illustrated in Fig. 3.8(a). A piston of area S is shown in one wall of the enclosure. When a force f is applied to the piston, it moves and compresses the air. Denote the piston displacement by x and its velocity by u. When the air is compressed, a restoring force is generated which can be written $f = k_M x$, where k_M is the spring constant. (This assumes that the displacement is not too large or the process cannot be modeled with linear equations.) The mechanical compliance is defined as the reciprocal of the spring constant, i.e. $C_M = 1/k_M$. Thus we can write

$$f = k_M x = \frac{x}{C_M} = \frac{1}{C_M} \int u\, dt \qquad (3.25)$$

This equation involves the mechanical variables f and u. We convert it to one that involves acoustic variables p and U by writing $f = pS$ and $u = U/S$ to obtain

$$p = \frac{1}{S^2 C_M} \int U\, dt = \frac{1}{C_A} \int U\, dt \qquad (3.26)$$

This equation defines the acoustic compliance C_A of the air in the volume. It is given by

$$C_A = S^2 C_M \;\mathrm{m}^5/\mathrm{N} \qquad (3.27)$$

$$(\mathrm{a}) \qquad\qquad\qquad\qquad (\mathrm{b})$$

Figure 3.8: (a) Closed volume of air that acts as acoustic compliance. (b) Analogous circuit.

An integration in the time domain corresponds to a division by $j\omega$ for phasor variables. It follows from Eq. (3.26) that the phasor pressure is related to the phasor volume velocity by $p = U/j\omega C_A$. Thus the acoustic impedance of the compliance is

$$Z_A = \frac{p}{U} = \frac{1}{j\omega C_A} \qquad (3.28)$$

An impedance which varies inversely with $j\omega$ is a capacitor. The analogous circuit is shown in Fig. 3.8(b). The figure shows one side of the capacitor connected to ground. This is because the pressure in a volume of air is measured with respect to zero pressure. One node of an acoustic compliance always connects to the ground node, i.e. the zero pressure node. If the maximum dimension of an enclosed volume of air is less than $\lambda/16$ at the operating frequency, the acoustic compliance of the volume of air is given by the expression for C_A in Eq. (3.19).

Example 3 *The piston in Fig. 3.8(a) has a radius $a = 6$ cm and vibrates sinusoidally at a frequency of 60 Hz. The SPL inside the enclosure is 120 dB. The enclosed volume is $V = 0.025\,\mathrm{m}^3$. Solve for the peak-to-peak displacement of the piston.*

Solution. The rms pressure in the volume is $p_{rms} = \left(2 \times 10^{-5}\right) 10^{120/20} = 20\,\mathrm{Pa}$. The enclosure compliance is $C_A = V/\rho_0 c^2 = 1.78 \times 10^{-7}\,\mathrm{m}^5/\mathrm{N}$. The phasor volume velocity emitted by the piston is $U = Su = Sj\omega x$, where u is the piston velocity and x is its displacement. The phasor pressure in the enclosure is given by $p = U/j\omega C_A = Sj\omega x/j\omega C_A = Sx/C_A$, which is independent of frequency. It follows that $x = pC_A/S$. The peak-to-peak piston displacement is $x_{p-p} = 2\sqrt{2}p_{rms}C_A/\pi a^2 = 0.89\,\mathrm{mm}$.

3.6 Acoustic Mass

Any volume of air that is accelerated without being compressed acts as an acoustic mass. Consider the cylindrical tube of air illustrated in Fig. 3.9(a) having a length ℓ and cross-section S. The mass of the air in the tube is $M_M = \rho_0 S \ell$. If the air is moved with a velocity u, the force required is given by $f = M_M du/dt$. The volume velocity of the air through the tube is $U = Su$ and the pressure difference between the two ends is $p = p_1 - p_2 = f/S$. It follows from these relations that the pressure difference p can be related to the volume velocity U as follows:

$$p = p_1 - p_2 = \frac{M_M}{S} \frac{du}{dt} = \frac{M_M}{S^2} \frac{dU}{dt} = M_A \frac{dU}{dt} \tag{3.29}$$

where M_A is the acoustic mass of the air in the volume that is given by

$$M_A = \frac{M_M}{S^2} = \frac{\rho_0 \ell}{S} \, \text{kg/m}^4 \tag{3.30}$$

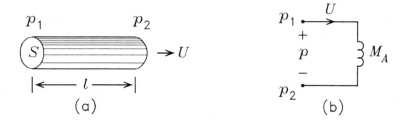

Figure 3.9: (a) Cylindrical tube of air which behaves as acoustic mass. (b) Analogous circuit.

A differentiation in the time domain corresponds to a multiplication by $j\omega$ for sinusoidal phasor variables. It follows from Eq. (3.29) that the phasor pressure is related to the phasor volume velocity by $p = j\omega M_A U$. Thus the acoustic impedance of the mass is

$$Z_A = \frac{p}{U} = j\omega M_A \tag{3.31}$$

An electrical impedance which is proportional to $j\omega$ is an inductor. The analogous circuit is shown in Fig. 3.9(b). For a tube of air to act as a pure acoustic mass, each particle of air in the tube must move with the same velocity. This is strictly true only if the frequency is low enough. Otherwise, the motion of the air particles must be modeled by a wave equation. An often used criterion that the air in the tube act as a pure acoustic mass is that its length must satisfy $\ell \leq \lambda/8$, where λ is the wavelength.

An acoustic mass is used to model the air in a vent tube in loudspeaker enclosures. The geometry of such a tube is shown in Fig. 3.10. The end of the tube that is installed in the enclosure wall is said to be flanged and the other end unflanged. When the air in the tube moves, there is an effective volume of air outside the tube on both ends that moves with the same velocity as the air inside the tube. To accurately model the total air motion, the two air volumes outside the tube must be added to the air volume inside the tube. The outside air volumes are called end corrections. We denote the effective length of the air outside the tube by ℓ_f for the flanged end and by ℓ_{uf} for the unflanged end. If S is the area of the tube, the end corrections are given by

$$\ell_f = 0.8488\sqrt{\frac{S}{\pi}} \qquad \ell_{uf} = 0.6132\sqrt{\frac{S}{\pi}} \tag{3.32}$$

Example 4 *Calculate the physical length of a tube of air that is flanged on one end and unflanged on the other end if it is to have an acoustic mass M_A.*

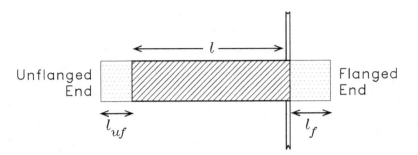

Figure 3.10: Flanged end correction ℓ_f and unflanged end correction ℓ_{uf} for a tube of air.

Solution. Let the length of the tube be denoted by ℓ and denote the area by S. The effective acoustic mass of the air in the tube is $M_A = \rho_0 \left(\ell + \ell_f + \ell_{uf}\right)/S = \rho_0 \left(\ell + 1.462\sqrt{S/\pi}\right)/S$. Solution for ℓ yields

$$\ell = \frac{M_A S}{\rho_0} - 1.462\sqrt{\frac{S}{\pi}} \tag{3.33}$$

Example 5 *Fig. 3.11(a) shows an enclosure with hollow tubes connected in two walls. Solve for the acoustical analogous circuit.*

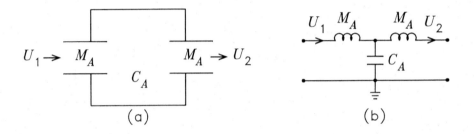

Figure 3.11: (a) Enclosure with tubes connected in two walls. (b) Acoustical analogous circuit.

Solution. The enclosure air acts as an acoustic compliance with one terminal grounded. The air in each tube acts as an acoustic mass. Fig. 3.11(b) shows the analogous circuit. It is in the form of an acoustic low-pass filter.

Example 6 *Fig. 3.12(a) shows the diagram of a Helmholtz resonator. It consists of a cavity of air with a tube that connects the air in the cavity to the outside. Solve for the acoustical analogous circuit of the system and the resonance frequency of the resonator.*

Solution. The analogous circuit is shown in Fig. 3.12(b). The impedance is given by $Z_A = j\omega M_A - j/\omega C_A$. The Helmholtz resonance frequency f_0 is the frequency at which $Z_A = 0$. It is given by

$$f_0 = \frac{\omega_0}{2\pi} = \frac{1}{2\pi\sqrt{M_A C_A}} \text{ Hz} \tag{3.34}$$

When excited at this frequency, the volume velocity in the tube increases markedly. A familiar example of this effect occurs when one blows over the neck of a jug, causing a resonant sound. When filled with a fibrous material such as fiberglass, a Helmholtz resonator acts as an acoustic absorber. Called an acoustic trap, such devices can be used to damp standing waves in rooms.

Figure 3.12: (a) Helmholtz resonator consisting of an acoustic mass and an acoustic compliance. (b) Analogous circuit.

3.7 Acoustic Impedance on a Piston in a Baffle

Fig. 3.13(a) illustrates a circular piston of radius a in an infinite baffle. A force f is applied to the piston which causes it to move with a velocity u. The acoustic impedance of the air load on one side of the piston is the ratio of the average acoustic pressure on that side to the volume velocity emitted. To calculate the pressure, we first calculate the force on the piston due to the air particles. The average pressure is then the force divided by the piston area.

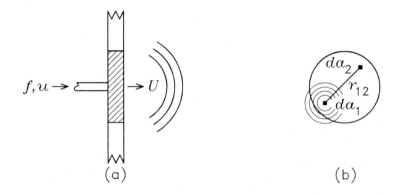

Figure 3.13: (a) Circular piston in an infinite baffle. (b) Front view of the piston.

Consider the front view of the piston shown in Fig. 3.13(b). We wish to write the expression for the force generated on area element da_2 due to the acoustic pressure radiated by da_1. Let r_{12} be the distance between the two elements. The volume velocity emitted by da_1 is $dU_1 = uda_1$. The pressure p_2 at da_2 due to the radiation from da_1 is that of a simple spherical wave radiated into a 2π-steradian load and is given by

$$p_2 = j\omega\rho_0 dU \frac{e^{-jkr_{12}}}{2\pi r_{12}} = j\omega\rho_0 uda \frac{e^{-jkr_{12}}}{2\pi r_{12}} \qquad (3.35)$$

The force on da_2 due to the radiation from da_1 is given by $df_2 = p_2 da_2$. The total force on the disk caused by the radiation from da_1 is given by the integral of df_2 over the surface of the disk. However, this is not the total force on the disk. To obtain the total force, the contributions of the radiation from all area elements must be summed. Thus the expression must be integrated a second time in da_1 to obtain the total force. It is given by

$$f = \frac{j\omega\rho_0 u}{2\pi} \int_S \left[\int_S \frac{e^{-jkr_{12}}}{r_{12}} da_2 \right] da_1 \qquad (3.36)$$

This is not a simple integral to evaluate. Only one of the two integrals can be evaluated in closed form, and this requires some skill in exploiting the symmetry of the problem. Fortunately, the final evaluation leads to functions which are tabulated in the literature. The force is given by

$$f = \pi a^2 \rho_0 cu \left[\left(1 - \frac{J_1(2ka)}{ka} \right) + j \frac{H_1(2ka)}{ka} \right] \tag{3.37}$$

where $k = \omega/c$, J_1 is the Bessel function of the first kind of order one, and H_1 is the Struve function of order one. These functions represent the infinite mathematical series

$$J_1(x) = \frac{x}{2} - \frac{x^3}{2^2 \times 4} + \frac{x^5}{2^2 \times 4^2 \times 6} - \cdots \tag{3.38}$$

$$H_1(x) = \frac{2}{\pi} \left[\frac{x^2}{3} - \frac{x^4}{3^2 \times 5} + \frac{x^6}{3^2 \times 5^2 \times 7} - \cdots \right] \tag{3.39}$$

The average pressure p on the front of the disk is given by $p = f/S$, where $S = \pi a^2$. The acoustic impedance of the air load on the piston is given by $Z_A = p/U$, where $U = Su$. It follows that Z_A is given by

$$Z_A = \frac{1}{S^2} \frac{f}{u} = \frac{\rho_0 c}{\pi a^2} \left[\left(1 - \frac{J_1(2ka)}{ka} \right) + j \frac{H_1(2ka)}{ka} \right] \tag{3.40}$$

For this result to be useful, we seek a circuit model which has an impedance that approximates Z_A. To obtain this, we write the normalized acoustic admittance as follows:

$$\frac{\rho_0 c Y_A}{\pi a^2} = \frac{\rho_0 c}{\pi a^2 Z_A} = \left[\left(1 - \frac{J_1(2\omega a/c)}{(\omega a/c)} \right) + j \frac{H_1(2\omega a/c)}{(\omega a/c)} \right]^{-1} \tag{3.41}$$

where $Y_A = G_A + jB_A$.

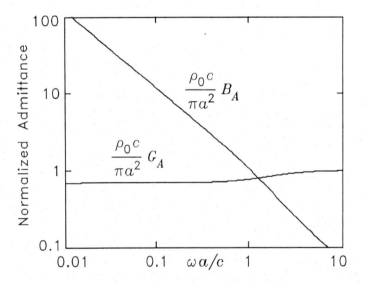

Figure 3.14: Plots of real and imaginary parts of normalized acoustic admittance seen by one side of plane circular piston in infinite baffle.

Plots of the normalized G_A and B_A as a function of normalized frequency are similar to the ones shown in Fig. 3.14. These are not exact plots because some of the ripples in the curves for $ka > 1$ which cannot be modeled by analogous circuits are smoothed out. However, the asymptotic behaviors of the curves are correct. We see that the imaginary part of the admittance exhibits a slope of -1 dec/dec. The analogous circuit which exhibits this behavior is an acoustic mass. The real part of the admittance exhibits a high-pass shelving transfer function. The analogous circuit which exhibits this behavior is an acoustic resistance in series with a parallel acoustic resistance and compliance. The completed circuit is shown in Fig. 3.15(a). It can be shown that the element values are given by

$$M_{A1} = \frac{8\rho_0}{3\pi^2 a} \qquad R_{A1} = \left(\frac{128}{9\pi^2} - 1\right)\frac{\rho_0 c}{\pi a^2} = \frac{0.4410\rho_0 c}{\pi a^2} \tag{3.42}$$

$$R_{A2} = \frac{\rho_0 c}{\pi a^2} \qquad C_{A1} = \frac{5.94 a^3}{\rho_0 c^2} \tag{3.43}$$

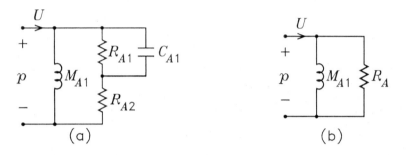

Figure 3.15: (a) Analogous circuit for radiation impedance on one side of circular piston in infinite baffle. (b) Circuit for $ka < 1$.

The piston range is defined as the frequency band for which $ka \leq 1$, or equivalently, $\lambda \geq 2\pi a = C$, where C is the circumference of the piston. In this range, the compliance C_{A1} is an open circuit so that the sum resistance $R_{A1} + R_{A2}$ can be considered to be a single resistor R_A. The analogous circuit for the piston range is given in Fig. 3.15(b), where R_A is given by

$$R_A = R_{A1} + R_{A2} = \frac{128\rho_0 c}{9\pi^3 a^2} \tag{3.44}$$

The circuits of Fig. 3.15 represent the acoustic load impedance on only one side of the piston. If the piston radiates into free air on both sides of the infinite baffle, the actual load impedance is doubled so that the inductor and resistors in the circuit are doubled and the capacitor is halved.

Example 7 *If the acoustic mass part of the air load impedance on one side of a plane circular piston in an infinite baffle is modeled as a tube of air, solve for the length of the tube. Assume that the tube has a cross section equal to that of the piston.*

Solution. Let the length of the tube be denoted by ℓ_f. To solve for ℓ_f, we equate the acoustic mass of the tube of air to M_{A1} in Eq. (3.42) to obtain $\rho_0 \ell_f / S = 8\rho_0 / 3\pi^2 a$. This can be solved for ℓ_f to obtain

$$\ell_f = \frac{8S}{3\pi^2 a} = \frac{8}{3\pi}\sqrt{\frac{S}{\pi}} = 0.8488\sqrt{\frac{S}{\pi}} \tag{3.45}$$

where $a = \sqrt{S/\pi}$. This is the same as ℓ_f in Eq. (3.32) for the flanged end correction for the acoustic mass of a tube mounted in an infinite baffle.

3.8   Acoustic Impedance on a Piston in a Tube

Fig. 3.16 illustrates a piston in the end of a long tube. Although it may seem that the solution for the radiation impedance for this case is as straightforward as that for the infinite baffle case, it is not. This is because the radiation from an area element on the piston cannot be modeled as a simple spherical wave into a 2π-steradian load as is done in Eq. (3.35). Indeed, a closed-form expression corresponding to that in Eq. (3.35) cannot be obtained.

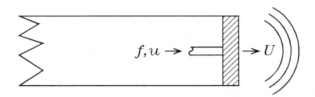

Figure 3.16: Plane circular piston in one end of a long tube.

It can be shown that the analogous circuit for the piston has the same form as that for the piston in an infinite baffle, only the element values are different. The circuit is given in Fig. 3.15(a). The element values are given by

$$M_{A1} = \frac{0.6133\rho_0}{\pi a} \qquad R_{A1} = \frac{0.5045\rho_0 c}{\pi a^2} \qquad R_{A2} = \frac{\rho_0 c}{\pi a^2} \qquad C_{A1} = \frac{0.55\pi^2 a^3}{\rho_0 c^2} \qquad (3.46)$$

At low frequencies where C_{A1} is an open circuit, the circuit for the piston is that given in Fig. 3.15(b), where R_A is given by

$$R_A = R_{A1} + R_{A2} = \frac{1.5045\rho_0 c}{\pi a^2} \qquad (3.47)$$

This is the piston range circuit that is valid when the wavelength is larger than the circumference of the piston.

Example 8 *If the acoustic mass part of the air load impedance on one side of a plane circular piston at the end of a long tube is modeled as a tube of air, solve for the length of the tube. Assume that the tube has a cross section equal to that of the piston.*

Solution. Let the length of the tube be denoted by ℓ_{uf}. To solve for ℓ_{uf}, we equate the acoustic mass of the tube to M_{A1} in Eq. (3.46) to obtain $\rho_0 \ell_{uf}/S = 0.6133\rho_0/\pi a$. This can be solved for ℓ_{uf} to obtain

$$\ell_{uf} = 0.6133\sqrt{\frac{S}{\pi}} \qquad (3.48)$$

where $a = \sqrt{S/\pi}$. This is the same as Eq. (3.32) for the unflanged end correction for the acoustic mass of a tube of air.

3.9   Radiation Impedance on a Piston in Free Air

When a loudspeaker is operated in free air without a baffle, the low-frequency radiation from the front and the back of the diaphragm tend to cancel so that the bass response is almost totally missing. At higher frequencies, the radiation from the two sides becomes directional and cancellation no longer occurs. A model that is often used for the loudspeaker diaphragm in this case is a flat piston in free air. Fig. 3.17(a) illustrates the piston geometry.

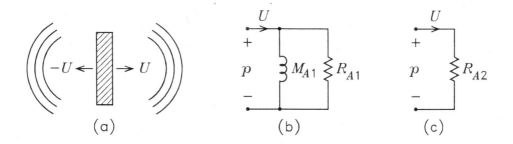

Figure 3.17: (a) Plane circular piston in free air. (b) Analogous circuit for radiation impedance on both sides of piston for $ka < 0.5$. (c) Analogous circuit for $ka > 5$.

It is not possible to model the acoustic radiation impedance on the piston with an analogous circuit that has frequency independent circuit elements. Also, there is no circuit model for the frequency range for which $0.5 < ka < 5$. For $ka < 0.5$, the circuit in Fig. 3.17(b) can be used to predict the radiation impedance on both sides of the piston. The element values are given by

$$M_{A1} = \frac{8\rho_0}{3\pi^2 a} \qquad R_{A1} = \frac{3.849\rho_0 c^3}{\omega^2 a^4} \tag{3.49}$$

where a is the radius of the piston. For $ka > 5$, the circuit in Fig. 3.17(c) holds. The acoustic resistor in this circuit is given by

$$R_{A2} = \frac{2\rho_0 c}{\pi a^2} \tag{3.50}$$

The circuit elements for the piston in free air are for the radiation impedance on both sides of the piston. In contrast, the elements given above for the piston in an infinite baffle are for one side only. The elements for the piston in a long tube are for the side of the piston that radiates outside the tube.

3.10 Problems

1. *(a)* A pulsating sphere has a nominal radius of 0.1 m. Calculate the acoustic admittance seen by the sphere for $f = 100\,\text{Hz}$. [$3.09 \times 10^{-4} - j1.70 \times 10^{-3}$] *(b)* Calculate the acoustic impedance. [$104 + j571$] *(c)* Calculate the acoustic impedance using the approximation given in Eq. (3.6). [$107 + j590$]

2. *(a)* An infinitely long tube has a diameter of 6 cm. Calculate the acoustic resistance seen looking into the tube. [1.44×10^5] *(b)* The tube is terminated with a rigid cap at a distance of 20 cm from the source. Calculate the acoustic compliance and acoustic mass seen looking into the tube. [4.03×10^{-9}, 27.8] *(c)* If the end cap is removed from the tube, calculate the acoustic mass seen looking into the tube. [83.5]

3. *(a)* A piston in the end of an infinitely long tube having a diameter of 6 cm radiates an average acoustic power of 1 mW into the tube. Calculate the SPL in the tube. [116 dB] *(b)* The tube is terminated with a rigid cap a distance of 20 cm from the piston. Calculate the SPL in the tube if the peak piston displacement is 1 mm and the frequency is 100 Hz. [148 dB] *(c)* Calculate the SPL in the 20 cm long tube if the end cap is removed. [130 dB]

4. A loudspeaker driver is located in one end of an infinitely long tube having a radius of 10 cm. At $f = 150\,\text{Hz}$, the loudspeaker produces an SPL of 100 dB inside the tube. If the loudspeaker radiates a simple spherical wave into 4π steradians outside the tube, calculate the SPL at a distance of 1 m from the loudspeaker. [56.7 dB]

5. A screen is to be used as the damping element in a loudspeaker port. The port is a tube with a diameter of 4 in. The acoustic resistance is to be $725\,\mathrm{N\,s/\,m^5}$. Use Table 3.1 to select a screen to achieve this resistance. Hint: multiply R_A by the port area S to obtain the table value. [50 wires per inch with a wire diameter of 0.022 cm]

6. A perforated sheet like the one shown in Fig. 3.7 has 9 holes with the dimensions $a = 0.5$ in and $b = 2$ in. It is desired to achieve an acoustic mass of $7\,\mathrm{kg/\,m^4}$ with the sheet. (a) What must be the thickness of the sheet? [0.428 in] (b) What is the acoustic resistance of the sheet at 50 Hz? [$63.1\,\mathrm{N\,s/\,m^5}$]

7. A sealed box with an internal volume V has a piston of area S in one wall. The piston undergoes a displacement x into the box. What is the force exerted by the air on the piston? [$\rho_0 c^2 S^2 x / V$]

8. (a) A tube of air has a cross-sectional area S and is unflanged on both ends. What is its length ℓ if it is to have an acoustic mass M_A? [$M_A S / \rho_0 - 1.226\sqrt{S/\pi}$] (b) If the tube is flanged on both ends, what is the length? [$M_A S / \rho_0 - 1.698\sqrt{S/\pi}$]

9. (a) Fig. 3.18(a) shows a musical jug, with a diameter of 10 in and a height of 12 in. Solve for the Helmholtz resonance frequency of the jug. Model the neck as a tube that is flanged on one end and unflanged on the other. [53.2 Hz] (b) Draw the acoustical analogous circuit of the system shown in Fig. 3.18(b).

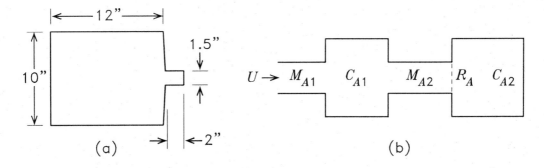

Figure 3.18: Figures for Problem 9.

10. The acoustic impedance seen by one side of a circular piston mounted in an infinite baffle for $ka \leq 1$ has the analogous circuit given in Fig. 3.15(b), where $k = \omega/c$, a is the radius of the piston, $M_{A1} = 8\rho_0/3\pi^2 a$, and $R_A = 128\rho_0 c/9\pi^3 a^2$. (a) Show that Z_A is given by

$$Z_A = \frac{j\omega M_{A1}}{1 + j\omega M_{A1}/R_A} = \frac{\omega^2 M_{A1}^2/R_A}{1 + \omega^2 M_{A1}^2/R_A^2} + j\omega \frac{M_{A1}}{1 + \omega^2 M_{A1}^2/R_A^2}$$

(b) For low frequencies such that $\omega^2 M_{A1}^2/R_A^2 \ll 1$, show that the expression reduces to

$$Z_A \simeq \frac{\omega^2 \rho_0}{2\pi c} + j\omega \frac{8\rho_0}{3\pi^2 a}$$

(c) Show that this impedance can be represented by an acoustic mass in series with a resistor which varies as the square of the frequency.

11. Fig. 3.19(a) shows two circular pistons in an infinite baffle. The upper piston has a radius a_1 and emits a volume velocity U_1. The average pressure at its surface is p_1. The lower piston has a radius a_2 and emits a volume velocity U_2. The average pressure at its surface is p_2. The center-to-center separation between the two pistons is d_{12}. Suppose the second piston is held stationary while the first piston is

driven. The pressure p_1 at the surface of the first piston is due to the force required to drive the air load to the right of that piston. At low frequencies, the ratio of p_1 to U_1 can be approximated by a pure mass reactance given by $p_1/U_1 = j\omega M_{A1}$, where $M_{A1} = 8\rho_0/3\pi^2 a_1$. Now suppose the first piston is blocked and the second piston is driven at the same frequency. The pressure at the first piston can be calculated from the spherical wave formula

$$p_1 = \frac{j\omega\rho_0 U_2}{2\pi d_{12}}e^{-jkd_{12}} \simeq \frac{j\omega\rho_0 U_2}{2\pi d_{12}}$$

where the approximation assumes that $d_{12} \ll \lambda$ so that $\exp(-jkd_{12}) \simeq 1$. Use superposition of U_1 and U_2 to show that the total pressure at the face of each piston is given by

$$p_1 = j\omega M_{A1}U_1 + \frac{j\omega\rho_0}{2\pi d_{12}}U_2 \qquad p_2 = j\omega M_{A2}U_2 + \frac{j\omega\rho_0}{2\pi d_{12}}U_1$$

where $M_{A2} = 8\rho_0/3\pi^2 a_2$.

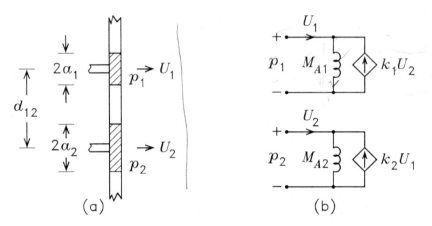

Figure 3.19: (a) Figure for problem 11. (b) Figure for problem 12.

12. From the equations for p_1 and p_2 in problem 11, show that the low-frequency analogous circuits for the two-piston system are the circuits given in Fig. 3.19(b). What are the equations for the mutual coupling coefficients k_1 and k_2? [$k_1 = 3\pi a_1/16d_{12}$, $k_2 = 3\pi a_2/16d_{12}$]

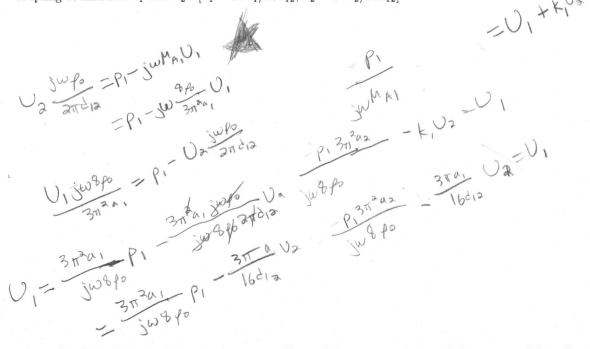

Chapter 4

Analogous Circuits of Mechanical Systems

A mechanical analogous circuit is an electrical circuit in which the currents and voltages are analogous to the forces and velocities in the mechanical system. The basic mechanical variables are force f and velocity u. The circuit is called an impedance analogous circuit if voltage is the analog of force and current is the analog of velocity. It is called a mobility analogous circuit if current is the analog of force and voltage is the analog of velocity.

4.1 Mechanical Sources

Fig. 4.1(a) shows the mechanical symbol for a force source. The two terminals move with the velocities u_1 and u_2, which are functions of the force and the external load. The mobility analogous circuit is given in Fig. 4.1(b). The impedance analogous circuit is given in Fig. 4.1(c). In the mobility circuit, the voltages at the two terminals are analogs of the velocities u_1 and u_2. In the impedance circuit, the current through the source is the analog of the velocity difference $u = u_1 - u_2$ so that the two velocities do not appear as separate variables in the circuit.

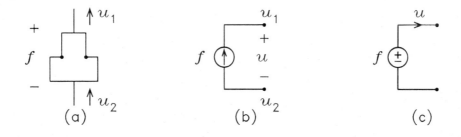

Figure 4.1: (a) Symbol for a force source. (b) Mobility analog. (c) Impedance analog.

Fig. 4.2(a) shows the mechanical symbol of a velocity source. The two terminals move with the velocities u_1 and u_2. The difference velocity $u = u_1 - u_2$ is independent of the external load. The mobility analogous circuit is given in Fig. 4.2(b). The impedance analogous circuit is given in Fig. 4.2(c). In the mobility circuit, the voltages at the two terminals are the analogs of the terminal velocities u_1 and u_2. In the impedance circuit, the current through the source is the analog of the velocity difference $u = u_1 - u_2$ so that the two velocities do not appear as separate variables in the circuit.

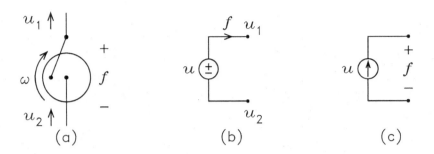

Figure 4.2: (a) Symbol for a velocity source. (b) Mobility analog. (c) Impedance analog.

4.2   Mass, Compliance, and Resistance

The three passive elements in mechanical systems are mass M_M, compliance C_M, and resistance R_M. The symbol for a mass is given in Fig. 4.3(a). The basic terminal equation is $f = M_M a$, where f is the force and a is the acceleration. Because acceleration is the time derivative of velocity, it follows that the force is related to the velocity by

$$f = M_M \frac{du}{dt} = M_M su = j\omega M_M u \qquad (4.1)$$

where M_M is the mass in kg, s is the complex frequency, and ω is the radian frequency.

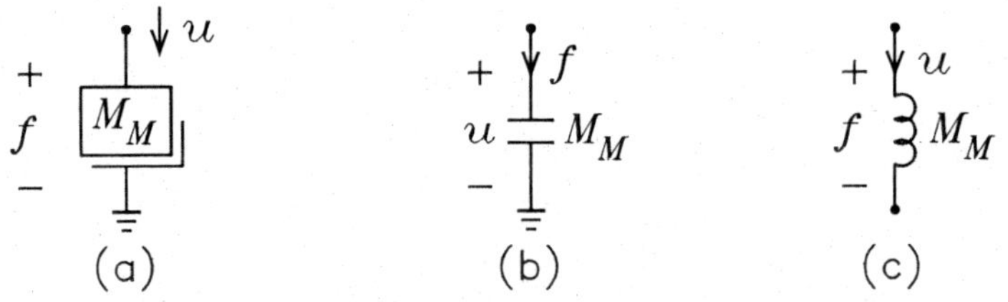

Figure 4.3: (a) Symbol for a mechanical mass. (b) Mobility analog. (c) Impedance analog.

It follows from Eq. (4.1) that the mobility analog for a mass is a capacitor and the impedance analog is an inductor. These are shown in Figs. 4.3(b) and 4.3(c). In the mobility analog, one side of the capacitor is always grounded. This follows because the velocity of a mass, which is analogous to the voltage on the capacitor, is a variable that is measured with respect to zero or rest velocity, which is represented by the ground node in the circuit. In the impedance analog, the velocity is analogous to the current in the inductor.

The symbol for a mechanical compliance is given in Fig. 4.4(a). A compliance is a spring for which the force f is related to the displacement x by the equation $f = k_M x$, where k_M is the spring constant. Alternately, we can write $x = C_M f$, where $C_M = 1/k_M$ is the mechanical compliance which has the units m/N. Let x_1 and x_2 be the displacements of the two sides the compliance. Let u_1 and u_2 be the velocities. The equation relating the force to the velocities is

$$f = \frac{x_1 - x_2}{C_M} = \frac{1}{C_M} \int (u_1 - u_2)\, dt = \frac{u}{C_M s} = \frac{u}{j\omega C_M} \qquad (4.2)$$

where $u = u_1 - u_2$, s is the complex frequency, and ω is the radian frequency.

It follows that the mobility analog for a compliance is an inductor and the impedance analog is a capacitor. These are shown in Figs. 4.4(b) and 4.4(c). In the mobility analog, the velocities u_1 and u_2 are analogous to the voltages at the two terminals of the inductor. In the impedance analog, the current in the capacitor is analogous to the velocity difference $u = u_1 - u_2$. Thus the two velocities do not appear as separate variables.

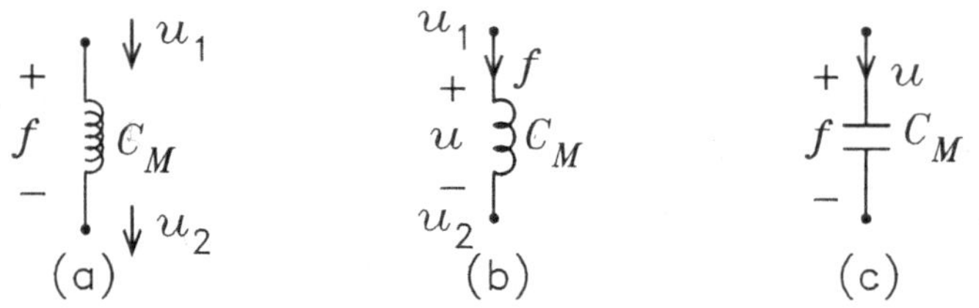

Figure 4.4: (a) Symbol for a mechanical compliance. (b) Mobility analog. (c) Impedance analog.

The symbol for a mechanical resistance is given in Fig. 4.5(a). A familiar device designed to act as a mechanical resistance is a shock absorber in a car suspension. The basic equation relating the force to the velocity is

$$f = R_M (u_1 - u_2) = R_M u \tag{4.3}$$

where $u = u_1 - u_2$ and R_M is the resistance which has the units $\mathrm{N\,s/m}$. The impedance analog for the mechanical resistor is a resistor with value R_M. The mobility analog is a resistor with value $1/R_M$. These are shown in Figs. 4.5(b) and 4.5(c). In the mobility analog, the velocities u_1 and u_2 are analogous to the voltages at the two terminals of the resistor. In the impedance analog, the current in the resistor is the velocity difference $u = u_1 - u_2$. Thus the two velocities do not appear as separate variables.

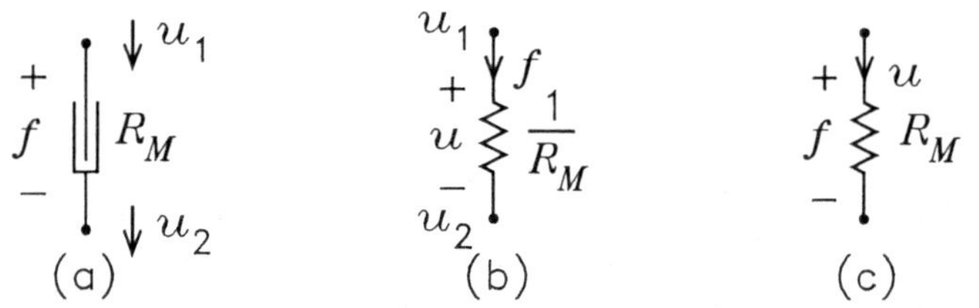

Figure 4.5: (a) Symbol for a mechanical resistance. (b) Mobility analog. (c) Impedance analog.

In practice, mechanical compliances and resistances are never completely linear as they are modeled here. For example, springs have softening or hardening characteristics which are nonlinear behaviors. Mechanical resistances can exhibit a friction component which is also non-linear. These effects are neglected here in order that linear circuit theory may be used for the analyses.

4.3 Mechanical Systems

Mechanical systems can be modeled by either mobility or impedance analogous circuits. To obtain an impedance analog, it is always necessary to form the mobility analog first. This is because the currents in the impedance circuits are not the analogs of individual velocities but velocity differences. The steps for forming the analogous circuits for a mechanical system are illustrated by the following example.

Fig. 4.6(a) shows an example system consisting of two masses M_{M1} and M_{M2} driven by a force source. The first mass slides on the second mass with mechanical resistance R_{M1}. The second mass slides on a horizontal surface with mechanical resistance R_{M2}. A spring with compliance C_M connects the second mass to a stationary support. To obtain the analogous circuits, a mechanical diagram for the system must be drawn. This is done by drawing horizontal bars to represent each velocity in the system, including a bar for zero velocity. The bars are then connected with the mechanical sources and elements. The mechanical diagram for the system is given in Fig. 4.6(b).

The steps for obtaining the analogous circuits are as follows:

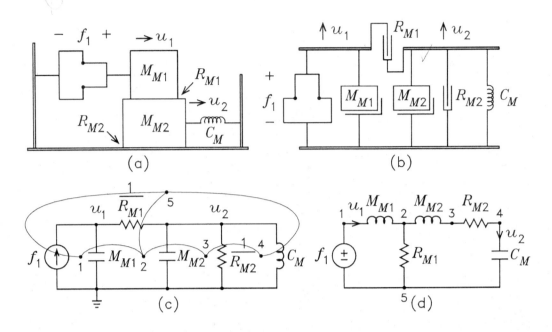

Figure 4.6: (a) Mechanical system. (b) Mechanical diagram. (c) Mobility analog. (d) Impedance analog.

1. Draw the mobility analog by replacing each element in the mechanical diagram with its mobility analog. Label the velocities and forces with the analogous voltages and currents. The mobility analog is given in Fig. 4.6(c).

2. Place a dot at the center of each mesh in the mobility analog and one dot outside all meshes. Number the dots. This is illustrated in Fig. 4.6(c). The dots represent the nodes in the impedance analog.

3. Connect the dots together with lines that pass through each element, using only one line per element. This is illustrated in Fig. 4.6(c).

4. Draw a new circuit such that each connecting line contains the dual of the element through which it passes. The dual of a resistor R is a resistor of value $1/R$. The dual of a capacitor C is an inductor of value C. The dual of an inductor L is a capacitor of value L. The circuit obtained is the impedance analog.

5. Label the velocities and forces with the analogous currents and voltages. The polarities must be chosen so that they correspond in the two circuits. The impedance analog for the system in Fig. 4.6(a) is shown in Fig. 4.6(d). The circuits in Fig. 4.6(c) and (d) are called dual circuits.

A second example mechanical system consisting of two masses M_{M1} and M_{M2} is shown in Fig. 4.7(a). The two masses slide on a horizontal surface with mechanical resistances R_{M1} and R_{M2}. A force source connects between the two masses. The mechanical diagram for the system is shown in Fig. 4.7(b). Note that the velocities are labeled so that u_1 is negative and u_2 is positive when f_1 is positive. The mobility analog is shown in Fig. 4.7(c) with the dots and lines needed to form the dual of the circuit. The impedance analog is shown in Fig. 4.7(d).

4.4   Moving-Coil Transducer

The moving-coil transducer, also called an electromagnetic-mechanical transducer, consists of a current carrying wire immersed in a magnetic field. This is the basic transducer which creates the force on the diaphragm of the familiar dynamic loudspeaker driver when a current is applied to the voice coil. It is also the transducer which converts the mechanical vibrations of the diaphragm of a dynamic microphone into an electrical signal.

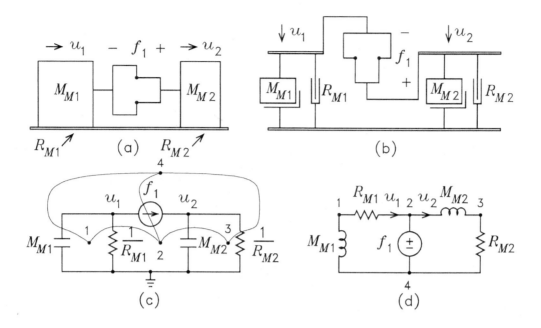

Figure 4.7: (a) Mechanical system. (b) Mechanical diagram. (c) Mobility analog. (d) Impedance analog.

To illustrate the voltage that is generated when a wire moves in a magnetic field, consider the system illustrated in Fig. 4.8(a). The figure shows an open-circuited wire that is moved with a velocity u in a magnetic field B. Let the effective length of the wire which cuts the magnetic field be denoted by ℓ. The voltage e generated in the wire is given by

$$e = B\ell u \tag{4.4}$$

This voltage is sometimes called the back emf, where emf stands for electromotive force.

A second equation is required to model the moving-coil transducer when a current flows in the wire. Fig. 4.8(b) illustrates a stationary wire in a magnetic field having a current i flowing in it. It follows from the Lorentz force law that the force generated in the wire is given by

$$f = B\ell i \tag{4.5}$$

Two analogous circuits for the moving-coil transducer are shown in Fig. 4.8(c) and (d). In one, the mechanical part is modeled with a mobility analog. In the other, the mechanical part is modeled with an impedance analog.

In a physical transducer, the length ℓ in the above formulas is not the actual length of the wire but the effective length that cuts the magnetic field B. Quite often, the magnetic field is not constant in which case ℓ cannot be specified as a physical length along the wire. Fortunately, in most equations the effective length appears multiplied by the magnetic field, i.e. the product $B\ell$. This is commonly called the $B\ell$ product of the transducer. Eq. (4.5) suggests a method for the measurement of the $B\ell$ product as the ratio of the force to the current in the wire.

Example 1 *Fig. 4.9(a) shows a moving-coil transducer connected to a mechanical circuit consisting of a mass, a mechanical resistance, and a spring. Solve for the equivalent circuit seen looking into the electrical terminals of the transducer.*

Solution. The mechanical diagram for the mechanical part of the system is shown in Fig. 4.9(b). The mobility analog is shown in Fig. 4.9(c). Fig. 4.9(d) shows the completed circuit with the mechanical part

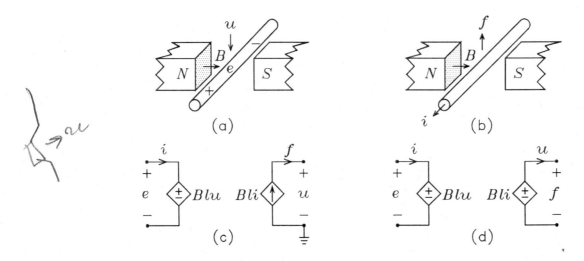

Figure 4.8: (a) Wire moving in a magnetic field. (b) Stationary current carrying wire in a magnetic field. (c) Mobility analog. (d) Impedance analog.

converted into an impedance analog. For this circuit, we can write

$$e = B\ell u = \frac{(B\ell)^2\, i}{M_M s + R_M + 1/C_M s} \tag{4.6}$$

It follows from this equation that the equivalent circuit seen looking into the electrical terminals is a parallel RLC circuit consisting of a resistor of value $(B\ell)^2/R_M$, an inductor of value $(B\ell)^2 C_M$, and a capacitor of value $M_M/(B\ell)^2$. The circuit is shown in Fig. 4.9(e).

Example 2 *Fig. 4.10(a) shows a source having an open-circuit voltage e_g and an output impedance Z_E connected to the electrical terminals of a moving-coil transducer. Solve for the Norton form of the analogous circuit seen looking into the mechanical terminals of the transducer.*

Solution: We can write

$$f = B\ell i = B\ell \frac{(e_g - B\ell u)}{Z_E} = \frac{B\ell e_g}{Z_E} - \frac{(B\ell)^2}{Z_E} u \tag{4.7}$$

It follows that the Thévenin form of the analogous circuit seen looking into the mechanical terminals is a force source of value $B\ell e_g/Z_E$ in series with an impedance of value $(B\ell)^2/Z_E$. The velocity source in the Norton form is obtained by dividing the force by the impedance to obtain $e_g/B\ell$. The circuit is shown in Fig. 4.10(b).

4.5 Crystal Transducer

The piezoelectric crystal is an example of a crystal transducer, also called an electrostatic-mechanical transducer. Fig. 4.11(a) illustrates a crystal transducer element mounted against a rigid wall. The figure shows two electrical terminals connected to capacitive plates on each side of a crystal. When a voltage e is applied to these terminals, a current i flows and a charge q is stored on the plates. This charge sets up an electric field inside the crystal which causes a deformation of the crystalline structure so as to cause a force f to be exerted as indicated in the figure. This is the force mechanism that is used when the crystal transducer is coupled to a loudspeaker diaphragm to form a loudspeaker. Although the available range of motion is small, the crystal element has been used in horn loaded tweeter loudspeakers.

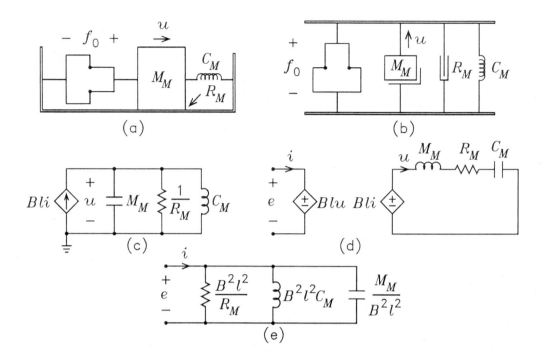

Figure 4.9: (a) Moving-coil transducer driving mechanical system. (b) Mechanical diagram. (c) Mobility analog for mechanical system. (d) Completed analogous circuit. (e) Electrical equivalent circuit.

If a force is applied to the element, an electric field is set up inside the crystal which induces a charge on the two plates, thus causing a voltage to appear across the terminals. This is the mechanism that is used when the crystal transducer is coupled to a microphone diaphragm to form a microphone.

If the crystal is blocked so that it cannot be deformed when a voltage is applied, i.e. $x = 0$, it can be shown that the force generated in the x-direction by a charge q on the plates is given by $f = \tau q$, where τ is the crystal coupling coefficient having the units N/C. Similarly, if the terminals are open-circuited so that $q = 0$ and the crystal is deformed a distance x, the restoring force is given by $f = -x/C_M$, where C_M is the mechanical compliance of the crystal. These two relations can be combined to obtain the general force relation

$$f = \tau q - \frac{x}{C_M} \tag{4.8}$$

If the terminals are open-circuited so that $q = 0$ and a force is applied to the crystal in the x-direction

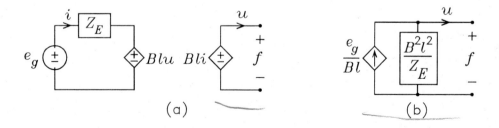

Figure 4.10: (a) Moving-coil transducer driven by a Thévenin source. (b) Norton form of the analogous circuit looking into the mechanical terminals.

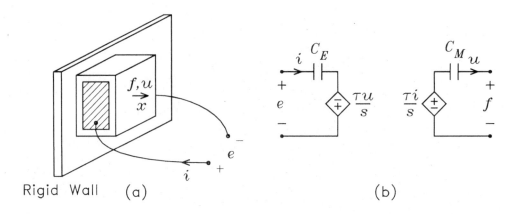

Figure 4.11: (a) Crystal transducer element mounted against a rigid wall. (b) Analogous circuit.

so as to deform it by an amount x, it can be shown that a voltage is generated across the capacitor plates is given by $e = -\tau x$. Similarly, if a charge q is applied to the capacitor plates with $x = 0$, a voltage is generated that is given by $v = q/C_E$, where C_E is the electrical capacitance between the plates. These two relations can be combined to obtain the general voltage relation

$$e = -\tau x + \frac{q}{C_E} \tag{4.9}$$

The two above equations are the basic electro-mechanical equations for the crystal transducer. However, not all of the variables in the equations are the standard ones for our circuit models. To put the equations into the desired form, we write $q = i/s$ and $x = u/s$, where s is the complex frequency, to obtain

$$f = \frac{\tau}{s}i - \frac{u}{C_M s} \qquad e = -\frac{\tau}{s}u + \frac{i}{C_E s} \tag{4.10}$$

The above two equations can be used to form the analogous circuit in Fig. 4.11(b), where an impedance analog is used in the mechanical circuit. In this circuit, the controlled sources are both functions of the complex frequency s. This dependence can be eliminated by making a Norton equivalent circuit of both sources. The new circuit is shown in Fig. 4.12(a). In Fig. 4.12(b), the mechanical circuit is converted to a mobility analog. The latter two circuits are the basic circuits for the crystal transducer.

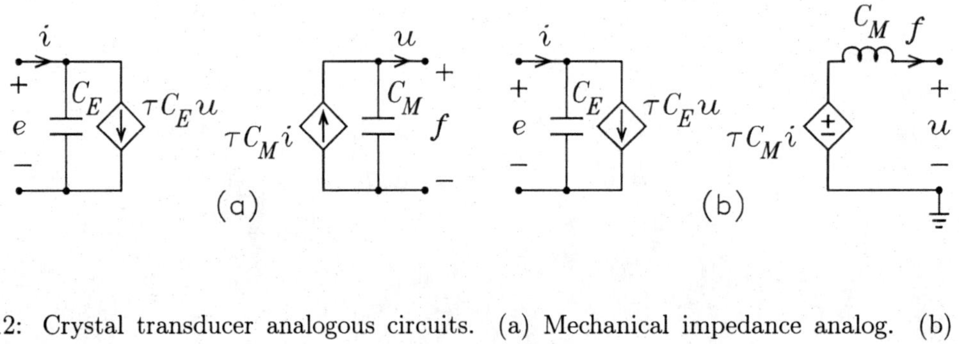

Figure 4.12: Crystal transducer analogous circuits. (a) Mechanical impedance analog. (b) Mechanical mobility analog.

4.6 Condenser Transducer

A second type of electrostatic-mechanical transducer is the condenser or capacitor transducer. This is the transducer that is used in condenser microphones and in electrostatic loudspeakers. The condenser microphone is considered to be the most accurate type of microphone and is the standard measuring microphone for precision acoustical measurements. Electrostatic loudspeakers are not seen that often in the consumer market because they are expensive and require high-voltage polarizing supplies which cause arcing problems that can damage the diaphragms of the loudspeaker elements. The popularity of these types of loudspeakers seems to cycle. When another electrostatic loudspeaker is introduced on the market, most consumers tend to think that it is a new type of loudspeaker. However, the basic design can be traced back into the 1920s, pre-dating the development of the so-called permanent-magnet (or PM) loudspeaker. Indeed, electrostatic tweeters have been used even in table-model vacuum-tube radios. The plate supply voltage in these radios typically ran in the range of 250 V to 350 V dc, ideal values for the polarizing voltage for the electrostatic tweeter. In full-range electrostatic loudspeakers, the polarizing voltage can be greater than 2000 V.

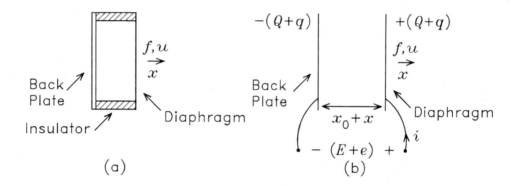

Figure 4.13: (a) Cross section of single-ended condenser transducer. (b) Parallel-plate capacitor model.

There are two types of condenser transducers: the single-ended and the push-pull. We first look at the single ended type. This is the type that is used in condenser microphones. It is also used in electrostatic loudspeakers which are not required to reproduce high sound pressure levels. The basic diagram of the single-ended condenser transducer as it might appear in a microphone design is illustrated in Fig. 4.13(a). The figure shows a thin conducting diaphragm suspended in front of a conducting back plate. Insulating material is used between the diaphragm and back plate so that a dc polarizing voltage can be applied between the two. We assume that the diaphragm is free to move against a mechanical compliance C_M and that the back plate is held stationary. In electrostatic loudspeakers, the back plate might be perforated so that the sound radiation can occur from both sides of the transducer.

In Fig. 4.13(b), the transducer is modeled as a parallel plate capacitor, where the right plate models the diaphragm and the left plate models the back plate. When the applied voltage is zero, denote the spacing between the plates by d. When a quiescent dc voltage E is applied between the plates, a charge $+Q$ is stored on the right plate and a charge $-Q$ is stored on the left plate. These two opposite charges attract each other, thus causing the diaphragm to be deflected against its mechanical compliance. This causes the distance between the plates to be decreased until the mechanical compliance of the diaphragm produces an opposing force that just balances the electrostatic force. Let the equilibrium distance between the plates with the applied voltage E be denoted by x_0, where $x_0 < d$. Let us denote small-signal, time-varying components of the spacing between the plates, the voltage on the diaphragm, and the charge on the diaphragm, respectively, by $x(t)$, $e(t)$, and $q(t)$. The total spacing is $x_0 + x(t)$, the total voltage is $E + e(t)$, and the total charge is $Q + q(t)$.

The electrical capacitance of the plates can be written

$$C_E = \frac{\epsilon_0 S}{x_0 + x(t)} = \frac{\epsilon_0 S/x_0}{1 + x(t)/x_0} = \frac{C_{E0}}{1 + x(t)/x_0} \tag{4.11}$$

where ϵ_0 is the permittivity of the air between the plates, S is the area of the plates, and $C_{E0} = \epsilon_0 S/x_0$ is the capacitance with $x(t) = 0$. The total voltage across the plates can be related to the total charge as follows:

$$E + e(t) = \frac{Q + q(t)}{C_E} \simeq Q\frac{1 + x(t)/x_0}{C_{E0}} + \frac{q(t)}{C_{E0}} \tag{4.12}$$

where the approximation neglects the term $q(t)x(t)/x_0$. If this second-order non-linear term is not neglected, the equation does not lead to a linear circuit model.

With $E = Q/C_{E0}$, the above equation can be solved for $e(t)$ to obtain

$$e(t) = E\frac{x(t)}{x_0} + \frac{q(t)}{C_{E0}} \tag{4.13}$$

The desired form of this equation is obtained by setting $x = u/s$ and $q = i/s$, where u is the velocity of the diaphragm, i is the current which flows in the external lead, and s is the complex frequency. We obtain

$$e = \frac{1}{C_{E0}s}i + \frac{E}{x_0 s}u \tag{4.14}$$

This is the first model equation for the single-ended condenser transducer. It is the equation that leads to the electrical part of the circuit model.

To obtain the second equation, we first solve for the total energy stored. It is given by the electrical energy (one-half the square of the total charge divided by the capacitance) plus the mechanical energy (one-half the square of the total displacement divided by the compliance) as follows:

$$\begin{aligned} W &= \frac{1}{2}\frac{[Q + q(t)]^2}{C_E} + \frac{1}{2}\frac{[x_0 + x(t) - d]^2}{C_M} \\ &\simeq \frac{1}{2}\left[Q^2 + 2Qq(t)\right]\frac{1 + x(t)/x_0}{C_{E0}} + \frac{1}{2}\frac{[x_0 + x(t) - d]^2}{C_M} \end{aligned} \tag{4.15}$$

where the approximation assumes that $q(t)^2$ can be neglected. This is necessary to obtain a linear circuit model.

By the principal of virtual work, the net force $f(t)$ exerted by the diaphragm is given by

$$f(t) = -\frac{\partial W}{\partial x} = -\left[\frac{1}{2}\frac{Q^2}{C_{E0}} - \frac{d - x_0}{C_M}\right] - \left[\frac{Qq(t)}{x_0 C_{E0}} + \frac{x(t)}{C_M}\right] \tag{4.16}$$

The first bracketed term on the right side of this equation is zero because it is the difference between the quiescent electrostatic force and the quiescent mechanical restoring force of the diaphragm suspension. Thus the small-signal component of the force is given by

$$f = -\frac{qQ}{x_0 C_{E0}} - \frac{x}{C_M} = -\frac{E}{x_0 s}i - \frac{1}{C_M s}u \tag{4.17}$$

where $Q = C_{E0}E$, $q = i/s$, and $x = u/s$ have been used in the simplification. This is the second equation for the single-ended condenser transducer. It is the equation that leads to the mechanical part of the circuit model.

The analogous circuit for the single-ended condenser transducer follows directly from Eqs. (4.14) and (4.17). The circuit is given in Fig. 4.14(a), where an impedance analog is used for the mechanical part. To eliminate the dependence of the controlled sources on the complex frequency s, Norton equivalents can be

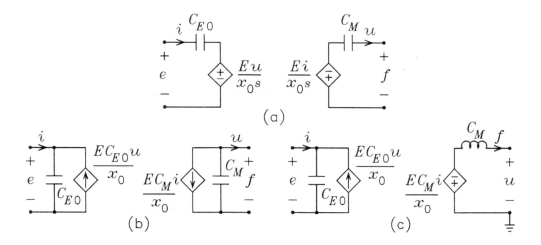

Figure 4.14: (a) Analogous circuit model for single-ended condenser transducer. (b) Circuit after making two Norton equivalents. (c) Circuit with mechanical mobility analog.

made of both parts. The resulting circuit is given in Fig. 4.14(b). In Fig. 4.14(c), the mechanical part of the circuit is converted to a mobility analog.

In modeling the single-ended condenser transducer, two approximations have been made in order to obtain linear model equations. If the deflection of the diaphragm is too large, the approximations are no longer valid and the transducer becomes non-linear. The push-pull condenser transducer extends the linear operating range by operating two back-to-back, single-ended transducers in series. The diagram of the basic push-pull transducer as it might appear in an electrostatic loudspeaker is shown in Fig. 4.15(a). The diaphragm is the center element. The two end plates are perforated to allow free movement of air particles on both sides of the diaphragm. With respect to the diaphragm, the dc polarizing voltages on the two end plates have the same polarity whereas the ac signal voltages are out of phase.

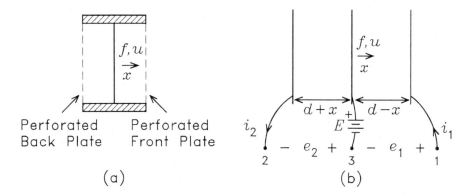

Figure 4.15: (a) Cross section push-pull condenser transducer. (b) Parallel-plate capacitor model.

Fig. 4.15(b) models the push-pull condenser transducer as two parallel plate capacitors which share a common center plate that is the diaphragm. Because same polarity polarizing voltages are applied to the two end plates, the quiescent force on the diaphragm is zero. Therefore, there is no quiescent displacement of the diaphragm when the polarizing voltages are applied. If small-signal, time-varying voltages e_1 and e_2 are applied out of phase between the two sides of the transducer as labeled in the figure, a net force is generated on the diaphragm. The analogous circuit for the transducer can be obtained by combining the circuits for two single-ended transducers as shown in Fig. 4.16(a), where an impedance analog is used for the mechanical part. In Fig. 4.16(b), a mobility analog is used for the mechanical part.

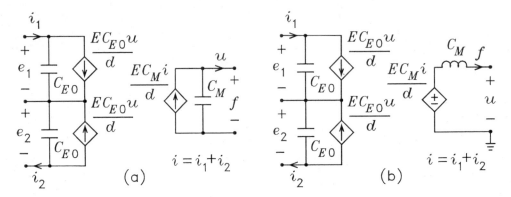

Figure 4.16: (a) Analogous circuit with mechanical impedance analog. (b) Analogous circuit with mechanical mobility analog.

When the push-pull condenser transducer is used as a loudspeaker, e_1 and e_2 are equal signal input voltages from a balanced source, e.g. an amplifier and a center-tapped transformer, so that the driving signal between the two sides of the transducer is a differential signal. When the transducer is used as a microphone, the output voltage must be derived by subtracting the voltages e_1 and e_2. This can be implemented with a transformer or a differential amplifier.

4.7   Mechano-Acoustic Transducer

The mechano-acoustic transducer is a piston that radiates an acoustic pressure when it is driven by a mechanical force. Fig. 4.17(a) illustrates a plane-piston transducer where S is the piston area, f is the force driving the piston, u is the velocity with which it moves, U is the volume velocity emitted from one side, and $p = p_F - p_B$ is the pressure difference between the front and back sides. We can write

$$f = S\,(p_F - p_B) = Sp \qquad U = Su \tag{4.18}$$

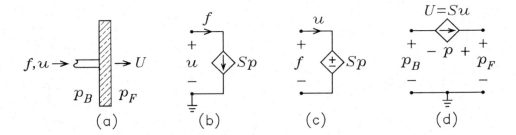

Figure 4.17: (a) Plane circular piston mechano-acoustic transducer. Analogous circuits: (b) Mechanical part with mobility analog. (c) Mechanical part with impedance analog. (d) Acoustical part.

Fig. 4.17(b) gives the mechanical mobility analogous circuit for the transducer. Fig. 4.17(c) gives the mechanical impedance analogous circuit. Fig. 4.17(d) shows the acoustical analogous circuit. Because u is the velocity with respect to zero velocity, one side of the force source in Fig. 4.17(b) must connect to ground, i.e. the zero velocity node.

Example 3 *Fig. 4.18 illustrates a moving-coil transducer connected in series with a crystal transducer to a plane piston mechano-acoustic transducer. The moving-coil transducer has a coil resistance R_E and a mechanical mass M_{M1}. The piezoelectric transducer is considered to be massless and has the parameters τ, C_E, and C_M. The piston has a mechanical mass M_{MD}, an area S_D, and a pressure difference across it of p_D. Let the air load impedances on the front and back of the piston, respectively, be Z_{AF} and Z_{AB}. Solve for the analogous circuits of the system. Use mobility analogs for the mechanical parts of the system.*

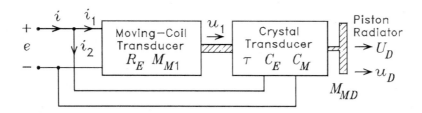

Figure 4.18: Series moving-coil and crystal transducers driving a plane circular piston.

Solution. The analogous circuits are obtained by combining the appropriate models for the moving-coil transducer, the crystal transducer, and the mechano-acoustic transducer. The circuits are shown in Fig. 4.19.

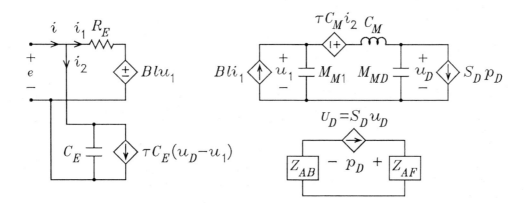

Figure 4.19: Analogous circuits.

4.8   Problems

1. Fig. 4.20 shows an impedance analogous circuit for a mechanical system. Solve for the mobility analog, the mechanical diagram, and the mechanical system.

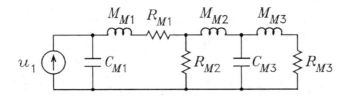

Figure 4.20: Circuit for problem 1.

2. An automobile and its suspension can be modeled by the mechanical diagram shown in Fig. 4.21. The velocity generator models bumps in the road. Form the mobility and the impedance analogous circuits for the system.

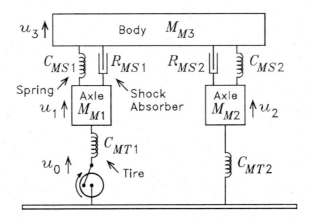

Figure 4.21: Figure for problem 2.

3. The two equations for the moving-coil transducer are $f = B\ell i$ and $e = B\ell u$, where f is the force generated when the current i flows and e is the back emf in the wire when it moves with a velocity u. We wish to use the ideal transformer in Fig. 4.22(a) to model these two equations. The transformer voltages and currents are related by $v_1/v_2 = n$ and $i_2/i_1 = n$, where n is the turns ratio. If $v_1 = e$ and $i_1 = i$, specify v_2, i_2, and n such that the transformer equations are the same as the transducer equations. [$v_2 = u$, $i_2 = f$, $n = B\ell$], (b) Can this circuit be used in place of the controlled source circuit in Fig. 4.8(c)? [Yes] Can it be used in place of the controlled source circuit in Fig. 4.8(d)? If not, why? [No, because the basic transformer equations force one to use a mobility analog for the mechanical side of the circuit.]

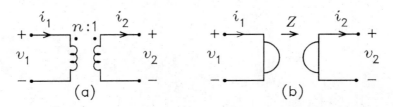

Figure 4.22: (a) Figure for problem 3. (b) Figure for problem 4.

4. A gyrator is a lossless two-port having the symbol in Fig. 4.22(b). Its equations are $v_1 = Zi_2$ and $v_2 = Zi_1$, where Z is the gyrator impedance. Let i_1 be the current i in a moving-coil transducer, v_1 the back emf e generated when the wire moves, v_2 the force f generated by the current in the wire, and i_2 the velocity u of the wire. (a) Draw the gyrator circuit for the transducer and label the variables on the drawing. (b) What is the impedance of the gyrator? [$Z = B\ell$] (c) Can the gyrator be used in place of the controlled source circuit in Fig. 4.8(c)? If not, why? [No, because the basic equations of the gyrator force one to use an impedance analog for the mechanical side of the circuit.] Can it be used in place of the controlled source circuit in Fig. 4.8(d)? [Yes]

5. The impedance Z_E in Fig. 4.10(a) consists of a resistor R_E in series with the parallel combination of an inductor L_E and a resistor R'_E. Solve for the impedance $(B\ell)^2 / Z_E$ in Fig. 4.10(b). [a resistor $(B\ell)^2 / R_E$ in parallel with a series capacitor $L_E / (B\ell)^2$ and resistor $(B\ell)^2 / R'_E$]

6. (a) Use the analogous circuits given in Fig. 4.14 to solve for the electrical input capacitance of the condenser microphone if the force on the diaphragm is zero, i.e. $f = 0$. [$C = C_{E0} / \left(1 - E^2 C_{E0} C_M / x_0^2\right)$] (b) Solve for the capacitance if the diaphragm is blocked so that its velocity is zero, i.e. $u = 0$. [$C = C_{E0}$]

7. Fig. 4.23 shows a combination mechanical and acoustical system that is coupled by a mechano-acoustic transducer of area S_D. Form the analogous circuits for the system using an impedance analog for the mechanical part. [Mechanical part: a parallel force source f_0 and compliance C_M in series with a mass M_M, a resistance R_M, and a force source $f_a = S_D p_D$. Acoustical part: a volume velocity source $U_D = S_D u_D$ in series with two air load impedances. Back air load impedance: a compliance C_{A1} to ground. Front air load impedance: a mass M_A in series with the parallel combination of a compliance C_{A2} to ground and a resistance R_A to ground.]

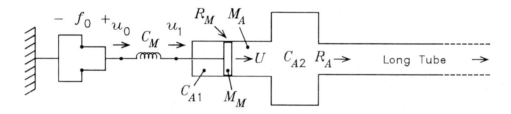

Figure 4.23: Figure for problem 7.

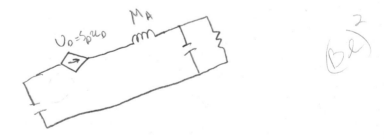

Chapter 5

Microphones

5.1 Classifications

A microphone is a transducer that converts acoustical power into electrical power. Microphones fall into one of two categories: cavity and free-field. A cavity microphone is designed to have an electrical output voltage that is proportional to the acoustic pressure at its diaphragm. A free-field microphone is designed to have an electrical output voltage that is proportional to the acoustic pressure which would exist at the position of the diaphragm in the absence of the microphone. The basic difference between the two types is that the free-field microphone is designed to compensate for the effects of acoustic reflections at its diaphragm whereas the cavity microphone is not.

Free-field microphones are used for sound recording in applications where the microphone is used on a stand or a boom that is not adjacent to any reflecting surfaces. Cavity microphones are used in applications where it is desired to measure the actual acoustic pressure at a point, usually inside an acoustic cavity device such as an artificial ear. The artificial ear is a device that is used to measure the frequency response of earphones and headphones. The earphone is attached to one side of the ear while a cavity microphone is inserted into the other end to act as a human eardrum. This is illustrated in Fig. 5.1(a). A cavity microphone can be used in sound recording applications if it is installed in a large flat plate, e.g. a sheet of plexiglass as shown in Fig. 5.1(b), so that the diaphragm is flush with one surface of the plate. The plate modifies the effect of reflections at the diaphragm and causes the microphone to respond as if it were installed in an infinite baffle. Cavity microphones used in this way are called "pressure-zone microphones."

A cavity microphone used in a free-field exhibits a high-frequency boost. That is, it produces a bright sounding signal that has a treble boost. This is caused by the reflections of high-frequency waves from the diaphragm which tend to boost the acoustic pressure. In contrast, low-frequency waves diffract around the diaphragm so that the microphone acts as a free-field device at low frequencies. A free-field microphone used as a pressure-zone microphone in a large plate of plexiglass produces a dull sounding signal that has a treble cut. This is because the plexiglass causes all frequencies to be reflected equally so that the pressure is increased at the diaphragm at all frequencies, not just the high frequencies.

There are three types of free-field microphones: pressure, pressure-gradient, and combination pressure and pressure-gradient. The pressure microphone is designed to respond to the acoustic pressure in a sound wave. The pressure gradient microphone is designed to respond the gradient or directional derivative of the acoustic pressure. The particle velocity in a wave is proportional to the gradient of the pressure. For this reason, pressure gradient microphones are also called velocity microphones. The combination pressure and pressure-gradient microphone has a response proportional to a linear combination of both the pressure and the particle velocity in the wave. Each of these types is examined in the following.

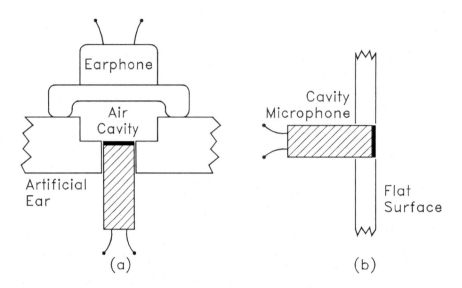

Figure 5.1: Cavity microphone (a) in an artificial ear measuring the frequency response of an earphone and (b) in a flat baffle as a pressure-zone microphone.

5.2 Modeling Diaphragm Reflections

When an acoustic wave is incident on a microphone diaphragm, a reflected wave is generated that causes the pressure at the diaphragm to be different from the free-field pressure in the absence of the microphone. An analogous circuit which can be used to model diaphragm reflections is developed in this section. The microphone is modeled as a diaphragm in the end of a long tube. The model is developed under the assumption that the diaphragm is blocked, i.e. it is restrained so that it cannot vibrate with the incident wave. This is analogous to solving for the open-circuit or Thévenin output voltage from a circuit. The mechanical mass of the diaphragm and the compliance and damping losses of its suspension are parameters that can be modeled in the mechanical circuit.

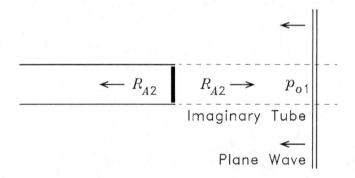

Figure 5.2: Plane wave incident on a lossless and massless piston in the end of an infinitely long tube.

Fig. 5.2 illustrates an acoustic plane wave of pressure amplitude p_{01} in free air that is incident from the left on a long thin-wall tube of radius a having a lossless and massless piston in its end. The plane wave that is coupled into the tube confronts an acoustic resistance $R_{A2} = \rho_0 c / S$, where $\rho_0 c$ is the specific impedance of the air and $S = \pi a^2$ is the area of the tube. (The symbol R_{A2} is used here because it is the same as the high-frequency limit of the external acoustic impedance seen by a piston in the end of a long tube discussed in Section 3.8.) The same wave would be coupled into the tube if an imaginary tube of the same area were extended to the right of the piston, as shown by the dashed lines in the figure, in which a plane wave of pressure amplitude p_{01} propagates. The acoustic output impedance of this imaginary source tube is $R_{A2} = \rho_0 c/S$. The analogous circuit which predicts the pressure amplitude p_D at the piston is a source of pressure $2p_{01}$ in series with a source resistance R_{A2} driving a load resistance R_{A2}. The analogous circuit is shown in Fig. 5.3(a). It follows by voltage division that $p_D = 2p_{01}R_{A2}/\left(R_{A2} + R_{A2}\right) = p_{01}$.

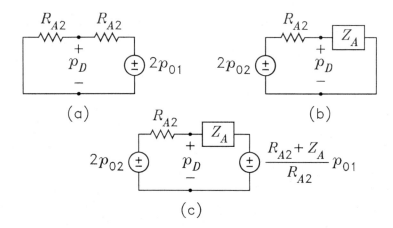

Figure 5.3: (a) Analogous circuit when the plane wave is incident from the free-air side. (b) Analogous circuit when the plane wave originates from the load end of the tube. (c) Analogous circuit for the plane wave incident from either side.

Let us consider the case where the source is moved so that the plane wave propagates to the right from the load end of the original tube. In this case, the wave that is radiated into free air by the piston is a spherical wave rather than a plane wave. Fig. 5.3(b) illustrates the circuit for this case, where the pressure source is now denoted by $2p_{02}$. For the pressure p_D at the piston to be correctly predicted by this circuit, the load impedance Z_A must be the impedance representing the air load on a piston in the end of a long tube given in Section 3.8. It follows by voltage division that $p_D = 2p_{02}Z_A/\left(R_{A2} + Z_A\right)$. We conclude, that the pressure source cannot be moved from one side of the circuit to the other without simultaneously changing the acoustic impedance for the free-air side of the circuit.

A circuit which can be used to predict the average pressure at the piston without changing the impedance in the free-air side of the circuit when the pressure source is moved is given in Fig. 5.3(c). The circuit shows two sources: one for the free-air part of the circuit and one for the original tube side. The pressure amplitude of the source on the free-air side of the circuit is multiplied by $T(s) = \left(R_{A2} + Z_A\right)/R_{A2}$, which is the reciprocal of the voltage divider $R_{A2}/\left(R_{A2} + Z_A\right)$. It follows from this circuit that the pressure at the piston when the source on the right is activated is $p_D = p_{01}$. Thus the correct pressure at the piston is predicted when either source is activated. Note that the high-frequency limit of Z_A from Section 3.8 is R_{A2} so that $|T(j\omega)| \to 2$ as ω increases.

The source circuit for the free-air side of the circuit of Fig. 5.3(c) is shown in Fig. 5.4(a) with the circuit for the acoustic impedance Z_A shown. The Norton equivalent of this circuit consists of two parallel volume velocity sources given by p_{01}/Z_A and p_{01}/R_{A2} and a parallel acoustic impedance Z_A. When a Thévenin equivalent circuit is made of the p_{01}/Z_A source and the parallel Z_A, the circuit of Fig. 5.4(b) results. We use the two circuits of Fig. 5.4 to model the pressure at a diaphragm for an incident plane wave. The transfer function $T(s)$ is given by

$$T(s) = \frac{R_{A2} + Z_A}{R_{A2}} = \frac{1 + b_1 s + b_2 s^2}{1 + c_1 s + c_2 s^2} \tag{5.1}$$

where b_1, b_2, c_1, and c_2 are given by

$$b_1 = (R_{A1} \| R_{A2}) C_{A1} + \frac{M_{A1}}{(R_{A1} + R_{A2}) \| R_{A2}} \qquad b_2 = \frac{2 R_{A1} M_{A1} C_{A1}}{R_{A1} + R_{A2}} \qquad (5.2)$$

$$c_1 = (R_{A1} \| R_{A2}) C_{A1} + \frac{M_{A1}}{R_{A1} + R_{A2}} \qquad c_2 = \frac{R_{A1} M_{A1} C_{A1}}{R_{A1} + R_{A2}} \qquad (5.3)$$

The expressions for M_{A1}, R_{A1}, R_{A2}, and C_{A1} are given in Section 3.8. The function $T(s)$ is a second-order transfer function that has unity gain at low frequencies and a gain of 2 (6 dB) at high frequencies. It represents the average effect of reflections on the pressure at the blocked piston. Example plots of $20 \log |T(j2\pi f)|$ as functions of frequency for piston radii of 1/4 in and 1/2 in are given in Fig. 5.5. This figure predicts the increase in pressure that would occur for 1/2-inch diameter and 1-inch diameter diaphragms.

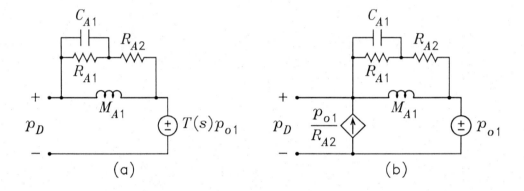

Figure 5.4: (a) Completed analogous circuit for a plane wave incident on a diaphragm in a long tube. (b) Alternate form of the circuit.

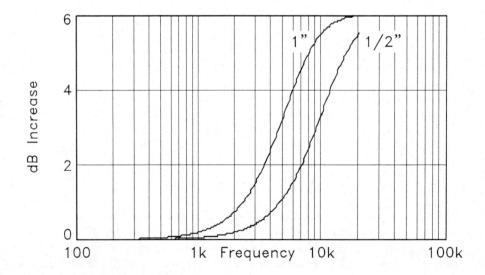

Figure 5.5: Plots of $20 \log |T(j2\pi f)|$ versus frequency for piston diameters of 1/2 inch and 1 inch.

5.3 Diaphragm Back Acoustical Load

A pressure microphone is constructed with its diaphragm mounted in a capsule so that an incident acoustic wave can exert a force on only one side of the diaphragm. This is illustrated in Fig. 5.6(a). In the analogous circuit for the air load on the back of the diaphragm, the air in the capsule is modeled as an acoustic compliance C_A. To equalize the static air pressure in the capsule with the external air pressure, one wall of the capsule normally has a small hole as is illustrated in Fig. 5.6(a). The hole exhibits an acoustic impedance that is modeled in the circuit by an acoustic resistance in series with an acoustic mass. If no other acoustic elements are in the capsule, the acoustic analogous circuit for the air load on the back of the diaphragm is the circuit given in Fig. 5.6(b). In the figure, p_B is the acoustic pressure in the capsule and $U_D = S_D u_D$, where u_D is the mechanical velocity of the diaphragm and S_D is its area.

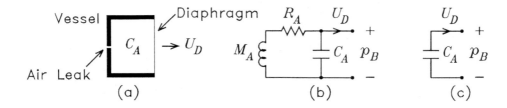

Figure 5.6: (a) Diaphragm in one wall of a microphone vessel. (b) Acoustical analogous circuit for the air on the back of the diaphragm. (c) Approximate acoustical analogous circuit.

The compliance C_A of the air in the capsule is given by

$$C_A = \frac{V_B}{\rho_0 c^2} \tag{5.4}$$

where V_B is the volume of air in the capsule, ρ_0 is the air density, and c is the velocity of sound. We model the hole in the capsule wall as a tube of very small diameter. The impedance of such a tube is given in Section 3.4. Both the resistance and mass component of the tube impedance increase rapidly as the radius of the tube is decreased. Because the air-leak tube normally has a very small radius, the acoustic impedance of the tube is very high. For this reason, it is normally neglected in the analogous circuit, i.e. it is replaced by an open circuit. The approximate circuit is shown in Fig. 5.6(c). It is this latter circuit which we use in the analysis of pressure microphones.

5.4 Diaphragm Mechanical Parameters

Fig. 5.6(a) illustrates the basic construction of a pressure microphone consisting of a capsule in which a diaphragm is installed in one wall. We assume that the diaphragm moves as a rigid body so that it can be modeled as a flat piston. The diaphragm exhibits a mechanical mass M_{MD}. Its suspension exhibits a damping resistance R_{MS} and a mechanical compliance C_{MS}. Let the mechanical force exerted on the diaphragm by the transducer be denoted by f_D. The force exerted by the air load on both sides of the diaphragm can be written

$$f_D = S_D p_D = S_D \left(p_F - p_B \right) \tag{5.5}$$

where S_D is the diaphragm area, p_D is the pressure difference across the diaphragm, p_F is the front pressure, and p_B is the back pressure. The mechanical circuits for the diaphragm are shown in Fig. 5.7. The circuit of Fig. 5.7(a) is an impedance circuit. The circuit of Fig. 5.7(b) is a mobility circuit.

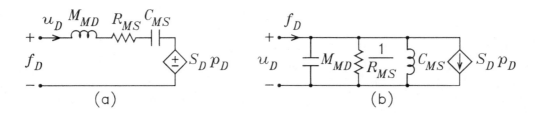

Figure 5.7: Circuits for the microphone mechanical system. (a) Impedance analog. (b) Mobility analog.

5.5   Condenser Microphone

The condenser microphone is considered to be the highest quality type. It is used in acoustical measurements where precision is required and in sound recording when high-fidelity reproduction is desired. The transducer mechanism is the condenser transducer that is developed in Section 4.6. The conventional condenser microphone uses an external power supply to provide the dc voltage to the transducer element while less expensive units use a permanently polarized diaphragm material that does not require an external supply. The latter type is called an electret condenser microphone. Although our analysis here concerns the conventional condenser microphone, it is applicable to the electret type with very little modification.

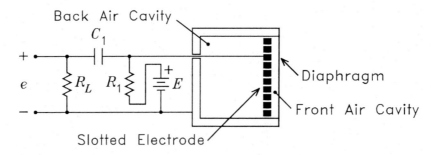

Figure 5.8: Basic construction of the condenser microphone.

The basic construction of the condenser microphone is illustrated in Fig. 5.8. The figure shows a cylindrical capsule with a diaphragm in one wall. Inside the capsule, a slotted electrode is suspended behind the diaphragm. The air in the slots acts as an acoustical resistance to provide damping of the diaphragm motion. A charge Q is applied to the electrode through a very large resistor R_1 in series with a dc voltage source E. When an acoustic wave is incident on the diaphragm, a force is exerted which causes the diaphragm to vibrate. This causes the spacing between the diaphragm and back electrode to alternately decrease and increase. This causes an ac voltage to be generated between the diaphragm and the electrode. This ac voltage is coupled through capacitor C_1 to the external load R_L. The voltage across R_L is the signal output voltage.

The transducer is the condenser transducer developed in Section 4.6. Fig. 5.9(a) through (c) show the ac analogous circuits. We assume that C_1 is an ac short circuit so that the effective load resistance is $R'_L = R_L \| R_1$. In the figure, e is the electrical output voltage, i is the electrical current which flows in the diaphragm circuit, p_D is the pressure difference across the diaphragm, E is the dc polarizing voltage, C_{E0} is the zero-signal capacitance between the diaphragm and electrode, x_0 is the zero-signal spacing between the diaphragm and the electrode, C_M is the mechanical compliance of the suspension, M_{MD} is the mechanical mass of the diaphragm, R_{MD} is the mechanical resistance of the suspension, S_D is the diaphragm area, R_{AS} is the acoustic resistance of the slots in the back electrode, C_{AB1} is the acoustic compliance of the air between the diaphragm and the electrode, and C_{AB2} is the acoustic compliance of the air cavity behind the

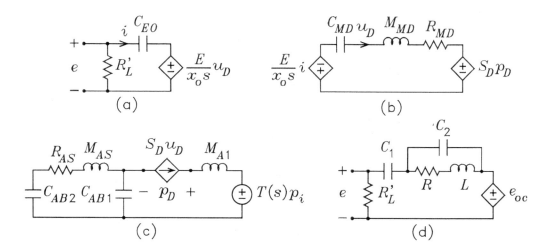

Figure 5.9: Condenser microphone analogous circuits: (a) electrical, (b) mechanical, (c) acoustical. (d) Equivalent circuit of the condenser microphone.

electrode.

We assume an incident plane wave of amplitude p_i that is incident normally on the diaphragm. The acoustical analogous circuit for the air load external to the diaphragm is modeled by the pressure source $T(s)p_i$ and acoustic mass M_{A1}. This is the low-frequency approximation to the circuit of Fig. 5.4(a) which assumes that the frequency is low enough so that the reactance of the acoustic mass M_{A1} is small compared to the impedance of the other elements in the circuit. Although the other elements are difficult to handle in deriving a transfer function, they can easily be included in a SPICE analysis of the circuits.

We wish to solve for the Thévenin equivalent circuit seen to the right of R'_L in Fig. 5.9(a). To do this, we assume that the compliance of the air cavity between the diaphragm and the electrode is small enough so that C_{AB1} can be approximated by an open circuit. In a microphone for which this approximation holds, C_{AB1} only affects the performance for frequencies above the upper cutoff frequency. For the circuits of Fig. 5.9, we can write

$$p_D = T(s)p_i + S_D u_D Z_A \qquad u_D = \frac{-1}{Z_M}\left(\frac{E}{x_0 s}i + S_D p_D\right) \tag{5.6}$$

$$e_{oc} = \frac{E}{x_0 s}u_D \qquad i_{sc} = -\frac{E}{x_0 s}u_D C_{E0}s = -\frac{E C_{E0}}{x_0}u_D \tag{5.7}$$

where e_{oc} is the open-circuit output voltage ($i = 0$), i_{sc} is the short-circuit output current ($e = 0$), and Z_A and Z_M are given by

$$Z_A = (M_{A1} + M_{AS})s + R_{AS} + \frac{1}{C_{AB2}s} \tag{5.8}$$

$$Z_M = M_{MD}s + R_{MD} + \frac{1}{C_{MD}s} \tag{5.9}$$

To solve for the transfer function for e_{oc}, we use the equations for p_D and u_D (with $i = 0$) in Eq. 5.6 to solve for u_D as a function of $T(s)p_i$. This is substituted into e_{oc} in Eq. (5.7) to obtain

$$\begin{aligned} e_{oc} &= -\frac{E S_D}{x_0 s\left(Z_M + S_D^2 Z_A\right)}T(s)p_i \\ &= -\frac{E C_{MT} S_D}{x_0} \times \frac{1}{\left(s/\omega_0\right)^2 + (1/Q)\left(s/\omega_0\right) + 1}T(s)p_i \end{aligned} \tag{5.10}$$

where ω_0 is the fundamental resonance frequency and Q is the quality factor. These are given by

$$\omega_0 = \frac{1}{\sqrt{M_{MT}C_{MT}}} \qquad Q = \frac{\omega_0 M_{MT}}{R_{MT}} = \frac{1}{\omega_0 R_{MT}C_{MT}} = \frac{1}{R_{MT}}\sqrt{\frac{M_{MT}}{C_{MT}}} \tag{5.11}$$

M_{MT}, R_{MT}, and C_{MT} are the total effective mechanical mass, resistance, and compliance given by

$$M_{MT} = M_{MD} + S_D^2\left(M_{A1} + M_{AS}\right) \qquad R_{MT} = R_{MD} + S_D^2 R_{AS} \tag{5.12}$$

$$C_{MT} = \left[\frac{1}{C_{MD}} + \frac{S_D^2}{C_{AB2}}\right]^{-1} \tag{5.13}$$

Aside from the function $T\left(s\right)$, Eq. (5.10) shows that the high-frequency response of the condenser microphone is characterized by a second-order low-pass transfer function. For $\omega > \omega_0$, the response rolls off at a rate of 40 dB /dec. The response at $\omega = \omega_0$ is determined by Q. For example, the response at resonance is down by 3 dB for $Q = 1/\sqrt{2}$. A typical range of values for Q might be from 0.5 to 1. For $Q < 0.5$, the high-frequency response would exhibit excessive attenuation. For $Q > 1$, the high-frequency response would exhibit undesirable peaking near the resonance frequency.

To solve for the transfer function for i_{sc}, we use the equations for p_D and u_D in Eq. (5.6) to solve for u_D as a function of i and $T\left(s\right)p_i$. This is substituted into i_{sc} in Eq. (5.7) to obtain

$$i_{sc} = \frac{EC_{E0}S_D}{x_0} \frac{1}{Z_M + S_D^2 Z_A - E^2 C_{E0}/x_0^2 s} T\left(s\right)p_i \tag{5.14}$$

The output impedance is then given by

$$Z_{out} = \frac{e_{oc}}{-i_{sc}} = \frac{1}{C_{E0}s} - \frac{E^2}{x_0^2 s^2 \left(M_{MT}s + R_{MT} + 1/C_{MT}s\right)} \tag{5.15}$$

With the aid of some algebra, this equation can be rewritten as follows:

$$Z_{out} = \left[\frac{1}{C_{E0}} - \frac{E^2 C_{MT}}{x_0^2}\right]\frac{1}{s} + \frac{E^2 R_{MT}C_{MT}^2}{x_0^2} \frac{\left(M_{MT}/R_{MT}\right)s + 1}{M_{MT}C_{MT}s^2 + R_{MT}C_{MT}s + 1} \tag{5.16}$$

After more algebra, this expression can be put into the form

$$Z_{out} = \frac{1}{C_1 s} + \left(\frac{1}{C_2 s}\right) \| \left(R + Ls\right) \tag{5.17}$$

where C_1, C_2, R, and L are given by

$$C_1 = \left[\frac{1}{C_{E0}} - \frac{E^2 C_{MT}}{x_0^2}\right]^{-1} \qquad C_2 = \frac{x_0^2}{E^2 C_{MT}} \tag{5.18}$$

$$R = \frac{E^2 R_{MT}C_{MT}^2}{x_0^2} \qquad L = \frac{E^2 M_{MT}C_{MT}^2}{x_0^2} \tag{5.19}$$

The equivalent circuit for the condenser microphone, including the external load resistor, is given in Fig. 5.9(d). In the audio frequency band, the output voltage e is independent of the output impedance provided $R_L' \gg \left|Z_{out}\right|$. In this case, we have $e = e_{oc}$. At very low frequencies, the magnitude of the impedance of capacitor C_1 becomes large. This causes the output voltage to decrease at a rate of 20 dB/dec as frequency is decreased.

It can be seen from Eq. (5.18) that C_1 can be made to be infinite if the polarizing voltage E has the value

$$E_{crit} = \frac{x_0}{\sqrt{C_{E0}C_{MT}}} \tag{5.20}$$

For this polarizing voltage, the low-frequency response is not limited by the output impedance. The voltage given by Eq. (5.20) is called the critical polarization voltage. Any voltage greater than this will pull the diaphragm the whole way to the back plate. For this reason, the polarization voltage must always be less than the critical voltage.

5.6 Condenser Microphone SPICE Simulation

An example application of the circuits for the condenser microphone is given in this section. The assumed specifications are: aluminum diaphragm material of density $\rho_1 = 2700\,\text{kg/m}^3$, diaphragm, electrode, and front air cavity radii $a = 1\,\text{cm}$, diaphragm thickness $t = 40\,\mu\text{m}$, diaphragm to back plate spacing $x_0 = 40\,\mu\text{m}$, diaphragm tension $T = 2 \times 10^4\,\text{N/m}$, back air cavity volume equal to 100 times front air cavity volume, polarizing voltage $E = 300\,\text{V}$, and total quality factor $Q = 1$ at the fundamental resonance frequency.

1. If we assume that the diaphragm vibrates in its fundamental mode, its mechanical mass M_{MD} and compliance C_{MD} are given by

$$M_{MD} = \frac{4}{3}\pi a^2 t \rho_1 = 4.52 \times 10^{-5}\,\text{kg} \qquad C_{MD} = \frac{1}{8\pi T} = 1.99 \times 10^{-6}\,\text{m/N}$$

The acoustic compliance of the front cavity is given by

$$C_{AB1} = \frac{V_{AF}}{\rho_0 c^2} = 8.95 \times 10^{-14}\,\text{m}^5/\text{N}$$

The compliance of the back cavity is $C_{AB2} = 100 C_{AB1} = 8.95 \times 10^{-12}\,\text{m}^5/\text{N}$. A diaphragm mechanical damping resistance $R_{MD} = 0.178\,\text{N s/m}$ is assumed. To set the quality factor at $Q = 1$, the screen perforations in the back plate must have an acoustic resistance $R_{AS} = 5.22 \times 10^7\,\text{N s/m}^5$. We will take the acoustic mass of the screen perforations to be $M_{AS} = 132\,\text{kg/m}^4$. The electrical capacitance is given by

$$C_{E0} = \frac{\epsilon_0 \pi a^2}{x_0} = 69.5\,\text{pF}$$

An effective load resistance of $R_L' = 20\,\text{M}\Omega$ is assumed for the simulation.

2. Fig. 5.10 shows the complete controlled source model. The circuit of Fig. 5.4(b) models the incident plane wave and the external air load. The pressure source p_i represents the acoustic pressure in an incident plane wave in the absence of the microphone. The volume velocity source p_i/R_{A2} (the Gpb source) models the effects of reflections from the diaphragm for a plane wave that is incident normally on the diaphragm. When the direction of incidence is in the plane of the diaphragm, this source is omitted. The resistor R_{AL} is included to prevent nodes 4, 5, and 6 from being floating nodes at dc. Without this resistor, SPICE would not run. The value of R_{AL} for the following simulations has been chosen to be large enough so that it is an open circuit for all practical purposes. The SPICE netlist for the circuit is given in Table 5.1. In the deck, the incident pressure is assumed to have the amplitude $p_i = 0.1\,\text{Pa}$ (1μbar) for which the *SPL* is 74 dB.

Table 5.1: SPICE Netlist for the Condenser Microphone

CONDENSER MIC EXAMPLE	Ca1 3 2 38.7p	LMas 5 4 132
RL 11 0 20Meg	Vd2 11 12 AC 0	Ras 6 5 52.2Meg
RaL 6 0 1E12	Vd1 10 0 AC 0	Gpb 0 3 1 0 772n
Rmd 8 9 0.178	Vpi 1 0 AC 0.1	Ra2 2 1 1.3Meg
Ra1 3 2 654k	FECe0u 0 12 Vd1 522u	LMa1 3 1 23
Ce0 12 0 69.5p	FECmi 7 0 Vd2 14.9	.ac dec 50 100 100k
CMd 7 0 1.99μ	ESdPd 9 10 3 4 314μ	.END
Cab2 6 0 8.95p	LMmd 7 8 45.2μ	
Cab1 4 0 89.5f	FSdUd 4 3 Vd1 314u	

Fig. 5.11 shows the calculated output voltages in dB as a function of frequency for the incident pressure of 0.1 Pa. The voltage output is shown for two cases: with the volume velocity source p_i/R_{A2} (the Gpb

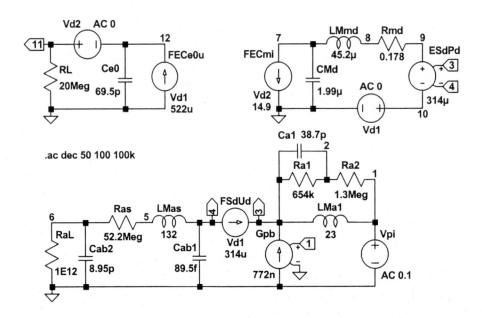

Figure 5.10: SPICE circuit for the condenser microphone.

source) that models reflections from the diaphragm omitted (lower curve) and with the source in the circuit (upper curve). The curves model the range of expected responses for angles of incidence between $0°$ and $90°$. The low-frequency rolloff is caused by the capacitor C_1 in the circuit. The figure illustrates the typical response of a pressure responding microphone in a free field environment. If the quality factor is decreased, the response for $0°$ incidence can be flattened out.

5.7   Condenser Microphone Buffer Amplifiers

Because the output impedance of the condenser microphone is so high, it is necessary to use an electronic buffer to interface the condenser element to the output cable and load. This buffer amplifier is normally part of the microphone. In microphones designed for recording, the power to the buffer amplifier is commonly supplied as a common-mode dc voltage on the balanced cable that connects the microphone to the remote preamplifier. This is called phantom powering. The audio signal on the cable is a differential signal.

Fig. 5.12 shows a typical arrangement. The condenser element is coupled through capacitor C_1 to JFET J_1, which is connected as a source-follower stage. The output from the source follower drives BJT Q_1, which is connected as an emitter-follower stage. The combination of the two stages gives an very high input impedance and a very low output impedance. The output from the emitter follower is coupled through capacitor C_2 to transformer T_1 which drives the balanced output line. The transformer is necessary to convert the unbalanced or single-ended signal from the emitter follower into a balanced or differential signal. The ac gain of the buffer amplifier and transformer is less than unity, a typical value might be 0.7.

The dc polarizing voltage to the condenser element in Fig. 5.12 is supplied through resistor R_1. This resistor connects to the output of a rectifier which converts the ac output voltage from an ultrasonic oscillator into a dc voltage. The ripple on the rectified voltage is filtered by R_2, C_3, and C_4. For simplicity, the oscillator circuit is not shown in the figure. The oscillator is powered by the same phantom voltage which powers the buffer amplifier circuit. In order to obtain a sufficiently high dc polarizing voltage for the condenser element, the ac output voltage from the oscillator must be stepped up by a transformer before the voltage is applied to the rectifying diode. The oscillator frequency must be well above the audio band in order to minimize the chance of interference with the output signal.

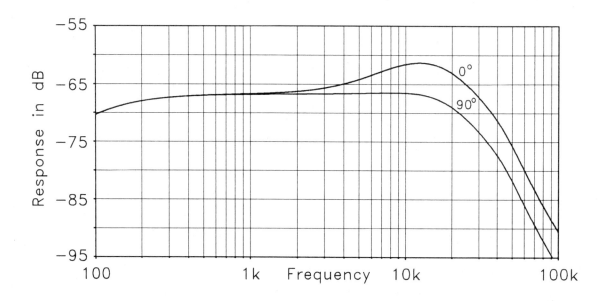

Figure 5.11: Calculated frequency responses for the condenser microphone. Lower curve is for incidence parallel to the diaphragm. Upper curve is for incidence perpendicular to the diaphragm.

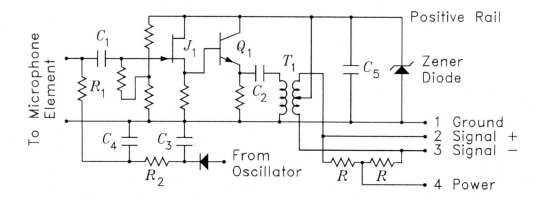

Figure 5.12: Circuit diagram of a typical condenser microphone buffer amplifier with phantom powering.

The output cable connects between terminals 1, 2, and 3 and the external preamplifier which contains the phantom power supply. Terminal 1 is the ground lead. The ac output signal is a differential or balanced signal between terminals 2 and 3. Terminal 4 is in the external preamplifier where phantom power is applied to the cable through two equal value resistors labeled R in the circuit. The phantom power is a common mode dc voltage on the cable which appears at the center tap of the secondary winding of transformer T_1 which connects to the positive rail for the circuit. The zener diode acts as a shunt voltage regulator. Capacitor C_5 is a decoupling capacitor which makes the positive rail an ac ground. Microphones which are designed to be operated with phantom power are designed so that they will work with a wide range of dc voltages applied to the resistors. Typically, this voltage might be in the range of 8 V to 50 V. The required resistor values are functions of this voltage.

5.8   Dynamic Microphone

The dynamic microphone is probably the most commonly used type in sound recording, broadcasting, and public address systems. It is very rugged and can be designed for high quality performance. Unlike the condenser microphone, it requires no power supply and its output impedance is low enough so that no active buffer amplifiers are required to interface it to a cable. The basic transducer mechanism is the moving-coil transducer discussed in Section 4.4.

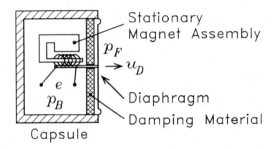

Figure 5.13: Construction of the dynamic microphone.

Fig. 5.13 shows the basic cross section of a typical dynamic microphone. It consists of a capsule with a diaphragm in one wall. Directly behind the diaphragm is a piece of felt which adds acoustical resistance to damp the diaphragm motion. Resistive elements employing narrow slits such as the one shown in Fig. 3.7(b) are also used for damping. The diaphragm is connected to a coil of wire which moves in a magnetic field set up by a stationary magnet assembly. When the diaphragm vibrates, an ac voltage is induced in the coil. In the figure, e is the voltage output of the coil, p_F and p_B, respectively, are the acoustic pressures on the front and back of the diaphragm, u_D is the mechanical velocity of the diaphragm, and $S_D = \pi a^2$ is its piston area. The net force on the diaphragm due to the pressure difference $p_D = p_F - p_B$ is given by $f_D = S_D p_D$, where the direction of this force is in the $-u_D$ direction.

The analogous circuits are given in Fig. 5.14. In the electrical circuit, R_L is the external load resistor and R_E is the resistance of the transducer coil. The coil also exhibits an inductance which we assume is negligible for the analysis here. The induced emf in the coil is given by $e_c = B\ell u_D$, where B is the magnetic flux that cuts the coil, ℓ is the effective length of wire cut by the flux, and u_D is the mechanical velocity of the diaphragm. In the mechanical circuit, M_{MD} is the effective moving mass of the diaphragm and coil assembly, R_{MS} is the mechanical damping resistance of the diaphragm suspension, and C_{MS} is the mechanical compliance of the suspension. In the acoustical circuit, R_{AF} is the acoustical resistance of the felt damping element, and C_{AB} is the acoustical compliance of the air in the cavity behind the diaphragm. The latter is given by $C_{AB} = V_{AB}/\rho_0 c^2$, where V_{AB} is the effective air volume in the cavity.

We assume a plane wave of amplitude p_i that is incident normally on the diaphragm. The acoustic analogous circuit for the air load external to the diaphragm is modeled in Fig. 5.14(c) by the pressure source

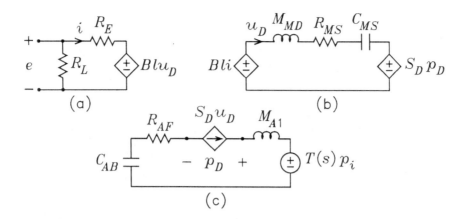

Figure 5.14: Analogous circuits for the dynamic microphone. (a) Electrical. (b) Mechanical. (c) Acousitcal.

$T(s)p_i$ and acoustic mass M_{A1}, where $T(s)$ is given by Eq. (5.1) and $M_{A1} = 0.6133\rho_0/\pi a$. This is the low-frequency approximation to the acoustical circuit of Fig. 5.4(a). It assumes that the frequency is low enough so that the reactance of acoustic mass M_{A1} is small compared to the impedance of the other elements in the circuit. Although the other elements are difficult to handle in deriving a transfer function, they can easily be included in a computer analysis of the circuits.

From Fig. 5.14, we can write

$$p_D = T(s)p_i + S_D u_D Z_A u_D = \frac{B\ell i - S_D p_D}{Z_M} \tag{5.21}$$

$$e = B\ell u_D \times \frac{R_L}{R_L + R_E} \qquad i = \frac{-B\ell u_D}{R_L + R_E} \tag{5.22}$$

where Z_A and Z_M are the impedances given by

$$Z_A = M_{A1}s + R_{AF} + \frac{1}{C_{AB}s} \qquad Z_M = M_{MD}s + R_{MS} + \frac{1}{C_{MS}s} \tag{5.23}$$

It is straightforward to solve these equations for the load voltage e to obtain

$$
\begin{aligned}
e &= \frac{-B\ell S_D R_L}{R_L + R_E} \frac{1}{Z_M + S_D^2 Z_A + (B\ell)^2/(R_L + R_E)} T(s)p_i \\
&= \frac{-B\ell S_D R_L}{R_L + R_E} \frac{1}{R_{MT}} \frac{(1/Q)(s/\omega_0)}{(s/\omega_0)^2 + (1/Q)(s/\omega_0) + 1} T(s)p_i
\end{aligned}
\tag{5.24}
$$

where ω_0 is the resonance frequency and Q is the quality factor. These are given by

$$\omega_0 = \frac{1}{\sqrt{M_{MT}C_{MT}}} \qquad Q = \frac{\omega_0 M_{MT}}{R_{MT}} = \frac{1}{\omega_0 R_{MT} C_{MT}} = \frac{1}{R_{MT}}\sqrt{\frac{M_{MT}}{C_{MT}}} \tag{5.25}$$

and M_{MT}, R_{MT}, and C_{MT} are given by

$$M_{MT} = M_{MD} + S_D^2 M_{A1} \qquad R_{MT} = R_{MS} + S_D^2 R_{AF} + \frac{(B\ell)^2}{R_L + R_E} \tag{5.26}$$

$$C_{MT} = \left[\frac{1}{C_{MD}} + \frac{S_D^2}{C_{AB}}\right]^{-1} \tag{5.27}$$

Aside from the function $T(s)$, Eq. (5.24) shows that the transfer function for e is a second-order band-pass filter having a radian resonance frequency ω_0 and a quality factor Q. Let $f_0 = \omega_0/2\pi$ and denote the lower and upper $-3\,\mathrm{dB}$ cutoff frequencies of the transfer function by f_a and f_b, respectively. It can be shown that f_0 and Q are related to the cutoff frequencies by

$$f_0 = \sqrt{f_a f_b} \qquad Q = \frac{f_0}{\Delta f} = \frac{f_0}{f_b - f_a} \tag{5.28}$$

For a given f_0, it can be seen from the latter equation that Q decreases as the bandwidth $\Delta f = f_b - f_a$ increases. For an acceptable bandwidth, the Q must be small. In general, $Q \leq 0.5$ for cases of interest. In this case, the poles of the transfer function for e are real. It can be seen from Eqs. (5.25) and (5.26) that Q is a function of the load resistor R_L. Thus the bandwidth of a dynamic microphone is a function of its load resistance. The bandwidth increases as R_L is decreased.

Example 1 *For a diaphragm diameter of* $1/2\,\mathrm{in}$, *the frequency at which reflections for normal incidence cause the response of a microphone to be boosted by* $3\,\mathrm{dB}$ *is approximately* $9\,\mathrm{kHz}$. *It is desired to design a dynamic microphone having a diaphragm diameter of* $1/2\,\mathrm{in}$ *such that* $f_b = 9\,\mathrm{kHz}$. *For* $f_a = 40\,\mathrm{Hz}$, *calculate the required resonance frequency and quality factor and plot the expected frequency response both for normal and parallel incidence of the sound wave.*

Solution. It follows from Eq. (5.28) that $f_0 = \sqrt{40 \times 9000} = 600\,\mathrm{Hz}$ and $Q = 490/(6000 - 40) = 0.06696$. The coefficients in the transfer function $T(s)$ given by Eq. (5.1) are calculated from Eqs. (5.2) and (5.3). For the 1/2-inch diameter diaphragm, the coefficients are $b_1 = 2.946 \times 10^{-3}$, $b_2 = 2.408 \times 10^{-9}$, $c_1 = 1.817 \times 10^{-5}$, and $c_2 = 1.204 \times 10^{-10}$. The plots for the frequency response are given in Fig. 5.15.

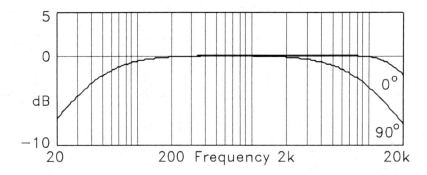

Figure 5.15: Dynamic microphone response plots.

5.9   Ribbon Microphone

Fig. 5.16(a) illustrates the construction of a ribbon microphone. A thin metal ribbon which acts as the diaphragm is suspended in a slot between two magnetic pole pieces that attach to a U-shaped magnet. The ribbon typically is 1 in long, 1/16 in wide, and 0.0001 in thick, with a clearance of 0.003 in at each side. A magnetic field fluxes through the slot between the pole pieces in a direction parallel to the width of the ribbon. When an acoustic wave is incident on the ribbon, it vibrates in a direction that is perpendicular to the magnetic field. This generates a force on the free electrons in the ribbon which causes them to move in a direction along its length. This causes an ac voltage to be generated across the ends of the ribbon. This voltage is the electrical output voltage.

The ribbon microphone differs from the condenser and dynamic types in that there is no capsule which isolates the back of the diaphragm from its front. Thus the pressure in an incident acoustic wave pushes

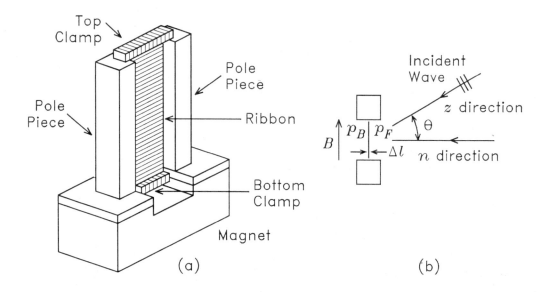

Figure 5.16: (a) Construction of the ribbon microphone. (b) Cross-section showing ribbon between pole pieces.

on both sides of the ribbon. This causes the net force on the ribbon to be proportional to the gradient or directional derivative of the pressure. For this reason, the ribbon microphone is sometimes called a gradient microphone. Because the particle velocity in a wave is proportional to the gradient of the pressure, the ribbon microphone is also called a velocity microphone.

Fig. 5.16(b) shows a cross section of the ribbon microphone with an incident sound wave. The pressure difference across the ribbon is given by $p_D = p_F - p_B$, where p_F is the pressure at the front and p_B is the pressure at the back. We assume that the dimensions of the microphone are small compared to the wavelength so that reflection effects can be neglected. This is equivalent to a low-frequency approximation for the analysis.

Let p_i be the amplitude of the incident wave at the front of the ribbon. At the back of the ribbon, the wave has the amplitude $p_i + \Delta p_i$, where Δp_i is given by

$$\Delta p_i \simeq \frac{\partial p_i}{\partial n}\Delta\ell = (\widehat{n}\cdot\nabla p_i)\,\Delta\ell = \frac{\partial p_i}{\partial z}\cos\theta\Delta\ell \qquad (5.29)$$

where $\Delta\ell$ is the effective distance between the two sides of the ribbon, n is the distance normal to the ribbon, $\widehat{n}$ is a unit vector in the n direction, and θ is the angle between the n and z directions. If we assume that the incident wave is a plane wave, we can write $p_i = p_0 exp\,(-jkz)$, where p_0 is a constant and $k = \omega/c$ is the wavenumber. In this case, Δp_i is given by

$$\Delta p_i = -jkp_0 e^{-jkz}\cos\theta\Delta\ell = -j\frac{\omega}{c}p_i\cos\theta\Delta\ell = -\frac{s}{c}p_i\cos\theta\Delta\ell \qquad (5.30)$$

where the relation $s = j\omega$ has been used.

We see from the above expression that the change in pressure is proportional to $\cos\theta$. It follows that the microphone does not respond to a sound wave that is incident from a direction parallel to the ribbon. This can be a useful feature when it is desired to reject noise that is incident from the sides.

The analogous circuits for the ribbon microphone are given in Fig. 5.17. The circuits assume that the frequency is low enough so that the dimensions of the ribbon are small compared to the wavelength. For the low-frequency analysis, the effects of reflections from the diaphragm are not modeled. In the acoustical circuit, p_F is the pressure on the front of the ribbon, p_B is the pressure on the back of the ribbon, M_{AA} is the acoustic mass of the air load on each side of the ribbon, and M_{AS} and R_{AS} represent the acoustic

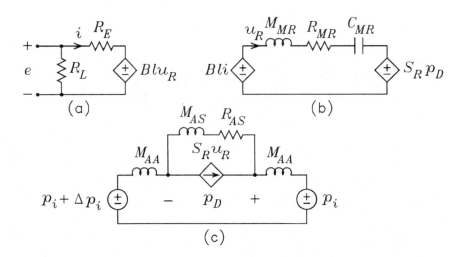

Figure 5.17: Low-frequency analogous circuits for the ribbon microphone. (a) Electrical. (b) Mechanical. (c) Acoustical.

mass and resistance of the two air slots between the edges of the ribbon and the pole pieces. In the analysis below, we assume that the impedance of the latter two elements is large enough so that the elements can be neglected.

In Figs. 5.17(b) and (c), a mechano-acoustic transducer connects the acoustical circuit to the mechanical circuit, where S_R is the area of the ribbon. In the mechanical circuit, u_R is the ribbon velocity, M_{MR} is the mechanical mass of the ribbon, R_{MR} is its mechanical damping resistance, and C_{MR} is its mechanical compliance. A moving-coil transducer connects the mechanical circuit to the electrical circuit, where B is the magnetic flux density between the pole pieces and ℓ is the effective length of the ribbon that is in this field. In the electrical circuit, R_E is the resistance of the ribbon and R_L is the load resistance.

To derive the low-frequency transfer function for the electrical output voltage e, the following equations can be written from the circuits:

$$p_D = \Delta p_i + S_R u_R 2 M_{AA} s \tag{5.31}$$

$$B\ell i - S_R p_R = u_R \left(M_{MR} s + R_{MR} + \frac{1}{C_{MR} s} \right) \tag{5.32}$$

$$e = B\ell u_R \frac{R_L}{R_L + R_E} \qquad i = -\frac{B\ell u_R}{R_L + R_E} \tag{5.33}$$

These equations can be solved for the output voltage to obtain

$$e = B\ell \frac{R_L}{R_L + R_E} \frac{s}{c} \cos\theta \Delta\ell p_i \frac{S_R C_{MR} s}{M_{MT} C_{MR} s^2 + R_{MT} C_{MR} s + 1} \tag{5.34}$$

where M_{MT} and R_{MT} are given by

$$M_{MT} = M_{MR} + 2 S_R M_{AA} \qquad R_{MT} = R_{MR} + \frac{(B\ell)^2}{R_L + R_E} \tag{5.35}$$

The transfer function in Eq. (5.34) can be put into the form

$$e = \frac{B\ell S_R R_L}{c M_{MT}} (R_L + R_E) \frac{(s/\omega_0)^2}{(s/\omega_0)^2 + (1/Q)(s/\omega_0) + 1} p_i \cos\theta \Delta\ell \tag{5.36}$$

where the resonance frequency ω_0 and the quality factor Q are given by

$$\omega_0 = \frac{1}{\sqrt{M_{MT}C_{MR}}} \qquad Q = \frac{1}{R_{MT}}\sqrt{\frac{M_{MT}}{C_{MR}}} \qquad (5.37)$$

We see that the transfer function for e is in the form of a second-order high-pass function. Thus a properly designed ribbon microphone should have a fundamental resonance frequency ω_0 that is lower than the lowest frequency to be reproduced. The frequency response near resonance is determined by the quality factor Q. For $Q = 1/\sqrt{2}$, the microphone exhibits a maximally-flat or Butterworth response. Any value of $Q > 1/\sqrt{2}$ causes the response to exhibit a peak near the resonance frequency.

In a typical unit, the fundamental resonance frequency is 15 Hz to 25 Hz. Above about 2 kHz, the effect of reflections comes into play in determining the response. The shape of the pole pieces on each side of the ribbon has a big effect on this. By properly shaping the pole pieces, good high-frequency response can be obtained to well over 10 kHz. A high-frequency analysis of the microphone is beyond the scope of our treatment here.

5.10 Proximity Effect

The analysis of the ribbon microphone in the preceding section assumes a plane-wave incident on the microphone. This is usually the case when the microphone is used in the far field of a source. When it is used near a talker, the wave is more accurately modeled as a spherical wave. In this case, the incident pressure is given by

$$p_i = K\frac{e^{-jkr}}{r} \qquad (5.38)$$

The change in incident pressure across the ribbon is given by

$$\Delta p_i \simeq \frac{\partial p_i}{\partial n}\Delta\ell = (\hat{n}\cdot\nabla p_i)\,\Delta\ell = \frac{\partial p_i}{\partial r}\cos\theta\Delta\ell \qquad (5.39)$$

which reduces to

$$\Delta p_i = -\left(\frac{1}{r} + jk\right)K\frac{e^{-jkr}}{r}\cos\theta\Delta\ell = -\left(\frac{1}{r} + \frac{j\omega}{c}\right)p_i\cos\theta\Delta\ell \qquad (5.40)$$

If we let $s = j\omega$, the above equation can be written

$$\Delta p_i = -\frac{s}{c}p_i\cos\theta\Delta\ell\left(1 + \frac{c}{sr}\right) \qquad (5.41)$$

When Eqs. (5.30) and (5.41) are compared, it follows that the pressure difference for the spherical wave case is equal to the pressure difference for the plane wave case multiplied by a transfer function which accounts for the proximity effect. This transfer function is given by

$$H_{prox}(s) = 1 + \frac{c}{sr} \qquad |H_{prox}(j\omega)| = \sqrt{1 + \left(\frac{c}{\omega r}\right)^2} \qquad (5.42)$$

For $s = j\omega$ and $c/\omega r \ll 1$, $H(j\omega) \simeq 1$ and the ribbon microphone has the same frequency response as for a plane wave. For $c/\omega r \gg 1$, $H(j\omega) \simeq c/j\omega$ and the ribbon microphone has a frequency response that varies as $1/\omega$ or $1/f$. This causes the bass frequencies to be boosted. This is called the proximity effect. Male radio announcers and singers often use this effect to introduce a "throaty" or "bassy" quality to their voice.

The break frequency below which the proximity effect causes the bass frequencies to be boosted is a function of the distance separating the microphone and the talker. The break frequency is given by

$$f_{prox} = \frac{c}{2\pi r} \qquad (5.43)$$

At this frequency, the boost due to the proximity effect is 3 dB. Below this frequency, the asymptotic slope is -6 dB /octave. For example, the distance $r = 1$ ft gives $f_{prox} = 180$ Hz. This break frequency is high enough to cause a perceptible bass boost in the lowest frequencies of the average male voice. The distance $r = 6$ in causes the break frequency to be doubled to $f_{prox} = 360$ Hz. This is high enough to produce a strong bass boost in the average male voice.

Example 2 *A ribbon microphone has a fundamental resonance frequency $f_0 = 20$ Hz and a quality factor $Q = 0.8$. Plot the frequency response at low frequencies for an incident plane wave and incident spherical waves for $r = c/80\pi = 4.5$ ft, $c/160\pi = 2.25$ ft, and $c/320\pi = 1.13$ ft.*

Solution. For the incident spherical wave, the normalized transfer function for the output voltage is given by

$$e = \left[1 + \frac{c}{j\omega r}\right] \frac{(s/\omega_0)^2}{(s/\omega_0)^2 + (1/Q)(s/\omega_0) + 1} \tag{5.44}$$

For the plane wave case, the transfer function in brackets is omitted. Fig. 5.18 shows the Bode magnitude plots for the three cases. The response is not calculated for frequencies higher than 2 kHz because diffraction effects have not been modeled.

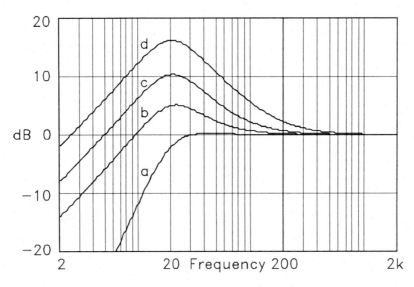

Figure 5.18: Ribbon microphone responses. (a) Incident plane wave. Incident spherical waves for (b) $r = 4.5$ ft, (c) $r = 2.25$ ft, and (d) $r = 1.13$ ft.

5.11   Combination Microphone

A combination pressure and pressure-gradient microphone is one which responds to both the pressure and the pressure gradient in an incident acoustic wave. The microphone is realized by placing a resistively loaded vent into one wall of the capsule of a pressure microphone. Such a microphone can be designed to exhibit a polar pickup pattern that is in the shape of a cardioid. For this reason, the combination pressure and pressure-gradient microphone is also called a cardioid microphone. The cardiod microphone was discovered quite by accident when the cover was left off of the access hole of a pressure microphone that was being tested in a anechoic chamber.

Fig. 5.19 shows the construction of a dynamic cardioid microphone. It consists of a capsule with a diaphragm in one wall, a moving-coil transducer, and a resistively loaded vent hole in another wall. The

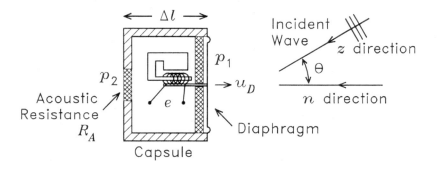

Figure 5.19: Construction of a dynamic cardiod microphone.

low-frequency circuits are shown in Fig. 5.20. In the acoustical circuit, p_i is the incident pressure at the diaphragm, $p_i + \Delta p_i$ is the incident pressure at the resistively loaded vent, M_{A1} is the acoustic mass of the air load seen by the diaphragm, R_A is the acoustic resistance of the material in the vent, C_{AB} is the acoustic compliance of the air in the capsule, and $\Delta \ell$ is the effective distance between the diaphragm and the vent. The circuit assumes that the frequency is low enough so that reflection effects can be neglected.

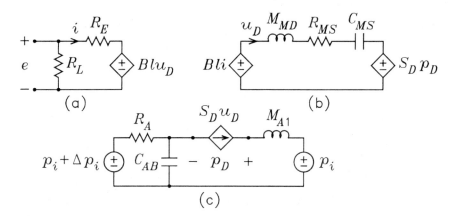

Figure 5.20: Low-frequency analogous circuits for the dynamic cardiod microphone. (a) Electrical. (b) Mechanical. (c) Acoustical.

We assume a plane wave incident on the diaphragm from the direction θ with respect to microphone axis. From Fig. 5.20(c), the pressure difference p_D across the diaphragm is given by

$$p_D = \left[p_i - (p_i + \Delta p_i) \frac{1}{1 + R_A C_{AB} s} \right] + S_D u_D \left(M_{A1} s + \frac{R_A}{1 + R_A C_{AB} s} \right) \tag{5.45}$$

It follows from Eqs. (5.29) and (5.30) that the pressure Δp_i can be written

$$\Delta p_i \simeq \frac{\partial p_i}{\partial n} \Delta \ell = -\frac{s}{c} p_i \cos \theta \Delta \ell \tag{5.46}$$

When this is substituted into Eq. (5.45), the equation reduces to

$$p_D = p_i \frac{R_A C_{AB} s}{1 + R_A C_{AB} s} (1 + B \cos \theta) + S_D u_D \left(M_{A1} s + \frac{R_A}{1 + R_A C_{AB} s} \right) \tag{5.47}$$

where B is given by

$$B = \frac{\Delta \ell}{R_A C_{AB} c} \tag{5.48}$$

The pressure p_i in Eq. (5.47) is multiplied by the function $(1 + B\cos\theta)$. It follows by linearity that the electrical output voltage must also proportional to this function. For $B = 1$, the function reduces to $(1 + \cos\theta)$, which represents a cardiod when it is plotted in polar coordinates. In this case, the microphone is said to exhibit a cardiod pattern. Fig. 5.21 shows the normalized plot of $(1 + \cos\theta)$ as a function of θ. The figure shows that the function is zero for $\theta = 180°$. Thus the response exhibits a null for sound that is incident from this direction. This is a very useful feature of the cardiod microphone when undesirable noise from a given direction is a problem in sound pickup. By pointing the null in the cardiod towards the noise source, the noise can be rejected. Cardiod microphones are popular in public address systems where audience noise is a problem.

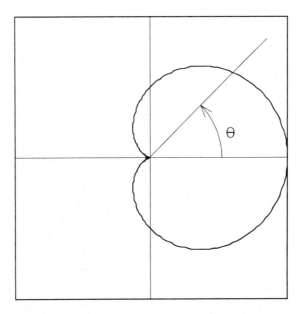

Figure 5.21: Illustration of normalized polar response of the cardiod microphone as a function of angle θ.

The transfer function for the output voltage from the cardiod microphone depends on the transducer mechanism and is more difficult to derive than for the microphones analyzed in the preceding. For example, for the moving-coil transducer, it can be shown that the transfer function is of the form of a third-order asymmetrical band-pass function that can be factored into the form of a first-order, high-pass function multiplied by a second-order, band-pass function. Although the transfer function is straightforward to derive, it is difficult to interpret because it cannot be easily factored into this form. Therefore, the derivation of the transfer function is omitted here.

Like the ribbon microphone, the cardiod microphone is affected by the proximity effect. It produces a throaty or "bassy" effect when used up close by a male talker or singer. Although this effect is preferred by many users, high-quality cardiod microphones usually have a bass cut switch to attenuate the low-frequency response when used up close.

Cardiod microphones are commonly thought to be useful in preventing feedback problems in public address systems. By directing the null toward the loudspeaker system, feedback can theoretically be eliminated. However, this can be a fallacy because it is virtually impossible to prevent users of microphones from moving them. Therefore, the directional characteristics of cardiod microphones should never be relied on as a method of controlling feedback.

5.12   Problems

1. For the condenser microphone example of Section 5.6: *(a)* Calculate the critical polarizing voltage. [3.44 kV] *(b)* Calculate the fundamental resonance frequency. [14.7 kHz]

2. A pressure microphone has a circular diaphragm. At 10 kHz, use Eq. 5.1 or Fig. 5.5 to determine the theoretical increase in the response due to reflections for a diaphragm diameter of *(a)* 1/2 in. [3.37 dB], *(b)* 1 in. [5.54 dB]

3. A simple model of a condenser microphone is a parallel plate capacitor having a constant charge $+Q$ on one plate and $-Q$ on the other. Let E be the voltage across the plates, S be the area of the plates, and x be the spacing between them. If x changes by an amount Δx show that E changes by an amount $\Delta E = Q\Delta x/\epsilon_0 S$ and that $\Delta E/E = \Delta x/x$.

4. A dynamic microphone is to be designed for the specifications: diaphragm diameter $d = 1/2$ in, lower cutoff frequency $f_a = 30$ Hz, and upper cutoff frequency $f_b = 8$ kHz. *(a)* Calculate the fundamental resonance frequency and quality factor. [490 Hz, 0.0615] *(b)* Plot the expected frequency response of the microphone for both normal and parallel incidence. By how much do reflections cause the high frequency response to peak up before it rolls off? [by about 1.4 dB at 7 kHz]

5. Calculate the frequency at which the proximity effect causes the output of a velocity microphone to be boosted by 6 dB compared to higher frequencies for a talker who is 2 ft from the microphone. [52 Hz]

6. A condenser microphone has a diaphragm radius of 1 cm that is stretched to a tension of 2×10^4 N/m. The spacing between the diaphragm and the slotted electrode behind it is 10 μm. The polarizing voltage is 350 V. Assume that $C_{MT} \simeq C_{MD}$. *(a)* If the effect of reflections can be neglected, calculate $|e_{oc}/p_i|$ in V/Pa, in V/μbar, and in dB re 1 V/μbar at midband. [0.0219, 0.00219, −53.2] *(b)* Calculate the peak diaphragm displacement x_p for an incident $SPL = 100$ dB. Neglect the effect of reflections. [17.8 μm]

7. For the numerical values given in the SPICE netlist in Table 5.1, determine the element values for the electrical equivalent circuit of the condenser microphone in Fig. 5.9(d) and the numerical values for the parameters in Eqs. (5.10) and (5.1) for the open circuit output voltage e_{oc}. Perform a SPICE simulation of the circuit with $T(s) = 1$ and $T(s)$ given by Eq. (5.1) for $p_i = 0.1$ Pa. Obtain the plot of the output voltage e_{oc} versus frequency and compare the results to those given in Fig. 5.11. To realize the transfer functions for e_{oc}, use the Analog Behavioral Modeling feature of *PSpice*.

Chapter 6

Moving-Coil Loudspeakers

6.1 Construction

The cross section of a typical moving-coil loudspeaker is illustrated in Fig. 6.1. The moving surface which radiates sound is called the diaphragm. Sometimes it is called the cone because of its cone shape. Some drivers are designed with flat diaphragms. However, the cone shape exhibits better rigidity and is usually the preferred geometry.

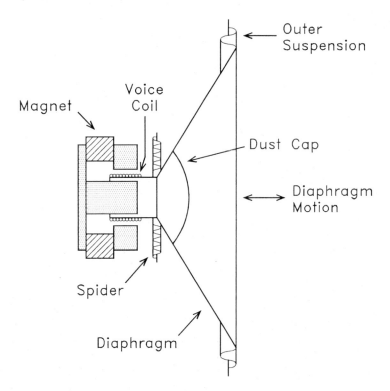

Figure 6.1: Cross section of a moving-coil driver.

The diaphragm is usually constructed of paper or a paper-felt material. Where deterioration due to weather or direct sunlight is a problem, a plastic based material is often used. The paper-felt materials usually exhibit better damping of mechanical resonant modes that can cause peaks and dips in the frequency

89

response in the upper frequency range. The diaphragm is supported by an inner suspension, called the spider, and an outer suspension. These permit diaphragm motion in the axial direction when a signal is applied while providing the restoring force to keep it centered in the absence of a signal.

There are two basic types of outer suspensions, the rolled and the accordion. The rolled suspension has a cross section that has the shape of an arc. It is very compliant and allows the diaphragm to move with relatively little restoring force. Drivers with rolled suspensions are better suited for closed-box systems where the spring constant of the air inside the enclosure dominates over that of the driver suspension. The accordion suspension has a cross section that resembles the folds of an accordion. It is stiffer than the rolled suspension and is used primarily for drivers designed for infinite baffle and vented-box systems.

The electrical input signal is applied to the voice coil. This is a coil of wire wound on a cylindrical form, called the former, which is glued to the diaphragm. A typical voice coil and former are illustrated in Fig. 6.2(a). A dome shaped dust cover prevents dust from entering the driver through the voice coil. The dust cover diameter is often larger than the diameter of the voice-coil former, a feature which can make the voice coil appear to be much larger from the front of the driver.

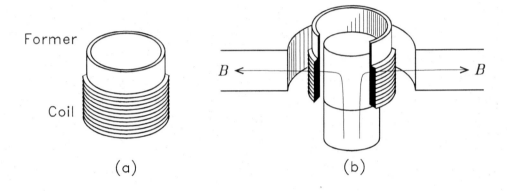

Figure 6.2: (a) Voice coil and voice-coil former. (b) Flux of the magnetic field B through the voice coil.

When current flows through the voice coil, a force is generated which causes the diaphragm to move and radiate sound. The mechanism which generates the force is an interaction of the current with a magnetic field that fluxes through the voice coil. For maximum force, the magnetic field must be perpendicular to the direction of current flow. The field is set up by a permanent magnet that is part of a magnet assembly which focuses the field through the voice coil. Fig. 6.2(b) shows a magnetic field B fluxing through the voice coil. The force generated when a current flows in the voice coil is in the axial direction in the figure.

The magnet assembly consists of the permanent magnet and several pole pieces. The magnet is normally made of an alnico (aluminum-nickel-cobalt) metal alloy, a magnetic ceramic material, or neodymium. Magnets made of neodymium are the strongest permanent magnets known. The pole pieces, made of a high permeability metal, form a low reluctance path to focus the magnetic field through the air gap. A cutaway view of a typical magnet assembly is shown in Fig. 6.3(a). The magnet has a cylindrical donut shape and is sandwiched between the top and bottom pole plates. The air gap is the space between the center pole and the top pole plate. Ceramic magnets normally have the shape shown in the figure while alnico magnets have a slug shape and occupy the position of the center pole piece.

Fig. 6.3(b) illustrates how the force is generated on the voice coil. The figure shows the cross section of one turn of voice-coil wire with the current flowing out of the page. The force is in the direction of the vector cross product $\vec{v} \times \vec{B}$, where $\vec{v}$ is the current velocity. It is upward in the figure. Because an audio signal is an ac signal, the force reverses direction each time the current reverses so that the force on the diaphragm causes it to move in and out with the signal.

The force on the diaphragm is linearly related to the current in the voice coil only if the total number of turns of wire in the magnetic field does not change when the diaphragm moves. Two methods by which

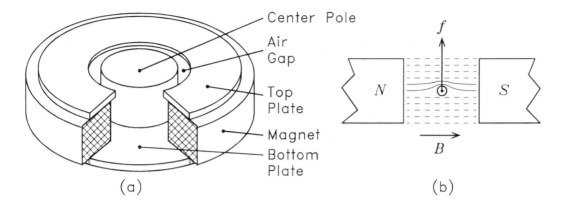

Figure 6.3: (a) Magnet assembly. (b) Force on a single turn of wire in the air gap.

this may be achieved are illustrated in Fig. 6.4. In Fig. 6.4(a), the voice coil is wound so that there is an overhang on each side of the air gap. When the voice coil moves, turns of wire leave the gap on one side while simultaneously the same number of turns enter the gap on the other side so that the total number of turns in the gap remains constant. This geometry is called the long voice coil. It is preferred in woofers and in higher power drivers because a greater diaphragm excursion can be obtained and the heat dissipation is better. Fig. 6.4(b) illustrates the short voice coil for which all turns of wire are located in the central portion of the air gap so that no turns leave the gap when the diaphragm moves. Because all turns are in the magnetic field, the efficiency of the driver can be improved. However, heat dissipation is poor because of the overlapping turns.

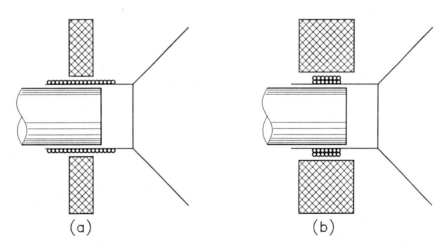

Figure 6.4: (a) Long voice coil. (b) Short voice coil.

There is a maximum distance the voice coil can move for either geometry before the number of turns in the magnetic field no longer remains constant. When this occurs, the driver becomes nonlinear and produces a distorted output. The maximum distance that the diaphragm can move from its zero rest position, either inward or outward before it becomes nonlinear is denoted by the symbol x_{max} and is called the diaphragm displacement limit.

Another nonlinear effect is caused by the inner and outer suspensions. The spring constant of these is constant only for small diaphragm displacements. As the displacement increases, the suspension becomes nonlinear. When the suspension bottoms out, the diaphragm cannot move further. In a well designed driver, the diaphragm displacement limit is reached before the suspension bottoms out.

In modeling the acoustic radiation from a driver, it is common to assume that the diaphragm can be modeled as a flat piston. The radius of this piston is called the piston radius of the driver. It is measured by taking one-half the diameter of the diaphragm aperture measured half-way into the outer suspension on each side. A rule of thumb is often used to relate the piston radius of a driver to its advertised diameter. The rule says that the piston radius in centimeters is approximately equal to the advertised diameter in inches.

The flat piston approximation fails at high frequencies. The frequency at which this occurs is a function of the piston radius, the depth of the diaphragm, and the diaphragm material. Although it is impossible to specify an exact relation for the upper-frequency limit, it is normal to take it to be the frequency at which the circumference of the equivalent flat piston is somewhere between $\lambda/2$ to λ, where λ is the wavelength. The depth of the diaphragm should not exceed about $\lambda/10$ at this frequency. Unless specified otherwise, the upper-frequency limit is taken here to be the frequency at which the circumference is λ. Above this frequency, the radiation from the diaphragm can become directional and exhibit undesirable peaks and dips as the frequency is increased.

6.2 Analogous Circuits

Fig. 6.5 shows the mechanical diagram for a loudspeaker. The source $f_D = B\ell i_c$ represents the force exerted on the diaphragm when the current i_c flows in the voice coil, where B is the magnetic flux density in the air gap and ℓ is the effective length of voice-coil wire cut by this flux. The polarity of f_D is chosen to make u_D increase when i_c is positive. The mass M_{MD} models the mechanical mass of the diaphragm and voice-coil assembly. The compliance C_{MS} models the mechanical compliance of the diaphragm suspension. The resistor R_{MS} models the mechanical losses in the suspension. The source $f_a = -S_D p_D$ represents the acoustic force on the diaphragm generated by the difference in pressure between its front and back, where S_D is the piston area of the diaphragm and p_D is the difference in acoustic pressure across the diaphragm. The polarity is chosen to make u_D decrease when p_D is positive.

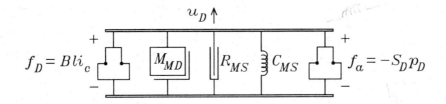

Figure 6.5: Mechanical diagram for the loudspeaker.

Fig. 6.6(a) shows the electrical circuit for the voice-coil. The amplifier which drives it is modeled by a voltage source with an open-circuit output voltage e_g and an output resistance R_g. R_E represents the voice-coil resistance. $L_E(\omega)$ represents the inductance of the voice coil. $R'_E(\omega)$ models the losses in the magnetic circuit. In general, both $L_E(\omega)$ and $R'_E(\omega)$ are functions of frequency. The source $e_c = B\ell u_D$ models the voltage induced in the voice coil when it moves with the mechanical velocity u_D.

To solve for the voice-coil current i_c, we assume that $R_g = 0$. A non-zero R_g can be accounted for by replacing R_E in any equation by $R_g + R_E$. The voice-coil current is given by

$$i_c = \frac{e_g - e_c}{Z_E} = \frac{e_g - B\ell u_D}{Z_E} = \frac{e_g}{Z_E} - \frac{B\ell}{Z_E}\frac{U_D}{S_D} \quad \text{where} \quad Z_E = R_E + R'_E(\omega) \| L_E(\omega) \quad (6.1)$$

The impedance analogous circuit of the mechanical diagram in Fig. 6.5 is obtained by the methods

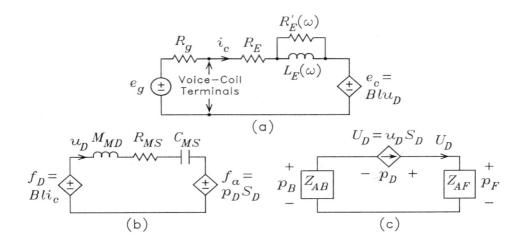

Figure 6.6: Analogous circuits. (a) Electrical. (b) Mechanical. (c) Acoustical.

described in Section 4.3. The circuit is shown in Fig. 6.6(b). The diaphragm velocity is given by

$$u_D = \frac{U_D}{S_D} = \frac{B\ell i_c - f_a}{Z_M} = \frac{B\ell i_c}{Z_M} - \frac{S_D p_D}{Z_M} \quad \text{where} \quad Z_M = M_{MD}s + R_{MS} + \frac{1}{C_{MS}s} \tag{6.2}$$

Fig. 6.6(c) shows the acoustical circuit. The source $U_D = S_D u_D$ represents the volume velocity emitted by the diaphragm. The impedances Z_{AF} and Z_{AB}, respectively, model the acoustic air load impedances on the front and the back of the diaphragm. The pressure difference between the front and rear of the diaphragm is given by

$$p_D = U_D \left(Z_{AF} + Z_{AB} \right) \tag{6.3}$$

For the infinite baffle analysis, we assume that Z_{AF} and Z_{AB} can both be modeled by the analogous circuit from Section 3.7 for the acoustic impedance seen by a flat circular piston in an infinite baffle.

6.3   Combination Analogous Circuit

The combination analogous circuit is a single circuit which relates U_D to e_g. To obtain it, we substitute i_c from Eq. (6.1) and p_D from Eq. (6.3) into Eq. (6.2) and multiply both sides by Z_M/S_D to obtain

$$U_D \left[\frac{(B\ell)^2}{S_D^2 Z_E} + \frac{Z_M}{S_D^2} + Z_{AF} + Z_{AB} \right] = \frac{B\ell e_g}{S_D Z_E} \tag{6.4}$$

Each term in the parentheses is an acoustic impedance. The first term is an impedance that is the dual of Z_E scaled by the factor $(B\ell)^2/S_D^2$. By Eq. (6.2), Z_M/S_D^2 represents three series impedances. Let the acoustical elements representing these be defined as follows:

$$M_{AD} = \frac{M_{MD}}{S_D^2} \qquad R_{AS} = \frac{R_{MS}}{S_D^2} \qquad C_{AS} = S_D^2 C_{MS} \tag{6.5}$$

We define M_{AD} as the acoustic mass of the diaphragm and voice-coil assembly, R_{AS} as the acoustic resistance that models mechanical losses in the suspension, and C_{AS} as the acoustic compliance of the suspension. With these definitions, it follows that $Z_M/S_D^2 = M_{AD}s + R_{AS} + 1/C_{AS}s$. When this relation is used in Eq. (6.4), the circuit of Fig. 6.7(a) follows. This is the Thévenin form of the combination analogous circuit.

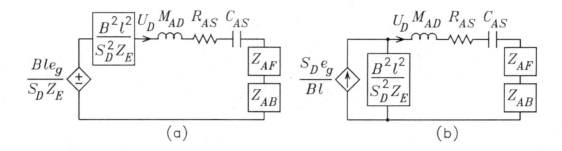

Figure 6.7: Combination analogous circuits. (a) Thévenin. (b) Norton.

The pressure source in Fig. 6.7(a) is inversely proportional to Z_E. A useful transformation can be made which transforms the pressure source into a volume velocity source that is not a function of Z_E. This transformation is to make a Norton equivalent circuit of the pressure source and the series impedance $(B\ell)^2/S_D^2 Z_E$. The circuit is transformed into the one given in Fig. 6.7(b). We refer to this as the Norton form of the combination analogous circuit.

6.4 Infinite Baffle Analogous Circuit

A baffle is any system which acoustically isolates the front of a driver from its back. The simplest loudspeaker baffle is an infinite baffle, i.e. an infinite wall that separates all of space into two halves. In practice, a driver mounted in a hole in a wall, a ceiling, or a door can be approximated by a driver in an infinite baffle. If a driver is mounted in an enclosure and the internal volume is large enough so that the air enclosed does not change the effective spring constant of the diaphragm suspension, the enclosure is often said to be an infinite baffle.

For an infinite baffle system, we model the air load on each side of the diaphragm with the circuit from Section 3.7 for the air load impedance on a flat circular disk in an infinite baffle. Because the circuit is the same for both sides of the diaphragm, the total air load impedance is double that for one side. The dual of the impedance Z_E is a resistor with the value $1/R_E$ in parallel with a series capacitor with the value $L_E(\omega)$ and resistor with the value $1/R_E'(\omega)$. The Norton form of the combination analogous circuit is given in Fig. 6.8(a), where R_{AE}, C_{AE}, and R_{AE}', are given by

$$R_{AE} = \frac{(B\ell)^2}{S_D^2 R_E} \qquad C_{AE} = \frac{S_D^2 L_E(\omega)}{(B\ell)^2} \qquad R_{AE}' = \frac{(B\ell)^2}{S_D^2 R_E'(\omega)} \tag{6.6}$$

6.5 Low-Frequency Solution for U_D

Several approximations can be made for a low-frequency analysis. Although these are strictly valid only for frequencies that are less than one-half the upper piston frequency limit, they are commonly used to predict the response for the entire piston range. The first approximation involves the capacitor C_{AE} of Fig. 6.8(a). At low frequencies, it is replaced by an open circuit. This is equivalent to the assumption that $L_E(\omega)$ is a short circuit in the electrical circuit.

The second approximation involves the air-load impedance. At low frequencies, the impedance of the acoustic mass $2M_{A1}$ in Fig. 6.8(a) is small compared to the impedance of the other air-load elements in parallel with it. Thus the air-load impedance at low frequencies can be approximated by the acoustic mass $2M_{A1}$. The low-frequency circuit is shown in Fig. 6.8(b). In this circuit, M_{AS} represents the total acoustic mass which is given by

$$M_{AS} = M_{AD} + 2M_{A1} = \frac{M_{MD}}{S_D^2} + 2\frac{8\rho_0}{3\pi^2 a} \tag{6.7}$$

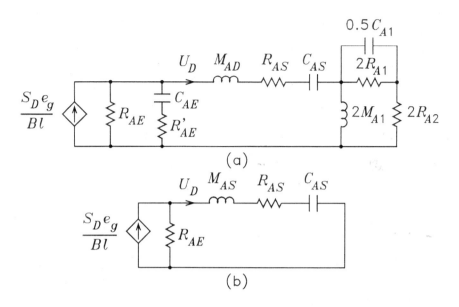

Figure 6.8: Combination analogous circuit. (a) General circuit. (b) Low-frequency approximation.

where a is the piston radius of the diaphragm. We denote the mechanical mass equivalent to M_{AS} by M_{MS}. It is given by

$$M_{MS} = S_D^2 M_{AS} = M_{MD} + 2S_D^2 M_{A1} = M_{MD} + 2S_D^2 \frac{8\rho_0}{3\pi^2 a} \tag{6.8}$$

In the circuit of Fig. 6.8(b), current division can be used to solve for the volume velocity emitted by the diaphragm to obtain

$$U_D = \frac{S_D e_g}{B\ell} \frac{R_{AE}}{R_{AT}} \frac{R_{AT} C_{AS} s}{M_{AS} C_{AS} s^2 + R_{AT} C_{AS} s + 1} \tag{6.9}$$

where R_{AT} is the total acoustic resistance given by

$$R_{AT} = R_{AE} + R_{AS} = \frac{(B\ell)^2}{S_D^2 R_E} + \frac{R_{MS}}{S_D^2} \tag{6.10}$$

To simplify the transfer function for U_D, we define the fundamental resonance frequency $\omega_S = 2\pi f_S$ and the total quality factor Q_{TS} as follows:

$$\omega_S = 2\pi f_S = \frac{1}{\sqrt{M_{AS} C_{AS}}} = \frac{1}{\sqrt{M_{MS} C_{MS}}} \tag{6.11}$$

$$Q_{TS} = \frac{1}{R_{AT}} \sqrt{\frac{M_{AS}}{C_{AS}}} = \frac{1}{R_{AE} + R_{AS}} \sqrt{\frac{M_{AS}}{C_{AS}}} = \frac{1}{\left[(B\ell)^2 / R_E\right] + R_{MS}} \sqrt{\frac{M_{MS}}{C_{MS}}} \tag{6.12}$$

With these definitions, the transfer function can be rewritten in the more compact form

$$U_D = \frac{S_D e_g}{B\ell} \frac{R_{AE}}{R_{AT}} \frac{(1/Q_{TS})(s/\omega_S)}{(s/\omega_S)^2 + (1/Q_{TS})(s/\omega_S) + 1} \tag{6.13}$$

6.6   Low-Frequency Bode Plots for U_D

Fig. 6.9 shows three Bode plots for $|U_D|$ for the cases $Q_{TS} = 1/\sqrt{2}$, 1.0, and $\sqrt{2}$. The maximum value is normalized to unity for each. The plots are made with a vertical axis that has a linear scale and a horizontal axis that has a log scale. The figure shows that the volume velocity is a maximum at the resonance frequency ω_S. For this reason, ω_S is called the velocity resonance frequency of the driver.

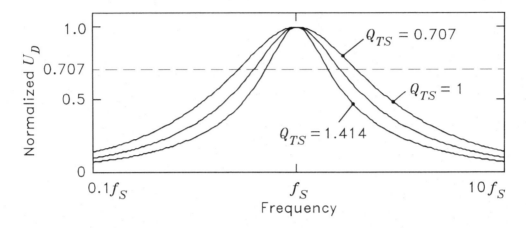

Figure 6.9: Normalized Bode magnitude plots for $|U_D|$.

The quality factor Q_{TS} can be interpreted as a measure of the relative width of the resonance curve. If we denote the two frequencies at which the volume velocity is down from its maximum value by a factor of $1/\sqrt{2}$ by ω_a and ω_b, it can be shown that the difference between these two frequencies is given by

$$\Delta\omega = \omega_b - \omega_a = \frac{\omega_S}{Q_{TS}} \tag{6.14}$$

The figure shows a horizontal dashed line that crosses the Bode plots at the $1/\sqrt{2}$ level. This line intersects each curve at the frequencies ω_a on the left and ω_b on the right. It can be concluded from Eq. (6.14) that the larger Q_{TS} is for a driver, the narrower the width of the resonance peak. For this reason, Q_{TS} is sometimes called a resonance magnification factor. The larger Q_{TS}, the more pronounced the resonance.

6.7   Small-Signal Parameters

There are five driver parameters referred to as the small-signal parameters. These are the velocity resonance frequency f_S, the total quality factor Q_{TS}, the electrical quality factor Q_{ES}, the mechanical quality factor Q_{MS}, and the volume compliance V_{AS}. The first two are defined in Eqs. (6.11) and (6.12). The other three are defined in this section. These parameters are called small-signal parameters because it is assumed that the driver diaphragm displacement is small enough so that non-linear effects can be neglected.

It follows from Eq. (6.10) that R_{AT} is the sum of two resistors, one which models electrical losses in the voice coil and the other which models mechanical losses in the suspension. Because Q_{TS} is a function of R_{AT}, Q_{TS} can be decomposed into two parts, one that is a function of the electrical losses and the other that is a function of the mechanical losses. The mechanical quality factor Q_{MS} and the electrical quality factor Q_{ES} are defined as follows:

$$Q_{MS} = \frac{1}{R_{AS}}\sqrt{\frac{M_{AS}}{C_{AS}}} = \frac{1}{R_{MS}}\sqrt{\frac{M_{MS}}{C_{MS}}} \qquad Q_{ES} = \frac{1}{R_{AE}}\sqrt{\frac{M_{AS}}{C_{AS}}} = \frac{R_E}{(B\ell)^2}\sqrt{\frac{M_{MS}}{C_{MS}}} \tag{6.15}$$

The total quality factor is related to the mechanical and the electrical quality factors by

$$Q_{TS} = \frac{Q_{MS}Q_{ES}}{Q_{MS} + Q_{ES}} \tag{6.16}$$

The fifth small-signal parameter is the volume compliance V_{AS}. This is the equivalent volume of air which, when compressed by a piston having the same piston area as the driver diaphragm, exhibits the same compliance or spring constant as the driver suspension. Fig. 6.10(a) illustrates the definition of the volume compliance. The volume compliance is related to C_{AS} and C_{MS} by

$$V_{AS} = \rho_0 c^2 S_D^2 C_{MS} = \rho_0 c^2 C_{AS} \tag{6.17}$$

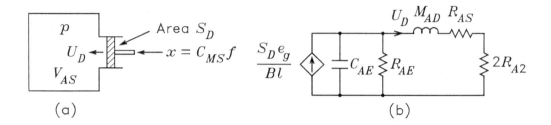

Figure 6.10: (a) Illustration for the definition of volume compliance. (b) High-frequency analogous circuit.

Example 1 *A driver with a rated diameter of* 12 in *(a* = 12 cm*) is mounted in an infinite baffle. Its parameters are:* $M_{MD} = 33.4$ g, $C_{MS} = 1.18 \times 10^{-3}$ m/ N, $R_{MS} = 1.85$ N s/ m, $B\ell = 11.4$ T m, $R_E = 7\,\Omega$, *and* $L_E = 1.8$ mH, *which is independent of frequency, and* $R'_E = \infty$. *Calculate* M_{MS}, f_S, Q_{MS}, Q_{ES}, Q_{TS}, *and* V_{AS}.

Solution. The calculations are summarized as follows:

$$M_{MS} = M_{MD} + 2\frac{8\rho_0}{3\pi^2 a}S_D^2 = 44.3 \text{ g} \qquad f_S = \frac{1}{2\pi\sqrt{M_{MS}C_{MS}}} = 22 \text{ Hz}$$

$$Q_{MS} = \frac{1}{R_{MS}}\sqrt{\frac{M_{MS}}{C_{MS}}} = 3.3 \qquad Q_{ES} = \frac{R_E}{(B\ell)^2}\sqrt{\frac{M_{MS}}{C_{MS}}} = 0.33$$

$$Q_{TS} = \frac{Q_{MS}Q_{ES}}{Q_{MS} + Q_{ES}} = 0.3 \qquad V_{AS} = \rho_0 c^2 S_D^2 C_{MS} = 0.34 \text{ m}^3 = 12 \text{ ft}^3$$

6.8 High-Frequency Solution for U_D

The high-frequency modeling of a loudspeaker driver is not as accurate as the low-frequency modeling because the diaphragm can cease to vibrate as a unit above its piston frequency range. When this happens, mechanical standing waves are set up on the diaphragm that cause its velocity distribution to be nonuniform. These effects cannot be modeled with analogous circuits. However, some understanding of the high-frequency behavior can be gained from the analogous circuits.

To simplify the solution, we neglect eddy current losses by setting $R'_E(\omega) = \infty$ in the electrical circuit. This makes $R'_{AE} = 0$ in Fig. 6.8. In addition, we assume that $L_E(\omega)$ is frequency independent. Next, we replace C_{AS} with a short circuit, $2M_{A1}$ with an open circuit, and $0.5C_{A1}$ with a short circuit. The circuit with the high-frequency approximations is shown in Fig. 6.10(b).

Current division can be used to solve for the high-frequency volume velocity transfer function to obtain

$$U_D = \frac{S_D e_g}{B\ell}\frac{1}{M_{AD}C_{AE}s^2 + (R_{AS} + 2R_{A2})C_{AE}s + [1 + (R_{AS} + 2R_{A2})/R_{AE}]} \tag{6.18}$$

This is the transfer function of a second-order low-pass filter. Thus the volume velocity becomes inversely proportional to the frequency squared at high frequencies. In contrast, Eq. (6.9), which is derived with the low-frequency approximations, predicts that the high-frequency volume velocity is inversely proportional to frequency.

We can obtain an idea of the frequency which divides the low and high-frequency approximations by letting $s = j\omega$ in Eqs. (6.9) and (6.18) and equating the magnitude of the asymptotic high-frequency responses predicted by each. This leads to the equation

$$\frac{S_D |e_g|}{B\ell} \frac{R_{AE}}{R_{AT}} \frac{R_{AT} C_{AS} \omega}{M_{AS} C_{AS} \omega^2} = \frac{S_D |e_g|}{B\ell} \frac{1}{M_{AD} C_{AE} \omega^2} \tag{6.19}$$

Let ω_{u1} be the frequency for which this equation is satisfied. It is given by

$$\omega_{u1} = 2\pi f_{u1} = \frac{M_{AS}}{M_{AD} R_{AE} C_{AE}} = \frac{R_E M_{AS}}{M_{AD} L_E} = \frac{M_{MS} R_E}{M_{MD} L_E} \tag{6.20}$$

If the Bode plots of Eqs. (6.9) and (6.18) are made on log-log scales, it follows that ω_{u1} is the frequency at which the -1 dec/dec asymptotic slope of Eq. (6.9) intersects the -2 dec/dec asymptotic slope of Eq. (6.18). We can conclude that the high-frequency effects can be approximately accounted for in Eqs. (6.9) and (6.13) by multiplying by the low-pass transfer function

$$T_{u1}(s) = \frac{1}{1 + s/\omega_{u1}} \tag{6.21}$$

Thus the volume velocity transfer function becomes

$$U_D = \frac{S_D e_g}{B\ell} \frac{R_{AE}}{R_{AT}} \frac{(1/Q_{TS})(s/\omega_S)}{(s/\omega_S)^2 + (1/Q_{TS})(s/\omega_S) + 1} \frac{1}{1 + s/\omega_{u1}} \tag{6.22}$$

The analysis must be considered somewhat qualitative because we have only predicted the ultimate high-frequency asymptote of the Bode plot. The shape of the actual plot between the low-frequency range and the high-frequency range has not been predicted. However, the result predicts that the high-frequency volume velocity is decreased by a pole in the transfer function that is inversely proportional to the voice-coil inductance. If the inductance is increased, this pole frequency decreases.

Example 2 *For the driver of Example 1, solve for the upper corner frequency f_{u1}.*

Solution: $f_{u1} = R_E M_{MS}/(2\pi L_E M_{MD}) = 7 \times 0.0443/(2\pi \times 0.0018 \times 0.0334) = 820\,\mathrm{Hz}$.

6.9   On-Axis Pressure

In Section 2.13, it is shown that the on-axis pressure radiated by a flat circular piston in an infinite baffle is given by

$$p(r) = j\omega\rho_0 U_D \frac{e^{-jkr}}{2\pi r} \tag{6.23}$$

where U_D is the volume velocity emitted by the piston, r is the distance from the piston to the observation point, and $k = \omega/c$. For the expression to be valid, the observation point must be in the far field region. This condition requires $r \geq 8a^2/\lambda$, where a is the piston radius and λ is the wavelength. At closer distances, Fresnel diffraction effects can cause the pressure to deviate from the value predicted by this equation.

The distance r in the denominator of Eq. (6.23) causes the pressure to drop by a factor of 2 (or by 6 dB) each time the distance is doubled. For purposes of defining a transfer function, we will assume $r = 1\,\mathrm{m}$, even though the distance to the far field may be greater than this. The complex exponential in the equation represents the phase delay caused by the propagation time delay from the piston to the observation point. Because the complex exponential has a magnitude of unity, we omit it in defining the pressure transfer function. Thus we write the normalized on-axis pressure as

$$p = \frac{\rho_0}{2\pi} j\omega U_D = \frac{\rho_0}{2\pi} s U_D \tag{6.24}$$

We see from this equation that the on-axis pressure is proportional to sU_D. In the frequency domain, a multiplication by the complex frequency s is equivalent to a time derivative in the time domain. Therefore, the on-axis pressure is proportional to the time derivative of the volume velocity, which is proportional to the piston acceleration. We conclude that in the far field we hear the acceleration of the piston. For a constant SPL to be radiated, the acceleration must be constant with frequency. Thus the displacement must be inversely proportional to the frequency squared. This means, for example, that the piston must move 100 times as far to radiate the same pressure at 20 Hz as it does at 200 Hz.

6.10   Pressure Transfer Function

To obtain the low-frequency on-axis pressure transfer function, we substitute the low-frequency transfer function for U_D given by Eq. (6.13) into Eq. (6.24) to obtain

$$p = \frac{\rho_0}{2\pi} \frac{S_D e_g}{B\ell} \frac{R_{AE}}{R_{AT}} \frac{R_{AT} C_{AS} s^2}{M_{AS} C_{AS} s^2 + R_{AT} C_{AS} s + 1} \tag{6.25}$$

This can be reduced to

$$p = \frac{\rho_0}{2\pi} \frac{B\ell e_g}{S_D R_E M_{AS}} \frac{(s/\omega_S)^2}{(s/\omega_S)^2 + (1/Q_{TS})(s/\omega_S) + 1} = \frac{\rho_0}{2\pi} \frac{B\ell e_g}{S_D R_E M_{AS}} G(s) \tag{6.26}$$

where $G(s)$ is the second-order high-pass transfer function given by

$$G(s) = \frac{(s/\omega_S)^2}{(s/\omega_S)^2 + (1/Q_{TS})(s/\omega_S) + 1} \tag{6.27}$$

At high frequencies, the response can be modeled approximately by multiplying the pressure transfer function by the low-pass function $T_{u1}(s)$ given by Eq. (6.21). When this is done, the function becomes

$$p = \frac{\rho_0}{2\pi} \frac{B\ell e_g}{S_D R_E M_{AS}} G(s) T_{u1}(s) \tag{6.28}$$

This expression shows that the on-axis pressure is proportional to the product of two transfer functions. $G(s)$ models the low-frequency behavior and $T_{u1}(s)$ models the high-frequency behavior. The high-frequency modeling is only approximate in the sense that it does not model the effects of mechanical resonances in the diaphragm structure. Despite this limitation, the high-frequency model does provide useful information about the response of the driver.

Example 3 *For the driver of Example 1, write the transfer function for the on-axis pressure.*

Solution. The transfer function follows from Eq. (6.28). It is given by

$$p = 0.312 e_g \frac{(s/138.2)^2}{(s/138.2)^2 + (1/0.3)(s/138.2) + 1} \times \frac{1}{1 + s/5158}$$

6.11   Bode Plots of On-Axis Pressure

The low-frequency transfer function $G(s)$ contains the information which predicts the lower cutoff frequency of the driver and the response near cutoff. To construct the Bode plot for $G(s)$, we first let $s = j\omega$. For $\omega \ll \omega_S$, the magnitudes of the first two terms in the denominator of Eq. (6.27) are small and can be neglected compared to the third term so that $G(j\omega) \simeq (j\omega/\omega_S)^2 = (\omega/\omega_S)^2 \angle + 180°$. Thus the Bode magnitude plot exhibits a slope of $+2$ dec/dec on log-log scales or $+12$ dB per octave on dB-log scales. For $\omega \gg \omega_S$, the magnitudes of the second and third terms in the denominator are small compared to the magnitude of the first so that $G(j\omega) \simeq 1$. The Bode magnitude plot exhibits a slope of zero. When $\omega = \omega_S$, $G(j\omega_S) = jQ_{TS} = Q_{TS}\angle + 90°$.

The high-frequency transfer function $T_{u1}(s)$ predicts the upper cutoff frequency of the driver. To construct the Bode plot for $T_{u1}(s)$, we first let $s = j\omega$. From Eq. (6.21), it can be seen that when $\omega \ll \omega_{u1}$, $T_{u1}(j\omega)$ can be approximated by $T_{u1}(j\omega) \simeq 1$. The Bode magnitude plot exhibits a slope of zero. For $\omega \gg \omega_{u1}$, we have $T_{u1}(j\omega) \simeq (\omega_{u1}/j\omega) = (\omega_{u1}/\omega)\angle - 90°$. The Bode magnitude plot exhibits a slope of -1 dec/dec or -6 dB per octave. For $\omega = \omega_{u1}$, $T_{u1}(j\omega) = 1/\sqrt{2}\angle - 45°$.

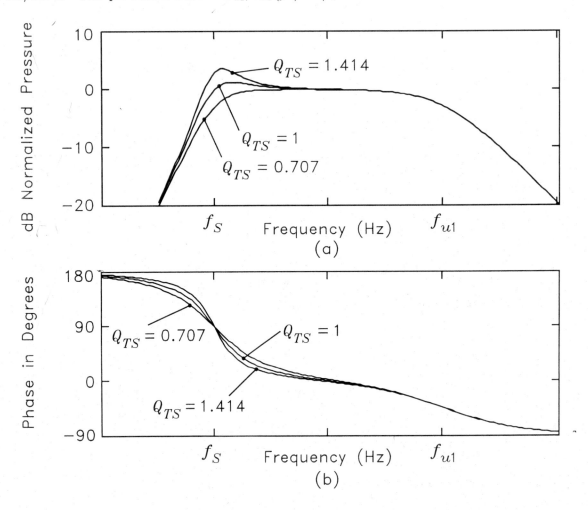

Figure 6.11: Bode (a) magnitude and (b) phase plots for the normalized on-axis pressure.

Three Bode magnitude plots for the product function $G(j2\pi f)T_{u1}(j2\pi f)$ are shown in Fig. 6.11(a). The plots are for $Q_{TS} = 1/\sqrt{2}$, 1.0, and $\sqrt{2}$, where log-log scales are used. The upper pole frequency f_{u1} is taken to be $50f_S$ Hz. The asymptotic slope is $+2$ dec/dec below f_S, zero between f_S and f_{u1}, and -1 dec/dec above f_{u1}. At f_S, the transfer function has a magnitude equal to Q_{TS}. At f_{u1}, it has a magnitude of $1/\sqrt{2}$. Between f_S and f_{u1}, the magnitude approaches unity. The horizontal line in the figure cuts the curves at the $1/\sqrt{2}$ or -3 dB level. It is obvious from the figure that the lower -3 dB cutoff frequency is determined by the resonance frequency f_S and the quality factor Q_{TS}. If $Q_{TS} \ll 1$, the response at resonance is weak and the cutoff frequency is greater than f_S. If $Q_{TS} > 1$, the response at resonance peaks up and the cutoff frequency is lower than f_S.

In the design of crossover networks, the phase response of a driver is a very important consideration. An analytical expression for the phase of the on-axis pressure transfer function is given by the sum of the phase of $G(j\omega)$ from Eq. (6.27) and the phase of $T_{u1}(j\omega)$ from Eq. (6.21). It is

$$\varphi(\omega) = 180° - \tan^{-1}\left[\frac{(1/Q_{TS})(\omega/\omega_S)}{1 - (\omega/\omega_S)^2}\right] - \tan^{-1}\left(\frac{\omega}{\omega_{u1}}\right) \tag{6.29}$$

The plots of $\varphi(2\pi f)$ versus f corresponding to the magnitude plots in Fig. 6.11 are shown in Fig. 6.11(b), where linear-log scales are used.

We see from Fig. 6.11(b) that the phase approaches $+180°$ for $f \ll f_S$, is $+90°$ at f_S, goes through zero between f_S and f_{u1}, is $-45°$ at f_{u1}, and approaches $-90°$ for $f \gg f_{u1}$. These values can be predicted from the slope of the magnitude plot given in Fig. 6.11(a) by using the two rules: (i) Well away from any break frequency, the phase on any asymptote is $90°$ multiplied by the log-log asymptotic slope of the magnitude plot. (ii) At a break frequency, the phase is $90°$ multiplied by the average of the slopes on the adjoining asymptotes. These two rules make it possible to qualitatively sketch a phase plot from the magnitude plot without forming the phase function.

For the qualitative rules of making phase plots to work, all poles and zeros of the transfer function must be in the left half of the complex plane. The transfer functions of physically stable systems always have the poles in the left-half plane. However, transfer functions can have zeros in the right-half plane. These are called non-minimum-phase transfer functions for which the above rules for forming the phase plots do not work.

6.12 Filter Theory Description of $G(s)$

Several descriptive terms from filter theory can be used to describe the low-frequency transfer function $G(s)$ for specific values of Q_{TS}. If $Q_{TS} < 0.5$, the transfer function is said to be overdamped . In this case, the poles are real and the denominator of $G(s)$ can be factored as follows:

$$\left(\frac{s}{\omega_S}\right)^2 + \left(\frac{1}{Q_{TS}}\right)\left(\frac{s}{\omega_S}\right) + 1 = \left(\frac{s}{\omega_1} + 1\right)\left(\frac{s}{\omega_2} + 1\right) \tag{6.30}$$

where ω_1 and ω_2 are given by

$$\omega_{1,2} = \omega_S\left(\frac{1}{2Q_{TS}} \pm \sqrt{\frac{1}{4Q_{TS}^2} - 1}\right) \tag{6.31}$$

If $Q_{TS} = 0.5$, it follows that $\omega_1 = \omega_2 = \omega_S$. In this case, the transfer function is said to be critically damped. If $Q_{TS} > 0.5$, the roots are complex and the transfer function is said to be underdamped. For $Q_{TS} = 1/\sqrt{2}$, $G(s)$ is said to have a Butterworth or maximally flat response. This is abbreviated B2, where the B stands for Butterworth and the 2 stands for second order. For $Q_{TS} > 1/\sqrt{2}$, $G(s)$ is said to have a Chebyshev or equal ripple alignment. This is abbreviated C2. If $Q_{TS} = 1/\sqrt{3}$, $G(s)$ is often said to have a Bessel alignment. For low-pass filters, Bessel alignments are also called linear phase alignments because they optimally approximate a constant time delay in the filter passband. However, it is not correct to say that a high-pass transfer function has a linear phase alignment because it cannot be used to approximate a constant time delay.

It should be obvious from Fig. 6.11 that very small or very large values of Q_{TS} are not desirable if the best frequency response is desired. If the driver is a woofer, a value of Q_{TS} that is too small results in weak bass reproduction near resonance. If Q_{TS} is too large, the bass reproduction near resonance is "boomy" and the driver exhibits poor transient response. The best values of Q_{TS} are probably in the range between $1/\sqrt{2}$ and 1.0 for an infinite baffle system.

Example 4 *For the driver of Example 1, solve for the two poles in the low-frequency response as given by Eq. (6.31). Express the answers in Hz.*

Solution. The frequencies are given by $f_{1,2} = 22\left(1/0.6 \pm \sqrt{1/0.6^2 - 1}\right) = 7.33$ Hz and 66 Hz.

6.13   Cutoff Frequencies

We denote the lower cutoff frequency of a driver by f_ℓ. This is the lower frequency at which the pressure is down by a factor of $1/\sqrt{2}$ or $-3\,\text{dB}$ compared to its midband response. The Bode plot in Fig. 6.11 shows that f_ℓ is a function of both f_S and Q_{TS}. To solve for it, we assume that $|T_{u1}\left(j2\pi f_\ell\right)| = 1$ and solve for the frequency f_ℓ such that $|G\left(j2\pi f_\ell\right)|^2 = 1/2$. If we write $x = f_\ell/f_S$, it follows that x must satisfy

$$\frac{x^4}{\left(1 - x^2\right)^2 + x^2/Q_{TS}^2} = \frac{1}{2} \tag{6.32}$$

It is straightforward to reduce the above equation to a quadratic in x^2 and to solve for the roots with the quadratic formula. Because $x^2 > 0$, the positive root must be chosen. When this is done, it follows that f_ℓ is given by

$$f_\ell = x f_S = f_S \left[\left(\frac{1}{2Q_{TS}^2} - 1\right) + \sqrt{\left(\frac{1}{2Q_{TS}^2} - 1\right)^2 + 1}\,\right]^{1/2} \tag{6.33}$$

This equation predicts $f_\ell = f_S$ when $Q_{TS} = 1/\sqrt{2}$, $f_\ell > f_S$ when $Q_{TS} < 1/\sqrt{2}$, and $f_\ell < f_S$ when $Q_{TS} > 1/\sqrt{2}$.

We denote the upper cutoff frequency by f_{u1}. This is the upper frequency at which the pressure is down by a factor of $1/\sqrt{2}$ or $-3\,\text{dB}$. To solve for it, we assume that $|G\left(j2\pi f_{u1}\right)| = 1$, $L_E\left(\omega\right)$ is independent of frequency, and that $R_E'\left(\omega\right) = \infty$. It follows that f_{u1} is the pole frequency of $T_{u1}\left(s\right)$ which is given by

$$f_{u1} = \frac{\omega_{u1}}{2\pi} = \frac{R_E M_{AS}}{2\pi L_E M_{AD}} \tag{6.34}$$

Example 5 *Solve for the lower and upper half-power cutoff frequencies for the driver of Example 1.*

Solution. From Eqs. (6.33) and (6.34), we have

$$f_\ell = 22 \left[\left(\frac{1}{2 \times 0.3^2} - 1\right) + \sqrt{\left(\frac{1}{2 \times 0.3^2} - 1\right)^2 + 1}\,\right]^{1/2} = 66.8\,\text{Hz}$$

$$f_{u1} = \frac{7 \times 0.0443}{2\pi \times 0.0018 \times 0.0334} = 820\,\text{Hz}$$

Example 6 *(a) If the value of $B\ell$ is changed for the driver of Example 1, calculate the value which will cause $f_\ell = f_S = 22\,\text{Hz}$. (b) By how many decibels does the mid-band on-axis pressure change with the new value of $B\ell$?*

Solution. (a) For $f_\ell = f_S$, the driver has a B2 alignment. This requires $Q_{TS} = 1/\sqrt{2}$. The change in $B\ell$ changes Q_{ES} and thus Q_{TS}. Denote the new Q_{ES} and Q_{TS} by Q_{ES}' and Q_{TS}'. We can write $Q_{ES}' = Q_{MS}Q_{TS}'/\left(Q_{MS} - Q_{TS}'\right) = 0.9$. Eq. (6.15) shows that $B\ell$ is inversely proportional to $\sqrt{Q_{ES}}$. Denote the new value of $B\ell$ by $\left(B\ell\right)'$. Thus $\left(B\ell\right)' = B\ell\sqrt{Q_{ES}/Q_{ES}'} = 6.9\,\text{T\,m}$. (b) Eq. (6.28) shows that the on-axis pressure is directly proportional to $B\ell$. The dB change in pressure is $20\log\left[\left(B\ell\right)'/B\ell\right] = -4.36\,\text{dB}$.

The above example illustrates how reducing the magnet strength of a driver can decrease its lower cutoff frequency, thus improving the bass response. It follows that the bass response of a driver cannot be judged by the size of its magnet. However, the magnet size effects its pressure output. Eq. (6.28) shows that the midband on-axis pressure is directly proportional to $B\ell$. Thus decreasing $B\ell$ reduces the pressure. This requires more power from the amplifier for the same SPL output.

6.14 Effect of Non-Zero Generator Resistance

A non-zero generator resistance, i.e. $R_g > 0$, increases Q_{ES} and Q_{TS} of a driver, thus decreasing the lower cutoff frequency f_ℓ. It also increases the upper cutoff frequency f_{u1}. One of the tricks that is often used to tweak the Q_{TS} of a driver is to add a resistor in series with the voice coil. This can be used to increase Q_{TS} if it is too small, but it cannot be used to decrease it. To investigate the effects of a non-zero R_g on Q_{ES}, we replace R_E in Eq. (6.15) with $R_g + R_E$ and denote the new Q_{ES} by Q'_{ES} to obtain

$$Q'_{ES} = \frac{R_g + R_E}{(B\ell)^2} \sqrt{\frac{M_{MS}}{C_{MS}}} = \left(1 + \frac{R_g}{R_E}\right) Q_{ES} \tag{6.35}$$

Let the new Q_{TS} be denoted by Q'_{TS}. It is given by

$$Q'_{TS} = \frac{Q_{MS} Q'_{ES}}{Q_{MS} + Q'_{ES}} \tag{6.36}$$

Because $Q'_{ES} > Q_{ES}$, the above equation predicts that $Q'_{TS} > Q_{TS}$. It follows from Eq. (6.33) that f_ℓ decreases as Q_{TS} increases. Thus, if a resistor is added in series with the voice coil to decrease f_ℓ, it can cause an undesirable peak to form in the pressure response at f_S. Eq. (6.28) shows that the on-axis pressure radiated by the driver is inversely proportional to R_E. Thus the addition of a resistor in series with the voice coil will decrease the pressure for a given voice-coil voltage. The pressure is decreased by the same factor that Q_{ES} is increased.

The effect of R_g on the upper cutoff frequency can be obtained from Eq. (6.34). When R_E is replaced by $R_g + R_E$ in this equation, the new upper cutoff frequency f'_{u1} is found to be

$$f'_{u1} = \frac{\omega'_{u1}}{2\pi} = \frac{(R_E + R_g) M_{AS}}{2\pi L_E M_{AD}} = \left(1 + \frac{R_g}{R_E}\right) f_{u1} \tag{6.37}$$

It can be seen that the effect of R_g is to increase the upper cutoff frequency by the same factor that Q_{ES} is increased.

Example 7 *A resistor is to be added in series with the voice coil of the driver of Example 1 to lower the half-power cutoff frequency to a value equal to the fundamental resonance frequency. (a) Solve for the value of the resistor. (b) Solve for the new upper cutoff frequency. (c) Solve for the number of decibels that the midband on-axis pressure drops.*

Solution. (a) For the driver to have a half-power cutoff frequency equal to its resonance frequency, it must have a B2 alignment. It is shown in Example 6 that this requires the electrical quality factor to be increased to $Q'_{ES} = 0.9$. Eq. (6.35) can be used to solve for the added resistor to obtain $R = R_E (Q'_{ES}/Q_{ES} - 1) = 12.1\,\Omega$. (b) The new upper cutoff frequency is $f'_{u1} = (1 + R/R_E) f_{u1} = 2.24\,\text{kHz}$. (c) Eq. (6.28) shows that the midband on-axis pressure is inversely proportional to R_E. Thus if a resistor R is added in series with R_E, the on-axis pressure drops by the factor $R_E / (R_E + R) = 7/19.1$ or $-8.7\,\text{dB}$.

6.15 Frequency of Peak Response

Fig. 6.11 shows that a peak can exist in the Bode plot of the low-frequency transfer function $G(j\omega)$ if $Q_{TS} > 1/\sqrt{2}$. We denote the peak frequency by f_{p1}. To solve for it, we set the derivative of $|G(j2\pi f)|^2$ equal to zero. If we let $x = f/f_S$, we obtain

$$\frac{d}{dx}\left[\frac{x^2}{(1 - x^2)^2 + x^2/Q_{TS}^2}\right] = 0 \tag{6.38}$$

It is straightforward to show that there is a real positive solution for x only if $Q_{TS} > 1/\sqrt{2}$. When this is true, it follows that f_{p1} and the relative magnitude of the peak response are given by

$$f_{p1} = x f_S = \frac{Q_{TS}}{\sqrt{Q_{TS}^2 - 0.5}} f_S \qquad |G(j2\pi f_{p1})| = \frac{Q_{TS}^2}{\sqrt{Q_{TS}^2 - 0.25}} \tag{6.39}$$

Example 8 *A driver mounted in an infinite baffle has the parameters* $f_S = 50\,\mathrm{Hz}$ *and* $Q_{TS} = 1.25$. *Calculate* f_ℓ, f_{p1}, *and the relative magnitude of the peak response at* f_{p1}.

Solution. From Eqs. (6.33) and (6.39), we have

$$f_\ell = 50 \left[\left(\frac{1}{2 \times 1.25^2} - 1 \right) + \sqrt{\left(\frac{1}{2 \times 1.25^2} - 1 \right)^2 + 1} \right]^{1/2} = 36.4\,\mathrm{Hz}$$

$$f_{p1} = \frac{50 \times 1.25}{\sqrt{1.25^2 - 0.5}} = 60.6\,\mathrm{Hz} \qquad |G| = \frac{1.25^2}{\sqrt{1.25^2 - 0.25}} = 1.36 \text{ or } 2.7\mathrm{dB}$$

6.16 Voice-Coil Impedance

The voice-coil impedance transfer function $Z_{VC}(s)$ is defined as the ratio of voice-coil voltage to voice-coil current. With reference to Fig. 6.6(a), it is given by

$$Z_{VC}(s) = \frac{e_g}{i_c} = R_E + L_E(\omega)s \| R'_E(\omega) + \frac{B\ell u_D}{i_c} \tag{6.40}$$

where we assume that $R_g = 0$.

To put this into the form of a transfer function, the transfer function for u_D/i_c must be known. To solve for this, we use Fig. 6.6(b) and Eqs. (6.2) and (6.3) to write

$$B\ell i_c = Z_M u_D + p_D S_D = \left[Z_M + (Z_{AF} + Z_{AB}) S_D^2 \right] u_D \tag{6.41}$$

where $U_D = S_D u_D$ has been used. This equation can be solved for u_D/i_c to obtain

$$\frac{u_D}{i_c} = \frac{B\ell/S_D^2}{Z_M/S_D^2 + Z_{AF} + Z_{AB}} \tag{6.42}$$

When this is used in Eq. (6.40), we obtain the following expression for the voice-coil impedance

$$Z_{VC}(s) = R_E + L_E s \| R'_E + \frac{(B\ell)^2/S_D^2}{Z_M/S_D^2 + Z_{AF} + Z_{AB}} \tag{6.43}$$

The first two terms in this equation represent the voice-coil impedance if the diaphragm is blocked, i.e. if $u_D = 0$. The third term represents the effect of the diaphragm velocity on the input impedance. We call this term the motional impedance term and denote it by $Z_{E(mot)}(s)$.

The effect of the motional impedance term on $Z_{VC}(s)$ is important only at the low frequencies where the fundamental velocity resonance occurs. To obtain an equivalent circuit, we use the low-frequency approximation to replace $Z_{AF} + Z_{AB}$ with $2M_{A1}s$, where M_{A1} is the acoustic mass of the air load on one side of the diaphragm. With this approximation, the expression for $Z_{E(mot)}(s)$ can be written

$$Z_{E(mot)}(s) \simeq \frac{(B\ell)^2/S_D^2}{Z_M/S_D^2 + 2M_{A1}s} = \frac{(B\ell)^2/S_D^2}{M_{AD}s + R_{AS} + 1/C_{AS}s + 2M_{A1}s} \tag{6.44}$$

It is straightforward to simplify this equation to obtain

$$Z_{E(mot)}(s) = R_{ES} \frac{(1/Q_{MS})(s/\omega_S)}{(s/\omega_S)^2 + (1/Q_{MS})(s/\omega_S) + 1} \tag{6.45}$$

where R_{ES} is given by

$$R_{ES} = \frac{(B\ell)^2}{S_D^2 R_{AS}} = \frac{(B\ell)^2}{R_{MS}} = R_E \frac{Q_{MS}}{Q_{ES}} \tag{6.46}$$

Thus we can write the voice-coil impedance function as

$$Z_{VC}(s) = R_E + L_E s \| R_E' + R_{ES} \frac{(1/Q_{MS})(s/\omega_S)}{(s/\omega_S)^2 + (1/Q_{MS})(s/\omega_S) + 1} \tag{6.47}$$

The above equation predicts that the dc impedance is R_E. If we assume that the reactance of the voice-coil inductance is negligible at the fundamental velocity resonance frequency f_S, it predicts that the impedance rises to a value $R_E + R_{ES}$ at f_S. At higher frequencies, it falls back toward R_E, and then the voice-coil inductances causes it to rise at high frequencies. Fig. 6.12 illustrates the variation of the impedance with frequency for a typical driver.

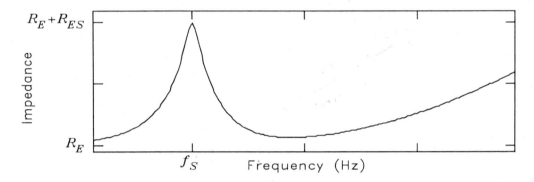

Figure 6.12: Example voice-coil impedance versus frequency.

To form the voice-coil equivalent circuit, we first form the equivalent circuit of the motional impedance term given by Eq. (6.45). Because it is of the form of a band-pass filter function, its equivalent circuit must be a parallel RLC circuit, where the resistor in the circuit is R_{ES} defined in Eq. (6.46). Let us denote the inductor and capacitor in this circuit by L_{CES} and C_{MES}, respectively. In order for the circuit to have the impedance given by Eq. (6.45), these are given by

$$L_{CES} = \frac{(B\ell)^2 C_{AS}}{S_D^2} = (B\ell)^2 C_{MS} = \frac{R_E}{2\pi f_S Q_{ES}} \qquad C_{MES} = \frac{S_D^2 M_{AS}}{(B\ell)^2} = \frac{M_{MS}}{(B\ell)^2} = \frac{Q_{ES}}{2\pi f_S R_E} \tag{6.48}$$

The completed equivalent voice-coil circuit is given in Fig. 6.13. Note that the inductor L_{CES} is proportional to the mechanical compliance C_{MS} and the capacitor C_{MES} is proportional to the mechanical mass M_{MS}. The first letter in the subscripts for L_{CES} and C_{MES} refer to the mechanical element that each is proportional to.

Example 9 *Write the expression for the voice-coil impedance of the driver of Example 1.*

Solution. The impedance function is given by

$$Z_{VC}(s) = 7 + 0.0018s + 70 \frac{(1/3.3)(s/138.2)}{(s/138.2)^2 + (1/3.3)(s/138.2) + 1}$$

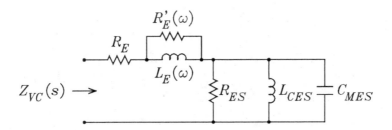

Figure 6.13: Voice coil equivalent circuit.

Example 10 *Solve for the element values in the equivalent circuit of the voice coil for the driver of Example 1.*

Solution. $R_{ES} = (Q_{MS}/Q_{ES}) R_E = 70\,\Omega$, $L_{CES} = (B\ell)^2 C_{MS} = 0.153\,\text{H}$, $C_{MES} = M_{MS}/(B\ell)^2 = 341\,\mu\text{F}$.

6.17   The Lossy Voice-Coil Inductance

At the higher audio frequencies, the inductive component of the voice-coil impedance can often be approximated by the impedance $Z_e(\omega)$ given by

$$Z_e(\omega) = (j\omega)^{n_e} L_e = \frac{\omega^{n_e} L_e}{(j)^{-n_e}} = \frac{\omega^{n_e} L_e}{\cos(n_e\pi/2) - j\sin(n_e\pi/2)} \tag{6.49}$$

where $0 < n_e < 1$. Note that the units of L_e are not henries unless $n_e = 1$. The corresponding admittance function is given by

$$\frac{1}{Z_e(\omega)} = \frac{\cos(n_e\pi/2)}{\omega^{n_e} L_e} - j\frac{\sin(n_e\pi/2)}{\omega^{n_e} L_e} = \frac{1}{R'_E(\omega)} + \frac{1}{j\omega L_E(\omega)} \tag{6.50}$$

It follows that the impedance $Z_e(\omega)$ can be represented by two parallel elements, a resistor $R'_E(\omega)$ and inductor $L_E(\omega)$ given by

$$R'_E(\omega) = \left[\frac{L_e}{\cos(n_e\pi/2)}\right]\omega^{n_e} \qquad L_E(\omega) = \left[\frac{L_e}{\sin(n_e\pi/2)}\right]\omega^{n_e-1} \tag{6.51}$$

For $n_e = 1$, $R'_E(\omega)$ is an open circuit and $L_E(\omega)$ is constant. In this case, the inductance is lossless. For $n_e = 0$, $R'_E(\omega)$ is constant and $L_E(\omega)$ is an open circuit. The inductance has degenerated into a resistance. It follows that the lossy inductance changes from an ideal inductor to a resistor as n_e decreases from 1 to 0.

For a given driver, n_e and L_e can often be determined from one measurement of the voice-coil impedance Z_{VC} at a frequency well above the fundamental resonance frequency. If the motional impedance of the voice coil can be neglected, the impedance of the lossy inductance is $Z_e = Z_{VC} - R_E$. The constants n_e and L_e can be calculated from

$$n_e = \frac{1}{90°}\arctan\left[\frac{\text{Im}(Z_e)}{\text{Re}(Z_e)}\right] \qquad L_e = \frac{|Z_e|}{\omega^{n_e}} \quad \text{where} \quad Z_e = Z_{VC} - R_E \tag{6.52}$$

Example 11 *At $f = 20\,\text{kHz}$, the voice-coil impedance of a 10-inch woofer is found to be $Z_{VC} = 41.7 + j66.6$. If $R_E = 5.1\,\Omega$, determine n_e and L_e.*

Solution. $\text{Re}(Z_e) = 41.7 - 5.1 = 36.6$, $\text{Im}(Z_e) = 66.6$, $n_e = (1/90)\arctan(66.6/36.6) = 0.680$, $L_e = \sqrt{36.6^2 + 66.6^2}/(2\pi \times 20\,\text{kHz})^{0.680} = 0.0259$.

6.18 On-Axis Pressure Sensitivity

The reference on-axis pressure sensitivity of a driver is defined as the magnitude of the midband on-axis pressure at $r = 1\,\mathrm{m}$ for a voice coil voltage $e_g = 1\,\mathrm{V}$ rms. We denote the pressure sensitivity by p_{sens}^{1V}. It is obtained from Eq. (6.28) by setting $e_g = 1$ and $|G(j\omega)\,T_{u1}(j\omega)| = 1$ and is given by

$$p_{sens}^{1V} = \frac{\rho_0}{2\pi}\frac{B\ell}{S_D R_E M_{AS}} = \frac{\sqrt{2\pi\rho_0}}{c} f_S^{3/2}\left(\frac{V_{AS}}{R_E Q_{ES}}\right)^{1/2} \tag{6.53}$$

The on-axis sensitivity is often specified as the SPL at $r = 1\,\mathrm{m}$ either for a voice-coil voltage of $e_g = 1\,\mathrm{V}$ rms or $e_g = \sqrt{R_E}\,\mathrm{V}$ rms. The latter is the rms voltage required for a power of $1\,\mathrm{W}$ into a resistor of value R_E, i.e. the voice-coil resistance. We denote the two SPL sensitivities by SPL_{sens}^{1V} and SPL_{sens}^{1W}, respectively. They are given by

$$SPL_{sens}^{1V} = 20\log\left(\frac{p_{sens}^{1V}}{p_{ref}}\right)\mathrm{dB} \qquad SPL_{sens}^{1W} = 20\log\left(\frac{p_{sens}^{1V}\sqrt{R_E}}{p_{ref}}\right)\mathrm{dB} \tag{6.54}$$

where $p_{ref} = 2\times 10^{-5}\,\mathrm{Pa}$.

Example 12 *For the driver of Example 1, calculate the on-axis pressure sensitivity p_{sens}^{1V} and the SPL_{sens}^{1V} without and with the resistor of Example 7.*

Solution. Without the resistor, the pressure sensitivity is evaluated in Example 3. It is $p_{sens}^{1V} = 0.312\,\mathrm{Pa}$. The corresponding SPL is $SPL_{sens}^{1V} = 20\log\left(0.312/2\times 10^{-5}\right) = 83.9\,\mathrm{dB}$. From Example 7, the added resistor causes the pressure sensitivity to drop by the factor $7/19.1$ to the value $p_{sens}^{1V} = 0.114\,\mathrm{Pa}$. The corresponding SPL is $SPL_{sens}^{1V} = 20\log\left(0.114/2\times 10^{-5}\right) = 75.1\,\mathrm{dB}$. Thus the resistor attenuates the output by $8.8\,\mathrm{dB}$.

Example 13 *If the power amplifier puts out $1\,\mathrm{W}$ of average sine-wave power (sometimes erroneously called $1\,\mathrm{W}$ rms), calculate the $1\,\mathrm{m}$ on-axis SPL_{sens}^{1W} for the driver of Example 1 with and without the resistor of Example 7.*

Solution. Without the resistor, $SPL_{sens}^{1W} = 20\log\left(0.312\sqrt{7}/2\times 10^{-5}\right) = 92.3\,\mathrm{dB}$. With the resistor, $SPL_{sens}^{1W} = 20\log\left(0.114\sqrt{19.1}/2\times 10^{-5}\right) = 87.9\,\mathrm{dB}$. Although the output is less by $4.4\,\mathrm{dB}$ with the resistor, the generator voltage for the two cases is different. The voltage output of the power amplifier must be increased to keep its output power at $1\,\mathrm{W}$. Therefore, thedB change does not correspond to the attenuation introduced by the resistor.

Example 14 *Calculate the $1\,\mathrm{m}$ on-axis pressure sensitivity p_{sens}^{1V} and the SPL_{sens}^{1V} for the driver of Example 1 with the new value of $B\ell$ obtained in Example 6.*

Solution. The original pressure sensitivity is evaluated in Example 3. It is $p_{sens}^{1V} = 0.312\,\mathrm{Pa}$. Eq. (6.53) shows that p_{sens}^{1V} is directly proportional to $B\ell$. Thus $p_{sens}^{1V} = 0.312\times 6.9/11.4 = 0.189\,\mathrm{Pa}$ and $SPL_{sens}^{1V} = 20\log\left(0.189/2\times 10^{-5}\right) = 79.5\,\mathrm{dB}$.

Example 15 *If the power amplifier puts out $1\,\mathrm{W}$ of average sine-wave power, calculate the $1\,\mathrm{m}$ on-axis SPL_{sens}^{1W} for the driver of Example 1 with the new value of $B\ell$ obtained in Example 6.*

Solution. $SPL_{sens}^{1W} = 20\log\left(0.189\sqrt{7}/2\times 10^{-5}\right) = 88\,\mathrm{dB}$.

6.19 Acoustic Power Response

The power output of a driver in an infinite baffle is defined as the acoustic power radiated to the front of the baffle. It is calculated as the power dissipated in the front air load impedance Z_{AF} in Fig. 6.7 and is given by $P_{AR} = (1/2)\,|U_D|^2\,\mathrm{Re}\,[Z_{AF}(j\omega)]$. First, we calculate the low-frequency power. At low frequencies, Eq.

(6.13) predicts that $|U_D|^2 \propto \omega^2$ for $\omega < \omega_S$ and $|U_D|^2 \propto 1/\omega^2$ for $\omega > \omega_S$. The low-frequency approximation to $\mathrm{Re}\,[Z_{AF}\,(j\omega)]$ is given in problem 10 of Chapter 3 and is $\mathrm{Re}\,[Z_{AF}\,(j\omega)] = \omega^2 \rho_0/2\pi c$. It follows that $P_{AR} \propto 1/\omega^4$ for $\omega < \omega_S$ and P_{AR} is constant for $\omega > \omega_S$.

To solve for the complete expression for the low-frequency power, we use the low-frequency approximation for $\mathrm{Re}\,[Z_{AF}\,(j\omega)]$ and Eq. (6.13) for U_D in the expression for P_{AR}. After some algebraic manipulations, the power can be expressed in terms of the transfer function $G\,(j\omega)$ defined in Eq. (6.27). The result is

$$P_{AR} = \frac{1}{2}\frac{\rho_0}{2\pi c}\frac{(B\ell)^2 |e_g|^2}{S_D^2 R_E^2 M_{AS}^2}|G\,(j\omega)|^2 \tag{6.55}$$

As the frequency is increased, the voice-coil inductance causes the volume velocity to decrease with increasing frequency. We model the effect of this on the power by multiplying $G\,(j\omega)$ in this equation by $T_{u1}\,(j\omega)$ in Eq. (6.21) to obtain

$$P_{AR} = \frac{1}{2}\frac{\rho_0}{2\pi c}\frac{(B\ell)^2 |e_g|^2}{S_D^2 R_E^2 M_{AS}^2}|G\,(j\omega)\,T_{u1}\,(j\omega)|^2 \tag{6.56}$$

As frequency is increased, $|G\,(j\omega)| \to 1$ and $|T_{u1}\,(j\omega)| \to \omega_{u1}/\omega$. Thus P_{AR} approaches the value

$$P_{AR} = \frac{1}{2}\frac{\rho_0}{2\pi c}\frac{(B\ell)^2 |e_g|^2}{S_D^2 R_E^2 M_{AS}^2}\frac{\omega_{u1}^2}{\omega^2} \tag{6.57}$$

This predicts that the high-frequency power is proportional to $1/\omega^2$. However, this is not correct, because we have not accounted for diffraction effects which cause the radiation pattern to narrow at high frequencies. It is shown below that the high-frequency power must be proportional to $1/\omega^4$. It follows that there must be another break frequency in the Bode plot to account for an additional factor of $1/\omega^2$.

To solve for the additional break frequency, we use the high-frequency circuit of Fig. 6.10(b) to calculate the high-frequency power. The power radiated to one side of the diaphragm is one-half the power dissipated in the resistance $2R_{A2}$ and is given by $P_{AR} = (1/2)|U_D|^2 R_{A2}$. When the high-frequency limit of Eq. (6.18) is used for U_D, it follows that P_{AR} must have the high-frequency asymptotic value

$$P_{AR} = \frac{1}{2}\frac{S_D^2 |e_g|^2}{(B\ell)^2}\frac{R_{A2}}{M_{AD}^2 C_{AE}^2 \omega^4} \tag{6.58}$$

This predicts that the high-frequency power is proportional to $1/\omega^4$ (a slope of -4 dec/dec or $-12\,\mathrm{dB}$ per octave).

The additional break frequency in the power transfer function must be the frequency at which the Bode magnitude plots of Eqs. (6.57) and (6.58) cross. We denote this frequency by ω_{u2}. It must satisfy

$$\frac{1}{2}\frac{\rho_0}{2\pi c}\frac{(B\ell)^2 |e_g|^2}{S_D^2 R_E^2 M_{AS}^2}\frac{\omega_{u1}^2}{\omega_{u2}^2} = \frac{1}{2}\frac{S_D^2 |e_g|^2}{(B\ell)^2}\frac{R_{A2}}{M_{AD}^2 C_{AE}^2 \omega_{u2}^4} \tag{6.59}$$

where $R_{A2} = \rho_0 c/\pi a^2$ and a is the diaphragm piston radius. Solution for ω_{u2} yields

$$\omega_{u2} = 2\pi f_{u2} = \frac{c}{a}\sqrt{2} \tag{6.60}$$

This is the frequency at which the circumference of the diaphragm is equal to $\sqrt{2}\lambda$.

We conclude that there are two break frequencies which model the high-frequency power rolloff. The break at ω_{u1} is caused by the voice-coil inductance. The break at ω_{u2} is caused by diffraction which causes the pressure to be radiated in a beam that becomes narrower as the frequency is increased, thus decreasing the output power. Let us define a second high-frequency transfer function which models the power rolloff above ω_{u2} by

$$T_{u2}\,(s) = \frac{1}{1 + s/\omega_{u2}} \tag{6.61}$$

Thus the complete power transfer function can be written

$$P_{AR} = \frac{1}{2} \frac{\rho_0}{2\pi c} \frac{(B\ell)^2 |e_g|^2}{S_D^2 R_E^2 M_{AS}^2} |G(j\omega) T_{u1}(j\omega) T_{u2}(j\omega)|^2 \qquad (6.62)$$

This expression is only approximate. It does not account for the effects of mechanical standing waves on the diaphragm which cause the diaphragm velocity distribution to be nonuniform. It assumes that the diaphragm can be modeled as a flat piston, an assumption that fails above the piston range for most drivers. Despite these limitations, the expression provides a basis for calculating the total power output to one side of an idealized driver as a function of frequency.

Example 16 *For the driver of Example 1, solve for the upper break frequency f_{u2} in the power response that is caused by diffraction.*

Solution. Eq. (6.60) gives $f_{u2} = (1/2\pi)(345\sqrt{2}/0.12) = 647\,\mathrm{Hz}$.

6.20   Reference Efficiency

The efficiency η of a driver is defined by

$$\eta = \frac{P_{AR}}{P_E} \qquad (6.63)$$

where P_{AR} is the acoustic power radiated to the front of the diaphragm and P_E is the electrical input power to the voice coil. This expression is a function of frequency. If the frequency is chosen to be in the midband region where the power radiated is flat and the voice-coil impedance can be approximated by R_E, a frequency independent ratio is obtained that is defined as the reference efficiency.

The midband power radiated is given by Eq. (6.62) with $|G(j\omega) T_{u1}(j\omega) T_{u2}(j\omega)| = 1$. The electrical power input to the voice coil at midband is $P_E = (1/2) |e_g|^2 / R_E$. It is straightforward to obtain the following equations for the reference efficiency:

$$\eta_0 = \frac{P_{AR}}{P_E} = \frac{\rho_0}{2\pi c} \frac{(B\ell)^2}{S_D^2 R_E M_{AS}^2} = \frac{\rho_0}{2\pi c} \frac{(B\ell)^2 S_D^2}{R_E M_{MS}^2} = \frac{4\pi^2}{c^3} \frac{f_S^3 V_{AS}}{Q_{ES}} \qquad (6.64)$$

The efficiency can be increased by increasing the $B\ell$ product, by increasing the diaphragm area, by decreasing the voice-coil resistance, and by decreasing the total moving mass. Increasing the diaphragm area, however, increases the moving mass, so that the change in efficiency may be canceled out. With the above definition of the reference efficiency, we can write the following alternate expression for the acoustic output power:

$$P_{AR} = \frac{1}{2} \frac{|e_g|^2}{R_E} \eta_0 |G(j\omega) T_{u1}(j\omega) T_{u2}(j\omega)|^2 \qquad (6.65)$$

Example 17 *Solve for the reference efficiency of the driver of Example 1.*

Solution. From Eq. (6.64), $\eta_0 = (4\pi^2/1131^3) \times 22^3 \times 12/0.33 = 1.05\%$.

6.21   Diaphragm Displacement Function

If a sinusoidal voltage is applied to the voice coil of a driver and the frequency is varied, the diaphragm displacement x_D will be a function of frequency. We can solve for the displacement transfer function using the relation between the displacement and the volume velocity. This relation is $x_D = U_D/sS_D$. When Eq. (6.13) is used for U_D, the following transfer function is obtained

$$x_D = e_g \left(\frac{V_{AS}}{\rho_0 c^2 S_D^2 R_E \omega_S Q_{ES}} \right)^{1/2} \frac{1}{(s/\omega_S)^2 + (1/Q_{TS})(s/\omega_S) + 1} \qquad (6.66)$$

This is the transfer function of a second-order low-pass filter. Bode plots for $|x_D|$ are shown in Fig. 6.14 for $Q_{TS} = 1/\sqrt{2}$, 1.0, and $\sqrt{2}$. The displacement is normalized so that it approaches unity at zero frequency. The horizontal line in the figure cuts the plots at the $1/\sqrt{2}$ or $-3\,\mathrm{dB}$ level.

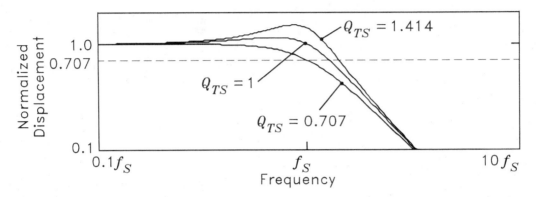

Figure 6.14: Bode magnitude plots of the normalized low-frequency diaphragm displacement.

The frequency at which $|x_D|$ is a maximum is the frequency for which

$$\frac{d}{dx}\left[\frac{1}{\left(1 - x^2\right)^2 + x^2/Q_{TS}^2}\right] = 0 \tag{6.67}$$

where $x = f/f_S$. Let this frequency be denoted by f_{p2}. It is straightforward to show that it is given by

$$f_{p2} = \frac{f_S}{Q_{TS}}\sqrt{Q_{TS}^2 - 0.5} \tag{6.68}$$

where the solution is valid only for $Q_{TS} \geq 1/\sqrt{2}$. For $Q_{TS} < 1/\sqrt{2}$, the solution is $f_{p2} = 0$.

When Eq. (6.66) is evaluated for $s = j2\pi f_{p2}$, the peak value of the displacement can be solved for. It is given by

$$|x_D|_{peak} = |e_g| \left(\frac{V_{AS}}{\rho_0 c^2 S_D^2 R_E \omega_S Q_{ES}}\right)^{1/2} \frac{Q_{TS}^2}{\sqrt{Q_{TS}^2 - 0.25}} \tag{6.69}$$

where again the solution is valid only for $Q_{TS} \geq 1/\sqrt{2}$. For $Q_{TS} < 1/\sqrt{2}$, the solution is the same as for $Q_{TS} = 1/\sqrt{2}$.

Example 18 *A driver in an infinite baffle has the parameters $f_S = 50\,\mathrm{Hz}$ and $Q_{TS} = 1.25$. Solve for the frequency f_{p2}. Solve for the factor by which the diaphragm displacement peaks up at f_{p2} compared to its value at lower frequencies.*

Solution. From Eq. (6.68), the frequency of maximum displacement is $f_{p2} = (50/1.25)\sqrt{(1.25)^2 - 0.5} = 41.2\,\mathrm{Hz}$. From Eq. (6.69), the displacement peaks up by the factor $Q_{TS}^2/\sqrt{Q_{TS}^2 - 0.25} = 1.36$ or $2.7\,\mathrm{dB}$.

6.22 Voice-Coil Electrical Power Rating

For linear operation, the peak value of the diaphragm displacement must be less than or equal to the displacement limit x_{max}. It follows from Eq. (6.69) that the maximum value of the applied voice-coil voltage for linear operation is related to the peak displacement limit by

$$|e_g|_{max} = \left(\frac{\rho_0 c^2 S_D^2 R_E \omega_S Q_{ES}}{V_{AS}}\right)^{1/2} x_{max}\frac{\sqrt{Q_{TS}^2 - 0.25}}{Q_{TS}^2} \tag{6.70}$$

The electrical power rating of the voice coil should be high enough so that a sine wave with the voltage given by this equation can be applied to the driver at any frequency in its operating range. Otherwise, maximum acoustic output power cannot be obtained before electrical failure occurs.

For a constant voltage drive, the electrical power input to the voice coil is a maximum at midband where the real part of voice-coil impedance has the minimum value R_E. It follows, therefore, that the electrical power rating of the voice coil must satisfy

$$P_{E(max)} \geq \frac{1}{2} \frac{|e_g|^2_{max}}{R_E} = \frac{1}{2} \frac{\rho_0 c^2 \omega_S Q_{ES}}{V_{AS}} V^2_{D(max)} \frac{Q^2_{TS} - 0.25}{Q^4_{TS}} \tag{6.71}$$

where $V_{D(max)} = S_D x_{max}$ is the maximum volume of air that the diaphragm can displace from its zero rest position.

Example 19 *A loudspeaker driver with an advertised diameter of* 12 in *(a = 12 cm) has the parameters* $f_S = 60$ Hz, $Q_{TS} = 0.8$, $Q_{MS} = 4$, *and* $V_{AS} = 3$ ft$^3 = 0.085$ m^3. *The driver uses a long voice-coil construction which has an overhang outside the air gap that is estimated to be* 0.4 cm *on each side, which can be assumed to be equal* x_{max}. *Calculate the minimum electrical power rating that the driver can have if it is to reach its mechanical displacement before it reaches its electrical limit.*

Solution. The maximum volume displacement for the driver is $V_{D(max)} = \pi \times 0.12^2 \times 0.004 = 1.81 \times 10^{-4}$ m^3. The electrical quality factor is $Q_{ES} = 4 \times 0.8/(4 - 0.8) = 1$. With $\omega_S = 2\pi \times 60 = 377$ in Eq. (6.71), we have

$$P_{E(max)} \geq \frac{1}{2} \frac{1.18 \times 345^2 \times 377 \times 1}{0.085} \left(1.81 \times 10^{-4}\right)^2 \frac{0.8^2 - 0.25}{0.8^4} = 9.72\,\text{W}$$

6.23 Displacement Limited Power Rating

Eq. (6.71) gives a lower bound for the electrical input power at midband for the maximum allowable voice-coil input voltage given by Eq. (6.70). When this power is multiplied by the reference efficiency given by Eq. (6.64), the product represents the acoustic output power of the driver at midband for the maximum allowable voice-coil voltage. We define this power as the displacement limited acoustic power rating and denote it by $P_{AR(max)}$. It is given by

$$P_{AR(max)} = \frac{1}{2} \frac{\rho_0 \omega_S^4}{2\pi c} V^2_{D(max)} \frac{Q^2_{TS} - 0.25}{Q^4_{TS}} = \frac{4\pi^3 \rho_0 f_S^4}{c} V^2_{D(max)} \frac{Q^2_{TS} - 0.25}{Q^4_{TS}} \tag{6.72}$$

Example 20 *A 12-inch driver (a = 12 cm) is to be designed that has an infinite baffle C2 alignment with* $Q_{TS} = 1$ *and a lower cutoff frequency* $f_\ell = 60$ Hz. *It is specified that the moving mass of the diaphragm including the air load is* 30 g. *The voice-coil resistance is* 7 Ω. *The driver must be capable of putting out an average sine-wave acoustic power to one side of the baffle of* 500 mW *in its midband region. Calculate the minimum electrical power rating of the voice coil, the minimum diaphragm displacement limit, and the minimum volume displacement of the diaphragm.*

Solution. From Eq. (6.33), the driver resonance frequency must be $f_S = 76.3$ Hz. For Q_{MS}, a typical value of 4 is assumed. The driver electrical quality factor is $Q_{ES} = Q_{MS}Q_{TS}/(Q_{MS} - Q_{TS}) = 1.33$. The volume compliance is $V_{AS} = \rho_0 c^2 S_D^2/\omega_S^2 M_{MS} = 0.0417$ m$^3 = 1.47$ ft^3. The reference efficiency is $\eta_0 = \left(4\pi^2/c^3\right)\left(f_S^3 V_{AS}/Q_{ES}\right) = 0.0134 = 1.34\%$. The peak voice-coil voltage required to put out a midband power of 500 mW is $|e_g| = \sqrt{2R_E P_{AR}/\eta_0} = 22.9$ V (16.2 V rms). The electrical input power for this applied voltage is $P_E = |e_g|^2/2R_E = 37.5$ W. This corresponds to the minimum value of $P_{E(max)}$. Eq. (6.69) can be used to calculate the minimum required value of x_{max}. It is $x_{max} = 4.77$ m. For this value of x_{max}, the maximum volume displacement of the driver is thus $V_D = S_D x_{max} = 2.16 \times 10^{-4}$ m^3.

Example 21 *Calculate the displacement limited acoustic power rating for the driver of Example 19.*

Solution. From Eq. (6.72), we have

$$P_{AR(max)} = \frac{4\pi^3 \times 1.18 \times 60^4}{345}\left(1.81 \times 10^{-4}\right)^2\frac{0.8^2 - 0.25}{0.8^4} = 0.145\,\text{W}$$

6.24 SPICE Models

All of the analyses so far in this chapter require some approximations to the analogous circuits in order to obtain a tractable solution. When one uses these approximations to design a loudspeaker, the question of how accurate they are always arises. This can usually be determined by a computer simulation with SPICE. In this section, several examples of the use of SPICE for the analysis of infinite baffle loudspeakers are presented. The examples are based on example numerical problems worked in this chapter. The simulations were made with LTSpice.

Example 22 *The driver of Example 1 has the parameters: $a = 12\,\text{cm}$, $M_{MD} = 33.4\,\text{g}$, $C_{MS} = 1.18 \times 10^{-3}\,\text{m/N}$, $R_{MS} = 1.85\,\text{N\,s/m}$, $B\ell = 11.4\,\text{T\,m}$, $R_E = 7\,\Omega$, $L_e = 0.00689$, and $n_e = 0.7$. Form the electrical, mechanical, and acoustical circuits for the driver when it is mounted in an infinite baffle. Use SPICE to calculate the on-axis SPL at $1\,\text{m}$ in front of the driver as a function of frequency over the frequency range from $10\,\text{Hz}$ to $10\,\text{kHz}$. Assume that the driver is driven by a power amplifier having an ac output voltage of $1\,\text{V}$ rms.*

Solution. The circuits are shown in Fig. 6.15. The power amplifier is represented by the independent voltage source e_g. The independent voltage sources Vd1 through Vd3 are used as ammeters in the circuits and have an assigned value of $0\,\text{V}$. The acoustical circuit shows the analogous circuit for one side of the piston with the mass and resistances doubled and the compliance halved in order to represent the air load impedance on both sides of the piston. The piston area of the diaphragm and the element values for one side of the acoustical circuit are calculated as follows:

$$S_D = \pi a^2 = 0.0452\,\text{m}^2 \qquad M_{A1} = 8\rho_0/3\pi^2 a = 2.66\,\text{kg/m}^4$$

$$R_{A2} = \rho_0 c/\pi a^2 = 9000\,\text{kg/m}^4\,\text{s} \qquad R_{A1} = 128\rho_0 c/9\pi^3 a^2 - R_{A2} = 3970\,\text{kg/m}^4\,\text{s}$$

$$C_{A1} = 5.94 a^3/\rho_0 c^2 = 7.31 \times 10^{-8}\,\text{m}^4\,\text{s}^2/\text{kg}$$

The SPICE nodes for the simulation are labeled in the figure. The SPICE netlist in Table 6.1 performs an ac analysis of the circuit in decades with 100 points per decade. Current-controlled voltage sources (H sources) are used to represent the $B\ell u_D$ and the $B\ell i_c$ sources. A voltage-controlled voltage source (E source) is used to represent the $S_D p_D$ source. A current-controlled current source (F source) is used to represent the $S_D u_D$. The first line is a title line and is required. Because an asterisk is used to indicate a comment line, the first line must not be preceded by an asterisk.

Table 6.1: LTSpice Netlist for the Simulation

Netlist for Example 22	Vd3 14 0 0 AC 0	EXd 18 0 17 0 Laplace=1/s
Veg 1 0 0 AC 1	Ra1f 11 13 3.97k	Ra1b 10 12 3.97k
Re 2 1 7	Ra2f 13 14 9k	Ra2b 12 0 9k
HBLu 3 4 Vd2 11.4	Ca1f 11 13 73n	Ca1b 10 12 73n
Vd1 4 0 0 AC 0	LMa1f 11 14 2.66	Lma1b 10 0 2.66
LMmd 5 6 33.4m	ESdPd 8 9 11 10 45.2m	FSdud 10 11 Vd2 45.2m
Rms 6 7 1.85	GZe 2 3 2 3 Laplace=1/(6.89m*s**0.7)	.ac dec 100 1 10k
Cms 7 8 1.18m	Hpd 15 0 Vd3 1	.end
HBLi 5 0 Vd1 11.4	Epd 16 0 15 0 Laplace=9390*s	
Vd2 9 0 0 AC 0	Hxd 17 0 Vd2 1	

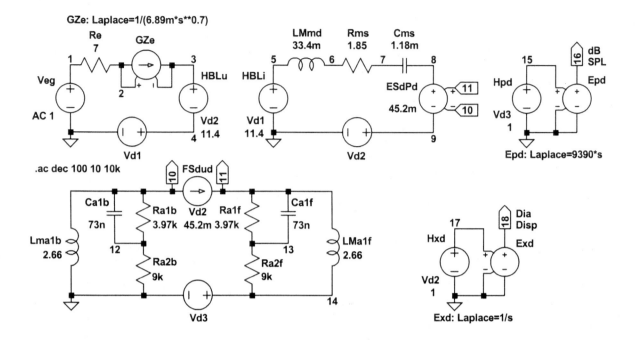

Figure 6.15: LTSpice circuit for the simulation.

The impedance $Z_e(\omega)$ of the lossy voice-coil inductance is realized with the analog behavioral modeling feature of LTSpice by the voltage-controlled current source GZe. The voltage that controls the source is multiplied by the term after the equal sign. The word Laplace indicates that the expression involves the complex frequency s. The current through GZe is calculated as the voltage V(2,3) divided by $6.89 \times 10^{-3} (s)^{0.7}$, where $s = j\omega$.

From Eq. (6.24), the rms on-axis pressure at 1 m in front of the driver is given by

$$p_{rms} = \frac{\rho_0}{2\pi} |s| \, U_{rms} = \frac{\rho_0}{2\pi} \omega U_{rms} \tag{6.73}$$

The SPL is given by

$$SPL = 20 \log \left(\frac{p_{rms}}{2 \times 10^{-5}} \right) = 20 \log \left(\frac{\rho_0 \omega U_{rms}}{2 \times 10^{-5}} \right) = 20 \log \left(9390 \omega U_{rms} \right) \tag{6.74}$$

The SPL is calculated by LTSpice as the dB voltage V(14). This is the voltage across the source Epd in the circuit. It is calculated by multiplying the current through Vd3 by $9390 \times s$. When the value of the source Veg is considered to be the rms value of the power amplifier output voltage, the magnitude of the current through the source Vd3 in the acoustical circuit is U_{rms}. The SPL versus frequency is given by curve **a** in Fig. 6.16.

Example 23 *In Example 7, it is shown that the addition of a $12.1\,\Omega$ resistor in series with the voice coil of the driver of Example 1 gives a B2 alignment for which $Q_{TS} = 1/\sqrt{2}$. Repeat the SPICE analysis for the driver with this resistor.*

Solution. The SPICE netlist for this example can be obtained by changing R_E in the deck for Example 22 to $7 + 12.1 = 19.1\,\Omega$. The SPL versus frequency is given by curve **b** in Fig. 6.16. Note the broad midrange region in the response. Before high-frequency rolloff occurs, the response peaks up by a small amount.

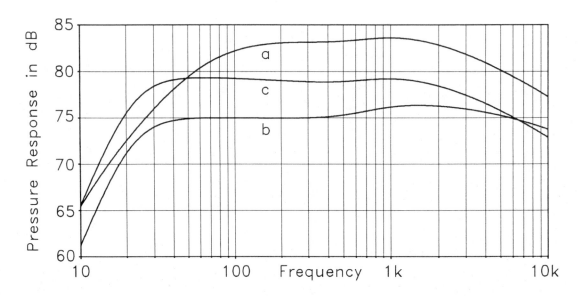

Figure 6.16: SPL in dB versus frequency. a – Example 22. b – Example 23. c – Example 24.

Example 24 *In Example 6, it is shown that a B2 alignment for which $Q_{TS} = 1/\sqrt{2}$ is obtained with the driver of Example 1 if $B\ell = 6.9\,\mathrm{T\,m}$. Repeat the SPICE analysis of Example 22 for the driver with this new value of $B\ell$.*

Solution. The SPICE netlist for this example can be obtained by changing $B\ell$ in the deck for Example 22 to 6.9. The *SPL* versus frequency is given by curve c in Fig. 6.16.

Fig. 6.16 illustrates how the bandwidth and the SPL_{sens}^{1V} of the driver vary for the three cases. The midband value of the *SPL* for each curve corresponds to the SPL_{sens}^{1V}. The rolloff above about $2\,\mathrm{kHz}$ is caused by the voice-coil inductance. The voice-coil impedance can be displayed in LTSpice with the trace of V(1)/I(VD1). The diaphragm velocity can be displayed with the trace of I(Vd3). The diaphragm displacement is the velocity divided by the complex frequency. It can be displayed with the trace of the voltage V(18).

6.25   Problems

1. *(a)* Modify the circuit of Fig. 6.8(a) to account for an inductor L_1 in series with the voice coil. [a compliance of value $C_1 = S_D^2 L_1 / (B\ell)^2$ is added in parallel with R_{AE}] *(b)* Explain how the inductor causes the high frequency response to be decreased. [the capacitor C_1 becomes a short circuit as frequency is increased, which decreases the upper cutoff frequency]

2. A loudspeaker driver in an infinite baffle has a diaphragm that can be modeled as a flat circular piston having a radius $a = 12\,\mathrm{cm}$. At what frequency is the wavelength equal to the piston circumference? [458 Hz]

3. A loudspeaker driver with an advertised diameter of 10 in ($a = 10\,\mathrm{cm}$) is mounted in an infinite baffle. The driver has the parameters $M_{MD} = 0.025\,\mathrm{kg}$, $C_{MS} = 2 \times 10^{-3}\,\mathrm{m/N}$, $R_{MS} = 1.5\,\mathrm{N\,s/m}$, $B\ell = 9\,\mathrm{T\,m}$, $R_E = 7\,\Omega$, and $L_E = 1\,\mathrm{mH}$, and $R_E' = \infty$. Calculate the element values in the low-frequency circuit of Fig. 6.8(b). [$R_{AE} = 11.7 \times 10^3\,\mathrm{N\,s/m^5}$, $M_{AS} = 31.7\,\mathrm{kg/m^4}$, $R_{AS} = 1.52 \times 10^3\,\mathrm{N\,s/m^5}$, $C_{AS} = 1.97 \times 10^{-6}\,\mathrm{m^5/N}$]

4. For the driver in problem 3, calculate the parameters f_S, Q_{MS}, Q_{ES}, Q_{TS}, and V_{AS}. [$f_S = 20.1\,\text{Hz}$, $Q_{MS} = 2.64$, $Q_{ES} = 0.342$, $Q_{TS} = 0.303$, $V_{AS} = 9.79\,\text{ft}^3$]

5. Given the driver parameters f_S, Q_{ES}, V_{AS}, and R_E, show that

$$C_{MS} = \frac{V_{AS}}{\rho_0 c^2 S_D^2} \qquad M_{MS} = \frac{1}{\left(2\pi f_S\right)^2 C_{MS}} \qquad B\ell = \sqrt{\frac{2\pi f_S M_{MS} R_E}{Q_{ES}}}$$

6. For the driver in problem 3, calculate the frequency f_{u1} which divides the low and high-frequency driver approximations. [$1.40\,\text{kHz}$]

7. For the driver of problems 3 and 6 *(a)* Calculate the distance to the far field at the frequency f_{u1} which divides the low and high-frequency driver approximations. [$0.323\,\text{m}$] *(b)* How does the distance change as the frequency is decreased? [it decreases]

8. *(a)* Using log-log scales, sketch the Bode magnitude plot for the on-axis pressure transfer function in Example 3. On the plot, label the break frequencies, the slopes, and the gain of the zero-slope asymptote. *(b)* Using linear-log scales, sketch the Bode phase plot for the on-axis pressure transfer function of Example 3. Label appropriate numerical values on the plot.

9. For the driver of problem 3 with $e_g = 1\,\text{V}$ rms: *(a)* Calculate the midband on-axis pressure p and the SPL at $r = 1\,\text{m}$. [$0.242\,\text{Pa}$, $81.7\,\text{dB}$] *(b)* Sketch the Bode magnitude plot for the on-axis SPL response. Label f_S, f_{u1}, the SPL at midband, and the SPL at f_S and at f_{u1}. [response at f_S is down by $10.4\,\text{dB}$, response at f_{u1} is down by $3\,\text{dB}$]

10. A loudspeaker driver has the parameters: $R_g = 1.5\,\Omega$, $R_E = 7.5\,\Omega$, $L_E = 0.3\,\text{mH}$, $R_E' = \infty$, $B = 2\,\text{T}$, $n = 50$ turns of wire on the voice coil, voice coil radius $= 2.5\,\text{cm}$, diaphragm piston radius $= 0.15\,\text{m}$, $M_{MD} = 30\,\text{g}$, $R_{MS} = 6\,\text{N}\,\text{s}/\,\text{m}$, and $C_{MS} = 6 \times 10^{-5}\,\text{m}/\,\text{N}$. The driver is to be mounted on an infinite baffle such that the air load mass is to be added to both sides of the diaphragm. *(a)* Calculate the parameters f_S, Q_{MS}, Q_{ES}, and Q_{TS}. Include the effect of R_g on the parameters. [$90.8\,\text{Hz}$, 4.87, 1.07, 0.875] *(b)* Calculate the upper cutoff frequency f_{u1}. [$8.16\,\text{kHz}$]

11. For the driver of problems 3 and 4: *(a)* What is the filter theory description for the transfer function $G(s)$? [overdamped] *(b)* Calculate the two pole frequencies in Hz for the transfer function. [$6.78\,\text{Hz}$, $59.6\,\text{Hz}$] *(c)* Verify that the geometric mean of the two pole frequencies is equal to the resonance frequency f_S.

12. For the driver in problems 3 and 4: *(a)* What value of resistor must be added in series with the voice coil to obtain a Butterworth alignment? [$12.8\,\Omega$] *(b)* What is the new lower $-3\,\text{dB}$ cutoff frequency? [$20.1\,\text{Hz}$] *(c)* By how many dBs would the resistor cause the midband on-axis SPL to drop? [$9.02\,\text{dB}$] *(d)* By what factor would the $B\ell$ product have to be changed to obtain a Butterworth alignment? [0.593] *(e)* By how many dBs would the change in $B\ell$ cause the midband on-axis SPL to drop? [$4.53\,\text{dB}$]

13. A loudspeaker driver on an infinite baffle has a resonance frequency $f_S = 55\,\text{Hz}$ and a total quality factor $Q_{TS} = 1.2$. The voice-coil inductance L_E can be neglected. *(a)* What is the lower $-3\,\text{dB}$ cutoff frequency? [$40.5\,\text{Hz}$] *(b)* What is the frequency of peak response? [$68.1\,\text{Hz}$] *(c)* What is the magnitude of the peak response in dB? [$2.41\,\text{dB}$] *(d)* Show that the pole frequencies in the transfer function for $G(s)$ are complex. [$1/4Q_{TS}^2 - 1$ is negative]

14. For the driver of problem 13: *(a)* Calculate the frequency at which the phase lead in the transfer function $G(s)$ is $+90°$. [$55\,\text{Hz}$] *(b)* Calculate the frequency at which the phase lead is $+45°$. [$82.5\,\text{Hz}$]

15. Explain why the SPL_{sens}^{1V} in Example 12 and the SPL_{sens}^{1W} in Example 13 do not drop by the same amount when the resistor is added in series with the voice coil of the driver. [One p_{sens} is proportional to R_E, the other to $R_E^{-1/2}$]

16. Does the SPL_{sens}^{1V} in Example 14 and the SPL_{sens}^{1W} in Example 15 drop by the same amount when the magnet weight is reduced? [p_{sens} is proportional to $B\ell$ for both cases]

17. For the driver in Examples 6 and 7, which method do you think is the most effective for lowering the half-power cutoff frequency, adding the resistor or decreasing the magnet weight, and why? [Decreasing the magnet weight is the most effective because the SPL_{sens}^{1W} is higher. Thus the efficiency is higher.]

18. For the driver of problems 3 and 4: *(a)* Calculate the 1 m on-axis pressure sensitivity p_{sens} given by the two formulas in Eq. (6.53). Verify that the two formulas give the same answer. [0.242 Pa] *(b)* Calculate the SPL_{sens}^{1V} and SPL_{sens}^{1W}. [81.7 dB, 90.1 dB]

19. The voice-coil inductance of a particular driver mounted on an infinite baffle is negligible. [follows from Eq. (6.49)] *(a)* At the fundamental resonance frequency of the driver, show that the voice-coil impedance is equal to $(1 + Q_{MS}/Q_{ES}) \times R_E$. *(b)* Show that the transfer function for $[Z_{VC}(s) - R_E]$ is a second-order band-pass function. [follows from Eq. (6.49)] *(c)* Compare the bandwidths of the bandpass function for U_D with the bandwidth of the $[Z_{VC}(s) - R_E]$ transfer function. [U_D has the quality factor Q_{TS} and $[Z_{VC}(s) - R_E]$ has the quality factor Q_{MS}. Because $Q_{MS} > Q_{TS}$, $[Z_{VC}(s) - R_E]$ has the smallest bandwidth.]

20. If L_E is neglected, show that $Q_{MS}/Q_{ES} = Z_{VC}(j\omega_S)/R_E - 1$, where $Z_{VC}(s)$ is the voice-coil impedance function for a driver in an infinite baffle. [follows from Eq. (6.47)]

21. Calculate the element values R_{ES}, L_{CES}, and C_{MES} in the circuit of Fig. 6.13 for the driver of problems 3 and 4. [$R_{ES} = 54.0\,\Omega$, $L_{CES} = 0.162\,H$, $C_{MES} = 3.87 \times 10^{-4}\,F$]

22. For the driver of problems 3 and 4, calculate the upper break frequency f_{u2} in the power response that is caused by diffraction. [777 Hz]

23. Explain why the pole at ω_{u2} in the acoustic power response of a loudspeaker driver does not appear in the transfer function for the on-axis pressure transfer function. [ω_{u2} models the effect on power radiated caused by the narrowing of the pressure beam at high frequencies.]

24. Calculate the reference efficiency for the driver in problems 3 and 4. [0.634%]

25. Calculate the reference efficiency for the driver in problem 10. [2.84%]

26. Starting with Eq. (6.63), derive the three expressions for η_0 in Eq. (6.64). [See Section 6.20]

27. A loudspeaker driver has the measured parameters R_E, f_S, Q_{ES}, Q_{MS}, and V_{AS}. *(a)* By what factor does each of these parameters change if a resistor R_1 is added in series with the voice coil? [Q_{ES} is multiplied by $(1 + R_1/R_E)$] *(b)* How does the driver efficiency change? [η_0 is divided by the same factor] *(c)* By what factor does each of these parameters change if a mechanical mass M_{M1} is attached to the diaphragm? [f_S is divided by $(1 + M_{M1}/M_{MS})^{1/2}$, Q_{ES} and Q_{MS} are multiplied by the same factor] *(d)* How does the efficiency change? [η_0 is divided by $(1 + M_{M1}/M_{MS})^2$]

28. A loudspeaker driver mounted in an infinite baffle has the parameters $f_S = 60\,Hz$ and $Q_{TS} = 1.4$. *(a)* Calculate the frequency at which the diaphragm displacement exhibits a maximum. [51.8 Hz] *(b)* Calculate the factor by which the diaphragm displacement peaks up compared to its lower frequency value. [1.50]

29. A loudspeaker driver has the parameters: piston radius $a = 10\,cm$, $f_S = 80\,Hz$, $Q_{TS} = 1$, $Q_{MS} = 5$, and $V_{AS} = 2.5\,ft^3$. The voice coil has an electrical power rating $P_{E(max)} = 15\,W$. *(a)* Calculate the minimum required peak voice coil displacement if the driver is not reach its electrical limit before its mechanical displacement limit. [5.70 mm] *(b)* Calculate the displacement limited acoustic power rating. [0.418 W]

30. High-frequency impedance measurements on a particular loudspeaker driver yields $Z_{VC} = 24.7\,\Omega + j26.2\,\Omega$ at $f = 20\,\text{kHz}$. The dc voice-coil resistance is $R_E = 7.5\,\Omega$. *(a)* Calculate n_e and L_e in Eq. (6.49). [$n_e = 0.630$, $L_e = \cancel{0.207}$] *(b)* Calculate R'_E and L_E at 20 kHz. [$57.1\,\Omega$, $13\,\text{mH}$]

.019

Chapter 7

Closed-Box Loudspeaker Systems

Closed-box loudspeakers are often called "acoustic suspension systems." This strictly holds only when the box is small enough so that the compliance of the air enclosed dominates over the compliance of the loudspeaker driver suspension. If the compliance of the driver suspension dominates over that of the air in the enclosure, the system is usually called an "infinite baffle system" even though the driver is not mounted in a true infinite baffle. This is discussed more in Section 7.2. Compared to drivers for an "infinite baffle" system, drivers for an "acoustic suspension" system usually have a lower resonance frequency and a lower total quality factor.

7.1 Modeling the Box

A loudspeaker driver operated in free air has poor bass response because the low-frequency volume velocities emitted from the front and the rear of the diaphragm are out of phase and tend to cancel. To prevent bass cancellation, the driver can be installed in an infinite baffle such as the wall between two non-connecting rooms. However, infinite baffle systems are not very practical because they are permanent installations. More practical systems employ a portable enclosure in which the driver is mounted. The simplest enclosure is the closed box. With the driver mounted in one wall of the box, the radiation from the back side of the diaphragm is into the box where it cannot cancel the radiation from the front of the diaphragm. To absorb standing waves inside the box, it is either filled or lined with an acoustical absorber or filling such as fiberglass.

In addition to absorbing standing waves inside the box, the filling has the effect of making the box look larger. The effect is a thermodynamic one which can be explained in two ways. With no filling, the acoustic wave inside the box is an adiabatic process. When filling is added, the acoustic wave is converted into an isothermal process, a process in which the air temperature does not vary with acoustic pressure. The velocity of sound for an isothermal process is slower than it is for an adiabatic process so that it takes longer for the wave to travel from the diaphragm to the back of the box. Thus the box appears bigger to the wave. The second explanation is based on a more fundamental thermodynamic argument. Suppose that the loudspeaker diaphragm is displaced into the box. This compresses the air which causes its temperature to rise. The filling absorbs the heat causing the air to be cooled. This causes the pressure to decrease, which makes the box appear larger. Similarly, when the diaphragm is displaced out of the box, the pressure drops and the air temperature decreases. The filling supplies heat to the air causing the pressure to increase, thus making the box appear larger. The effect is frequency dependent, working only at the lower frequencies for which the period is long enough to allow the heat exchange to occur.

This chapter covers the low-frequency modeling and performance of closed-box loudspeaker systems. The analysis is aimed primarily at woofer systems. With minor modifications, it is applicable to the low-frequency analysis of closed-box midrange and tweeter drivers. To calculate the acoustic pressure radiated by the driver, we assume that the box is recessed into an infinite wall so that the front of the diaphragm radiates into one hemisphere. Fig. 7.1(a) illustrates the system.

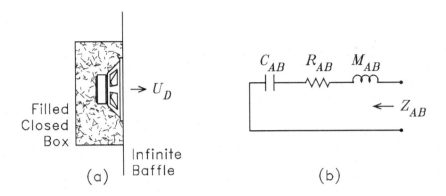

Figure 7.1: (a) Closed-box system. (b) Low-frequency analogous circuit for the air load impedance on the back of the diaphragm.

Compared to the loudspeaker in an infinite baffle, only the acoustical impedance of the air load on the rear of the diaphragm is changed by the box. If the box is lossless and its maximum dimension is no larger than about $\lambda/10$, the acoustic impedance of the air in the box is represented by a compliance. A physical box, however, presents an acoustical impedance that exhibits a compliance, a mass, and a resistance, all of which are a function of the box and the amount of filling used. The compliance and mass components can be calculated, but the resistance component must be estimated.

Let the internal volume of the enclosure be written $V_B = S_B \times d$, where S_B is the inside area of the wall on which the driver is mounted and d is the internal depth of the box behind the driver. Fig. 7.1(b) gives the low-frequency approximation to the acoustical analogous circuit for the air load on the rear of the diaphragm. The compliance C_{AB} and mass M_{AB} are given by

$$C_{AB} = \frac{V_{AB}}{\rho_0 c^2} \qquad M_{AB} = \frac{B\rho}{\pi a} \tag{7.1}$$

where ρ_0 is the air density, ρ is the effective density of the combined air and filling in the box, V_{AB} is the effective acoustic volume of the air in the box that accounts for the effects of the filling, and B is the mass loading factor. The latter three can be estimated from the relations

$$\rho_0 \le \rho \le \rho_0 \left(1 - \frac{V_f}{V_B}\right) + \rho_f \frac{V_f}{V_B} \tag{7.2}$$

$$V_{AB} = V_B \left(1 - \frac{V_f}{V_B}\right) \left[1 + \frac{\gamma - 1}{1 + \gamma \left(V_B/V_f - 1\right) \rho_0 c_v/\rho_f c_f}\right] \tag{7.3}$$

$$B = \frac{d}{3}\sqrt{\frac{\pi}{S_D}} \left(\frac{S_D}{S_B}\right)^2 + \frac{8}{3\pi}\left[1 - \frac{S_D}{S_B}\right] \tag{7.4}$$

where S_D is the piston area of the diaphragm. A typical value of B that is often used in example calculations is $B = 0.65$.

In the above expressions, ρ_f is the bulk density of the filling fibers, V_f is the volume in the box occupied by the filling, $\gamma = 1.4$ is the ratio of the specific heat of air at constant pressure to the specific heat of air at constant volume, c_v is the specific heat of air at constant volume, and c_f is the specific heat of the filling material. The lower bound in the inequality for ρ assumes that the box is unfilled. The upper bound represents the average density of the air and the filling in the box. It is an approximation to model the effective density by the average density because the filling fibers do not necessarily move with the same velocity as the air particles in the box.

With $\gamma = 1.4$, Eq. (7.3) predicts that the maximum increase in box volume due to the effect of the filling can never be greater than 40%. This maximum value can never be achieved in practice. To illustrate this, consider fiberglass of the type that is commonly used in home construction as a filling material. When a box is filled with uncompressed fiberglass, the ratio of the box volume V_B to the volume V_f occupied by the fiberglass is $V_B/V_f \simeq 400$. For the values $\rho_0 = 1.18\,\text{kg}/\text{m}^3$, $\rho_f \simeq 2400\,\text{kg}/\text{m}^3$, $c_v = 717\,\text{J}/\text{kg}\,^\circ\text{C}$, and $c_f = 670\,\text{J}/\text{kg}\,^\circ\text{C}$, Eq. (7.3) predicts that $V_{AB} \simeq 1.31 V_B$. Therefore, the effect of the fiberglass is to increase the volume of the box by about 31%. In practice, the increase is probably never more than about 20%.

Example 1 *A loudspeaker enclosure has internal dimensions with the ratios $0.6 \times 1.0 \times 1.6$. A 12-inch woofer with the diaphragm piston radius $a = 0.12\,\text{m}$ is mounted on the panel having the dimension ratios 1.0×1.6. If $S_D/S_B = 1/3$, calculate the mass loading factor B.*

Solution. Let h and w, respectively, be the height and width of the box. We have $S_D = hw/3 = (1.6d/0.6)\,(d/0.6)\,/3 = 1.482d^2$. Thus Eq. (7.4) gives

$$B = \frac{d}{3}\sqrt{\frac{\pi}{1.482d^2}}\left(\frac{1}{3}\right)^2 + \frac{8}{3\pi}\left[1 - \frac{1}{3}\right] = 0.620$$

Example 2 *A closed-box enclosure is filled with uncompressed fiberglass of the type used in home construction. The filling occupies $1/400$ of the total volume of the box. If the bulk density of the filling fibers is $2400\,\text{kg}/\text{m}^3$, calculate the lower and upper bounds for the effective density of the air plus filling in the box.*

Solution. We can use Eq. (7.2) to solve for the bounds on ρ as follows:

$$1.18\,\text{kg}/\text{m}^3 \le \rho \le 1.18\left(1 - \frac{1}{400}\right) + \frac{2400}{400} = 7.18\,\text{kg}/\text{m}^3$$

7.2 The Analogous Circuits

Figs. 7.2(a) through (c) show the low-frequency electrical, mechanical, and acoustical analogous circuits for a closed-box system. These circuits can be used to determine the effect of the box on the lower cutoff frequency. The circuits are the same as those for the infinite baffle system in Fig. 6.6 except that the generator resistance and the voice-coil inductance are neglected in the electrical circuit, the front air load impedance in the acoustical circuit is approximated with the acoustic mass M_{A1}, and the rear air load impedance in the acoustical circuit is approximated with the box circuit of Fig. 7.1(b).

The low-frequency Norton form of the combination analogous circuit for the closed-box system is obtained in a way similar to the way that the corresponding infinite-baffle circuit in Fig. 6.8(b) is obtained. The circuit is given in Fig. 7.2(d). The circuit element values are given by

$$R_{AE} = \frac{(B\ell)^2}{S_D^2 R_E} \qquad M_{AC} = M_{AD} + M_{AB} + M_{A1} \tag{7.5}$$

$$R_{AC} = R_{AS} + R_{AB} \qquad C_{AT} = \frac{C_{AS}C_{AB}}{C_{AS} + C_{AB}} = \frac{C_{AS}}{1 + \alpha} = \frac{\alpha C_{AB}}{1 + \alpha} \tag{7.6}$$

where $M_{A1} = 8\rho_0/3\pi^2 a$, the expressions for M_{AD}, R_{AS}, and C_{AS} are given in Eq. (6.5), and α is the box compliance ratio given by

$$\alpha = \frac{C_{AS}}{C_{AB}} = \frac{V_{AS}}{V_{AB}} \tag{7.7}$$

It is convenient to define the total volume compliance V_{AT} of the system as the volume of air having the acoustic compliance C_{AT} given in Eq. (7.6). It is given by

$$V_{AT} = \frac{V_{AS}V_{AB}}{V_{AS} + V_{AB}} = \frac{V_{AS}}{1 + \alpha} = \frac{\alpha V_{AB}}{1 + \alpha} \tag{7.8}$$

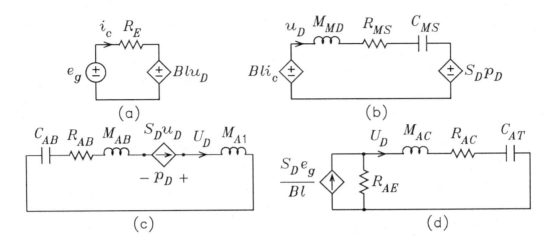

Figure 7.2: Low-frequency (a) electrical, (b) mechanical, and (c) acoustical analogous circuits for the closed-box system. (d) Norton form of the combination acoustical analogous circuit.

Closed-box systems can be classified according to the value of the compliance ratio. For $\alpha = 1$, the compliance of the diaphragm suspension is equal to the compliance of the air in the enclosure. For $\alpha < 1$, the compliance of the suspension dominates and the system tends to respond as an infinite baffle system. Large-volume, closed-box systems which use a low-compliance driver, i.e. one having a stiff suspension, are typically called infinite baffle systems. For $\alpha > 1$, the compliance of the air in the enclosure dominates and the system is said to be an air suspension or acoustic suspension system. Such systems typically have a compliance ratio in the range $3 \leq \alpha \leq 10$. To achieve a compliance ratio in this range, the driver suspension must usually be very loose, thus resulting in a very low free-air resonance frequency.

7.3   The Volume Velocity Transfer Function

The low-frequency combination analogous circuits for the infinite-baffle and the closed-box systems are identical with the exception that the subscripts on some of the circuit elements are different. It follows that the transfer function for the volume velocity U_D emitted by the closed-box driver can be obtained by modifying the subscripts in Eq. (6.13) for U_D for the infinite-baffle system. In this equation, we substitute R_{ATC} for R_{AT}, ω_C for ω_S, and Q_{TC} for Q_{TS} to obtain

$$U_D = \frac{S_D e_g}{B\ell} \frac{R_{AE}}{R_{ATC}} \frac{(1/Q_{TC})(s/\omega_C)}{(s/\omega_C)^2 + (1/Q_{TC})(s/\omega_C) + 1} \qquad (7.9)$$

where ω_C is the closed-box resonance frequency, Q_{TC} is the closed-box total quality factor, and R_{ATC} is the total acoustical resistance in the circuit. These are given by

$$\omega_C = 2\pi f_C = \frac{1}{\sqrt{M_{AC}C_{AT}}} \qquad Q_{TC} = \frac{1}{R_{ATC}}\sqrt{\frac{M_{AC}}{C_{AT}}} \qquad R_{ATC} = R_{AE} + R_{AC} \qquad (7.10)$$

The Bode magnitude plots for the volume velocity transfer function are similar to those for the infinite-baffle transfer function in Fig. 6.9.

The closed-box resonance frequency ω_C can be related to the infinite baffle resonance frequency ω_S as follows:

$$\omega_C = \frac{1}{\sqrt{M_{AC}C_{AT}}} = \frac{\sqrt{1+\alpha}}{\sqrt{M_{AC}C_{AS}}} = \sqrt{\frac{M_{AS}}{M_{AC}}}\sqrt{1+\alpha}\,\omega_S \qquad (7.11)$$

where $M_{AS} = M_{AD} + 2M_{A1}$ is the acoustic mass of the diaphragm and air load on both sides of the diaphragm for the driver mounted in an infinite baffle. An often used approximation for ω_C is to assume that $M_{AS} \simeq M_{AC}$ so that ω_C and f_C can be written

$$\omega_C \simeq \sqrt{1 + \alpha}\omega_S \qquad \text{and} \qquad f_C \simeq \sqrt{1 + \alpha}f_S \tag{7.12}$$

As with the case of the infinite baffle system, the total quality factor Q_{TC} for the closed-box system can be broken into two parts, the mechanical quality factor Q_{MC} and the electrical quality factor Q_{EC}, such that

$$Q_{TC} = \frac{Q_{MC}Q_{EC}}{Q_{MC} + Q_{EC}} \tag{7.13}$$

The expressions for Q_{MC} and Q_{EC} are

$$Q_{MC} = \frac{1}{R_{AC}}\sqrt{\frac{M_{AC}}{C_{AT}}} = \frac{R_{AS}}{R_{AS} + R_{AB}}\sqrt{\frac{M_{AC}}{M_{AS}}}\sqrt{1 + \alpha}Q_{MS} \tag{7.14}$$

$$Q_{EC} = \frac{1}{R_{AE}}\sqrt{\frac{M_{AC}}{C_{AT}}} = \sqrt{\frac{M_{AC}}{M_{AS}}}\sqrt{1 + \alpha}Q_{ES} \tag{7.15}$$

If we assume that $M_{AC} \simeq M_{AS}$, approximate expressions for Q_{MC} and Q_{EC} are

$$Q_{MC} \simeq \frac{R_{AS}}{R_{AS} + R_{AB}}\sqrt{1 + \alpha}Q_{MS} \leq \sqrt{1 + \alpha}Q_{MS} \qquad Q_{EC} \simeq \sqrt{1 + \alpha}Q_{ES} \tag{7.16}$$

We see from the above results that the closed-box resonance frequency and electrical quality factor can be related to the infinite baffle resonance frequency and electrical quality factor if the system compliance ratio α is known and it is assumed that $M_{AC} \simeq M_{AS}$. It is not possible to relate the mechanical quality factors so simply because the acoustic resistor R_{AB} which models losses in the box is not known. If $R_{AB} = 0$ and $M_{AC} \simeq M_{AS}$, an upper bound on the mechanical quality factor is $Q_{MC} = \sqrt{1 + \alpha}Q_{MS}$. For $R_{AB} > 0$, Q_{MC} is less than this upper bound value. An often used rule of thumb for Q_{MC} is as follows:

$$\text{For Unfilled Systems: } 5 \leq Q_{MC} \leq 10 \qquad \text{For Filled Systems: } 2 \leq Q_{MC} \leq 5 \tag{7.17}$$

The larger the closed-box, the higher the losses and the lower the mechanical quality factor. In design procedures where the box size is not known beforehand, the average of the lower and upper values is often assumed for Q_{MC}, i.e. $Q_{MC} \simeq 7.5$ for unfilled systems and $Q_{MC} \simeq 3.5$ for filled systems. In any case, the assumed value for Q_{MC} must not exceed the upper bound value of $\sqrt{1 + \alpha}Q_{MS}$.

7.4 The On-Axis Pressure Transfer Function

The on-axis pressure transfer function for the closed-box system is defined in the same way that it is defined for the infinite baffle system. In terms of the volume velocity U_D emitted by the driver diaphragm, the low-frequency pressure can be written

$$p = \frac{\rho_0}{2\pi}sU_D = \frac{\rho_0}{2\pi}\frac{Ble_g}{S_D R_E M_{AC}}G_C(s) \tag{7.18}$$

where $G_C(s)$ is the low-frequency on-axis pressure transfer function for the closed-box system given by

$$G_C(s) = \frac{(s/\omega_C)^2}{(s/\omega_C)^2 + (1/Q_{TC})(s/\omega_C) + 1} \tag{7.19}$$

Similar to the case for the driver in an infinite baffle, the high-frequency response of the closed-box system can accounted for by multiplying Eq. (7.18) by a first-order, low-pass filter function given by

$$T_{u1}(s) = \frac{1}{1 + s/\omega_{u1}} \tag{7.20}$$

where ω_{u1} for the closed-box system is given by

$$\omega_{u1} = \frac{R_E M_{AC}}{L_E M_{AD}} \tag{7.21}$$

and R_E and L_E, respectively, are the voice-coil resistance and inductance. The Bode magnitude plots for the on-axis pressure for the closed-box system are similar to those for the infinite-baffle system in Fig. 6.11.

Table 7.1: Infinite-Baffle to Closed-Box Substitutions

$M_{AS} \longrightarrow M_{AC}$	$C_{AS} \longrightarrow C_{AT}$	$R_{AT} \longrightarrow R_{ATC}$	$V_{AS} \longrightarrow V_{AT}$
$\omega_S \longrightarrow \omega_C$	$f_S \longrightarrow f_C$	$Q_{TS} \longrightarrow Q_{TC}$	$Q_{MS} \longrightarrow Q_{MC}$
$Q_{ES} \longrightarrow Q_{EC}$	$R_{ES} \longrightarrow R_{EC}$	$L_{CES} \longrightarrow L_{CEC}$	$C_{MES} \longrightarrow C_{MEC}$
$2M_{A1} \longrightarrow (M_{A1} + M_{AB})$			

Most of the material in Chapter 6 for infinite-baffle systems applies with minor modifications to closed-box systems. In order for the infinite-baffle formulas to apply to the closed-box system, the substitutions given in Table 7.1 must be made, where the arrows in the table are read "is replaced by." As an example of a formula conversion, Eq. (6.53) for the on-axis pressure sensitivity for the infinite baffle system can be converted into a closed-box formula to obtain

$$p_{sens}^{1V} = \frac{\rho_0}{2\pi}\frac{B\ell}{S_D R_E M_{AC}} = \frac{\sqrt{2\pi\rho_0}}{c} f_C^{3/2} \left[\frac{V_{AT}}{R_E Q_{EC}}\right]^{1/2} \tag{7.22}$$

7.5   Effect of the Box on the System Response

To examine the effects of the box volume on the low-frequency response of the closed-box system, we assume that the box losses can be neglected and that the diaphragm acoustic mass load is the same as for the infinite-baffle system. That is, we assume that $R_{AB} \simeq 0$ and $M_{AC} \simeq M_{AS}$. These assumptions greatly simplify the analysis and lead to a better intuitive understanding of the relationships involved. The equations below that are based on the assumption that $R_{AB} = 0$ should never be used for design purposes.

If $R_{AB} \simeq 0$ and $M_{AC} = M_{AS}$, the mechanical quality factor can be written $Q_{MC} \simeq \sqrt{1+\alpha}Q_{MS}$. Because the total quality factor Q_{TC} is related to the electrical and mechanical quality factors by $Q_{TC} = Q_{EC}Q_{MC}/(Q_{EC} + Q_{MC})$, it follows from Eqs. (7.15) for Q_{EC}, the approximate equation for Q_{MC}, and Eq. (7.12) that Q_{TC} is given by

$$Q_{TC} \simeq \sqrt{1+\alpha}Q_{TS} \simeq \frac{Q_{TS}}{f_S}f_C \tag{7.23}$$

Thus, if box losses are neglected, the closed-box total quality factor Q_{TC} is directly proportional to the closed-box resonance frequency f_C.

The transfer function $G_C(s)$ is a second-order, high-pass filter function. On log-log scales, its Bode magnitude plot exhibits an asymptotic slope of $+2\,\mathrm{dec/dec}$ for frequencies lower than the resonance frequency f_C and an asymptotic slope of $0\,\mathrm{dec/dec}$ for frequencies greater than f_C. The actual response at f_C is equal to the total quality factor Q_{TC}. Suppose that Bode magnitude plots are constructed for $G_C(s)$ for different box volumes. It follows from Eq. (7.23) that a line connecting the points with coordinates (f_C, Q_{TC}) on the plots exhibit a slope of $+1\,\mathrm{dec/dec}$. This observation makes the construction of the Bode plots simple. This is illustrated for three box sizes in Fig. 7.3, where curve a is for the largest enclosure for which $f_C = 30\,\mathrm{Hz}$ and $Q_{TC} = 0.35$. Curve b is for the next smallest enclosure for which $f_C = 60\,\mathrm{Hz}$ and $Q_{TC} = 0.71$. Curve c is for the smallest enclosure for which $f_C = 120\,\mathrm{Hz}$ and $Q_{TC} = 1.4$. The line of slope $m = +1\,\mathrm{dec/dec}$ which passes through the points (f_C, Q_{TC}) is shown as a dashed line.

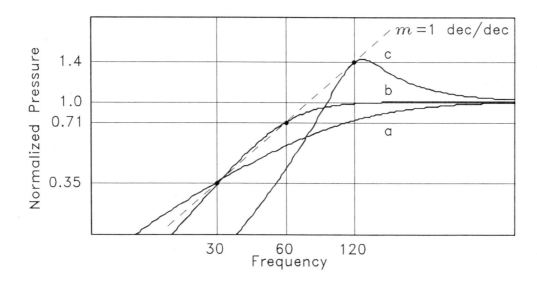

Figure 7.3: Plots of $|G_C(j2\pi f)|$ versus f for three sizes of enclosures. Curve a is for largest. Curve c is for smallest.

It can be seen from Fig. 7.3 that too large a box results in a weak bass response whereas a box that is too small can result in a bass response that exhibits an undesirable peak and then cuts off rapidly below the peak. An optimum size box is one which minimizes the lower half-power or $-3\,\mathrm{dB}$ cutoff frequency of the system. The lower cutoff frequency is given by

$$f_\ell = f_C \left[\left(\frac{1}{2Q_{TC}^2} - 1 \right) + \sqrt{ \left(\frac{1}{2Q_{TC}^2} - 1 \right)^2 + 1 } \right]^{1/2} \tag{7.24}$$

From Eq. (7.23), we can write $f_C \simeq Q_{TC} f_S / Q_{TS}$. It is left as an exercise to replace f_C in Eq. (7.24) with this expression, square the resulting equation for f_ℓ, take the derivative with respect to Q_{TC}, and show that it exhibits a minimum for the value $Q_{TC} = 1/\sqrt{2}$. This value of Q_{TC} results in a Butterworth or maximally-flat alignment. This is abbreviated a B2 alignment, where the 2 denotes second-order. A value of $Q_{TC} > 1/\sqrt{2}$ corresponds to a Chebyshev or equal-ripple alignment that is abbreviated C2.

7.6 Sensitivity of the Lower Cutoff Frequency

To a good approximation, the lower $-3\,\mathrm{dB}$ cutoff frequency of a closed-box system is minimized if the box volume is chosen so that $Q_{TC} \simeq 1/\sqrt{2}$. Suppose that a system is to be designed with this value of Q_{TC} as a target. We might ask how much will the lower cutoff frequency differ from the minimum value if the target value of Q_{TC} is not realized? We investigate this by means of an example. Suppose that we have a driver with the following parameters: $f_S = 20\,\mathrm{Hz}$, $Q_{TS} = 0.2$, and $V_{AS} = 20\,\mathrm{ft}^3$. Let the driver be installed in a lossless closed-box baffle ($R_{AB} = 0$), and let us assume that the acoustic mass load on the driver is the same as in an infinite baffle, i.e. that $M_{AC} = M_{AS}$. We wish to calculate the compliance ratio α, the effective acoustic box volume V_{AB}, the fundamental resonance frequency f_C, and the lower half-power cutoff frequency f_ℓ as a function of the total quality factor Q_{TC}.

The lower cutoff frequency f_ℓ is given by Eq. (7.24). With the approximations $R_{AB} \simeq 0$ and $M_{AC} \simeq M_{AS}$, the relations for α, V_{AB}, and f_C are

$$\alpha \simeq \left(\frac{Q_{TC}}{Q_{TS}} \right)^2 - 1 \qquad V_{AB} = \frac{V_{AS}}{\alpha} \qquad f_C \simeq \sqrt{1+\alpha}\, f_S \tag{7.25}$$

The calculations for several values of Q_{TC} are summarized in Table 7.2. It can be seen from the table that f_ℓ is a minimum for $Q_{TC} = 0.7$ and that f_ℓ varies very little from its minimum value for changes in Q_{TC} of ± 0.1 about the optimum value of 0.7 (a $\pm 14.3\%$ change). It can be concluded that a value of Q_{TC} in the range from 0.6 to 0.8 gives optimum bass response for the closed-box system. This assumes that the system design is for a given driver and that the box volume is the only variable in the design.

Table 7.2: Data for the Closed-Box System

Q_{TC}	α	V_{AB} (ft^3)	f_C (Hz)	f_ℓ (Hz)
0.2	0	∞	20	96.0
0.3	1.25	16	30	91.1
0.4	3	6.67	40	84.6
0.5	5.25	3.81	50	77.7
0.6	8	2.5	60	72.5
0.7	11.25	1.78	70	70.7
0.8	15	1.33	80	71.8
0.9	19.25	1.04	90	74.7
1.0	24	0.83	100	78.6

7.7   System Design with a Given Driver

The first step in designing a closed-box system for a given driver is to select the driver. The ones which give the best response have a very low resonance frequency. The next step is to measure the small-signal driver parameters. Manufacturers' test data should not be used unless the parameters cannot be measured. If two drivers are measured for a stereo system, it is not unusual for the parameters to differ by 10% to 15%. In this case, it is acceptable to average the parameters and base the system design on the averages. The parameters required for the design are f_S, V_{AS}, Q_{TS}, Q_{MS}, and Q_{ES}. The design procedure is as follows:

1. Specify the desired Q_{TC}. The driver must have a Q_{TS} that is lower than the desired Q_{TC}, otherwise it cannot be used. Q_{TC} should be selected in the range of 0.6 to 0.8 if the low-frequency response is to be optimized. A higher value results in a smaller enclosure which can be an important consideration if the system size matters.

2. Estimate the mechanical quality factor Q_{MC}. The rule of thumb given in Eq. (7.17) can be used to do this. For a filled system, it is typical to guess the value $Q_{MC} = 3.5$.

3. Calculate the electrical quality factor Q_{EC}, the compliance ratio α, and the effective acoustic box volume V_{AB}.

$$Q_{EC} = \frac{Q_{MC}Q_{TC}}{Q_{MC} - Q_{TC}} \qquad \alpha = \left(\frac{Q_{EC}}{Q_{ES}}\right)^2 - 1 \qquad V_{AB} = \frac{V_{AS}}{\alpha} \qquad (7.26)$$

4. Calculate the fundamental resonance frequency $f_C = f_S\sqrt{1+\alpha}$ and the lower half-power cutoff frequency f_ℓ from Eq. (7.24).

The internal box volume V_B should be calculated to account for the effect of the filling. For a filled enclosure, V_B is smaller than V_{AB} by about 20%, i.e. $V_B \simeq V_{AB}/1.2$. There are two sets of ratios of the internal dimensions that are often used. These ratios are

$$0.6 \times 1.0 \times 1.6 \qquad \text{and} \qquad 0.8 \times 1.0 \times 1.25 \qquad (7.27)$$

The first ratios give a more rectangular shaped box while the second ratios give a more cubic shaped box. When the box is built, it should be properly braced inside. Allowance for the volume occupied by both the bracing and the drivers should be made. An empirical relation for the volume occupied by a woofer inside the box is

$$V_{driver} \simeq 6 \times 10^{-6} \times d^4 \, \text{ft}^3 \tag{7.28}$$

where d is the advertised diameter of the driver in inches. For example, the volume occupied by a 12 in driver is approximately $0.12 \, \text{ft}^3$.

Example 3 *A 12 in driver has the parameters: $f_S = 19\,\text{Hz}$, $Q_{MS} = 3.7$, $Q_{ES} = 0.35$, and $V_{AS} = 19\,\text{ft}^3$. The voice-coil electrical power rating is $P_{E(max)} = 25\,\text{W}$, the peak linear voice-coil displacement is $x_{max} = 6\,\text{mm}$ (1/4 in), and the diaphragm piston radius is $a = 0.12\,\text{m}$. (a) If $Q_{MC} \simeq 3.5$, calculate V_{AB} and V_B for $Q_{TC} = 1/\sqrt{2}$. Assume $V_B = V_{AB}/1.2$. (b) Calculate the lower half-power cutoff frequency f_ℓ. (c) Calculate the displacement limited maximum acoustic output power $P_{AR(max)}$. (d) Calculate the efficiency η_0 and the corresponding electrical power input P_E required to achieve the maximum acoustic output power.*

Solution. (a) $Q_{EC} = Q_{MC}Q_{TC}/(Q_{MC} - Q_{TC}) = 0.89$, $\alpha = (Q_{EC}/Q_{ES})^2 - 1 = 5.47$, $V_{AB} = V_{AS}/\alpha = 3.47\,\text{ft}^3$, $V_B = 3.47/1.2 = 2.89\,\text{ft}^3$. (b) $f_C = \sqrt{1 + \alpha}f_S = 48.3\,\text{Hz}$. For the B2 alignment, the lower half-power cutoff frequency is equal to f_C so that $f_\ell = 48.3\,\text{Hz}$. (c) The maximum volume of air that the diaphragm can displace is $V_{D(max)} = x_{max}\pi a^2 = 2.7 \times 10^{-4}\,\text{m}^3$. The maximum displacement limited acoustic output power is

$$P_{AR(max)} = \frac{4\pi^3 \rho_0 f_C^4}{c} V_{D(max)}^2 \frac{Q_{TC}^2 - 0.25}{Q_{TC}^4} = 0.17\,\text{W} \tag{7.29}$$

(This expression is valid only for $Q_{TC} \geq 1/\sqrt{2}$. For $Q_{TC} < 1/\sqrt{2}$, the solution is the same as for $Q_{TC} = 1/\sqrt{2}$.) The system efficiency is

$$\eta_0 = \frac{4\pi^2}{c^3} \times \frac{f_C^3 V_{AT}}{Q_{EC}} = 0.010 \text{ or } 1\% \tag{7.30}$$

The electrical input power required to radiate $P_{AR(\, \text{J/kg} \, ^\circ\text{C})}$ is $P_E = P_{AR(max)}/\eta_0 = 17\,\text{W}$. Because this is less than $P_{E(max)}$, the system can deliver its maximum acoustic output power before electrical failure occurs.

Example 4 *Design the enclosure for the system of Example 3. Assume that the internal dimensions of the box have the ratios $0.6 \times 1.0 \times 1.6$ and that the box has bracing in each corner between all internal walls so that it forms a rectangular frame inside the box. The bracing has cross section dimensions of 1.5 in by 1.5 in (commonly called two-by-two bracing).*

Solution. Denote the internal width, height, and depth of the box, respectively, by w, h, and d. Let the height be the longest dimension and the depth be the shortest. Thus $w = h/1.6 = 0.625h$ and $d = 0.6w = 0.375h$. The volume occupied by the driver in the box is estimated to be $0.12\,\text{ft}^3$ so that the total internal volume of the unfilled box is $2.89 + 0.12 = 3.01\,\text{ft}^3$. The volume occupied by each piece of bracing is equal to its cross-sectional area times its length. In cubic feet, this is given by $(1.5/12)^2 \times L$, where L is the length in feet. There are 12 bracing pieces. Let the 4 vertical pieces have a length equal to h. Thus 4 pieces are required having a length $(w - 3/12)$ ft and four pieces are required having a length $(d - 3/12)$ ft. The following equation can be written for the box height h:

$$
\begin{aligned}
3.01 =\ & (0.625h) \times h \times (0.375h) - 4(1.5/12)^2 \times h - 4(1.5/12)^2 \times (0.625h - 3/12) \\
& -4(1.5/12)^2 \times (0.375h - 3/12) = 0.234375h^3 - 0.1251h + 0.03125
\end{aligned} \tag{7.31}
$$

This equation can be solved for h to obtain $h = 2.41\,\text{ft}$. The width and depth are $w = h/1.6 = 1.51\,\text{ft}$ and $d = 0.6w = 0.904\,\text{ft}$.

7.8 System Verification

To verify a system design, any crossover network must be disconnected. The parameters f_C and Q_{TC} must be measured. These can be determined by the techniques described in Section 11.7. The lower $-3\,\text{dB}$ frequency of the system can then be calculated from Eq. (7.24).

7.9 System Design From Specifications

A closed-box system design from specifications starts with the specification of the system resonance frequency f_C and the total quality factor Q_{TC}. Once these are specified, either the enclosure volume V_B or the system efficiency η_0 may be specified, but not both. Finally, the power capacity may be specified in terms of either the voice-coil electrical power rating $P_{E(max)}$ or the displacement limited acoustic power rating $P_{AR(max)}$. A typical design from specifications might start with the desired values of f_C, Q_{TC}, V_B (or equivalently V_{AB}), and $P_{AR(max)}$. Because the enclosure is effectively specified by V_B (or V_{AB}), the design problem is to specify the driver.

The design process begins by assigning values to the mechanical quality factor Q_{MC} and the compliance ratio α. Because $Q_{MC} \gg Q_{EC}$ for most systems, the electrical quality factor dominates and the mechanical quality factor has only a minor effect on the performance. The rule of thumb given in Eq. (7.17) can be used to estimate Q_{MC}. For lack of a better value, the average of the values in the rule of thumb can be used, i.e. $Q_{MC} \simeq 3.5$ for a filled system and $Q_{MC} \simeq 7.5$ for an unfilled system. Once Q_{TC} is specified and Q_{MC} is estimated, the required value for Q_{EC} can be calculated from Eq. (7.26).

The system efficiency is given by Eq. (7.30). This can be expressed as a function of the system compliance ratio α and the effective acoustic volume of the enclosure V_{AB} as follows:

$$\eta_0 = \frac{4\pi^2}{c^3} \frac{f_C^3 V_{AT}}{Q_{EC}} = \frac{4\pi^2}{c^3} \frac{f_C^3 V_{AB}}{Q_{EC}} \frac{\alpha}{1+\alpha} \tag{7.32}$$

It can be seen from this equation that once f_C, V_{AB}, and Q_{EC} are specified, the efficiency of the system is a function only of the compliance ratio α. Maximum efficiency occurs for $\alpha = \infty$. We conclude that α should be chosen as large as possible consistent with physical realizability of the driver. If α is chosen too large, the driver will be found to require unrealistically high compliance which could lead to poor mechanical stability of the suspension.

A suitable choice for α is usually in the range of 3 to 10. For $\alpha = 3$, the above equation predicts that η_0 is 75% of its maximum value. For $\alpha = 10$, η_0 is 91% of its maximum value. Once α is specified, the driver can be designed to meet the specifications. This process is illustrated by the following numerical example.

Example 5 *It is desired to design a closed-box system having a B2 alignment ($Q_{TC} = 1/\sqrt{2}$) with a lower half-power cutoff frequency of $40\,\text{Hz}$. The effective acoustic volume of the box is $V_{AB} = 2\,\text{ft}^3$ ($0.0566\,\text{m}^3$) and the maximum average sine-wave acoustic power output is $P_{AR} = 80\,\text{mW}$ with expected short term peak powers of $5\,\text{dB}$ above this. The enclosure is to be filled and the estimated system mechanical quality factor is $Q_{MC} = 3.5$. The system compliance ratio is specified to be $\alpha = 5$. Design the driver for the system.*

Solution. A 15-inch driver having a voice-coil resistance of $7\,\Omega$ and an effective piston radius $a = 0.15\,\text{m}$ is assumed. For the B2 alignment, the fundamental resonance frequency must equal the lower $-3\,\text{dB}$ cutoff frequency so that the system must have the resonance frequency $f_C = 40\,\text{Hz}$. The maximum diaphragm volume displacement is

$$V_{D(max)} = \left[P_{AR(max)} \frac{c}{4\pi^3 \rho_0 f_C^4} \frac{Q_{TC}^4}{Q_{TC}^2 - 0.25} \right]^{1/2} = 2.71 \times 10^{-4}\,\text{m}^3 \tag{7.33}$$

(This expression is valid only for $Q_{TC} \geq 1/\sqrt{2}$. For $Q_{TC} < 1/\sqrt{2}$, the solution is the same as for $Q_{TC} = 1/\sqrt{2}$.) To accommodate a peak power that is $5\,\text{dB}$ greater than $80\,\text{mW}$, $V_{D(max)}$ must be multiplied by the factor $10^{5/20} = 1.78$ to obtain $V_{D(max)} = 4.82 \times 10^{-4}\,\text{m}^3$. This is only 0.85% of the effective box volume

V_{AB} so that linearity of the compliance in the box should not be a problem. The maximum diaphragm peak displacement is $x_{max} = V_{D(max)}/\pi a^2 = 6.82\,\text{mm} = 0.27\,\text{in}$. The total peak-to-peak displacement, i.e. the voice-coil throw, must be twice this value or $13.6\,\text{mm} = 0.54\,\text{in}$.

The system electrical quality factor is

$$Q_{EC} = \frac{Q_{MC}Q_{TC}}{Q_{MC} - Q_{TC}} = \frac{3.5/\sqrt{2}}{3.5 - 1/\sqrt{2}} = 0.886 \tag{7.34}$$

From Eq. (7.32), the system reference efficiency is

$$\eta_0 = \frac{4\pi^2}{c^3}\frac{f_C^3 V_{AB}}{Q_{EC}}\frac{\alpha}{1+\alpha} = \frac{4\pi^2}{1131^3}\frac{40^3 \times 2}{0.886}\frac{5}{1+5} = 0.00329 \text{ or } 0.329\% \tag{7.35}$$

(This equation is an example of one in which English units can be used for V_{AB} and c.) The average voice-coil electrical power rating must satisfy $P_E \geq P_{AR}/\eta_0 = 24.3\,\text{W}$. The voice coil must be able to handle short term peak powers 5 dB greater than this, or 76.8 W.

The driver volume compliance is $V_{AS} = \alpha V_{AB} = 10\,\text{ft}^3 = 0.283\,\text{m}^3$. The diaphragm mechanical compliance C_{MS} and the total mechanical mass M_{MC} including the air load are

$$C_{MS} = \frac{C_{AS}}{S_D^2} = \frac{V_{AS}}{\rho_0 c^2 (\pi a^2)^2} = 4.03 \times 10^{-4}\,\text{m/N} \tag{7.36}$$

$$M_{MC} = \frac{S_D^2}{(2\pi f_C)^2 C_{AT}} = \frac{(\pi a^2)^2 (1+\alpha)\rho_0 c^2}{(2\pi f_C)^2 V_{AS}} = 0.236\,\text{kg} \tag{7.37}$$

To obtain the mechanical mass of the diaphragm, the mass of the two air loads must be subtracted. We assume that the front air load mass is that for a piston mounted in an infinite baffle given by $M_{A1} = 8\rho_0/3\pi^2 a = 2.13\,\text{kg/m}^4$. For the rear air load mass, let us assume the typical value $B = 0.65$ in Eq. (7.1). For the density ρ, let us assume the average of the lower and upper bounds given in Eq. (7.2), i.e. $\rho = 4.18\,\text{kg/m}^3$. Thus $M_{AB} = B\rho/\pi a = 5.77\,\text{kg/m}^4$. The required mechanical mass of the diaphragm and voice coil is given by

$$M_{MD} = M_{MC} - (M_{A1} + M_{AB}) \times \pi^2 a^4 = 0.197\,\text{kg} \tag{7.38}$$

The design is completed by specifying $B\ell$. It is given by

$$B\ell = \left[\frac{S_D^2 R_E}{Q_{EC}}\sqrt{\frac{M_{AC}}{C_{AT}}}\right]^{1/2} = \left[\frac{\pi a^2 c R_E}{Q_{EC}}\sqrt{\frac{\rho_0(1+\alpha)M_{MC}}{V_{AS}}}\right]^{1/2} = 21.6\,\text{T m} \tag{7.39}$$

7.10 A SPICE Simulation Example

Fig. 7.4 shows the LTSpice circuit for a closed-box system. The electrical and mechanical circuits are the same as those for the infinite baffle system given in Fig. 6.15. In the acoustical circuit, the external air-load impedance on the diaphragm is represented by the elements M_{A1}, R_{A1}, R_{A2}, and C_{A1}. The box is modeled by the elements M_{AB}, R_{AB}, and C_{AB}. To prevent node 15 from being a floating node, the resistor R_{AL} must be included in parallel with C_{AB}. The value of this resistor can be made large enough so that it effectively appears as an open circuit in the analysis. Alternately, R_{AL} can be used to model an air leak in the box.

The simulation given in this section is based on Example 5. In the electrical circuit, it is assumed that the impedance of the lossy voice-coil inductance is given by $Z_e(j\omega) = 0.00689(j\omega)^{0.7}$, where the value $L_e = 0.00689$ has been chosen so that $|Z_e|$ at $f = 1\,\text{kHz}$ is the same as the magnitude of the impedance of a 0.5 mH inductor. In addition, the value $Q_{MS} = 3$ is assumed. The following circuit element values are taken from the example: $R_E = 7\,\Omega$, $B\ell = 21.6\,\text{T m}$, $M_{MD} = 0.197\,\text{kg}$, $C_{MS} = 4.03 \times 10^{-4}\,\text{m/N}$, $M_{A1} = 2.13\,\text{kg/m}^4$, and $M_{AB} = 5.77\,\text{kg/m}^4$. The other elements in the circuit are calculated as follows:

$$R_{A2} = \frac{\rho_0 c}{\pi a^2} = 5760\,\text{N s/m}^5 \qquad R_{A1} = \frac{128\rho_0 c}{9\pi^3 a^2} - R_{A2} = 2540\,\text{N s/m}^5$$

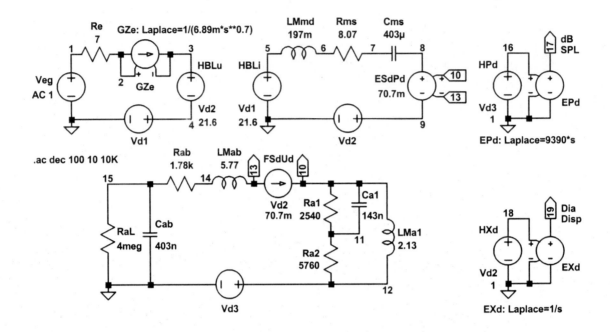

Figure 7.4: LTSpice circuit for the closed-box simulation.

$$C_{A1} = \frac{5.94a^3}{\rho_0 c^2} = 1.43 \times 10^{-7} \, \text{m}^5/\text{N} \qquad R_{MS} = \frac{1}{Q_{MS}} \sqrt{\frac{M_{MC}}{C_{MS}}} = 8.07 \, \text{N s}/\text{m}$$

$$S_D = \pi a^2 = 0.0707 \, \text{m}^2 \qquad C_{AB} = \frac{V_{AB}}{\rho_0 c^2} = 4.03 \times 10^{-7} \, \text{m}^5/\text{N}$$

$$R_{AB} = \left(\frac{\sqrt{1+\alpha} Q_{MS}}{Q_{MC}} - 1 \right) \frac{R_{MS}}{S_D^2} = 1780 \, \text{N s}/\text{m}^5$$

The LTSpice netlist for the circuit is given in Table 7.3. The value given for R_{AL} is $R_{AL} = 4 \times 10^6 \, \text{N s}/\text{m}^5$. This value is chosen to make R_{AL} an open circuit compared to C_{AB} for frequencies above about 0.1 Hz. The impedance $Z_e(j\omega)$ of the lossy voice-coil inductance is realized with the voltage-controlled current source Gze described in Section 6.24.

Figs. 7.5 through 7.7 show the calculated system responses. In each case, curve **a** is calculated with the $Z_e(j\omega)$ given by Eq. (6.49). Curve b is calculated with $Z_e(j\omega)$ replaced with a lossless 0.5 mH inductor. The magnitude of the impedance of both inductors is the same at $f = 1$ kHz. Fig. 7.5 shows the SPL responses. Note that the effect of the lossy inductor is to depress the response at midband but cause an increased response at higher frequencies. Because $e_g = 1$ V rms, the midband SPL corresponds to the SPL_{sens}^{1V} for the driver. The SPL is displayed as the voltage at node 17.

Fig. 7.6 shows the calculated input impedances for the system. The input impedance is given by the ratio of the generator voltage to the voice-coil current, i.e. V(1)/I(Vd1). Fig. 7.7 shows the diaphragm displacement in meters given by V(19) as a function of frequency. This is calculated by using the analog behavioral modeling of LTSpice to divide the diaphragm velocity I(Vd2) by the complex frequency s. If the value of the source voltage Veg is considered to be an rms value, the diaphragm displacement x_D is an rms value which must be multiplied by $\sqrt{2}$ to obtain the peak value.

Table 7.3: SPICE Netlist for the Closed Box Simulation

CLOSED-BOX EXAMPLE	ESdPd 8 9 10 13 70.7m	LMa1 10 12 2.13
Veg 1 0 0 AC 1	GZe 2 3 2 3 Laplace=1/(6.89m*s**0.7)	LMab 14 13 5.77
Re 2 1 7	HPd 16 0 Vd3 1	Rab 14 15 1.78k
HBLu 3 4 Vd2 21.6	EPd 17 0 16 0 Laplace=9390*s	Cab 15 0 403n
Vd1 4 0 0 AC 0	HXd 18 0 Vd2 1	RaL 15 0 4meg
LMmd 5 6 197m	EXd 19 0 18 0 Laplace=1/s	Vd3 12 0 0 AC 0
Rms 6 7 8.07	FSdUd 13 10 Vd2 70.7m	.ac dec 100 10 10K
Cms 7 8 403μ	Ra1 10 11 2540	.end
HBLi 5 0 Vd1 21.6	Ra2 11 12 5760	
Vd2 9 0 0 AC 0	Ca1 10 11 143n	

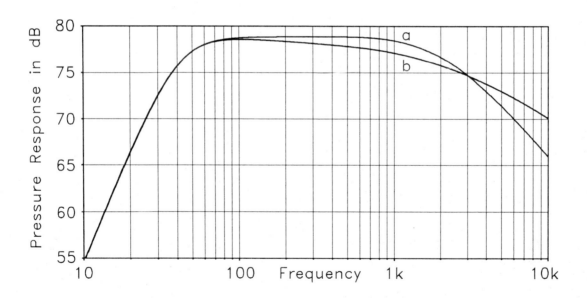

Figure 7.5: SPL in dB versus frequency. a – lossy inductor. b – lossless inductor.

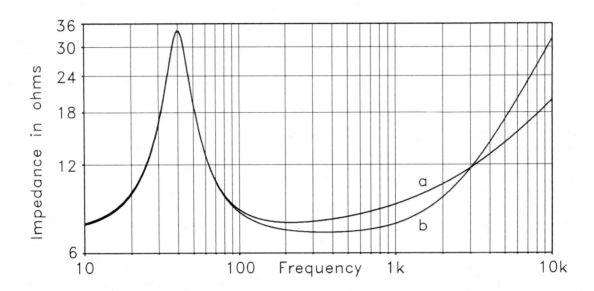

Figure 7.6: Input impedance in ohms versus frequency – 1/I(VD1). a – lossy inductor. b – lossless inductor.

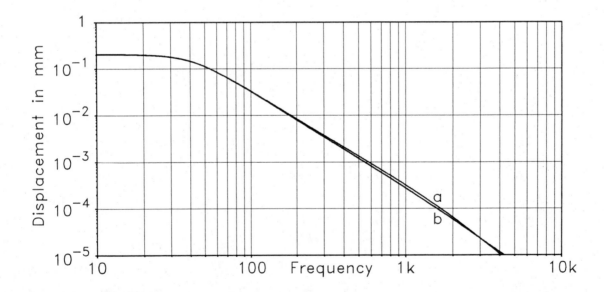

Figure 7.7: Diaphram displacement in mm versus frequency. a – lossy inductor. b – lossless inductor.

7.11 Problems

1. A loudspeaker enclosure has internal dimensions with the ratios $0.8 \times 1.0 \times 1.25$. A 10-inch woofer with the diaphragm piston radius $a = 10\,\mathrm{cm}$ is mounted on the panel having the dimensions ratios 1.0×1.25. The piston area of the diaphragm is $1/4$ the area of the panel. Calculate the mass loading factor B. [0.689]

2. *(a)* Express the driver volume compliance V_{AS} as a function of V_{AT} and V_{AB}. [$V_{AS} = V_{AB}V_{AT} \div (V_{AB} - V_{AT})$] *(b)* What compliance ratio makes $V_{AT} = V_{AB}/3$? [$\alpha = 0.5$]

3. A loudspeaker driver is mounted in a lossless closed-box baffle ($R_{AB} = 0$). It can be assumed that $M_{AC} = M_{AS}$. For this case, we have $Q_{TC} = \sqrt{1 + \alpha}\,Q_{TS}$ and $f_C = \sqrt{1 + \alpha}\,f_S$. Prove that the lower half-power (or $-3\,\mathrm{dB}$) cutoff frequency is minimized for $Q_{TC} = 1/\sqrt{2}$. [In the equation for f_ℓ, let $f_C = f_S Q_{TC}/Q_{TS}$. Set $df_\ell/dQ_{TC} = 0$ and solve for Q_{TC}.]

4. A driver has the parameters $f_S = 20\,\mathrm{Hz}$, $Q_{TS} = 0.28$, $Q_{ES} = 0.30$, and $V_{AS} = 20\,\mathrm{ft}^3$. *(a)* Specify the volume of a filled closed-box for $Q_{TC} = 0.8$. Assume $Q_{MC} = 3.5$ and that the filling increases the effective volume by 15%. [$1.59\,\mathrm{ft}^3$] *(b)* What is the lower $-3\,\mathrm{dB}$ system frequency? [$62.0\,\mathrm{Hz}$]

5. A driver with an advertised diameter of $12\,\mathrm{in}$ is to be designed for a closed-box system having the specifications: $V_{AB} = 3\,\mathrm{ft}^3$, $f_\ell = 30\,\mathrm{Hz}$, $\alpha = 3$, $Q_{TC} = 1.0$, $R_E = 7\,\Omega$, and $Q_{MC} = 4$. It can be assumed that $M_{AC} = M_{AS}$. *(a)* Solve for the parameters f_S, Q_{ES}, and V_{AS}. [$19.1\,\mathrm{Hz}$, 0.667, $9\,\mathrm{ft}^3$] *(b)* Solve for the parameters M_{MC}, C_{MS}, and $B\ell$. [$78.5\,\mathrm{g}$, $8.87 \times 10^{-4}\,\mathrm{m/N}$, $9.94\,\mathrm{T\,m}$] *(c)* What is the driver reference efficiency? [0.255%]

6. A closed-box system has the parameters f_C, Q_{EC}, and $V_{AT} = V_{AS}\|V_{AB}$. If $M_{AC} = M_{AS}$, prove that the system reference efficiency calculated from these parameters reduces to the reference efficiency expression for the driver, i.e. in terms of f_S, V_{AS}, and Q_{ES}.

7. A closed-box system has the parameters f_C, Q_{EC}, and V_{AB}. *(a)* If $M_{AC} = M_{AS}$, prove that the reference efficiency is given by

$$\eta_0 = \frac{4\pi^2}{c^3} \frac{f_C^3 V_{AB}}{Q_{EC}} \frac{\alpha}{1 + \alpha}$$

(b) If α is the only variable, what is the maximum value of η_0 and what value of α gives this maximum? [$\alpha \to \infty$] *(c)* What value of α would make η_0 exactly $1\,\mathrm{dB}$ less than its maximum value? [Because η_0 is a power ratio, use $10\log$. $\alpha = 3.86$]

8. A closed-box system is to be designed for a C2 alignment with $Q_{TC} = 1$. It is to use a driver with a $12\,\mathrm{in}$ advertised diameter. It is to be designed for the specifications $V_{AB} = 2\,\mathrm{ft}^3$ and $f_\ell = 35\,\mathrm{Hz}$. If $Q_{MC} = 4.0$ and $\alpha = 6$, specify the required driver parameters C_{MS}, M_{MC}, and $B\ell$. [$1.18 \times 10^{-3}\,\mathrm{m/N}$, $75.7\,\mathrm{g}$, $9.17\,\mathrm{T\,m}$] What is the driver reference efficiency? [0.309%]

9. Show that the diaphragm displacement function for a driver in a closed-box system is given by

$$x_D = \frac{e_g}{B\ell} \frac{R_{AE}}{R_{ATC}} \frac{1}{\omega_C Q_{TC}} \frac{1}{(s/\omega_C)^2 + (1/Q_{TC})(s/\omega_C) + 1}$$

Chapter 8

Vented-Box Loudspeaker Systems

Vented-box loudspeaker systems differ from closed-box systems in that a vent or port is installed in one wall of the enclosure. The acoustic mass of the air in the vent in combination with the acoustic compliance of the air in the enclosure forms a Helmholtz resonator which can extend the lower cutoff frequency of the system to provide better bass response. Compared to drivers which are suitable for acoustic suspension closed-box systems, drivers which are most suitable for vented-box systems are those that have a stiffer suspension. This is because the restoring force provided by the compliance of the air in the enclosure is greatly reduced below the Helmholtz resonance frequency. This can lead to excessive diaphragm displacement at infrasonic frequencies with drivers that have loosely suspended diaphragms.

8.1   Modeling the Enclosure

Fig. 8.1(a) illustrates a vented-box loudspeaker system recessed into an infinite baffle. The vent or port is usually a tube with a circular cross section which is installed in the front wall of the enclosure near the woofer and away from the side walls. The air in the vent is modeled as an acoustic mass. This mass and the compliance of the air in the enclosure form a Helmholtz resonator which can improve the bass response of the system. Vented-box enclosures are not normally filled because the filling can interfere with the air flow in the vent. To prevent standing waves in the enclosure, the box is normally lined with filling such as a 1 in layer of fiberglass.

There are two major comparisons between closed-box and vented-box systems. First, if a given driver is used in both a properly designed closed-box and a properly designed vented-box, the vented-box enclosure will be larger and its lower $-3\,\text{dB}$ cutoff frequency will be lower. Both systems will have the same efficiency. Second, if a properly designed closed-box system and a properly designed vented-box system have the same enclosure volume and the same lower $-3\,\text{dB}$ cutoff frequency, the vented-box system will be more efficient. However, the two systems require different drivers.

The low-frequency electrical, mechanical, and acoustical analogous circuits for a vented-box system are shown in Figs. 8.1(b) through (d). The electrical and the mechanical circuits are the same as those for the closed-box system. In the acoustical circuit, the resistance R_{AL} models air-leak losses in the enclosure. The mass M_{AP} models the air in the port. We assume that the port is a tube with a cross-section S_P and a length L_P and assume that the tube is flanged at one end and unflanged at the other. The acoustic mass of the air in the port is given by

$$M_{AP} = \frac{\rho_0}{S_P}\left(L_P + 1.462\sqrt{\frac{S_P}{\pi}}\right) \tag{8.1}$$

The system Helmholtz frequency is given by

$$\omega_B = 2\pi f_B = \frac{1}{\sqrt{M_{AP}C_{AB}}} \tag{8.2}$$

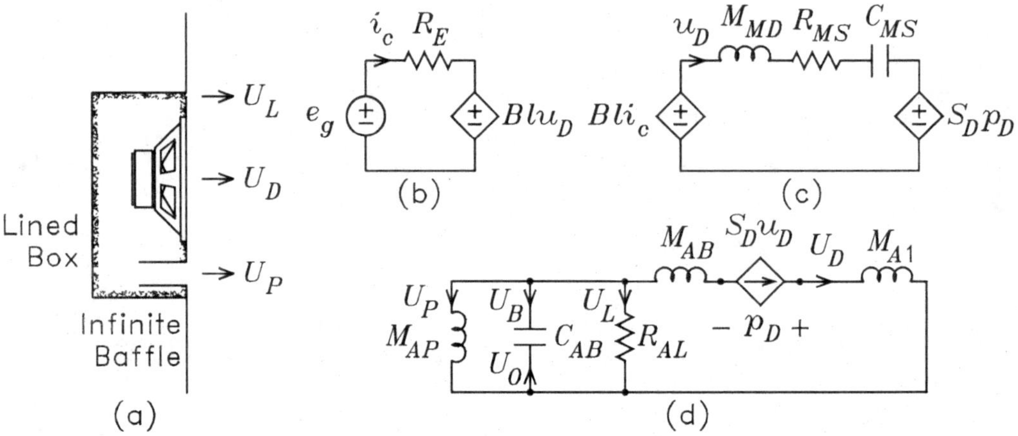

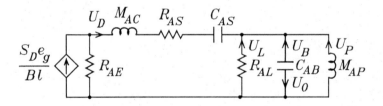

Figure 8.1: (a) Vented-box system in an infinite baffle. Low-frequency (b) electrical, (c) mechanical, and (d) acoustical analogous circuits.

where C_{AB} is the compliance of the air in the enclosure given by

$$C_{AB} = \frac{V_{AB}}{\rho_0 c^2} \tag{8.3}$$

and V_{AB} is the effective acoustic volume of air in the enclosure.

The low-frequency Norton form of the combination analogous circuit for the vented-box system can be obtained in a way similar to the way that the corresponding circuits are obtained for the infinite baffle system and closed-box system. The circuit is given in Fig. 8.2. The elements R_{AE}, R_{AS}, and C_{AS} are the same as for the infinite-baffle circuit in Fig. 6.8(b). The element M_{AC} is the same as for the closed-box circuit in Fig. 7.2(d). The value of R_{AL} depends on the box size. It is determined by specifying the box quality factor Q_L as described in Section 8.3.

Figure 8.2: Norton form of the combination acoustical analogous circuit.

8.2 Effect of the Vent

The compliance C_{AB} and the mass M_{AP} in Fig. 8.2 form a parallel resonant circuit. The resonance frequency is the Helmholtz frequency given by Eq. (8.2). At this frequency, the combined impedance of M_{AP} and C_{AB} is an open circuit so that the impedance of the parallel elements R_{AL}, M_{AP}, and C_{AB} is R_{AL}. If R_{AL} is large, i.e. the enclosure losses are small, it follows from Fig. 8.2 that the volume velocity U_D is small, with $U_D \to 0$ as $R_{AL} \to \infty$. It follows that the acoustic radiation from the driver becomes small at the Helmholtz frequency. This means that the system output predominantly comes from the port at the Helmholtz frequency.

The effect of the vent can be easily demonstrated by driving a vented-box system with a sine wave. When the frequency of the sine wave is equal to the Helmholtz frequency, the motion of the diaphragm can be seen to exhibit a null and a large flow of air can be felt in the port. Indeed, a dramatic demonstration is to let the air flow in the port blow out a candle.

If a book is held over the port when the system is driven at its Helmholtz frequency, the motion of the driver diaphragm can be seen to increase when the book is in place. It follows that the mechanical forces on the diaphragm are greater for input signals near the Helmholtz frequency compared to the forces on the diaphragm in a closed-box system. Thus a driver can be more susceptible to mechanical failure in a vented-box system. An example of this failure might be a detached glue joint between the voice-coil former and the diaphragm.

The null in the diaphragm velocity at the Helmholtz frequency has an important effect on the input impedance. Because there is no back emf generated in the driver voice coil if its velocity is zero, the driver input impedance exhibits a null at the Helmholtz frequency. The minimum value that this impedance can achieve is the voice-coil resistance R_E. Because the system draws more current when the impedance decreases, it follows that the electrical input power increases at the Helmholtz frequency. For strong bass input signals near this frequency, the power dissipated in the voice coil is greater than the power dissipated for the driver in a closed box. Therefore, a driver in a vented-box can be more susceptible to electrical failure compared to the same driver in a closed box.

8.3 The On-Axis Pressure Transfer Function

Let U_0 be the total volume velocity emitted by the system of Fig. 8.1. This is the sum of the volume velocities emitted from the diaphragm, the port, and the air leaks. From Fig. 8.2, it is given by

$$U_0 = U_D + U_P + U_L = -U_B \tag{8.4}$$

where U_B is the net volume velocity entering the enclosure. This relation follows from application of Kirchhoff's current law to the analogous circuit.

To solve for the volume velocity transfer function, it is convenient to first define the complex impedance Z_{A1} and the complex admittance Y_{A2} as follows:

$$Z_{A1} = M_{AC}s + R_{AE} + R_{AS} + \frac{1}{C_{AS}s} = \frac{M_{AC}C_{AS}s^2 + R_{AT}C_{AS}s + 1}{C_{AS}s} \tag{8.5}$$

$$Y_{A2} = C_{AB}s + \frac{1}{R_{AL}} + \frac{1}{M_{AP}s} = \frac{M_{AP}C_{AB}s^2 + M_{AP}s/R_{AL} + 1}{M_{AP}s} \tag{8.6}$$

where

$$R_{AT} = R_{AE} + R_{AS} \tag{8.7}$$

To simplify the expression for Z_{A1}, we assume that $M_{AC} \simeq M_{AS} = M_{AD} + 2M_{A1}$. That is, we assume that the total acoustic mass load is the same as for the infinite baffle case. With the definitions of ω_S and Q_{TS} from Section 6.5, the expression for Z_{A1} can then be written

$$Z_{A1} = \frac{(s/\omega_S)^2 + (1/Q_{TS})(s/\omega_S) + 1}{C_{AS}s} \tag{8.8}$$

To simplify the expression for Y_{A2}, denote the quality factor of the parallel R_{AL}, M_{AP}, and C_{AB} circuit by Q_L. It is given by

$$Q_L = \frac{R_{AL}}{\omega_B M_{AP}} = \omega_B R_{AL} C_{AB} = R_{AL}\sqrt{\frac{C_{AB}}{M_{AP}}} \tag{8.9}$$

Thus Y_{A2} can be written

$$Y_{A2} = \frac{(s/\omega_B)^2 + (1/Q_L)(s/\omega_B) + 1}{M_{AP}s} \tag{8.10}$$

With these definitions, we can use current division in the circuit of Fig. 8.2 to solve for the total system volume velocity output as follows:

$$U_0 = \frac{S_D e_g}{B\ell} \frac{R_{AE}}{Z_{A1} + 1/Y_{A2}} \frac{C_{AB}s}{Y_{A2}} = \frac{S_D e_g}{B\ell} \frac{R_{AE} C_{AB}s}{1 + Z_{A1} Y_{A2}} \tag{8.11}$$

Note that R_{AE} does not occur in the denominator because it is included in Z_{A1}. It can be shown that this expression reduces to

$$U_0 = \frac{B\ell e_g}{S_D R_E M_{AS}} \frac{s^3/\omega_0^4}{(s/\omega_0)^4 + a_3 (s/\omega_0)^3 + a_2 (s/\omega_0)^2 + a_1 (s/\omega_0) + 1} \tag{8.12}$$

where the frequency ω_0 and the coefficients a_1, a_2, and a_3 are given by

$$\omega_0 = 2\pi f_0 = \sqrt{\omega_S \omega_B} = \omega_S \sqrt{h} = \frac{\omega_B}{\sqrt{h}} \tag{8.13}$$

$$a_1 = \frac{1}{Q_L \sqrt{h}} + \frac{\sqrt{h}}{Q_{TS}} \qquad a_2 = \frac{\alpha + 1}{h} + h + \frac{1}{Q_L Q_{TS}} \qquad a_3 = \frac{1}{Q_{TS} \sqrt{h}} + \frac{\sqrt{h}}{Q_L} \tag{8.14}$$

In these equations, α is the system compliance ratio and h is the Helmholtz tuning ratio given by

$$\alpha = \frac{C_{AS}}{C_{AB}} = \frac{V_{AS}}{V_{AB}} \qquad h = \frac{\omega_B}{\omega_S} = \frac{f_B}{f_S} \tag{8.15}$$

The normalized on-axis pressure is given by $p = \rho_0 s U_0 / 2\pi$. When the expression for U_0 is used in the equation for p, we obtain after some simplification

$$p = \frac{\rho_0}{2\pi} \frac{B\ell e_g}{S_D R_E M_{AS}} G_V(s) \tag{8.16}$$

where $G_V(s)$ is the vented-box on-axis pressure transfer function given by

$$G_V(s) = \frac{(s/\omega_0)^4}{(s/\omega_0)^4 + a_3 (s/\omega_0)^3 + a_2 (s/\omega_0)^2 + a_1 (s/\omega_0) + 1} \tag{8.17}$$

The pressure transfer function is a fourth-order, high-pass filter function. At low frequencies, the Bode magnitude plot exhibits an asymptotic slope of $+4$ dec/dec ($+24$ dB per octave) compared to a slope of $+2$ dec/dec ($+12$ dB per octave) for the closed-box system.

The shape of the Bode plot is a function of the coefficients a_1, a_2, and a_3. The numerical values of these coefficients define the vented-box system alignment. Examination of Eq. (8.14) shows that the coefficients are functions of the four system parameters α, h, Q_{TS}, and Q_L. Thus if the three a-coefficients are specified for a particular alignment, one of the four system parameters must be assumed before the other three can be calculated. That parameter is usually taken to be Q_L. A lossless box is modeled by choosing $Q_L = \infty$. Values of Q_L which are representative of real enclosures are $Q_L = 20$, 10, 7, 5, and 3. For systems with an internal box volume in the $1\,\text{ft}^3$ to $4\,\text{ft}^3$ range, Q_L is typically between 5 and 10, becoming smaller with increasing enclosure volume. For enclosures of moderate size, the value $Q_L = 7$ is usually assumed as a starting point for design purposes.

8.4 Voice-Coil Impedance Function

If it is assumed that the air mass load on the diaphragm is the same as its infinite-baffle value, i.e. $M_{AC} = M_{AS}$, it can be shown that the voice-coil impedance of a driver in a vented-box system is given by

$$Z_{VC}(s) = R_E + R'_E \| L_E s + R_{ES} \frac{(1/Q_{MS})(s/\omega_S)[(s/\omega_B)^2 + (1/Q_L)(s/\omega_B) + 1]}{(s/\omega_0)^4 + b_3(s/\omega_0)^3 + b_2(s/\omega_0)^2 + b_1(s/\omega_0) + 1} \quad (8.18)$$

where $R_{ES} = R_E Q_{MS}/Q_{ES}$ and the equations for b_1, b_2, and b_3, respectively, are the same as those for a_1, a_2, and a_3 in the pressure transfer function with the exception that Q_{TS} in the a coefficients is replaced by Q_{MS} in the b coefficients. Fig. 8.3 shows the voice-coil equivalent circuit. The elements are given by

$$R_{ES} = \frac{Q_{MS}R_E}{Q_{ES}} \qquad R_{EL} = \frac{hR_E}{\alpha Q_{ES}Q_L} \qquad L_{CES} = \frac{R_E}{2\pi f_S Q_{ES}} \quad (8.19)$$

$$L_{CEB} = \frac{R_E}{2\pi f_S \alpha Q_{ES}} \qquad C_{MES} = \frac{Q_{ES}}{2\pi f_S R_E} \qquad C_{MEP} = \frac{\alpha Q_{ES}}{2\pi f_S h^2 R_E} \quad (8.20)$$

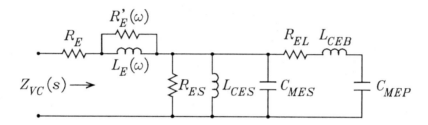

Figure 8.3: Equivalent voice-coil circuit for the vented-box driver.

The Bode magnitude plot of the voice-coil impedance for a typical driver in a vented-box enclosure is shown in Fig. 8.4. The figure shows the impedance with the vent closed and opened. With the vent closed, there is a single resonance peak and the resonance frequency is labeled f_C. With the vent open, there are two impedance peaks. The Helmholtz frequency is the frequency of the null between the peaks and is labeled f_B. The figure corresponds to the case where the Helmholtz frequency is approximately equal to the fundamental resonance frequency of the driver, i.e. $f_B \simeq f_S$. For this case, the two impedance peaks have approximately the same magnitude. A method of tuning the vent that has been widely used is to adjust its length and/or area until the two peaks are equal. This method results in a proper design only if $Q_{TS} \simeq 0.4$.

8.5 The Magnitude-Squared Function

The alignment of a vented-box system is specified with reference to the magnitude-squared function defined by $|G_V(j\omega)|^2$, where $\omega = 2\pi f$. It follows from Eq. (8.17) that $|G_V(j2\pi f)|^2$ is given by

$$|G_V(j2\pi f)|^2 = \frac{(f/f_0)^8}{(f/f_0)^8 + A_3(f/f_0)^6 + A_2(f/f_0)^4 + A_1(f/f_0)^2 + 1} \quad (8.21)$$

where $\omega_0 = 2\pi f_0$ and the A coefficients are given by

$$A_3 = a_3^2 - 2a_2 \qquad A_2 = 2 + a_2^2 - 2a_1 a_3 \qquad A_1 = a_1^2 - 2a_2 \quad (8.22)$$

For any given alignment, the A coefficients are first specified. From these, the a coefficients can be solved for. The small-signal system parameters can then be determined.

Once the A and a coefficients are determined for any particular alignment, a value for the box quality factor Q_L must be assumed. Then the basic steps for determining the system parameters are:

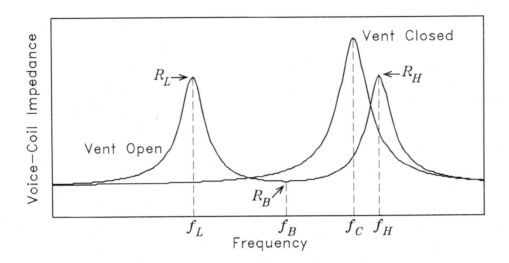

Figure 8.4: $|Z_{VC}|$ versus frequency with the vent open and the vent closed.

1. Solve for the positive real roots of the equation

$$d^4 - A_3 d^3 - A_2 d^2 - A_1 d - 1 = 0 \qquad (8.23)$$

This polynomial is obtained from the equation $|G_V(j2\pi f_\ell)|^2 = 1/2$, where $d = (f_\ell/f_0)^2$ and f_ℓ is the lower $-3\,\mathrm{dB}$ frequency of the system.

2. Solve for the positive real roots of the equation

$$r^4 - (a_3 Q_L) r^3 + (a_1 Q_L) r - 1 = 0 \qquad (8.24)$$

This equation is obtained by eliminating Q_{TS} between a_1 and a_3 in Eq. (8.14) and setting $r = \sqrt{h} = \sqrt{f_B/f_S}$. In the case that $Q_L \to \infty$, there is only one root given by $r = \sqrt{a_1/a_3}$.

3. Use the values of d and r to calculate the system parameters

$$h = \frac{f_B}{f_S} = r^2 \qquad q = \frac{f_\ell}{f_S} = r\sqrt{d} \qquad Q_{TS} = \frac{r^2 Q_L}{a_1 r Q_L - 1} \qquad (8.25)$$

$$\alpha = \frac{V_{AS}}{V_{AB}} = r^2 \left(a_2 - \frac{1}{Q_L Q_{TS}} - r^2 \right) - 1 \qquad (8.26)$$

If there is more than one positive root for r, the root which makes α and Q_{TS} positive must be used. If there is more than one positive root for d, the correct root depends on the value of r. For $r < 1$, pick the root that satisfies $d \leq r^2$. For $r > 1$, pick the root that satisfies $d \geq r^2$.

8.6   The B4 Alignment

The B4 or $4th$-order Butterworth vented-box alignment has a $|G_V(j2\pi f)|^2$ given by

$$|G_V(j2\pi f)|^2 = \frac{(f/f_0)^8}{1 + (f/f_0)^8} \qquad (8.27)$$

When this is compared to Eq. (8.21), it follows that $A_1 = A_2 = A_3 = 0$. For these values, it follows from Eq. (8.22) that

$$a_2 = 2 + \sqrt{2} \qquad a_1 = a_3 = \sqrt{2a_2} = 2.6131 \qquad (8.28)$$

Table 8.1 summarizes the values of α, h, Q_{TS}, and q for six values of Q_L for the B4 alignment. Because $h = 1$ for each value of Q_L, the Helmholtz resonance frequency f_B is equal to the driver resonance frequency f_S. The B4 alignment is the only vented-box alignment for which this holds. Another characteristic of the B4 alignment is that the lower half-power or $-3\,$dB cutoff frequency f_ℓ is equal to f_S, i.e. $q = 1$.

Table 8.1: B4 Alignment Data

Q_L	α	h	Q_{TS}	q
∞	1.414	1	0.383	1
20	1.286	1	0.390	1
10	1.163	1	0.398	1
7	1.061	1	0.405	1
5	0.932	1	0.414	1
3	0.654	1	0.439	1

For a given Q_L, there is only one value of Q_{TS} for the B4 alignment. In contrast, for the closed-box systems, a Butterworth or B2 alignment can be realized for any value of $Q_{TS} < 1/\sqrt{2}$. This illustrates a basic difference between the closed-box and vented-box systems. For the closed-box case, the B2 alignment can be specified independently of the driver, as long as $Q_{TS} < Q_{TC}$. This is not the case with the vented-box system.

8.7 The QB3 Alignments

For drivers that have a Q_{TS} that is lower than the value required for the B4 alignments, the QB3 or quasi-Butterworth 3rd-order alignments are commonly used. These alignments have a $|G_V(j2\pi f)|^2$ given by

$$|G_V(j2\pi f)|^2 = \frac{(f/f_0)^8}{1 + B^2 (f/f_0)^2 + (f/f_0)^8} \qquad (8.29)$$

where B is a parameter. For $B = 0$, the QB3 alignment is the same as the B4 alignment. The alignment is called quasi-Butterworth 3rd-order because, for large values of B, the Bode magnitude plots appear to exhibit a $+3$ dec/dec slope (log-log scales) in the cutoff region, increasing to $+4$ dec/dec well below cutoff. All of the QB3 alignments result in a lower half-power or $-3\,$dB cutoff frequency that is higher than the driver resonance frequency, i.e. $f_\ell > f_S$.

When Eq. (8.29) is compared to Eq. (8.21), it can be seen that $B^2 = A_1$ and $A_2 = A_3 = 0$. For these values, it follows from Eq. (8.22) that

$$B^2 = a_1^2 - 2a_2 \qquad a_1 = \frac{a_2^2 + 2}{2a_3} \qquad a_2 > 2 + \sqrt{2} \qquad a_3 = \sqrt{2a_2} \qquad (8.30)$$

The procedure for solving for the QB3 alignment data is summarized as follows:

1. Specify a value for $B > 0$.

2. When a_1 and a_3 are eliminated, the equation for B^2 in Eq. (8.30) can be reduced to

$$a_2^4 - 12a_2^2 - 8B^2 a_2 + 4 = 0 \qquad (8.31)$$

Solve for the positive real root of this equation which satisfies the inequality $a_2 > 2 + \sqrt{2}$.

3. Calculate a_3 and a_1 from

$$a_3 = \sqrt{2a_2} \qquad a_1 = \frac{a_2^2 + 2}{2a_3} \tag{8.32}$$

These equations come from Eq. (8.30).

4. Calculate the alignment data from Eqs. (8.23) through (8.26).

8.8   The Chebyshev Alignments

For drivers that have a value of Q_{TS} that is higher than the value required for the B4 alignments, the C4 or Chebyshev equal-ripple alignments can be used. These alignments have a $|G_V(j2\pi f)|^2$ given by

$$|G_V(j2\pi f)|^2 = \frac{1 + \epsilon^2}{1 + \epsilon^2 C_4^2(f_n/f)} \tag{8.33}$$

where ϵ is a parameter (similar to the B in the QB3 alignments), $C_4(f_n/f)$ is the fourth-order Chebyshev polynomial given by

$$C_4(f_n/f) = 8(f_n/f)^4 - 8(f_n/f)^2 + 1 \tag{8.34}$$

and f_n is a normalization frequency that is related to the lower $-3\,\text{dB}$ cutoff frequency f_ℓ by

$$f_n = \frac{f_\ell}{2} \left[2 + \sqrt{2 + 2\sqrt{2 + \frac{1}{\epsilon^2}}} \right]^{1/2} \tag{8.35}$$

Note that the argument of the Chebyshev function is inversely proportional to the frequency f.

After some algebra, the magnitude-squared function can be put into the form

$$|G_V(j2\pi f)|^2 = \frac{\left[(1 + \epsilon^2)/(64\epsilon^2)\right](f/f_n)^8}{\left[(1+\epsilon^2)/(64\epsilon^2)\right](f/f_n)^8 - 0.25(f/f_n)^6 + 1.25(f/f_n)^4 - 2(f/f_n)^2 + 1} \tag{8.36}$$

It follows from this expression that f_0 and the A coefficients are given by

$$f_0 = \left(\frac{64\epsilon^2}{1 + \epsilon^2} \right)^{1/8} f_n \tag{8.37}$$

$$A_3 = -0.25 \left(\frac{64\epsilon^2}{1 + \epsilon^2} \right)^{3/4} \qquad A_2 = 1.25 \left(\frac{64\epsilon^2}{1 + \epsilon^2} \right)^{1/2} \qquad A_1 = -2 \left(\frac{64\epsilon^2}{1 + \epsilon^2} \right)^{1/4} \tag{8.38}$$

For $f \geq f_n$, $|G_V(j2\pi f)|^2$ ripples between the values 1 and $1 + \epsilon^2$. The parameter ϵ is related to the dB ripple by

$$\epsilon = \sqrt{10^{\text{dB}/10} - 1} \qquad \text{or} \qquad \text{dB} = 10\log(1 + \epsilon^2) \tag{8.39}$$

A parameter k that is used in calculation of the C4 alignment data is related to ϵ by

$$k = \tanh\left[\frac{1}{4}\sinh^{-1}\left(\frac{1}{\epsilon} \right) \right] \qquad \text{or} \qquad \epsilon = \left[\sinh(4\tanh^{-1} k) \right]^{-1} \tag{8.40}$$

All of the C4 alignments result in a lower half-power or $-3\,\text{dB}$ cutoff frequency that is lower than the driver resonance frequency, i.e. $f_\ell < f_S$.

For $k = 1$, the C4 alignment is the same as the B4 alignment. The alignments are C4 for $k < 1$. The dB ripple for $k = 0.5$ is 0.21 dB while it is 1.1 dB for $k = 0.33$. Thus for k in the range of 0.5 to 1, the C4 alignments have very little ripple. The dB ripple begins to increase rapidly for k less than 0.5.

The procedure for calculating C4 alignment data is as follows:

1. Specify the dB ripple, then calculate ϵ and k from Eqs. (8.39) and (8.40).

2. Calculate D from

$$D = \frac{k^4 + 6k^2 + 1}{8} \tag{8.41}$$

3. Use the values of k and D to calculate the a coefficients from

$$a_1 = \frac{k\sqrt{4 + 2\sqrt{2}}}{D^{1/4}} \qquad a_2 = \frac{1 + k^2\left(1 + \sqrt{2}\right)}{D^{1/2}} \qquad a_3 = \frac{a_1}{D^{1/2}}\left(1 - \frac{1 - k^2}{2\sqrt{2}}\right) \tag{8.42}$$

4. Calculate the alignment data from Eqs. (8.23) through (8.26).

8.9   Example Pressure Responses

Fig. 8.5 shows example Bode magnitude plots for the B4, the QB3, and the C4 alignments. The f_0 for each curve has been chosen to be different so that the curves are shifted from each other in the horizontal direction to make it easier to see the differences in shapes. The B4 alignment corresponds to the middle curve. The two curves to the left are for C4 alignments ($k = 0.5$ and $k = 0.33$) while the two curves to the right are for QB3 alignments ($B = 2$ and $B = 4$). Note the ripple in the two C4 alignments. It can be seen that the slope of the plots below the cutoff frequency is steepest for the small-k C4 alignments and is more gradual for the large-B QB3 alignments. As B increases, the slope of the QB3 alignments just below the cutoff frequency approaches $+3$ on log-log scales.

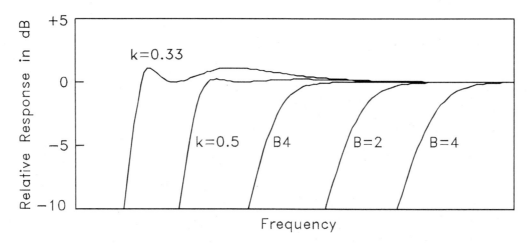

Figure 8.5: Bode magnitude plots for the on-axis pressure for B4, C4, and QB3 alignments. Curves are displaced horizontally for clarity.

8.10   Design with a Given Driver

The vented-box design procedure for a given driver requires a knowledge of the driver parameters f_S, Q_{TS}, and V_{AS}. A value for Q_L must be assumed. The rule of thumb that is commonly used is to assume the value $Q_L = 7$ for the initial design. After the required box volume is determined, it can be assumed that the value for Q_L is correct if the box volume is in the medium range, i.e. $2\,\text{ft}^3$ to $3\,\text{ft}^3$. For smaller volumes, a larger value of Q_L should be assumed and the design procedure repeated. For larger volumes, a smaller value of Q_L should be assumed and the design procedure repeated.

Vented-box design charts for $Q_L = \infty$, 20, 10, 7, 5, and 3 are given in Figs. 8.6 through 8.11. The procedure for using these charts is as follows:

1. On the left ordinate of the appropriate chart, locate the value of Q_{TS} for the driver. Draw a horizontal line through this value which intersects the Q_{TS} curve on the chart. Draw a vertical line through this intersection that cuts the abscissa.

2. Read the value of the box compliance ratio α from the intersection of the vertical line with the abscissa. Calculate the required box volume $V_{AB} = V_{AS}/\alpha$.

3. Read the value of the Helmholtz tuning ratio $h = f_B/f_S$ from the right ordinate corresponding to the point that the vertical line in step 1 crosses the h curve on the chart. Calculate the Helmholtz frequency $f_B = hf_S$.

4. Read the value $q = f_\ell/f_S$ from the right ordinate corresponding to the point that the vertical line in step 1 crosses the q curve on the chart. Calculate the system lower half-power or $-3\,\mathrm{dB}$ cutoff frequency $f_\ell = qf_S$.

5. For a vent or port of cross section S_P, calculate its length from the formula

$$L_P = \left(\frac{c}{2\pi f_B}\right)^2 \frac{S_P}{V_{AB}} - 1.463\sqrt{\frac{S_P}{\pi}} \tag{8.43}$$

The selection of the vent area is an important consideration. For a given f_B, it can be seen from Eq. (8.43) that the vent length increases as its area is increased. As a general rule, the vent area should be chosen as large as possible to minimize noise caused by turbulent air flow. If the area is too large, however, the vent will extend too far into the enclosure and might have its unflanged end too close to the back wall. Ideally, the vent should extend to about one-half the depth of the box. In the event that it is too long to fit in the enclosure, an elbow shaped vent can be used. Round PVC tubing makes a good vent material. To increase the vent area, two or more equal length vent tubes can be used. In this case, the length is calculated as if the tubes are a single tube having a cross-sectional area equal to the total area of all the tubes. There is only one Helmholtz frequency when multiple vents are used.

After a system is designed and built, the Helmholtz frequency can be measured by connecting the system to the parameter measurement test set described in Section 11.7. At the Helmholtz frequency, the system exhibits a null in its input impedance so that the voice-coil voltage exhibits a null. Often, it will be found that the measured frequency will not correspond to the desired frequency. There is a simple procedure which can be used to tune the port length. Cut the port 20% longer than the value predicted by Eq. (8.43). Denote this length by L'_P. Measure the Helmholtz frequency for this length. Denote this by f'_B (which is less than f_B). The amount which L'_P must be reduced to make the Helmholtz frequency increase from f'_B to f_B is given by

$$\Delta L_P = L'_P - L_P = \left(\frac{c}{2\pi}\right)^2 \frac{S_P}{V_{AB}} \left[\frac{1}{f_B'^2} - \frac{1}{f_B^2}\right] \tag{8.44}$$

Example 1 *A driver has the parameters $Q_{TS} = 0.3$, $f_S = 28\,\mathrm{Hz}$, $V_{AS} = 6\,\mathrm{ft}^3$, and $R_E = 7\,\Omega$. The inductor in the crossover network has the dc resistance $R_g = 1\,\Omega$ that is in series with the woofer. Design a vented-box enclosure for the driver.*

Solution. In order to account for R_g, we need the electrical quality factor Q_{ES} of the driver. Because this is not given, the value of Q_{MS} must be estimated and then Q_{ES} calculated. Let us assume that $Q_{MS} \simeq 4$. Thus we have

$$Q_{ES} = \frac{Q_{MS}Q_{TS}}{Q_{MS} - Q_{TS}} = 0.324 \tag{8.45}$$

Q_{ES} and Q_{TS} with R_g in series with the driver are

$$Q'_{ES} = Q_{ES}\left(1 + \frac{R_g}{R_E}\right) = 0.371 \qquad Q'_{TS} = \frac{Q'_{ES}Q_{MS}}{Q'_{ES} + Q_{MS}} = 0.339 \tag{8.46}$$

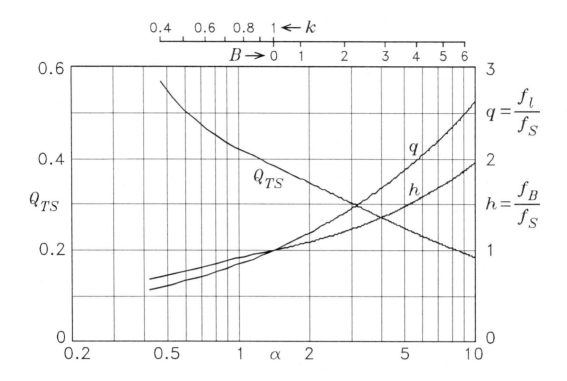

Figure 8.6: Vented-box alignment chart for $Q_L = \infty$.

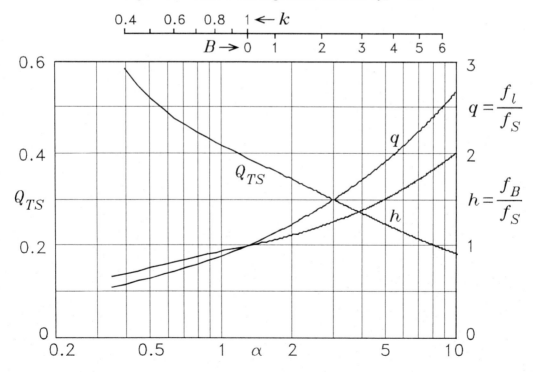

Figure 8.7: Vented-box alignment chart for $Q_L = 20$.

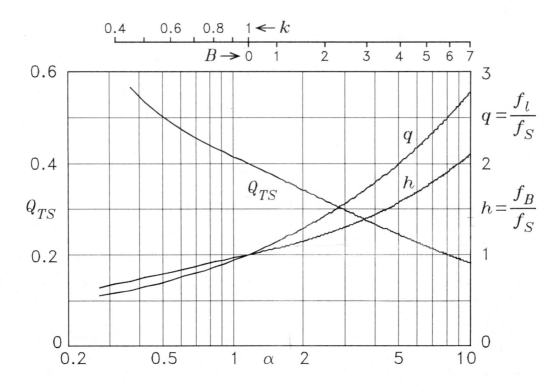

Figure 8.8: Vented-box alignment chart for $Q_L = 10$.

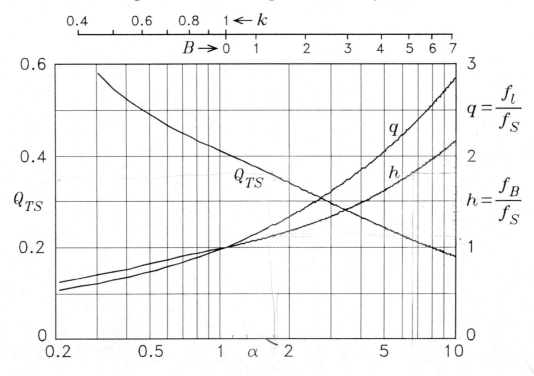

Figure 8.9: Vented-box alignment chart for $Q_L = 7$.

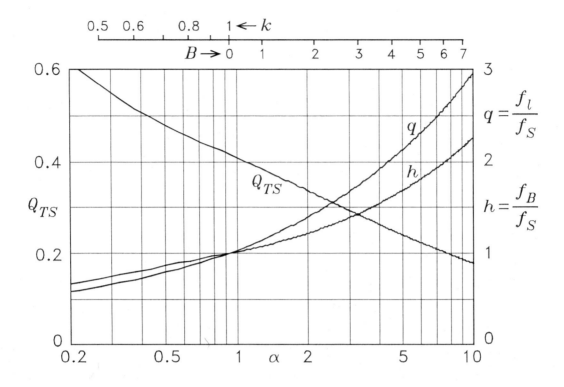

Figure 8.10: Vented-box alignment chart for $Q_L = 5$.

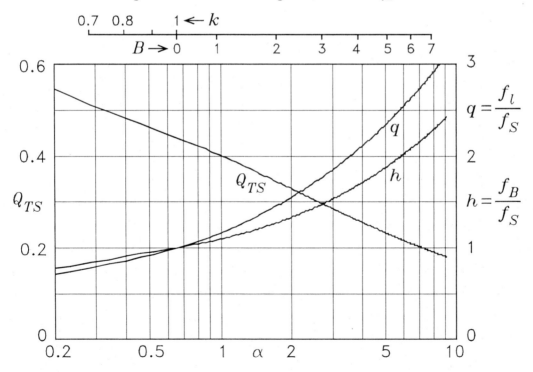

Figure 8.11: Vented-box alignment chart for $Q_L = 3$.

From the $Q_L = 7$ design chart, we have $\alpha = 2$, $h = 1.2$, and $f_3/f_S = 1.3$. Thus $V_{AB} = V_{AS}/\alpha = 3\,\text{ft}^3$, $f_B = h f_S = 33.6\,\text{Hz}$, and $f_\ell = q f_S = 36.4\,\text{Hz}$. Let us assume a vent tube that has a circular cross section with a diameter of 3 in. The length of the vent is given by

$$L_P = \left[\frac{1131}{2\pi 33.6}\right]^2 \frac{\pi (1.5/12)^2}{3} - 1.463\,(1.5/12) = 0.2867\,\text{ft} = 3.441\,\text{in} \tag{8.47}$$

8.11   System Verification

To verify a system design, any crossover network must be disconnected. The frequencies f_L, f_B, and f_H shown in Fig. 8.4 must be measured. At these frequencies, the voice-coil impedance is real and is labeled R_L, R_B, and R_H in the figure. The value of R_B must also be measured. These can be determined by the techniques described in Section 11.7. The frequencies f_L, f_B, and f_H are most easily determined as the frequencies where the phase crosses zero. However, enclosure losses and the voice-coil inductance can perturb the phase more than the magnitude, so that it is preferable to determine f_L and f_H at the maximum impedance and f_B at the minimum. From these measurements, the driver resonance frequency f_{SB} for the air load mass presented by the enclosure, the compliance ratio α, and the vent tuning ratio h can be calculated from the relations

$$f_{SB} = \frac{f_L f_H}{f_B} \qquad a = \left[\left(\frac{f_B}{f_L}\right)^2 - 1\right]\left[1 - \left(\frac{f_B}{f_H}\right)^2\right] \qquad h = \frac{f_B}{f_{SB}} \tag{8.48}$$

To determine the box quality factor Q_L, the driver voice-coil resistance R_E, its resonance frequency f_S, and its quality factors Q_{ES} and Q_{MS} must be known. First, adjust the quality factors for the air load mass presented by the enclosure using the relations $Q_{ESB} = Q_{ES} \times f_S/f_{SB}$ and $Q_{MSB} = Q_{MS} \times f_S/f_{SB}$. The box quality factor is given by

$$Q_L = \frac{h}{\alpha}\left[\frac{R_E}{Q_{ESB}\,(R_B - R_E)} - \frac{1}{Q_{MSB}}\right] \tag{8.49}$$

8.12   Design from Specifications

This section illustrates an example design of a driver for a vented-box system. We assume a 10-inch driver with a piston radius of 10 cm. Let the system specifications be as follows:

B4 Alignment	$f_\ell = 35\,\text{Hz}$	$P_{AR(max)} = 300\,\text{mW}$ on peaks
$V_{AB} = 2\,\text{ft}^3 = 0.0566\,\text{m}^3$	$R_E = 7\,\Omega$	Peak-to-Ave. Ratio= 5 dB

We will assume that $Q_L = 7$ for the enclosure and $Q_{MS} = 3.5$ for the driver. From Table 8.1, we have $\alpha = 1.061$, $h = 1$, $Q_{TS} = 0.405$, and $q = 1$. The driver must have the parameters

$$V_{AS} = \alpha V_{AB} = 2.12\,\text{ft}^3 = 6.01 \times 10^{-2}\,\text{m}^3 \qquad f_S = \frac{f_\ell}{q} = 35\,\text{Hz} \qquad Q_{ES} = \frac{Q_{MS}Q_{TS}}{Q_{MS} - Q_{TS}} = 0.458$$

The driver efficiency is

$$\eta_0 = \frac{4\pi^2}{c^3}\frac{f_S^3 V_{AS}}{Q_{ES}} = 0.541\%$$

On program peaks, the voice coil must dissipate the power

$$P_{E(max)} = \frac{P_{AR(max)}}{\eta_0} = 55.5\,\text{W}$$

For a peak-to-average power ratio of 5 dB, the minimum average thermal rating for the voice coil must be

$$P_{E(ave)} = \frac{55.5}{10^{(\text{dB}/10)}} = 17.5\,\text{W}$$

For a driver in a vented box, it can be shown that the maximum volume of air displaced by the diaphragm is related to the maximum acoustic power radiated by

$$V_{D(max)} = \frac{1}{f_\ell^2} \sqrt{\frac{P_{AR(max)}}{k_p}}$$

where $k_p \simeq 3$. This equation gives $V_{D(\text{max})} = 2.58 \times 10^{-4} \, \text{m}^3$. For a piston radius $a = 10 \, \text{cm}$, the maximum diaphragm displacement is

$$x_{max} = \frac{V_{D(max)}}{\pi a^2} = 8.22 \, \text{mm}$$

The mechanical compliance and mass are

$$C_{MS} = \frac{V_{AS}}{\rho_0 c^2 S_D^2} = 4.33 \times 10^{-4} \, \text{m/N} \qquad M_{MS} = \frac{1}{(2\pi f_S)^2 C_{MS}} = 0.0477 \, \text{kg}$$

The diaphragm and voice-coil mass is obtained by subtracting the air load masses from M_{MS} to obtain

$$M_{MD} = M_{MS} - S_D^2 \left(\frac{8\rho_0}{3\pi^2 a} + \frac{B\rho_0}{\pi a} \right) = 0.0422 \, \text{kg}$$

where the value $B = 0.65$ in Eq. (7.4) is assumed for the back air-load mass. The $B\ell$ product is

$$B\ell = \sqrt{\frac{2\pi f_S R_E M_{MS}}{Q_{ES}}} = 12.7 \, \text{T m}$$

8.13 Vented-Box SPICE Example

A SPICE simulation of the system designed above is described in this section. Fig. 8.12 shows the system geometry. We assume that the system radiates into half space, i.e. into a 2π-steradian load. In the figure, a_p is the radius of the port, d_1 is the spacing between the centers of the diaphragm and port, d_w is the diameter of the woofer frame, and L_P is the length of the port. Fig. 8.13 gives the complete LTSpice controlled-source circuit model with nodes numbered. Zero voltage sources (labeled Vdn, where n is an integer) are included in the circuit where needed as ammeters for the current controlled sources. At a distance $r = 1 \, \text{m}$, the rms value of the on-axis acoustic pressure of the system is given by

$$p_{rms} = \rho_0 f U_{0(rms)} \tag{8.50}$$

where $U_{0(rms)}$ is the rms value of the total system output volume velocity and f is the frequency.

For the simulation, we will assume the following values: woofer frame diameter $d_w = 10 \, \text{in}$, woofer piston radius $a_w = 0.10 \, \text{m}$, port radius $a_p = 3.81 \, \text{cm}$ (3 in diameter port), woofer-port spacing of 1.6 times the woofer frame radius so that $d_1 = 1.6 d_w/2 = 8 \, \text{in} = 0.203 \, \text{m}$, and lossy voice-coil inductance impedance $Z_e(j\omega) = 0.00689 (j\omega)^{0.7}$. The element values not given above are calculated as follows:

$$R_{MS} = \frac{1}{2\pi f_S C_{MS} Q_{MS}} = 3.00 \, \text{N s/m} \qquad S_W = \pi a_w^2 = 0.0314 \, \text{m}^2$$

$$M_{AB} = \frac{B\rho_0}{\pi a_w} = 2.44 \, \text{kg/m}^4 \qquad C_{AB} = \frac{V_{AB}}{\rho_0 c^2} = 4.03 \times 10^{-7} \, \text{m}^5/\text{N}$$

$$R_{AL} = \frac{Q_L}{2\pi f_B C_{AB}} = 7.89 \times 10^4 \, \text{N s/m}^5 \qquad M_{A1P} = \frac{8\rho_0}{3\pi^2 a_p} = 8.39 \, \text{kg/m}^4$$

$$M'_{AP} = \frac{1}{(2\pi f_B)^2 C_{AB}} - M_{A1P} = 42.9 \, \text{kg/m}^4 \qquad R_{A2P} = \frac{\rho_0 c}{\pi a_p^2} = 8.97 \times 10^4 \, \text{N s/m}^5$$

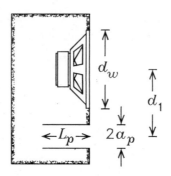

Figure 8.12: System geometry.

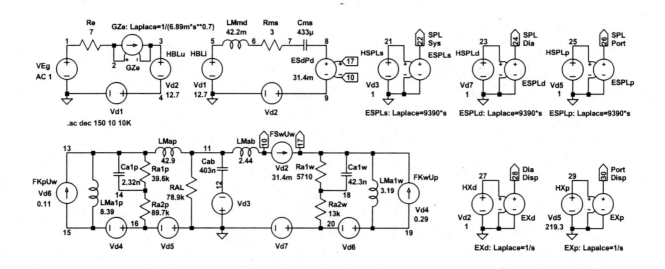

Figure 8.13: LTSpice circuit.

$$R_{A1P} = \frac{128\rho_0 c}{9\pi^3 a_p^2} - R_{A2P} = 3.96 \times 10^4 \,\mathrm{N\,s/\,m^5} \qquad C_{A1P} = \frac{5.94 a_p^3}{\rho_0 c^2} = 2.32 \times 10^{-9}\,\mathrm{m^5/\,N}$$

$$k_p = \frac{3\pi a_p}{16 d_1} = 0.110 \qquad S_P = \pi a_p^2 = 4.56 \times 10^{-3}\,\mathrm{m^2} \qquad M_{A1W} = \frac{8\rho_0}{3\pi^2 a_w} = 3.19\,\mathrm{kg/\,m^4}$$

$$R_{A2W} = \frac{\rho_0 c}{\pi a_w^2} = 1.30 \times 10^4\,\mathrm{N\,s/\,m^5} \qquad R_{A1W} = \frac{128\rho_0 c}{9\pi^3 a_w^2} - R_{A2W} = 5.71 \times 10^3\,\mathrm{N\,s/\,m^5}$$

$$C_{A1W} = \frac{5.94 a_w^3}{\rho_0 c^2} = 4.23 \times 10^{-8}\,\mathrm{m^5/\,N} \qquad k_w = \frac{3\pi a_w}{16 d_1} = 0.290$$

where the typical value $B = 0.65$ has been used for the mass loading factor in calculating M_{AB}. The equation for B is given by Eq. (7.4).

The constants k_p and k_w are mutual coupling coefficients that are defined in problems 11 and 12 in Chapter 3. The coupling coefficient from the woofer to the port is k_p. The coupling coefficient from the port to the woofer is k_w. Because the volume velocity emitted by the diaphragm exhibits a null at the Helmholtz frequency where the port volume velocity is a maximum, the mutual coupling effects play a minor role in the simulation.

The LTSpice netlist is given in Table 8.2. Fig. 8.14 shows the calculated SPL frequency responses of the system. The figure shows the total system output, the woofer diaphragm output, and the vent output. The SPL is displayed as the voltages at nodes 22 (system), 24 (diaphragm), and 26 (port). Fig. 8.15 shows the calculated input impedance. The input impedance is calculated in the graphics routine of LTSpice with the expression V(1)/I(Vd1). The null in the impedance plot is at the Helmholtz resonance frequency f_B. The two approximately equal impedance peaks are a characteristic of the B4 alignment.

Table 8.2: SPICE Netlist for the Vented-Box Simulation

VENTED-BOX SIMULATION	EXd 28 0 27 0 Laplace=1/s	Vd5 0 16 0 AC 0
VEg 1 0 0 AC 1	FSwUw 10 17 Vd2 31.4m	Vd4 16 15 0 AC 0
Re 2 1 7	Ra1w 17 18 5710	Vd6 19 20
HBLu 3 4 Vd2 12.7	Ra2w 18 20 13k	Vd3 0 12 0 AC 0
Vd1 4 0 0 AC 0	Ca1w 17 18 42.3n	FKpUw 15 13 Vd6 0.11
LMmd 5 6 42.2m	LMa1w 17 19 3.19	FKwUp 19 17 Vd4 0.29
Rms 6 7 3	LMab 11 10 2.44	HSPLp 25 0 Vd5 1
Cms 7 8 433μ	Vd7 20 0 0 AC 0	ESPLp 26 0 25 0 Laplace=9390*s
HBLi 5 0 Vd1 12.7	Cab 11 12 403n	HXp 29 0 Vd5 219.3
Vd2 9 0 0 AC 0	RAL 11 0 78.9k	EXp 30 0 29 0 Laplace=1/s
ESdPd 8 9 17 10 31.4m	LMap 13 11 42.9	HSPLd 23 0 Vd7 1
GZe 2 3 2 3 Laplace=1/(6.89m*s**0.7)	Ra1p 13 14 39.6k	ESPLd 24 0 23 0 Laplace=9390*s
HSPLs 21 0 Vd3 1	Ra2p 14 16 89.7k	.ac dec 150 10 10K
ESPLs 22 0 21 0 Laplace=9390*s	Ca1p 13 14 2.32n	.end
HXd 27 0 Vd2 1	LMa1p 13 15 8.39	

Curve **a** in Fig. 8.16 shows the diaphragm displacement in mm as a function of frequency. It is the voltage at node 28. Curve **b** shows the displacement of the air in the vent in mm as a function of frequency. It is the voltage at node 30. If the voice-coil voltage is considered to be an rms value, the displacements are also rms values which must be multiplied by $\sqrt{2}$ to obtain peak values.

The diaphragm displacement exhibits a null at the Helmholtz frequency. Below that frequency, the displacement increases to a value that is limited by the diaphragm compliance and not by the enclosure. This is the primary reason that drivers having a high-compliance suspension are not recommended for vented-box systems. In contrast, the low-frequency limit of the diaphragm displacement for a closed-box system is

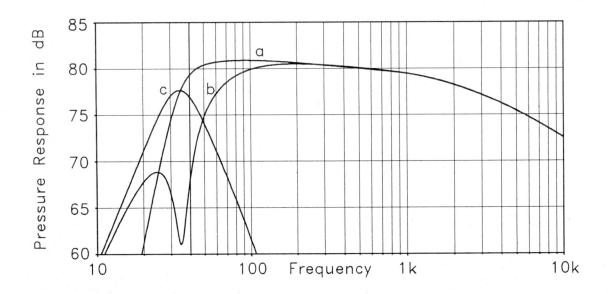

Figure 8.14: SPL responses versus frequency. a – Woofer and vent. b – Woofer. c – Vent.

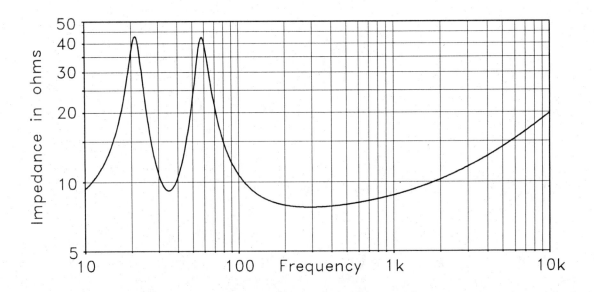

Figure 8.15: System impedance in ohms versus frequency.

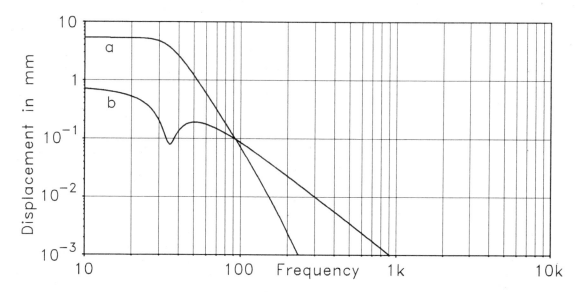

Figure 8.16: (a) Diaphragm displacement in mm versus frequency. (b) Port air displacement in mm versus frequency.

determined by the suspension compliance and the air in the box. In air suspension or acoustic suspension closed-box systems where the compliance ratio is typically in the range $3 \leq \alpha \leq 10$, the low-frequency limit is primarily determined by the air in the box.

Fig. 8.16 shows that the displacement of the air in the vent is greater than the diaphragm displacement for all frequencies below approximately 90 Hz. The vent air displacement can be decreased by increasing the area of the port. To minimize vent noises due to turbulent air flow, the port area should be as large as possible. However, increasing the port area also increases its length, thus making the unflanged end of the port closer to the back panel which can restrict the air flow. An elbow shaped port may be used to solve this problem.

8.14   Problems

1. A vented-box system has an internal acoustic volume V_{AB}. A port or vent tube installed in one wall of the enclosure has a cross-sectional area S_P and a length L_P. (a) Neglecting end corrections, solve for the mechanical mass of the air in the vent. Convert this into an acoustic mass. $[M_{MP} = \rho_0 S_P L_P,$ $M_{AP} = \rho_0 L_P / S_P]$ (b) Use the box analogous circuit to show that the Helmholtz resonance frequency of the acoustic mass of the air in the port and the acoustic compliance of the air in the box is given by

$$f_B = \frac{c}{2\pi} \sqrt{\frac{S_P}{L_P V_{AB}}}$$

Solve this equation for L_P as a function of f_B, S_P, and V_{AB}. (c) For a circular port, the flanged end correction is $L_f = 0.850a$, where a is the radius of the port. The unflanged end correction is $L_{uf} = 0.613a$. For a non-circular port, it is common to replace the port radius a by the radius of a circular port which has the same area. With the end corrections, show that the port length formula becomes

$$L_P = \left[\frac{c}{2\pi f_B} \right]^2 \frac{S_P}{V_{AB}} - 1.463 \sqrt{\frac{S_P}{\pi}}$$

2. If end corrections are neglected show that *(a)* both the mechanical mass and the acoustic mass of the air in a vent tube are doubled if the length is doubled, *(b)* the mechanical mass is doubled but the acoustic mass is halved if the area is doubled, and *(c)* two vent tubes of the same length are acoustically equivalent to one tube having an area equal to the sum of the two areas.

3. A driver with a rated diameter of 12 in is to be designed for a vented-box system having the specifications: $V_{AB} = 3\,\text{ft}^3$, $f_\ell = 30\,\text{Hz}$, and $R_E = 7\,\Omega$. If $M_{AC} = M_{AS}$ and $Q_{MS} = 3.0$, use the vented-box design procedures to solve for f_S, Q_{ES}, V_{AS}, η_0, and f_B for *(a)* a C4 alignment with $k = 0.7$ and $Q_L = 7$ [$f_S = 37.9\,\text{Hz}$, $Q_{ES} = 0.551$, $V_{AS} = 1.80\,\text{ft}^3$, $\eta_0 = 0.485\%$, $f_B = 32.9\,\text{Hz}$], *(b)* a B4 alignment with $Q_L = 7$ [$f_S = 30\,\text{Hz}$, $Q_{ES} = 0.468$, $V_{AS} = 3.18\,\text{ft}^3$, $\eta_0 = 0.500\%$, $f_B = 30\,\text{Hz}$], and *(c)* a QB3 alignment with $B = 3$ and $Q_L = 7$ [$f_S = 17.4\,\text{Hz}$, $Q_{ES} = 0.307$, $V_{AS} = 10.4\,\text{ft}^3$, $\eta_0 = 0.484\%$, $f_B = 24.5\,\text{Hz}$]

4. A vented box loudspeaker system is to be designed for an internal volume of $3\,\text{ft}^3$. The Helmholtz resonance frequency is to be 34 Hz. The system driver has a rated diameter of 12 in. The box material is to have a wall thickness of 3/4 in. The volume occupied by the driver inside the box can be estimated from the formula $V_{\text{driver}} = 6 \times 10^{-6} d^4\,\text{ft}^3$, where d is the rated diameter in inches. *(a)* For a port or vent tube with an internal diameter of 4 in and a wall thickness of 3/16 in, what is the required length of the port and what internal box volume does it occupy? Note that the port projects into the box a distance equal to its length minus the box wall thickness. [$L_P = 6\text{-}7/8\,\text{in}$, $V_P = 0.0531\,\text{ft}^3$] *(b)* To what volume must the box be constructed? [$3.18\,\text{ft}^3$] *(c)* The internal box dimensions are to have the ratios $0.6 \times 1.0 \times 1.6$. If the internal bracing can be neglected, what are the internal dimensions? [10-3/4 in, 1 ft 5-7/8 in, 2 ft 4-5/8 in] *(d)* The box is to be internally braced with bracing that has a cross section of 1.5 in by 1.5 in. The bracing is to be installed in each corner between the internal walls so that it forms a rectangular frame inside the box. If the internal ratios are to be the same as those given in part (c), use the methods of Example 4 to calculate the internal dimensions of the box. [11 in, 1 ft 6-3/8 in, 2 ft 5-3/8 in]

5. A vented-box loudspeaker system uses a driver with the small-signal parameters $f_S = 32\,\text{Hz}$, $Q_{TS} = 0.35$, and $V_{AS} = 3\,\text{ft}^3$. The internal volume of the enclosure is $1.7\,\text{ft}^3$ and the Helmholtz resonance frequency is 38 Hz. The box quality factor is estimated to be $Q_L = 7$. *(a)* What are the system parameters α and h? [1.77, 1.19] *(b)* What are the parameters a_1, a_2, a_3, and f_0 in the vented-box transfer function $G_V(s)$? Write out the transfer function with the numerical values for a_1, a_2, a_3, and f_0. [$a_1 = 3.25$, $a_2 = 3.92$, $a_3 = 2.78$, $f_0 = 34.9\,\text{Hz}$] *(c)* Calculate the magnitude and phase of $G_V(s)$ for $s = j2\pi f_0$. [0.505, 194°]

6. It is desired to realize a vented-box loudspeaker system having the transfer function of a 5*th* order Butterworth high-pass filter given by

$$T(p) = \frac{p^5}{(p+1)\left[p^2 + (2\cos 36°)p + 1\right]\left[p^2 + (2\cos 72°)p + 1\right]}$$

where $p = s/\omega_0$ is the normalized frequency and $\omega_0 = 2\pi f_0$ is the lower $-3\,\text{dB}$ cutoff frequency. *(a)* Factor out the first-order transfer function $T_1(p) = p/(p+1)$ and show that it can be realized by a passive high-pass RC filter preceding the power amplifier. *(b)* From the remaining fourth-order transfer function, determine the constants a_1, a_2, and a_3 for the vented-box transfer function. [$a_1 = a_3 = 2.236$, $a_2 = 3.0$] *(c)* If $Q_L = 7$, solve for the system parameters α, h, and Q_{TS}. [$\alpha = 0.701$, $h = 1$, $Q_{TS} = 0.478$] *(d)* Sketch the Bode magnitude plots for the system, the auxiliary filter, and the loudspeaker without the auxiliary filter. [Both the system and the filter are down by 3 dB at ω_0. Thus the relative response of the loudspeaker is 0 dB at ω_0. The loudspeaker alone exhibits a peak in its response just above ω_0.]

7. For the analogous circuit in Fig. 8.2, show that the transfer function for the volume velocity U_D is given by

$$U_D = \frac{B\ell e_g}{S_D R_E} \frac{\left[(s/\omega_B)^2 + (1/Q_L)(s/\omega_B) + 1\right]C_{AS}s}{(s/\omega_0)^4 + a_3(s/\omega_0)^3 + a_2(s/\omega_0)^2 + a_1(s/\omega_0) + 1}$$

where ω_B, Q_L, ω_0, and the a coefficients are defined in Section 8.3. Make the same approximations used in the derivation of Eq. 8.11.

8. Use the result in problem 7 to show that the transfer function for the diaphragm displacement x_D is given by

$$x_D = \frac{e_g}{B\ell\omega_S Q_{ES}} \frac{(s/\omega_B)^2 + (1/Q_L)(s/\omega_B) + 1}{(s/\omega_0)^4 + a_3(s/\omega_0)^3 + a_2(s/\omega_0)^2 + a_1(s/\omega_0) + 1}$$

9. It is desired to design a vented-box system having a QB3 alignment with $B = 4$. It can be assumed that $Q_L = 7$. *(a)* Use the procedure described in Section 8.7 to solve for a_1, a_2, and a_3. [5.26, 5.82, 3.41] *(b)* Use the procedure described in Section 8.5 to solve for Q_{TS}, α, h, and q. [0.245, 4.80, 1.59, 2.01]

10. It is desired to design a vented-box system having a C4 alignment with a dB ripple of 0.5 dB. It can be assumed that $Q_L = 7$. *(a)* Use the procedure described in Section 8.8 to solve for a_1, a_2, and a_3. [1.53, 2.79, 2.12] *(b)* Use the procedure described in Section 8.5 to solve for Q_{TS}, α, h, and q. [0.607, 0.267, 0.674, 0.582]

11. Set $|G_V(j2\pi f_\ell)|^2 = 1/2$ in Eq. (8.33) and solve for f_n/f_ℓ to verify Eq. (8.35).

12. For $\epsilon \to 0$ in the C4 alignment, show that $f_n \to f_\ell/\left(2^{3/4}\epsilon^{1/4}\right)$ in Eq. (8.35), $C_4(f_n/f) \to (f_\ell/f)^4/\epsilon$ in Eq. (8.34), $|G_V(j2\pi f)|^2 \to 1/\left[1 + (f_\ell/f)^8\right]$ in Eq. (8.33), and $f_0 \to f_\ell$ in Eq. (8.37). Show that the magnitude-squared function for the C4 alignment reduces to $|G_V(j2\pi f)|^2 = (f/f_0)^8/\left[1 + (f/f_0)^8\right]$, which is that for the B4 alignment given in Eq. (8.27).

Chapter 9

Acoustic Horns

In general, horn loaded systems exhibit a higher efficiency than direct radiator systems. This is because the horn acts as an acoustic transformer to provide a better impedance match between the loudspeaker diaphragm and the external air load. This chapter investigates some of the important aspects of horns and horn loaded systems.

9.1 The Webster Horn Equation

Fig. 9.1 shows the cross section of an acoustic horn of length L that is aligned with the z axis. Let the cross-sectional area be denoted by $S(z)$, where z is the distance into the horn. If the pressure p is assumed to be uniform across the cross section, it satisfies the Webster horn equation given by

$$\left\{\frac{d^2}{dz^2} + \frac{1}{4S(z)^2}\left[S'(z)^2 - 2S(z)S''(z)\right] - \frac{s^2}{c^2}\right\}\left[\sqrt{S(z)}p(z)\right] = 0 \tag{9.1}$$

where s is the complex frequency and c is the velocity of sound. The primes denote differentiation with respect to z, i.e. $S'(z) = dS(z)/dz$ and $S''(z) = d^2S(z)/dz^2$. The volume velocity $U(z)$ satisfies the Euler equation

$$\rho_0 s U(z) = -S(z)\frac{dp(z)}{dz} \tag{9.2}$$

where ρ_0 is the density of air.

9.2 Salmon's Family of Horns

Solutions to the Webster equation can be readily obtained if the following condition holds:

$$\frac{1}{4S(z)^2}\left[S'(z)^2 - 2S(z)S''(z)\right] = -m^2 \tag{9.3}$$

where m is a constant. Horns which satisfy this condition belong to Salmon's family. The Webster equation for this case reduces to

$$\left[\frac{d^2}{dz^2} - \left(m^2 + \frac{s^2}{c^2}\right)\right]\left[\sqrt{S(z)}p(z)\right] = 0 \tag{9.4}$$

Eq. (9.3) leads to solutions for $S(z)$ of the form

$$
\begin{aligned}
S(z) &= S_T\left[1 + \left(\frac{S_T'}{2S_T}\right)z\right]^2 && \text{for } m = 0 \\
&= S_T\left[\cosh mz + M\sinh mz\right]^2 && \text{for } m > 0
\end{aligned}
\tag{9.5}
$$

157

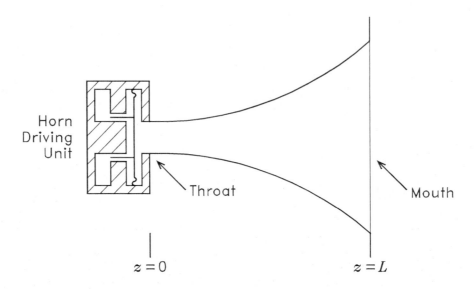

Figure 9.1: Cross section of a horn loudspeaker.

where $S_T = S(0)$ is the area at the throat and M is a constant.

The values of m and M define the type of horn in Salmon's family. These are defined in Table 9.1. For the exponential horn, the area equation simplifies to

$$S(z) = S_T \exp(2mz) \tag{9.6}$$

Fig. 9.2 shows the upper half of example longitudinal cross sections of the four horns as a function of z. The distance above the z axis represents the radius of the cross section. The throat and the mouth areas are the same for each horn.

Table 9.1: Categories of Horns

Conical	Catenoidal		Exponential		Hyperbolic	
$m = 0$	$m > 0$	$M = 0$	$m > 0$	$M = 1$	$m > 0$	$0 < M < 1$

For any of the horns in Salmon's family, the solutions for $p(z)$ and $U(z)$ are given by

$$p(z) = \left[\frac{S_T}{S(z)}\right]^{1/2} \left(p_a e^{-\gamma z} + p_b e^{\gamma z}\right) \tag{9.7}$$

$$U(z) = \left[\frac{S_T}{S(z)}\right]^{1/2} \left[Y_a(z) p_a e^{-\gamma(s)z} - Y_b(z) p_b e^{\gamma(s)z}\right] \tag{9.8}$$

where p_a and p_b are constants, $\gamma(s)$ is the propagation constant, and $Y_a(z)$ and $Y_b(z)$ are acoustic admittances. The latter three are given by

$$\gamma(s) = \sqrt{m^2 + (s/c)^2} \qquad Y_a(z) = \frac{S(z)}{\rho_0 s}\left[\gamma + \frac{S'(z)}{2S(z)}\right] \qquad Y_b(z) = \frac{S(z)}{\rho_0 s}\left[\gamma - \frac{S'(z)}{2S(z)}\right] \tag{9.9}$$

Note that the two admittances are functions of the distance z into the horn.

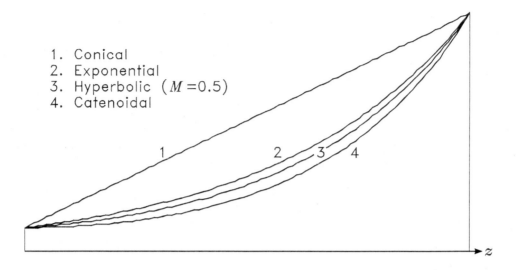

1. Conical
2. Exponential
3. Hyperbolic $(M = 0.5)$
4. Catenoidal

Figure 9.2: Upper cross sections of example horns.

For $s = j\omega$, the propagation constant can be written

$$
\begin{aligned}
\gamma(j\omega) &= \sqrt{m^2 - (\omega/c)^2} && \text{for } \frac{\omega}{c} < m \\
&= j\sqrt{(\omega/c)^2 - m^2} && \text{for } \frac{\omega}{c} > m
\end{aligned}
\tag{9.10}
$$

For $\omega/c < m$, γ is real and the term $\exp(-\gamma z)$ represents an attenuation. The horn is said to be cut off and acoustic power does not propagate. For $\omega/c > m$, γ is imaginary and the term $\exp(-\gamma z)$ represents a phase delay. In this case, acoustic power propagates in the horn. The cutoff frequency ω_c is defined as the frequency for which $\gamma = 0$. It is given by

$$
\omega_c = mc \,\mathrm{rad/\,s}
\tag{9.11}
$$

This is usually expressed in hertz as $f_c = \omega_c/2\pi = mc/2\pi$.

For $\omega > \omega_c$, the solutions for $p(z)$ and $U(z)$ each represent traveling waves, one propagating from the source in the $+z$ direction and a reflected wave propagating toward the source in the $-z$ direction. The reflected wave is generated when the forward wave is incident on the discontinuity at the mouth of the horn. At $z = 0$, the amplitude of the forward pressure wave is p_a and the amplitude of reflected wave is p_b. If $L = \infty$, there is no reflected wave and $p_b = 0$. In this case, the acoustic admittance seen looking into the throat is $Y_a(0)$ which is given by

$$
Y_a(0) = \frac{S_T}{j\omega\rho_0}\left[j\sqrt{(\omega/c)^2 - m^2} + \frac{S_T'}{2S_T}\right] = \frac{S_T}{\rho_0 c}\sqrt{1 - (\omega_c/\omega)^2} + \frac{S_T'}{j\omega 2\rho_0}
\tag{9.12}
$$

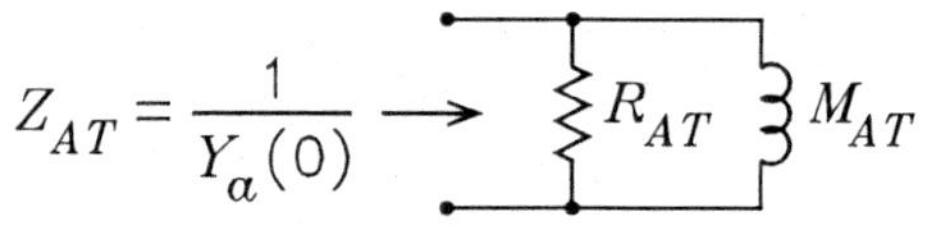

$$
Z_{AT} = \frac{1}{Y_a(0)} \longrightarrow \quad \lessgtr R_{AT} \quad \rbrace M_{AT}
$$

Figure 9.3: Analogous circuit for the throat impedance for the infinite length horn.

The analogous circuit for Z_{AT} is a parallel acoustic resistor and acoustic mass. The circuit is shown in Fig. 9.3. The element values are given by

$$R_{AT} = \frac{\rho_0 c}{S_T \sqrt{1 - (\omega_c/\omega)^2}} \qquad M_{AT} = \frac{2\rho_0}{S_T'} \tag{9.13}$$

For the case $m > 0$, it can be shown that $S_T' = 2mMS_T$. In this case the expression for M_{AT} reduces to

$$M_{AT} = \frac{\rho_0}{mMS_T} = \frac{\rho_0 c}{\omega_c MS_T} \tag{9.14}$$

For the catenoidal horn, $M = 0$ and $M_{AT} = \infty$. For the exponential horn, $M = 1$ and M_{AT} is fixed by the cutoff frequency and the throat area. For the hyperbolic horn, $0 < M < 1$ and M_{AT} can be adjusted to any positive value by the choice of M. When this is done to cancel an acoustic compliance in the analogous circuit for the horn driving unit, it is called reactance annulling. An example of this is presented in the following in the design of low-frequency horn systems.

9.3   Finite Length Horn

Depending on the baffle in which it is mounted, the radiation from the mouth of a horn can be modeled as the radiation from a flat piston either in an infinite baffle or in a long tube. The size of the mouth must be chosen so that the air load impedance seen by the piston is resistive over the frequency range of interest. We have seen in Sections 3.7 and 3.8 that a flat circular piston in an infinite baffle or in the end of a tube sees an air load impedance that is approximately resistive if $ka > 1$, where a is the piston radius and $k = 2\pi f/c$ is the wavenumber. Thus we have the condition $2\pi fa/c > 1$ or, equivalently, $a > c/2\pi f$. Let S_M be the area of the mouth. It follows that a general condition on S_M can be written

$$S_M = \pi a^2 > \pi \left(\frac{c}{2\pi f}\right)^2 = \frac{1}{\pi}\left(\frac{c}{2f}\right)^2 \tag{9.15}$$

Although not strictly correct, this equation is often applied to horns with a square or rectangular cross section.

The above condition on S_M should hold at the lowest frequency in the range of interest. A good rule of thumb to follow in horn design is to design for an effective mouth area that satisfies the equality in this equation at the horn cutoff frequency f_c and cross the horn over so that it is operated at frequencies $2f_c$ and above.

Example 1 *A circular exponential horn is to be designed for a lower crossover frequency of* 600 Hz. *The cutoff frequency is to be* 1/2 *this value, or* 300 Hz. *If the throat diameter is* 1 in, *specify the flare constant* m, *the mouth area* S_M, *and the length* L. *Assume that the equality in Eq. (9.15) is to hold at the cutoff frequency.*

Solution. From Eq. (9.11), the flare constant is $m = 2\pi 300/345 = 5.464$. The mouth area is $S_M = (1/\pi)(345/2 \times 300)^2 = 0.1052\,\text{m}^2 = 163.1\,\text{in}^2$. For a circular mouth, this corresponds to the mouth diameter $d_M = 0.3661\,\text{m} = 14.41\,\text{in}$. For the exponential horn, $S_M = S_T e^{2mL}$. This can be solved for L to obtain $L = (1/2m)\ln(S_M/S_T) = 0.4883\,\text{m} = 1.602\,\text{ft}$.

9.4   A Horn Analogous Circuit

Let the values of p, U, S, Y_a, and Y_b at $z = 0$ be denoted by p_1, U_1, S_1, Y_{a1}, and Y_{b1}. Let the values at $z = L$ be denoted by p_2, U_2, S_2, Y_{a2}, and Y_{b2}. (S_1 is the same as S_T and S_2 is the same as S_M.) It follows from Eqs. (9.7) and (9.8) that

$$p_1 = p_a + p_b \qquad U_1 = Y_{a1}p_a - Y_{b1}p_b \tag{9.16}$$

$$p_2 = \left(\frac{S_1}{S_2}\right)^{1/2} \left(p_a e^{-\gamma L} + p_b e^{+\gamma L}\right) \qquad U_2 = \left(\frac{S_1}{S_2}\right)^{1/2} \left(Y_{a2} p_a e^{-\gamma L} - Y_{b2} p_b e^{+\gamma L}\right) \tag{9.17}$$

It is straightforward to use the above equations to write p_1 and p_2 as follows:

$$p_1 = U_1 Z_{11} + T_1 [p_2 - U_2 Z_{12}] \qquad p_2 = T_2 [p_1 + U_1 Z_{21}] - U_2 Z_{22} \tag{9.18}$$

where T_i is a transfer function and Z_{ij} is an acoustic impedance. These are given by

$$T_1 = \left(\frac{S_2}{S_1}\right)^{1/2} \frac{\gamma + S_2'/2S_2}{\gamma + S_1'/2S_1} e^{-\gamma L} \qquad T_2 = \left(\frac{S_1}{S_2}\right)^{1/2} \frac{\gamma - S_1'/2S_1}{\gamma - S_2'/2S_2} e^{-\gamma L} \tag{9.19}$$

$$Z_{11} = \frac{\rho_0 s}{S_1 (\gamma + S_1'/2S_1)} \qquad Z_{12} = \frac{\rho_0 s}{S_2 (\gamma + S_2'/2S_2)} \tag{9.20}$$

$$Z_{21} = \frac{\rho_0 s}{S_1 (\gamma - S_1'/2S_1)} \qquad Z_{22} = \frac{\rho_0 s}{S_2 (\gamma - S_2'/2S_2)} \tag{9.21}$$

A circuit which models the equations is given in Fig. 9.4.

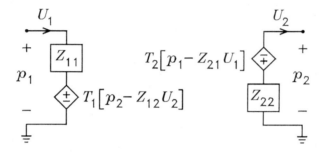

Figure 9.4: Analogous circuit for the horn.

The horn circuit can be implemented in LTSpice as shown in Fig. 9.5. The LTSpice netlist for the circuit is given in Table 9.2. Continuation lines are preceded by a + sign followed by a space. There are several constants in the netlist which must be assigned numerical values. These are denoted in the table by kj, where j is an integer. The constants are defined as follows:

$$k_1 = \sqrt{\frac{S_2}{S_1}} \qquad k_2 = \frac{1}{k_1} \qquad k_3 = \frac{S_1'}{2S_1} \qquad k_4 = \frac{S_2'}{2S_2} \qquad k_5 = k_4 - k_3 \qquad k_6 = \frac{\rho_0}{S_1} \tag{9.22}$$

$$k_7 = \frac{\rho_0}{S_2} \qquad k_8 = c \qquad k_9 = c^2 \qquad k_{10} = m^2 \qquad k_{11} = L \qquad k_{12} = \frac{L}{c} \tag{9.23}$$

9.5 SPICE Examples

The SPICE horn model can be used to calculate the acoustic impedance seen looking into the throat and the transfer function from throat pressure to on-axis far-field pressure. Fig. 9.6 shows a circuit for doing this that incorporates the horn circuit in Fig. 9.5. The throat is driven by a volume velocity (current) source labeled I1 which is assigned a value of unity. The throat impedance is equal to the pressure (voltage) at node 1. The far-field pressure divided by the pressure at node 1 is the transfer function. We assume that the horn has a circular cross section and that its mouth is terminated in an infinite baffle. The acoustic load impedance on the mouth of the horn is the impedance seen by one side of a flat circular piston in an infinite baffle that is covered in Section 3.7 [Eqs. (3.42) and (3.43)]. The resistor RMA1 is not part of the piston

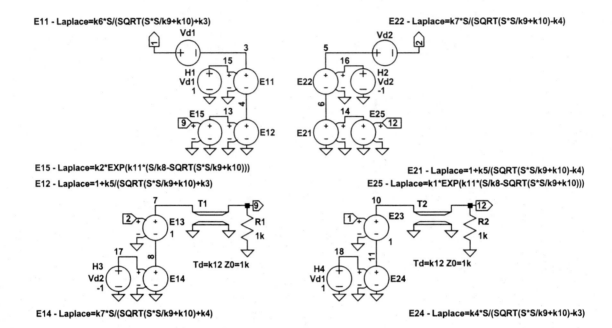

Figure 9.5: LTSpice implementation of the horn.

Table 9.2: SPICE Netlist for the Horn Implementation

Vd1 1 3 0 AC 0	R2 12 0 1k
E11 3 4 15 0 Laplace	T2 10 0 12 0 Td=k12 Z0=1k
+ =k6*S/(SQRT(S*S/k9+k10)+k3)	E13 7 8 2 0 1
H1 15 0 Vd1 1	E14 8 0 17 0 Laplace
H2 16 0 Vd2 -1	+ =k7*S/(SQRT(S*S/k9+k10)+k4)
E12 4 0 13 0 Laplace	E23 10 11 1 0 1
+ =1+k5/(SQRT(S*S/k9+k12)+k3)	E24 11 0 18 0 Laplace
E22 5 6 16 0 Laplace	+ =k4*S/(SQRT(S*S/k9+k10)-k3)
+ =k7*S/(SQRT(S*S/k9+k10)-k4)	E15 13 0 9 0 Laplace
E21 6 0 14 0 Laplace	+ =k2*EXP(k11*(S/k8-SQRT(S*S/k9+k10)))
+ =1+k5/(SQRT(S*S/k9+k10)-k4)	E25 14 0 12 0 Laplace
Vd2 5 2 0 AC 0	+ =k1*EXP(k11*(S/k8-SQRT(S*S/k9+k10)))
T1 7 0 9 0 Td=k12 Z0=1k	H3 17 0 Vd2 -1
R1 9 0 1k	H4 18 0 Vd1 1

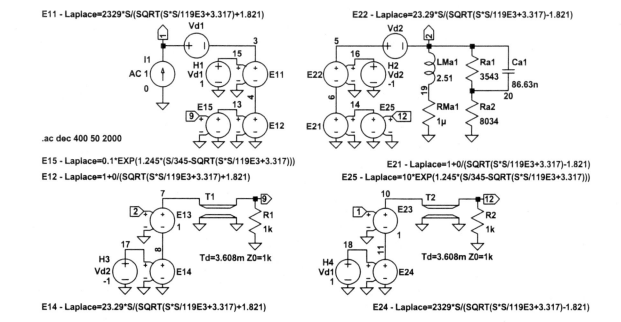

Figure 9.6: LTSpice circuit for example horn A.

impedance circuit. It must be included in the SPICE circuit to prevent a loop with zero resistance. This resistor can be assigned a very small value, e.g. 1 $\mu\Omega$, so that it looks like a short circuit for all practical purposes.

Let us consider two exponential circular horns, each having the cutoff frequency $f_c = 100\,\text{Hz}$ and a throat diameter of 1 in but different mouth diameters. The latter means that the horns will not have the same length. For both horns, we have $M = 1$, $m = 2\pi f_c/c = 1.821\,\text{m}^{-1}$, $S_1 = \pi(0.5 \times 0.0254)^2 = 5.067 \times 10^{-4}\,\text{m}^2$, and $S_1' = dS_1'/dz = 2mM_1 = 1.846 \times 10^{-3}\,\text{m}$. Let the mouth diameter of horn A be 10 in and that of horn B be 40 in. For the exponential horn, the mouth diameter d_2 is related to the throat diameter d_1 by $d_2 = d_1 \exp(mL)$. It follows from this relation that the lengths of the two horns are 49.78 in and 79.74 in, respectively. Horn A has the netlist constants:

$$k_1 = 10 \qquad k_2 = 0.1 \qquad k_3 = k_4 = 1.821 \qquad k_5 = 0 \tag{9.24}$$

$$k_6 = 2329 \qquad k_7 = 23.29 \qquad k_8 = 345 \qquad k_9 = 119 \times 10^3 \tag{9.25}$$

$$k_{10} = 3.317 \qquad k_{11} = 1.245 \qquad k_{12} = 3.608 \times 10^{-3} \tag{9.26}$$

$$M_{A1} = 2.510 \qquad R_{A1} = 3543 \qquad R_{A2} = 8034 \qquad C_{A1} = 86.63 \times 10^{-9} \tag{9.27}$$

Horn B has the same values with the following exceptions:

$$k_1 = 40 \qquad k_2 = 0.025 \qquad k_7 = 1.455 \qquad k_{11} = 2.007 \qquad k_{12} = 5.816 \times 10^{-3} \tag{9.28}$$

$$M_{A1} = 0.6276 \qquad R_{A1} = 221.5 \qquad R_{A2} = 502.1 \qquad C_{A1} = 5.545 \times 10^{-6} \tag{9.29}$$

The SPICE netlist for an ac analysis of horn A is given in Table 9.3. Continuation lines are preceded by a + sign followed by a space.

Fig. 9.7 shows the real and imaginary parts of the normalized throat impedance of horn A as a function of frequency, where the normalization factor is the high frequency limit of the impedance given by $\rho_0 c/S_1 = 803.4 \times 10^3$. The impedances are calculated in the graphics routine of LTSpice with the lines

Table 9.3: SPICE Netlist for the Horn Simulation

EXAMPLE HORN A	T1 7 0 9 0 Td=3.608m Z0=1k
Vd1 1 3 0 AC 0	R1 9 0 1k
I1 0 1 0 AC 1	R2 12 0 1k
LMa1 2 19 2.51	T2 10 0 12 0 Td=3.608m Z0=1k
RMa1 19 0 1μ	E13 7 8 2 0 1
Ra1 2 20 3543	E14 8 0 17 0 Laplace
Ra2 20 0 8034	+ =23.29*S/(SQRT(S*S/119E3+3.317)+1.821)
Ca1 2 20 86.63n	E23 10 11 1 0 1
E11 3 4 15 0 Laplace	E24 11 0 18 0 Laplace
+ =2329*S/(SQRT(S*S/119E3+3.317)+1.821)	+ =2329*S/(SQRT(S*S/119E3+3.317)-1.821)
H1 15 0 Vd1 1	E15 13 0 9 0 Laplace
H2 16 0 Vd2 -1	+ =0.1*EXP(1.245*(S/345-SQRT(S*S/119E3+3.317)))
E12 4 0 13 0 Laplace	E25 14 0 12 0 Laplace
+ =1+0/(SQRT(S*S/119E3+3.317)+1.821)	+ =10*EXP(1.245*(S/345-SQRT(S*S/119E3+3.317)))
E22 5 6 16 0 Laplace	H3 17 0 Vd2 -1
+ =23.29*S/(SQRT(S*S/119E3+3.317)-1.821)	H4 18 0 Vd1 1
E21 6 0 14 0 Laplace	.ac dec 400 50 2000
+ =1+0/(SQRT(S*S/119E3+3.317)-1.821)	.end
Vd2 5 2 0 AC 0	

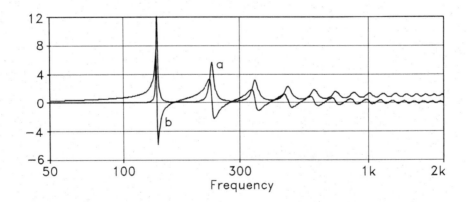

Figure 9.7: Throat impedance versus frequency for horn A. a – real part. b – imaginary part.

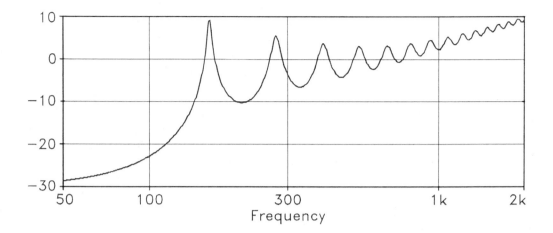

Figure 9.8: Magnitude in dB of the pressure transfer function for horn A versus frequency.

Real Part   Re(V(1))/803.4k
Imaginary Part   Im(V(1))/803.4k

where V(1) is the voltage at node 1.

Let p_3 be the far-field on-axis pressure radiated by the horn. It is given by

$$p_3 = \frac{j\rho_0 f U_2}{r} e^{-j\omega r/c} \tag{9.30}$$

where f is the frequency and r is the distance from the mouth to the far-field point. Fig. 9.8 shows the magnitude of the pressure transfer function $|p_3/p_1|$ in dB for horn A for $r = 1$ m. It is displayed in LTSpice by displaying

20*log10(1.18*frequency*I(Vd2)/V(1))

where I(Vd2) is the magnitude of the current through voltage source Vd2. The plots for horn B are shown in Figs. 9.9 and 9.10.

Comparison of the figures for the two horns shows that both the impedance and the pressure transfer function for horn A vary much more with frequency than for horn B. This is because the reflected wave that travels in the $-z$ direction is much stronger in the shorter horn A than it is in the longer horn B. The pressure transfer function for horn B has a magnitude that is approximately 35 dB greater than that for horn A. The pressure transfer functions exhibit an asymptotic slope of $+20$ dB/dec. To obtain flat pressure response, the horn driving unit must produce a throat pressure that has a slope of -20 dB/dec.

9.6 Horn Driving Units

The horn driving unit is a small loudspeaker that radiates into the throat of the horn. This is illustrated in Fig. 9.1. The cross section of a typical driving unit that might be used with midrange and tweeter horns is shown in Fig. 9.11. The diaphragm is in the shape of a sector of a sphere which radiates into the throat through a phase correction plug. The plug is designed to make the phase of the acoustic pressure wave constant across the cross section of the throat. It does this by equalizing the path distances from points on the diaphragm to the throat cross section.

Fig. 9.12 shows the analogous circuits for the driving unit. Figs. 9.12(a) and 9.12(b), respectively, show the electrical and mechanical circuits. These are the same as those given in Section 6.2 for the moving coil

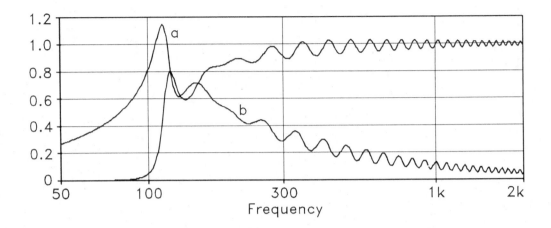

Figure 9.9: Throat impedance versus frequency for horn B. a – real part. b - imaginery part.

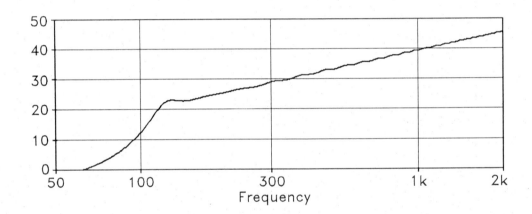

Figure 9.10: Magnitude in dB of the pressure transfer function for horn B versus frequency.

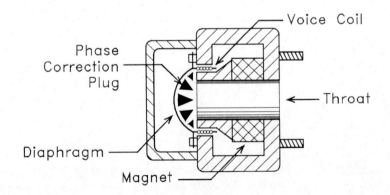

Figure 9.11: Cross section of horn driving unit.

driver. In the acoustical circuit of Fig. 9.12(c), the volume velocity emitted by the diaphragm is $U_D = S_D u_D$ where S_D is its piston area and u_D is its mechanical velocity. The acoustic impedance of the air in the cavity behind the diaphragm is modeled by M_{AB}, R_{AB}, and C_{AB}. The compliance C_{AF} models the compliance of the air space between the front of the diaphragm and the throat. The impedance Z_{AT} is the acoustic impedance seen looking into the throat of a horn connected to the unit. In the following, we assume that the source has negligible output resistance, i.e. that $R_g = 0$ in the electrical circuit.

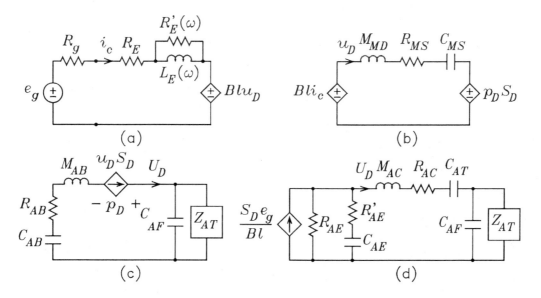

Figure 9.12: Analogous circuits for the horn driving unit. (a) Electrical. (b) Mechanical. (c) Acoustical. (d) Combination acoustical analogous circuit.

The three circuits in Fig. 9.12(a) through (c) can be combined to form the single circuit shown in Fig. 9.12(d) which we call the combination acoustical analogous circuit. The elements are given by

$$R_{AE} = \frac{(B\ell)^2}{S_D^2 R_E} \qquad R'_{AE} = \frac{(B\ell)^2}{S_D^2 R'_E} \qquad R_{AC} = \frac{R_{MS}}{S_D^2} + R_{AB} \tag{9.31}$$

$$M_{AC} = \frac{M_{MS}}{S_D^2} + M_{AB} \qquad C_{AT} = \frac{C_{AS}}{1 + \alpha} \tag{9.32}$$

where C_{AS} and α are given by

$$C_{AS} = S_D^2 C_{MS} \qquad \alpha = \frac{C_{AS}}{C_{AB}} \tag{9.33}$$

9.7 Mid-Frequency Range

If the horn is long enough so that the backward traveling wave in it is negligible, the throat impedance Z_{AT} is the impedance given in Fig. 9.3. The mid-frequency range is the range for which C_{AE}, C_{AF}, and M_{AT} can be approximated with open circuits and Z_{AT} can be approximated by its high-frequency limit

$$R_{AT} = \frac{\rho_0 c}{S_T} \tag{9.34}$$

The combination analogous circuit for the mid-frequency range is shown in Fig. 9.13(a).

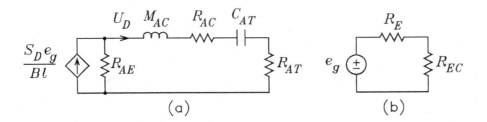

Figure 9.13: (a) Mid-frequency acoustical analogous circuit. (b) Equivalent electrical input circuit at $\omega = \omega_0$.

The power radiated by the horn is the power dissipated in the resistor R_{AT}. It is straightforward to show that this is given by

$$P_{AR} = \frac{1}{2} \frac{|e_g|^2}{R_E} \frac{R_{AE} R_{AT}}{(R_{AE} + R_{AC} + R_{AT})^2} |F_M(j\omega)|^2 \tag{9.35}$$

where $F_M(s)$ is the transfer function

$$F_M(s) = \frac{(1/Q_T)(s/\omega_0)}{(s/\omega_0)^2 + (1/Q_T)(s/\omega_0) + 1} = \frac{(1/Q_T)(s/\omega_0)}{(1 + s/\omega_\ell)(1 + s/\omega_u)} \tag{9.36}$$

The resonance frequency ω_0 and quality factor Q_T are given by

$$\omega_0 = \frac{1}{\sqrt{M_{AC} C_{AT}}} \qquad Q_T = \frac{1}{R_{AE} + R_{AC} + R_{AT}} \sqrt{\frac{M_{AC}}{C_{AT}}} \tag{9.37}$$

The transfer function $F_M(s)$ is a second-order band-pass function for which $|F_M(j\omega_0)| = 1$. We assume that $Q_T \leq 0.5$ so that the poles ω_ℓ and ω_u are real. These are related to ω_0 and Q_T by

$$\omega_0 = \sqrt{\omega_\ell \omega_u} \qquad Q_T = \frac{\omega_0}{\omega_\ell + \omega_u} \tag{9.38}$$

The quality factor Q_T is a function of three acoustical resistances. We can define three additional quality factors which are a function of only one resistor each. These are the electrical quality factor Q_E, the mechanical quality factor Q_M, and the acoustical quality factor Q_A given by

$$Q_E = \frac{1}{R_{AE}} \sqrt{\frac{M_{AC}}{C_{AT}}} \qquad Q_M = \frac{1}{R_{AC}} \sqrt{\frac{M_{AC}}{C_{AT}}} \qquad Q_A = \frac{1}{R_{AT}} \sqrt{\frac{M_{AC}}{C_{AT}}} \tag{9.39}$$

With these definitions, it follows that

$$Q_T = \left(\frac{1}{Q_E} + \frac{1}{Q_M} + \frac{1}{Q_A} \right)^{-1} \tag{9.40}$$

9.8   Condition for Maximum P_{AR}

It can be seen from Eq. (9.35) that $P_{AR} = 0$ for either $R_{AT} = 0$ or $R_{AT} = \infty$. Thus there is a value of R_{AT} that maximizes P_{AR}. Let $\omega = \omega_0$ so that $|F(j\omega_0)|^2 = 1$. The value of R_{AT} which maximizes P_{AR} at ω_0 can be obtained by setting $dP_{AR}/dR_{AT} = 0$ and solving for R_{AT}. It is straightforward to show that this is given by

$$R_{AT} = R_{AE} + R_{AC} = \frac{1}{2\omega_c Q_T C_{AT}} \tag{9.41}$$

This condition can be achieved in the design of a system by varying the area of the horn throat, i.e. by varying S_T in Eq. (9.13).

9.9 The Horn Efficiency

The efficiency of the horn system is defined as the ratio of the acoustic output power P_{AR} to the electrical input power P_E at the frequency $\omega = \omega_0$. The input power can be calculated from the electrical circuit obtained by reflecting all mechanical and acoustical elements in Fig. 9.12 back into the electrical circuit. For $\omega = \omega_0$, this circuit is given in Fig. 9.13(b), where R_{EC} is given by

$$R_{EC} = \frac{(B\ell)^2}{S_D^2 (R_{AC} + R_{AT})} = \frac{(B\ell)^2}{R_{MS} + S_D^2 (R_{AB} + R_{AT})} \tag{9.42}$$

It follows from the circuit that the electrical input power at $\omega = \omega_0$ is given by

$$P_E = \frac{1}{2} \frac{|e_g|^2}{R_E + R_{EC}} = \frac{1}{2} \frac{|e_g|^2}{R_E} \frac{R_{AC} + R_{AT}}{R_{AE} + R_{AC} + R_{AT}} \tag{9.43}$$

The system efficiency is given by

$$\eta = \frac{P_{AR}}{P_E} = \frac{R_{AE} R_{AT}}{(R_{AE} + R_{AC} + R_{AT}) (R_{AC} + R_{AT})} = \frac{Q_T^2}{Q_A (Q_E - Q_T)} \tag{9.44}$$

For $R_{AT} = R_{AE} + R_{AC}$, i.e. the condition that maximizes P_{AR}, this expression reduces to

$$\eta = \frac{R_{AE}}{2 (R_{AC} + R_{AT})} = \frac{Q_T}{2 (Q_E - Q_T)} \tag{9.45}$$

9.10 The Low-Frequency Range

The low-frequency approximation to the combination acoustical analogous circuit is shown in Fig. 9.14(a). This circuit is valid only for frequencies above the horn cutoff frequency, i.e. for $\omega > \omega_c$. A method for increasing the acoustic output power for frequencies just above the horn cutoff frequency is to choose the acoustic mass M_{AT} so that its reactance is the negative of the reactance of C_{AT} at the cutoff frequency, i.e. choose M_{AT} such that $\omega_c M_{AT} = 1/\omega_c C_{AT}$. This is called reactance annulling. When Eq. (9.14) is used for M_{AT}, the reactance annulling condition yields

$$\omega_c M_{AT} = \frac{\rho_0 c}{M S_T} = \frac{1}{\omega_c C_{AT}} \tag{9.46}$$

In horn system design, this condition can be imposed by the choice of the parameter M in the hyperbolic family of horns. The required value of M is

$$M = \omega_c \frac{\rho_0 c}{S_T} C_{AT} = \frac{\omega_c V_{AS}}{c S_T (1 + \alpha)} \tag{9.47}$$

9.11 The High-Frequency Range

The high-frequency approximation to the combination acoustical analogous circuit is shown in Fig. 9.14(b). It is straightforward to show that the acoustic power delivered to R_{AT} is given by

$$P_{AR} = \frac{1}{2} \frac{(B\ell)^2 |e_g|^2}{S_D^2 R_E^2} \frac{R_{AT}}{(R_{AE} + R_{AC} + R_{AT})^2} |F_H (j\omega)|^2 \tag{9.48}$$

where $F_H (s)$ is the second-order low-pass transfer function

$$F_H (s) = \frac{1}{(s/\omega_a)^2 + (1/Q_a) (s/\omega_a) + 1} \tag{9.49}$$

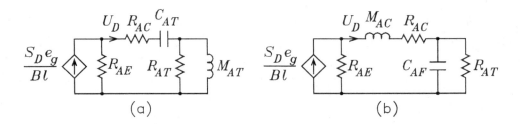

Figure 9.14: Low-frequency analogous circuit. (b) High-frequency analogous circuit.

The resonance frequency ω_a and quality factor Q_a are given by

$$\omega_a = \frac{1}{\sqrt{M_{AC}C_{AF}}}\sqrt{1 + \frac{R_{AE} + R_{AC}}{R_{AT}}} \tag{9.50}$$

$$Q_a = \sqrt{1 + \frac{R_{AE} + R_{AC}}{R_{AT}}}\left[(R_{AE} + R_{AC})\sqrt{\frac{C_{AF}}{M_{AC}}} + \frac{1}{R_{AT}}\sqrt{\frac{M_{AC}}{C_{AF}}}\right]^{-1} \tag{9.51}$$

The upper -3 dB frequency for $F_H(s)$ would correspond to that for $F_M(s)$ if $C_{AF} = 0$. (This assumes that the impedance of C_{AT} in Fig. 9.14(a) can be neglected at this frequency.)

Proper choice of C_{AF} can extend the high-frequency response of a horn system. The upper -3 dB cutoff frequency of $F_H(s)$ is given by

$$\omega_3^2 = \frac{1}{8}\left(\frac{R_{AE} + R_{AC} + R_{AT}}{M_{AC}}\right)^2\left[\left(2 - \frac{1}{Q_a^2}\right) + \sqrt{\left(2 - \frac{1}{Q_a^2}\right)^2 + 4}\right]$$

$$\times \left[\frac{1}{Q_a} + \sqrt{\frac{1}{Q_a^2} - \frac{4}{1 + R_{AT}/(R_{AE} + R_{AC})}}\right]^2 \tag{9.52}$$

If C_{AF} is varied, the only variable in this expression is Q_a. To determine the optimum value of C_{AF}, the value of Q_a that maximizes ω_3 must be solved for. Once this is done, the required value of C_{AF} can be calculated from

$$C_{AF} = 4Q_A Q_T C_{AT}\left[\frac{1}{Q_a} + \sqrt{\frac{1}{Q_a^2} - \frac{4}{1 + R_{AT}/(R_{AE} + R_{AC})}}\right]^{-2} \tag{9.53}$$

If the system is designed for maximum P_{AR}, i.e. $R_{AT} = R_{AE} + R_{AC}$, it can be shown that ω_3 is maximized when $Q_a = 0.5$. In this case, the required value for C_{AF} and the resulting upper -3 dB cutoff frequency are given by

$$C_{AF} = 0.6863Q_T^2 C_{AT} \qquad \omega_3 = \frac{1.099\omega_0}{Q_T} \tag{9.54}$$

These expressions assume that the reactance of the voice-coil inductance is negligible at ω_3.

9.12   Low-Frequency System Design

The design procedures described here can be used to design horn-loaded systems for low frequency applications. At higher frequencies, the design becomes more complicated when phase correction plugs must be designed to be used between the horn driver and the throat of the horn.

Design with a Given Driver

Specifications of the system pole frequencies ω_ℓ and ω_u and the small-signal parameters of the driver are sufficient to determine all system parameters. Let the driver have the parameters ω_S, V_{AS}, Q_{ES}, Q_{MS}, and Q_{TS}. For the procedure, we will assume that $M_{AC} = M_{AS}$, i.e. the acoustic mass of the driver diaphragm plus air load is the same in the horn system as it is on an infinite baffle. The design procedure is as follows:

1. *Calculate the system resonance frequency ω_0 and total quality factor Q_T. These are given in Eq. (9.38).*

2. *Calculate the compliance ratio α. If the change in mass loading on the driver diaphragm can be neglected when it is mounted into the horn system, α is given by $\alpha = (\omega_0/\omega_S)^2 - 1$.*

3. *Calculate the acoustic volume of air behind the diaphragm $V_{AB} = V_{AS}/\alpha$.*

4. *Calculate the electrical quality factor Q_E. Under the assumption stated in step 2, this is given by $Q_E = \sqrt{1+\alpha}\,Q_{ES}$.*

5. *Calculate the acoustical quality factor $Q_A = (1/Q_T - 1/Q_E - 1/Q_M)^{-1}$.*

6. *To evaluate this, a value for Q_M must be assumed. For zero losses in the box, i.e. $R_{AB} = 0$, Q_M is given by $Q_M = (1+\alpha)^{1/2}Q_{MS}$. The box will limit Q_M to a lower value because of the losses in R_{AB}. A rule of thumb for estimating Q_M is described in Section 7.3 where the parameter has the symbol Q_{MC}.*

7. *Calculate the throat area $S_T = \omega_0 V_{AS} Q_A/(1+\alpha)\,c$.*

8. *Calculate the electrical input resistance at ω_0 given by $R_E + R_{EC} = R_E \left[1 + Q_E^{-1}/\left(Q_M^{-1} + Q_A^{-1}\right)\right]$.*

9. *Calculate the system efficiency η. This is given by Eq. (9.44).*

10. *Calculate the front cavity volume V_{AF}. This is done by determining the value of Q_a that maximizes ω_3 in Eq. (9.52). C_{AF} is then calculated from Eq. (9.53) and V_{AF} is given by $V_{AF} = \rho_0 c^2 C_{AF}$. The optimum value of Q_a is a function of*

$$\frac{R_{AT}}{R_{AE} + R_{AC}} = \frac{Q_T}{Q_A - Q_T}$$

11. *Calculate the upper -3 dB frequency. This is given by Eq. (9.52).*

12. *Design the horn for reactance annulling. This is achieved with a hyperbolic horn having a M given by Eq. (9.47).*

Example System Design

A driver has the parameters $f_S = 45\,\text{Hz}$, $Q_{TS} = 0.20$, $Q_{ES} = 0.21$, $Q_{MS} = 6$, $V_{AS} = 0.17\,\text{m}^3$, and $R_E = 7\,\Omega$. Design the horn system for $f_\ell = 40\,\text{Hz}$ and $f_u = 400\,\text{Hz}$. Assume $Q_M = 10$. The calculations are summarized as follows:

1. $f_0 = \sqrt{40 \times 400} = 126.5\,\text{Hz}$, $Q_T = 126.5/(40 + 400) = 0.29$

2. $\alpha = (126.5/45)^2 - 1 = 6.90$

3. $V_B = 0.17/6.90 = 2.46 \times 10^{-2}\,\text{m}^3$

4. $Q_E = (1 + 6.90)^{1/2} \times 0.21 = 0.59$

5. $Q_A = (1/0.29 - 1/0.59 - 1/10)^{-1} = 0.60$

6. $S_T = 2\pi 126.5 \times 0.17 \times 0.60/\left[(1 + 6.90)\,345\right] = 0.0296\,\text{m}^2$

7. $R_E + R_{EC} = 7\left[1 + 0.59^{-1}/\left(10^{-1} + 0.6^{-1}\right)\right] = 13.7\,\Omega$

8. $\eta = 0.29^2/\left[0.6\,(0.59 - 0.29)\right] = 46.7\%$

9. $R_{AT}/\left(R_{AE} + R_{AC}\right) = 0.29/\left(0.6 - 0.29\right) = 0.94$, ω_3 is maximized when $1/Q_a^2 = 4.1$, Eq. (9.53) gives $C_{AF} = 8.97 \times 10^{-9}$, thus $V_{AF} = 1.18 \times 345^2 \times 8.97 \times 10^{-6} = 1.26 \times 10^{-3}\,\text{m}^3$

10. Eq. (9.52) gives $f_3 = 376\,\text{Hz}$

11. $M = 2\pi 40 \times 0.17/\left[345 \times 0.0296 \times (1 + 6.9)\right] = 0.530$

System Design from Specifications

The procedure described in this section allows the designer to design the driver from system specifications. The procedure yields a maximum P_{AR} design. Specifications of the system pole frequencies ω_ℓ and ω_u, the box acoustic volume V_{AB}, the driver piston area S_D, the horn throat area S_T, the system electrical input resistance at ω_0, and the driver voice-coil resistance R_E are required. It is assumed that $M_{AC} = M_{AS}$, i.e. the acoustic mass of the driver diaphragm plus air load is the same in the horn as it is on an infinite baffle. The design procedure is as follows:

1. *Calculate the system resonance frequency ω_0 and quality factor Q_T. These are given in Eq. (9.38).*

2. *Calculate the system electrical quality factor Q_E. For a maximum P_{AR} design, Q_E is given by $Q_E = \left[1/2Q_T - 1/Q_M\right]^{-1}$*

3. *Calculate the total volume compliance $V_{AT} = cS_T/2Q_T\omega_0$.*

4. *Calculate the compliance ratio $\alpha = V_{AT}/\left(V_{AB} - V_{AT}\right)$.*

5. *Calculate the driver electrical quality factor $Q_{ES} = Q_E/\sqrt{1 + \alpha}$.*

6. *Calculate the driver resonance frequency $\omega_S = \omega_0/\sqrt{1 + \alpha}$.*

7. *Calculate the driver volume compliance $V_{AS} = \alpha V_{AB}$.*

8. *Calculate the driver mechanical compliance $C_{MS} = V_{AS}/\rho_0 c^2 S_D^2$.*

9. *Calculate the driver mechanical mass $M_{MS} = 1/\omega_S^2 C_{MS}$*

10. *Calculate the $B\ell$ product of the driver.*

$$B\ell = \left[S_D^2\left(R_{in} - R_E\right)\left(\frac{1}{Q_T} - \frac{1}{Q_E}\right)\frac{\rho_0 c^2}{\omega_0 V_{AT}}\right]^{1/2}$$

11. *Calculate the system efficiency η. This is given by Eq. (9.45).*

12. *Calculate the front cavity volume $V_{AF} = 0.6863 Q_T^2 V_{AT}$.*

13. *Calculate the new upper -3 dB frequency $f_3 = 1.099 f_0/Q_T$.*

14. *Design the horn for reactance annulling. This is achieved with a hyperbolic horn having a M given by Eq. (9.47).*

Example System Design

A horn and driver are to be designed for the system parameters: $V_{AB} = 0.015\,\text{m}^3$, $S_D = 0.073\,\text{m}^2$, $S_T = 0.018\,\text{m}^2$, $f_\ell = 40\,\text{Hz}$, $f_u = 400\,\text{Hz}$, $R_{in} = 8\,\Omega$, and $R_E = 4\,\Omega$. The calculations are summarized as follows:

1. $f_0 = \sqrt{40 \times 400} = 126.5\,\text{Hz}$, $Q_T = 126.5/(40+400) = 0.29$

2. $Q_E = [1/(2 \times 0.29) - 1/10]^{-1} = 0.62$ (assume $Q_M = 10$)

3. $V_{AT} = 345 \times 0.018/(2 \times 0.29 \times 2\pi126.5) = 0.0135\,\text{m}^3$

4. $\alpha = 0.0135/(0.015 - 0.0135) = 8.81$

5. $Q_{ES} = 0.62/\sqrt{1+8.81} = 0.20$

6. $f_S = 126.5/\sqrt{1+8.81} = 40.4\,\text{Hz}$

7. $V_{AS} = 8.81 \times 0.015 = 0.132\,\text{m}^3$

8. $C_{MS} = 0.132/\left(1.18 \times 345^2 \times 0.073^2\right) = 1.76 \times 10^{-4}\,\text{m/N}$

9. $M_{MS} = 1/\omega_S^2 C_{MS} = 1/\left[(2\pi40.4)^2 \times 1.76 \times 10^{-4}\right] = 0.0882\,\text{kg}$

10. $B\ell = 0.073^2 \times (8-4) \times \left(\frac{1}{0.29} - \frac{1}{0.62}\right) \times 1.18 \times 345^2/(2\pi126.5 \times 0.0135) = 22.6\,\text{T m}$

11. $\eta = 0.29/(0.62 - 0.29) = 43.9\%$

12. $V_{AF} = 0.6863 \times 0.29^2 \times 0.0135 = 7.79 \times 10^{-4}\,\text{m}^3$

13. $f_3 = 1.099 \times 126.5/0.29 = 479\,\text{Hz}$

14. $M = 2\pi40 \times 0.132/[345 \times 0.018 \times (1+8.81)] = 0.545$

9.13 Problems

1. An exponential horn is to be designed to be crossed over at 400 Hz. Its cutoff frequency is to be 200 Hz. If the throat diameter is 1 in, specify the flare constant m, the mouth diameter S_M, and the length L.

2. Use SPICE to display the real and imaginary parts of the throat impedance and the magnitude of the pressure transfer function for the following horns: *(a)* Cutoff frequency $f_c = 100\,\text{Hz}$, mouth diameter $d_M = 0.225\lambda_c$. *(b)* Cutoff frequency $f_c = 100\,\text{Hz}$, mouth diameter $d_M = 0.15\lambda_c$.

3. A 10-inch loudspeaker driver has the parameters: effective piston radius $= 10\,\text{cm}$, total quality factor $Q_{TS} = 0.43$, electrical quality factor $Q_{ES} = 0.49$, volume compliance $V_{AS} = 2.6\,\text{ft}^3$, and voice-coil resistance $R_E = 5.1\,\Omega$. Design a low-frequency horn system for the specifications $f_\ell = 30\,\text{Hz}$ and $f_h = 500\,\text{Hz}$. Assume $Q_M = 10$.

4. Design a horn and driver for the following system parameters: $V_{AB} = 0.05\,\text{m}^3$, $S_D = 0.073\,\text{m}^3$, $S_T = 0.025\,\text{m}^2$, $f_\ell = 30\,\text{Hz}$, $f_h = 500\,\text{Hz}$, $R_{in} = 7\,\Omega$, and $R_E = 3.5\,\Omega$. Assume $Q_M = 10$.

5. An exponential hour has a length of 0.5 m, a throat radius of 1.5 cm, and a mouth radius of 0.25 m. *(a)* Solve for the flare constant m. $[5.63\,\text{m}^{-1}]$ *(b)* Calculate the cutoff frequency f_c. $[309\,\text{Hz}]$ *(c)* If the acoustic output power at midband is 0.5 W, calculate the rms volume velocity emitted into the throat. $[9.32 \times 10^{-4}\,\text{m}^3/\text{s}]$ *(d)* If the driver diaphragm has a piston radius of 3 cm, calculate the peak-to-peak diaphragm displacement at the frequency $2f_c$ for the value of U_{rms} found in part (c). $[0.24\,\text{mm}]$

Chapter 10

Crossover Networks

10.1 Role of Crossover Networks

Crossover networks are electrical filters which divide the audio signal into frequency bands suitable for driving the different loudspeaker drivers in a system. For example, there are two drivers in a two-way system, a woofer which reproduces the low frequencies and a tweeter which reproduces the high frequencies. A low-pass filter is used in series with the woofer and a high-pass filter is used in series with the tweeter. A two-way system is converted to a three-way system by adding a midrange (sometimes called a squawker) which reproduces the mid frequencies. A band-pass filter is used in series with the midrange. Crossover networks in popular priced consumer systems often consist of nothing more than one or two capacitors.

The crossover frequency between two drivers connected to a crossover network is the frequency at which the two drivers radiate equal on-axis pressures. In a two-way system, the crossover frequency between the woofer and the tweeter is typically in the range from 1.5 kHz to 2 kHz. In a three-way system, the crossover frequency between the woofer and the midrange is typically 300 Hz to 800 Hz and that between the midrange and the tweeter is typically 3 kHz to 5 kHz.

The order of a crossover network refers to the slope of the Bode magnitude plot for its voltage gain transfer function. For example, a $1st$-order network has a slope of ± 1 dec/dec (± 20 dB/dec), a $2nd$-order network has a slope of ± 2 dec/dec (± 40 dB/dec), etc. A crossover system may have mixed orders. For example, in a two-way system, a $1st$-order low-pass filter may be used with the woofer and a $2nd$-order high-pass filter may be used with the tweeter. Similarly, the band-pass filter used on the midrange might consist of a $2nd$-order high-pass filter in cascade with a $1st$-order low-pass filter.

The crossover frequencies should preferably be chosen so that no driver is used outside its piston range, i.e. above the frequency for which the circumference of its diaphragm is equal to the wavelength. For example, a 10-inch woofer having the piston radius $a = 10$ cm should have a crossover frequency less than $c/2\pi a = 549$ Hz. The upper piston-range frequency for a midrange with the piston radius $a = 4.25$ cm is $f = 1.3$ kHz. This is lower than the upper crossover frequency typically used with most midranges. When used above its piston frequency limit, the frequency response of the driver is an important consideration.

Depending on its order, the cutoff frequency of a crossover network is calculated as the frequency at which the response is down by a factor of $1/\sqrt{2}$ (3 dB) or down by a factor of $1/2$ (6 dB). It is calculated under the assumption that the load on the network is a resistor equal to the loudspeaker voice-coil resistance R_E. Because the voice-coil impedance is not purely resistive, the actual cutoff frequency with a driver connected to the network can differ significantly. In addition, the frequency response of the network can be significantly altered.

10.2   Passive Crossover Networks

Passive crossover networks can be designed so that the drivers and their corresponding crossover network elements are driven in parallel or in series. The series connections utilize the voice-coil impedance of each driver as part of the crossover network for the other drivers. If the voice-coil impedances are resistive, there is no advantage of either connection. Because they are not resistive, the frequency dependence of the voice-coil impedance of one driver can affect the frequency response of the crossover networks for the other drivers with the series connections. For this reason, the parallel connections are preferred.

First Order

The simplest crossover networks are $1st$-order networks. The Bode magnitude plots exhibit a slope of ± 1 dec/dec or ± 20 dB/decade in the cutoff bands. Fig. 10.1 shows the circuit diagrams of $1st$-order parallel-connected and series-connected crossover networks for a three-way system. The loudspeaker loads are modeled by the voice-coil resistance. The woofer and tweeter networks are true $1st$-order filters because they contain only one energy storage element. However, the midrange network contains two energy storage elements. Therefore, it is really a $2nd$-order filter. However, it is usually called first order because it exhibits $1st$-order slopes. The slope of the Bode magnitude plot is $+1$ dec/dec in the low-frequency cutoff band and -1 dec/dec in the upper cutoff band.

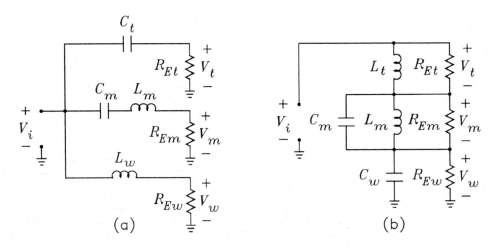

Figure 10.1: First-order crossover networks for a three-way system. (a) Parallel connection. (b) Series connection.

Denote the voltage-gain transfer functions for the woofer, the midrange, and the tweeter, respectively, in Fig. 10.1(a) by $T_w(s)$, $T_m(s)$, and $T_t(s)$. If each voice coil is modeled by its voice-coil resistance, it is straightforward to use voltage division to show that the transfer functions are given by

$$T_w(s) = \frac{1}{1 + s/\omega_w} \qquad T_m(s) = \frac{s/\omega_{m1}}{1 + s/\omega_{m1}}\frac{1}{1 + s/\omega_{m2}} \qquad T_t(s) = \frac{s/\omega_t}{1 + s/\omega_t} \qquad (10.1)$$

where $\omega_w = 2\pi f_w$ is the -3 dB frequency of the woofer network, $\omega_{m1} = 2\pi f_{m1}$ and $\omega_{m2} = 2\pi f_{m2}$, respectively, are the lower and upper -3 dB frequencies of the midrange network, and $\omega_t = 2\pi f_t$ is the -3 dB frequency of the tweeter network.

The element values in Fig. 10.1(a) are given by

$$L_w = \frac{R_{Ew}}{2\pi f_w} \qquad C_m = \frac{1}{2\pi f_{m1} R_{Em}} \qquad L_m = \frac{R_{Em}}{2\pi f_{m2}} \qquad C_t = \frac{1}{2\pi f_t R_{Et}} \qquad (10.2)$$

For the midrange network elements, the expressions assume that L_m is a short circuit at f_{m1} and that C_m is a short circuit at f_{m2}. This assumption holds if $f_{m2} \gg f_{m1}$. The Bode magnitude plots for the transfer functions are given in Fig. 10.2. The figure assumes that $f_w = f_{m1}$ and $f_{m2} = f_t$. It is left as an exercise to determine the element values for the series-connected networks.

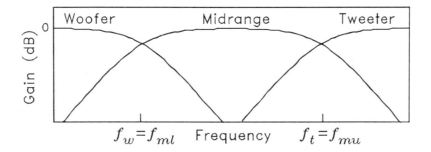

Figure 10.2: Bode magnitude plots for first-order crossover networks.

Fig. 10.1 shows that the inductors in the woofer and midrange crossover networks are in series with the driver voice coils. This makes it possible to utilize the voice-coil inductances of these two drivers as part or all of the crossover network inductance. In most applications, the voice-coil inductance is not large enough by itself so that series inductors must be used. Because the voice-coil inductance is lossy, its use as a crossover network element may require some experimentation.

Example 1 *A two-way loudspeaker system uses a woofer with a voice-coil resistance $R_{Ew} = 7.5\,\Omega$ and a tweeter with a voice-coil resistance $R_{Et} = 6.2\,\Omega$. Calculate the element values for 1st-order crossover networks for the drivers if the crossover frequency is 1.8 kHz for each.*

Solution: From Eqs. (10.2), we have $L_w = 7.5/(2\pi1800) = 0.66\,\mathrm{mH}$ and $C_t = 1/(2\pi6.2 \times 1800) = 14\,\mu\mathrm{F}$.

Second Order

Although 1*st*-order crossover networks are the simplest and the cheapest, the Bode magnitude plots do not have very steep cutoff slopes. Most tweeters and midranges can be damaged if strong signals are applied to the voice coils below the fundamental resonance frequency of the driver. To protect the drivers from failure, 2*nd*-order (or higher) high-pass crossover networks are often used. Second-order low-pass networks are also useful in controlling high-frequency peaking problems in woofers and midranges that are due to cone breakup above the piston range of the driver.

Fig. 10.3 shows the circuit diagrams of parallel-connected and series-connected crossover networks in which a 2*nd*-order low-pass filter is used on the woofer, a 2*nd*-order high-pass filter and a 2*nd*-order low-pass filter are used on the midrange, and a 2*nd*-order high-pass filter is used on the tweeter. The Bode magnitude plots for the voltage-gain transfer functions are similar to the plots of Fig. 10.2 with the exception that the asymptotic slopes in the cutoff bands are ± 2 dec/dec or ± 40 dB/dec.

If the voice-coil impedance of each driver is assumed to be equal to the dc voice-coil resistance, it can be shown that the voltage-gain transfer functions of the networks in Fig. 10.3(a) are given by

$$T_w(s) = \frac{1}{(s/\omega_w)^2 + (1/Q_w)(s/\omega_w) + 1} \tag{10.3}$$

$$T_m(s) = \frac{(s/\omega_{m1})^2}{(s/\omega_{m1})^2 + (1/Q_{m1})(s/\omega_{m1}) + 1} \times \frac{1}{(s/\omega_{m2})^2 + (1/Q_{m2})(s/\omega_{m2}) + 1} \tag{10.4}$$

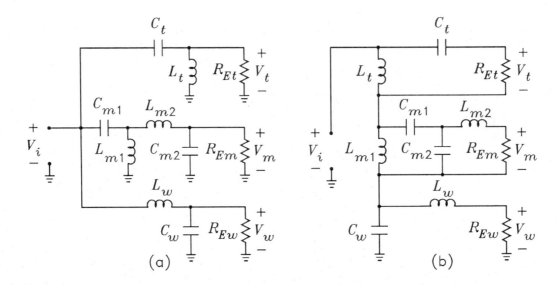

Figure 10.3: Second-order crossover networks for a three-way system. (a) Parallel connection. (b) Series connection.

$$T_t(s) = \frac{(s/\omega_t)^2}{(s/\omega_t)^2 + (1/Q_t)(s/\omega_t) + 1} \tag{10.5}$$

where $\omega_w = 2\pi f_w$, $\omega_{m1} = 2\pi f_{m1}$, $\omega_{m2} = 2\pi f_{m2}$, and $\omega_t = 2\pi f_t$. The element values in Fig. 10.3(a) are related to the resonance frequencies and quality factors as follows:

$$L_w = \frac{R_{Ew}}{2\pi f_w Q_w} \qquad C_w = \frac{Q_w}{2\pi f_w R_{Ew}} \qquad L_{m1} = \frac{R_{Em}}{2\pi f_{m1} Q_{m1}} \qquad C_{m1} = \frac{Q_{m1}}{2\pi f_{m1} R_{Em}} \tag{10.6}$$

$$L_{m2} = \frac{R_{Em}}{2\pi f_{m2} Q_{m2}} \qquad C_{m2} = \frac{Q_{m2}}{2\pi f_{m2} R_{Em}} \qquad L_t = \frac{R_{Et}}{2\pi f_t Q_t} \qquad C_t = \frac{Q_t}{2\pi f_t R_{Et}} \tag{10.7}$$

The midrange formulas assume that $f_{m2} \gg f_{m1}$. It is left as an exercise to determine the element values for the series-connected networks.

The 2nd-order functions have two parameters each, a resonance frequency and a quality factor. In each case, the relative response at the resonance frequency is equal to the quality factor. When the quality factor has the value $1/\sqrt{2}$, the resonance frequency corresponds to the $-3\,\text{dB}$ frequency. This corresponds to a Butterworth or maximally-flat alignment. For a quality factor of 0.5, the alignment is said to be critically damped and the resonance frequency corresponds to the $-6\,\text{dB}$ frequency. Second-order networks are usually designed with $f_w = f_{m1}$ and $f_{m2} = f_t$. In addition, the quality factors of the networks are all chosen to be $Q = 0.5$.

Example 2 *A two-way loudspeaker system uses a woofer with a voice-coil resistance $R_{Ew} = 7.5\,\Omega$ and a tweeter with a voice-coil resistance $R_{Et} = 6.2\,\Omega$. Calculate the element values for 2nd-order crossover networks for the drivers if the crossover frequency is 1.8 kHz and $Q = 0.5$ for each.*

Solution: From Eqs. (10.6) and (10.7), we have

$$L_w = 7.5/(2\pi 1800 \times 0.5) = 1.3\,\text{mH} \qquad C_w = 0.5/(2\pi 1800 \times 7.5) = 5.9\,\mu\text{F}$$

$$L_t = 6.2/(2\pi 1800 \times 0.5) = 1.1\,\text{mH} \qquad C_t = 0.5/(2\pi 1800 \times 6.2) = 7.1\,\mu\text{F}$$

Third Order

Third-order high-pass filters are commonly used with midrange and tweeter drivers when the power handling of the system is a major concern, e.g. with horn midranges and tweeters in public address systems. In the cutoff region, the slope of the Bode magnitude plot for such a filter is $+3$ dec/dec or $+60$ dB/dec. The circuit diagram of a $3rd$-order high-pass filter is given in Fig. 10.4(a). If the load impedance on the filter is a resistor R_E, the network elements for a Butterworth response are related to R_E and the -3 dB cutoff frequency f_c as follows:

$$C_1 = \frac{1}{3\pi f_c R_E} \qquad C_2 = 3C_1 \qquad L = \frac{3R_E}{8\pi f_c} \qquad (10.8)$$

At the frequency f_c, the transfer function has a magnitude of $1/\sqrt{2}$.

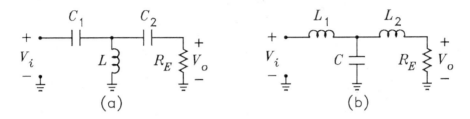

Figure 10.4: Third-order (a) high-pass and (b) low-pass filters.

The circuit diagram of a $3rd$-order low-pass filter is shown in Fig. 10.4(b). Like the $1st$-order low-pass filter, the $3rd$-order low-pass filter can be designed so that the voice-coil inductance of the driver is part of L_2. If the load impedance on the filter is a resistor R_E, the network elements for a Butterworth response are related to R_E and the -3 dB frequency f_c as follows:

$$L_2 = \frac{R_E}{4\pi f_c} \qquad L_1 = 3L_2 \qquad C = \frac{2}{3\pi f_c R_E} \qquad (10.9)$$

At $f = f_c$, the transfer function has a magnitude of $1/\sqrt{2}$.

Example 3 *A two-way loudspeaker system consisting of a direct-radiator woofer and a horn-loaded high-frequency driver is to use 3rd-order crossover networks. The crossover frequency is to be 800 Hz. The voice-coil resistance of each driver is 7 Ω. (a) Calculate the elements C_1, C_2, and L for the high-pass filter. (b) Calculate the elements L_1, L_2, and C for the low-pass filter.*

Solution. (a) From Eq. (10.8), $C_1 = 18.9\,\mu\text{F}$, $C_2 = 56.8\,\mu\text{F}$, and $L = 1.04\,\text{mH}$. (b) From Eq. (10.9), $L_1 = 2.09\,\text{mH}$, $L_2 = 0.696\,\text{mH}$, and $C = 37.9\,\mu\text{F}$.

10.3 L-Pad Design

If each driver in a system does not have the same pressure sensitivity p_{sens}^{1V}, the frequency response of the system will not be flat. To correct this, resistive voltage dividers called L-pads can be used to decrease the voltage applied to the voice coils of the drivers which have the higher p_{sens}^{1V}. Because adding resistors in series with a driver increases its Q_{ES}, L-pads should not be used with the woofer unless its Q_{ES} is to be increased intentionally, for this affects the enclosure design. Thus the midrange and tweeter drivers in a system should have a p_{sens}^{1V} greater than or equal to that of the woofer. The effect of the resistors in the midrange and tweeter L-pads on the Q_{ES} of these drivers can usually be compensated for by experimental adjustment or tweaking of the crossover network.

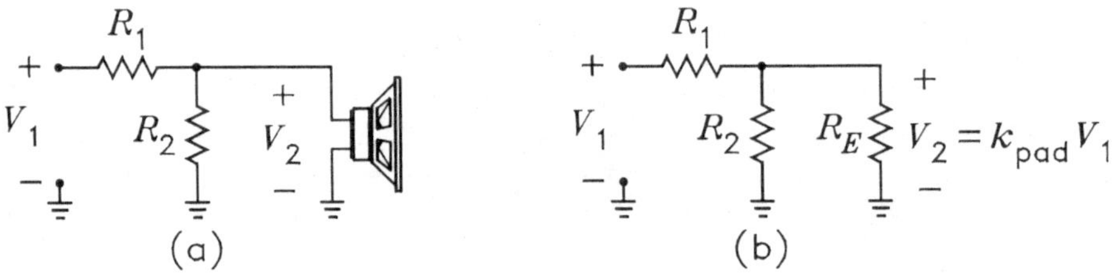

Figure 10.5: (a) L-pad and driver. (b) L-pad with the driver modeled by its voice-coil resistance R_E.

Fig. 10.5(a) illustrates an L-pad connected to a driver. In Fig. 10.5(b), the driver is modeled by its voice-coil resistance R_E. For a desired voltage gain $k_{pad} = V_2/V_1$ and input resistance R_{in}, the L-pad elements are given by

$$R_2 = \frac{R_{in}R_E}{(R_E/k_{pad}) - R_{in}} \qquad R_1 = R_{in} - R_2\|R_E \tag{10.10}$$

Suppose two drivers have the pressure sensitivities p_{sens1}^{1V} and p_{sens2}^{1V}, where $p_{sens1}^{1V} < p_{sens2}^{1V}$, the efficiencies η_{01} and η_{02}, and the voice-coil resistances R_{E1} and R_{E2}. The value of k_{pad} for a L-pad in series with driver 2 to make it have the same effective p_{sens}^{1V} as driver 1 is given by

$$k_{pad} = \frac{p_{sens1}^{1V}}{p_{sens2}^{1V}} = \sqrt{\frac{R_{E2}}{R_{E1}} \times \frac{\eta_{01}}{\eta_{02}}} \tag{10.11}$$

If the SPL sensitivities of the drivers are given, the value of k_{pad} is

$$k_{pad} = 10^{\left(SPL_{sens1}^{1V} - SPL_{sens2}^{1V}\right)/20} = \sqrt{\frac{R_{E2}}{R_{E1}}} 10^{\left(SPL_{sens1}^{1W} - SPL_{sens2}^{1W}\right)/20} \tag{10.12}$$

Example 4 *The woofer, midrange, and tweeter drivers for a three-way system each have a dc voice-coil resistance of $7\,\Omega$. The tweeter and the midrange each have an SPL_{sens}^{1V} that is $3\,dB$ higher than that for the woofer. Specify the elements in the crossover network of Fig. 10.6 such that $f_w = f_{m1} = 400\,Hz$, $f_{m2} = f_t = 4\,kHz$, and $Q_w = Q_{m1} = Q_{m2} = Q_t = 0.5$. Resistive L-pads are to be used between the tweeter and its crossover network and between the high-pass and low-pass sections of the midrange crossover network to make the effective SPL_{sens}^{1V} of these drivers equal to the that of the woofer. The L-pads are to be designed to have a $7\,\Omega$ input resistance when terminated in a $7\,\Omega$ load. Neglect the amplifier output resistance and the series resistance of the inductors in the crossover network.*

Solution. We assume that each network is loaded with a resistor having the value $R_E = 7\,\Omega$. From Eq. (10.6), $L_w = R_{Ew}/(2\pi f_w Q_w) = 5.57\,mH$ and $C_w = Q_w/(2\pi f_w R_{Ew}) = 28.4\,\mu F$. For the tweeter L-pad, $k_{pad} = 1/\sqrt{2}$. From Eq. (10.10), $R_{t2} = R_{Et}^2/[(R_{Et}/k_{pad}) - R_{Et}] = 16.9\,\Omega$ and $R_{t1} = R_{Et} - R_{t2}\|R_{Et} = 2.05\,\Omega$. The midrange L-pad resistors have the same values. For the tweeter network, from Eq. (10.7) $L_t = R_{Et}/(2\pi f_t Q_t) = 0.557\,mH$ and $C_t = Q_t/(2\pi f_t R_{Et}) = 2.84\,\mu F$. For the midrange network, the values of L_{m2} and C_{m2} are the same as for L_t and C_t.

Because the midrange L-pad precedes the midrange low-pass filter, the source impedance seen by the low-pass section of the midrange network is not zero. Therefore, Eq. (10.7) cannot be used to calculate L_{m2} and C_{m2}. For L_{m1} an open circuit and C_{m1} a short circuit, the effective source resistance seen by the low-pass section is $R_g = R_{m1}\|R_{m2}$. In this case, it can be shown that C_{m2} and L_{m2} are given by

$$C_{m2} = \frac{1}{4\pi f_{m2} Q_{m2}(R_g\|R_{Em})}\left[1 \pm \sqrt{1 - \frac{4Q_{m2}^2}{1 + R_{Em}/R_g}}\right] \tag{10.13}$$

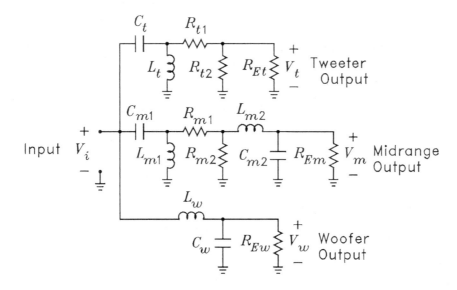

Figure 10.6: Example crossover network with two L-pads.

$$L_{m2} = \frac{1 + R_g/R_{Em}}{(2\pi f_{m2})^2 C_{m2}} \tag{10.14}$$

With $f_{m2} = 4\,\text{kHz}$, $Q_{m2} = 0.5$, $R_{Em} = 7\,\Omega$, $R_{m1} = 2.05\,\Omega$, and $R_{m2} = 16.9\,\Omega$, these two equations yield $L_{m2} = 0.664\,\text{mH}$ and $C_{m2} = 3.01\,\mu\text{F}$, where the minus sign has been used in Eq. (10.13).

In the above example, the L-pad for the midrange is between the high-pass and the low-pass sections of the midrange network. This often is preferable because it provides some isolation between the two sections of the network and improves their frequency response. The resistors in the pads for both drivers should be power resistors. These are usually available in 5, 10, and 25 W ratings, and higher. In systems designed for home use, 10 W resistors in the midrange and tweeter pads are usually adequate.

10.4   Effect of the Voice-Coil Impedance

The voice-coil impedance of a driver is not purely resistive. This can have a major perturbation on the performance of crossover networks. At high frequencies, the voice-coil impedance becomes inductive. For odd-order crossover networks, this inductance can be utilized as part of the crossover network. Because the inductance is lossy, some experimentation may be necessary. For even-order networks, the inductance can be canceled by using a simple RC matching network as discussed below.

The impedance rise near the resonance frequency of closed-box midrange and tweeter drivers can have a major perturbation on the performance of the high-pass crossover networks. The effect is to cause a peak to appear in the pressure output of the driver at or near its resonance frequency. It can be very difficult to pull down this peak without causing a depression in the frequency response over a much wider band. To minimize the problem, the lower crossover frequency for the midrange and the tweeter should be greater than the fundamental resonance frequency of the drivers. The matching network described below can be used to cancel the impedance rise, but the element values may not be practical.

A matching network, sometimes called a Zobel network, between the crossover network and the voice-coil terminals of a driver can be used to cause the effective load on the crossover network to be resistive. Fig. 10.7 shows the network connected to the voice-coil equivalent circuit for a closed-box driver. The high-frequency part of the network consists of R_1, C_1, R_2, and C_2. This network can be designed to correct for the lossy voice-coil inductance in an equal ripple sense between two specified frequencies in the band where the impedance is dominated by $Z_e(\omega)$. At the fundamental resonance frequency of the driver, L_1 and C_3 resonate and put R_3 in parallel with the voice coil. This cancels the rise in impedance at the fundamental resonance frequency f_C.

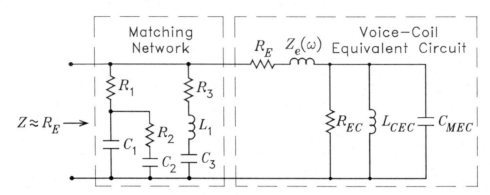

Figure 10.7: Voice-coil equivalent circuit with matching networks.

Let the lossy voice coil inductance have the impedance $Z_e(\omega) = L_e(j\omega)^{n_e}$, where L_e and n_e are defined in Section 6.16. Let the network consisting of R_1, C_1, R_2, and C_2 correct for the lossy voice-coil inductance over the frequency band from f_1 to f_2. The frequency f_1 might be chosen to be the frequency above the fundamental resonance frequency f_C where the voice-coil impedance exhibits a minimum before the high-frequency rise caused by the voice-coil inductance. This minimum is illustrated in Fig. 6.12 for a driver in an infinite baffle. The frequency f_2 might be chosen to be 20 kHz. In order for the input impedance to the network plus the driver to be approximately equal to R_E at all frequencies, the matching network elements are given by

$$R_1 = R_E \qquad C_1 = \frac{L_e}{(2\pi)^{(1-n_e)} R_E^2 \left[f_1^{n_e} f_2^{(2+n_e)} \right]^{\frac{(1-n_e)}{2(1+n_e)}}} \qquad (10.15)$$

$$C_2 = \frac{L_e}{(2\pi)^{(1-n_e)} R_E^2 \left[f_1^{(2+n_e)} f_2^{n_e} \right]^{\frac{(1-n_e)}{2(1+n_e)}}} - C_1 \qquad R_2 = \frac{1}{2\pi f_1^{\frac{1}{(1+n_e)}} f_2^{\frac{n_e}{(1+n_e)}} C_2} \qquad (10.16)$$

$$R_3 = R_E \left(1 + \frac{Q_{EC}}{Q_{MC}} \right) \qquad L_1 = \frac{R_E Q_{EC}}{2\pi f_C} \qquad C_3 = \frac{1}{2\pi f_C R_E Q_{EC}} \qquad (10.17)$$

where R_E is the voice-coil resistance, f_C is the closed-box resonance frequency, Q_{EC} is the electrical quality factor, and Q_{MC} is the mechanical quality factor.

The above equations are derived under the assumption that C_1 and C_2 are open circuits in the low-frequency range where R_3, C_3, and L_1 are active and that L_1 is an open circuit in the high-frequency range where R_1, C_1, R_2, and C_2 are active. For a lossless inductor, n_e has the value $n_e = 1$. In this case, $C_1 = L_e/R_E^2$, and both R_2 and C_2 are open circuits.

Example 5 *A closed-box midrange driver has the parameters $R_E = 7.5\,\Omega$, $L_e = 0.00689$, $n_e = 0.7$, $f_C = 250\,\text{Hz}$, $Q_{EC} = 1.1$, and $Q_{MC} = 4$. For the high-frequency network, assume $f_1 = 733\,\text{Hz}$ and $f_2 = 20\,\text{kHz}$. Calculate the element values for the matching network which will make the driver impedance look like a $7.5\,\Omega$ resistor to the crossover network.*

Solution: From Eqs. (10.15) - (10.17), we have $R_1 = 7.5\,\Omega$, $C_1 = 4.44\,\mu\text{F}$, $R_2 = 15.8\,\Omega$, $C_2 = 3.52\,\mu\text{F}$, $R_3 = 9.56\,\Omega$, $L_1 = 5.25\,\text{mH}$, and $C_3 = 77.2\,\mu\text{F}$. Curve a in Fig. 10.8 shows the plot of the voice-coil impedance without the matching network. Curve b shows the impedance with the network. The frequency f_1 was chosen to be the frequency at which curve a exhibits a minimum in its midband region. The figure shows evidence of some interaction between the two networks.

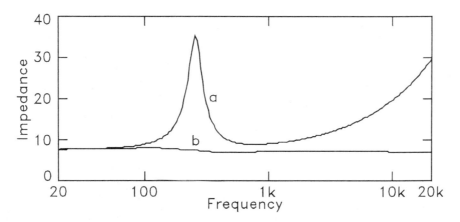

Figure 10.8: Figure for Example 5.

10.5 Effect of the Driver Phase Response

A loudspeaker system should be designed so that phase cancellation cannot occur in the on-axis pressure caused by two drivers operating out of phase at the crossover frequency. To explain this effect, let us first consider how the phase of a transfer function is related to its Bode magnitude plot. Our discussion is limited to the case of minimum-phase transfer functions which have no poles or zeros in the right-half of the complex plane. The rule for predicting the phase is as follows:

Rule for Transfer Function Phase. At a frequency well removed from a break frequency on a Bode magnitude plot, the phase of the transfer function is approximately given by the slope in dec/dec multiplied by 90°. At a break frequency, the phase is approximately given by the average value of the predicted slopes on each side of the break frequency.

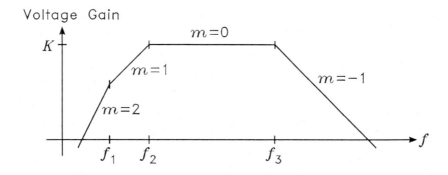

Figure 10.9: Asymptotic Bode magnitude plot for the example phase calculation.

As an example, consider the asymptotic Bode magnitude plot shown in Fig. 10.9. The transfer function has high-pass poles at f_1 and f_2, a midband gain constant of K, and a low-pass pole at f_3. Denote the phase by φ. We have

$$\varphi \simeq 2 \times 90° = 180° \text{ for } f < f_1 \qquad \varphi \simeq (180° + 90°)/2 = 135° \text{ for } f = f_1$$
$$\varphi \simeq 1 \times 90° = 90° \text{ for } f_1 < f < f_2 \qquad \varphi \simeq (90° + 0°)/2 = 45° \text{ for } f = f_2$$
$$\varphi \simeq 0° \text{ for } f_2 < f < f_3 \qquad \varphi \simeq (0° - 90°)/2 = -45° \text{ for } f = f_3$$
$$\varphi \simeq -1 \times 90° = -90° \text{ for } f > f_3$$

First-Order Networks

Let us consider the crossover between a closed-box woofer and a closed-box midrange. We assume that both drivers have the same p_{sens}^{1V} and are mounted in separate closed-box baffles. Let a 1st-order low-pass filter be used on the woofer and a 1st-order high-pass filter on the midrange. Assume the crossover frequency is equal to the midrange resonance frequency and that this frequency is in the midband region for the woofer. In addition, let the midrange transfer function have a quality factor $Q_{TC} = 1$ so that its on-axis pressure transfer function has a relative value of unity at the crossover frequency.

Fig. 10.10 shows the Bode magnitude plots for the on-axis transfer functions for both drivers and for the transfer functions of the two crossover networks. At the crossover frequency, the woofer on-axis pressure transfer function has a relative magnitude of unity and a phase of $0°$. The woofer crossover network has a magnitude response of $1/\sqrt{2}$ and a phase of $-45°$. Thus the phasor representing the pressure output from the woofer has a relative magnitude of $1/\sqrt{2}$ and a phase of $-45°$. This phasor is shown in Fig. 10.11(a).

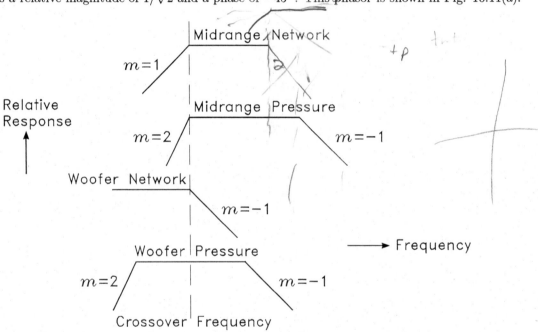

Figure 10.10: Asymptotic Bode magnitude plots for the woofer, the midrange, and the crossover networks for the example system.

At the crossover frequency, the midrange on-axis pressure transfer function has a relative magnitude of unity and a phase of $+90°$. The midrange crossover network has a magnitude response of $1/\sqrt{2}$ and a phase of $+45°$. Thus the on-axis pressure from the midrange has a relative magnitude of $1/\sqrt{2}$ and a phase of $+135°$. The pressure phasors for the midrange alone, for the midrange crossover alone, and the combination of the two are shown in Fig. 10.11(a). The figure shows that the woofer and midrange phasors have equal magnitudes, but they are $180°$ out of phase. Thus the pressure outputs from the two drivers cancel at the crossover frequency. The effect would be the same as using a graphic equalizer to notch out the frequency response at the crossover frequency.

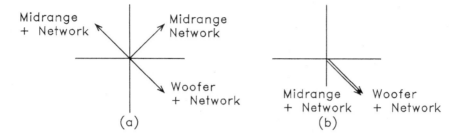

Figure 10.11: Phasor diagrams for the woofer and the midrange pressure outputs for the example first-order crossover networks. (a) Same-polarity and (b) opposite-polarity connections.

The solution to the cancellation problem is to reverse the electrical polarity of the midrange voice coil connection to the crossover network. This inverts the pressure output from the midrange, i.e. multiplies it by -1, thus causing the midrange and woofer pressure outputs to be in phase at the crossover frequency. Fig. 10.11(b) shows the system phasors for the out-of-phase connection. Reversing the polarity of the voice coil flops the midrange phasor about the origin. If a bump forms in the response, the crossover frequencies for the two drivers can be pulled apart. That is, the woofer crossover frequency can be decreased and the midrange crossover frequency can be increased to even out the bump.

Second-Order Networks

A $2nd$-order low-pass filter exhibits $90°$ of phase lag at its resonance frequency whereas a $2nd$-order high-pass filter exhibits $90°$ of phase lead. At the crossover frequency between the woofer and the midrange, we again assume that the phase of the woofer pressure transfer function is $0°$. Let us assume that the crossover frequency is equal to or greater than the fundamental resonance frequency of the midrange. In this case, the phase lead in the midrange pressure transfer function is between $90°$ and $0°$. Fig. 10.12(a) illustrates the phasor diagrams for the system for the voice coils connected with the same polarity. It can be seen that phase cancellation occurs in the pressure output of the system. Fig. 10.12(b) illustrates the phasor diagrams with the polarity of the midrange voice coil reversed. It can be seen that cancellation no longer occurs. Therefore, we conclude that the woofer and the midrange should be connected to $2nd$-order crossover networks with the polarity of one driver reversed. This driver is normally the midrange.

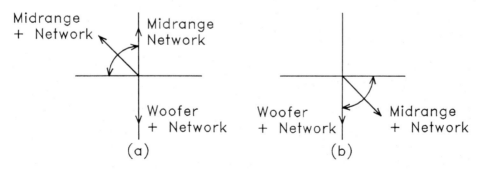

Figure 10.12: Phasor diagrams for the woofer and the midrange pressure outputs for second-order networks. (a) Same-polarity and (b) opposite-polarity connections.

A Mixed-Order Network

Suppose that the crossover network for a midrange and a tweeter consists of a $1st$-order low-pass filter on the midrange and $2nd$-order high-pass filter on the tweeter. At the crossover frequency, the $1st$-order low-pass network exhibits $45\,°$ of phase lag. The $2nd$-order high-pass network exhibits $90\,°$ of phase lead. We assume that the crossover frequency is such that the phase lead in the midrange pressure transfer function is $0\,°$. If the crossover frequency is at or above the resonance frequency of the tweeter, the phase lead in its pressure transfer function is between $90\,°$ and $0\,°$. The phasor diagrams for the pressure outputs from both drivers are shown in Fig. 10.13(a) for the case where both voice coils are connected with the same polarity. Because the phasors are out of phase, it is obvious that phase cancellation occurs. This does not occur when the polarity of the midrange voice coil is reversed as is illustrated in Fig. 10.13(b). Thus the midrange and the tweeter voice coils should be connected with opposite polarity to the crossover networks.

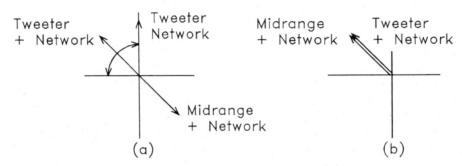

Figure 10.13: Phasor diagrams for the midrange and the tweeter pressure outputs for a first-order crossover network on the midrange and a second-order network on the tweeter. (a) Same-polarity and (b) opposite-polarity connections.

If a bump forms in the system frequency response at the crossover frequency when $2nd$-order crossover networks are used, the bump can be minimized in two ways. As with the $1st$-order networks, the crossover frequencies can be pulled apart. To improve the power handling of the higher frequency driver, it would be preferable to achieve this by increasing crossover frequency of the higher frequency driver. A second way is to reduce the quality factors of the networks. This reduces the gain of the networks at the crossover frequency.

Third-Order Networks

A $3rd$-order woofer low-pass network exhibits a $135\,°$ phase lag at the crossover frequency. A $3rd$-order midrange high-pass network exhibits a $135\,°$ phase lead. We assume that the phase lead in the woofer on-axis pressure transfer function is $0\,°$ at the crossover frequency and that the phase lead in the midrange on-axis pressure transfer function is between $90\,°$ and $0\,°$. Fig. 10.14(a) shows the system phasor diagrams for the same polarity connection of the voice coils to the crossover networks. Fig. 10.14(b) shows the phasor diagrams for the reversed polarity. It is obvious that the same polarity connections prevent phase cancellation in the system response.

Fourth-Order Networks

A $4th$-order low-pass network exhibits $180\,°$ of phase lag at the crossover frequency. A $4th$-order high-pass network exhibits $180\,°$ of phase lead. Thus the outputs are in phase. If the phase lead in the woofer on-axis pressure transfer function is $0\,°$ at this frequency and the phase lead in the midrange on-axis pressure transfer function is between $90\,°$ and $0\,°$, it follows that the two drivers must be connected in phase to the crossover networks. An out-of-phase connection would result in an angle between the woofer and midrange phasors between $90\,°$ and $180\,°$.

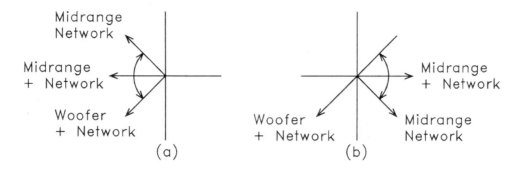

Figure 10.14: Phasor diagrams for the woofer and the midrange pressure outputs for third-order crossover networks. (a) Same-polarity and (b) opposite-polarity connections.

In summary, the acoustic pressures radiated by two drivers at a crossover frequency can cancel and cause a dip in the frequency response of the system at that frequency. To prevent this problem, the phase of the pressure outputs from the drivers at the crossover frequency must be examined by means of phasor diagrams. At a crossover frequency, the angle between two phasors must be $90°$ or less to prevent cancellation. If the angle between phasors is greater than $90°$, the polarity of the voice coil connection of one of the drivers to the crossover network should be reversed.

10.6 Constant-Voltage and All-Pass Functions

Crossover networks are often designed to satisfy either a constant-voltage condition or an all-pass condition. To see how these are derived, let $D_n(s)$ be a polynomial in s of the form

$$D_n(s) = 1 + a_1(s/\omega_0) + a_2(s/\omega_0)^2 + \cdots + (s/\omega_0)^n \qquad (10.18)$$

where ω_0 is the crossover frequency. The transfer functions of low-pass and high-pass filters can be written

$$T_{LP}(s) = \frac{1}{D_n(s/\omega_0)} \qquad T_{HP}(s) = \frac{(s/\omega_0)^n}{D_n(s/\omega_0)} \qquad (10.19)$$

In the following, the equations are simplified by assuming that $\omega_0 = 1\,\text{rad/s}$, i.e. the crossover frequency is normalized to $1\,\text{rad/s}$.

For $s = j\omega$, we wish to investigate the conditions for which

$$|T_{LP}(j\omega) \pm T_{HP}(j\omega)| = 1 \qquad (10.20)$$

where the minus sign represents a reversal of the polarity of the high-frequency driver to the network. Networks which satisfy this condition are called all-pass networks. In the case that $T_{LP}(s) + T_{HP}(s) = 1$, the network is called a constant-voltage network.

The generation of all-pass transfer functions requires factorization of the polynomial $1 \pm (s)^n$ into the product of first and second-order polynomials having real coefficients. For $n = 1$, the polynomial is already factored. The factored polynomials for the cases $2 \leq n \leq 4$ are as follows:

$$1 - s^2 = (1 + s)(1 - s) \qquad 1 + s^3 = (1 + s)(1 - s + s^2) \qquad (10.21)$$

$$1 + s^4 = \left(1 + \sqrt{2}s + s^2\right)\left(1 - \sqrt{2}s + s^2\right) \qquad (10.22)$$

The denominator polynomial for $T_{LP}(s)$ and $T_{HP}(s)$ is obtained by taking the factors of $1 \pm s^n$, changing the signs of all negative coefficients of s, and multiplying the factors. It follows that

$$D_2(s) = (1 + s)^2 \qquad D_3(s) = (1 + s)(1 + s + s^2) \qquad D_4(s) = \left(1 + \sqrt{2}s + s^2\right)^2 \qquad (10.23)$$

It is straightforward to obtain orders higher than 4 by factoring the $1 \pm s^n$ polynomial. The cases that cannot be used are those for which a factor of the polynomial is $1 + s^2$, for this leads to poles on the $j\omega$ axis. For example, this occurs with $1 + s^6$ but not with $1 - s^6$.

First Order

For $n = 1$, we have

$$T_{LP}(s) = \frac{1}{1+s} \qquad T_{HP}(s) = \frac{s}{1+s} \qquad T_{LP}(s) \pm T_{HP}(s) = \frac{1 \pm s}{1+s} \tag{10.24}$$

It is obvious that $T_{LP}(s) + T_{HP}(s) = 1$, so that the $1st$-order crossover is constant voltage. This is the only order for which the network is constant voltage. For $s = j\omega$, the magnitude of the difference is

$$|T_{LP}(j\omega) - T_{HP}(j\omega)| = \left| \frac{1 - j\omega}{1 + j\omega} \right| = \frac{\sqrt{1 + \omega^2}}{\sqrt{1 + \omega^2}} = 1 \tag{10.25}$$

Thus the $1st$-order function is all-pass if the difference connection is used.

At the crossover frequency, i.e. for $\omega = 1$, $T_{LP}(j1) = 1/\sqrt{2}\angle - 45°$ and $T_{HP}(j1) = 1/\sqrt{2}\angle + 45°$. The angle between the phasors is $90°$. If crossover occurs near the resonance frequency of the high-frequency driver, its phase lead causes the phase difference to be greater than $90°$ for the sum connection and less than $90°$ for the difference connection. To prevent phase cancellation, this angle should be no greater than $90°$ so that the difference connection is the proper one.

Second Order

For $n = 2$, we have

$$T_{LP}(s) = \frac{1}{(1+s)^2} \qquad T_{HP}(s) = \frac{s^2}{(1+s)^2} \qquad T_{LP}(s) \pm T_{HP}(s) = \frac{1 \pm s^2}{(1+s)^2} \tag{10.26}$$

For $s = j\omega$, it is obvious that the sum connection exhibits a null at $\omega = 1$. For the difference connection, the numerator can be factored to obtain $(1 + s)(1 - s)$. For $s = j\omega$, we have

$$|T_{LP}(j\omega) - T_{HP}(j\omega)| = \left| \frac{(1 - j\omega)(1 + j\omega)}{(1 + j\omega)^2} \right| = \left| \frac{1 - j\omega}{1 + j\omega} \right| = 1 \tag{10.27}$$

Thus the difference connection is all-pass.

At the crossover frequency, i.e. for $\omega = 1$, $T_{LP}(j1) = 0.5\angle - 90°$ and $T_{HP}(j1) = 0.5\angle + 90°$. The angle between the phasors is $180°$ so that $T_{LP}(j1) + T_{HP}(j1) = 0$. For the difference connection, the angle between the phasors is $0°$ and $T_{LP}(j1) - T_{HP}(j1) = 1\angle 0°$. If crossover occurs near the resonance frequency of the high-frequency driver, its phase lead causes the phase difference to be between $90°$ and $180°$ for the sum connection and less than $90°$ for the difference connection. To prevent phase cancellation, this angle should be no greater than $90°$ so that the difference connection is preferred.

Third Order

For $n = 3$, we have

$$T_{LP}(s) = \frac{1}{(1+s)(1+s+s^2)} \qquad T_{HP}(s) = \frac{s^3}{(1+s)(1+s+s^2)} \tag{10.28}$$

The sum and difference are

$$T_{LP}(s) \pm T_{HP}(s) = \frac{1 \pm s^3}{(1+s)(1+s+s^2)} = \frac{(1 \pm s)(1 \mp s + s^2)}{(1+s)(1+s+s^2)} \tag{10.29}$$

For the sum connection, the $(1 + s)$ factors cancel. For $s = j\omega$, the magnitude of the sum is

$$|T_{LP}(j\omega) + T_{HP}(j\omega)| = \left| \frac{1 - j\omega - \omega^2}{1 + j\omega - \omega^2} \right| = \frac{\sqrt{(1 - \omega^2)^2 + \omega^2}}{\sqrt{(1 - \omega^2)^2 + \omega^2}} = 1 \qquad (10.30)$$

which is $2nd$-order all-pass.

For the difference connection, the $(1 + s + s^2)$ factors cancel. For $s = j\omega$, the magnitude of the difference is

$$|T_{LP}(j\omega) - T_{HP}(j\omega)| = \left| \frac{1 - j\omega}{1 + j\omega} \right| = \frac{\sqrt{1 + \omega^2}}{\sqrt{1 + \omega^2}} = 1 \qquad (10.31)$$

which is $1st$-order all-pass.

At the crossover frequency, i.e. for $\omega = 1$, $T_{LP}(j1) = 1/\sqrt{2}\angle-135°$ and $T_{HP}(j1) = 1/\sqrt{2}\angle+135°$. The angle between the phasors is $90°$. If crossover occurs near the resonance frequency of the high-frequency driver, its phase lead causes the phase difference to be less than $90°$ for the sum connection and greater than $90°$ for the difference connection. To prevent phase cancellation, this angle should be no greater than $90°$ so that the sum connection is the proper one.

Fourth Order

For $n = 4$, we have

$$T_{LP}(s) = \frac{1}{\left(1 + \sqrt{2}s + s^2\right)^2} \qquad T_{HP}(s) = \frac{s^4}{\left(1 + \sqrt{2}s + s^2\right)^2} \qquad (10.32)$$

The sum is

$$T_{LP}(s) + T_{HP}(s) = \frac{1 + s^4}{\left(1 + \sqrt{2}s + s^2\right)^2} = \frac{\left(1 + \sqrt{2}s + s^2\right)\left(1 - \sqrt{2}s + s^2\right)}{\left(1 + \sqrt{2}s + s^2\right)^2} \qquad (10.33)$$

The $\left(1 + \sqrt{2}s + s^2\right)$ factors cancel yielding

$$T_{LP}(s) + T_{HP}(s) = \frac{1 - \sqrt{2}s + s^2}{1 + \sqrt{2}s + s^2} \qquad (10.34)$$

For $s = j\omega$, the magnitude of the sum is

$$|T_{LP}(j\omega) + T_{HP}(j\omega)| = \left| \frac{1 - j\sqrt{2}\omega - \omega^2}{1 + j\sqrt{2}\omega - \omega^2} \right| = \frac{\sqrt{(1 - \omega^2)^2 + 2\omega^2}}{\sqrt{(1 - \omega^2)^2 + 2\omega^2}} = 1 \qquad (10.35)$$

Thus the sum connection is $2nd$-order all-pass.

The difference is

$$T_{LP}(s) - T_{HP}(s) = \frac{1 - s^4}{\left(1 + \sqrt{2}s + s^2\right)^2} = \frac{\left(1 - s^2\right)\left(1 + s^2\right)}{\left(1 + \sqrt{2}s + s^2\right)^2} \qquad (10.36)$$

For $s = j1$, i.e. $\omega = 1$, it follows that $T_{LP}(j1) - T_{HP}(j1) = 0$. Thus the difference connection is not all-pass.

At the crossover frequency, i.e. for $\omega = 1$, $T_{LP}(j1) = 0.5\angle-180°$ and $T_{HP}(j1) = 0.5\angle+180°$. The angle between the phasors is $0°$ so that $T_{LP}(j1) + T_{HP}(j1) = 1$. For the difference connection, the angle between the phasors is $180°$ and $T_{LP}(p) - T_{HP}(p) = 0$. If crossover occurs near the resonance frequency of the high-frequency driver, its phase lead causes the phase difference to be between $0°$ and $90°$ for the sum connection and between $90°$ and $180°$ for the difference connection. To prevent phase cancellation, this angle should be no greater than $90°$ so that the sum connection is preferred.

A Three-Way Network

For an example that might be applied to 3-way systems, consider the transfer function

$$T\left(s\right) = \frac{1}{1 + s/Q + s^2} \pm \frac{s/Q}{1 + s/Q + s^2} + \frac{s^2}{1 + s/Q + s^2} = \frac{1 \pm s/Q + s^2}{1 + s/Q + s^2} \tag{10.37}$$

$T\left(s\right)$ consists of three functions: low-pass, band-pass, and high-pass. These might be the crossover network functions for the woofer, the midrange, and the tweeter, respectively, in a 3-way system. If the $+$ sign is used, $T\left(s\right)$ is a constant voltage function. If the $-$ sign is used, the numerator of $T\left(j\omega\right)$ is the conjugate of the denominator and $\left|T\left(j\omega\right)\right| = 1$. In this case, $T\left(s\right)$ is an all-pass function. The $-$ sign can be achieved in a design by reversing the terminals of the midrange connection to the crossover network. For $s = j\omega/\omega_0$, the $-3\,\mathrm{dB}$ crossover frequency ω_1 between the woofer and midrange and the $-3\,\mathrm{dB}$ crossover frequency ω_2 between the midrange and the tweeter are related to Q and ω_0 by $\omega_2 - \omega_1 = \omega_0/Q$ and $\omega_1\omega_2 = \omega_0^2$. The effects of driver phase shifts are not so obvious with this crossover. Computer simulation or experimental measurements can be used to determine the polarities of the driver connections which result in the best frequency response.

10.7   Active Crossover Networks

If a separate power amplifier is used for each driver in a system, the crossover networks can precede the power amplifiers. In this case, active operational amplifier filters can be used for the networks. A system which uses two amplifiers, one to drive the woofer and the other to drive both the midrange and the tweeter, is called a bi-amplified system. In bi-amplified systems, passive crossover networks are used to cross the midrange over to the tweeter while active networks are used to cross the woofer over to the combination midrange and tweeter. A system which uses three amplifiers, one each for the woofer, the midrange, and the tweeter, is called a tri-amplified system. In this case, active crossover networks are used for all three drivers.

One of the most common filter topologies used in active crossover networks is the non-inverting Sallen-Key filter. Compared to the inverting topologies, these networks are preferable because the op amps exhibit a greater bandwidth. For example, when operated at unity gain, the non-inverting op amp has twice the bandwidth of the inverting op amp. The networks described in this section are unity-gain Sallen-Key low-pass and high-pass filters. Band-pass filters can be realized by cascading a high-pass filter with a low-pass filter.

Second Order

Fig. 10.15(a) shows the diagram of a $2nd$-order Sallen-Key low-pass filter with unity voltage gain in its passband. This filter has the transfer function

$$\frac{V_{o\ell}}{V_i} = \frac{1}{\left(s/\omega_\ell\right)^2 + \left(1/Q_\ell\right)\left(s/\omega_\ell\right) + 1} \tag{10.38}$$

where ω_ℓ is the radian resonance frequency and Q_ℓ is the quality factor. Let $f_\ell = \omega_\ell/2\pi$, Q_ℓ, $C_{1\ell}$ and $C_{2\ell}$ be specified. The values of $R_{1\ell}$ and $R_{2\ell}$ are given by

$$R_{1\ell}, R_{2\ell} = \frac{1}{4\pi f_\ell Q_\ell C_{2\ell}} \left[1 \pm \sqrt{1 - 4Q_\ell^2 \frac{C_{2\ell}}{C_{1\ell}}}\right] \tag{10.39}$$

where the $+$ sign is used for $R_{1\ell}$ and the $-$ sign is used for $R_{2\ell}$, or vice versa. That is, the values of $R_{1\ell}$ and $R_{2\ell}$ are interchangeable. The filter is often designed with $R_{1\ell} = R_{2\ell}$. In this case, $C_{1\ell} = 4Q_\ell^2 C_{2\ell}$.

Fig. 10.15(b) shows the circuit diagram of a $2nd$-order Sallen-Key high-pass filter with unity voltage gain in its passband. This filter has the transfer function

$$\frac{V_{oh}}{V_i} = \frac{\left(s/\omega_h\right)^2}{\left(s/\omega_h\right)^2 + \left(1/Q_h\right)\left(s/\omega_h\right) + 1} \tag{10.40}$$

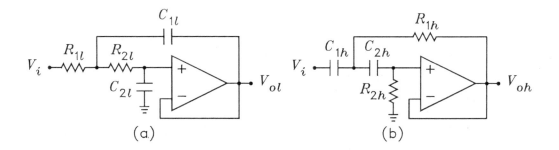

Figure 10.15: Second-order Sallen-Key (a) low-pass and (b) high-pass filters.

where ω_h is the radian resonance frequency and Q_h is the quality factor. Let $f_h = \omega_h/2\pi$, Q_h, C_{1h} and C_{2h} be specified. The values of R_{1h} and R_{2h} are given by

$$R_{1h} = \frac{1}{2\pi f_h \left(C_{1h} + C_{2h}\right) Q_h} \qquad R_{2h} = \frac{Q_h}{2\pi f_h} \left(\frac{1}{C_{1h}} + \frac{1}{C_{2h}}\right) \qquad (10.41)$$

Note that interchanging the values of C_{1h} and C_{2h} has no effect on the values of R_{1h} and R_{2h}. Thus the values of C_{1h} and C_{2h} are interchangeable.

The 2*nd*-order networks are usually designed with $f_\ell = f_h$ and $Q_\ell = Q_h = 0.5$. This makes the difference between the low-pass and the high-pass functions a 2*nd*-order all-pass transfer function. For $Q = 0.5$, the $-6\,\mathrm{dB}$ cutoff frequency of each filter is equal to its resonance frequency. At the resonance frequency, the output of the low-pass filter is lagging by $90°$ and the output of the high-pass filter is leading by $90°$. The phase difference between the outputs is $180°$ at all frequencies. To minimize phase cancellation at the crossover frequency, the voice coil of one of the drivers should be connected with its polarity reversed compared to the voice coil polarity of the other driver.

Third Order

Fig. 10.16 shows the diagrams of 3*rd*-order Sallen-Key low-pass and high-pass filters with unity gain in the passbands. These filters are usually designed to have Butterworth responses with equal $-3\,\mathrm{dB}$ cutoff frequencies. In this case, the sum of the high-pass and low-pass transfer functions is a 2*nd*-order all-pass function while the difference is a 1*st*-order all-pass function. At the $-3\,\mathrm{dB}$ cutoff frequency, the output of the low-pass filter is lagging by $135°$ and the output of the high-pass filter is leading by $135°$. The phase difference between the two filter outputs is $90°$ at all frequencies. To minimize phase cancellation at the crossover frequency, the voice coils of the two drivers should usually be connected with the same polarity. Let f_ℓ and f_h, respectively, be the $-3\,\mathrm{dB}$ cutoff frequencies for the low-pass and the high-pass filters. Let values for R_ℓ and C_h be specified. The design equations for the other capacitors and resistors are

$$C_{1\ell} = \frac{0.20245}{2\pi f_\ell R_\ell} \qquad C_{2\ell} = \frac{3.5465}{2\pi f_\ell R_\ell} \qquad C_{3\ell} = \frac{1.3926}{2\pi f_\ell R_\ell} \qquad (10.42)$$

$$R_{1h} = \frac{4.93949}{2\pi f_h C_h} \qquad R_{2h} = \frac{0.28194}{2\pi f_h C_h} \qquad R_{3h} = \frac{0.71808}{2\pi f_h C_h} \qquad (10.43)$$

Fourth Order

Fig. 10.17 shows the diagrams of 4*th*-order Sallen-Key low-pass and high-pass filters with unity gain in the passbands. These filters are usually designed to have a response equal to the square of a 2*nd*-order Butterworth response, with the same resonance frequency for all four sections. At the resonance frequency, each section has a response that is down by $3\,\mathrm{dB}$. Thus the output of each filter is $-6\,\mathrm{dB}$ at that frequency.

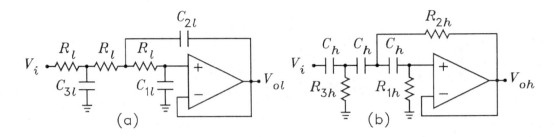

Figure 10.16: Third-order Sallen-Key (a) low-pass and (b) high-pass filters.

The output of the low-pass filter is lagging by $180°$ and the output of the high-pass filter is leading by $180°$. The two filter outputs are in phase at all frequencies. To minimize phase cancellation at the crossover frequency, the voice coils of the two drivers should be connected with the same polarity. Eq. (10.39) applies to the two sections of the low-pass filter and Eq. (10.41) applies to the two sections of the high-pass filter. The sections are normally designed with $f_\ell = f_h$ and $Q_\ell = Q_h = 1/\sqrt{2}$.

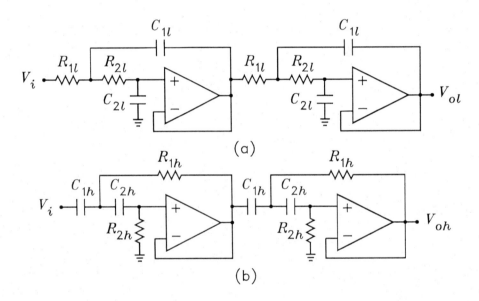

Figure 10.17: Fourth-order Sallen-Key (a) low-pass and (b) high-pass filters.

10.8   A SPICE Modeling Example

This section illustrates the application of SPICE modeling to the evaluation of crossover networks for a woofer and a midrange. The vented-box loudspeaker modeled in Section 8.13 is used as the woofer in the system. For the midrange, a closed-box driver is assumed. The system is illustrated in Fig. 10.18. To simplify the example, the mutual coupling between the midrange and the woofer and between the midrange and the port are neglected. It is assumed that the midrange has the same p_{sens}^{1V} as the woofer and has the following parameters: $R_E = 7\,\Omega$, lossless $L_E = 0.2\,\text{mH}$, diaphragm piston radius $a_m = 0.04\,\text{m}$, $f_C = 259\,\text{Hz}$, $Q_{EC} = 1.0$, $Q_{MC} = 4$, $Q_{TC} = 0.8$, $V_{AT} = 0.323$ liters, $\alpha = 3$, $Q_{MS} = 3$, and mass loading factor $B = 0.449$.

The midrange circuit elements are calculated as follows:

$$R_{A2M} = \frac{\rho_0 c}{\pi a_m^2} = 8.10 \times 10^4 \,\mathrm{N\,s/m^5}$$

$$R_{A1M} = \left(\frac{128}{9\pi^2} - 1\right) R_{A2M} = 3.57 \times 10^4 \,\mathrm{N\,s/m^5}$$

$$M_{A1M} = \frac{8\rho_0}{3\pi^2 a_m} = 7.97 \,\mathrm{kg/m^4} \qquad C_{A1M} = \frac{5.94 a_m^3}{\rho_0 c^2} = 2.71 \times 10^{-9} \,\mathrm{m^5/N}$$

$$C_{AB} = \frac{(1+\alpha)\,V_{AT}}{\alpha \rho_0 c^2} = 3.07 \times 10^{-9} \,\mathrm{m^5/N} \qquad M_{AB} = \frac{B\rho_0}{\pi a_m} = 4.22 \,\mathrm{kg/m^4}$$

$$R_{MS} = \frac{\pi a_m^4 \rho_0 c^2}{2 f_C Q_{MS} V_{AT} \sqrt{1+\alpha}} = 1.13 \,\mathrm{N\,s/m}$$

$$R_{AB} = R_{MS} \frac{\sqrt{1+\alpha}\, Q_{MS}/Q_{MC} - 1}{\pi^2 a_m^4} = 2.23 \times 10^4 \,\mathrm{N\,s/m^5}$$

$$M_{MD} = \left[\frac{\rho_0 c^2}{(2\pi f_C)^2 V_{AT}} - M_{A1M} - M_{AB}\right] \pi^2 a_m^4 = 3.84 \times 10^{-3} \,\mathrm{kg}$$

$$C_{MS} = \frac{(1+\alpha)\,V_{AT}}{\pi^2 a_m^4 \rho_0 c^2} = 3.64 \times 10^{-4} \,\mathrm{m/N} \qquad B\ell = \pi a_m^2 c \sqrt{\frac{R_E \rho_0}{2\pi f_C V_{AT} Q_{EC}}} = 6.87 \,\mathrm{T\,m}$$

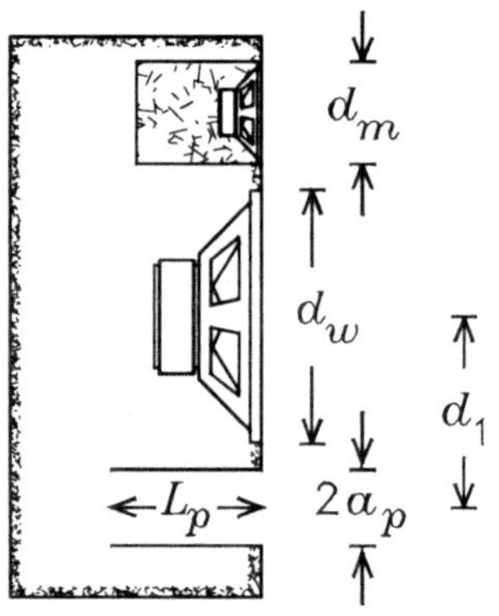

Figure 10.18: Vented-box woofer and closed-box midrange.

Figures 10.19 and 10.20 give the complete LTSpice circuit model of the woofer and midrange with the SPICE node numbers labeled. Fig. 10.19 shows a 2*nd*-order high-pass crossover network preceding the midrange voice coil. A 2*nd*-order low-pass crossover network is shown for the woofer. This network connects to the woofer system circuit given in Section 8.13. Two volume velocity summing networks are shown, one which adds the volume velocity outputs from the woofer system and the midrange and the other which subtracts the volume velocity outputs. These networks allow the simultaneous simulation of the system responses with the voice coils of the two drivers connected in electrical phase and out of electrical phase. If mutual coupling effects between the drivers are included, the simultaneous simulations would not be possible. In this case, the voice-coil connections for one driver would have to be reversed at the crossover network for the out-of-phase simulation.

The crossover frequency is chosen to be $f_{co} = 450\,\mathrm{Hz}$. This is approximately the frequency at which the wavelength is equal to the circumference of the woofer diaphragm. The crossover network elements are

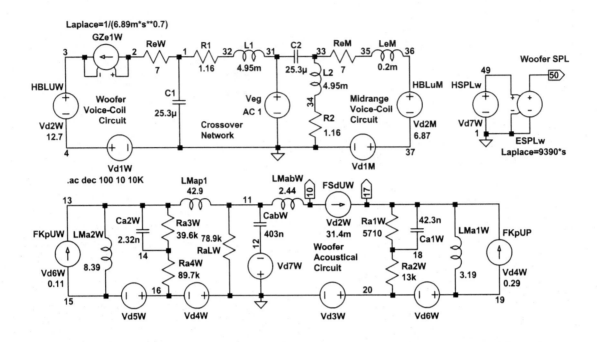

Figure 10.19: Part one of the SPICE circuit for the midrange and two crossover networks.

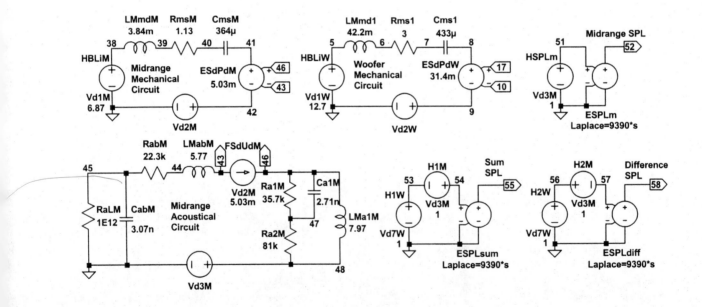

Figure 10.20: Part two of the SPICE circuit for the midrange and two crossover networks.

calculated for a quality factor $Q_{co} = 0.5$ under the assumption that each network has a resistive load equal to the voice-coil resistance R_E of the driver. From Eq. (10.6), the element values are given by

$$C_1 = C_2 = \frac{Q_{co}}{2\pi f_{co} R_E} = 25.3\,\mu\text{F} \qquad L_1 = L_2 = \frac{R_E}{2\pi f_{co} Q_{co}} = 4.95\,\text{mH}$$

Resistors R_1 and R_2, respectively, represent the dc resistances of L_1 and L_2. To calculate these, we assume that the resistance of the inductors varies as the square root of the inductance and that a 2.5 mH inductor has a dc resistance of $1\,\Omega$. This is a typical value for an air-core inductor wound with #18 gauge wire. Thus we have $R_1 = R_2 = 0.9 \times \sqrt{4.95/3} = 1.16\,\Omega$. The LTSpice netlist in Table 10.1 can be used to calculate the on-axis SPL of the system, where the omitted woofer netlist is the same as that given for the SPICE simulation in Section 8.13. Continuation lines are preceded by a + sign followed by a space.

Table 10.1: SPICE Netlist for the Simulation

CROSSOVER EXAMPLE	L2 33 34 4.95m	LMap1 13 11 42.9
Veg 31 0 0 AC 1	R2 34 0 1.16	Ra3W 13 14 39.6k
ReM 35 33 7	C2 31 33 25.3μ	Ra4W 14 16 89.7k
HBLuM 36 37 Vd2M 6.87	HBLUW 3 4 Vd2W 12.7	Ca2W 13 14 2.32n
Vd1M 37 0 0 AC 0	Vd1W 4 0 0 AC 0	LMa2W 13 15 8.39
LMmdM 38 39 3.84m	LMmd1 5 6 42.2m	Vd4W 0 16 0 AC 0
RmsM 39 40 1.13	Rms1 6 7 3	Vd5W 16 15 0 AC 0
CmsM 40 41 364μ	Cms1 7 8 433μ	Vd6W 19 20
HBLiM 38 0 Vd1M 6.87	HBLiW 5 0 Vd1W 12.7	Vd7W 0 12 0 AC 0
Vd2M 42 0 0 AC 0	Vd2W 9 0 0 AC 0	FKpUW 15 13 Vd6W 0.11
ESdPdM 41 42 46 43 5.03m	ESdPdW 8 9 17 10 31.4m	FKpUP 19 17 Vd4W 0.29
FSdUdM 43 46 Vd2M 5.03m	GZe1W 2 3 2 3	Esum 55 0 54 0
Ra1M 46 47 35.7k	+ Laplace=1/(6.89m*s**0.7)	+ Laplace=9390*s
Ra2M 47 48 81k	HSPLw 49 0 Vd7W 1	Ediff 58 0 57 0
Ca1M 46 47 2.71n	ESPLw 50 0 49 0	+ Laplace=9390*s
LMa1M 46 48 7.97	+ Laplace=9390*s	H1W 53 0 Vd7W 1
LMabM 44 43 5.77	FSdUW 10 17 Vd2W 31.4m	H2W 56 0 Vd7W 1
RabM 44 45 22.3k	Ra1W 17 18 5710	H1M 54 53 Vd3M 1
CabM 45 0 3.07n	Ra2W 18 20 13k	H2M 56 57 Vd3M 1
RaLM 45 0 1E12	Ca1W 17 18 42.3n	HSPLm 51 0 Vd3M 1
Vd3M 48 0 0 AC 0	LMa1W 17 19 3.19	ESPLm 52 0 51 0
L1 32 31 4.95m	LMabW 11 10 2.44	+ Laplace=9390*s
R1 1 32 1.16	Vd3W 20 0 0 AC 0	ReW 1 2 7
C1 1 0 25.3μ	CabW 11 12 403n	.ac dec 100 10 10K
LeM 35 36 0.2m	RaLW 11 0 78.9k	.end

At a distance $r = 1\,\text{m}$, the value of the on-axis acoustic pressure of the system is given by

$$p_{rms} = \rho_0 f \left(U_{0rms} + U_{Mrms} \right) \tag{10.44}$$

where U_{0rms} is the rms volume velocity emitted by the woofer system and U_{Mrms} is the rms volume velocity emitted by the midrange. Fig. 10.21 shows the calculated responses for the woofer plus crossover network, the midrange plus crossover network, the total system output with the drivers operating in phase, and the total system output with the drivers operating out of phase. The out of phase connection results in the flattest overall frequency response. However, many of the typical problems that are normally encountered in crossover system design are evident in the plot. The response could be improved by careful tweaking of the crossover network elements. A better response might be obtained with different order networks. Fig. 10.22 shows the response with the addition of the matching networks of Problem 12. Note the absence of the peak in the midrange response at its resonance frequency.

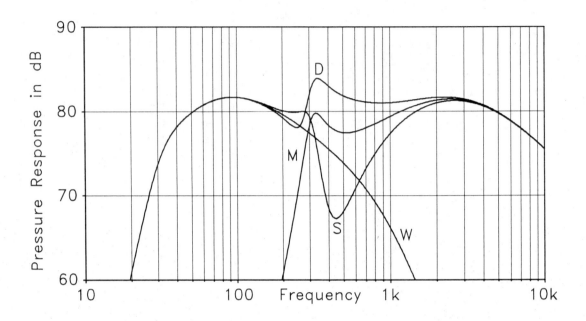

Figure 10.21: SPL responses in dB versus frequency. W – woofer. M – midrange. S – sum. D – difference.

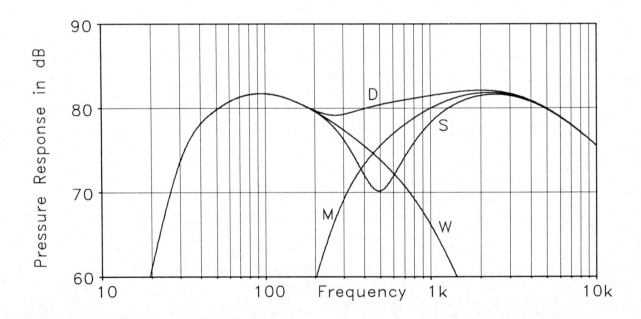

Figure 10.22: SPL responses in dB versus frequency with the matching networks of Problem 12. W – woofer. M – midrange. S – sum. D – difference.

10.9 Problems

1. *(a)* What value inductor is required with a $7.5\,\Omega$ woofer to obtain a $1st$-order crossover with a $-3\,\mathrm{dB}$ cutoff frequency of $400\,\mathrm{Hz}$? $[2.98\,\mathrm{mH}]$ *(b)* Calculate the lower and upper $-3\,\mathrm{dB}$ crossover frequencies of a midrange network consisting of a $25\,\mu\mathrm{F}$ capacitor in series with a $0.3\,\mathrm{mH}$ inductor. Assume a midrange voice-coil resistance of $7.5\,\Omega$. $[849\,\mathrm{Hz}$ and $3.98\,\mathrm{kHz}]$ *(c)* Design a $2nd$-order Butterworth high-pass crossover network for a $7.5\,\Omega$ tweeter. The $-3\,\mathrm{dB}$ crossover frequency is to be $4.5\,\mathrm{kHz}$. $[C = 3.33\,\mu\mathrm{F}$ and $L = 0.375\,\mathrm{mH}]$

2. If the woofer is to be connected in electrical phase to the crossover network of problem 1, specify the phase of the connections for the midrange and the tweeter. Neglect the woofer phase shift at the woofer-to-midrange crossover frequency and the midrange phase shift at the midrange-to-tweeter crossover frequency. [midrange out of phase and tweeter in phase]

3. A closed-box midrange has the parameters $f_C = 200\,\mathrm{Hz}$ and $Q_{TC} = 1.0$. It is desired to cross it over to a woofer at the frequency at which the phase of the midrange pressure transfer function is leading by $45\,^\circ$. The midrange crossover network is to have a slope of $12\,\mathrm{dB/octave}$ below this frequency. *(a)* If the midrange L_E is neglected, use the phase expression in Eq. 6.29 to calculate the crossover frequency. Neglect the contribution of the term involving ω_{u1}. $[324\,\mathrm{Hz}]$ *(b)* Specify the order and alignment of the lowest order network that can be used with the woofer if both drivers are to be connected in phase to the networks. What must be the alignment of the midrange network? Neglect the woofer phase shift at the crossover frequency. [$3rd$-order Butterworth network on woofer. Connect both drivers in phase to the networks. Design the midrange network for $Q = 1/\sqrt{2}$.] *(c)* Specify the components for the networks. Assume that $R_E = 8\,\Omega$ for both drivers. [Woofer: $L_1 = 5.9\,\mathrm{mH}$, $L_2 = 2.0\,\mathrm{mH}$, and $C = 82\,\mu\mathrm{F}$. Midrange: $L = 5.6\,\mathrm{mH}$ and $C = 43.5\,\mu\mathrm{F}$.]

4. It is desired to use the Sallen-Key active high-pass filter circuit of Fig. 10.15(b) as an infrasonic filter to block inaudible low-frequency signals from the input of a power amplifier which drives a public address loudspeaker system. The filter transfer function is given by Eq. (10.40). *(a)* Show that the lower $-3\,\mathrm{dB}$ or half-power cutoff frequency is given by

$$f_\ell = f_2 \left[\frac{1}{2Q_2^2} - 1 + \sqrt{\left(\frac{1}{2Q_2^2} - 1\right)^2 + 1} \right]^{1/2}$$

where $f_2 = \omega_2/2\pi$. *(b)* Let the two capacitors in the filter have a value of $0.1\,\mu\mathrm{F}$. Calculate the values of R_1 and R_2 which will give $f_\ell = 40\,\mathrm{Hz}$ and $Q_2 = 1/\sqrt{2}$. $[R_1 = 28.1\,\mathrm{k\Omega}, R_2 = 56.3\,\mathrm{k\Omega}]$ *(c)* Sketch the asymptotic and actual Bode magnitude plots using log-log scales and label the slopes.

5. A woofer voice coil has the values $R_E = 7\,\Omega$, and lossless $L_E = 0.8\,\mathrm{mH}$. It is desired to design a two-pole low-pass filter crossover network for the woofer which has one pole at $400\,\mathrm{Hz}$ and the other at $800\,\mathrm{Hz}$. *(a)* What value inductor must be added in series with the voice coil to obtain a pole frequency of $800\,\mathrm{Hz}$? $[0.59\,\mathrm{mH}]$ *(b)* A series RC network is to be added in parallel with the inductor plus the voice coil to cancel the total inductance. Calculate the value of R and C if the input resistance is to be $7\,\Omega$. $[7\,\Omega$ in series with $28\,\mu\mathrm{F}]$ *(c)* A second inductor is to be used in series with the combination driver, first inductor, and RC network, to set the pole at $400\,\mathrm{Hz}$. What is its value? $[2.8\,\mathrm{mH}]$

6. A midrange driver with the voice-coil resistance $R_E = 7\,\Omega$ has the reference efficiency $\eta_0 = 1.5\%$. It is to be used in a loudspeaker system with a woofer which has a reference efficiency of $\eta_0 = 0.8\%$ and a voice-coil resistance $R_E = 8\,\Omega$. Design a two resistor L-pad attenuator for the midrange which will cause it to have the same effective SPL_{sens}^{1V} as the woofer. The L-pad is to have an input resistance of $8\,\Omega$ with the midrange connected as its load. [a $2.54\,\Omega$ series resistor and a $24.9\,\Omega$ shunt resistor]

7. A tweeter which can be modeled as a closed-box driver mounted in an infinite baffle has a resonance frequency $f_C = 1.5\,\mathrm{kHz}$ and a total quality factor $Q_{TC} = 1.2$. *(a)* Write the expression for the transfer

function from voice-coil voltage to acoustic output pressure and solve for the expression for the phase of the transfer function as a function of frequency. Assume that the voice-coil inductance can be neglected. *(b)* Use the phase function to calculate the frequency at which the phase lead of the transfer function is $\varphi = +45\,°$. [2.25 kHz] *(c)* Calculate the magnitude of the transfer function at the frequency found in the previous part and plot a phasor diagram for the tweeter output at this frequency. [magnitude is 1.27 or +2.1 dB]

8. A woofer has a voice-coil resistance $R_E = 7\,\Omega$ and a lossless voice-coil inductance $L_E = 0.5\,\mathrm{mH}$. *(a)* What is the highest crossover frequency which can be obtained if a 3*rd*-order Butterworth low-pass filter is to be used with the woofer? (1.1 kHz) *(b)* Design the 3*rd*-order crossover network if the −3 dB crossover frequency is to be 500 Hz. [$L_1 = 3.3\,\mathrm{mH}$, $L_2 = 0.61\,\mathrm{mH}$, $C = 61\,\mu\mathrm{F}$] *(c)* Draw the phasor diagram for the woofer output at the crossover frequency. [lagging by 135 °]

9. Consider the 3*rd*-order transfer functions given in Eq. (10.28). *(a)* In a bi-amplified system, $T_{LP}(p)$ is to be used for the low-pass crossover network on the woofer. $T_{HP}(p)$ is to be factored into the product of the 2*nd*-order closed-box transfer function $G_C(p)$ of the tweeter multiplied by a 1*st*-order high-pass transfer function $T'_{HP}(p)$ that is to be used for the tweeter crossover network. For both the sum and difference polarities, what must be the tweeter quality factor Q_{TC}? [$Q_{TC} = 1$] What is the transfer function $T'_{HP}(p)$? [$p/(1+p)$] How would one determine the crossover frequency? [$\omega_0 = \omega_C$, where ω_C is the tweeter resonance frequency] Sketch the Bode plots of $T_{LP}(j\omega)$ and $T'_{HP}(j\omega)$ and label the break frequencies and slopes. *(b)* If the polarity of the combination of $T_{LP}(p)$ and $T_{HP}(p)$ is to be determined in such a way so as to minimize the total variation in the phase angle of the combination as a function of frequency, which polarity would be preferable, the sum or the difference? [the difference]

10. Repeat problem 9 for the 4*th*-order transfer functions given in Eq. (10.32). Show that the difference connection results in a null at $\omega = \omega_0$ so that the sum is preferred.

11. A closed-box midrange loudspeaker driver has the parameters $Q_{MC} = 4$, $Q_{EC} = 0.8$, $f_C = 250\,\mathrm{Hz}$, $R_E = 7\,\Omega$, $L_e = 0.023$, and $n = 0.62$. Design an impedance matching network to be placed in parallel with the voice coil of the driver so that it will present a resistive load to the crossover network. For the lossy voice-coil inductance compensation, assume $f_1 = 655\,\mathrm{Hz}$ and $f_2 = 20\,\mathrm{kHz}$. [$R_1 = 7\,\Omega$, $C_1 = 6.95\,\mu\mathrm{F}$, $R_2 = 7.69\,\Omega$, $C_2 = 8.54\,\mu\mathrm{F}$, $R_3 = 8.4\,\Omega$, $L_1 = 3.57\,\mathrm{mH}$, $C_3 = 114\,\mu\mathrm{F}$]

12. Design an impedance matching network for the midrange in the SPICE example of Section 10.8. Because L_E is lossless, $n = 1$ in Eqs. (10.15) and (10.16). [$R_1 = 7\,\Omega$, $C_1 = 4.08\,\mu\mathrm{F}$, $R_3 = 8.75\,\Omega$, $L_1 = 4.30\,\mathrm{mH}$, $C_3 = 87.7\,\mu\mathrm{F}$]

13. *(a)* By factoring the polynomial $(s^5 - 1)$, show that the denominator $D_5(s)$ for a 5*th*-order all-pass crossover network is given by

$$D_5(s) = (1+s)\left(1 + a_1 s + s^2\right)\left(1 + a_2 s + s^2\right)$$

where $a_1 = \left(\sqrt{5}+1\right)/2$ and $a_2 = \left(\sqrt{5}-1\right)/2$. *(b)* Let $T_{LP}(s) = 1/D_5(s)$ and $T_{HP}(s) = s^5/D_5(s)$. Show that the sum is a 2*nd*-order all-pass function and the difference is a 3*rd*-order all-pass function given by

$$T_{LP}(s) + T_{HP}(s) = \frac{1 - a_1 s + s^2}{1 + a_1 s + s^2} \qquad T_{LP}(s) - T_{HP}(s) = \frac{(1-s)\left(1 - a_2 s + s^2\right)}{(1+p)\left(1 + a_2 s + s^2\right)}$$

14. In the crossover networks of Figs. 10.1 and 10.3, let $R_{Ew} = R_{Em} = R_{Et} = R_E$. Show that the series connected networks are the duals of the parallel connected networks with all element values scaled by the factor R_E^2. Note that the dual of a resistor R_E scaled by a factor R_E^2 is a resistor of value R_E, the dual of a capacitor C scaled by a factor R_E^2 is an inductor of value $R_E^2 C$, and the dual of an inductor L scaled by a factor R_E^2 is a capacitor of value L/R_E^2.

Chapter 11

A Loudspeaker Potpourri

11.1 The Isobaric Connection

Fig. 11.1(a) shows two identical loudspeaker drivers connected together on a common baffle in what is called an isobaric connection. Such a connection is often used in compact loudspeaker systems where it is desired to make the internal volume of the system enclosure as small as possible. The electrical polarity of the voice coils must be chosen so that both diaphragms move in the same direction. If both move with the same velocity, no net force is exerted to compress or expand the air trapped between the diaphragms. In this case, the region between the diaphragms is a constant pressure or isobaric region.

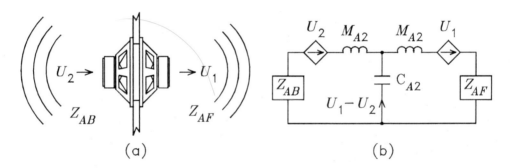

Figure 11.1: (a) Isobaric connection. (b) Acoustical analogous circuit.

The two drivers can be connected so that the voice coils are either in series or in parallel. Compared to a single driver, the series connection has an impedance that is doubled. The parallel connection has an impedance that is halved. In the following, we assume that the drivers are connected in parallel so that voice-coil voltage of each driver is equal to the amplifier output voltage e_g.

11.1.1 The Acoustical Analogous Circuit

Fig. 11.1(b) shows the acoustical analogous circuit for the drivers. The masses labeled M_{A2} and the compliance C_{A2} model the air cavity between the diaphragms. These elements are given by

$$M_{A2} = \frac{\rho_0 V_2}{2S_D^2} \qquad C_{A2} = \frac{V_2}{\rho_0 c^2} \tag{11.1}$$

where V_2 is the volume of air trapped between the diaphragms and S_D is the diaphragm piston area. Note that M_{A2} is simply one-half the acoustic mass of the volume of air trapped between the diaphragms.

Let the two drivers be mounted in an infinite baffle. In this case, the low-frequency circuit for Z_{AF} and Z_{AB} is an acoustic mass $M_{A1} = 8\rho_0/3\pi^2 a$, where a is the piston radius of the drivers. The low-frequency analogous circuit is shown in Fig. 11.2(a). Each mass labeled M'_{AS} is given by

$$M'_{AS} = M_{AD} + M_{A1} + M_{A2} \tag{11.2}$$

It follows by symmetry from the figure that $U_2 = U_1$ so that the volume velocity through the acoustic compliance C_{A2} is zero. Thus C_{A2} can be replaced by an open circuit.

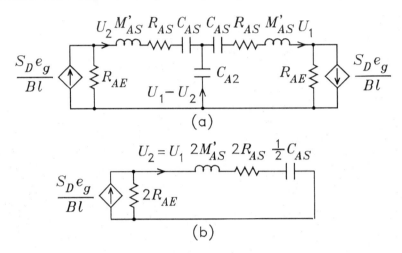

Figure 11.2: (a) Circuit with the low-frequency approximation to the air load impedances. (b) Final circuit.

11.1.2   The Small-Signal Parameters

If the current through C_{A2} is neglected, the circuit in Fig. 11.2(a) can be reduced to the one shown in Fig. 11.2(b). Except for the labels on the elements, it is identical to the circuit for a single driver given in Chapter 6. It follows that the two drivers can be modeled as a single driver. By analogy to the equations in Chapter 6, the resonance frequency, quality factors, and volume compliance are given by

$$\omega_S = \frac{1}{\sqrt{2M'_{AS}C_{AS}/2}} = \frac{1}{\sqrt{M'_{AS}C_{AS}}} \qquad Q_{MS} = \frac{1}{2R_{AS}}\sqrt{\frac{2M'_{AS}}{C_{AS}/2}} = \frac{1}{R_{AS}}\sqrt{\frac{M'_{AS}}{C_{AS}}} \tag{11.3}$$

$$Q_{ES} = \frac{1}{2R_{AE}}\sqrt{\frac{2M'_{AS}}{C_{AS}/2}} = \frac{1}{R_{AE}}\sqrt{\frac{M'_{AS}}{C_{AS}}} \qquad V_{AS} = \frac{\rho_0 c^2 C_{AS}}{2} \tag{11.4}$$

If we assume that $M'_{AS} \simeq M_{AS}$, the isobaric small-signal parameters are the same as of a single driver with the exception that V_{AS} which is halved.

When the drivers are mounted in an enclosure, $Z_{AF} \neq Z_{AB}$. In this case, the volume velocity through C_{A2} in Fig. 11.2(a) is not zero. This makes $U_1 \neq U_2$, which alters the system response. In particular, C_{A2} might result in a resonance which can cause peaks or dips in the midband system response. To minimize this, the volume of air trapped between the two drivers should be as small as possible and the crossover frequency should be as low as possible.

11.1.3   SPICE Simulation Example

Let the system of Section 7.10 be converted into an isobaric connection. The single driver system requires an internal box volume of $2\,\text{ft}^3$. The isobaric system requires two drivers with an internal box volume of $1\,\text{ft}^2$.

The LTSpice analogous circuit for the acoustical part of the system is given in Fig. 11.3. The electrical and mechanical circuits for each driver are identical to the ones given in Fig. 7.4. The LTSpice netlist for the acoustical part is given in Table 11.1, where the subscripts for the added driver end with the letter **a**. The netlist for the electrical and mechanical circuits is identical to that given in Table 7.3 with the exception that there must be separate circuits for each driver. For example, the subscripts for the added driver might end with the letter **a**. The elements M_{A2} and C_{A2} in Fig. 11.1 were estimated from measurements on a typical 15-inch driver. R_{AL2} prevents node 21 from being a floating node and is calculated so that $1/(2\pi R_{AL2}C_{A2}) < 2\,\mathrm{Hz}$.

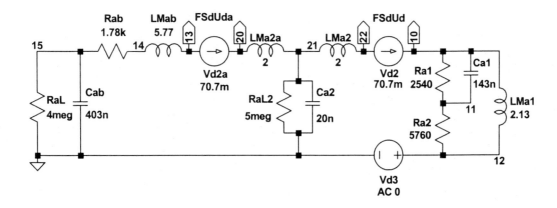

Figure 11.3: LTSpice acoustical circuit for the isobaric simulation.

Table 11.1: SPICE Netlist for the Acoustical Circuit

*ACOUSTICAL CIRCUIT	LMab 14 13 5.77	FSdUda 13 20 Vd2a 70.7m
FSdUd 22 10 Vd2 70.7m	Rab 14 15 1.78k	Ca2 21 0 20n
Ra1 10 11 2540	Cab 15 0 403n	RaL2 21 0 5meg
Ra2 11 12 5760	RaL 15 0 4meg	LMa2a 20 21 2
Ca1 10 11 143n	Vd3 12 0 0 AC 0	.END
LMa1 10 12 2.13	LMa2 21 22 2	

The calculated on-axis SPL responses with $e_g = 1\,\mathrm{V}$ rms are shown in Fig. 11.4 for the parallel and series voice-coil connections. The responses are displayed by displaying the voltage at node 17 in the circuit of Fig. 7.4. With the exception of the dips just below 300 Hz and the 6 dB difference between the two, the responses are essentially identical to that in Fig. 7.5. The dips are caused by a resonance in the air cavity between the two diaphragms. It is more pronounced for the series connection because of non-equal division of the amplifier voltage across the two voice coils.

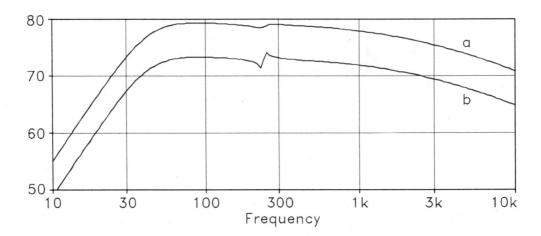

Figure 11.4: SPL responses in dB versus frequency. a – parallel connection. b – series connection.

11.2   4th-Order Bandpass Systems

11.2.1   System Description

Fig. 11.5(a) shows a hybrid closed-box vented-box system which has an on-axis pressure transfer function that is the form of a 4th-order band-pass filter. The driver is mounted on an internal wall that separates the enclosure into two parts. The air cavity behind the driver is a closed-box. The air cavity in front of the driver is a vented-box. Only the vent in the front air cavity radiates into the external air load. Fig. 11.5(b) - (d) shows the low-frequency analogous circuits for the system. The elements M_{AB1}, R_{AB1}, and C_{AB1} model the closed-box air load on the back of the diaphragm. The elements M_{AB2}, C_{AB2}, R_{AL2}, and M_{AP2} model the vented-box air load on the front of the diaphragm. These models are developed in Chapters 7 and 8.

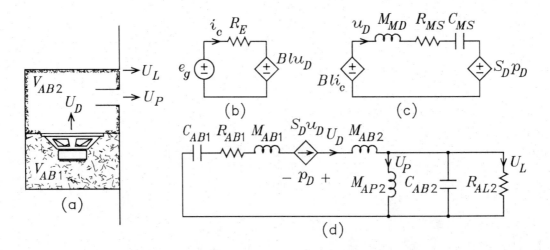

Figure 11.5: (a) System geometry. Analogous circuits: (b) Electrical, (c) Mechanical, and (d) Acousitcal.

The combination acoustical analogous circuit for the system can be obtained by reflecting the electrical and mechanical circuits into the acoustical circuit. It is given in Fig. 11.6. The elements in this circuit are given by

$$R_{AE} = \frac{(B\ell)^2}{S_D^2 R_E} \qquad M_{AC} = M_{AD} + M_{AB1} + M_{AB2} \qquad R_{AC} = R_{AS} + R_{AB1} \qquad (11.5)$$

$$C_{AT} = \frac{C_{AS}C_{AB1}}{C_{AS} + C_{AB1}} = \frac{C_{AS}}{1 + \alpha_1} \qquad \alpha_1 = \frac{C_{AS}}{C_{AB1}} = \frac{V_{AS}}{V_{AB1}} \qquad (11.6)$$

where α_1 is the compliance ratio.

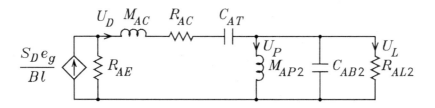

Figure 11.6: Combination acoustical circuit.

11.2.2 Output Volume Velocity

The total output volume velocity is $U_P + U_L$ in Fig. 11.6, where U_P is the volume velocity in the vent and U_L is the air leak volume velocity. We assume that $U_L \ll U_P$ so that the output volume velocity can be approximated by U_P. To solve for this, we define

$$R_{ATC} = R_{AE} + R_{AC} = R_{AE} + R_{AS} + R_{AB1} \qquad (11.7)$$

$$Z_{A1} = M_{AC}s + R_{ATC} + \frac{1}{C_{AT}s} = \frac{(s/\omega_C)^2 + (1/Q_{TC})(s/\omega_C) + 1}{C_{AT}s} \qquad (11.8)$$

$$Y_{A2} = C_{AB2}s + \frac{1}{R_{AL2}} + \frac{1}{M_{AP2}s} = \frac{(s/\omega_B)^2 + (1/Q_L)(s/\omega_B) + 1}{M_{AP2}s} \qquad (11.9)$$

where ω_C and Q_{TC}, respectively, are the resonance frequency and total quality factor for the closed-box part of the system and ω_B and Q_L, respectively, are the Helmholtz frequency and quality factor for the vented-box part. These are given by

$$\omega_C = 2\pi f_C = \frac{1}{\sqrt{M_{AC}C_{AT}}} = \frac{\sqrt{1 + \alpha_1}}{\sqrt{M_{AC}C_{AS}}} \qquad (11.10)$$

$$Q_{TC} = \frac{1}{R_{ATC}}\sqrt{\frac{M_{AC}}{C_{AT}}} = \frac{1}{R_{ATC}}\sqrt{1 + \alpha_1}\sqrt{\frac{M_{AC}}{C_{AS}}} \qquad (11.11)$$

$$\omega_B = 2\pi f_B = \frac{1}{\sqrt{M_{AP2}C_{AB2}}} \qquad Q_L = R_{AL2}\sqrt{\frac{C_{AB2}}{M_{AP2}}} = \omega_B R_{AL2} C_{AB2} \qquad (11.12)$$

With reference to Fig. 11.6, U_P can be written

$$
\begin{aligned}
U_P &= \frac{S_D e_g}{B\ell} \frac{R_{AE}}{Z_{A1} + 1/Y_{A2}} \frac{1}{Y_{A2}M_{AP}s} \\
&= \frac{B\ell e_g}{S_D R_E M_{AC}} \frac{s/\omega_C^2}{(s/\omega_0)^4 + a_3(s/\omega_0)^3 + a_2(s/\omega_0)^2 + a_1(s/\omega_0) + 1} \qquad (11.13)
\end{aligned}
$$

where the frequency ω_0 and the coefficients a_3, a_2, and a_1 are given by

$$\omega_0 = \sqrt{\omega_C \omega_B} = \omega_C \sqrt{h} \qquad a_3 = \frac{1}{Q_{TC}\sqrt{h}} + \frac{\sqrt{h}}{Q_L} \tag{11.14}$$

$$a_2 = \frac{1 + \alpha_2/\left(1 + \alpha_1\right)}{h} + h + \frac{1}{Q_L Q_{TC}} \qquad a_1 = \frac{1}{Q_L \sqrt{h}} + \frac{\sqrt{h}}{Q_{TC}} \tag{11.15}$$

In these equations, α_2 is the compliance ratio for the vented-box part of the system and h is the vented-box tuning ratio given by

$$\alpha_2 = \frac{C_{AS}}{C_{AB2}} = \frac{V_{AS}}{V_{AB2}} \qquad h = \frac{\omega_B}{\omega_C} = \frac{f_B}{f_C} \tag{11.16}$$

11.2.3   On-Axis Pressure

The on-axis pressure transfer function is obtained by multiplying the volume velocity transfer function by $\rho_0 s / 2\pi$. It is given by

$$p = \frac{\rho_0}{2\pi} \frac{B\ell e_g}{S_D R_E M_{AC}} G_{BP4}\left(s\right) \tag{11.17}$$

where $G_{BP4}\left(s\right)$ is the transfer function

$$G_{BP4}\left(s\right) = \left(\frac{\omega_0}{\omega_C}\right)^2 \frac{\left(s/\omega_0\right)^2}{\left(s/\omega_0\right)^4 + a_3\left(s/\omega_0\right)^3 + a_2\left(s/\omega_0\right)^2 + a_1\left(s/\omega_0\right) + 1} \tag{11.18}$$

This is a fourth-order band-pass transfer function. The slope of the Bode magnitude plot is $+2$ dec/dec at low frequencies and -2 dec/dec at high frequencies.

11.2.4   Fourth-Order Band-Pass Functions

A general $4th$-order bandpass transfer function is obtained by making a frequency transformation on a second-order low-pass transfer function. The low-pass transfer function and the frequency transformation are given by

$$T\left(s\right) = \frac{K}{\left(s/\omega_1\right)^2 + \left(1/Q_1\right)\left(s/\omega_1\right) + 1} \qquad \frac{s}{\omega_1} \rightarrow B\left(\frac{s}{\omega_1} + \frac{\omega_1}{s}\right) \tag{11.19}$$

where K is a constant and the symbol "$\rightarrow$" is read "is replaced by." The quality factor Q_1 sets the alignment of the band-pass filter. For example, it is Butterworth for $Q_1 = 1/\sqrt{2}$, Chebyshev for $Q_1 > 1/\sqrt{2}$, critically damped for $Q_1 = 0.5$, and overdamped for $Q_1 < 0.5$. The parameter B sets the bandwidth of the filter.

When the frequency transformation is made in Eq. (11.19), it follows that the bandpass transfer function is given by

$$T\left(s\right) = \frac{K}{B^2} \frac{\left(s/\omega_1\right)^2}{\left(s/\omega_1\right)^4 + b_3\left(s/\omega_1\right)^3 + b_2\left(s/\omega_1\right)^2 + b_1\left(s/\omega_1\right) + 1} \tag{11.20}$$

where the coefficients b_1, b_2, and b_3 are given by

$$b_1 = b_3 = \frac{1}{Q_1 B} \qquad b_2 = 2 + \frac{1}{B^2} \tag{11.21}$$

The half-power or -3 dB bandwidth for the band-pass function is given by

$$BW = \frac{f_0}{B}\left\{1 - \frac{1}{2Q_1^2} + \left[\left(1 - \frac{1}{2Q_1^2}\right)^2 + 1\right]^{1/2}\right\}^{1/2} \tag{11.22}$$

For $Q_1 > 1/\sqrt{2}$, the dB ripple in the Bode magnitude plot is given by

$$\text{dB ripple} = 20\log\left(\frac{Q_1^2}{\sqrt{Q_1^2 - 0.25}}\right) \tag{11.23}$$

11.2.5 System Parameters

When Eqs. (11.18) and (11.20) are equated, it follows that $\omega_0 = \omega_1$, $a_1 = b_1$, $a_2 = b_2$, and $a_3 = b_3$. For these conditions to be satisfied, it is straightforward to show that h, α_2, and Q_{TC} must be given by

$$h = 1 \qquad \alpha_2 = (1 + \alpha_1)\left[\frac{1}{B^2} + \frac{1}{Q_L^2} - \frac{1}{Q_1 B Q_L}\right] \qquad Q_{TC} = \left[\frac{1}{Q_1 B} - \frac{1}{Q_L}\right]^{-1} \tag{11.24}$$

Because $h = 1$, it follows that $\omega_C = \omega_B = \omega_0$.

For $s = j\omega_0$, it is straightforward to show that G_{BP4} has the value

$$G_{BP4}(j\omega_0) = \left[\frac{\alpha_2}{1 + \alpha_1} + \frac{1}{Q_L Q_{TC}}\right]^{-1} = B^2 \tag{11.25}$$

The on-axis pressure sensitivity into 2π steradians at $r = 1$ meter for $e_g = 1\,\mathrm{V}$ rms is given by

$$p_{\mathrm{sens}}^{1V} = \frac{\rho_0}{2\pi} \frac{B\ell}{S_D R_E M_{AC}} G_{BP4}(j\omega_0) = \frac{\sqrt{2\pi\rho_0}}{c} f_S^{3/2} \left[\frac{V_{AS}}{R_E Q_{ES}}\right]^{1/2} B^2 \tag{11.26}$$

This equation shows that the pressure sensitivity is that of the driver in an infinite baffle that is derived in Chapter 6 multiplied by the factor B^2. Because the bandwidth is inversely proportional to B, it follows that the on-axis pressure decreases rapidly as the bandwidth is increased, decreasing by 12 dB each time the bandwidth is doubled.

In the design of a band-pass system, the closed-box part should be filled with a filling such as fiberglass to minimize the effect of standing waves inside the box. The filling also has the advantage of increasing the acoustic volume of the box as is discussed in Chapter 7. The vented-box part should be lined with fiberglass. A typical thickness is one inch. The lining should not cover the driver diaphragm or the vent opening. To minimize vent noise, the area of the vent should be as large as possible.

11.2.6 Design with a Given Driver

Let a driver have the parameters f_S, Q_{ES}, and V_{AS}. A possible design procedure is described as follows:

1. Specify the lower cutoff frequency f_1 and the upper cutoff frequency f_2. Use the rule of thumb described in Chapter 7 to assume a value for the closed-box mechanical quality factor Q_{MC}. Use the rule of thumb described in Chapter 8 to assume a value for the vented-box quality factor Q_L.

2. Calculate the center frequency f_0, the closed-box compliance ratio α_1, the closed-box electrical quality factor Q_{EC}, and the closed-box total quality factor Q_{TC} from the equations

$$f_0 = \sqrt{f_1 f_2} \qquad \alpha_1 = \left(\frac{f_0}{f_S}\right)^2 - 1 \qquad Q_{EC} = Q_{ES}\sqrt{1 + \alpha_1} \qquad Q_{TC} = \frac{Q_{EC} Q_{MC}}{Q_{EC} + Q_{MC}} \tag{11.27}$$

3. Calculate A, Q_1, and B from the equations

$$A = \frac{f_2 - f_1}{f_0} \times \frac{Q_L Q_{TC}}{Q_L + Q_{TC}} \qquad Q_1 = \left[A\left(\sqrt{2A^2 + 1} - A\right)\right]^{1/2} \tag{11.28}$$

$$B = \frac{f_0}{f_2 - f_1}\left\{1 - \frac{1}{2Q_1^2} + \left[\left(1 - \frac{1}{2Q_1^2}\right)^2 + 1\right]^{1/2}\right\}^{1/2} \tag{11.29}$$

4. Calculate α_2 from Eq. (11.24). Calculate the acoustic volumes V_{AB1} and V_{AB2} of the two boxes and the vent length L_P as follows:

$$V_{AB1} = \frac{V_{AS}}{\alpha_1} \qquad V_{AB2} = \frac{V_{AS}}{\alpha_2} \qquad L_p = \left(\frac{c}{2\pi f_0}\right)^2 \frac{S_P}{V_{AB2}} - 1.463\sqrt{\frac{S_P}{\pi}} \qquad (11.30)$$

where S_P is the area of the vent.

Example 1 *A driver has the parameters $f_S = 30\,\mathrm{Hz}$, $Q_{ES} = 0.4$, and $V_{AS} = 4\,\mathrm{ft}^3$. It is desired to use the driver in a 4th-order bandpass system that has the cutoff frequencies $30\,\mathrm{Hz}$ and $150\,\mathrm{Hz}$. A 3-inch diameter vent pipe is to be used for the system. (a) Solve for the acoustic volume of the two boxes, the length of the vent, specify the alignment of the system, and the dB ripple if the system has a Chebyshev alignment. (b) Plot the normalized graph of the SPL response of the system versus frequency.*

Solution. (a) We assume $Q_{MC} = 3.5$ and $Q_L = 7$. From Eqs. (11.27) through (11.29) and Eq. (11.24), we have $f_0 = 67.08\,\mathrm{Hz}$, $\alpha_1 = 4$, $Q_{EC} = 0.8944$, $Q_{TC} = 0.7124$, $A = 1.157$, $Q_1 = 0.9379$, $B = 0.6894$. and $\alpha_2 = 9.518$. From Eq. (11.30), we have $V_{AB1} = 1\,\mathrm{ft}^3$, $V_{AB2} = 0.420\,\mathrm{ft}^3$, and $L_P = 8.03\,\mathrm{in}$. Because $Q_1 > 0.71$, the system has a Chebyshev alignment. From Eq. (11.23), the dB ripple $0.9\,\mathrm{dB}$. (b) The graph of the relative SPL response of the system is given in Fig. 11.7. The SPL at $f = f_0$ is normalized to $0\,\mathrm{dB}$.

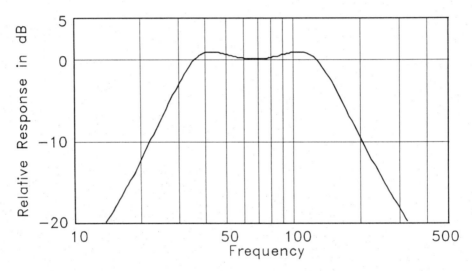

Figure 11.7: Calculated system response.

11.3 6th-Order Bandpass Systems

11.3.1 System Transfer Function

A 6th-order band-pass system consists of a loudspeaker driver mounted in a wall that separates two vented-box enclosures. Another name for such a system is a dual-Helmholtz system. Fig. 11.8(a) illustrates the geometry. The low-frequency Norton form of the combination acoustical analogous circuit is shown in Fig. 11.8(b). The circuit is simplified in that box and vent losses are neglected. This makes it possible to express the transfer function in the form of a 6th-order quasi-band-pass filter. The transfer function is not a true band-pass function because it does not have symmetrical slopes.

The circuit in Fig. 11.8(b) is obtained by taking the Norton form of the low-frequency combination acoustical analogous circuit for a driver and connecting it between the acoustical analogous circuits for two

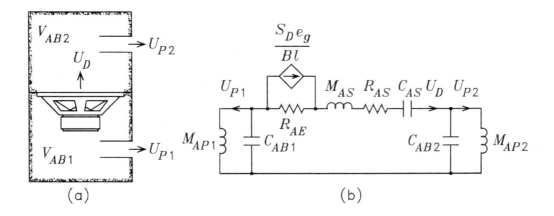

Figure 11.8: (a) System geometry. (b) Combination acoustical analogous circuit.

vented boxes. The elements in the driver circuit are defined in Chapter 6. The mass M_{AS} here represents the sum of the acoustical masses of the diaphragm and the front and rear air load masses. The elements in the circuits for the two vented boxes are defined in Chapter 8.

The system output volume velocity is given by $U_{P1} + U_{P2}$. The the low-frequency on-axis pressure transfer function at $r = 1$ m can be written

$$p = \frac{\rho_0}{2\pi} s \left(U_{P1} + U_{P2} \right) \tag{11.31}$$

From Fig. 11.8(b), it follows by current division that U_{P1} and U_{P2} are given by

$$U_{P1} = -U_D \frac{Z_{AB1}}{M_{AP1}s} \qquad U_{P2} = U_D \frac{Z_{AB2}}{M_{AP2}s} \tag{11.32}$$

where Z_{AB1}, Z_{AB2}, and U_D are given by

$$Z_{AB1} = \frac{M_{AP1}s}{M_{AP1}C_{AB1}s^2 + 1} \qquad Z_{AB2} = \frac{M_{AP2}s}{M_{AP2}C_{AB2}s^2 + 1} \tag{11.33}$$

$$U_D = \frac{S_D e_g}{B\ell} \frac{R_{AE}}{R_{AE} + M_{AC}s + R_{AS} + 1/C_{AS}s + Z_{AB1} + Z_{AB2}} \tag{11.34}$$

When these equations are solved for the on-axis pressure transfer function, the following expression is obtained:

$$p = \frac{\rho_0}{2\pi} \frac{B\ell e_g}{S_D R_E M_{AS}} \left(\frac{1}{\omega_{B1}^2} - \frac{1}{\omega_{B2}^2} \right) \frac{s^4/\omega_S^2}{A_6 s^6 + A_5 s^5 + A_4 s^4 + A_3 s^3 + A_2 s^2 + A_1 s + 1} \tag{11.35}$$

The constants in this equation are given by

$$\omega_S^2 = \frac{1}{M_{AS}C_{AS}} \qquad \omega_{B1}^2 = \frac{1}{M_{AP1}C_{AB1}} \qquad \omega_{B2}^2 = \frac{1}{M_{AP2}C_{AB2}} \tag{11.36}$$

$$A_6 = \frac{1}{\omega_S^2 \omega_{B1}^2 \omega_{B2}^2} \qquad A_5 = \frac{1}{\omega_S Q_{TS} \omega_{B1}^2 \omega_{B2}^2} \tag{11.37}$$

$$A_4 = \frac{1}{\omega_{B1}^2 \omega_{B2}^2} + \frac{1}{\omega_{B1}^2 \omega_{2S}^2} + \frac{1}{\omega_{B2}^2 \omega_{1S}^2} + \frac{1}{\omega_S^2} \left(\frac{1}{\omega_{B1}^2} + \frac{1}{\omega_{B2}^2} \right) \tag{11.38}$$

$$A_3 = \frac{1}{\omega_S Q_{TS}} \left(\frac{1}{\omega_{B1}^2} + \frac{1}{\omega_{B2}^2} \right) \tag{11.39}$$

$$A_2 = \frac{1}{\omega_S^2} + \frac{1}{\omega_{B1}^2} + \frac{1}{\omega_{B2}^2} + \frac{1}{\omega_{1S}^2} + \frac{1}{\omega_{2S}^2} \qquad A_1 = \frac{1}{\omega_S Q_{TS}} \tag{11.40}$$

where

$$Q_{TS} = \frac{1}{R_{AE} + R_{AS}} \sqrt{\frac{M_{AS}}{C_{AS}}} \qquad \omega_{1S}^2 = \frac{1}{M_{AP1} C_{AS}} \qquad \omega_{2S}^2 = \frac{1}{M_{AP2} C_{AS}} \tag{11.41}$$

The Helmholtz resonance frequencies of the two boxes are ω_{B1} and ω_{B2}. It can be seen from Eq. (11.35) that the output of the system is zero if $\omega_{B1} = \omega_{B2}$. In this case, the output volume velocities from the two vents cancel. If acceptable efficiency is to be obtained from the system, the two Helmholtz frequencies must not be too close together.

The transfer function in Eq. (11.35) is a 6*th*-order quasi-band-pass function. At low frequencies, the slope of the Bode plot is +4 dec/dec. At high frequencies, the slope is −2 dec/dec. If it were a true band-pass function, the power of s in the numerator would be 3 and the Bode plot would have symmetrical slopes of ±3 dec/dec. A true band-pass transfer function having symmetrical slopes would be obtained by performing a low-pass to band-pass transformation on a 3*rd*-order low-pass function. The alignment of the band-pass function would be the same as that of the 3*rd*-order function, i.e. Butterworth, Chebyshev, etc. Because a low-pass to band-pass transformation cannot produce a transfer function of the form of Eq. (11.35), it is impossible to specify an alignment for the 6*th*-order system in the usual sense.

11.3.2   System Alignment Functions

The transfer function can be factored into the product of a 4*th*-order high-pass function multiplied by a 2*nd*-order low-pass function. Aside from a gain constant, the product function can be written

$$G(s) = G_a(s) \times G_b(s) \tag{11.42}$$

where

$$G_a(s) = \frac{(s/\omega_a)^4}{(s/\omega_a)^4 + a_3 (s/\omega_a)^3 + a_2 (s/\omega_a)^2 + a_1 (s/\omega_a) + 1} \tag{11.43}$$

$$G_b(s) = \frac{1}{(s/\omega_b)^2 + (1/Q_b)(s/\omega_b) + 1} \tag{11.44}$$

With these definitions, Eq. (11.35) can be written

$$p = \frac{\rho_0}{2\pi} \frac{B\ell e_g}{S_D R_E M_{AS}} \left(\frac{1}{\omega_{B1}^2} - \frac{1}{\omega_{B2}^2} \right) \frac{\omega_a^4}{\omega_S^2} G_a(s) \times G_b(s) \tag{11.45}$$

The transfer functions $G_a(s)$ and $G_b(s)$ determine the alignment of the system. For example, $G_a(s)$ might be one of the B4, C4, or QB3 alignments described in Chapter 8. For $Q_b \leq 0.5$, $G_b(s)$ has real poles. For $Q_b = 0.5$, it is critically damped. For $Q_b > 0.5$, it has complex poles with a Butterworth response for $Q = 1/\sqrt{2}$ and a Chebyshev response for $Q_b > 1/\sqrt{2}$.

If ω_a and ω_b are not too close together, $|G_a(j\omega) \times G_b(j\omega)|$ should be close to unity in the midband frequency region. In this case, the system reference sensitivity for $e_g = 1\,\mathrm{V}$ rms can be approximated by

$$p_{sens}^{1V} \simeq \frac{\rho_0}{2\pi} \frac{B\ell}{S_D R_E M_{AS}} \left(\frac{1}{\omega_{B1}^2} - \frac{1}{\omega_{B2}^2} \right) \frac{\omega_a^4}{\omega_S^2} \tag{11.46}$$

This differs from the reference sensitivity for a driver in an infinite baffle by the factor

$$k_{sens} = \left(\frac{1}{\omega_{B1}^2} - \frac{1}{\omega_{B2}^2} \right) \frac{\omega_a^4}{\omega_S^2} \tag{11.47}$$

11.3.3 System Design from Specifications

Because the algebra is so tedious, a procedure for the design for a given driver is difficult to formulate. However, it is straightforward to design a system from specifications. This might be accomplished with the steps described below.

1. Specify the desired total effective acoustic volume V_{AB} of the two enclosures. The total compliance is then given by

$$C_{AB1} + C_{AB2} = \frac{V_{AB}}{\rho_0 c^2} \tag{11.48}$$

2. Specify ω_a, a_1, a_2, a_3, ω_b, and Q_b in the two transfer functions $G_a(s)$ and $G_b(s)$. The specification of these parameters defines the alignment of the system and the cutoff frequencies.

3. Calculate the A coefficients from

$$A_6 = \frac{1}{\omega_a^4 \omega_b^2} \qquad A_5 = \frac{1}{Q_b \omega_a^4 \omega_b} + \frac{a_3}{\omega_a^3 \omega_b^2} \qquad A_4 = \frac{1}{\omega_a^4} + \frac{a_3}{Q_b \omega_a^3 \omega_b} + \frac{a_2}{\omega_a^2 \omega_b^2} \tag{11.49}$$

$$A_3 = \frac{a_3}{\omega_a^3} + \frac{a_2}{Q_b \omega_a^2 \omega_b} + \frac{a_1}{\omega_a \omega_b^2} \qquad A_2 = \frac{a_2}{\omega_a^2} + \frac{a_1}{Q_b \omega_a \omega_b} + \frac{1}{\omega_b^2} \qquad A_1 = \frac{a_1}{\omega_a} + \frac{1}{Q_b \omega_b} \tag{11.50}$$

These equations are obtained by equating Eqs. (11.35) and (11.45).

4. Solve for the system parameters from the relations

$$\omega_S = \sqrt{\frac{A_5}{A_1 A_6}} \qquad Q_{TS} = \frac{1}{A_1 \omega_S} \tag{11.51}$$

$$\omega_{B1}^2 = \frac{A_3}{2A_5} + \sqrt{\left(\frac{A_3}{2A_5}\right)^2 - \frac{A_1}{A_5}} \qquad \omega_{B2}^2 = \frac{A_3}{2A_5} - \sqrt{\left(\frac{A_3}{2A_5}\right)^2 - \frac{A_1}{A_5}} \tag{11.52}$$

$$\omega_{1S}^2 = \frac{1 - \omega_{B1}^2/\omega_{B2}^2}{A_2 - \omega_{B1}^2 \left(A_4 - 1/\omega_S^2 \omega_{B2}^2\right) - 1/\omega_{B1}^2} \qquad \omega_{2S}^2 = \frac{1}{A_2 - 1/\omega_S^2 - 1/\omega_{B1}^2 - 1/\omega_{B2}^2 - 1/\omega_{1S}^2} \tag{11.53}$$

$$C_{AS} = \frac{V_{AB}/\rho_0 c^2}{\omega_{1S}^2/\omega_{B1}^2 + \omega_{2S}^2/\omega_{B2}^2} \qquad M_{AS} = \frac{1}{\omega_S^2 C_{AS}} \qquad R_{AE} + R_{AS} = \frac{1}{Q_{TS}} \sqrt{\frac{M_{AS}}{C_{AS}}} \tag{11.54}$$

$$M_{AP1} = \frac{1}{\omega_{1S}^2 C_{AS}} \qquad C_{AB1} = \frac{1}{\omega_{B1}^2 M_{AP1}} \qquad M_{AP2} = \frac{1}{\omega_{2S}^2 C_{AS}} \qquad C_{AB2} = \frac{1}{\omega_{B2}^2 M_{AP2}} \tag{11.55}$$

These relations are obtained from Eqs. (11.36) through (11.41).

5. To solve for R_{AE}, R_{AS}, and $B\ell$, a typical value of Q_{MS} must be assumed. This can be used to calculate $Q_{ES} = Q_{MS}Q_{TS}/(Q_{MS} - Q_{TS})$. Then R_{AE}, R_{AS}, and $B\ell$ are given by

$$R_{AE} = \frac{1}{Q_{ES}} \sqrt{\frac{M_{AS}}{C_{AS}}} \qquad R_{AS} = \frac{1}{Q_{MS}} \sqrt{\frac{M_{AS}}{C_{AS}}} \qquad B\ell = \left[\frac{S_D^2 R_E}{Q_{ES}} \sqrt{\frac{M_{AS}}{C_{AS}}}\right]^{1/2} \tag{11.56}$$

11.3.4 Example System Design

Let $G_a(s)$ be a $k = 0.7$ Chebyshev function with a lower cutoff frequency $f_\ell = 30\,\text{Hz}$. The dB ripple for this alignment is $0.2\,\text{dB}$. The equations for calculating f_a, a_1, a_2, and a_3 are given in Chapter 8. The values are

$$f_a = \frac{\omega_a}{2\pi} = 35.38\,\text{Hz} \qquad a_1 = 2.150 \qquad a_2 = 3.013 \qquad a_3 = 2.438$$

In the transfer function $G_b(s)$, let $f_b = \omega_b/2\pi = 100\,\text{Hz}$ and $Q_b = 1/1.1$. This is a Chebyshev alignment with a dB ripple of $20\log\left(Q_b^2/\sqrt{Q_b^2 - 0.25}\right) = 0.74\,\text{dB}$. Eqs. (11.49) and (11.50) give

$$A_6 = 1.037 \times 10^{-15} \qquad A_5 = 1.279 \times 10^{-12} \qquad A_4 = 9.525 \times 10^{-10}$$

$$A_3 = 3.532 \times 10^{-7} \qquad A_2 = 8.044 \times 10^{-5} \qquad A_1 = 1.142 \times 10^{-2}$$

Let the driver have the piston radius $a = 12$ cm, the voice-coil resistance $R_E = 7\,\Omega$, and the mechanical quality factor $Q_{MS} = 3$. The system parameters can be calculated from Eqs. (11.51) through (11.56) to obtain

$$f_S = \frac{\omega_S}{2\pi} = 38.5\,\text{Hz} \qquad V_{AS} = 2.14\,\text{ft}^3 \qquad Q_{TS} = 0.266 \qquad Q_{ES} = 0.292$$

$$f_{B1} = \frac{\omega_{B1}}{2\pi} = 30.8\,\text{Hz} \qquad f_{B2} = \frac{\omega_{B2}}{2\pi} = 77.7\,\text{Hz}$$

$$V_{AB1} = 2.475\,\text{ft}^3 \qquad V_{AB2} = 0.525\,\text{ft}^3$$

The pressure sensitivity is reduced by the factor $k_{sens} = 0.51$ or -5.9 dB compared to the driver in an infinite baffle, closed box, or vented box. The low-frequency analogous circuit for the LTSpice simulation is shown in Fig. 11.9. The netlist is given in Table 11.2.

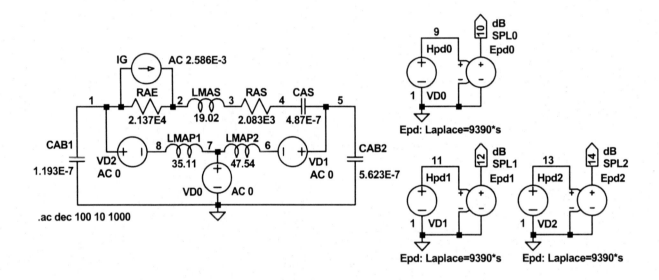

Figure 11.9: Low-frequency LTSpice circuit for the 6th order band-pass system.

Table 11.2: SPICE Netlist for the Example System

6TH ORDER BANDPASS EXAMPLE	LMAP1 8 7 35.11	Epd2 14 0 13 0 Laplace=9390*s
IG 1 2 AC 2.586E-3	LMAP2 7 6 47.54	Hpd1 11 0 VD1 1
RAE 2 1 2.137E4	LMAS 2 3 19.02	Epd1 12 0 11 0 Laplace=9390*s
RAS 4 3 2.083E3	VD0 7 0 AC 0	VD1 5 6 AC 0
CAB1 0 1 1.193E-7	Hpd0 9 0 VD0 1	VD2 1 8 AC 0
CAB2 5 0 5.623E-7	Epd0 10 0 9 0 Laplace=9390*s	.ac dec 100 10 1000
CAS 5 4 4.87E-7	Hpd2 13 0 VD2 1	.end

Fig. 11.10 shows the calculated SPL response of the system at $r = 1\,\mathrm{m}$ with $e_g = 1\,\mathrm{V}$ rms. The SPL responses of the two ports are also shown. For purposes of comparison, the driver in a vented-box with an internal volume $V_{AB} = 0.544\,\mathrm{ft}^3$ would have a QB3 alignment with a lower $-3\,\mathrm{dB}$ cutoff frequency $f_\ell = 70.5\,\mathrm{Hz}$. Its efficiency would be $5.9\,\mathrm{dB}$ higher.

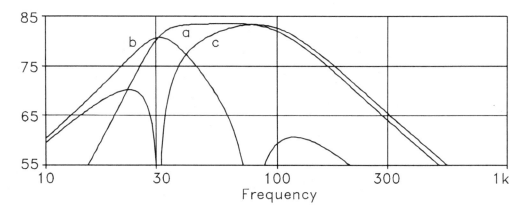

Figure 11.10: SPL responses in dB versus frequency. a – total system output. b – port 1 output. c – port 2 output.

11.4 Passive Radiator Systems

11.4.1 System Transfer Function

A passive radiator replaces the vent in a vented-box system with a passive driver, i.e. one with no voice coil. It is sometimes called a drone-cone system. The diagram of the system is shown in Fig. 11.11(a). The low-frequency Norton form of the combination acoustical analogous circuit is shown in Fig. 11.11(b). The circuit differs from that of a vented box in that the port mass is replaced by a series mass M_{AP}, resistance R_{AP}, and compliance C_{AP} representing the acoustical analogous circuit of the passive radiator.

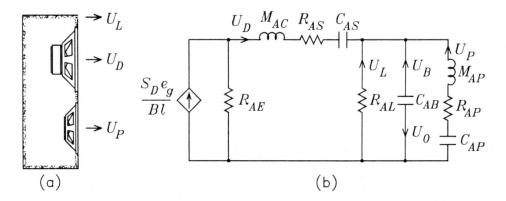

Figure 11.11: (a) System diagram. (b) Analogous circuit.

Like the vented-box system, the system output volume velocity is calculated as the volume velocity that flows in the box compliance C_{AB}. By current division, it is given by

$$U_0 = \frac{S_D e_g}{B\ell} \frac{R_{AE}}{Z_{A1} + 1/Y_{A2}} \frac{C_{AB}s}{Y_{A2}} = \frac{S_D e_g}{B\ell} \frac{R_{AE} C_{AB}s}{1 + Z_{A1} Y_{A2}} \tag{11.57}$$

where

$$Z_{A1} = M_{AC}s + R_{AE} + R_{AS} + \frac{1}{C_{AS}s} \tag{11.58}$$

$$Y_{A2} = C_{AB}s + \frac{1}{R_{AL}} + \frac{1}{M_{AP}s + R_{AP} + 1/C_{AP}s} \tag{11.59}$$

In the following, we assume that $M_{AC} \simeq M_{AS}$, i.e. that the acoustic mass of the diaphragm and its air load is the same as for an infinite baffle. In this case the impedance Z_{A1} can be written

$$Z_{A1} = \frac{(s/\omega_S)^2 + (1/Q_{TS})(s/\omega_S) + 1}{C_{AS}s} \tag{11.60}$$

where

$$\omega_S = \frac{1}{\sqrt{M_{AS}C_{AS}}} \qquad Q_{TS} = \frac{1}{\omega_S R_{AT} C_{AS}} \qquad R_{AT} = R_{AE} + R_{AS} \tag{11.61}$$

The admittance Y_{A2} can be written

$$Y_{A2} = \left(1 + \frac{1}{\delta}\right) \frac{(s/\omega_B)^2 + (1/Q_L)(s/\omega_B)}{M_{AP}s} + \frac{(s/\omega_P)^2}{M_{AP}s \left[(s/\omega_P)^2 + (1/Q_{MP})(s/\omega_P) + 1\right]} \tag{11.62}$$

where

$$\omega_P = \frac{1}{\sqrt{M_{AP}C_{AP}}} \qquad Q_{MP} = \frac{1}{\omega_P C_{AP} R_{AP}} \tag{11.63}$$

$$\delta = \frac{C_{AP}}{C_{AB}} \qquad \omega_B = \omega_P \sqrt{1 + \delta} \qquad Q_L = \omega_B C_{AB} R_{AL} \tag{11.64}$$

If $C_{AP} \to \infty$ and $R_{AP} \to 0$, the equation for Y_{A2} reduces to that for the vented-box system covered in Chapter 8.

With $R_{AE} = (B\ell)^2 / S_D^2 R_E$, the on-axis pressure at $r = 1$ m is given by

$$p = \frac{\rho_0}{2\pi} s U_0 = \frac{\rho_0}{2\pi} \frac{B\ell e_g}{S_D R_E} \frac{C_{AB}s^2}{1 + Z_{A1} Y_{A2}} = \frac{\rho_0}{2\pi} \frac{B\ell e_g}{S_D R_E M_{AS}} G_P(s) \tag{11.65}$$

where $G_P(s)$ is a 5th-order transfer function. This makes it difficult to compare the system to the vented-box system which has a 4th-order transfer function. One way of circumventing this problem is to neglect the box losses by setting $R_{AL} = \infty$ so that $Q_L \to \infty$. This leads to a 4th-order on-axis pressure transfer function which can be compared to the $Q_L = \infty$ vented-box case. An additional assumption which simplifies the analysis is to neglect the mechanical losses in the passive radiator by setting $R_{AP} = 0$ so that $Q_{MP} \to \infty$. With these approximations, the transfer function $G_P(s)$ can be written

$$\begin{aligned}
G_P(s) &= \frac{(s/\omega_0)^2 \left[(s/\omega_0)^2 + (\omega_P/\omega_0)^2\right]}{(s/\omega_0)^4 + b_3 (s/\omega_0)^3 + b_2 (s/\omega_0)^2 + b_1 (s/\omega_0) + 1} \\
&= \frac{(s/\omega_0)^2 \left[(s/\omega_0)^2 + y/\sqrt{1 + \alpha + \delta}\right]}{(s/\omega_0)^4 + b_3 (s/\omega_0)^3 + b_2 (s/\omega_0)^2 + b_1 (s/\omega_0) + 1}
\end{aligned} \tag{11.66}$$

where

$$\omega_0 = \omega_S \sqrt{y}\,(1 + \alpha + \delta)^{1/4} \qquad y = \frac{\omega_P}{\omega_S} \qquad \alpha = \frac{C_{AS}}{C_{AB}} \qquad b_3 = \frac{1}{(1 + \alpha + \delta)^{1/4} \sqrt{y} Q_{TS}} \tag{11.67}$$

$$b_2 = \frac{1}{\sqrt{1+\alpha+\delta}}\left[(1+\delta)\,y + \frac{1+\alpha}{y}\right] \qquad b_1 = \frac{(1+\delta)\sqrt{y}}{(1+\alpha+\delta)^{3/4}\,Q_{TS}} \qquad (11.68)$$

In the limit as $\delta \to \infty$, $G_P(s)$ approaches the vented-box transfer function $G_V(s)$ in Chapter 8 for the case $Q_L = \infty$.

The on-axis transfer function in Eq. (11.66) has a 4*th*-order denominator which is similar to that of the vented-box system. But unlike the vented-box system, two of the zeros of the numerator are not at the origin, i.e. not at $s = 0$. It is the location of these zeros which is the major reason that the passive-radiator system differs from the vented-box system. Indeed, for $R_{AP} = 0$, the transfer function is zero for $\omega = \omega_P$ ($s = j\omega_P$), i.e. it exhibits a null. For $R_{AL} > 0$, the system response exhibits a notch or dip at $\omega = \omega_P$, the depth of which depends on the value of R_{AL}. In a properly designed system, the notch frequency should be well below the system cutoff frequency.

Passive-radiator systems are an alternative to vented-box systems, especially when a compact enclosure is desired where a vent would be too long to fit into the box. For best response, the suspension compliance C_{AP} should be as large as possible and the resistance R_{AP} should be as small as possible. The piston area of the passive radiator should be greater than or equal to that of the driver. Because its volume displacement requirement is normally larger than that of the driver, its displacement limit $x_{\max}$ should be as large as possible.

It is difficult to specify alignments for $G_P(s)$ because the transfer function cannot be put into the form of a standard filter function. Like an elliptic filter function, $G_P(s)$ has complex conjugate zeros on the $j\omega$ axis. A 4*th* order elliptic function has two pairs of complex conjugate zeros on the $j\omega$ axis. Because $G_P(s)$ only has one pair on the $j\omega$ axis, is not of the form of an elliptic filter. If the 4*th* order denominator is factored into the product of two 2*nd* order polynomials, the function can be written as the product of a 2*nd* order high-pass function and a biquad function. In contrast, a 4*th* order elliptic filter function is written as the product of two biquad functions.

11.4.2 Example System Design

A possible procedure for the design of a system is to pick the coefficients of the denominator polynomial of $G_P(s)$ the same way that they are picked for the vented-box function $G_V(s)$ with the aim of making ω_P lower than the system cutoff frequency. The effect of the notch at ω_P is then to sharpen the corner of the frequency response curve near the cutoff frequency and to give a steeper initial cutoff compared to the equivalent vented-box system. Once the denominator coefficients b_3, b_2, and b_1 are specified, the system parameters which must be solved for are α, δ, y, and Q_{TS}. It follows that one of the four parameters must be specified before the others can be solved for.

As an example system design, let $b_2 = 2 + \sqrt{2}$ and $b_1 = b_3 = \sqrt{2b_2}$. These correspond to the coefficients of the Butterworth vented-box or B4 alignment covered in Chapter 8. Let us assume that the passive radiator has the same diaphragm suspension as the driver so that $\delta = \alpha$. It is desired to specify the driver parameters for a system with the lower $-3\,\text{dB}$ cutoff frequency $f_\ell = 35\,\text{Hz}$ and the box volume $V_{AB} = 2\,\text{ft}^3$.

With the assumption that $\delta = \alpha$, the parameters α, y, and Q_{TS} can be solved for. For the assumed b coefficients, the equations are

$$\frac{1+\alpha}{\sqrt{1+2\alpha}}\left(y + \frac{1}{y}\right) = 2 + \sqrt{2} \qquad \frac{1}{(1+2\alpha)^{1/4}\sqrt{y}Q_{TS}} = \frac{(1+\alpha)\sqrt{y}}{(1+2\alpha)^{3/4}Q_{TS}} = \sqrt{2\left(2+\sqrt{2}\right)} \qquad (11.69)$$

When y is eliminated from the first relation in Eq. (11.69), the following equation in α is obtained:

$$(1+\alpha)^2 + \left(\sqrt{2}-1\right)(1+2\alpha) = 0 \qquad (11.70)$$

There are two solutions to this equation. The one which corresponds to the smallest value of y is the desired one because it makes the notch frequency lower. It is $\alpha = 2.18$. The corresponding values of y and Q_{TS} are

$$y = \frac{\sqrt{1+2\alpha}}{1+\alpha} = 0.728 \qquad Q_{TS} = \frac{(1+\alpha)\sqrt{y}}{\sqrt{2\left(2+\sqrt{2}\right)}(1+2\alpha)^{3/4}} = 0.295 \qquad (11.71)$$

For the above numerical values, it follows that $|G_P(j\omega)|^2$ is given by

$$|G_P(j\omega)|^2 = \frac{(\omega/\omega_0)^4 \left[0.3145 - (\omega/\omega_0)^2\right]^2}{(\omega/\omega_0)^8 + 1}$$

The lower $-3\,\mathrm{dB}$ cutoff frequency is obtained by setting $|G_P(j\omega)|^2 = 1/2$. This equation reduces to

$$x^4 - 0.1978x^2(0.3145 - x)^2 + 1 = 0$$

where $x = (\omega_\ell/\omega_0)^2 = (f_\ell/f_0)^2$. The solution is $x = 1.449$, thus $f_\ell = f_0\sqrt{1.449} = 1.204f_0$. Note that for a true B4 alignment $f_\ell = f_0$. Thus the effect of the notch is to move the lower cutoff frequency up. For $f_\ell = 35\,\mathrm{Hz}$, it follows that $f_0 = 35/1.204 = 29.07\,\mathrm{Hz}$. The driver resonance frequency and volume compliance must be

$$f_S = \frac{f_0}{\sqrt{y}(1 + \alpha + \delta)^{1/4}} = 22.4\,\mathrm{Hz} \qquad V_{AS} = \alpha V_{AB} = 5.55\,\mathrm{ft}^3$$

The passive radiator must have the resonance frequency

$$f_P = yf_S = 16.3\,\mathrm{Hz}$$

Plots of $|G_P(j2\pi f)|$ versus frequency are given in Fig. 11.12. Curve a shows the response if the losses in the box and the passive radiator are neglected. Curve b includes these losses, where it is assumed that $Q_L = 7$ and $Q_{MP} = 4$. It is of interest to note that the same driver in a vented-box enclosure having the effective internal volume $V_{AB} = 1.87\,\mathrm{ft}^3$ and the Helmholtz frequency $f_B = 29.9\,\mathrm{Hz}$ would have a QB3 alignment with the lower cutoff frequency $f_\ell = 35.9\,\mathrm{Hz}$.

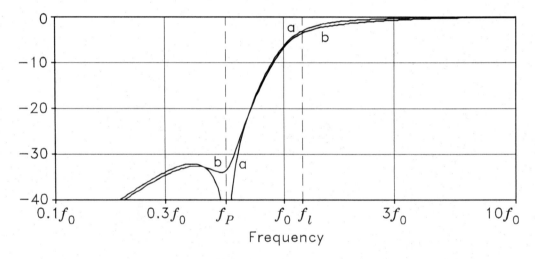

Figure 11.12: SPL responses versus frequency. a – Box and radiator losses neglected. b – Box and radiator losses included.

11.5   Assisted Vented-Box Alignments

11.5.1   System Transfer Functions

Let $T(s)$ be a high-pass transfer function with the order $n \geq 5$. If n is odd, $T(s)$ can be written

$$T(s) = \frac{b_{(n+1)/2}s/\omega_c}{1 + b_{(n+1)/2}s/\omega_c} \prod_{i=1}^{(n-1)/2} \frac{(b_i s/\omega_c)^2}{(b_i s/\omega_c)^2 + (1/c_i)(b_i s/\omega_c) + 1} \qquad (11.72)$$

If n is even, $T(s)$ can be written

$$T(s) = \prod_{i=1}^{n/2} \frac{(b_i s/\omega_c)^2}{(b_i s/\omega_c)^2 + (1/c_i)(b_i s/\omega_c) + 1} \tag{11.73}$$

In these expressions, the b and c coefficients are constants that determine the alignment of the filter. The frequency ω_c is called the cutoff frequency. For the Butterworth filter, it is the $-3\,\mathrm{dB}$ frequency. For the Chebyshev filter, the $-3\,\mathrm{dB}$ frequency is lower than ω_c.

Let $T(s)$ be expressed in the form

$$T(s) = G_E(s) \times G_V(s) \tag{11.74}$$

where $G_V(s)$ is the $4th$-order transfer function for the low-frequency response of a vented-box system. If an electrical filter having the transfer function $G_E(s)$ precedes the amplifier that drives the system, it follows that the overall response is that of $T(s)$. The system alignment is said to be assisted because the filter acts as an equalizer to improve the frequency response of the vented-box system.

The cases described here are for $n = 5$ and $n = 6$. The methods can be extended for higher orders. For $n = 5$, there are two $2nd$-order factors in $T(s)$. Both of these must be assigned to $G_V(s)$. The remaining $1st$-order factor determines the equalizer. In this case, the equalizer can be realized by a passive RC high-pass filter. For $n = 6$, there are three $2nd$-order factors in $T(s)$. Any one can be assigned to $G_E(s)$ and the remaining two to $G_V(s)$. Thus there are three possible ways to realize the system. These are called Type 1, Type 2, and Type 3 alignments. The c coefficient in $G_E(s)$ corresponds to the quality factor or Q of the equalizer. For $Q > 0.5$, the equalizer has complex poles and must be realized as an active filter. For $Q \leq 0.5$, the equalizer can be realized with either a passive or an active filter. The Type 1 alignment puts the highest Q term in the equalizer. The Type 3 alignment puts the lowest Q term in the equalizer.

The transfer function $G_V(s)$ has the form

$$G_V(s) = \frac{(s/\omega_0)^4}{(s/\omega_0)^4 + a_3(s/\omega_0)^3 + a_2(s/\omega_0)^2 + a_1(s/\omega_0) + 1} \tag{11.75}$$

where ω_0 and the a coefficients are defined in Chapter 8. Once these parameters are specified, the vented-box system parameters Q_{TS}, α, and h can be determined. Let the subscripts of the b and c parameters in Eqs. (11.72) and (11.73) that are assigned to $G_V(s)$ be denoted by x and y. It follows that ω_0 and the a coefficients are given by

$$\omega_0 = \frac{\omega_c}{\sqrt{b_x b_y}} \qquad a_3 = \frac{1}{(b_x b_y)^{3/2}} \left(\frac{b_x^2 b_y}{c_y} + \frac{b_x b_y^2}{c_x} \right) \tag{11.76}$$

$$a_2 = \frac{1}{b_x b_y} \left(b_x^2 + b_y^2 + \frac{b_x b_y}{c_x c_y} \right) \qquad a_1 = \frac{1}{\sqrt{b_x b_y}} \left(\frac{b_x}{c_x} + \frac{b_y}{c_y} \right) \tag{11.77}$$

11.5.2 $5th$-Order Alignments

Butterworth

The coefficients in Eq. (11.72) for the $5th$-order Butterworth function are

$$b_1 = b_2 = b_3 = 1 \tag{11.78}$$

$$c_1 = \frac{1}{2\sin 18°} = 1.6180 \qquad c_2 = \frac{1}{2\sin 54°} = 0.6180 \qquad c_3 = 1 \tag{11.79}$$

It follows that ω_0 and the a coefficients are

$$\omega_0 = \frac{\omega_c}{\sqrt{b_1 b_2}} = \omega_c \qquad a_3 = \frac{1}{(b_1 b_1)^{3/2}} \left(\frac{b_1^2 b_2}{c_2} + \frac{b_1 b_2^2}{c_1} \right) = 2.2361 \tag{11.80}$$

$$a_2 = \frac{1}{b_1 b_2}\left(b_1^2 + b_2^2 + \frac{b_1 b_2}{c_1 c_2}\right) = 3 \qquad a_1 = \frac{1}{\sqrt{b_1 b_2}}\left(\frac{b_1}{c_1} + \frac{b_2}{c_2}\right) = 2.2361 \tag{11.81}$$

The equalizer transfer function is given by

$$G_E(s) = \frac{s/\omega_c}{1 + s/\omega_c} \tag{11.82}$$

Chebyshev

For the Chebyshev alignment, the dB ripple must be specified. This determines the parameters ϵ and k given by

$$\epsilon = \left[10^{dB/10} - 1\right]^{1/2} \qquad k = \tanh\left[\frac{1}{n}\sinh^{-1}\frac{1}{\epsilon}\right] \tag{11.83}$$

where $n = 5$. To relate the $-3\,dB$ frequency to ω_c, first solve for the positive real root of the polynomial

$$16x^5 - 20x^3 + 5x - \frac{1}{\epsilon} = 0 \tag{11.84}$$

The lower $-3\,dB$ frequency is then given by

$$\omega_\ell = \frac{\omega_c}{x} \tag{11.85}$$

The coefficients in Eq. (11.72) for the 5th-order Chebyshev function are given by

$$b_1 = \left(\frac{1}{1 - k^2} - \sin^2 18°\right)^{1/2} \qquad b_2 = \left(\frac{1}{1 - k^2} - \sin^2 54°\right)^{1/2} \qquad b_3 = \frac{k}{\sqrt{1 - k^2}} \tag{11.86}$$

$$c_1 = \frac{1}{2}\left(1 + \frac{1}{k^2 \tan^2 18°}\right)^{1/2} \qquad c_2 = \frac{1}{2}\left(1 + \frac{1}{k^2 \tan^2 54°}\right)^{1/2} \tag{11.87}$$

For any value of k, ω_0 and the a coefficients can be calculated with Eqs. (11.76) and (11.77). The equalizer transfer function is given by

$$G_E(s) = \frac{b_3 s/\omega_c}{1 + b_3 s/\omega_c} \tag{11.88}$$

11.5.3   6th-Order Alignments

Butterworth

The coefficients in Eq. (11.73) for the 6th-order Butterworth function are

$$b_1 = b_2 = b_3 = 1 \qquad c_1 = \frac{1}{2 \sin 15°} = 1.9319 \tag{11.89}$$

$$c_2 = \frac{1}{2 \sin 45°} = 0.7071 \qquad c_3 = \frac{1}{2 \sin 75°} = 0.5176 \tag{11.90}$$

The equalizer subscript is assigned $z = 1$ for the Type 1 alignment, $z = 2$ for the Type 2, and $z = 3$ for the Type 3. The equalizer transfer function is given by

$$G_E(s) = \frac{(s/\omega_c)^2}{(s/\omega_c)^2 + (1/c_z)(s/\omega_c) + 1} \tag{11.91}$$

ω_0 and the a coefficients are given by Eqs. (11.76) and (11.77).

Chebyshev

For the Chebyshev alignment, the dB ripple must be specified. This determines the parameters ϵ and k given by Eq. (11.83) with $n = 6$. To solve for the $-3\,\mathrm{dB}$ frequency, first solve for the positive real root of the polynomial

$$32x^6 - 48x^4 + 18x^2 - 1 - \sqrt{\frac{1}{\epsilon^2} + 2} = 0 \tag{11.92}$$

The lower $-3\,\mathrm{dB}$ frequency is then given by Eq. (11.85).

The coefficients in Eq. (11.73) for the $6th$-order Chebyshev function are given by

$$b_1 = \sqrt{\frac{1}{1-k^2} - \sin^2 15^\circ} \qquad b_2 = \sqrt{\frac{1}{1-k^2} - \sin^2 45^\circ} \qquad b_3 = \sqrt{\frac{1}{1-k^2} - \sin^2 75^\circ} \tag{11.93}$$

$$c_1 = \frac{1}{2}\sqrt{1 + \frac{1}{k^2 \tan^2 15^\circ}} \qquad c_2 = \frac{1}{2}\sqrt{1 + \frac{1}{k^2 \tan^2 45^\circ}} \qquad c_3 = \frac{1}{2}\sqrt{1 + \frac{1}{k^2 \tan^2 75^\circ}} \tag{11.94}$$

For any value of k, ω_0 and the a coefficients are given by Eqs. (11.76) and (11.77). The equalizer is assigned the subscript $z = 1$ for the Type 1 alignment, $z = 2$ for the Type 2, and $z = 3$ for the Type 3. The equalizer transfer function is given by

$$G_E(s) = \frac{(b_z s/\omega_c)^2}{(b_z s/\omega_c)^2 + (1/c_z)(b_z s/\omega_c) + 1} \tag{11.95}$$

11.5.4 The Vented-Box System Parameters

The Butterworth and Chebyshev transfer functions determine the b parameters. From these, the a coefficients in the vented-box transfer function can be calculated. Once these are determined, use the rule of thumb given in Chapter 8 to assume a value for Q_L. Solve for the positive real roots of the equation

$$r^4 - (a_3 Q_L) r^3 + (a_1 Q_L) r - 1 = 0 \tag{11.96}$$

The vented-box system parameters are then given by

$$h = \frac{f_B}{f_S} = r^2 \qquad Q_{TS} = \frac{r^2 Q_L}{a_1 r Q_L - 1} \qquad \alpha = \frac{V_{AS}}{V_{AB}} = r^2\left(a_2 - \frac{1}{Q_L Q_{TS}} - r^2\right) - 1 \tag{11.97}$$

If there is more than one positive root for r, the largest root which makes α and Q_{TS} positive must be used. The value of ω_c in the transfer function is related to the driver resonance frequency ω_S by

$$\omega_c = r\omega_S \sqrt{b_x b_y} = \omega_S \sqrt{h b_x b_y} \tag{11.98}$$

11.5.5 Example Design from Specifications

A $6th$-order Type 1 Chebyshev system is to be designed for the following specifications: $f_\ell = 30\,\mathrm{Hz}$, $V_{AB} = 3\,\mathrm{ft}^3$, dB ripple $= 0.5\,\mathrm{dB}$, and $R_E = 7\,\Omega$. Solve for the system parameters. Assume the box loss quality factor $Q_L = 7$.

From Eq. (11.83), we have $\epsilon = 0.3493$ and $k = 0.2874$. Thus Eq. (11.92) becomes

$$32x^6 - 48x^4 + 18x^2 - 4.1930 = 0$$

The positive real root is $x = 1.0468$. It follows that $f_c = 1.0468 \times 30 = 31.4\,\mathrm{Hz}$. From Eqs. (11.93) and (11.94), the b and c coefficients are $b_1 = 1.0114$, $b_2 = 0.7681$, $b_3 = 0.3962$, $c_1 = 6.5128$, $c_2 = 1.8104$, and $c_3 = 0.6836$. From Eqs. (11.76) and (11.77), the a coefficients are $a_3 = 2.4334$, $a_2 = 3.2624$, and $a_1 = 1.8197$. Eq. (11.96) becomes

$$r^4 - 17.0336r^3 + 12.7377r - 1 = 0$$

The positive real root which makes α and Q_{TS} positive is $r = 0.84481$. Thus, from Eq. (11.97), $\alpha = 0.6198$, $Q_{TS} = 0.5118$, and $h = 0.7137$. The driver volume compliance is $V_{AS} = \alpha V_{AB} = 1.8594\,\text{ft}^3$. From Eq. (11.98) the driver resonance frequency is $f_S = 67.38\,\text{Hz}$. The box Helmholtz frequency is $f_B = hf_S = 48.09\,\text{Hz}$.

The equalizer is a 2nd-order high pass filter having the resonance frequency $f_0 = f_c/b_1 = 31.05\,\text{Hz}$ and the quality factor $Q = c_1 = 6.513$. The circuit can be realized with the Sallen-Key high-pass filter described in Section 10.7. Let us assume that $C_1 = C_2 = 0.22\,\mu\text{F}$ in this circuit. It follows from Eq. (10.41) that R_1 and R_2 are given by

$$R_1 = \frac{1}{2\pi f_0 Q\,(C_1 + C_2)} = 1.79\,\text{k}\Omega \qquad R_2 = \frac{Q}{2\pi f_0}\left(\frac{1}{C_1} + \frac{1}{C_2}\right) = 303\,\text{k}\Omega$$

The equalizer circuit is shown in Fig. 11.13. The first op amp acts as a unity gain buffer to isolate the source impedance from the input circuit from the filter. The peak boost in the filter response is $20\log\left[Q^2/\sqrt{Q^2 - 0.25}\right] = 16.3\,\text{dB}$, occurring at the frequency $f_{\text{peak}} = f_0 Q/\sqrt{Q^2 - 0.5} = 31.2\,\text{Hz}$. Because this is lower than the Helmholtz frequency, noise caused by turbulent air flow in the vent would be expected to be a problem.

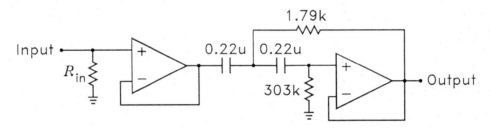

Figure 11.13: Active equalizer circuit.

Fig. 11.14 shows the simulated low-frequency responses of the loudspeaker system by itself, the equalizer by itself, and the combined responses of the loudspeaker and the equalizer, where all responses are normalized to 0 dB. The equalizer boosts the signal by 16.3 dB at 31 Hz. Its gain is less than unity for frequencies lower than about 22 Hz. Thus it acts as an infrasonic filter below that frequency. The $-3\,\text{dB}$ frequency of the loudspeaker by itself is approximately 56 Hz. The on-axis pressure sensitivity of the system is 87.8 dB at 1 m with a voice-coil voltage of 1 V rms. This system has the very undesirable feature that the maximum boost in the equalizer occurs at a frequency well below the Helmholtz resonance frequency where the radiation from the diaphragm and the port tend to cancel.

11.6   A Closed-Box System Equalizer

11.6.1   Equalizer Transfer Function

The low-frequency response of a closed-box system can be extended if an equalizer is installed preceding the power amplifier that drives it. To prevent the overdrive of the amplifier and speaker by infrasonic signals, the equalizer should roll off at low frequencies, i.e. it should exhibit the response of a high-pass filter. An equalizer based on the overall response of a 4th-order Butterworth filter is described here.

The transfer function of a 4th-order Butterworth high-pass filter can be written in the product form

$$T(s) = T_1(s) \times T_2(s) \tag{11.99}$$

where $T_1(s)$ and $T_2(s)$ are given by

$$T_1(s) = \frac{(s/\omega_0)^2}{(s/\omega_0)^2 + b_1(s/\omega_0) + 1} \qquad T_2(s) = \frac{(s/\omega_0)^2}{(s/\omega_0)^2 + b_2(s/\omega_0) + 1} \tag{11.100}$$

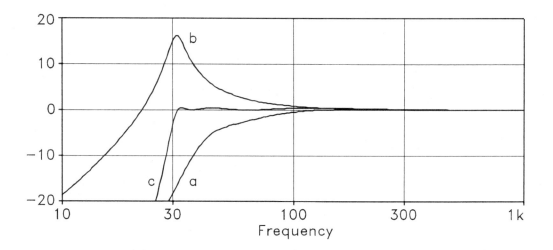

Figure 11.14: a – Unequalized system SPL response in dB versus frequency. b – dB response of equalizer. c – Equalized system SPL response in dB.

$$b_1 = 2\sin 22.5^\circ = 0.7654 \qquad b_2 = 2\sin 67.5^\circ = 1.8478 \tag{11.101}$$

The frequency ω_0 is the lower $-3\,$dB frequency of the transfer function.

Let $G_C(s)$ be the second-order high-pass function for the low-frequency response of a closed-box system given by

$$G_C(s) = \frac{(s/\omega_C)^2}{(s/\omega_C)^2 + (1/Q_{TC})(s/\omega_C) + 1} \tag{11.102}$$

The parameters ω_C and Q_{TC}, respectively, are the closed-box resonance frequency and total quality factor.. It follows from a simple algebraic manipulation that $T_1(s)$ can be written

$$T_1(s) = \frac{1}{1-k}\left[1 - kT_1(s) + m_1\left(\frac{\omega_0}{s}\right)T_1(s)\right]G_C(s) \tag{11.103}$$

where

$$k = 1 - \left(\frac{\omega_0}{\omega_C}\right)^2 \qquad m_1 = \frac{\omega_0}{Q_{TC}\omega_C} - b_1 \tag{11.104}$$

Let the transfer function $G_E(s)$ be defined by

$$G_E(s) = \frac{1}{1-k}\left[1 - kT_1(s) + m_1\left(\frac{\omega_0}{s}\right)T_1(s)\right]T_2(s) \tag{11.105}$$

It follows that $T(s) = G_E(s)G_C(s)$. Therefore, if an equalizer having the transfer function $G_E(s)$ precedes the power amplifier, the combined transfer function of the loudspeaker plus equalizer will be the $4th$-order Butterworth transfer function $T(s)$.

Note that the subscripts 1 and 2 can be interchanged in Eq. (11.105) without affecting the frequency response of the equalizer. Thus an alternate equalizer transfer function is given by

$$G_E(s) = \frac{1}{1-k}\left[1 - kT_2(s) + m_2\left(\frac{\omega_0}{s}\right)T_2(s)\right]T_1(s) \tag{11.106}$$

where

$$m_2 = \frac{\omega_0}{Q_{TC}\omega_C} - b_2 \tag{11.107}$$

11.6.2   Equalizer Circuit

Fig. 11.15 shows the circuit diagram of a possible realization for $G_E\left(s\right)$. The switch positions shown in the figure are for $m > 0$. For $m < 0$, both switch positions must be reversed. A special case is the one for which $m = 0$. In this case, R_6 and R_9 are open circuits. This leaves the output of A_3 disconnected from the circuit. Thus A_3, R_7, R_{11}, C_3, and C_4 can be omitted from the circuit for $m = 0$. If values are assigned to C_1 through C_3, R_6, and R_{10}, it can be shown that

$$R_5 = |m_{1,2}|\, R_6 \qquad R_7 = \frac{1}{2\pi f_0 C_3} \qquad R_9 = R_{10}\frac{1-k}{|m_{1,2}|} \qquad R_8 = R_{10}\frac{1-k}{k} \qquad (11.108)$$

$$R_2 = \frac{b_{2,1}}{4\pi f_0 C_1} \qquad R_1 = \frac{4R_2}{b_{2,1}^2} \qquad R_4 = \frac{b_{1,2}}{4\pi f_0 C_2} \qquad R_3 = \frac{4R_4}{b_{1,2}^2} \qquad (11.109)$$

where either the first subscripts are used in all equations or the second subscripts are used in all equations.

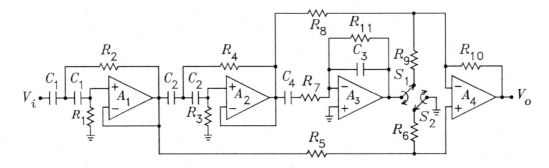

Figure 11.15: Equalizer circuit diagram.

The circuit realizes the equalizer transfer function only if resistor R_{11} is an open circuit and capacitor C_4 is a short circuit. In this case, op amp A_3 operates as an inverting integrator. R_{11} and C_4 are added to provide dc feedback to A_3. Without them, the dc offset at the output of A_3 would not be stable. R_{11} and C_4 must be chosen to be large enough so that A_3 acts as an integrator for frequencies well below the lower cutoff frequency of the system. Let ω_0/n be the frequency above which A_3 is to act as an integrator. This condition can be met if

$$R_{11} \geq 2nR_7 \qquad C_4 \geq 2nC_3 \qquad (11.110)$$

For example, the circuit might be realized with $n = 50$.

11.6.3   Example Realization

For an example design, consider the closed-box system described in Example 5 of Chapter 7. The system consists of a 15-inch woofer in a closed-box with an effective internal volume of $2\,\text{ft}^3$. The system alignment is Butterworth with a lower $-3\,\text{dB}$ frequency of $40\,\text{Hz}$. Let the box volume be halved to $1\,\text{ft}^3$. The equalizer is to be designed to decrease the $-3\,\text{dB}$ frequency to $30\,\text{Hz}$. The smaller box size causes the closed-box alignment to be Chebyshev so that it exhibits a peak in its response. Therefore, the equalizer must have a dip to compensate for this peak. The equalizer response must then peak up at lower frequencies to decrease the $-3\,\text{dB}$ cutoff frequency to $f_0 = 30\,\text{Hz}$.

Let the system parameters of Chapter 7 be designated with the subscript 1. These are $f_{C1} = 40\,\text{Hz}$, $Q_{TC1} = 1/\sqrt{2}$, $Q_{MC1} = 3.5$, $Q_{EC1} = 0.886$, $V_{AB1} = 2\,\text{ft}^3$, and $\alpha_1 = 5$. Let the system parameters for the smaller box be designated with the subscript 2. If V_{AB} is reduced to $1\,\text{ft}^3$, then the compliance ratio is doubled to the value $\alpha_2 = 10$. The closed-box resonance frequency and electrical quality factor are both increased by the factor $\sqrt{(1 + \alpha_2) / (1 + \alpha_1)}$ to $f_{C2} = 54.16$ Hz and $Q_{EC2} = 1.20$. The smaller box should have less losses, so let us assume that $Q_{MC2} = 4$. It follows that $Q_{TC2} = 4 \times 1.4 / (4 + 1.2) = 0.9230$.

The equalizer is to be realized with the first subscripts in the design equations and $n = 50$. Eq. (11.104) gives $k = 0.7870$ and $m_1 = -0.4577$. Let $C_1 = C_2 = C_3 = 0.15$ μF and $R_6 = R_{10} = 10$ kΩ. From Eqs. (11.109) and (11.110), it follows that $R_5 = 1.65$ kΩ, $R_7 = 35.4$ kΩ, $R_9 = 18.6$ kΩ, $R_8 = 4.43$ kΩ, $R_2 = 32.7$ kΩ, $R_1 = 38.3$ kΩ, $R_4 = 13.5$ kΩ, $R_3 = 92.4$ kΩ, $R_{11} = 2nR_7 = 3.54$ MΩ, $C_4 = 2nC_3 = 15$ μF. Because m is negative, the switch positions in Fig. 11.15 must be reversed.

Fig. 11.16 shows the simulated low-frequency responses of the loudspeaker system by itself, the equalizer by itself, and the combined responses of the loudspeaker and the equalizer, where all responses are normalized to 0 dB. The equalizer boosts the signal by 6.7 dB at 30 Hz and cuts it by 0.65 dB at 87 Hz. Its gain is less than unity for frequencies lower than about 17 Hz. Thus it acts as an infrasonic filter below that frequency. The -3 dB frequency of the loudspeaker by itself is approximately 44 Hz.

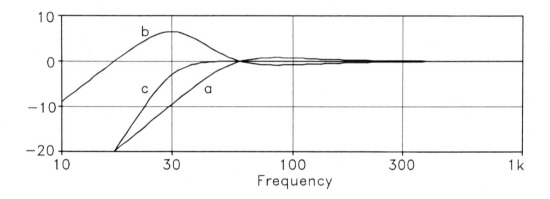

Figure 11.16: a – Unequalized system SPL response in dB versus frequency. b – dB response of equalizer. c – Equalized system SPL response in dB.

Let us compare the equalized vented-box system of Section 11.5 to the system described here. Both have the same lower -3 dB frequency of 30 Hz and the same voice-coil resistance of 7 Ω. Well above the boost range of the equalizers, the vented-box system has a pressure sensitivity that is approximately 9 dB greater than the closed-box system. However, it requires a box volume that is three times as large. At 30 Hz, the vented-box equalizer has 9.6 dB more boost than the closed-box equalizer. When we adjust this for the 9 dB difference in pressure sensitivities, it follows that the vented-box system would require about the same input voltage at 30 Hz to reproduce the same *SPL*.

The comparison is not complete unless the effects of vent noise and non-linear effects are discussed. The vented-box system is driven very hard below its Helmholtz resonance frequency where the radiation from the vent and the diaphragm are out of phase and tend to cancel. Thus we would expect vent noise to be a problem. The closed-box system does not suffer from this. Because the box volume is small for the closed-box system, non-linear effects in the compression and rarefaction of the air inside the box could cause a rise in distortion. Because distortion is harmonically related to the signal and vent noise is not, the vent noise problem would be expected to be of more concern when comparing the two.

An additional comparison is the lower -3 dB cutoff frequency of the systems if the active equalizers are not used. For the vented-box system, it is 56 Hz. For the closed-box system, it is 44 Hz.

11.7   Driver Parameter Measurements

11.7.1   Basic Theory

The five small-signal loudspeaker parameters defined in Chapter 6 are the velocity resonance frequency f_S, the total quality factor Q_{TS}, the electrical quality factor Q_{ES}, the mechanical quality factor Q_{MS}, and the volume compliance V_{AS}. In the following, methods are described which can be used to measure these. In addition, methods are described which can be used to measure the frequency dependent voice-coil inductance $L_E(\omega)$ and inductor loss resistance $R'_E(\omega)$. The measurements are summarized on the Parameter Measurement Summary Sheet at the end of the chapter.

The measurement procedures for the low-frequency parameters assume that the rise in impedance due to the voice-coil inductance occurs at a frequency much higher than the velocity resonance frequency so that $L_E(\omega)$ can be considered to be short circuit at low frequencies. When this is true, the low-frequency voice-coil impedance can be written

$$Z_{VC}(j2\pi f) = R_E + R_{ES}\frac{j(1/Q_{MS})(f/f_S)}{1 - (f/f_S)^2 + j(1/Q_{MS})(f/f_S)} \tag{11.111}$$

where $R_{ES} = R_E Q_{MS}/Q_{ES}$. This equation predicts that $|Z_{VC}(0)| = R_E$, $|Z_{VC}(j2\pi f_S)| = R_E + R_{ES}$ and $|Z_{VC}(j2\pi f)| = R_E$ for $f \gg f_S$.

A plot of $|Z_{VC}(j2\pi f)|$ versus f on log-log scales is a symmetrical function about the resonance frequency f_S. Let R_1 be a resistance such that $R_E < R_1 < R_E + R_{ES}$. It follows that there are two frequencies f_1 and f_2 such that $f_1 f_2 = f_S^2$ and $|Z_{VC}(j2\pi f_1)| = |Z_{VC}(j2\pi f_2)| = R_1$. If f_1 and f_2 are measured for a particular R_1, the data can be used to solve for Q_{MS} by substituting Eq. (11.111) into the relation $|Z_{VC}(j2\pi f_1)| + |Z_{VC}(j2\pi f_2)| = 2R_1$ and solving for Q_{MS}. It is straightforward to show that the equation reduces to

$$Q_{MS} = \frac{f_S}{f_2 - f_1}\sqrt{\frac{(R_E + R_{ES})^2 - R_1^2}{R_1^2 - R_E^2}} \tag{11.112}$$

In measuring f_1 and f_2 for a given driver, a convenient value to choose for R_1 is the geometric mean between R_E and $R_E + R_{ES}$. That is, R_1 is chosen to have the value

$$R_1 = \sqrt{R_E(R_E + R_{ES})} \tag{11.113}$$

This choice for R_1 causes it to lie one-half way between R_E and $(R_E + R_{ES})$ on a log scale. For this value of R_1, Q_{MS} is given by

$$Q_{MS} = \frac{f_S}{f_2 - f_1}\sqrt{\frac{R_E + R_{ES}}{R_E}} \tag{11.114}$$

Given Q_{MS} from this equation, Q_{ES} and Q_{TS} can be determined from the equations

$$Q_{ES} = Q_{MS} \times \frac{R_E}{R_{ES}} \qquad Q_{TS} = \frac{R_E}{R_E + R_{ES}} \times Q_{MS} \tag{11.115}$$

11.7.2   The Measurement Test Set

The measurement test set consists of a dc resistance bridge, an oscillator or a function generator, two ac voltmeters, an oscilloscope that is capable of $x - y$ operation, and a frequency counter. A digital multimeter that is capable of measuring resistance to two or preferably three significant figures can substitute for the dc bridge. A single ac voltmeter can be used, but it must be switched between points in the circuit several times during the procedure. A circuit diagram of the measurement setup is shown in Fig. 11.17. The output of the oscillator or function generator is floating in this circuit, i.e. it does not have a ground reference. Some oscillators and function generators have the signal ground connected to the chassis which is connected to the ac power cord safety ground, i.e. to the third prong on the cord. In this case, a "two-prong" isolator plug must be used on the generator cord to isolate the ground. However, it is preferable to use a generator with balanced or floating outputs to minimize phase errors at the higher frequencies caused by the capacitance between the generator signal ground and other leads in the circuit. Some of the older vacuum tube oscillators with a transformer coupled output are ideal for the measurements.

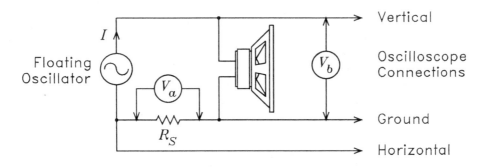

Figure 11.17: The measurement test set.

Fig. 11.17 shows a current sampling resistor R_S in series with the loudspeaker with a voltmeter connected across the resistor. The voltage V_a is proportional to the current which flows in the voice-coil. The voice-coil current is held constant during the measurement procedures. An ac current of 10 mA rms is a good value for the measurements of most drivers. For example, for $R_S = 100\ \Omega$, the ac voltage across it would be held at 1 V rms. A second voltmeter connects across the voice coil. The voice-coil impedance at any frequency is the ratio of V_b to the current $I = V_a/R_S$. It follows that the magnitude of the impedance is given by

$$|Z_{VC}(j2\pi f)| = \frac{V_b}{I} = R_S \times \frac{V_b}{V_a} \tag{11.116}$$

The figure shows the oscilloscope horizontal or x-input connected in parallel with the resistor R_S and the vertical or y-input connected in parallel with the loudspeaker. The oscilloscope ground must be connected to the node between R_S and the voice coil. This connection causes the display to show the voice-coil voltage on the vertical axis and the negative of the voice-coil current on the horizontal axis. The display is a Lissajou figure which contains information from which the phase of the impedance can be calculated. In the procedures described here, the oscilloscope display is used only to locate the frequency at which the voice-coil impedance is real. In this case, the Lissajou figure collapses to a straight line.

The driver should be mounted on an infinite baffle for the measurements. Because this is impractical in most cases, the driver is normally measured unbaffled, i.e. it is supported without a baffle. This changes the air load on the diaphragm and can perturb the measurements. The most significant change in the air load impedance is in the acoustical mass of the air load. The infinite baffle air load mass is $2 \times M_{A1(\text{ib})}$, where $M_{A1(\text{ib})} = 8\rho_0/3\pi^2 a$ and a is the piston radius of the diaphragm. For an unbaffled driver in free air, the air load mass is $1 \times M_{A1(\text{fa})}$, where $M_{A1(\text{fa})} = 0.2705\rho_0/a$. It follows then that the acoustic mass of the air load on the diaphragm is lower by a factor of $\left(16/3\pi^2\right)/0.2705 = 2$ for the unbaffled driver compared to the infinite baffle driver. In the following, a method is described for correcting the measurements to account for the change in air load mass.

Fig. 11.18(a) illustrates a driver mounted on a test support with its diaphragm aperture vertical. The loudspeaker parameters should be measured in this position if possible. If it is horizontal, the diaphragm will sag and the parameters can change. (For this same reason, a loudspeaker system should never be designed with the diaphragm aperture horizontal. The suspension will sag over a period of time until the voice coil is no longer centered properly in the magnet assembly.) The driver should be located so that there are no obstructions near the diaphragm. Mechanical vibrations of the support structure, such as those caused by building heating and air conditioning systems, and loud sounds in the room should be avoided. If these cause any motion of the diaphragm, a back emf will be generated which can be seen as a noise on the oscilloscope.

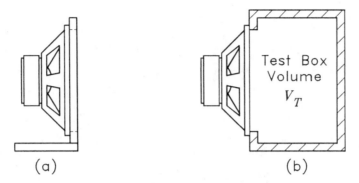

Figure 11.18: Driver mounted (a) on test support and (b) on compliance box.

11.7.3 Measuring R_E, f_S, Q_{MS}, Q_{ES}, and Q_{TS}

The first step in measuring the small-signal parameters is to measure the voice-coil resistance R_E. A dc bridge is preferred for this measurement. If an electronic bridge or multimeter is used, it must not use an ac current because the voice-coil impedance at the test frequency will not be equal to its dc value. If clip-on connectors are used, the contacts must be clean and make good connection. After R_E is measured, the driver is connected to the measurement system shown in Fig. 11.17. The fundamental velocity resonance frequency f_S is located as the frequency at which the oscilloscope Lissajou figure collapses to a straight line. The voltage V_a should be monitored and held constant each time the generator frequency is changed. There will be at least two frequencies where the Lissajou figure collapses to a straight line. The higher of the two is caused by the voice-coil inductance L_E. It should not be mistaken for f_S.

Once f_S is located, the voice-coil voltage V_b is read and recorded. The resistance at resonance $R_E + R_{ES}$ is calculated from Eq. (11.116). Eq. (11.113) is used to calculate R_1. Eq. (11.116) can then be used to calculate the voltage V_b for $|Z_{VC}(j\omega)| = R_1$. With this information, the two frequencies f_1 and f_2 can be experimentally located and recorded. Again, V_a must be held constant when the frequency is changed. Once f_1 and f_2 are determined, the geometric mean should be calculated and compared to f_S as a check. The percentage difference between these should be no larger than about 5% or an error in measurement can be suspected. If the inductance of L_E is not negligible at the test frequencies, this error can increase. With the measured data, Q_{MS}, Q_{ES}, and Q_{TS} can be calculated from Eqs. (11.114) and (11.115).

11.7.4 Measuring V_{AS}

To measure V_{AS}, the driver is mounted on an airtight, unlined, and unfilled test box which we will refer to as a compliance box. This is illustrated in Fig. 11.18(b). In most cases, it is simpler to mount the driver so that the magnet is on the outside of the box so that electrical connections can be made without running wires through the box walls. The internal volume of the box should be known accurately. Therefore, it is important to account for any internal bracing and the increase in volume caused by the driver mounted outside the box. It is important also that there be an air-tight seal between the driver and the box. The driver can be mounted to the box with machine screws that mate with T-nuts installed in the mounting holes inside the box. Any air leaks can be sealed with plumbers rope caulk. An alternate procedure is to apply closed-cell foam tape to the box surface around the hole over which the driver is mounted. An air-tight seal is achieved by pressing the driver against the tape. It should be verified that the diaphragm can move freely without contacting the tape. In this case, it is more convenient to turn the box so that the driver sits on the top of the box and the weight of the driver holds it against the tape. Any error caused by a sagging of the diaphragm should be minor.

With the driver mounted on the box, the measurements described above are repeated. Denote the on-box parameters by f_{CT}, Q_{MCT}, Q_{ECT}, and Q_{TCT}, where the subscripts CT imply that the measurements are made on a closed test box. A good choice of compliance box volume would cause the resonance frequency on the box to be larger than the resonance frequency in free air by approximately a factor of 2. If f_{CT} is too close to f_S, the accuracy of the calculations can be affected. If f_{CT} is too high, the effect of L_E on the measurements will be more pronounced. The internal dimensions of the test box should not exceed $\lambda/16$ to $\lambda/8$ at the test frequencies.

For the driver mounted on the box, the equations for f_{CT}, Q_{ECT}, and the total acoustic compliance C_{AT} of the driver and box are given by

$$f_{CT} = \frac{1}{2\pi\sqrt{M_{ACT}C_{AT}}} \qquad Q_{ECT} = \frac{1}{R_{AE}}\sqrt{\frac{M_{ACT}}{C_{AT}}} \qquad C_{AT} = \frac{V_{AT}}{\rho_0 c^2} = \frac{1}{\rho_0 c^2}\frac{V_{AS}V_T}{V_{AS}+V_T} \qquad (11.117)$$

where M_{ACT} is the acoustic mass of the diaphragm plus air load on the box (which is not equal to the infinite-baffle mass M_{AS}) and V_T is the internal volume of the test box.

It follows that the products $f_C Q_{ECT}$ and $f_S Q_{ES}$ are given by

$$f_C Q_{ECT} = \frac{1}{2\pi R_{AE}C_{AT}} = \frac{\rho_0 c^2}{2\pi R_{AE}V_{AS}}\left(1+\frac{V_{AS}}{V_T}\right) \qquad f_S Q_{ES} = \frac{1}{2\pi R_{AE}C_{AS}} = \frac{\rho_0 c^2}{2\pi R_{AE}V_{AS}} \qquad (11.118)$$

The equation for V_{AS} is obtained by taking the ratio of these two equations to obtain

$$V_{AS} = V_T\left(\frac{f_C}{f_S}\frac{Q_{ECT}}{Q_{ES}}-1\right) \qquad (11.119)$$

11.7.5 Conversion to Infinite-Baffle Parameters

The above procedures give the parameters of the driver in free air, i.e. not in an infinite baffle. Because only the air-load mass is different for the two cases, the parameters can be converted to the infinite baffle parameters by dividing f_S by the mass correction factor $k_M = \left(M_{AS(ib)}/M_{AS(fa)}\right)^{1/2}$ and by multiplying Q_{MS}, Q_{ES}, and Q_{TS} by the same factor, where $M_{AS(fa)}$ is the acoustic mass of the diaphragm plus air load in free air and $M_{AS(ib)}$ is the acoustic mass of the diaphragm plus air load in an infinite baffle. These are related as follows:

$$M_{AS(fa)} - M_{A1(fa)} = M_{AS(ib)} - 2M_{A1(ib)} \qquad (11.120)$$

where where $M_{A1(fa)}$ is given in Eq. (3.49) and $M_{A1(ib)}$ is given in Eq. (3.42). Because

$$M_{AS(fa)} = \frac{\rho_0 c^2}{\left(2\pi f_{S(fa)}\right)^2 V_{AS}} \qquad (11.121)$$

it follows that the correction factor is given by

$$k_M = \left(\frac{M_{AS(ib)}}{M_{AS(fa)}}\right)^{1/2} = \left[1 + 0.2699\frac{\left(2\pi f_{S(fa)}\right)^2 V_{AS}}{c^2 a}\right]^{1/2} \qquad (11.122)$$

After k_M is calculated, the low-frequency parameters measured in free air can be converted to the infinite baffle parameters as described above. The correction has a minor effect on the parameters in most cases.

11.7.6 Measuring the Voice-Coil Inductance

To a good approximation, the impedance of the lossy voice-coil inductance can be written

$$Z_e\left(\omega\right) = \left[(j\omega)^{n_e} L_e\right] = \omega^{n_e} L_e\left[\cos\left(\frac{n_e\pi}{2}\right) + j\sin\left(\frac{n_e\pi}{2}\right)\right] \qquad (11.123)$$

where n_e and L_e are constants. It follows that $|Z_e\left(\omega\right)| = \omega^{n_e} L_e$ and $\arg\left[Z_e\left(\omega\right)\right] = n_e \times 90°$. To experimentally determine n_e and L_e, the measurement test set shown in Fig. 11.17 can be used with the exception that a capacitor C_1 is connected in series with one lead of the driver. So that the motional impedance term of the voice coil impedance can be neglected, the capacitor should be chosen so that it resonates with the voice-coil inductance at a frequency well above the driver fundamental resonance frequency f_S. For example, the frequency might be chosen to be close to 20 kHz.

At the frequency $\omega_1 = 2\pi f_1$ where the Lissajou figure collapses to a straight line, the impedance of the voice-coil inductance is given by

$$Z_e\left(j\omega_1\right) = R_e\left(\omega_1\right) + jX_e\left(\omega_1\right) = \left(R_S \times \frac{V_b}{V_a} - R_E\right) + j\frac{1}{\omega_1 C_1} \tag{11.124}$$

where R_E is the voice-coil resistance. It follows that n_e and L_e can be calculated from

$$n_e = \frac{1}{90^\circ}\arctan\left[\frac{X_e\left(\omega_1\right)}{R_e\left(\omega_1\right)}\right] \qquad L_e = \frac{\sqrt{\left[R_e\left(\omega_1\right)\right]^2 + \left[X_e\left(\omega_1\right)\right]^2}}{\omega_1^{n_e}} \tag{11.125}$$

where the arctan function is evaluated in degrees.

A more accurate procedure is to use a linear regression analysis to estimate n_e and L_e from a series of measurements. Let the magnitude and phase of the voice-coil impedance be measured at N points in the frequency range from f_1 to f_2, where f_1 might be in the range $2\,\mathrm{kHz} \le f_1 \le 5\,\mathrm{kHz}$ and f_2 might be 20 kHz. The value of f_1 must be well above resonance where the impedance of the voice-coil inductance dominates. The inductor impedance can be calculated from the measured data as follows:

$$Z_e\left(j\omega\right) = Z_{VC}\left(j\omega\right) - R_E \tag{11.126}$$

A linear regression analysis can be used to show that the best estimates for n_e and L_e are given by

$$n_e = \frac{1}{\Delta}\left\{\sum_i \ln\left|Z_e\left(j\omega_i\right)\right|\ln\left(\omega_i\right) - \frac{1}{N}\sum_i \ln\left|Z_e\left(j\omega_i\right)\right| \times \sum_i \ln\left(\omega_i\right) + \frac{\pi}{2}\sum_i \arg\left[Z_e\left(j\omega_i\right)\right]\right\} \tag{11.127}$$

$$\ln\left(L_e\right) = \frac{1}{N}\left[\sum_i \ln\left|Z_e\left(j\omega_i\right)\right| - n_e\sum_i \ln\left(\omega_i\right)\right] \tag{11.128}$$

where $\ln\left|Z_e\left(j\omega_i\right)\right|$ is the natural logarithm of $\left|Z_e\left(j\omega_i\right)\right|$, $\arg\left[Z_e\left(j\omega_i\right)\right]$ is the radian angle of $Z_e\left(j\omega_i\right)$, and Δ is given by

$$\Delta = \sum_i \left[\ln\left(\omega_i\right)\right]^2 - \frac{1}{N}\left[\sum_i \ln\left(\omega_i\right)\right]^2 + N\left(\frac{\pi}{2}\right)^2 \tag{11.129}$$

All summations have the limits $1 \le i \le N$. Many drivers exhibit diaphragm resonances at high frequencies which cause the measured impedance magnitude and phase to exhibit ripples. The ripples are easily identified from plots of $\ln\left|Z_e\left(j\omega_i\right)\right|$ and $\arg\left[Z_e\left(j\omega_i\right)\right]$ versus $\ln\left(\omega_i\right)$. The data in the ranges around such ripples should be smoothed or excluded from the calculations.

For the case where the measurements are made at only two frequencies ω_1 and ω_2, the solutions for n_e and L_e reduce to

$$n_e = \frac{\ln\left|Z_2/Z_1\right| \times \ln\left(\omega_2/\omega_1\right) + \pi\left[\arg\left(Z_1\right) + \arg\left(Z_2\right)\right]}{\left[\ln\left(\omega_2/\omega_1\right)\right]^2 + \pi^2} \qquad L_e = \sqrt{\frac{\left|Z_1\right| \times \left|Z_2\right|}{\omega_1^{n_e} \times \omega_2^{n_e}}} \tag{11.130}$$

The two measurement frequencies should be chosen to be well above the fundamental resonance frequency of the driver. For example, the frequencies might be chosen to be 10 kHz and 20 kHz. At these frequencies, the motional impedance $Z_{E(mot)}\left(j\omega\right)$ for a woofer is small and can often be neglected in calculating $Z_e\left(j\omega\right)$. However, R_E must be subtracted from the real part of the impedance to obtain the real part of the lossy inductor impedance.

Example 2 *At $f = 10\,\text{kHz}$, the voice-coil impedance of a 10-inch driver is found to be $Z_{VC} = 27.6 + j41.2$. The impedance at $f = 20\,\text{kHz}$ is $Z_{VC} = 41.6 + j66.6\ \Omega$. If $R_E = 5.1\ \Omega$ and $Z_{E(mot)}\,(j\omega)$ can be neglected, determine n_e and L_e from the impedance data at the two frequencies.*

Solution. $f_1 = 10\,\text{kHz}$, $Z_{e1} = 27.6 - 5.1 + j41.2 = 22.5 + j41.2$, $|Z_{e1}| = 46.94$, $\arg(Z_{e1}) = 1.071\,\text{rad}$, $f_2 = 20\,\text{kHz}$, $Z_{e2} = 41.6 - 5.1 + j66.6 = 36.5 + j66.6$, $|Z_{e2}| = 75.95$, $\arg(Z_{e2}) = 1.070\,\text{rad}$. Eq. (11.130) yields $n_e = 0.682$ and $L_e = 0.0255$.

It is straightforward to model the lossy inductor in LTSpice with the use of a frequency dependent voltage-controlled current source. For example, let the inductor connect between nodes 2 and 3 in the circuit. The LTSpice netlist line for Z_e is as follows:

$$\text{GZe 2 3 2 3 Laplace} = 1/(L_e \ast \text{s} \ast \ast n_e) \tag{11.131}$$

where numerical values for L_e and n_e must be used.

Fig. 11.19 shows 21 values of the magnitude and phase of Z_e in the range from $2\,\text{kHz}$ to $20\,\text{kHz}$ for the driver of Example 2. The circles are the values calculated with Eq. (11.126) from measured data. The solid lines are the approximating functions calculated with Eq. (11.123). The parameter values estimated with Eqs. (11.127) through (11.129) are $n_e = 0.688$ and $L_e = 0.0235$. These are close to those calculated in Example 2 where only two data points are used and the effect of $Z_{E(mot)}$ are neglected.

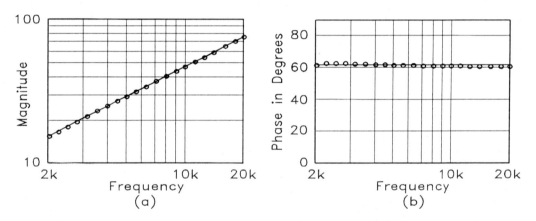

Figure 11.19: (a) Magnitude and (b) phase of Z_e versus frequency over the band from $2\,\text{kHz}$ to $20\,\text{kHz}$.

11.8   Parameter Measurement Summary Sheet

Driver Make and Model: _____

Test Performed By: _____ Date: _____

Voice-Coil Resistance: $R_E = $ _____ Piston Radius: $a = $ _____

Off Box Resonance Frequency: $f_S = $ _____ On Box: $f_{CT} = $ _____

Off Box at Resonance: $V_B/V_A = $ _____ On Box: $V_B/V_A = $ _____

Off Box: $R_E + R_{ES} = R_S \times V_B/V_A = $ _____ On Box: $R_E + R_{ECT} = $ _____

Off Box: $R_1 = \sqrt{R_E(R_E + R_{ES})} = $ _____ On Box: $R_1 = $ _____

Off Box: $V_B = V_A \times \dfrac{R_1}{R_S} = $ _____ On Box: $V_B = $ _____

Off Box: $f_1 = $ _____ On Box: $f_1 = $ _____

Off Box: $f_2 = $ _____ On Box: $f_2 = $ _____

Off Box: $f_{\text{check}} = \sqrt{f_1 f_2} = $ _____ On Box: $f_{check} = $ _____

Off Box: $Q_{MS} = \dfrac{f_S}{f_2 - f_1} \sqrt{\dfrac{R_E + R_{ES}}{R_E}} = $ _____ On Box: $Q_{MCT} = $ _____

Off Box: $Q_{ES} = \dfrac{R_E}{R_{ES}} Q_{MS} = $ _____ On Box: $Q_{ECT} = $ _____

Off Box: $Q_{TS} = \dfrac{R_E}{R_E + R_{ES}} Q_{MS} = $ _____ On Box: $Q_{TCT} = $ _____

Test Box Volume: $V_T = $ _____ $V_{AS} = V_T \left[\dfrac{f_{CT}}{f_S} \dfrac{Q_{ECT}}{Q_{ES}} - 1 \right] = $ _____

Mass Correction Factor: $k_M = \sqrt{1 + 10.65 \dfrac{f_S^2 V_{AS}}{c^2 a}} = $ _____

$\dfrac{f_S}{k_M} = $ _____ $Q_{MS} \times k_M = $ _____

$Q_{ES} \times k_M = $ _____ $Q_{TS} \times k_M = $ _____

Efficiency: $\eta_0 = \dfrac{4\pi^2}{c^3} \dfrac{f_S^3 V_{AS}}{Q_{ES}} = $ _____

Voice-Coil Inductance: $C_1 = $ _____ $f_1 = $ _____ $R_e = \left(R_S \times \dfrac{V_b}{V_a} - R_E \right) = $ _____

$X_e = \dfrac{1}{2\pi f C_1} = $ _____ $n_e = \dfrac{1}{90} \arctan \left[\dfrac{X_e}{R_e} \right] = $ _____ $L_e = \dfrac{\sqrt{R_e^2 + X_e^2}}{(2\pi f_1)^{n_e}} = $ _____

Chapter 12

Audio Power Amplifiers

The notation for variables in this chapter corresponds to that used in electronics texts. Dc variables are denoted by an upper-case letter with upper-case subscripts, e.g. V_{BE}. Small-signal ac variables are denoted by a lower-case letter with lower case subscripts, e.g. v_{be}. The sum of the dc and ac values is denoted by a lower-case letter with upper-case subscripts, e.g. $v_{BE} = V_{BE} + v_{be}$. Phasor and root-mean-square (rms) variables are denoted by an upper-case letter with lower-case subscripts, e.g. V_{be} and $V_{o(rms)}$.

12.1 Power Specifications

In a sound system, the power amplifier supplies power to the loudspeaker. The typical loudspeaker input impedance is low, usually in the $4\,\Omega$ to $8\,\Omega$ range. The power amplifier must be able to supply the high peak currents required to drive a low impedance. For example, an amplifier rated at $100\,\mathrm{W}$ into $8\,\Omega$ must deliver peak currents of $5\,\mathrm{A}$.

An ideal power amplifier has zero output impedance. In practice, all amplifiers have a non-zero output impedance. The impedance should be small compared to the loudspeaker impedance, otherwise the amplifier voltage gain is a function of the loudspeaker impedance, which is a function of frequency. Should the amplifier be an ideal current source, its output impedance is infinite and its voltage gain at any frequency is directly proportional to the loudspeaker impedance. This would have a very undesirable effect on the loudspeaker frequency response.

Power rating is a basic amplifier specification. The test load resistance must be specified as part of the rating. Resistor values most commonly used are $4\,\Omega$, $8\,\Omega$, and $16\,\Omega$. Because the lower impedances draw more current, the power rating increases as the load impedance decreases. Therefore, an amplifier power rating is highest with the $4\,\Omega$ load and lowest with the $16\,\Omega$ load. The $8\,\Omega$ load is the most commonly used value. In the case of amplifiers designed for use in vehicles, load impedances as low as $2\,\Omega$ are common.

The standard test signal for power measurements is a sine wave having a frequency in the $20\,\mathrm{Hz}$ to $20\,\mathrm{kHz}$ band. The power rating is obtained by increasing the input level until the output is just below clipping. Fig. 12.1(a) shows the diagram of an amplifier with a resistive load. Let the output voltage be written $v_O(t) = V_P \sin(2\pi t/T)$ where T is the period. The average power delivered to the load is given by

$$P_{L(ave)} = \frac{1}{T}\int_0^T \frac{v_O^2(t)}{R_L}dt = \frac{1}{T}\frac{V_P^2}{R_L}\int_0^T \sin^2\left(\frac{2\pi t}{T}\right)dt = \frac{V_P^2}{2R_L} = \frac{V_{o(rms)}^2}{R_L} \qquad (12.1)$$

where the units are watts (W) and $V_{o(rms)} = V_P/\sqrt{2}$ is the root-mean-square or rms output voltage. The average power is often incorrectly called rms power or watts rms. It is correct to say volts rms and amps rms but watts rms is incorrect.

A method that is used to make an amplifier seem to have a more impressive power rating is to rate the

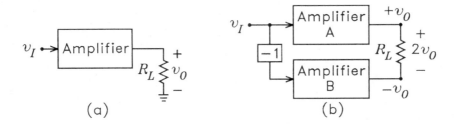

Figure 12.1: (a) Amplifier with load resistor. (b) Bridged amplifier configuration.

peak sine-wave output power. It is given by

$$P_{L(peak)} = \frac{V_P^2}{R_L} = 2P_{L(ave)} \tag{12.2}$$

which is twice the average power. For a square-wave test signal, the average power and the peak power are the same and are given by

$$P_{L(ave)} = P_{L(peak)} = \frac{V_P^2}{R_L} \tag{12.3}$$

The increased power drawn from the power supply with a square-wave signal usually results in a lower V_P compared to the sine-wave signal. This is because the output impedance of the power supply causes its voltage to drop when the current drawn from it increases.

Example 1 *An amplifier is rated at* $100\,\mathrm{W}$ *into* $8\,\Omega$. *At full power, calculate (a) the peak and rms sine-wave output voltages and currents, (b) the sine-wave average power rating into* $4\,\Omega$ *and* $16\,\Omega$, *and (c) the square-wave average power rating into* $8\,\Omega$. *Assume* V_P *is the same for each case.*

Solution. (a) $V_P = \sqrt{2R_L P_{L(ave)}} = 40\,\mathrm{V}$, $V_{o(rms)} = V_P/\sqrt{2} = 28.3\,\mathrm{V}$, $I_P = V_P/R_L = 5\,\mathrm{A}$, $I_{o(rms)} = I_P/\sqrt{2} = 3.54\,\mathrm{A}$. (b) The $4\,\Omega$ power rating is twice the $8\,\Omega$ rating or $200\,\mathrm{W}$. The $16\,\Omega$ rating is one-half the $8\,\Omega$ rating or $50\,\mathrm{W}$. (c) The square wave rating into $8\,\Omega$ is twice the sine wave rating or $200\,\mathrm{W}$.

A method of delivering more power to a load without using higher power supply voltages is to use a bridged or strapped configuration. When the two channels of a stereophonic amplifier are bridged, it becomes a monophonic amplifier. Fig. 12.1(b) shows the basic configuration. Both amplifiers are driven by the same signal, but the signal to amplifier B is inverted, i.e. multiplied by -1. Let the output voltage from amplifier A be $v_O(t)$. It follows that the output voltage from amplifier B is $-v_O(t)$ and the voltage across the load is $2v_O(t)$. Because the voltage across the load is doubled, the load current is doubled and the load power is quadrupled. The effective load impedance seen by each amplifier is $R_L/2$. For example, a stereo amplifier rated at $100\,\mathrm{W}$ per channel into $8\,\Omega$ would deliver $400\,\mathrm{W}$ when bridged. Each channel would see a $4\,\Omega$ load. In practice, the output power from a bridged amplifier is less than 4 times the power rating per channel because the increased load current causes the power supply voltages to drop.

Example 2 *An amplifier is to be designed for use in vehicles where the available dc voltage is* $12\,\mathrm{V}$. *The load resistance is* $4\,\Omega$. *Calculate the maximum average sine-wave power that can be obtained with (a) an unbridged amplifier and (b) with a bridged amplifier.*

Solution. (a) The maximum peak ac output voltage from an unbridged amplifier is one-half the dc supply voltage or $6\,\mathrm{V}$. With a $4\,\Omega$ load, the output power is $P_{L(ave)} = 6^2/(2 \times 4) = 4.5\,\mathrm{W}$. (b) For a bridged amplifier, the maximum peak output voltage is $12\,\mathrm{V}$. The power is $P_{L(ave)} = 12^2/(2 \times 4) = 18\,\mathrm{W}$. Each amplifier in the bridged configuration sees a $2\,\Omega$ load. In such applications, where a single power supply is used, an unbridged amplifier must be ac coupled to the loudspeaker load. The ac coupling capacitor can be eliminated with the bridged configuration by biasing the amplifiers so that each has the same dc output voltage. For example, this might be $6\,\mathrm{V}$ for the car amplifier with a power supply voltage of $12\,\mathrm{V}$.

12.2 Effects of Feedback

The negative feedback amplifier was discovered by Harold S. Black in 1927. He was taking the Hudson River Ferry to his office at Bell Laboratories in New York City when he suddenly thought of a solution to the problem of distortion in amplified signals, a fundamental obstacle to economical long-distance telephone service. Having nothing else to write on, he sketched his idea on a copy of The New York Times and then signed and dated it. His discovery led to the development of negative feedback amplifiers for use in the burgeoning telephone system network that was covering the globe. The amplifying devices at that time were vacuum tubes. One of motivations for the development of feedback amplifiers was to make the amplifiers less dependent on non-ideal characteristics of tubes. Although most amplifiers today are solid state, the effects of feedback are essentially the same.

12.2.1 Feedback Amplifier Gain

As with operational amplifiers, negative feedback is used in most power amplifiers to set the voltage gain. Fig. 12.2(a) shows an amplifier model consisting of an input subtracting stage followed by a gain stage. The gain A is called the open-loop gain or the gain before feedback. The output voltage is sampled by a feedback network having a gain b, where b is called the feedback factor. We assume here that A and b are real and that the feedback network contains only resistors so that $0 \le b \le 1$. The output from the feedback network is subtracted from the input to form the error voltage v_E which drives the gain stage.

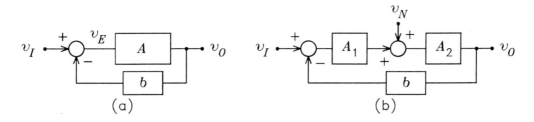

Figure 12.2: (a) Model for calculating the gain. (b) Model with intra-loop noise and distortion added.

The amplifier output voltage is given by

$$v_O = Av_E = A\left(v_I - bv_O\right) \tag{12.4}$$

This can be solved for the voltage gain to obtain

$$\frac{v_O}{v_I} = \frac{A}{1 + bA} \tag{12.5}$$

This is called the closed-loop gain or the gain after feedback. It is lower than the open-loop gain by the factor $(1 + bA)$ which is called the amount of feedback. This is often expressed in dB as $20 \log (1 + bA)$.

Negative feedback amplifiers are designed so that the open-loop gain is larger than the desired gain. Feedback is then used to reduce the gain to the desired value. If A can be made large enough so that $bA \gg 1$, it follows from Eq. (12.5) that the gain can be approximated by

$$\frac{v_O}{v_I} \simeq \frac{1}{b} \tag{12.6}$$

This approximation is often called the op-amp approximation because it is also used to predict the gain of operational amplifier circuits. It shows that the amplifier gain can be made independent of the open-loop gain as long as bA is large enough. This is very desirable because a feedback network that contains only linear passive elements results in a linear voltage gain characteristic.

Example 3 *Feedback is to be added to an amplifier with an open-loop voltage gain of 200 to reduce its gain to 20. Calculate the required value of the feedback factor b.*

Solution. We have $20 = 200/(1 + 200b)$. Solution yields $b = 9/200 = 0.045$.

12.2.2 Effect of Feedback on Distortion and Noise

Distortion is an undesired signal in an amplifier output which is present only when an input signal is applied. For example, let the input signal be a sine wave with a frequency of 1 kHz. If the output contains an unwanted 3 kHz sine wave in addition to the desired 1 kHz sine wave, the amplifier is said to generate third-order harmonic distortion. Harmonic distortion is generated by nonlinearity in the circuit. All active amplifier devices have nonlinear transfer characteristics which cause the generation of distortion.

Noise is an undesired signal in an amplifier output that is present when the input is removed. Random noise is generated in all active devices and resistors in a circuit. It is due to the thermal agitation and random flow of current carriers in devices. Generally, the random noise generated in the amplifier input stage dominates because it is amplified by the full gain of the amplifier. Random noise is usually modeled as white noise although most active devices produce excess noise at low frequencies compared to pure white noise. Non-random noise can also be present at an amplifier output. An example is low-frequency hum induced by the power supply. The frequency is related to the power-line frequency and is normally 60 Hz, 120 Hz, or a combination of the two.

Distortion and noise can be generated anywhere in a circuit. A desirable feature of negative feedback is that it reduces both. Consider the block diagram circuit of Fig. 12.2(b). The gain stage is divided into two stages such that $A = A_1 A_2$. To model distortion and noise generated in the circuit, an external signal v_N is added between the stages. It is straightforward to show that the output voltage is given by

$$v_O = \frac{A_1 A_2}{1 + bA} v_I + \frac{A_2}{1 + bA} v_N \tag{12.7}$$

It follows that both the distortion and noise in the output are reduced by the amount of feedback.

Eq. (12.7) shows that the ratio of the signal to the distortion plus noise is independent of the amount of feedback. This seems to imply that adding feedback does not improve the signal-to-noise ratio or the percent distortion in the output signal. However, if the input voltage is increased when feedback is added so that the desired signal at the output remains constant, the output noise and distortion can be made smaller when expressed as a fraction of the output voltage. It is this way that the percent distortion is decreased and the signal-to-noise ratio is increased with negative feedback.

Example 4 *An amplifier has an open-loop voltage gain of 200. When driven with a sine wave input to an output voltage of 10 V rms, the percent distortion in the output is 1%. (a) Calculate the ac rms input voltage. (b) Feedback is added to reduce the gain to 20. The input is increased to obtain the same 10 V rms output voltage. Calculate the new values of the input voltage and the percent distortion in the output.*

Solution. (a) To obtain an output of 10 V rms without feedback, the required input voltage is $10/200 = 50$ mV rms. (b) When feedback is added, the required input voltage for the same output is $10/20 = 500$ mV rms. The percent distortion is $1\% \div 10 = 0.1\%$.

12.2.3 Effect of Feedback on Output Resistance

Fig. 12.3 shows an amplifier block diagram with a gain stage that has an output resistance R_o. The overall output resistance R_{out} is given by the ratio of the open-circuit output voltage to the short-circuit output current. If the load resistor is replaced by an open circuit and the current drawn by the feedback network is negligible, the open-circuit output voltage $v_{O(oc)}$ is given by Eq. (12.5).

If the load resistor is replaced by a short circuit, the amplifier loses feedback and the short-circuit output current is given by

$$i_{O(sc)} = \frac{Av_I}{R_o} \tag{12.8}$$

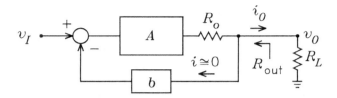

Figure 12.3: Circuit for calculating the output resistance.

Thus the output resistance with feedback is given by

$$R_{out} = \frac{v_{O(oc)}}{i_{O(sc)}} = \frac{R_o}{1 + bA} \tag{12.9}$$

Compared to the amplifier without feedback, the output resistance is reduced by the amount of feedback. Thus feedback makes the amplifier look more like an ideal voltage amplifier with zero output resistance. In practical amplifiers, A is a complex function of frequency so that the output impedance is complex. In general, $|A|$ decreases with frequency so that the output impedance increases with frequency.

The damping factor is the ratio of the load resistance to the output resistance. It is given by

$$DF = \frac{R_L}{R_{out}} \tag{12.10}$$

An ideal amplifier has a damping factor that is infinite. In practical amplifiers, the damping factor decreases with frequency because the output impedance increases.

Example 5 *The output resistance of an amplifier can normally be neglected if it is less than one-tenth the load resistance. What is the minimum acceptable damping factor for an amplifier with an $8\,\Omega$ loudspeaker load if its output resistance is to be negligible?*

Solution. From Eq. (12.10), it follows that $DF \geq 8/0.8 = 10$.

Damping factors in excess of 100 are common in most contemporary solid-state amplifiers. Vacuum tube amplifiers commonly have a damping factor that is less than 10. This is a major reason for the difference in sound between vacuum tube and solid state amplifiers. The higher output impedance of a tube amplifier causes its frequency response to be a function of the loudspeaker load impedance. The major effect is to cause a boost at low frequencies near the loudspeaker resonance frequency resulting in what has been described as the warm sound of tubes. It has been said that a $2\,\Omega$ resistor in series with the output of a solid-state amplifier can be used to give it the warm sound of vacuum tubes.

12.3 Amplifier Model

A feedback power amplifier has two inputs and one output. The input signal is applied to the non-inverting input and the feedback signal is applied to the inverting input. The circuit is designed so that the output voltage is proportional to the difference between the two voltages. In general, an amplifier can be modeled as a three-stage circuit as shown in Fig. 12.4. The non-inverting input is v_{I1}. The inverting input is v_{I2}. The feedback network, which is not shown, would connect between v_O and v_{I2}. The input stage is a differential amplifier (Q_1 and Q_2). The diff amp tail supply is the dc current source I_Q which can be realized with a transistor. In some circuits, it is simply a resistor. The second stage is a high-gain stage having an inverting or negative gain. A capacitor connects the output of this stage to its input. This capacitor is called the compensating capacitor. Other names for it are lag capacitor, Miller capacitor, and pole-splitting capacitor. It sets the bandwidth of the circuit to a value so that the amplifier is stable, i.e. so that it does not oscillate. The output stage is a unity-gain stage which provides the current gain to drive the low impedance of a loudspeaker load.

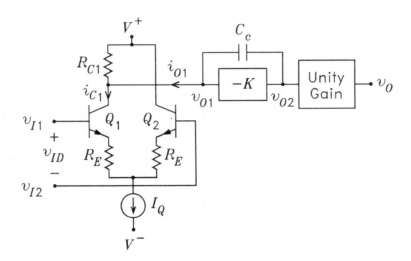

Figure 12.4: Amplifier model.

12.3.1   Open-Loop Transfer Function

Phasor notation for voltages and currents is used in this section. We wish to solve for the transfer function for V_o/V_{id}, where V_{id} is the difference voltage between the two inputs. First, we solve for the current I_{c1} as a function of V_{id}. For the diff amp, let us assume that the transistors are matched, that $I_{E1} = I_{E2} = I_Q/2$, the Early effect can be neglected, and the base currents are zero. In this case, the small-signal ac emitter equivalent circuit of the diff amp is the circuit given in Fig. 12.5(a). In this circuit, r_{e1} and r_{e2} are the intrinsic emitter resistances given by

$$r_{e1} = r_{e2} = r_e = \frac{V_T}{I_E} = \frac{2V_T}{I_Q} \tag{12.11}$$

Note that the dc tail supply I_Q does not appear in this circuit because it is not an ac source. From the emitter equivalent circuit, it follows that

$$I_{c1} = I_{e1} = \frac{V_{i1} - V_{i2}}{2\left(r_e + R_E\right)} = \frac{V_{id}}{2\left(r_e + R_E\right)} \tag{12.12}$$

where $I_{c1} = I_{e1}$ because we have assumed zero base currents.

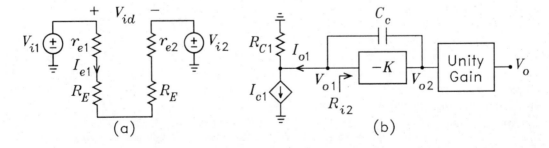

Figure 12.5: (a) Circuit for calculating I_{e1}. (b) Circuit for calculating V_o.

Fig. 12.5(b) shows the equivalent circuit which we use to calculate V_o. We can write the following node equation at the V_{o1} node:

$$I_{c1} + \frac{V_{o1}}{R_{C1}} + \frac{V_{o1}}{R_{i2}} + (V_{o1} - V_{o2}) C_c s = 0 \tag{12.13}$$

But $V_{o1} = -V_{o2}/K = -V_o/K$. Thus it follows that the equation can be rewritten

$$I_{c1} - \frac{V_o}{K} \left[\frac{1}{R_{eq}} + C_{eq}s \right] = 0 \tag{12.14}$$

where $R_{eq} = R_{C1} \| R_{i2}$ and $C_{eq} = (1 + K) C_c$. Note that C_c appears to be increased by the factor $(1 + K)$. This is called the Miller effect. When Eq. (12.12) is used for I_{c1}, Eq. (12.14) can be solved for the voltage gain $G(s) = V_o/V_{id}$ to obtain

$$G(s) = \frac{V_o}{V_{id}} = \frac{K R_{eq}}{2 (r_e + R_E)} \frac{1}{1 + R_{eq}C_{eq}s} \tag{12.15}$$

This is of the form

$$G(s) = \frac{A}{1 + s/\omega_1} \tag{12.16}$$

where A and ω_1 are given by

$$A = \frac{K R_{eq}}{2 (r_e + R_E)} \qquad \omega_1 = 2\pi f_1 = \frac{1}{R_{eq}C_{eq}} \tag{12.17}$$

12.3.2 Gain Bandwidth Product

The asymptotic Bode magnitude plot for $|G(j\omega)|$ is shown in Fig. 12.6(a). Above the pole frequency ω_1, the plot has a slope of -1 dec/dec or -20 dB/dec. The frequency at which $|G(j\omega)| = 1$ is called the unity-gain frequency or the gain-bandwidth product. It is labeled ω_x in the figure and is given by

$$\omega_x = 2\pi f_x = A\omega_1 = \frac{K R_{eq}}{2 (r_e + R_E)} \frac{1}{R_{eq}C_{eq}} = \frac{K}{1 + K} \frac{1}{2 (r_e + R_E) C_c} \simeq \frac{1}{2 (r_e + R_E) C_c} \tag{12.18}$$

where the approximation holds for $K \gg 1$. It follows that an alternate expression for $G(s)$ is

$$G(s) = \frac{A}{1 + sA/\omega_x} \tag{12.19}$$

For maximum bandwidth, f_x should be as large as possible. However, if f_x is too large, the amplifier can oscillate. A value of 8 MHz is typical for an amplifier that exhibits good stability.

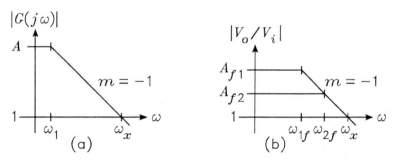

Figure 12.6: Asymptotic Bode magnitude plots. (a) Without feedback. (b) With feedback.

Example 6 *An amplifier is to be designed for $f_x = 8$ MHz and $I_Q = 3.24$ mA. If $R_E = 0$, calculate the required value for C_c.*

Solution. $C_c = 1/(4\pi f_x r_e) = I_Q/(8\pi f_x V_T) = 622$ pF, where we assume that $V_T = 0.0259$ V.

12.3.3 Slew Rate

The amplifier slew rate SR is the maximum value of the time derivative of its output voltage. In general, the positive and negative slew rates can be different. The simple model of Fig. 12.4 predicts that the two are equal so that we can write

$$-SR \leq \frac{dv_O}{dt} \leq +SR \tag{12.20}$$

To solve for the slew rate, Eq. (12.14) can be put into the form

$$\left[\frac{1}{KR_{eq}} + \left(\frac{1}{K} + 1\right)C_c s\right] V_o = I_{c1} \tag{12.21}$$

For KR_{eq} large and $K \gg 1$, this equation reduces to

$$sV_o = \frac{I_{c1}}{C_c} \tag{12.22}$$

The s operator in a phasor equation becomes the d/dt operator in a time-domain equation. Thus we can write

$$\frac{dv_O}{dt} = \frac{i_{c1}}{C_c} \tag{12.23}$$

It follows that the slew rate is determined by the maximum value of i_{c1}. The total collector current in Q_1 is the sum of the dc value plus the small-signal ac value. Thus we can write $i_{C1} = I_Q/2 + i_{c1}$. This current has the limits $0 \leq i_{C1} \leq I_Q$. It follows that the small-signal ac component has the limits $-I_Q/2 \leq i_{c1} \leq I_Q/2$. Thus we can write

$$\frac{-I_Q}{2C_c} \leq \frac{dv_O}{dt} \leq \frac{+I_Q}{2C_c} \tag{12.24}$$

It follows that the slew rate is given by

$$SR = \frac{I_Q}{2C_c} \tag{12.25}$$

Example 7 *Calculate the slew rate of the amplifier of Example 6.*

Solution. $SR = I_Q/2C_c = 2.60 \, \text{V}/\mu\text{S}$.

12.3.4 Relations between Slew Rate and Gain-Bandwidth Product

If C_c is eliminated between Eqs. (12.18) and (12.25), we obtain the relation

$$SR = 2\pi f_x I_Q (r_e + R_E) = 4\pi f_x V_T \left(1 + \frac{I_Q R_E}{2V_T}\right) \tag{12.26}$$

This equation clearly shows that the slew rate is fixed by the gain-bandwidth product if $R_E = 0$. If $R_E > 0$, the slew rate and gain bandwidth product can be specified independently.

Example 8 *Emitter resistors with the value $R_E = 300 \, \Omega$ are added to the input diff amp in the amplifier of Example 6. If f_x is to be held constant, calculate the new value of the slew rate and the new value of C_c.*

Solution. $SR = 2\pi f_x I_Q (r_e + R_E) = 51.5 \, \text{V}/\mu\text{S}$. $C_c = I_Q/2SR = 31.5 \, \text{pF}$. The slew rate is greater by a factor of about 20 and C_c is smaller by the same factor.

The above example illustrates how the slew rate of an amplifier can be increased without changing its gain-bandwidth product. When R_E is added, ω_x decreases. To make ω_x equal to its original value, C_c must be decreased, and this increases the slew rate. It can be seen from Eq. (12.26) that the slew rate can also be increased by increasing I_Q. However, this causes ω_x to increase. To make ω_x equal to its original value, R_E must also be increased. Therefore, the general rule for increasing the slew rate is to either decrease C_c, increase I_Q, or both. All of these make ω_x increase. To bring ω_x back down to its original value, R_E must be increased. The change in R_E does not affect the slew rate.

12.3.5 Closed-Loop Transfer Function

Fig. 12.7(a) shows the amplifier with a two resistor voltage divider connected as a feedback network. The amplifier is modeled with the op amp symbol. The output voltage can be written

$$V_o = G(s)(V_i - V_f) = G(s)(V_i - bV_o) \qquad (12.27)$$

where b is the voltage division ratio given by

$$b = \frac{V_f}{V_o} = \frac{R_1}{R_1 + R_F} \qquad (12.28)$$

Note that $0 \le b \le 1$. Eq. (12.27) can be solved for V_o/V_i to obtain

$$\frac{V_o}{V_i} = \frac{G(s)}{1 + bG(s)} = \frac{A_f}{1 + s/\omega_{1f}} \qquad (12.29)$$

where Eq. (12.19) is used for $G(s)$. The dc gain A_f and the pole frequency ω_{1f} are given by

$$A_f = \frac{A}{1 + bA} \simeq \frac{1}{b} \qquad \omega_{1f} = 2\pi f_{1f} = (1 + bA)\omega_1 = (1 + bA)\frac{\omega_x}{A} = \frac{\omega_x}{A_f} \simeq b\omega_x \qquad (12.30)$$

where the f in the subscript implies "with feedback" and the approximations assume that $bA \gg 1$.

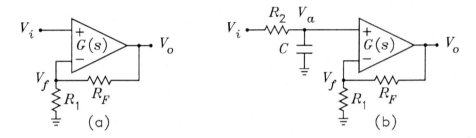

Figure 12.7: (a) Amplifier with feedback. (b) Amplifier with feedback preceded by a low-pass filter.

It can be seen from these equations that

$$A_f \omega_{1f} = A\omega_1 = \omega_x \qquad (12.31)$$

Fig. 12.6(b) shows the Bode plot for $|V_o/V_i|$ for two values of A_f. As b is increased, A_f decreases and the bandwidth ω_{1f} increases so that the product of the two remain constant. This illustrates why ω_x is called the gain-bandwidth product.

Example 9 *An amplifier has the gain bandwidth product $f_x = 8\,\text{MHz}$. Calculate the upper $-3\,\text{dB}$ frequency f_u if the amplifier is operated at a voltage gain of 21.*

Solution. The upper $-3\,\text{dB}$ frequency is equal to the pole frequency of the closed-loop transfer function. Thus $f_u = f_{1f} = f_x/A_f = 381\,\text{kHz}$.

12.3.6 Transient Response

Let the input voltage to the amplifier in Fig. 12.7(a) be a step of amplitude V_1. We can write $v_I(t) = V_1 u(t)$, where $u(t)$ is the unit step function. The Laplace transform of $v_I(t)$ is $V_i(s) = V_1/s$. The Laplace transform of the output voltage is given by

$$V_o(s) = \frac{V_1}{s} \frac{A_f}{1 + s/\omega_{1f}} \qquad (12.32)$$

The time domain output voltage is obtained by taking the inverse Laplace transform to obtain

$$v_O(t) = A_f V_1 \left[1 - \exp(-\omega_{1f} t)\right] u(t) \tag{12.33}$$

A plot of $v_O(t)$ is shown in Fig. 12.8(a).

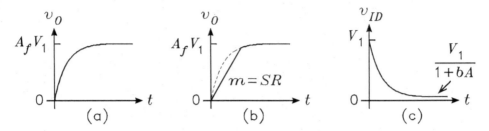

Figure 12.8: (a) No slewing step response. (b) Step response with slewing. (c) Differential input voltage.

The maximum time derivative of $v_O(t)$ occurs at $t = 0$ and is given by

$$\left.\frac{dv_O}{dt}\right|_{max} = A_f V_1 \frac{d}{dt} \left\{ \left[1 - \exp(-\omega_{1f} t)\right] u(t) \right\}\bigg|_{t=0} = A_f \omega_{1f} V_1 = \omega_x V_1 \tag{12.34}$$

If the derivative exceeds the amplifier slew rate, the output voltage will be distorted as shown in Fig. 12.8(b), where the non-slewing response is shown by the dashed curve. The maximum value of V_1 before the amplifier slews is given by

$$V_{1(max)} = \frac{SR}{\omega_x} = \frac{SR}{2\pi f_x} = I_Q (r_e + R_E) \tag{12.35}$$

Example 10 *Calculate the maximum value of V_1 for the amplifiers of Examples 7 and 8.*

Solution. For Example 7, $V_{1(max)} = 2.6 \times 10^6 / \left(2\pi \times 8 \times 10^6\right) = 51.8\,\text{mV}$. For Example 8, $V_{1(max)} = \left(51.5 \times 10^6\right) \div \left(2\pi \times 8 \times 10^6\right) = 1.02\,\text{V}$. This is greater by about a factor of 20, which is the ratio of the two slew rates.

12.3.7   Input Stage Overload

For the step input signal to the amplifier with feedback in Fig. 12.7(a), the differential input voltage is given by

$$v_{ID}(t) = v_I(t) - bv_O(t) = \frac{V_1}{1 + bA}\left[1 + bA_0 \exp(-b\omega_x t)\right] u(t) \tag{12.36}$$

It follows that $v_{ID}(0) = V_1$ and $v_{ID}(\infty) = V_1 / (1 + bA)$. A plot of $v_{ID}(t)$ is shown in Fig. 12.8(c). The peak voltage occurs at $t = 0$. If the amplifier is not to slew, the diff amp input stage must not overload with this voltage.

If base currents are neglected, the emitter and collector currents in Q_1 and Q_2 can be written

$$i_{E1} = i_{C1} = I_S \exp\left(\frac{v_{BE1}}{V_T}\right) \qquad i_{E2} = i_{C2} = I_S \exp\left(\frac{v_{BE2}}{V_T}\right) \tag{12.37}$$

where I_S is the BJT saturation current. The differential input voltage can be written

$$v_{ID} = (v_{BE1} - v_{BE2}) + (i_{E1} - i_{E2}) R_E \tag{12.38}$$

With the relation $i_{E2} = I_Q - i_{E1}$, these equations can be solved to obtain

$$v_{ID} = V_T \ln\left(\frac{i_{C1}}{I_Q - i_{C1}}\right) + (2i_{C1} - I_Q) R_E \tag{12.39}$$

The same equation holds for i_{C2} except v_{ID} is replaced with $-v_{ID}$.

Both i_{C1} and i_{C2} must satisfy the inequality $0 \leq i_C \leq I_Q$. At either limit of this inequality, one transistor in the diff amp is cut off. Let us consider the diff-amp active range to be the range for which i_{C1} and i_{C2} satisfy $0.05I_Q \leq i \leq 0.95I_Q$. This is the 5% to 95% range for the currents. When the diff amp is operated in this range, it follows from Eq. (12.39) that v_{ID} must satisfy

$$-v_{ID(max)} \leq v_{ID} \leq +v_{ID(max)} \qquad (12.40)$$

where $v_{ID(max)}$ is given by

$$v_{ID(max)} = V_T \ln 19 + 0.9 I_Q R_E \qquad (12.41)$$

If v_{ID} lies in this range, neither transistor in the diff amp can cut off and the amplifier cannot exhibit slewing.

Example 11 *Calculate $v_{ID(max)}$ for $I_Q = 3.24$ mA for the two cases $R_E = 0$ and $R_E = 300\,\Omega$. Plot i_{C1} and i_{C2} as a function of v_{ID} for both cases. Assume $V_T = 0.0259$ V.*

Solution. For $R_E = 0$, we have $v_{ID(max)} = V_T \ln 19 = 76.3$ mV. For $R_E = 300\,\Omega$, $v_{ID(max)} = 0.0763 + 0.9 \times 0.00324 \times 300 = 951$ mV. These values differ from the values of $V_{1(max)}$ calculated in Example 10 because the analysis here is based on the BJT large signal behavior. The plots of i_{C1} and i_{C2} as functions of v_{ID} are shown in Fig. 12.9. Dots on each curve indicate the limits where the collector currents are equal to $0.05I_Q$ and $0.95I_Q$. The curves for $R_E = 300\,\Omega$ show better linearity over the active range of the diff amp.

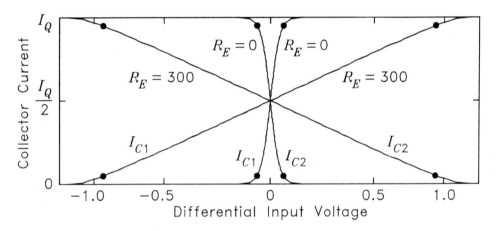

Figure 12.9: Plots of i_{C1} and i_{C2} as a function of v_{ID} for $I_Q = 3.24$ mA.

12.3.8 Full Power Bandwidth

Fig. 12.10 shows the output voltage of an amplifier with a sine wave input for two cases, one where the amplifier is not slewing and the other where the amplifier is driven into full slewing. The full slewing waveform is a triangle wave. The slew-limited peak voltage is given by the slope multiplied by one-fourth the period, i.e.

$$V_{Pslew} = SR \times \frac{T}{4} = \frac{SR}{4f} \qquad (12.42)$$

where $T = 1/f$. When the amplifier is driven into full slewing, an increase in the amplitude of the input signal causes no change in the amplitude of the output signal. If the frequency is doubled, the amplitude of the output signal is halved.

Let the input voltage to the amplifier be a sine wave. If the amplifier does not slew and is not driven into peak clipping, the output voltage can be written $v_O(t) = V_P \sin 2\pi f t$. The time derivative is given by

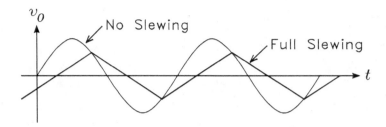

Figure 12.10: Non-slewing and full slewing output voltage waveforms.

$dv_O/dt = 2\pi f V_P \cos 2\pi ft$. The maximum value of $|dv_O/dt|$ occurs at $2\pi ft = n\pi$, where n is an integer, and is given by $|dv_O/dt|_{max} = 2\pi f V_P$. For a physical amplifier, this cannot exceed the slew rate, i.e. $2\pi f V_P < SR$. It follows that the maximum frequency that the amplifier can put out the sine wave without slewing and the peak output voltage without slewing are given by

$$f_{max} = \frac{SR}{2\pi V_P} \qquad V_{P(max)} = \frac{SR}{2\pi f} \qquad (12.43)$$

Let V_{clip} be the amplifier clipping voltage at midband frequencies. If an amplifier is driven at this level and the frequency is increased, the amplifier will eventually slew and the maximum output voltage will decrease as the frequency is increased. The full power bandwidth frequency is defined as the highest frequency at which the amplifier can put out a sine wave with a peak voltage equal to V_{clip}. It is given by

$$f_{FPBW} = \frac{SR}{2\pi V_{clip}} \qquad (12.44)$$

Fig. 12.11 shows the peak output voltage versus frequency for a sine wave input signal. At low frequencies, the peak voltage is limited to the amplifier clipping voltage V_{clip}. As frequency is increased, the peak voltage becomes inversely proportional to frequency when the amplifier is driven into full slewing and is given by Eq. 12.42. The figure also gives the peak voltage at the threshold of slewing. It is given in Eq. 12.43.

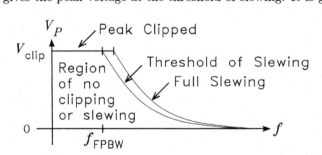

Figure 12.11: Maximum sine-wave output voltage as a function of frequency.

Example 12 *The amplifiers of Examples 7 and 8 are rated at* 120 W *into* 8 Ω. *Calculate the full power bandwidth frequency if the amplifiers are not to slew at full power.*

Solution. The midband clipping voltage is $V_{clip} = \sqrt{P_{ave} \times 2R_L} = 43.8$ V. For the amplifier of Example 7, $f_{FPBW} = 2.6 \times 10^6 / (2\pi 43.8) = 9.45$ kHz. For the amplifier of Example 8, $f_{FPBW} = 51.5 \times 10^6 / (2\pi 43.8) = 187$ kHz.

12.3.9   Effect of an Input Low-Pass Filter

Step Input Signal

Fig. 12.7(b) shows the amplifier with a low-pass filter preceding its input. By voltage division, the transfer function for the voltage gain of the filter is

$$\frac{V_a}{V_i} = \frac{1/Cs}{R_2 + 1/Cs} = \frac{1}{1 + R_2Cs} = \frac{1}{1 + s/\omega_a} \tag{12.45}$$

where $\omega_a = 1/R_2C$. It follows that the overall transfer function for the voltage gain of the amplifier and filter is

$$\frac{V_o}{V_i} = \frac{A_f}{(1 + s/\omega_a)(1 + s/\omega_{1f})} \tag{12.46}$$

The transfer function for the differential input voltage is given by

$$\frac{V_{id}}{V_i} = \frac{V_a - bV_o}{V_i} = \frac{V_a}{V_i}\left(1 - b\frac{V_o}{V_a}\right) \tag{12.47}$$

With the aid of Eqs. (12.29) – (12.30), (12.45), and (12.46), this can be reduced to

$$\frac{V_{id}}{V_i} = \frac{A_f(1 + s/\omega_1)}{(1 + s/\omega_a)(1 + s/\omega_{1f})} \tag{12.48}$$

Let the input voltage be a step of amplitude V_1. Its Laplace transform is $V_i(s) = V_1/s$. It follows that the Laplace transform for V_{id} is

$$V_{id}(s) = \frac{A_f V_1(1 + s/\omega_1)}{s(1 + s/\omega_a)(1 + s/\omega_{1f})} \tag{12.49}$$

For the case $\omega_a \neq \omega_{1f}$, the inverse transform of this is

$$v_{ID}(t) = V_1\left[\frac{\omega_1}{\omega_{1f}} + \frac{\omega_a - \omega_1}{\omega_{1f} - \omega_a}\exp(-\omega_a t) - \frac{\omega_a}{\omega_{1f}} \times \frac{\omega_{1f} - \omega_1}{\omega_{1f} - \omega_a}\exp(-\omega_{1f}t)\right] \tag{12.50}$$

The maximum value of $v_{ID}(t)$ occurs at the time t_1 which satisfies $dv_{ID}(t_1)/dt = 0$. It is straightforward to show that t_1 is given by

$$t_1 = \frac{1}{\omega_{1f} - \omega_a}\ln\left(\frac{\omega_{1f} - \omega_1}{\omega_a - \omega_1}\right) \tag{12.51}$$

The value of $v_{ID}(t_1)$ is

$$v_{ID}(t_1) = V_1\left[\frac{\omega_1}{\omega_{1f}} + \left(1 - \frac{\omega_1}{\omega_{1f}}\right)\left(\frac{\omega_a - \omega_1}{\omega_{1f} - \omega_1}\right)^{\omega_{1f}/(\omega_{1f} - \omega_a)}\right] \tag{12.52}$$

If the diff amp is not to leave its linear region, this voltage must not exceed $v_{ID(max)}$ given by Eq. (12.41). When this is true, the amplifier cannot slew with the step input signal.

Example 13 *An amplifier rated at 120 W into 8 Ω has the open-loop bandwidth $f_1 = 2\,\text{kHz}$, the closed-loop gain $A_f = 21$, and the closed-loop bandwidth $f_{1f} = 400\,\text{kHz}$. The amplifier is preceded by a low-pass filter having a bandwidth $f_a = 150\,\text{kHz}$. The amplifier input is a voltage step which drives the output to the clipping level. Calculate t_1 and $v_{ID}(t_1)$.*

Solution. The output clipping voltage is calculated in Example 12 and is $V_{clip} = 43.8\,\text{V}$. The amplitude of the input step is thus $V_1 = 43.8/21 = 2.09\,\text{V}$. Eqs. (12.51) and (12.52) give $t_1 = 0.63\ \mu\text{S}$ and $v_{ID}(t_1) = 0.437\,\text{V}$. A plot of $v_{ID}(t)$ versus t is shown in Fig. 12.12. The low-pass filter has reduced the peak overload of the diff amp by the factor $2.09/0.437 = 4.78$ or by $13.6\,\text{dB}$.

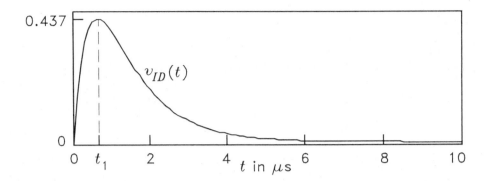

Figure 12.12: Plot of v_{ID} as a function of t for Ex. 13.

Example 14 *The amplifier of Example 13 has a diff amp that is biased at $I_Q = 3.24\,\text{mA}$. Calculate the minimum value of R_E if the diff amp is not to leave its linear region for the value of $v_{ID}(t_1)$. Assume that C_c is adjusted so that f_{1f} does not change with R_E.*

Solution. In Eq. (12.41), we let $v_{ID(max)} = v_{ID}(t_1) = 0.437\,\text{V}$. For $V_T = 0.0259\,\text{V}$, R_E is given by $R_E = (0.437 - V_T \ln 19)/0.9 I_Q = 124\,\Omega$.

Square-Wave Input Signal

The transient examples that we have looked at so far assume that the amplifier input voltage is a step and that the initial value of the output voltage is zero. Transient response measurements on amplifiers are usually made with a square-wave input signal, not a step. A square wave can be written as a series of steps. Thus it may seem that the results obtained for the step can be applied directly for the square wave. This is true only if the calculations are modified to account for the non-zero initial value of the amplifier output voltage.

Let a square wave be applied to an amplifier that switches from its negative level to its positive level at $t = 0$. The input and output voltage waveforms are illustrated in Fig. 12.13(a), where it is assumed that no low-pass filter precedes the amplifier input. At $t = 0^-$, let the input voltage be $-V_1$. The output voltage is $-A_f V_1$. At $t = 0^+$, the input voltage switches to $+V_1$, but the output voltage is still at $-A_f V_1$. Thus the differential input voltage at $t = 0^+$ is $v_{ID} = V_1 - v_O/A_f = 2V_1$. It follows from this result that the results obtained for the step input apply to the square wave input if the amplitude of the step is doubled. This is equivalent to saying that the amplitude of the step must equal the total change in voltage of the square wave between its negative and positive levels. The same conclusion holds when the amplifier is preceded by a low-pass filter.

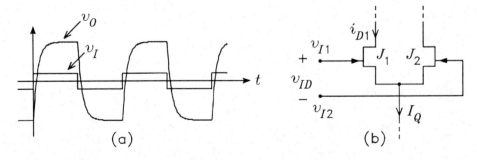

Figure 12.13: (a) Square wave input and output voltages. (b) JFET diff amp input stage.

Example 15 *The amplifier of Example 14 has emitter resistors with the value $R_E = 300\,\Omega$. The amplifier is driven to its clipping level with a square wave input signal. Determine if the diff amp input stage leaves its linear range with this signal.*

Solution. For the step input of Example 14, the maximum differential input voltage is 0.437 V. For the square wave input, it is doubled to the value 0.874. Eq. (12.41) gives $v_{ID(max)} = V_T \ln 19 + 0.9 \times 0.00324 \times 300 = 0.951\,\text{V}$. Because this is larger than 0.874 V. the diff amp does not leave its linear range. Because the square wave is a worst case signal, it follows that the amplifier cannot slew before it clips.

12.3.10 JFET Diff Amp

We have seen above that the addition of emitter resistors to the diff amp transistors reduces the gain bandwidth product of the amplifier. If the compensation capacitor is then reduced to bring the gain bandwidth product back up to its original value, the slew rate is increased. Another method of accomplishing this is to replace the BJTs with JFETs. A JFET diff amp is shown in Fig. 12.13(b). For a specified bias current, the JFET has a much lower transconductance than the BJT. In effect, this makes it look like a BJT with emitter resistors. For this reason, resistors in series with the JFET sources are omitted in the figure. The analysis in this section also applies to the MOSFET diff amp.

The JFET drain current can be written

$$i_D = I_{DSS}\left(1 - \frac{v_{GS}}{V_{TO}}\right)^2 \tag{12.53}$$

where I_{DSS} is the drain-source saturation current (the value of i_D with $v_{GS} = 0$), V_{TO} is the threshold voltage (which is negative), v_{GS} is the gate to source voltage, and $V_{TO} \le v_{GS} \le 0$. For the drain current in either JFET to be in the range of $0.05I_Q$ to $0.95I_Q$, the maximum differential input voltage is given by

$$v_{ID(max)} = |V_{TO}|\left(\sqrt{0.95} - \sqrt{0.05}\right)\sqrt{\frac{I_Q}{I_{DSS}}} = 0.751\,|V_{TO}|\sqrt{\frac{I_Q}{I_{DSS}}} \tag{12.54}$$

The JFET transconductance is given by

$$g_m = \frac{dI_D}{dV_{GS}} = \frac{2I_{DSS}}{-V_{TO}}\left(1 - \frac{V_{GS}}{V_{TO}}\right) = \frac{2}{|V_{TO}|}\sqrt{I_D I_{DSS}} \tag{12.55}$$

To convert a formula derived for the amplifier with a BJT diff amp into a corresponding formula for the JFET diff amp, the BJT intrinsic emitter resistance r_e is replaced with $1/g_m$ for the JFET. Thus the gain bandwidth product of the amplifier with the JFET diff amp is given by

$$\omega_x = 2\pi f_x = \frac{g_m}{2C_c} \tag{12.56}$$

where it is assumed that $R_E = 0$.

Example 16 *An amplifier with a JFET diff amp input stage is to be designed for $f_x = 8\,\text{MHz}$ and $I_Q = 2\,\text{mA}$. The diff amp transistors have the parameters $I_{DSS} = 2\,\text{mA}$ and $V_{TO} = -2\,\text{V}$. Calculate the required value for C_c and the amplifier slew rate.*

Solution. Eq. (12.55) gives $g_m = \sqrt{2} \times 10^{-3}$ S. Eq. (12.56) gives $C_c = 28.1\,\text{pF}$. The slew rate is $SR = I_Q/2C_c = 35.5\,\text{V}/\mu\text{S}$.

Example 17 *Calculate $v_{ID(max)}$ for the diff amp of Example 16.*

Solution. Eq. (12.54) gives $v_{ID(max)} = 0.751 \times 2 = 1.50\,\text{V}$.

Example 18 *If the JFET diff amp in Example 16 is replaced with a BJT diff amp, what value of R_E is required to make the circuit have the same gain bandwidth product? Assume I_Q splits equally between the two diff amp transistors.*

Solution. We set $r_e + R_E$ for the BJT equal to $1/g_m$ for the JFET and solve for R_E. For the BJT, $r_e = 2V_T/I_Q = 25.9\,\Omega$. For the JFET, $1/g_m = 707.1\,\Omega$. It follows that $R_E = 707.1 - 25.9 = 681.2\,\Omega$.

For several reasons, the JFET is at a disadvantage compared to the BJT in audio amplifier design. First, JFET parameters vary widely from unit to unit of the same part number. This makes it difficult to obtain closely matched pairs unless they are fabricated as a pair. In contrast, the match between two BJTs with emitter resistors is insensitive to mismatch between the BJTs. It is determined mainly by the resistors. Second, JFETs with a high breakdown voltage are not that common. This can complicate the design of high-power amplifiers which use power supply voltages as high as $\pm 100\,\text{V}$. Third, the drain-source saturation current I_{DSS} of most JFETs fabricated for use in small-signal amplifiers is usually in the low mA range. Because I_{DSS} must be larger than the bias current I_Q, the choice of JFETs may be limited because of this requirement.

The depletion mode MOSFET is similar to the JFET and the above equations apply to it as well. Unlike the JFET, it has an insulated gate so that gate current cannot flow if $i_D > I_{DSS}$. The enhancement mode MOSFET differs in that its threshold voltage V_{TO} is positive. Thus it is not conducting with $v_{GS} = 0$. The above equations apply to the enhancement mode device, but I_{DSS} cannot be interpreted as the drain-source current with $v_{GS} = 0$. Compared to the JFET, the MOSFET generates more low frequency noise. This noise is commonly called excess noise or $1/f$ noise.

12.3.11   Diff Amp with Current-Mirror Load

Fig. 12.14 shows the amplifier model of Fig. 12.4 with the resistive load on the input diff amp replaced with a current mirror. If we assume that Q_1 and Q_2 are matched, that Q_3 and Q_4 are matched, that base currents can be neglected, and that the Early effect can be neglected, we can write for i_{O1}

$$i_{O1} = i_{C1} - i_{C3} = i_{C1} - i_{C4} = i_{C1} - i_{C2} \tag{12.57}$$

But $i_{C1} + i_{C2} = I_Q$ and $i_{C1} = I_Q/2 + i_{c1}$. Thus we obtain

$$i_{O1} = 2i_{C1} - I_Q = 2i_{c1} \tag{12.58}$$

The factor of 2 in Eq. 12.58 causes both the gain-bandwidth product ω_x and the slew rate SR to be doubled compared to the case with the resistive load on the diff amp. In addition, the high output resistance of the current mirror causes the gain A to be much larger and the pole frequency ω_1 to be much smaller. The gain-bandwidth product and the slew rate are given by

$$\omega_x = 2\pi f_x = A\omega_1 = \frac{K}{1+K}\frac{1}{(r_e + R_E)\,C_c} \simeq \frac{1}{(r_e + R_E)\,C_c} \qquad SR = \frac{I_Q}{C_c} \tag{12.59}$$

A current mirror load on the input diff amp cannot be used to double the slew rate without doubling the gain-bandwidth product. To hold the gain-bandwidth product constant, I_Q must be decreased, C_c increased, or R_E increased. Decreasing I_Q or increasing C_c both decrease the slew rate. This is not the case if R_E is increased. For a specified gain-bandwidth product, a current mirror can be used to double the slew rate if R_E is increased to hold the gain-bandwidth product constant. A current mirror load on the diff amp is commonly used in design of integrated circuit op amps. The current mirror gives a much higher open-loop gain at dc, thus making it possible to use the op amp with feedback to realize high-gain dc circuits. Compared to a resistive load, the current mirror generates more noise. For this reason, resistive loads are commonly used in low-noise op amps. Because audio amplifiers are not operated at high gains, neither noise nor an insufficient open-loop gain at dc are common problems. There is one case in which the current mirror load cannot be used in either an op amp or an audio amplifier. That is the case of a fully complementary circuit which uses complementary diff amps in parallel for the input stage. The bias currents in the stage following the diff amps are not stable with the current mirror loads. An example circuit is examined in detail in the following.

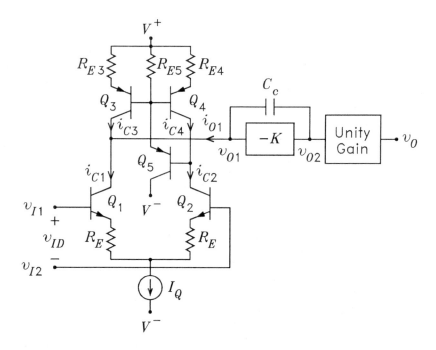

Figure 12.14: Amplifier model with a current mirror load on the input diff amp.

12.4 Signal Tracing

Signal tracing a circuit can lead to a great deal of insight in understanding its operation. When a circuit is signal traced, an assumed signal polarity at its input is traced through each stage to the output. If there is more than one parallel path from input to output, each path must be traced to verify that all paths cause the output to change with the same polarity. The output signal is then traced back through the feedback network to the input stage where it can be verified that the feedback is negative.

The four basic rules for signal tracing BJT and FET circuits are as follows: (a) Never trace into the BJT collector or into the FET drain. (b) Never trace out of the BJT base or out of the FET gate. (c) The BJT common-emitter (CE) and the FET common-source (CS) stages are the only inverting stages. (d) Never trace backward through any path, e.g. never trace backward through a feedback network. The first three rules are straightforward to apply. The fourth can sometimes be confusing. However, with practice, the common mistakes of signal tracing can be avoided.

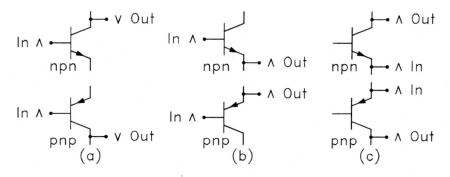

Figure 12.15: Signal tracing for single-stage BJT amplifiers. (a) CE. (b) CC. (c) CB.

Fig. 12.15 illustrates the signal tracing of BJT npn and pnp single stages. We refer to each upward pointing arrow in the figure as an "up" and to each downward pointing arrow as a "down." The up at each input indicates that the input voltage is assumed to increase. The only stage which inverts the signal is the CE stage. Thus the arrow symbol at its output is a down. For FETs, the drain, gate, and source leads, respectively, are analogous to the BJT collector, base, and emitter leads.

Consider the two-stage CE amplifier of Fig. 12.16(a). To trace the circuit, we assume an up at the input. This is traced to the base of Q_1 as an up. If we trace out of the emitter of Q_1, we end up at the negative rail which is an ac ground. Thus we must trace out of the collector. For signals into the base and out of the collector, Q_1 is a CE amplifier which inverts. Thus the up on the base of Q_1 makes a down at its collector which is applied to the base of Q_2. Because Q_2 is a CE stage, the down its base produces an up at its collector which is coupled to the output as an up. Thus, the circuit is a non-inverting amplifier.

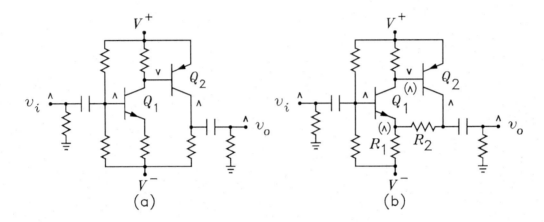

Figure 12.16: (a) Amplifier without feedback. (b) Amplifier with feedback.

Fig. 12.16(b) shows the circuit with feedback added from its output back to the emitter of Q_1. The feedback network consists of R_1 and R_2. There are two choices in signal tracing Q_1. We can go out of the emitter with an up or out of the collector with a down. If we go out of the emitter, we would be forced to go backward through the feedback network to reach the output. Thus we must go out of the collector.

Tracing the signal through Q_1 and Q_2 via the same path used in the amplifier without feedback, we see that an up at the input produces an up at the output. The up at the output is fed back through R_2 to appear as a feedback up at the emitter of Q_1, where the feedback up is enclosed in parentheses in the figure. Because we cannot trace out of the base of Q_1, the feedback up at its emitter must be traced to the collector. Thus Q_1 acts as a CB amplifier for the feedback signal. The feedback up at its emitter produces a feedback up at its collector. This up polarity is opposite to the down polarity caused by the input signal. We conclude that the feedback is negative.

For another example, consider the circuit of Fig. 12.17. We assume an up at the base input of Q_1. If we trace this out of the emitter of Q_1, we could only go into the emitter of Q_2 and out of its collector. The latter is an ac ground point due to the parallel Zener diode and capacitor. Thus we must go out of the collector of Q_1 with a down. This is traced into the emitter of Q_3 and out of its collector as a down. The down is traced to the base of Q_4 which has two signal outputs. The output at the emitter of Q_4 is a down while the output at the collector is an up. The down at the emitter is applied to the base of Q_5 which is traced out of its collector as an up. We see that both Q_4 and Q_5 are forcing the base of Q_6 to go up. This is traced to the emitter of Q_6 as an up and to the output as an up. Thus the circuit is a non-inverting amplifier. Because a signal cannot be traced into the collector of Q_7, we conclude that Q_7 is not part of the signal path. It is a constant current source which sinks the currents in Q_4 through Q_6 to the negative rail.

The feedback network consists of R_1, R_2, and C. By voltage division, the voltage gain of the feedback

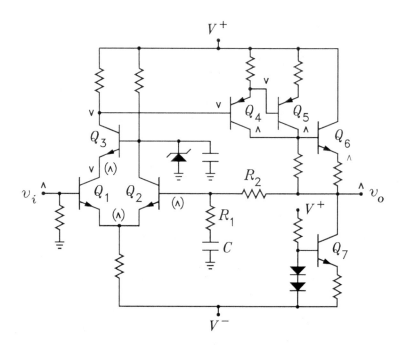

Figure 12.17: More complicated circuit for signal tracing.

network is given by

$$H\left(s\right) = \frac{R_1 + 1/Cs}{R_1 + R_2 + 1/Cs} = \frac{1 + R_1 Cs}{1 + \left(R_1 + R_2\right) Cs} \qquad (12.60)$$

At very low frequencies, C is an open circuit which causes $\left|H\left(j\omega\right)\right| \to 1$. The circuit is said to have 100% dc feedback. It is common to use 100% dc feedback in audio amplifier circuits because it provides better dc bias stability. Any change in the circuit which would cause a dc bias current or voltage to change gets fed back on itself and tends to be canceled by the negative feedback. If C is replaced by a short circuit, the loop gain at dc would be lower by the factor $R_1/\left(R_1 + R_2\right)$, and the bias stability would be degraded by that factor.

If we assume that the op-amp approximation holds, the closed-loop gain of the circuit is $\left[H\left(s\right)\right]^{-1}$. The Bode plot of this is given in Fig. 12.18. At very low frequencies, the gain is unity. As frequency is increased, the gain increases to the value $1 + R_2/R_1$. This is the midband ac gain of the amplifier. The lower cutoff frequency is $f_\ell = 1/2\pi R_1 C$. This should be lower than the lowest frequency to be amplified for flat response in the audio signal band. Although not indicated on the Bode plot, the gain at high frequencies must decrease because the transistors do not have infinite bandwidth.

To prevent oscillations in the amplifier with feedback, the frequency compensation techniques discussed in the following section can be applied. The dc gain constant can be reduced by adding resistors in series with the emitters of Q_1 and Q_2. The dominant pole frequency can be decreased by adding a capacitor from collector to base of Q_4. Lead compensation can be applied by adding a capacitor in parallel with R_2.

12.5 The Stability Criterion

After Black's invention of the negative feedback amplifier, a serious problem was discovered. Namely, when feedback was added, an amplifier would tend to put out a signal with no input signal. The undesired signal was in the audio band and the amplifiers were said to exhibit singing. Attempts to solve this problem by application of the Routh stability criterion (developed by E. J. Routh in 1877) of control theory failed. In

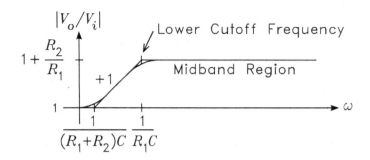

Figure 12.18: Bode magnitude plot for the amplifier.

1932, H. Nyquist showed that stability could be determined from an experimentally obtained plot which is today called a Nyquist diagram. In 1945, H. W. Bode built on Nyquist's work. His method was also based on an experimentally obtained plot which is today called a Bode plot. The stability criterion developed by Bode is described in the following and methods of applying it to modern solid-state power amplifiers are described. These amplifiers tend to oscillate at an ultrasonic frequency that can be as high as $1\,\text{MHz}$. This can be a serious problem because an oscillating amplifier can blow loudspeakers. Oscillations can also cause overheating so that expensive power output transistors can fail. Also, the distortion performance can be seriously degraded.

12.5.1   The Bode Stability Theorem

Oscillations result from phase shifts which cause the feedback to become positive at some frequency. The phase shifts are usually caused by capacitances, e.g. c_π and c_μ in the small-signal BJT model, which cause the gain to roll off at high frequencies. Vacuum-tube amplifiers can oscillate at either low or high frequencies. Low-frequency oscillations are often called motorboating because the sound resembles that of a distant motorboat on a lake. They result from phase shifts in transformers and coupling capacitors used to isolate the dc bias voltages between stages. The analysis here assumes that all circuits are dc coupled so that only high-frequency stability is a concern.

Fig. 12.19(a) shows the diagram of an amplifier with feedback, where the op amp symbol is used to represent the amplifier. $G(s)$ is the open-loop gain transfer function. $H(s)$ is the transfer function of the feedback network. The output voltage is given by $V_o = G(s)[V_i - H(s)V_o]$. This can be solved for the closed-loop gain to obtain

$$\frac{V_o}{V_i} = \frac{G(s)}{1 + G(s)H(s)} \tag{12.61}$$

With $s = j\omega$, it follows from this expression that the gain is undefined if there is an ω such that $G(j\omega)H(j\omega) = -1$. If this condition is satisfied at any frequency, the amplifier will oscillate at that frequency. We define $G(s)H(s)$ as the loop-gain transfer function. Note that this is really the negative of the gain around the loop.

Fig. 12.19(b) shows the amplifier input grounded, the feedback network disconnected from the output, and a source with an output voltage $v_1(t) = V_1 \cos \omega t$ driving the feedback network. The output voltage is given by

$$v_O(t) = -|G(j\omega)H(j\omega)| V_1 \cos(\omega t + \varphi) \tag{12.62}$$

where φ is the phase angle of $G(j\omega)H(j\omega)$. Suppose there is a frequency for which $|G(j\omega)H(j\omega)| = 1$ and $\varphi = -180°$, i.e. $G(j\omega)H(j\omega) = -1$. Under this condition, Eq. (12.62) predicts that $v_O(t) = v_1(t)$. With the source set to this frequency, the switch position in Fig. 12.19(b) could be changed and the output signal would not change. The amplifier becomes an oscillator that puts out a sine wave with no external input signal.

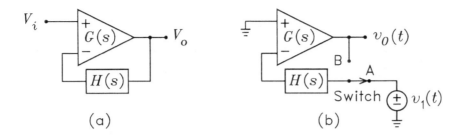

Figure 12.19: (a) Diagram of a feedback amplifier. (b) Circuit used to determine the unity gain frequency.

The two conditions which must be satisfied for an amplifier to act as an oscillator at some frequency are $|G(j\omega)H(j\omega)| = 1$ and $\varphi = -180\,^\circ$. Consider the case where the second condition is met but the first one is not. Suppose there is a frequency for which $\varphi = -180\,^\circ$ and $|G(j\omega)H(j\omega)| > 1$. With the generator set to this frequency, the amplifier output signal would begin to increase with time when the switch position is changed. The amplifier would be unstable. If $|G(j\omega)H(j\omega)| < 1$ at the frequency for which $\varphi = -180\,^\circ$, the output signal would decrease or damp out with time. The amplifier is stable.

Let $\varphi(\omega)$ be the phase of $G(j\omega)H(j\omega)$. Without a formal proof, the Bode stability theorem can be stated as follows:

Bode Stability Theorem Given an amplifier for which the Bode plot for $|G(j\omega)H(j\omega)|$ passes through unity only once in the downward direction, a necessary and sufficient condition for closed-loop stability is that $\varphi(\omega)$ be more positive than $-180\,^\circ$ at the unity-gain crossover frequency. This is the frequency for which $|G(j\omega)H(j\omega)| = 1$. The open-loop amplifier is assumed to be stable.

It is convenient to specify stability in terms of what is called the amplifier phase margin φ_m. Let the unity-gain crossover frequency be denoted by ω_x. The phase margin is given by

$$\varphi_m = 180\,^\circ + \varphi(\omega_x) \tag{12.63}$$

where $\varphi(\omega_x)$ is the phase of $G(j\omega_x)H(j\omega_x)$. The phase margin is a measure of how close the phase of $G(j\omega_x)H(j\omega_x)$ comes to the unstable $-180\,^\circ$ value. For example, if $\varphi(\omega_x) = -135\,^\circ$, the phase margin is $\omega_x = 180\,^\circ - 135\,^\circ = 45\,^\circ$. In most cases, amplifiers with a phase margin $\geq 45\,^\circ$ exhibit acceptable stability. In calculating the phase margin for a transfer function, the asymptotic Bode plot is often used to obtain an approximate value for ω_x. This is illustrated in the following example.

Example 19 *Calculate the phase margin for*

$$G(s)H(s) = \frac{A}{(1 + s/\omega_1)(1 + s/\omega_2)(1 + s/\omega_3)} \tag{12.64}$$

where $A = 100\sqrt{10}$, $\omega_1 = \sqrt{10}$, $\omega_2 = 10\sqrt{10}$, and $\omega_3 = 1000$.

Solution. The asymptotic Bode magnitude plot is given in Fig. 12.20(a). Because log-log scales are used, the ratio of the gains at any two frequencies on an asymptote is equal to the ratio of the frequencies raised to a power equal to the slope. This rule gives the gains at ω_2 and ω_3 that are labeled in the figure. To solve for ω_x, we assume that the actual plot can be approximated by the asymptotic plot. Because the asymptotic slope between ω_2 and ω_3 is -2, it follows by ratios that $10\sqrt{10} \div 1 = \left(\omega_x \div 10\sqrt{10}\right)^2$. This can be solved to obtain $\omega_x = 100\,(10)^{1/4} = 177.83\,\mathrm{rad/s}$. The phase at ω_x is

$$\begin{aligned}
\varphi(\omega_x) &= -\tan^{-1}\left[\frac{\omega_x}{\omega_1}\right] - \tan^{-1}\left[\frac{\omega_x}{\omega_2}\right] - \tan^{-1}\left[\frac{\omega_x}{\omega_3}\right] \\
&= -89.43\,^\circ - 84.29\,^\circ - 17.55\,^\circ = -179.0\,^\circ
\end{aligned} \tag{12.65}$$

The phase margin is

$$\varphi_m = 180\,° - 179.0\,° = 1.0\,° \tag{12.66}$$

This is too close to zero for acceptable stability.

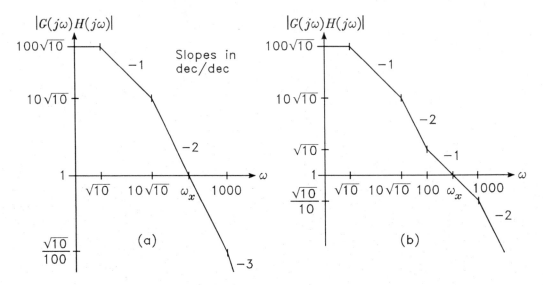

Figure 12.20: (a) Bode magnitude plot for Example 19. (b) Bode magnitude plot for Example 20.

Example 20 *Calculate the phase margin for*

$$G\left(s\right)H\left(s\right) = \frac{A\left(1 + s/\omega_4\right)}{\left(1 + s/\omega_1\right)\left(1 + s/\omega_2\right)\left(1 + s/\omega_3\right)} \tag{12.67}$$

where A, ω_1, ω_2, and ω_3 are given in Example 19 and $\omega_4 = 100$.

Solution. The asymptotic Bode magnitude plot is given in Fig. 12.20(b). We assume that the actual plot can be approximated by the asymptotic plot. It follows from the plot that $\omega_x = 100\sqrt{10}$. The phase at ω_x is

$$
\begin{aligned}
\varphi\left(\omega_x\right) &= -\tan^{-1}\left[\frac{\omega_x}{\omega_1}\right] - \tan^{-1}\left[\frac{\omega_x}{\omega_2}\right] + \tan^{-1}\left[\frac{\omega_x}{\omega_4}\right] - \tan^{-1}\left[\frac{\omega_x}{\omega_3}\right] \\
&= -89.43\,° - 84.29\,° + 72.45\,° - 17.55\,° = -118.8\,°
\end{aligned} \tag{12.68}
$$

The phase margin is

$$\varphi_m = 180\,° - 118.8\,° = 61.2\,° \tag{12.69}$$

This is large enough so that the amplifier should exhibit good stability.

The two examples above illustrate how the slope of the Bode plot at the unity-gain crossover frequency affects the phase margin. The plot in Fig. 12.20(a) crosses unity gain with a slope of -2 whereas the plot in Fig. 12.20(b) crosses with a slope of -1. A basic design rule for good stability is to design for a -1 slope at the unity-gain frequency. The -1 slope in Example 20 is achieved by adding the term $(1 + s/\omega_4)$ to the numerator of the transfer function of Example 19. This has the effect of increasing the high-frequency loop gain. Because it adds phase lead, it is called lead compensation. In the present case, more than $60\,°$ of phase lead is added to the phase margin.

12.5.2 Single-Pole Amplifier

The amplifier model analyzed in Section 12.3 results in a single-pole transfer function. The open-loop transfer function is given by Eq. (12.16). For the resistive feedback network shown in Fig. 12.7(a), the feedback ratio is a positive real quantity which we denote by b and is given by Eq. (12.28). The closed-loop gain is given by Eqs. (12.29) and (12.30). The loop-gain transfer function is

$$G(s)H(s) = bG(s) = \frac{bA}{1 + s/\omega_1} \tag{12.70}$$

The asymptotic Bode magnitude plot for $G(j\omega)H(j\omega)$ is shown in Fig. 12.21(a). Because the unity-gain crossover frequency occurs on a -1 slope, we can use ratios to write $bA \div 1 = \omega_x \div \omega_1$. Solution for ω_x yields

$$\omega_x = bA\omega_1 \tag{12.71}$$

The phase margin is

$$\varphi_m = 180° + \varphi(\omega_x) = 180° - \tan^{-1}\left(\frac{\omega_x}{\omega_1}\right) = 180° - \tan^{-1}(bA) \tag{12.72}$$

Because $0° \le \tan^{-1}(bA) \le 90°$, it follows that $90° \le \varphi_m \le 180°$. Thus the minimum φ_m is twice the $45°$ value for acceptable stability. The single-pole amplifier exhibits excellent stability.

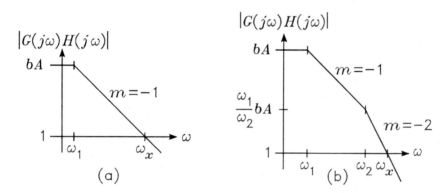

Figure 12.21: Asymptotic Bode-magnitude plots of loop-gain transfer function. (a) Single-pole amplifier. (b) Two-pole amplifier.

12.5.3 Two-Pole Amplifier

All amplifiers exhibit more than one pole in the open-loop transfer function. Compared to the single-pole amplifier, the next more complicated model is the two-pole amplifier. A basic understanding of this model is usually sufficient in understanding the steps of stabilizing amplifiers with more than two poles. A two-pole amplifier has an open-loop transfer function of the form

$$G(s) = \frac{A}{(1 + s/\omega_1)(1 + s/\omega_2)} \tag{12.73}$$

where A is the gain constant and ω_1 and ω_2 are the two pole frequencies. We assume that $\omega_1 < \omega_2$ so that ω_1 is the first or dominant pole. Let the amplifier with resistive feedback in Fig. 12.7(a) have this transfer function. The loop-gain transfer function is

$$G(s)H(s) = bG(s) = \frac{bA}{(1 + s/\omega_1)(1 + s/\omega_2)} \tag{12.74}$$

where b is given by Eq. (12.28).

The asymptotic Bode magnitude plot for $|G(j\omega)H(j\omega)|$ is shown in Fig. 12.21(b), where it is assumed that the gain at ω_2 is greater than unity. Thus the unity-gain crossover frequency occurs on a -2 slope. We can use ratios to write, $(bA\omega_1/\omega_2) \div 1 = (\omega_x \div \omega_2)^2$. Solution for ω_x yields

$$\omega_x = \sqrt{bA\omega_1\omega_2} \tag{12.75}$$

Unlike ω_x for the single-pole amplifier, this cannot be interpreted as a gain-bandwidth product. The phase margin is given by

$$\varphi_m = 180° + \varphi(\omega_x) = 180° - \tan^{-1}\left(\frac{\omega_x}{\omega_1}\right) - \tan^{-1}\left(\frac{\omega_x}{\omega_2}\right) \tag{12.76}$$

For $\omega_x \gg \omega_2$, this equation predicts that $\varphi_m \to 0°$ and the two-pole amplifier becomes unstable. If $\omega_x = \omega_2$ and $\omega_2 \gg \omega_1$, the equation predicts that $\varphi_m \simeq 45°$ and the amplifier exhibits acceptable stability. We can conclude that the magnitude of the loop-gain at ω_2 should be less than or equal to 1 for acceptable stability. An equivalent statement is that the slope of the asymptotic plot for $|G(j\omega)H(j\omega)|$ at $\omega = \omega_x$ should not be more negative than -1 dec/dec or $-20\,\text{dB/dec}$. The same conclusion usually applies to amplifiers having more than two poles.

It is straightforward to show that the closed-loop gain of the two-pole amplifier is given by

$$\frac{V_o}{V_i} = \frac{G(s)}{1 + bG(s)} = \frac{A_f}{(s/\omega_0)^2 + (1/Q)(s/\omega_0) + 1} \tag{12.77}$$

where A_f, ω_0, and Q are given by

$$A_f = \frac{A}{1 + bA} \qquad \omega_0 = \sqrt{(1 + bA)\omega_1\omega_2} \qquad Q = \frac{\omega_0}{\omega_1 + \omega_2} \tag{12.78}$$

The poles of the transfer function are the roots of the denominator quadratic. The poles are complex if $Q > 0.5$ and real if $Q \le 0.5$. The complex pole case represents the case where the phase margin is the smallest.

With $s = j\omega_0$, it follows from Eq. (12.77) that $|V_o/V_i| = Q_f A_f$. Thus if $Q_f > 1$, the Bode plot exhibits gain peaking at $\omega = \omega_0$. Fig. 12.22(a) shows a typical Bode magnitude plot for the case $Q = 2$. The gain peaking is associated with a phase margin that is less than $45°$. The figure shows that the frequency at which the gain is the highest is slightly less than ω_0. As the phase margin approaches zero, the gain peak approaches infinity and the peak frequency approaches ω_0.

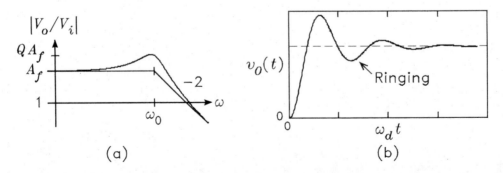

Figure 12.22: (a) Bode magnitude plot of closed-loop gain. (b) Step response.

The gain peaking in the Bode plot, can be related to ringing in the amplifier transient response. The higher the gain peak, the more the ringing. Let a voltage step of amplitude V_1 be applied to the input. It can be shown the output voltage is given by

$$v_O(t) = A_f V_1 \left[1 - \left(\frac{\omega_0}{\omega_d} \right) \exp \left(\frac{-\omega_0 t}{2Q} \right) \cos (\omega_d t - \theta) \right] u_{-1}(t) \tag{12.79}$$

where $u_{-1}(t)$ is the unit step function and ω_d and θ are given by

$$\omega_d = \omega_0 \sqrt{1 - \frac{1}{4Q^2}} \qquad \theta = \sin^{-1} \left(\frac{1}{2Q} \right) \tag{12.80}$$

The graph of $v_O(t)$ versus $\omega_d t$ is given in Fig. 12.22(b) for the case $Q = 2$. The figure shows that there is an initial time delay after the input step occurs before the output voltage begins to rise. The voltage then rises, overshoots the final value, and exhibits a damped oscillation before it settles. The damped oscillation is called ringing.

The presence of ringing in the square-wave response indicates that the amplifier is marginally stable. One criterion for good stability is that the peak overshoot not exceed 1.1 times the final value of the waveform. This is called a 10% peak overshoot. It can be shown that the peak overshoot in the voltage waveform is 10% or less when $Q \leq 0.64$. The peak overshoot in Fig. 12.22(b) is 45%. If an amplifier under test has an input low-pass filter for the rejection of ultrasonic signals, it must be disabled to measure the peak overshoot or it will limit the rise time of the input signal and mask the effects of marginal stability.

12.5.4 An Alternate Stability Criterion

An alternate form of the Bode stability theorem can be stated in terms of the Bode plots of $|G(j\omega)|$ and $|H(j\omega)|^{-1}$ rather than the plot of $|G(j\omega) H(j\omega)|$. The phase of $G(j\omega) H(j\omega)$ is the phase of $G(j\omega)$ plus the phase of $H(j\omega)$. But the phase of $H(j\omega)$ is the negative of the phase of $[H(j\omega)]^{-1}$. Therefore, stability requires the phase of $G(j\omega)$ minus the phase of $[H(j\omega)]^{-1}$ to be more positive than $-180\,°$ at $\omega = \omega_x$.

To solve for ω_x, construct the Bode plot for $|H(j\omega)|^{-1}$ on the plot for $|G(j\omega)|$. The two plots intersect at ω_x. We have seen that an amplifier is usually stable if the asymptotic slope of the plot for $|G(j\omega_x) H(j\omega_x)|$ is -1 dec/dec at ω_x. This slope can be written as the difference between the slopes of the plot for $|G(j\omega)|$ and the plot for $|H(j\omega)|^{-1}$. The amplifier is unstable if the difference is more negative than -1 dec/dec.

Example 21 *A two-pole amplifier has a dc gain constant $A = 10^4$ and pole frequencies at $f_1 = 100\,\text{Hz}$ and $f_2 = 10.1\,\text{kHz}$. Use the alternate stability theorem to determine stability when the amplifier is used with the feedback network of Fig. 12.23(a). The network element values are $R_1 = 1\,\text{k}\Omega$, $R_2 = 10\,\text{k}\Omega$, $C_1 = 100\,\mu\text{F}$, and $C_2 = 0.001\,\mu\text{F}$.*

Solution. We assume that the break frequencies caused by C_1 and C_2 are spaced widely enough so that the effect of each can be considered separately. At very low frequencies, both capacitors are open circuits and $H(s) = 1$. As frequency is increased, C_1 becomes a short circuit before C_2. With C_2 an open circuit, it follows by voltage division that the low-frequency $H(s)$ is given by

$$H_1(s) = \frac{R_1 + 1/C_1 s}{R_1 + 1/C_1 s + R_2} = \frac{1 + R_1 C_1 s}{1 + (R_1 + R_2) C_1 s} \tag{12.81}$$

At higher frequencies where C_1 is a short circuit, it follows by voltage division that $H(s)$ becomes

$$H_2(s) = \frac{R_1}{R_1 + R_2 \| (1/C_2 s)} = \frac{R_1}{R_1 + R_2} \frac{1 + R_2 C_2 s}{1 + (R_1 \| R_2) C_2 s} \tag{12.82}$$

Note that the factor $R_1 / (R_1 + R_2)$ is the high-frequency limit of $H_1(s)$. It follows that this factor must be omitted when $H_1(s)$ and $H_2(s)$ are combined to obtain $H(s)$. It is given by

$$H(s) = \frac{(1 + R_1 C_1 s)(1 + R_2 C_2 s)}{[1 + (R_1 + R_2) C_1 s][1 + (R_1 \| R_2) C_2 s]} \tag{12.83}$$

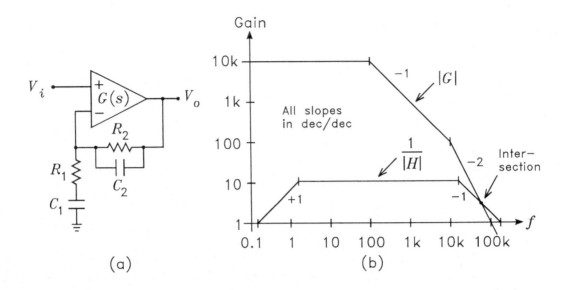

Figure 12.23: (a) Circuit for Example 21. (b) Bode plots.

The break frequencies in the Bode plot for $|H(j\omega)|$ are

$$f_1 = \frac{1}{2\pi(R_1+R_2)C_1} = 0.145\,\text{Hz} \qquad f_2 = \frac{1}{2\pi R_1 C_1} = 1.59\,\text{Hz}$$

$$f_3 = \frac{1}{2\pi R_2 C_2} = 15.9\,\text{kHz} \qquad f_4 = \frac{1}{2\pi(R_1\|R_2)C_2} = 175\,\text{kHz}$$

The asymptotic plots for $|G(j\omega)|$ and $|H(j\omega)|^{-1}$ are given in Fig. 12.23(b). At the intersection, the slope of $|G(j\omega)|$ is -2 and the slope of $|H(j\omega)|^{-1}$ is -1. The difference between these slopes is -1. Thus the amplifier should be stable. Note that C_1 does not affect the stability because its break frequencies are located far below the intersection. If C_2 is either too small or too large, the intersection would occur on a 0 slope of $|H(j\omega)|^{-1}$ and the difference in the slopes would be -2. The amplifier would then have insufficient phase margin for good stability. It is left as an exercise to show that the phase margin is $66.6\,^\circ$

Capacitor C_2 in the above example is called a lead compensation capacitor. It is called this because it increases the high-frequency loop gain and adds phase lead at f_x to improve the phase margin. The example shows that lead compensation in the feedback network can be tricky because it can cause the amplifier to become unstable if the lead capacitor is too large or too small.

12.6   Techniques for Compensating Feedback Amplifiers

Suppose an amplifier has an open-loop transfer function given by Eq. (12.73). Let us assume a resistive feedback network with the transfer function $H(s) = b$, where $b < 1$. Typical Bode plots for $|G(j\omega)|$ and $|H(j\omega)|^{-1} = 1/b$ are given in Fig. 12.24(a), where we remember that $1/b$ is the op-amp approximation to the closed-loop gain. It is assumed in the figure that ω_x occurs on the -2 dec/dec slope portion on the plot for $|G(j\omega)|$. The phase margin is given by Eq. (12.76).

Let us assume that $\omega_2 \gg \omega_1$ and that $\omega_x = \omega_2$. For this case, it follows from Eq. (12.76) that the phase margin is

$$\varphi_m = 180\,^\circ - \tan^{-1}\left[\frac{\omega_2}{\omega_1}\right] - \tan^{-1}(1) \simeq 180\,^\circ - 90\,^\circ - 45\,^\circ = 45\,^\circ \qquad (12.84)$$

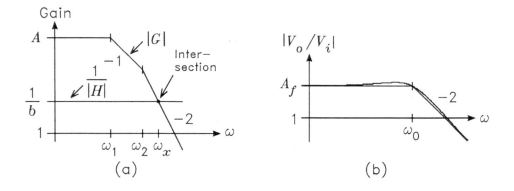

Figure 12.24: (a) Bode magnitude plots for $|G|$ and $|H|^{-1}$. (b) Bode magnitude plot of closed-loop gain.

where $\tan^{-1}(\omega_2/\omega_1) \simeq \tan^{-1}(\infty) = 90°$. If $\omega_x > \omega_2$, it follows that $\varphi_m < 45°$. For a minimum acceptable phase margin of $45°$, we can conclude that the maximum value for the unity-gain crossover frequency is $\omega_x = \omega_2$. This corresponds to the condition that the break between the -1 and the -2 slopes on the asymptotic plot for $|G(j\omega)|$ occur at or below the $1/b$ level.

The poles in the transfer function for the two-pole amplifier with feedback are complex if $Q > 0.5$, where Q is given in Eq. (12.78). Let us solve for the value of Q for the case where $\omega_2 = \omega_x$ in Fig. 12.24. This corresponds to the case above for which $\varphi_m = 45°$. It follows by ratios from Fig. 12.24 that $\omega_2 \div \omega_1 = A \div (1/b)$, or $bA = \omega_2/\omega_1$. This relation and ω_0 from Eq. (12.78) can be used to solve for Q to obtain

$$Q_f = \frac{\sqrt{(1 + \omega_2/\omega_1)\,\omega_1\omega_2}}{\omega_1 + \omega_2} = \sqrt{\frac{\omega_2}{\omega_1 + \omega_2}} \simeq 1 \qquad (12.85)$$

where the approximation assumes that $\omega_2 \gg \omega_1$.

Thus $45°$ of phase margin for the two-pole amplifier corresponds to $Q_f \simeq 1$. The actual and asymptotic Bode plots for $|V_o/V_i|$ for this case are given in Fig. 12.24(b). These plots are to be compared to the ones in Fig. 12.22(a) where $Q_f = 2$. For $Q_f = 1$, the gain peaking in the actual plot is absent for all practical purposes. It can be concluded that an amplifier with a phase margin of $45°$ or more exhibits very little gain peaking in its voltage gain.

For the amplifier with the Bode plots of Fig. 12.24(a), it is clear from the preceding discussion that $\varphi_m < 45°$. For $\varphi_m = 45°$, we must have $\omega_x = \omega_2$. There are four methods which can be used to achieve this without changing the feedback factor b. These are gain constant reduction, first pole lag compensation, and second pole lead compensation. A fourth method called feedforward compensation involves bypassing an internal stage in the amplifier at high frequencies. These four methods are described in the following. Note that changing the feedback factor b causes the amplifier gain to change. For this reason, it is assumed in the following that b is held constant.

12.6.1 Gain Constant Reduction

This method involves reducing the gain constant A. With reference to Fig. 12.24(a), let A be reduced to the value $A' < A$ such that $|G(j\omega_2)| = 1/b$. The asymptotic Bode plots for the modified amplifier are given in Fig. 12.25(a). It follows by ratios from the plot that A' is given by

$$A' = \frac{\omega_2}{b\omega_1} \qquad (12.86)$$

The amplifier with this gain constant has a phase margin $\varphi_m \simeq 45°$.

The gain reduction must be accomplished without changing ω_1 and ω_2. This is best accomplished by reducing the gain of the input subtraction stage. In most amplifiers, this is either a differential amplifier or a

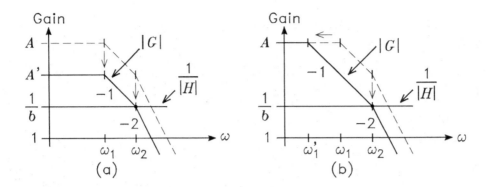

Figure 12.25: (a) Bode plots for gain constant reduction. (b) Bode plots for first-pole lag compensation.

common-emitter stage similar to the ones shown in Fig. 12.26. In the differential amplifier of Fig. 12.26(a), the error output is the small-signal current i_{c1}. Let us assume that the dc tail current I_Q splits equally between Q_1 and Q_2 and that the current gains of the transistors are large. The error current is given by

$$i_{c1} = \frac{v_i - bv_o}{2\,(r_e + R_E)} \tag{12.87}$$

where b is the feedback factor and r_e is the intrinsic emitter resistance. These are given by

$$b = \frac{R_1}{R_1 + R_F} \qquad r_e = \frac{V_T}{I_E} = \frac{2V_T}{I_Q} \tag{12.88}$$

where V_T is the thermal voltage which has the value $V_T = 0.0259\,\text{V}$ at $T = 27\ ^{\circ}\text{C}$.

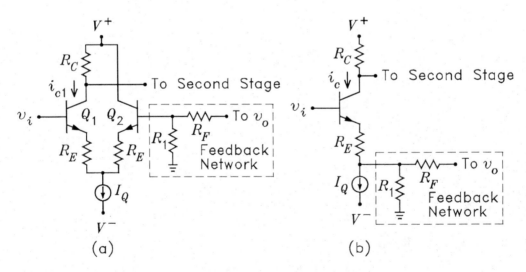

Figure 12.26: Typical input subtraction stages. (a) Diff amp. (b) Common-emitter stage.

The gain of the differential amplifier is inversely proportional to $r_e + R_E$. The gain of the stage can be reduced by increasing the value of R_E. If R'_E is the value to which R_E is increased, it follows by ratios that

$$\frac{A'}{A} = \frac{r_e + R_E}{r_e + R'_E} \tag{12.89}$$

A second way that A may be reduced is to decrease I_Q so that r_e increases. This is not the preferred method because reducing the tail current reduces the amplifier slew rate.

For the common-emitter circuit of Fig. 12.26(b), the error current is given by

$$i_c = \frac{v_i - bv_o}{r_e + R_E + R_1 \| R_F} \tag{12.90}$$

where $r_e = V_T/I_E$ and I_E is the quiescent emitter current. (Note that I_E and I_Q are not be equal if a dc current flows in R_1 and R_F). If I_E is held constant, the gain of the input stage can be reduced by increasing R_E or by increasing $R_1 \| R_F$. However, any change in $R_1 \| R_F$ must be done in a way that does not change the feedback factor b. If R_E is increased to R'_E and $R_1 \| R_F$ is increased to $R'_1 \| R'_F$ such that $R_1/(R_1 + R_F) = R'_1/(R'_1 + R'_F)$, it follows by ratios that

$$\frac{A'}{A} = \frac{r_e + R_E + R_1 \| R_F}{r_e + R'_E + R'_1 \| R'_F} = \frac{r_e + R_E + bR_F}{r_e + R'_E + bR'_F} \tag{12.91}$$

12.6.2 First Pole Lag Compensation

This method of compensation is also known as dominant pole compensation. It involves reducing the frequency of the first or dominant pole. It is called lag compensation because a phase lag is introduced when the bandwidth is reduced. With reference to Fig. 12.24(a), let ω_1 be reduced to the value $\omega'_1 < \omega_1$ such that $|G(j\omega_2)| = 1/b$. The asymptotic Bode plots for the modified amplifier are given in Fig. 12.25(b). It follows by ratios from the Bode plot that ω'_1 is given by

$$\omega'_1 = \frac{\omega_2}{bA} \tag{12.92}$$

The amplifier with this first pole has a phase margin $\varphi_m \simeq 45°$.

The first pole frequency reduction should be accomplished without changing A or ω_2, unless ω_2 is increased. The first pole is usually set by the stage that follows the input subtraction stage. In most circuits, it is a common-emitter stage, a compound common-emitter stage, or a cascode stage similar to the ones shown in Fig. 12.27. The figures show a compensating capacitor C_c connected from the output to the input of each circuit. This capacitor is also called a lag capacitor or a Miller capacitor. It provides negative feedback that reduces the high-frequency gain of the stage.

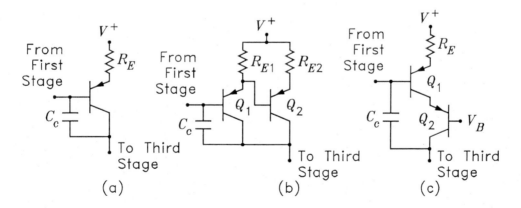

Figure 12.27: Second gain stages. (a) Common emitter. (b) Compound common emitter. (c) Cascode.

In Fig. 12.27(a), C_c is effectively in parallel with the internal collector-base capacitance c_μ of the transistor. The pole frequency is approximately inversely proportional to the total capacitance $C_c + c_\mu$. If the pole is to be reduced from ω_1 to ω_1' by increasing C_c to C_c', it follows by ratios that

$$\frac{\omega_1'}{\omega_1} = \frac{C_c + c_\mu}{C_c' + c_\mu} \qquad (12.93)$$

This equation approximately holds for the compound common-emitter stage of Fig. 12.27(b), where c_μ is the collector-to-base capacitance of Q_1. For the cascode circuit of Fig. 12.27(c), the formula approximately holds with $c_\mu = 0$.

For the circuits of Figs. 12.27(a) and (b), it can be shown that the compensation capacitor not only decreases ω_1 but also increases the second pole frequency of the stage. This is called pole splitting and the capacitor is often referred to as a pole-splitting capacitor. This effect improves the stability of the amplifier, especially if ω_2 is caused by that stage.

12.6.3 Second Pole Lead Compensation

This method involves increasing ω_2. It is called lead compensation because a phase lead is introduced when the bandwidth is increased. With reference to Fig. 12.24(a), let ω_2 be increased to the value $\omega_2' > \omega_2$ such that $|G(j\omega_2)| = 1/b$. The asymptotic Bode plots for the modified amplifier are given in Fig. 12.28(a). It follows by ratios from the Bode plots that ω_2' is given by

$$\omega_2' = bA\omega_1 \qquad (12.94)$$

The amplifier with this second pole has a phase margin $\varphi_m \simeq 45\,°$.

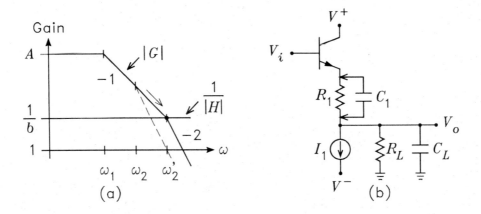

Figure 12.28: (a) Bode plots for second-pole lead compensation. (b) Example circuit.

Lead compensation can be difficult to implement in the open-loop amplifier unless a stage can be found where adding a capacitor cancels a pole. Such a circuit is shown in Fig. 12.28(b). Without capacitor C_1, the transfer function for V_o/V_i is a low-pass function. With the addition of C_1, the pole in the low-pass function can be canceled or moved to a higher frequency. The increase in high frequency gain adds phase lead to the open-loop transfer function of the amplifier. Thus C_1 is called a phase-lead capacitor.

Lead compensation is often implemented in the feedback network. This is illustrated in Example 21 where C_2 in Fig. 12.23 causes the plot of $|H(j\omega)|^{-1}$ to have a -1 slope at ω_x in Fig. 12.23. C_2 is called a lead capacitor because it increases the bandwidth of the loop. When C_2 becomes a short circuit at high frequencies, the feedback factor increases to unity. This causes the closed-loop gain to decrease at high frequencies, thus decreasing the closed-loop bandwidth. In order for C_2 to not affect the gain at audio frequencies, ω_2 should be well above the audio band. In most applications, the lead capacitor is arrived at experimentally. It is shown in Example 21 that too small or too large a value of C_2 can cause the amplifier to be unstable. Therefore, lead compensation must be approached with care.

12.6.4 Feedforward Compensation

Feedforward compensation is a technique that involves bypassing an amplifier gain stage at high frequencies with a resistor-capacitor network. The method is commonly used in circuits which have two high-gain stages in cascade to achieve a very high open-loop gain. To improve stability, the second high-gain stage is bypassed at high frequencies by a resistor-capacitor network so that the overall amplifier behaves like it has only one high-gain stage at ω_x. Fig. 12.29 illustrates the concept of feedforward compensation. At low frequencies, C_1 and C_2 are open circuits so that the signal is amplified by the two stages in cascade. At high frequencies, C_1 and C_2 become short circuits and the signal is amplified by the first stage only.

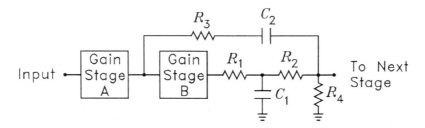

Figure 12.29: Technique of feedforward compensation.

Feedforward compensation techniques are commonly used in the design of low-noise IC op-amps. In audio amplifiers, feedforward compensation around the output stage can be used to improve the amplifier stability with capacitive loads. This is covered in an example amplifier design in the following.

12.7 Output Stage Topologies

To investigate the typical circuits of the stages in the amplifier modeled in Fig. 12.4, we start with the power output stage that drives the loudspeaker load and work backward to the differential amplifier input stage. The power output stage supplies current to the loudspeaker load. High power transistors must be used to supply this current. These transistors must be mounted on heat sinks to dissipate the heat. Because of the size of the output transistors, they have higher internal capacitances compared to lower power transistors. To maximize their bandwidth, it is preferable to operate them in a configuration that has a low voltage gain. The unity-gain CC configuration is preferred. Should the output transistors be operated in the CE configuration, local negative feedback must be used to reduce the stage gain to unity for maximum bandwidth. A desirable characteristic of the output stage is a low open-loop output resistance. The CC configuration exhibits the lowest output resistance. This is another reason that it is preferred over the CE configuration.

12.7.1 Common-Collector Stage

A complementary CC output stage is shown in Fig. 12.30(a). The two output transistors are Q_{14} and Q_{15}. Both must be mounted on a suitable heat sink. Positive load current is supplied by Q_{14}. Negative load current is supplied by Q_{15}. The series emitter resistors provide local negative feedback, help stabilize the quiescent dc bias current, and act as current sense resistors for the protection circuits (discussed in a following section). To increase the current rating of the output stage, additional transistors can be added in parallel with Q_{14} and Q_{15}. To ensure equal sharing of current between transistors, separate resistors must be used in series with the emitter of each. A typical value for the emitter resistors is $0.33\,\Omega$.

Q_{10} through Q_{13} are called driver transistors. These provide the necessary current gain to drive the bases of Q_{14} and Q_{15}. Q_{10} and Q_{12} operate as a cascade CC stage which drives the base of Q_{14}. Q_{11} and Q_{13} operate as a cascade CC stage which drives the base of Q_{15}. Another name for the cascade CC stage is the Darlington connection. For best thermal stability, the driver transistors should never be mounted on the

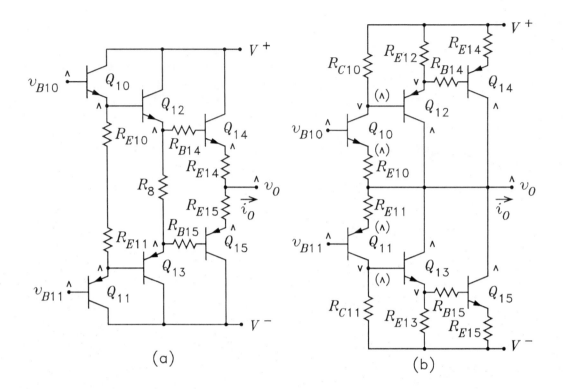

Figure 12.30: (a) Complementary common-collector output stage. (b) Common-emitter output stage.

heat sinks with the output transistors. Q_{12} and Q_{13} normally require individual heat sinks to dissipate the heat generated.

The current gain of a CC stage is the ratio of the emitter current to the base current. It is $1 + \beta$, where β is the BJT current gain. Because each side of the output stage consists of three CC stages in cascade, the current gain of the output stage is given by the product of three current gains. If all BJTs have the same β, the current gain of the stage is $(1 + \beta)^3$. The voltage gain of the output stage is the product of the gains of three CC stages. Because the gain of a single CC stage is less than unity, the overall gain of the output stage is less than unity. A typical value might be 0.95.

Series base resistors R_{B14} and R_{B15} help prevent what are called parasitic oscillations. Typical values are $3\,\Omega$ to $10\,\Omega$. A parasitic oscillation is a burst of high-frequency oscillation that occurs at the peak of the output voltage waveform when the amplifier drives a load.

There are two inputs v_{B10} and v_{B11} to the output stage in Fig. 12.30. The signal tracing arrows show that the circuit is a non-inverting stage. The two inputs are driven by the same ac signal but must have different dc voltages applied to them. The dc voltage sets the bias currents in the output transistors. The two input voltages are of the form $v_{B10} = v_S + V_B/2$ and $v_{B11} = v_S - V_B/2$, where v_S is the audio signal voltage and V_B is a dc bias voltage. Under quiescent conditions, the load current is zero and $I_{E14} = I_{E15}$. The dc bias voltage V_B can be written

$$V_B = V_{BE10} + V_{BE12} + V_{BE14} + I_{E14}R_{E14} + I_{E15}R_{E15} + V_{EB15} + V_{EB13} + V_{EB11} \tag{12.95}$$

Crossover Distortion

If $V_B = 0$, all transistors in the output stage are quiescently off. Fig. 12.31(a) shows the graph of the output voltage v_O as a function of the input voltage v_S for both $V_B = 0$ and for $V_B > 0$. Fig. 12.31(b) shows the corresponding output signals for v_S a sine wave. The distortion illustrated in Fig. 12.31(b) is called crossover distortion or center clipping. It is caused by the non-zero threshold voltages of the driver and output transistors. Typically, the threshold voltage for these transistors is approximately 0.5 V. Thus Q_{10}, Q_{12}, and Q_{14} turn on when $v_S > 1.5$ V and Q_{11}, Q_{13}, and Q_{15} turn on when $v_S < -1.5$ V so that the width of the crossover region in Fig. 12.31(a) is approximately 3 V.

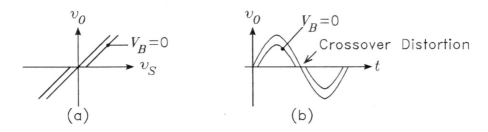

Figure 12.31: (a) Plot of v_O versus v_S for $V_B = 0$ and $V_B > 0$. (b) Sine wave responses.

Although crossover distortion is partially canceled by negative feedback, it is not possible to completely eliminate all of it with feedback. To minimize it, Q_{14} and Q_{15} must have a quiescent bias current that is non-zero so that both transistors are conducting in the crossover region. Typically, the required bias current is 25 to 30 mA. To obtain this current, V_B must be approximately 3.3 V. This is calculated as 0.6 V for Q_{10} and Q_{11}, 0.55 V for Q_{12} and Q_{13}, and 0.5 V for Q_{14} and Q_{15}. The higher the current rating, the lower the threshold voltage. When driving a load, the output transistors heat up and the bias current increases. This can lead to what is called thermal runaway in the output stage if V_B is not decreased with temperature. This is discussed in more detail in the next section.

Example 22 *For the output stage in Fig. 12.30, it is given that $R_{E14} = R_{E15} = 0.33\,\Omega$, $R_{B14} = R_{B15} = 3.3\,\Omega$, and $R_{E10} = R_{E11}$. The specified bias currents are $I_{C14} = I_{C15} = 25$ mA and $I_{C10} = I_{C11} = I_{C12} = I_{C13} = 4$ mA. The dc junction voltages can be assumed to be $V_{BE14} = -V_{EB15} = 0.5$ V, $V_{BE12} = -V_{EB13} = 0.55$ V, $V_{BE10} = -V_{EB11} = 0.6$ V. Solve for R_{E10}, R_{E11}, and R_8. Neglect all base currents.*

Solution. The voltage drop across R_8 is $0.025 \times 2 \times 0.33 + 2 \times 0.5 = 1.02$ V. Thus $R_8 = 1.02/0.004 = 254\,\Omega$. The voltage drop across $R_{E10} + R_{E11}$ is $1.02 + 2 \times 0.55 = 2.12$ V. Thus $R_{E10} = R_{E11} = 0.5 \times (2.12/0.004) = 265\,\Omega$.

Class of Operation

The class of operation is defined by the quiescent bias current in the output transistors. In a class-C amplifier, V_B is smaller than the value required to cut on Q_{14} and Q_{15} and crossover distortion is visible on the output. In a class-B amplifier, V_B is just large enough to quiescently put Q_{14} and Q_{15} at the threshold of conduction. In this case, crossover distortion is just barely visible. In a class-AB amplifier, V_B is large enough to quiescently bias Q_{14} and Q_{15} into conduction at a typical current of 25 to 30 mA. When the output voltage goes positive, Q_{14} supplies the load current and Q_{15} gradually cuts off. When the output voltage goes negative, Q_{15} supplies the load current and Q_{14} gradually cuts off.

In a class-A amplifier, V_B is large enough so that the quiescent current in Q_{14} and Q_{15} is large enough so that neither cuts off. The bias current must be greater than one-half the peak loudspeaker load current. When the output stage is biased this way, crossover distortion cannot be generated by either Q_{14} or Q_{15} cutting on and off with the signal. This argument assumes a resistive load. With a reactive load, the bias current may have to be even larger. All loudspeakers present a reactive load.

Class-A amplifiers are considered to be the lowest distortion amplifiers. However, there is a large penalty to be paid. Suppose a class-A amplifier is designed to deliver 100 W to an 8 Ω load. The peak load voltage is 40 V and the peak load current is 5 A. Thus Q_{14} and Q_{15} must be biased at $5/2 = 2.5$ A or greater. The power supply voltages must be greater than 40 V. Let us assume voltages of ±50 V and a bias current of 2.5 A. For a stereo amplifier, the quiescent power dissipated is $2 \times 100 \times 2.5 = 500$ W. This is typical of the output of an electric heater when set on low. If the amplifier is biased for a $4\,\Omega$ load, the quiescent power would be 1000 W, or about what an electric heater puts out when set on medium or high. Thus a class-A amplifier can be expensive to operate, especially if the heat it produces must be removed by a home air conditioning system.

Feedback from the Output Stage

Feedback is taken from one or more points in the output stage and fed back to the amplifier input stage where it is subtracted from the input signal to form the error signal. In Fig. 12.30, feedback can be taken from two points. The main feedback is taken from the junction of R_{E14} and R_{E15}. When feedforward compensation around the output stage is used, high-frequency feedback can be taken from the junction of R_{E10} and R_{E11}. The connection of the feedback network to these two points is illustrated in a following example.

12.7.2 Common-Emitter Stage

Fig. 12.30(b) shows an output stage in which the two output transistors Q_{14} and Q_{15} are operated in the common-emitter configuration. Driver transistors Q_{12} and Q_{13} operate as common-collector stages to provide current gain to drive the bases of Q_{14} and Q_{15}. Pre-driver transistors Q_{10} and Q_{11} operate as common-emitter stages to drive the bases of Q_{12} and Q_{13}. Negative feedback is taken from the collectors of Q_{12} through Q_{15} to the emitters of Q_{10} and Q_{11}. The signal flow through the circuit is shown by the signal tracing symbols, where the symbols in parenthesis represent feedback. The connection of Q_{10} and Q_{12} and the connection of Q_{11} and Q_{13} are sometimes called Sziklai or complementary Darlington connections.

The negative feedback from the collectors of Q_{12} through Q_{15} to the emitters of Q_{10} and Q_{11} is disabled if the common node between R_{E10} and R_{E11} is connected to ground and the branch to the right of that node is open circuited. In this case, the output stage would exhibit a high voltage gain, a low bandwidth, and a high output impedance. The negative feedback reduces the gain of the stage to approximately unity, widens the bandwidth, and lowers the output impedance. In general, the common-emitter output stage exhibits a higher output impedance than the common-collector stage. In addition, the feedback around the stage can cause stability problems if the feedback becomes positive at some frequency.

12.7.3 Quasi-Complementary Output Stage

Fig. 12.32(a) shows what is called a quasi-complementary output stage. The upper half of the circuit is the same as the common-collector stage while the lower half is the same as the common-emitter stage. The feature of this topology is that the output transistors Q_{14} and Q_{15} and the driver transistors Q_{12} and Q_{13} are all npn types. Because high power npn transistors are often more rugged and can supply more current than pnp types, this stage has been used in many amplifiers.

12.7.4 MOSFET Output Stages

The output stages in Figs. 12.32(b) and 12.33 are MOSFET equivalents of the BJT circuits. The MOSFET gate current is so small that only two driver transistors are shown in each circuit. At high frequencies, the gate-source and gate-drain capacitances in the MOSFET cause gate current to flow. The driver transistors supply this current. The MOSFET symbols in the figures are for enhancement mode devices. Like the BJT, these devices are quiescently cutoff. A dc bias voltage V_B across the bases of Q_{10} and Q_{11} sets the quiescent current in the output transistors. Unlike the BJT, the MOSFET has a current at which its temperature coefficient is zero. If it is biased below this current, its current will increase with temperature. If it is biased above this current, its current will decrease with temperature. Biasing it at the zero temperature coefficient current eliminates the need for temperature compensating the bias supply. In some devices, however, this current is large, causing a high quiescent power dissipation in the heat sinks.

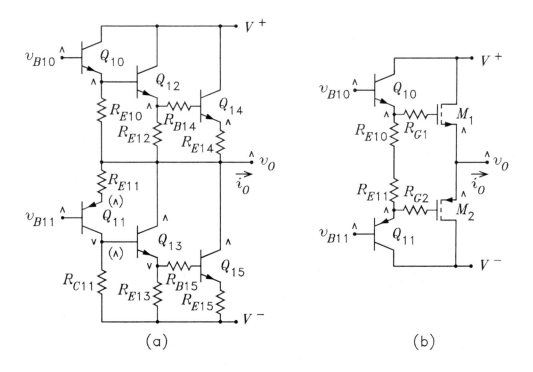

Figure 12.32: (a) Quasi-complementary output stage. (b) Common-drain output stage.

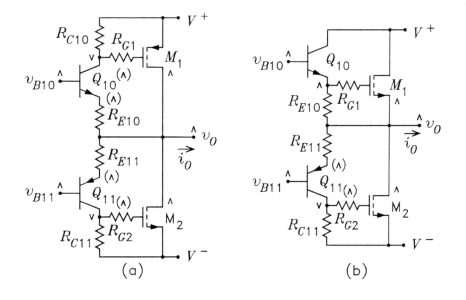

Figure 12.33: (a) Common-source output stage. (b) Quasi-complementary output stage.

As with the BJT output stages, transistors can be added in parallel with the output devices to increase the current rating of the MOSFET output stages. If the output devices are biased at a current for which the bias current decreases with temperature, the currents in the parallel devices tend to equalize without the aid of resistors in series the source leads. However, this can make the problem of a high quiescent power dissipation in the heat sinks even more serious.

12.8 Voltage Gain Stage

Fig. 12.34 shows the circuit of the typical voltage gain stage which precedes the output stage. Q_7 and Q_8 are operated as CE stages to obtain a high gain. Signal tracing shows that the circuit is an inverting stage. C_4 and C_5 are lag compensation capacitors which set the dominant pole. A typical value for these is 10 pF to 100 pF. R_{E7} and R_{E8} provide local negative feedback for improved linearity and bias stability. The quiescent currents in Q_7 and Q_8 flow through the circuit associated with Q_9. This circuit is called a V_{BE} multiplier. It sets the dc voltage V_B between the two outputs and thus sets the bias currents in the output stage. Potentiometer R_p provides adjustment to set the voltage V_B.

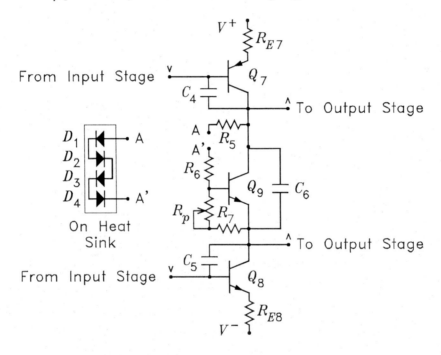

Figure 12.34: Second gain stage.

The four diodes in Fig. 12.34 are mounted on the heat sinks with the output transistors. When the amplifier drives a load, the heat sinks warm up due to the power dissipated in the output transistors. This warms up the diodes which decreases the voltage across the V_{BE} multiplier. (The voltage across a diode decreases approximately 2 mV for each 1° C increase in temperature.) Without this negative thermal feedback, the bias current in the output transistors would increase as the heat sink temperature increases. This would cause the heat sinks to heat up further and increase the bias current still more. This positive feedback phenomenon is called thermal runaway. An alternate circuit puts Q_9 on the heat sink with the output transistors. In this case, the diodes are not needed.

MOSFETs have a positive thermal coefficient at low current levels and a negative thermal coefficient at high levels. The current at which the coefficient is zero is called the threshold current. Thus thermal runaway is not a problem with a MOSFET output stage if the devices are biased at or above the threshold current.

For many devices, the threshold current is relatively large, thus requiring a high bias current compared to a BJT output stage. This increases power dissipation in the heat sinks.

The quiescent collector-to-emitter voltage across Q_9 in Fig. 12.34 is the bias voltage V_B. To solve for this, we neglect the base current in Q_9. The current through R_p and R_7 is given by $V_{BE9}/(R_p + R_7)$. This current flows through R_5, the four diodes, and R_6. The bias voltage is given by

$$V_B = 4V_D + \frac{V_{BE9}}{R_p + R_7}(R_5 + R_6) + V_{BE9} = 4V_D + V_{BE9}\left[1 + \frac{R_5 + R_6}{R_p + R_7}\right] \tag{12.96}$$

where V_D is the voltage across each diode.

For best voltage regulation, I_{C9} should be greater than the current through its base bias circuit. In addition, the current through the base bias circuit should be large compared to I_{B9}. For example, I_{C9} might be chosen to be $0.9I_{C7}$ and the current through R_5 to be $0.1I_{C7}$. The four diodes should be glued into holes in the same wall of the heat sink on which the power output transistors are mounted. The leads which connect the diodes to the amplifier circuit board exhibit capacitance to ground. To minimize this, the lead lengths should be kept short. R_5 and R_6 help to isolate this capacitance from the circuit board.

Example 23 *The V_{BE} multiplier in Fig. 12.34 is to be designed for a nominal voltage of 3.3 V. Q_7 and Q_8 are biased at 4 mA. If $V_{BE9} = 0.65$ V, $I_{C9} = 0.9I_{C7}$, and $V_D = 0.5$ V, solve for $R_5 + R_6$ and $R_p + R_7$, where R_p is the adjusted value of the potentiometer.*

Solution. The current in the base bias network is $0.1 \times 4\,\text{mA} = 0.4\,\text{mA}$. If I_{B9} is neglected, $R_p + R_7 = 0.65/0.4 = 1.625\,\text{k}\Omega$. From Eq. (12.96), we have $3.3 = 4 \times 0.5 + 0.65\,[1 + (R_5 + R_6)/1625]$. Solution yields $R_5 + R_6 = 1.625\,\text{k}\Omega$.

Example 24 *The V_{BE} multiplier circuit of Example 23 is to be adjusted over the range from 3 V to 3.6 V. Solve for R_p and R_7, where R_p is the full value of the potentiometer.*

Solution. Maximum voltage occurs with $R_p = 0$ and minimum voltage occurs with R_p set at its full value. From Eq. (12.96), we have

$$3.6 = 2 + 0.65\,(1 + 1625/R_7) \qquad 3 = 2 + 0.65\,[1 + 1625/(R_p + R_7)]$$

Simultaneous solution yields $R_7 = 1112\,\Omega$ and $R_p = 3018\,\Omega$.

12.9 Input Stage

Fig. 12.35 shows the diagram of a typical differential amplifier input stage. There are two complementary diff-amps which are operated in parallel to obtain two outputs. There are two inputs, one for the input signal and one for the feedback signal. The signal flow through the circuit is shown by the signal tracing symbols, where the symbols in parenthesis represent feedback. The symbol polarities show that the input and feedback signals are out of phase at the collectors of Q_1 and Q_3, which represents negative feedback.

Q_5 and Q_6 are operated as CB stages. C_2, C_3, and zener diodes D_5 and D_6 provide an ac signal ground reference for the bases of Q_5 and Q_6. In addition, D_5 and D_6 act as voltage regulators to maintain the base voltages constant if the power supply voltage varies. Because the current gain of a CB stage is approximately unity, the addition of Q_5 and Q_6 to the diff-amp stage does not change its gain. These transistors serve to increase the breakdown voltage rating of the input stage. R_{C5} and R_{C6} are the diff-amp load resistors. The tail current in the npn diff-amp is set by R_4 and the voltage on C_3. Similarly, the tail current in the pnp diff-amp is set by R_3 and the voltage on C_2. R_{E1} through R_{E4} set the diff-amp transconductance. Let I_Q be the tail current in each diff-amp and let $R_E = R_{E1} = R_{E2} = R_{E3} = R_{E4}$. If the β of the transistors is large, the transconductance of the diff amps is given by

$$G_m = \frac{i_{c5}}{v_i - v_f} = \frac{-i_{c6}}{v_i - v_f} = \frac{1}{2\,(R_E + r_e)} \tag{12.97}$$

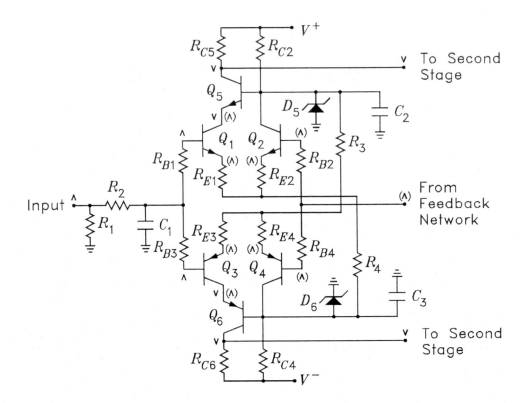

Figure 12.35: Complementary diff amp input stage.

where v_i is the input voltage, v_f is the feedback voltage, and r_e is the intrinsic emitter resistance given in Eq. (12.88).

R_1 sets the amplifier input resistance. R_2 and C_1 form a single-pole low-pass input filter. The purpose of this filter is to reduce the amplitude of any rf signal that might be present at the input. Such signals are often picked up when radio or television transmitters are nearby. In addition, the filter can be designed to prevent the amplifier from slewing before it exhibits peak clipping. If base currents are neglected, the cutoff frequency of this filter is $f_c = 1/[2\pi(R_2 + R_S)C_1]$, where R_S is the source resistance. A typical value for this frequency is 100 kHz to several hundred kHz. R_{B1} through R_{B4} serve to isolate the BJT bases. These have a typical value of $100\,\Omega$ to several hundred ohms.

Example 25 *The tail current in each diff-amp in Fig. 12.35 is to be 4 mA. The transconductance gain is specified to be $G_m = 3.2 \times 10^{-3}$. Calculate the value of the emitter resistors R_{E1} through R_{E4}.*

Solution. From Eqs. (12.97) and (12.88), we have $3.2 \times 10^{-3} = 1/(R_E + 2 \times 0.0259/0.004)$. Solution yields $R_E = 300\,\Omega$.

Example 26 *The voltage on C_2 in Fig. 12.35 is $+40\,V$. The voltage on C_3 is $-40\,V$. For the value of the emitter resistors calculated in Example 25, calculate the required values for the tail bias resistors R_3 and R_4. Assume that both inputs to the diff amps are grounded and that $V_{BE1} = V_{BE2} = -V_{EB3} = -V_{EB4} = 0.65\,V$. Neglect base currents.*

Solution. By symmetry, $R_3 = R_4$. We can write $0.004 = [-0.65 - (-40)]/(R_4 + 300/2)$. Solution yields $R_4 = R_3 = 9688\,\Omega$.

12.10 Completed Amplifier Circuit

Fig. 12.36 shows the diagram of the amplifier with the three stages connected together. A feedback network consisting of R_{F1} through R_{F4} and C_{F1} and C_{F2} connect the output stage back to the input stage. In the audio band, C_{F1} is a short circuit and C_{F2} and C_{F3} are open circuits causing the feedback to be taken from the v_O node. The feedback factor b is given by

$$b = \frac{R_{F1}}{R_{F1} + R_{F2} + R_{F3}} \tag{12.98}$$

The closed-loop voltage gain is approximately $1/b$. At infrasonic frequencies, C_{F1} becomes an open circuit. This gives the amplifier 100% dc feedback for improved bias stability.

Above the audio band, C_{F2} and C_{F3} become short circuits. This causes the high-frequency feedback to be taken from the v_O' node, thus bypassing Q_{12} through Q_{15} in the loop-gain transfer function. This is called feedforward compensation of the output stage because the high-frequency feedback is taken from a point in the loop that is forward of the point where the low-frequency feedback is taken. The feedback factor should not change when C_{F2} and C_{F3} become short circuits. This is true if

$$R_{F4} = \frac{R_{F2} + R_{F3} + (1 - k) R_{F1}}{k (1 + R_{F1}/R_{F2})} \tag{12.99}$$

where $k = v_o/v_o'$, i.e. the small-signal gain from the v_o' node to the v_o node. A typical value might be $k = 0.95$. Let f_f be the frequency at which the feedforward compensation becomes active. It can be shown that C_{F2} and C_{F3} are given by

$$C_{F2} = \frac{R_{F1} + R_{F2} + R_{F3}}{2\pi f_f R_{F1} R_{F2} R_{F3}} \times R_{F1} \| R_{F2} \| R_{F4} \qquad C_{F3} = \frac{R_{F2} \| R_{F3}}{R_{F4}} C_{F2} \tag{12.100}$$

A typical value for f_f might be in the range from 150 kHz to 200 kHz.

The lower closed-loop cutoff frequency is determined by C_{F1} and R_{F1} and is given by $f_\ell = 1/2\pi R_{F1} C_{F1}$. A typical value might be in the range from 1 Hz to 2 Hz. C_{F1} typically has a value of several hundred μF. Electrolytic capacitors must be used for capacitors this large. A non-polar capacitor is preferred. A non-polar electrolytic can be realized with two polar electrolytics of twice the desired value connected in series with the negative terminals of each connected together. C_{F1} should have a high quality capacitor connected in parallel with it to improve its high-frequency performance. Typically, a $0.1\,\mu$F polyester capacitor is used for this purpose.

Fig. 12.36 shows a parallel resistor R_9 and inductor L_1 in series with the loudspeaker output and a series resistor R_{10} and capacitor C_7 in parallel with the output. These elements help suppress continuous and parasitic high-frequency oscillations. L_1 and R_9 isolate shunt capacitance in the loudspeaker load from the amplifier at high frequencies. R_{10} and C_7 maintain a resistive load on the amplifier at high frequencies. The latter network is often called a Zobel network. At audio frequencies, L_1 is a short circuit and C_7 is an open circuit so that the networks have no effect. Typical values are 1 to 5 μH for L_1, 3 to 10 Ω for R_9 and R_{10}, and $0.1\,\mu$F for C_7. The ground connection for C_7 should never be made to the amplifier circuit board or induced oscillations can occur. A preferred location for the $R_{10} - C_7$ network is on the loudspeaker output jacks. In this case, C_7 is grounded to the central power supply ground through the loudspeaker ground wire.

Example 27 *The feedback network in Fig. 12.36 is to be designed so that the amplifier gain in the audio band is 21 (26.4 dB). The lower cutoff frequency is to be 1 Hz. The frequency at which the feedforward compensation becomes active is to be 150 kHz. If $R_{F1} = 1.1$ kΩ, $R_{F2} = R_{F3}$, and $k = v_O/v_O' = 0.96$, solve for the other elements in the feedback network.*

Solution. For a gain of 21, $b = 1/21$. With $R_{F2} = R_{F3}$, Eq. (12.98) can be used to obtain $R_{F2} = R_{F3} = (21 - 1) R_{F1}/2 = 11$ kΩ. For $f_\ell = 1$ Hz, we have $C_{F1} = 1/2\pi R_{F1} = 145\,\mu$F. Eq. (12.99) gives $R_{F4} = (22 + 0.04 \times 1.1) / [0.96 (1 + 1.1/11)] = 20.9$ kΩ. Eq. (12.100) gives $C_{F2} = 176$ pF and $C_{F3} = 46.3$ pF.

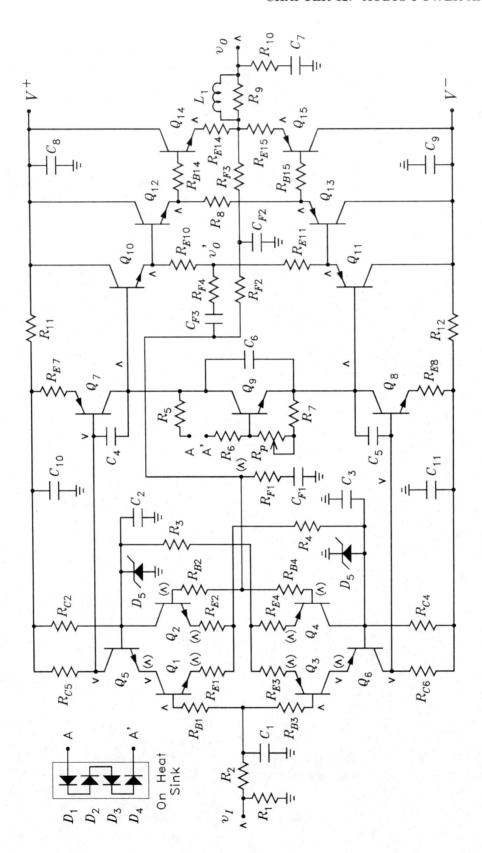

Figure 12.36: Completed amplifier circuit.

12.11 Protection Circuits

Protection circuits are designed to protect the amplifier output transistors from failure in the event that an overload condition develops. The simplest type of protection circuit is a fuse in series with the loudspeaker output. If the output leads are accidentally shorted together or if the amplifier is used to drive too low an impedance, the fuse should blow before any of the transistors in the amplifier do. However, a blown fuse causes a dead amplifier until the fuse can be replaced. This is not acceptable in many applications.

Current limit circuits were used in early amplifier designs to protect the output transistors from failure. Although these circuits have been replaced in most designs by voltage-current sensing limiters, the current limiter is still used in some designs. These circuits activate to limit the maximum current output from the amplifier. Unlike a fuse, they do not require replacement after being activated.

BJT Current Limiter Circuits

Fig. 12.37 shows a simplified version of the output stage of Fig. 12.30 with a protection circuit added. First, we consider the operation of the circuit with the elements R_{17}, R_{18}, D_{11}, and D_{12} omitted. In this case, the protection circuit acts as a current limiter. Q_{16} and Q_{17} are connected so that they sense the voltage across R_{E14} and R_{E15}. Because all output current flows through these resistors, the voltage across them is proportional to the load current. With the proper design, Q_{16} and Q_{17} can be made to turn on when the load current exceeds a desired threshold. Q_{16} turns on for positive i_O and Q_{17} turns on for negative i_O. When either transistor turns on, base drive current to Q_{10} or Q_{11} is removed and the amplifier goes into current limit. R_{13} through R_{16} form voltage dividers which set the current limit thresholds. Typically, R_{13} and R_{14} have a value in the range of 100 to 300 Ω. R_{15} and R_{16} are calculated to obtain the desired voltage division ratio.

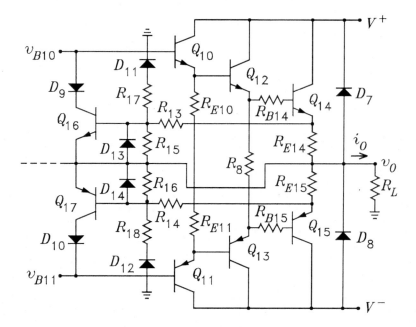

Figure 12.37: Output stage with VI limiter protection circuit. The circuit operates as a current limiter with R_{17}, R_{18}, D_{11}, and D_{12} omitted.

Current limit circuits can oscillate when activated. These oscillations can be suppressed by adding capacitors, typically 0.01 μF, in parallel with R_{13} and R_{14}. To prevent activation on fast transients, capacitors can be added in parallel with R_{15} and R_{16}. A typical value for these is 0.1 μF.

D_7 through D_{10} protect the amplifier circuit from voltage transients which can occur when driving an inductive load such as a loudspeaker. Suppose the current limiter is activated when driving an inductive load. This causes the amplifier output stage to cut off and the source impedance seen by the load inductance increases abruptly. Because the current in an inductor cannot change instantaneously, the load current does not change at the instant that the current limit occurs. This causes the amplifier output voltage to change rapidly. If it should increase to a value greater than the rail voltage, an output transistor can fail. D_7 and D_8 prevent this by shunting the inductive load current into one of the rails. D_9 and D_{10} prevent the base-collector junctions of Q_{16} and Q_{17} from being forward biased when this happens. D_{13} and D_{14} prevent reverse breakdown of the base-emitter junctions of Q_{16} and Q_{17}.

BJT Safe Operating Area

The maximum safe current that any transistor can deliver to a load is a function of the voltage across it. The maximum current for any voltage can be obtained from the safe operating area curves specified by the manufacturer. A typical curve for a power BJT is shown in Fig. 12.38. For $V_{CE} < V_1$, the transistor can supply a maximum current I_1 which is determined by the mechanical bonds that attach the internal leads to the semiconductor material. For $V_1 < V_{CE} < V_2$, the current decreases with increasing voltage. The maximum current in this region is determined by the maximum power dissipation inside the transistor. For $V_{CE} > V_2$, the current rapidly approaches zero. The maximum current here is determined by a phenomenon called second breakdown. If this occurs, the transistor will fail, usually developing an internal collector-emitter short circuit. The VI limiter is a protection circuit which can be designed to limit the BJT to its safe operating area. It is described below.

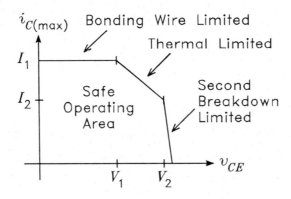

Figure 12.38: Typical BJT safe operating area.

BJT VI Limiter Circuit

Without the elements R_{17}, R_{18}, D_{11}, and D_{12} in the circuit of Fig. 12.37, the circuit acts as a current limiter. The addition of these elements causes the circuit to act as a voltage-current limiter or VI limiter. The elements modify the current limiter circuit to cause it to sense the output voltage v_O as well as the output current i_O. The circuit can be designed to constrain the operation of the output transistors to stay within the safe operating area.

To explain the operation of the VI limiter, first consider the case of a short circuited output, i.e. $R_L = 0$. In this case, $v_O = 0$ and the emitters of Q_{16} and Q_{17} are grounded. Under this condition, Q_{16} and Q_{17} have the same limit threshold as the basic current limiter. The elements D_{11}, R_{17}, D_{12}, and R_{18} have little effect on the threshold of the current limit because the threshold voltage of D_{11} and D_{12} is approximately the same as that of Q_{16} and Q_{17}. Because R_{17} and R_{18}, respectively, are in series with D_{11} and D_{12}, there is a higher available voltage to saturate Q_{16} and Q_{17} than there is to turn on D_{11} and D_{12}.

Next, consider the case for $R_L > 0$ so that $|v_O| > 0$. For $i_O > 0$, the drop across R_{E14} tends to forward bias the base-to-emitter junction of Q_{16} while v_O at the emitter of Q_{16} tends to reverse bias the junction. This reverse bias action causes the value of i_O at which Q_{16} saturates to increase as v_O increases. Because $V_{CE14} \simeq V^+ - v_O$, the VI limiter has a threshold that increases as the voltage across Q_{14} decreases. Proper design of the circuit prevents Q_{14} and Q_{15} from leaving their safe operating area while allowing them to pass a maximum current to the load. To prevent the circuit from oscillating, capacitors can be added in parallel with R_{13} and R_{14} (typically $0.01\,\mu\mathrm{F}$). To prevent activation on fast transients, capacitors can be added in parallel with R_{15} and R_{16} (typically $0.1\,\mu\mathrm{F}$).

D_{11} and D_{12} play a second role in the operation of the circuit. D_{12} prevents Q_{17} from saturating when $v_O > 0$. To see how this works, suppose D_{12} is a short circuit. When v_O goes positive, $v_{B17} < v_{E17}$ because current flows from the base node of Q_{17} to ground through R_{18}. If v_{B17} drops below v_{E17} by more than the turn-on threshold, then Q_{17} will turn on and limit i_O. D_{12} prevents this from happening by preventing R_{18} from conducting when $i_O > 0$. This causes Q_{17} to limit only for $v_O < 0$. Similarly, D_{11} causes Q_{16} to limit only for $v_O > 0$. D_{13} and D_{14} prevent reverse voltage breakdown of the base-to-emitter junctions of Q_{16} and Q_{17}.

As an example of a VI limiter design, consider the MJ15003 for Q_{14} and the MJ15004 for Q_{15} in an amplifier which is to be designed for $100\,\mathrm{W}$ average sine wave power into $8\,\Omega$. The peak output voltage must be $40\,\mathrm{V}$. For purposes of illustration, consider the power supply to have unloaded voltages of $\pm52\,\mathrm{V}$, and let the values of R_{E14} and R_{E15} be $0.33\,\Omega$. We calculate the element values for the MJ15003 limiter. The corresponding values for the MJ15004 limiter are the same.

With $R_L = 0$, Q_{14} has a maximum worst case V_{CE} of $52\,\mathrm{V}$. The safe operating characteristics published for the MJ15003 gives a maximum i_C of slightly less than $5\,\mathrm{A}$ for $v_{CE} = 52\,\mathrm{V}$. To be on the safe side, the limiter will be designed to limit at $4\,\mathrm{A}$ with $R_L = 0$. Thus, with reference to Fig. 12.37 with $R_L = 0$, if we assume that all of i_{E14} flows through R_{E14}, we have the design equation

$$0.33\ \Omega \times 4\,\mathrm{A} \times \frac{R_{15}}{R_{13} + R_{15}} = 0.6\,\mathrm{V} \tag{12.101}$$

where the $0.6\,\mathrm{V}$ is the estimated v_{BE} threshold for Q_{16}. Let us choose $R_{15} = 270\,\Omega$. Eq. (12.101) then can be used to calculate $R_{13} = 324\,\Omega$, the closest 5% value is $330\,\Omega$. Similarly, $R_{14} = 330\,\Omega$ and $R_{16} = 270\,\Omega$. To prevent oscillations, $0.01\,\mu\mathrm{F}$ capacitors can be used in parallel with R_{13} and R_{14} as described above.

For an average sine wave power of $100\,\mathrm{W}$ into $8\,\Omega$, the peak load voltage is $40\,\mathrm{V}$. At maximum instantaneous load voltage, $v_{CE14} \simeq V^+ - 40\,\mathrm{V}$. Although V^+ is less than the no-load value of $52\,\mathrm{V}$ (because the power supply voltage always drops when loaded), we will use the worst case no load voltage for our calculations. Thus v_{CE14} under worst case full load voltage is approximately $12\,\mathrm{V}$. The MJ15003 specifications gives a maximum safe current of $20\,\mathrm{A}$ at $v_{CE} = 12\,\mathrm{V}$. Thus the protection circuit must limit i_O to $20\,\mathrm{A}$ when $v_O = 40\,\mathrm{V}$. To be on the safe side, we will design the circuit to limit at $16\,\mathrm{A}$. Thus $v_{B16} = 40.6\,\mathrm{V}$ at this point so that v_{BE16} will be at the conduction threshold of $0.6\,\mathrm{V}$. R_{17} sets this voltage. Fig. 12.39(a) shows the circuit for calculating R_{17}. We estimate the forward bias voltage across D_{11} to be $0.6\,\mathrm{V}$. The voltage at the node above R_{E14} is given by $v_O + i_O \times R_{E14} = 45.28\,\mathrm{V}$.

At the threshold of conduction for Q_{16}, we assume that $i_{B16} = 0$. To calculate v_{B16}, we neglect the loading effects of R_{13} and R_{15} in parallel with R_{E14} by assuming that a negligible fraction of the $16\,\mathrm{A}$ flows into R_{13}. Thus we can write

$$\frac{v_{B16} - 0.6}{R_{17}} + \frac{v_{B16} - 40}{R_{15}} + \frac{v_{B16} - 45.28}{R_{13}} = 0 \tag{12.102}$$

For $v_{B16} = 40.6\,\mathrm{V}$, this equation can be solved for R_{17} to obtain

$$R_{17} = \frac{40}{(4.68/R_{13}) - (0.6/R_{15})} = 3.34\,\mathrm{k\Omega} \tag{12.103}$$

The closest 5% resistor value is $3.3\,\mathrm{k\Omega}$. The same value should be used for R_{18}. Both should have a power rating of $1/2\,\mathrm{W}$. The completes the design of the VI limiter. To prevent the circuit from limiting on fast transients, $0.1\,\mu\mathrm{F}$ capacitors can be put in parallel with R_{15} and R_{16}.

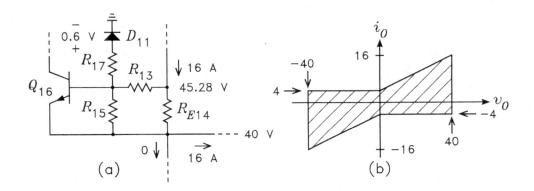

Figure 12.39: (a) Circuit used to calculate R_{17}. (b) Region in which the VI limiter does not operate.

We can obtain the v_O versus i_O region to which the limiter constrains the amplifier to operate if we assume a that a straight line connects the two design points in our example. For Q_{14}, these points in an i_O versus v_O graph are $(4,0)$ and $(16,40)$. For Q_{15}, they are $(-4,0)$ and $(-16,-40)$. The graph is shown in Fig. 12.39(b). The shaded area indicates the region in the i_O versus v_O plane where the limiter does not operate. With a reactive load, a sine wave input signal results in an elliptical load line that is centered on the origin in the i_O versus v_O plane. If this ellipse tries to leave the shaded area, the VI limiter is activated. If the ellipse remains inside the shaded area, the protection circuit is not activated.

If N output transistors in parallel are used on each side of the output stage, each should have a resistor connected from its emitter to the base of the VI limiter transistor. The value of these resistors is given by $N \times R_{13}$ (or $N \times R_{14}$). All other resistor in the limiter circuit are unchanged. Only one resistor on each side of the output stage should have the parallel 0.01 μF capacitor. For example, if two npn and two pnp output transistors are used in the circuit of Fig. 12.37, the value of R_{13} and R_{14} for each should be $2 \times 324 = 648\,\Omega$. The closest 5% value is $620\,\Omega$.

The limiter circuits involve transistors which when saturated produce a short circuit between the input to a driver transistor and the amplifier output. Thus, in the event of a short circuited load, the stage which drives the driver transistors can be shorted to ground through the protection circuit transistors. In the circuit of Fig. 12.36, this stage is the Q_7 and Q_8 gain stage. To protect Q_7 and Q_8, their maximum current must be limited. Fig. 12.40(a) shows possible circuits for achieving this. Q_{18} and Q_{19}, respectively, sense the emitter current in Q_7 and Q_8. If the current becomes excessive, one or both of Q_{18} and Q_{19} will saturate, thus removing base drive current from Q_7 and Q_8. The threshold at which this occurs is set by R_{E7A} and R_{E8A}. For example, the resistors might be chosen so that Q_{18} and Q_{19} turn on when the current in Q_7 and Q_8 is 10 mA. This could be achieved with $R_{E7A} = R_{E8A} \simeq 62\,\Omega$.

MOSFET Protection Circuits

Enhancement mode MOSFETs in an output stage are normally protected by limiting the maximum gate-source voltage with zener diodes. Fig. 12.40(b) shows the MOSFET output stage of Fig. 12.32(b) with these zener diodes. Under normal operation, the zener diodes are open circuits. Their breakdown voltage is selected so that they conduct in order to limit the output current from exceeding the maximum safe current. This current is normally specified by the manufacturer. Gate resistors R_{G1} and R_{G2} suppress parasitic oscillations. These are typically in the 100 to 1000 Ω range. Some manufacturers recommend a ferrite bead around the MOSFET gate lead in place of the resistor. In some MOSFETs, the gate-to-source zener diode is fabricated as part of the device.

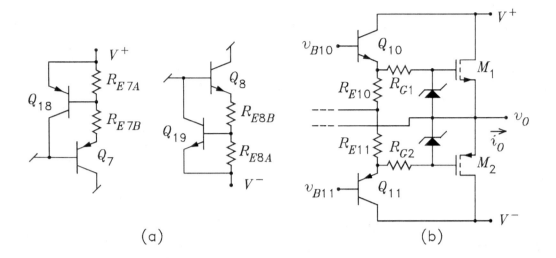

Figure 12.40: (a) Circuit showing the current limiter transistors for Q_7 and Q_8. (b) MOSFET output stage with the zener diode current limit protection circuit.

12.12 Power Supply Design

Fig. 12.41 shows the circuit diagram of a typical amplifier power supply. The ground symbol represents what is called the central chassis ground. This is a single point on the metal chassis to which all ground connections are made. The standard color codes for the three ac line cord leads are: black – hot, green – safety ground, and white – neutral. The safety ground is connected to the central ground, the neutral is connected to one lead of the transformer primary, and the hot is connected through a fuse and switch to the other lead of the transformer primary.

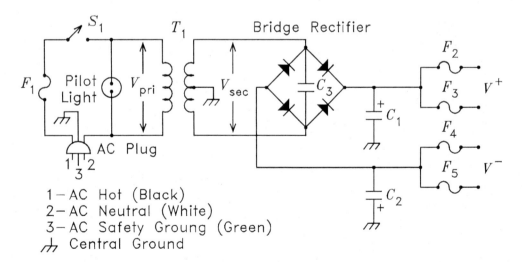

Figure 12.41: Power supply for a two-channel amplifier.

The transformer secondary has three leads. The center lead is called the center tap which connects to central ground. The two outside leads connect to the ac inputs of a diode bridge rectifier. A capacitor C_3 is shown connected across the bridge rectifier inputs. This capacitor is for suppression of rf radiation that can be produced by the switching of the diodes. A typical value for C_3 is $0.1\,\mu F$. It should have a voltage rating greater than $\sqrt{2}V_{sec}$, where V_{sec} is the secondary rms voltage.

The power supply voltages in Fig. 12.41 are labeled V^+ and V^-, where we assume that $V^- = -V^+$. If $v_O(t)$ is the instantaneous amplifier output voltage, it must satisfy the inequality $V^- \leq v_O(t) \leq V^+$. For a sine-wave output, an upper bound on the average power output of the amplifier is $(V^+)^2/2R_L$, where R_L is the load resistance. In practice, this upper bound cannot be realized because the amplifier cannot put out a peak voltage equal to V^+. The maximum peak output voltage is called the clipping voltage which is several volts less than V^+.

The no-load power supply voltages must be greater than the midband clipping voltage given by

$$V_{clip} = \sqrt{2R_L P_{ave}} \tag{12.104}$$

where R_L is the load resistance and P_{ave} is the average output power. The required no-load power supply voltages can be estimated by adding the drop across the output transistors at full load to V_{clip} and then multiplying the sum by a factor to correct for the no-load to full-load regulation of the transformer. For example, an amplifier rated at $120\,W$ into $8\,\Omega$ would be required to put out a peak voltage of $43.8\,V$. The amplifier may require power supply voltages of $\pm(43.8 + 9.4) \div 0.95 = \pm 56\,V$. This calculation assumes a $9.4\,V$ drop across the output transistors and a loaded voltage that is 5% lower than the no load voltage.

If V_{sec} is the ac rms secondary voltage of the transformer in Fig. 12.41, the dc power supply voltages are given by

$$V^+ = -V^- = \frac{V_{sec}}{\sqrt{2}} - V_{BR} \tag{12.105}$$

where V_{BR} is the effective dc voltage drop in the bridge rectifier. Typically this might be $V_{BR} = 3\,V$. Eq. (12.105) can be used to calculate the required transformer secondary voltage rating if V^+ is specified. For example, the $120\,W$ amplifier with $V^+ = 56\,V$ would require a transformer with $V_{sec} = (56 + 3)\sqrt{2} = 83.4\,V$.

The method described above for calculating V_{sec} gives the no load value. The secondary voltage of most transformers is specified at full rated current into a resistive load. For example, the current rating might be specified as the value at which the secondary voltage drops by 5% from its no load value. In this case, the loaded secondary voltage is the no load voltage multiplied by 0.95. Thus the transformer which has a no load $V_{sec} = 83.4\,V$ might have a rated secondary voltage $V_{sec} = 0.95 \times 83.4 = 79.2\,V$.

The transformer volt-ampere or VA rating is the product of the rated rms secondary voltage and current. This product must be greater than the average power rating of the amplifier divided by the efficiency of the amplifier output stage. (A typical efficiency is 0.6 or 60%.) If the power supply is used to power a stereo amplifier, the sum of the output powers from the two channels must be used in determining the minimum VA rating. A conservatively designed power supply might have a transformer VA rating equal to twice the total amplifier power rating. Thus the transformer in a stereo amplifier rated at $120\,W$ average power per channel might have a VA rating of $480\,W$ or greater.

Example 28 *It is desired to design a stereo amplifier that will put out $100\,W$ of average power per channel into two $8\,\Omega$ loads. It is estimated that the power supply voltage drops 10% at maximum power output and that the amplifier clipping voltage is $7\,V$ lower than the power supply voltage. Calculate the required no-load power supply voltages.*

Solution: From Eq. (12.104), the peak clipping voltage is $V_{clip} = (2 \times 8 \times 100)^{1/2} = 40\,V$. The power supply voltages are thus given by $\pm(43.8 + 5) \div 0.9 = \pm 52.2\,V$.

Example 29 *If the effective dc voltage drop across the rectifier diodes is estimated to be $3\,V$, calculate the no load secondary rms voltage rating for the transformer in Example 28.*

Solution. From Eq. (12.105), $V_{sec} = \sqrt{2} \times (52.2 + 3) = 78\,V$.

Fig. 12.41 shows five fuses. The ac line fuse F_1 is normally a slow blow fuse to prevent its being blown at turn on by the current rush into C_1 and C_2. Output fuses F_2 through F_5 are normally fast blow fuses.

The power switch must be a high-current switch. A common problem with the switch is that its contacts can be welded together by the large current flow at turn on. Toggle switches which make a loud click when turned on and off do not seem to exhibit this problem as much as other switches.

The bridge rectifier in Fig. 12.41 consists of four high-current diodes mounted in a common package. It should be mounted on the amplifier metal chassis to dissipate the heat generated in the diodes. The reverse breakdown voltage rating of the diodes must be greater than $2V^+$. In a conservative design, the average current rating of each diode should be greater than the peak amplifier load current. For a stereo amplifier, the peak load current is twice that for a single channel.

C_1 and C_2 are the power supply filter capacitors. These must have a large value to minimize ripple on the power supply rails. Typical values are in the range from $1000\,\mu F$ to $10,000\,\mu F$. Capacitors this large must be electrolytic types. The positive signs in Fig. 12.41 show the proper polarities. The voltage rating of the capacitors must be greater than V^+. A common figure of merit is to quote the total energy stored in the filter capacitors. This is calculated as follows:

$$\text{Energy} = 2 \times \left[\frac{1}{2}C\left(V^+\right)^2\right] = C\left(V^+\right)^2 \tag{12.106}$$

where the units are joules (J). For example, if $V^+ = 56\,V$ and $C = 10,000\,\mu F$, the energy is 31.4 J. This is enough energy to raise a 10 pound dog a distance of about 2.3 feet off the floor.

High peak currents can flow in the power supply circuit. Heavy gauge wiring should be used to minimize the wiring resistance. Typical wire sizes are #18 or #16 gauge stranded conductor wire. Solid conductor wire should never be used because it is difficult to route and easy to break.

12.13 Decoupling and Grounding

The main source of electromagnetic interference in any amplifier is the power supply. The large peak currents which flow from the transformer through the bridge rectifier and into the filter capacitors must not be allowed to flow in a signal ground lead or hum can be induced in the signal circuit. To minimize this, a central power supply ground should be used. This is a single point on the metal chassis to which the transformer center tap, the filter capacitor grounds, the ac safety ground, the circuit board grounds, and the loudspeaker grounds connect. Separate leads must be used to connect each of these to the central ground. In this way, the ground return currents for each circuit flows in only one lead.

A central ground also eliminates what are called ground loops in the ground system. A ground loop consists of two parallel ground paths through which an ac magnetic field can flux, e.g. the magnetic fields external to the power supply transformer. When an ac magnetic field fluxes through a ground loop, a voltage is generated around the loop (by Faraday's law) which causes a current to flow. This current can couple into the amplifier signal circuit and cause a hum in the loudspeaker. Thus ground loops must be avoided.

The external magnetic field around the power transformer should be minimized. Toroidal core transformers have a very low leakage field and are used in applications where magnetic field coupling effects are to be minimized. External magnetic fields around rectangular shaped transformers can be minimized by shielding the transformer and installing a hum canceling copper strap around it. The external magnetic field induces currents in the strap which set up a magnetic field that tends to cancel the original field.

Switching noise in the power supply bridge rectifier can cause radio frequency noise which can interfere with nearby radio and TV receivers. This problem is worse with AM and short wave radios. The problem can usually be eliminated by installing a small capacitor, typically 0.01 to $0.1\,\mu F$, across the AC inputs to the bridge rectifier. This capacitor is labeled C_3 in Fig. 12.41. The voltage rating for the capacitor should be greater than $2V^+$ to prevent voltage breakdown.

Positive feedback can occur in an amplifier ground system which can cause oscillations. Let us consider the case where the chassis is isolated from the amplifier circuit as illustrated in Fig. 12.42(a). C_1 represents the capacitance from the signal input lead to the chassis, C_2 represents the capacitance from the signal output lead to the chassis, and C_3 through C_5 represent the capacitance from the amplifier ground leads to the chassis. All of these are distributed capacitances. Fig. 12.42(b) shows the circuit redrawn to show the

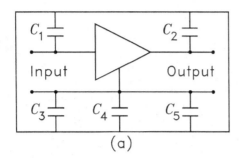 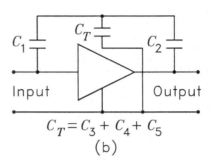

$$C_T = C_3 + C_4 + C_5$$

Figure 12.42: (a) Amplifier circuit showing the capacitances to the chassis. (b) Equivalent circuit.

feedback path through the capacitors. The signal fed back through this circuit can cause positive feedback which causes the amplifier to oscillate.

The only way to break the feedback path is to place a short circuit across C_T, i.e. a short circuit across the distributed capacitances to ground by shorting C_3 through C_5. This requires a short circuit from input ground to chassis, a short circuit from circuit board ground to chassis, and a short circuit from output ground to chassis. It can be seen from Fig. 12.42(a) that placing a short circuit across C_3, C_4, and C_5 would cause two ground loops that can cause hum pickup. To eliminate the loops, a wire should be used for one of the shorts and capacitors with a typical value of $0.1\,\mu$F for the others. At high frequencies, the added capacitors short out the feedback signal. At low frequencies, the capacitors are open circuits, which breaks the ground loops. Small value resistors are often used in place of the capacitors. The values are chosen to be small enough to short out the feedback but large enough to suppress ground loop currents. A typical value is $10\,\Omega$. The lead lengths of these components should be kept as short a possible.

For safety, the amplifier chassis should be grounded to the ac power safety ground. This is normally accomplished with a three-wire line cord. The safety ground on the ac plug connects to the green wire in the line cord. The green wire should connect to the amplifier central chassis ground. Safety requires the black or ac hot lead to be the one which connects through the line fuse to the power switch. The white or ac neutral lead connects directly to the transformer primary. Any component connected to the amplifier input will have its chassis grounded to the amplifier chassis through the ground shield of the connecting signal cable. Three-wire ac line cords should not be used on these components for ground loops would result that could cause hum in the loudspeaker.

The leads which connect the power supply filter capacitors to the amplifier circuit boards have undesirable series inductance which causes the impedance of the power supply leads to increase with frequency. This can cause positive feedback through the power supply rails, resulting in oscillations. To prevent this, the power supply leads should have decoupling capacitors to ground at the point where the leads connect to the circuit board. Typical values are in the range from 1 to $100\,\mu$F. Electrolytic capacitors should have a $0.1\,\mu$F polyester capacitor in parallel with each for better high-frequency performance. The decoupling capacitors in the amplifier example of Fig. 12.36 are C_8 and C_9.

Ripple on the power supply leads can couple into the low-level amplifier input stages and cause hum in the loudspeaker. Low-pass filters on the power supply rails should be used to prevent this. Typically, this filter consists of a series resistor and a capacitor to ground on each power supply rail. In the amplifier circuit of Fig. 12.36, these filters consist of R_{11}, R_{12}, C_{10}, and C_{11}. Typical values are $100\,\Omega$ for the resistors and $100\,\mu$F for the capacitors. A $0.1\,\mu$F polyester capacitor should be used in parallel with each electrolytic capacitor. The resistors should not drop more than one to two volts or the power rating of the amplifier could be decreased.

An improperly grounded amplifier can oscillate or hum may be audible in the loudspeaker. To minimize these problems, the circuit board should have separate ground traces for the signal grounds and the grounds for the decoupling capacitors. In the amplifier of Fig. 12.36, R_1, C_1, C_{F1}, and C_{F2} should connect to the signal ground trace. C_2, C_3, and C_8 through C_{11} should connect to the ground trace for the decoupling capacitors. Each trace should connect to central ground with separate wires. The traces should be connected together on the circuit board with a capacitor (typically $0.1\,\mu$F) to maintain the two grounds at the same potential at high frequencies. Sometimes a small value resistor (typically $100\,\Omega$) is used instead of the capacitor. R_{10} and C_7 should be mounted on the loudspeaker output jacks so that C_7 is grounded through the loudspeaker ground lead. The loudspeaker ground lead should never connect to the amplifier circuit board.

12.14   Power Dissipation and Efficiency

The heat sinks for the output transistors must be large enough to dissipate the maximum power dissipation in the output stage. To calculate this power, let us assume a class-B output stage. The answer should be very close to correct for a class-AB stage. Let the output voltage be $v_O = V_P \sin{(2\pi t/T)}$, where V_P is the peak voltage and T is the period. The output current is v_O/R_L, where R_L is the load resistance. For $0 \le t \le T/2$, the side of the output stage connected to the positive rail, i.e. to V^+, conducts the current. The voltage across these transistors is $V^+ - v_O$. For $T/2 \le t \le T$, the side of the output stage connected to the negative rail, i.e. to V^-, conducts the current. The voltage across these transistors is $v_O - V^-$. The average power dissipated in the heat sinks over one period is given by

$$P_D = \frac{1}{T}\left[\int_0^{T/2}\left(V^+ - v_O\right)\times\frac{v_O}{R_L}dt + \int_{T/2}^{T}\left(v_O - V^-\right)\times\frac{v_O}{R_L}dt\right] \qquad (12.107)$$

For $V^- = -V^+$, the two integrals are equal and the expression can be written as twice the first integral to obtain

$$P_D = \frac{2}{T}\int_0^{T/2}\left[V^+ - V_P\sin\left(\frac{2\pi t}{T}\right)\right]\times\frac{V_P}{R_L}\sin\left(\frac{2\pi t}{T}\right)dt = \frac{2V^+ V_P}{\pi R_L} - \frac{V_P^2}{2R_L} \qquad (12.108)$$

The value of V_P which maximizes P_D is obtained by setting $dP_D/dV_P = 0$ and solving for V_P. It is $V_P = 2V^+/\pi$. The corresponding power dissipated is

$$P_{D(max)} = \frac{2\left(V^+\right)^2}{\pi^2 R_L} \qquad (12.109)$$

The corresponding power delivered to the load is $P_L = V_P^2/2R_L$ which is equal to $P_{D(max)}$.

For the class-B amplifier, the average power delivered to the load when the power dissipated in the heat sinks is a maximum is often expressed as a fraction of the maximum load power, where the maximum load power is calculated with $V_P = V^+$. This fraction is given by

$$\frac{2\left(V^+\right)^2/\left(\pi^2 R_L\right)}{\left(V^+\right)^2/\left(2R_L\right)} = \frac{4}{\pi^2} = 0.4053 \qquad (12.110)$$

Thus it is often said that the heat sinks get the hottest when the load power is about 40% of its maximum. In practice, however, an amplifier cannot put out a peak voltage equal to the rail voltage. Therefore, the maximum load power is always less than $\left(V^+\right)^2/\left(2R_L\right)$. Thus the 0.4053 represents a lower bound. This is illustrated in the following example.

Example 30 *A class-B amplifier rated at* $120\,$W *into* $8\,\Omega$ *has the rail voltages* $V^+ = -V^- = 56\,$V. *Calculate the maximum power dissipated in the heat sink, the corresponding load power for a sine wave signal, and the ratio of this load power to the rated load power. Assume the power supply voltages do not drop under load.*

Solution. By Eq. (12.109), $P_{D(max)} = 2\times 56^2/\left(\pi^2\times 8\right) = 79.4\,$W. The corresponding load power is also $79.4\,$W. The ratio of load power to maximum load power is $79.4/120 = 0.662$ or 66.2%.

The efficiency of an amplifier is defined as the ratio of the average power delivered to the load divided by the average power consumed from the power supply. The latter is often approximated by the sum of the power delivered to the load and the power dissipated in the heat sinks. Thus, for a sine wave output signal having a peak value V_P, the efficiency can be written

$$\eta = \frac{P_{L(ave)}}{P_{L(ave)} + P_{D(ave)}} = \frac{V_P^2/2R_L}{[V_P^2/(2R_L)] + [2V^+V_P/(\pi R_L) - V_P^2/(2R_L)]} = \frac{\pi V_P}{4V^+} \qquad (12.111)$$

Note that this is independent of R_L. An upper bound for η can be calculated with $V_P = V^+$. In this case, $\eta = 0.7854$ or 78.54%.

Example 31 *For a sine-wave signal, calculate the efficiency of the amplifier in Example 30 when it is delivering maximum power to the $8\,\Omega$ load.*

Solution. The peak voltage is $V_P = \sqrt{2 \times 8 \times 120} = 43.8\,\text{V}$. By Eq. (12.111), $\eta = \pi \times 43.8/(4 \times 56) = 0.614$ or 61.4%.

12.15   The Class-D Amplifier

A class-D amplifier is one in which the output transistors are operated as switches. When a transistor is off, the current through it is zero. When it is on, the voltage across it is small, ideally zero. In each case, the power dissipation is very low. This increases the efficiency, thus requiring less power from the power supply and smaller heat sinks for the amplifier. These are important advantages in portable battery-powered equipment. The "D" in class-D is sometimes said to stand for "digital." This is not correct because the operation of the class-D amplifier is based on analog principles. There is no digital coding of the signal. Before the advent of the class-D amplifier, the standard classes were class-A, class-AB, class-B, and class-C. The "D" is simply the next letter in the alphabet after "C." Indeed, the earliest work on class-D amplifiers involved vacuum tubes and can be traced to a 1930 patent by Burnice D. Bedford.

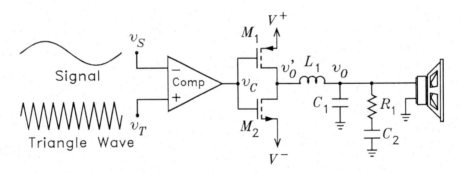

Figure 12.43: Basic class-D amplifier.

Fig. 12.43 shows the basic simplified circuit of a class-D amplifier. We assume a bipolar power supply so that $V^- = -V^+$. The amplifier consists of a comparator driving complementary MOSFET transistors which operate as switches. The comparator has two inputs. One is a triangle wave, the other is the audio signal. The frequency of the triangle wave must be much higher than that of the audio input. The voltage output of the comparator can be written

$$v_C = -V_1 \quad \text{for} \quad v_S > v_T \quad \text{and} \quad v_C = +V_1 \quad \text{for} \quad v_S < v_T \qquad (12.112)$$

This voltage is applied to the input of a complementary common-source MOSFET output stage. Each transistor operates as a switch. For $v_C = -V_1$, M_1 is on and M_2 is off. If the voltage drop across M_1 is negligible, then $v_O' = V^+$. Similarly, for $v_C = +V_1$, M_2 is on, M_1 is off, and $v_O' = V^-$. In practice, there is a small voltage drop across the on MOSFET switch so that the peak output voltage is less than the power supply voltage. For the case $v_S = 0$, v_O' is a symmetrical square wave. The low-pass filter consisting of L_1 and C_1 passes the average value of the square wave to the loudspeaker, which is zero. Thus $v_O = 0$ for $v_S = 0$. The network consisting of R_1 and C_2 compensates for the inductive impedance of the loudspeaker voice coil so that the filter sees a resistive load at high frequencies. This is discussed in Section 10.4.

Fig. 12.44 shows the circuit waveforms for the case where v_S is a sine wave. For purposes of illustration, the sine wave frequency is $f_S = 1\,\text{kHz}$ and the triangle wave frequency is $f_T = 20\,\text{kHz}$. The sine wave amplitude is $0.75 V_{TP}$. For $v_S > 0$, the duty cycle of the square wave changes so that v_O' spends more time at its positive level than at its negative level. This causes v_O' to have a positive average value. Similarly, for $v_S < 0$, v_O' has a negative average value. The waveform for v_O' is said to be pulse-width-modulated. The passive filter consisting of L_1 and C_1 passes the average or low-frequency value of v_O' to the loudspeaker load and rejects the higher-frequency harmonics of the switching waveform.

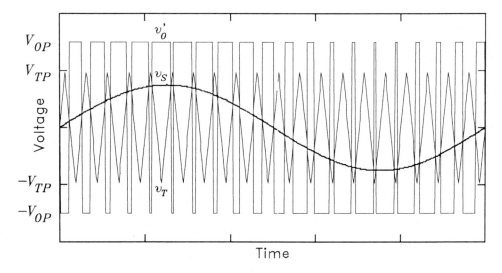

Figure 12.44: Amplifier voltage waveforms.

The effective gain of the amplifier can be determined by applying a dc voltage at the input and calculating the ratio of $\langle v_O' \rangle$ to v_S, where $\langle v_O' \rangle$ denotes the low-frequency time average of v_O'. If v_S is increased, $\langle v_O' \rangle$ increases linearly until it reaches the level V_{OP}, which corresponds to the positive clipping voltage at the output. This occurs when $v_S = V_{TP}$. It follows that the effective gain k is given by

$$k = \frac{\langle v_O' \rangle}{v_S} = \frac{V_{OP}}{V_{TP}} \qquad (12.113)$$

Fig. 12.45 shows the waveforms of the output voltage v_O for two values of the cutoff frequency of the LC filter. The transfer function of the filter is

$$\frac{V_o}{V_o'} = \frac{1}{(s/\omega_c)^2 + (1/Q_c)(s/\omega_c) + 1} \qquad (12.114)$$

where $\omega_c = 2\pi f_c = 1/\sqrt{L_1 C_1}$ is the resonance frequency and $Q_c = 1/(\omega_c R_L C_1)$ is the quality factor. The load resistance R_L is the effective high-frequency resistance of the loudspeaker voice coil in parallel with the matching network consisting of R_1 and C_2. The quality factor is $Q_c = 1/\sqrt{2}$ for the waveforms in Fig. 12.45 so that the gain is down by $3\,\text{dB}$ at ω_c. The signal frequency is $f_S = 1\,\text{kHz}$. The filter resonance frequency for the v_{O1} waveform is $f_c = 1\,\text{kHz}$. For the v_{O2} waveform, it is $f_c = 8\,\text{kHz}$. The harmonics of the pulse-width-modulated signal are clearly visible on the v_{O2} waveform.

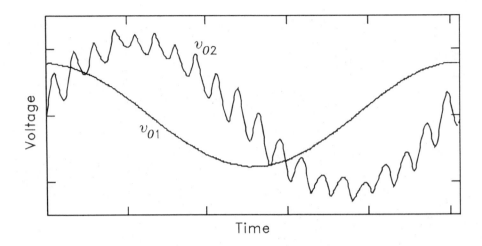

Figure 12.45: Output voltage waveforms for two different LC filter cutoff frequencies.

For minimum distortion, the frequency of the triangle wave should be as high as possible compared to the cutoff frequency of the filter. Because the filter resonance frequency corresponds to the signal frequency for the v_{O1} waveform in Fig. 12.45, the phase lag is $90°$. The phase lag for the v_{O2} waveform is less because the resonance frequency is greater than the signal frequency. A higher-order filter can be used to more effectively remove the high-frequency switching harmonics. For example, the third-order filter in Fig. 10.4(b) or a fourth-order filter consisting of the cascade of two second-order LC filters could be used.

Fig. 12.46 shows the spectrum of the v_O' waveform. It contains a fundamental at f_S. Above f_S, the significant switching harmonics are at f_T, $f_T \pm 2f_S$, $2f_T \pm f_S$, $2f_T \pm 3f_S$, etc. The lowest of these is at the frequency $f_T - 2f_S$. The triangle wave frequency must be chosen high enough so that the lowest significant harmonic is well above the highest signal frequency of interest. Thus we have the requirement $f_T - 2f_S \gg f_S$ or $f_T \gg 3f_S$. To minimize ripple on the output, the cutoff frequency of the LC filter should be much lower than f_T. For example, in a wideband amplifier with a maximum signal frequency of 20 kHz, the switching frequency should ideally be 600 kHz or greater. Because of limitations imposed by a high switching frequency, a more practical value might be 300 kHz. The -3 dB frequency of the LC filter should be much lower than the switching frequency. For example, it might be 30 kHz for a 300 kHz switching frequency. Note that the amplitude of the harmonic at f_T is larger than that of the signal. At the signal clipping level, the signal harmonic becomes 1.5 times as large as the harmonic at f_T.

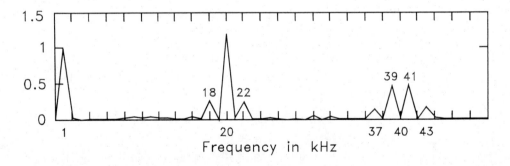

Figure 12.46: Unfiltered spectrum of the output voltage.

Negative feedback can be used around the basic amplifier circuit to improve its performance. Fig. 12.47

shows such a circuit. The input op amp acts as an integrator to set the bandwidth. For a sinusoidal input signal with a frequency much lower than the switching frequency, the effective transfer function for the circuit and its pole frequency are given by

$$\frac{V_o'}{V_s} = -\frac{R_F}{R_2}\frac{1}{1+s/\omega_0} \qquad \omega_0 = 2\pi f_0 = \frac{k}{R_F C_F} \qquad (12.115)$$

The pole frequency must be greater than the highest frequency to be amplified but lower than the switching frequency. Because the integrator has a very high gain at dc, it acts to minimize dc offsets at the output. For a wide band amplifier, a typical value of f_0 might be 60 kHz.

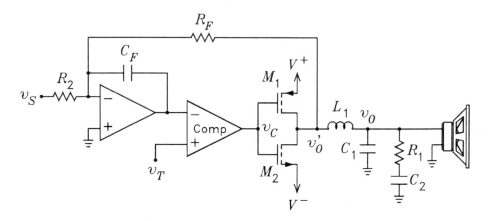

Figure 12.47: Amplifier with negative feedback.

Class-D amplifiers are often operated in a bridged configuration to increase the output power without increasing the power supply voltages. A bridged output stage is shown in Fig. 12.48. A typical input circuit is shown in Fig. 12.49. The feedback voltage v_F is proportional to the difference voltage $v_{O1}' - v_{O2}'$. The bridge circuit is often designed with $V^- = 0$ and a dc offset at each output of $V^+/2$ V, thus eliminating the need for a bipolar power supply.

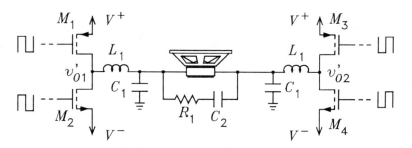

Figure 12.48: Bridged output stage.

In the circuit of Fig. 12.49, a diff amp is used to subtract v_{O2}' from v_{O1}'. The capacitors labeled C_3 act as low-pass filters to limit the rise time of the signals applied to the op amp to prevent slewing. The transfer function for the diff amp and its pole frequency are given by

$$\frac{V_f}{V_{o1}' - V_{o2}'} = \frac{R_5}{R_3+R_4}\frac{1}{1+s/\omega_1} \qquad \omega_1 = 2\pi f_1 = \frac{1}{(R_3\|R_4)C_3} \qquad (12.116)$$

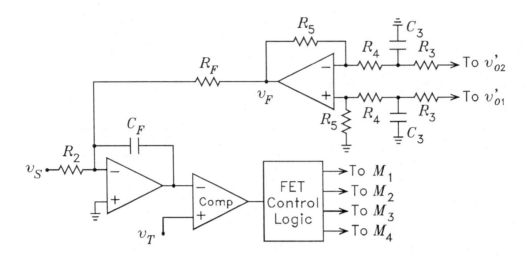

Figure 12.49: Input stage to the bridged amplifier with feedback.

The overall transfer function for the amplifier is given by

$$
\begin{aligned}
\frac{V'_{o1} - V'_{o2}}{V_s} &= -\frac{R_F}{R_2}\frac{R_3 + R_4}{R_5}\frac{1 + s/\omega_1}{s^2/\omega_1\omega_2 + s/\omega_2 + 1}\\
&= -\frac{R_F}{R_2}\frac{R_3 + R_4}{R_5}\frac{1 + s/\omega_1}{(s/\omega_0)^2 + (1/Q_0)(s/\omega_0) + 1}
\end{aligned}
\tag{12.117}
$$

where ω_2, ω_0, and Q_0 are given by

$$
\omega_2 = 2\pi f_2 = \frac{R_5}{R_3 + R_4}\frac{k}{R_F C_F} \qquad \omega_0 = 2\pi f_0 = \sqrt{\omega_1\omega_2} \qquad Q_0 = \sqrt{\frac{\omega_2}{\omega_1}}
\tag{12.118}
$$

The amplifier should exhibit good stability for $Q_0 \leq 1$. Thus we have the condition $\omega_1 \geq \omega_2$. However, the simple model used here neglects higher order poles. Because the existence of such poles degrades stability, a conservative approach might be to design for $Q_0 \leq 0.5$ so that the poles in Eq. (12.117) are real. This requires $\omega_1 \geq 4\omega_2$. For example, in a wideband amplifier utilizing a switching frequency of 300 kHz, f_1 might be chosen to be equal to the switching frequency and f_2 might be chosen to be 75 kHz.

An example triangle wave generator circuit is shown in Fig. 12.50. The circuit consists of an integrator driving a comparator that is connected as a Schmitt trigger. The output of the comparator drives the input to the integrator. Let the comparator output voltages be $+V_1$ and $-V_1$. When the voltage is at the $-V_1$ level, the triangle wave output rises with the slope $m = V_1/R_6C_4$. Let the peak values of the triangle wave be $+V_{TP}$ and $-V_{TP}$. It follows that $2V_{TP} = mT/2 = V_1/2f_T R_6 C_4$, where $T = 1/f_T$ is the period of the triangle wave. The comparator switches states when the voltage at its non-inverting input goes through zero. This occurs when $V_1/R_8 = V_{TP}/R_7$. Solution for f_T and V_{TP} yields

$$
f_T = \frac{R_8}{4R_6 R_7 C_4} \qquad V_{TP} = \frac{R_7}{R_8}V_1
\tag{12.119}
$$

A problem called "shoot through" can reduce the efficiency of class-D amplifiers and lead to potential failure of the output devices. This occurs during the transition when one device is being cut off and another is being cut on. During the transition, both devices are on and a large current pulse can flow through the two. This can be eliminated by driving the gates of the MOSFETs with asymmetrical square waves such that one device is cut off before the other is cut on. One way of achieving this in the circuit of Figs. 12.43 and 12.47 is to use two comparators, one for each MOSFET. A positive dc offset is added to the triangle

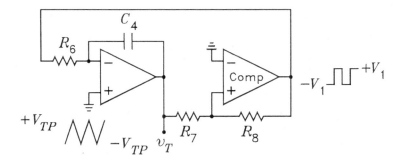

Figure 12.50: Triangle wave generator.

wave input to the comparator which drives M_1 and a negative dc offset is added to the triangle wave input to the comparator which drives M_2. This effectively adds crossover distortion to the v'_O output waveform, but the frequency components are above the switching frequency, thus outside the audio band.

The high switching frequency used in class-D amplifiers is a potential source of rf interference with other electronic equipment. The amplifiers must be properly shielded and grounded to prevent radiation of the switching harmonics. In addition, low-pass filters must be used on all input and output leads, including the power supply leads.

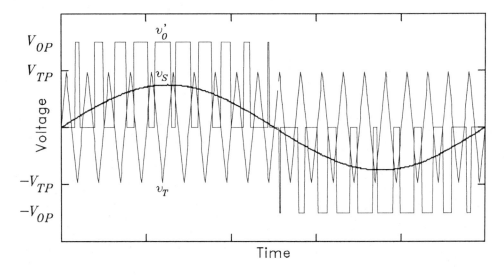

Figure 12.51: Amplifier voltage waveforms.

A variation of the class-D amplifier is called a filterless class-D amplifier. In the absence of an input signal, its output signal is zero rather than a symmetrical square wave. This eliminates the need of a low-pass filter to prevent application of the square wave to the loudspeaker. When the input voltage goes positive, the output voltage is a train of pulse width modulated pulses which switch between 0 and $+V_{OP}$. When the input voltage goes negative, the output voltage is a train of pulse width modulated pulses which switch between 0 and $-V_{OP}$. This is illustrated in Fig. 12.51. The loudspeaker responds to the average value of the signal, which is the audio signal. Because there is no filter, rf interference problems require the amplifier to be mounted as close to the loudspeaker as possible. The spectrum of the output signal is shown in Fig. 12.52. One problem with the filterless class-D amplifier is crossover distortion. To eliminate this, the FET control logic must be designed so that the amplifier puts out very narrow alternating positive and negative pulses in the absence of an input signal. In effect, this biases the amplifier in the class-AB mode.

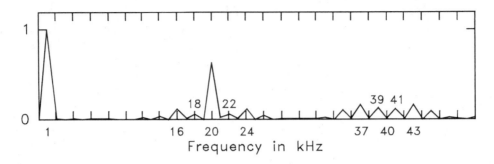

Figure 12.52: Spectrum of the output voltage v'_O.

12.16   Amplifier Measurements

Power Rating

The basic test setup for measuring an amplifier power rating is shown in Fig. 12.53. The amplifier is driven by an oscillator or a function generator. The most commonly used value for the load resistor R_L is $8\,\Omega$. Other values that are also used are $16\,\Omega$, $4\,\Omega$, and $2\,\Omega$. A sine wave is applied to the input at a typical frequency of $1\,\text{kHz}$ and the output is monitored on an oscilloscope. The amplitude of the sine wave is increased until the oscilloscope reveals clipping on the peaks. The clipping should be symmetrical in a properly designed amplifier. The amplitude of the sine wave is then decreased until the clipping just disappears. The output power is given by

$$P_L = \frac{V^2_{o(peak)}}{2R_L} = \frac{V^2_{o(rms)}}{R_L} \tag{12.120}$$

where $V_{o(peak)}$ is the peak output voltage read from the oscilloscope and $V_{o(rms)}$ is the rms output voltage read from the voltmeter. Power ratings usually specify that the amplifier is capable of putting out the rated power for any frequency in the audio band from $20\,\text{Hz}$ to $20\,\text{kHz}$.

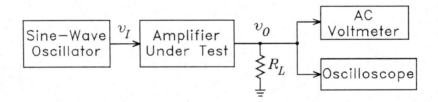

Figure 12.53: Test setup for measuring output power.

Care must be taken in making power measurements on high power amplifiers. The load resistor should have a power rating that is greater than or equal to the amplifier output power. Both the amplifier and the load resistor can get quite hot during the tests. The heat sinks on which the output transistors are mounted must be capable of dissipating the heat or the output transistors can fail. Full power measurements above $20\,\text{kHz}$ can cause amplifier failure. Therefore, high frequency power measurements should be made with care.

Voltage Gain

The amplifier gain refers to its voltage gain, not its power gain. With reference to Fig. 12.53, the voltage gain A_v is given by

$$A_v = \frac{v_O}{v_I} \tag{12.121}$$

The input and output voltages can be measured with either an ac voltmeter or an oscilloscope. The voltage gain is sometimes specified in dB. This is given by $A_{v(\mathrm{dB})} = 20\log(A_v)$. The gain is usually specified at a frequency of 1 kHz. A typical value is 20 (26 dB).

Frequency Response

Frequency response is measured by determining the lower and upper frequencies where the gain is 3 dB down (a factor of $1/\sqrt{2}$) from the midband value. There are two types of measurements. These are small-signal response and large-signal response. The small-signal response is measured at a level that is low enough so that the upper -3 dB frequency is not limited by slewing. A typical level might be 1 V peak at the amplifier output. In some cases, the small-signal bandwidth is measured at an output power of 1 W into an 8 Ω load resistor. The output voltage in this case is $\sqrt{8}$ V rms or 4 V peak. The large-signal bandwidth is measured at full power. It can be less than the small-signal bandwidth because the amplifier may exhibit slew rate limiting. A properly designed amplifier should not slew before it peak clips in the 20 Hz to 20 kHz band.

Output Resistance and Damping Factor

Fig. 12.54 shows a basic setup for measuring the output resistance R_{out}. If the amplifier is a stereo unit, one channel can be driven from the other channel with the load resistor connected between the two. If the amplifier is a mono unit, a second amplifier is required. With reference to the figure, we can write

$$i = \frac{v_A - v_B}{R_L} = \frac{v_B}{R_{out}} \tag{12.122}$$

This equation can be solved for R_{out} to obtain

$$R_{out} = \frac{R_L}{(v_A/v_B) - 1} \tag{12.123}$$

The output resistance of an ideal amplifier is zero. The voltages v_A and v_B can be measured with either an ac voltmeter or an oscilloscope.

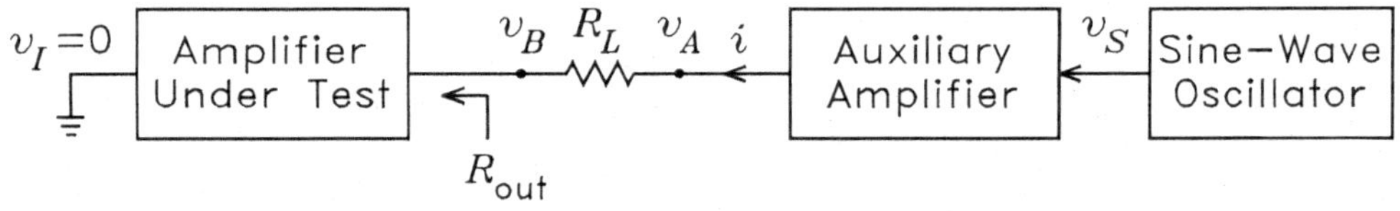

Figure 12.54: Test setup for measuring output resistance and damping factor.

The damping factor DF is given by

$$DF = \frac{R_L}{R_{out}} = \frac{v_A}{v_B} - 1 \tag{12.124}$$

The damping factor of an ideal amplifier is infinite. A typical value is $DF = 100$ for $R_L = 8\,\Omega$. This corresponds to $R_{out} = 0.08\,\Omega$.

In practice, the output impedance is complex and varies with frequency. In this case, Eq. (12.123) gives the magnitude of the output impedance, i.e. $|Z_{out}|$.

Slew Rate

To measure the slew rate, a high-frequency square wave is applied to the amplifier input. A typical frequency might be in the range of 10 kHz to 20 kHz. The output voltage is observed on an oscilloscope. The amplitude of the square wave is increased until the slopes of the rise and fall portions of the wave appear to be independent of the amplitude. Fig. 12.55 illustrates a typical output voltage waveform. The slew rate is measured as the slope of the rise and fall portions of the waveform. It may be necessary to drive the amplifier into clipping to make the measurements and the two slopes may not the same. A typical slew rate might be in the range from 5 to 40 V/μS. Slew rate tests should be performed with care because components in some amplifiers overheat when driven with a high-frequency square wave.

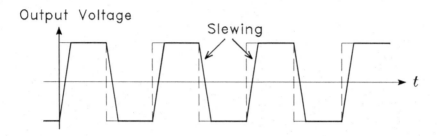

Figure 12.55: Waveform showing slewing with a square wave input signal.

Signal-to-Noise Ratio

The noise output from an amplifier is measured with its input terminals shorted. Let the rms noise output voltage be denoted by $V_{no(rms)}$. When the amplifier is driven with a sine wave, let the maximum rms output voltage before peak clipping be denoted by $V_{so(rms)}$. The signal-to-noise ratio is given by

$$SNR = 20 \log \left[\frac{V_{so(rms)}}{V_{no(rms)}} \right] \tag{12.125}$$

A typical SNR is 90 dB or greater. Often the noise is measured with an A-weighting filter preceding the voltmeter. The A-weighted SNR is always greater than the unweighted SNR. For this reason, the SNR should not be specified without specifying the weighting filter used in its measurement.

Total Harmonic Distortion

A sine wave applied to the input of an ideal amplifier will produce a sine wave at the output. If the amplifier is not ideal, its output will be a distorted sine wave that can be represented by a Fourier series consisting of a fundamental plus harmonics. The total harmonic distortion, or THD, is the ratio of the total rms voltage of the harmonics to the rms voltage of the fundamental. It is usually specified as a percent by multiplying the ratio by 100%.

Fig. 12.56 shows a simplified block diagram of a harmonic distortion analyzer. The amplifier input signal is a sine wave having an rms voltage $V_{i(rms)}$. (The signal generator must be a low distortion sine-wave oscillator. A function generator puts out a synthesized sine wave that may contain more distortion components than the amplifier generates.) The output signal consists of a sine wave of rms voltage $V_{so(rms)} = A_v V_{i(rms)}$, where A_v is the voltage gain, plus distortion having an rms voltage $V_{do(rms)}$. The distortion has frequency components that are harmonically related to the frequency of the sine wave. For example, if the sine wave has a frequency of 1 kHz, the distortion has frequency components at 2 kHz, 3 kHz, 4 kHz, etc. The output voltage is applied to a notch filter which is tuned to the frequency of the fundamental. The notch filter rejects the fundamental and passes only the distortion components. A meter is used to read the

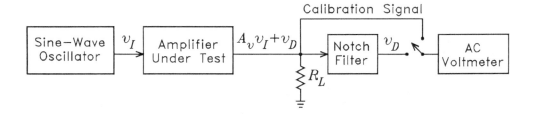

Figure 12.56: Diagram of harmonic distortion analyzer.

rms value of the distortion. The meter can be switched to read the total rms output voltage so that the distortion can be read as a percent of the output voltage.

The THD is given by $\left[V_{do(rms)}/V_{so(rms)}\right] \times 100\%$. Distortion analyzers are commonly calibrated to read the THD as a percent of the total output voltage

$$THD = \frac{V_{do(rms)}}{V_{so(rms)} + V_{do(rms)}} \times 100\% \tag{12.126}$$

For $V_{do(rms)}$ small compared to $V_{so(rms)}$, there is little difference between the two.

The THD generated by an amplifier is a function of both the frequency and the power level. At midband (e.g. 1 kHz) and mid power levels, the THD can be typically as low as 0.005% to 0.01%. As the power level is increased, the THD increases slowly until it is typically 0.15% just below the amplifier clipping level. As the amplifier is driven into clipping, the THD increases very rapidly as the power level is increased.

In general, the THD generated by an amplifier which is not driven into clipping is inversely proportional to the amount of feedback. Above the first pole frequency in the open-loop transfer function, the amount of feedback decreases as frequency is increased. This causes the THD to increase at high frequencies. Thus the rise in THD at high frequencies can be used as an indicator of the amount of feedback in an amplifier. An unusually low high-frequency distortion can be an indicator that the amplifier is not properly frequency compensated.

For example, an amplifier having a dominant pole at $f = 2$ kHz might have a THD of 0.015% at 1 kHz and a THD of 0.15% at 20 kHz. If the compensation capacitor which sets the dominant pole is decreased, the dominant pole frequency is increased. This increases the amount of feedback at high frequencies so that the THD at 20 kHz decreases. Decreasing the emitter resistors R_E in the input diff amp has a similar effect. However, the phase margin of the amplifier is decreased and this makes it more susceptible to oscillations. This illustrates how optimizing a parameter (e.g. THD) can result in a degradation in another parameter (e.g. stability).

In general, a well designed amplifier will have a THD that increases at high frequencies. This indicates that the amplifier has good stability. An increased high-frequency THD has no effect on the sound quality as long as the distortion components lie outside the audio band. For example, at 20 kHz, the lowest harmonic distortion component is at 40 kHz. Most solid-state amplifiers generate mostly odd-order harmonics. In this case, the lowest harmonic distortion component is at 60 kHz.

Intermodulation Distortion

When the sum of two sine waves is applied to the input of an ideal amplifier, its output signal consists of a sum of only two sine waves. If the amplifier is not ideal, its output signal contains sine wave components at frequencies other than those of the input signal. This is called intermodulation distortion. Let the frequency components of the input signal be denoted by f_1 and f_2. In general, the frequency components of the output intermodulation components will be $(nf_1 \pm mf_2)$, where n and m are positive integers.

As an example, let the instantaneous amplifier output voltage be given by

$$v_O = Av_I + Bv_I^2 \tag{12.127}$$

where v_I is the input voltage and $B = 0$ for an ideal amplifier. For $B \neq 0$, the amplifier is said to have a second-order non-linearity. In general, amplifiers exhibit more non-linear terms than just second-order. Let $v_I = V_1 \sin \omega_1 t + V_2 \sin \omega_2 t$, where $\omega_1 > \omega_2$. It follows that v_O is given by

$$
\begin{aligned}
v_O &= A\left(V_1 \sin \omega_1 t + V_2 \sin \omega_2 t\right) + B\left(V_1 \sin \omega_1 t + V_2 \sin \omega_2 t\right)^2 \\
&= A\left(V_1 \sin \omega_1 t + V_2 \sin \omega_2 t\right) + v_D
\end{aligned}
\tag{12.128}
$$

where v_D is the distortion component given by

$$
\begin{aligned}
v_D &= 0.5\left(V_1^2 + V_2^2\right) - 0.5 V_1 \cos 2\omega_1 t + 0.5 V_2 \cos 2\omega_2 t \\
&\quad + V_1 V_2 \cos\left(\omega_1 - \omega_2\right) t - V_1 V_2 \cos\left(\omega_1 + \omega_2\right) t
\end{aligned}
\tag{12.129}
$$

The first term in the expression for v_D represents a dc term. It can be interpreted as a perturbation in the dc bias at the amplifier output. The second and third terms represent harmonic distortion components at the frequencies $2\omega_1$ and $2\omega_2$. The third and fourth terms represent intermodulation distortion terms at the frequencies $\omega_1 - \omega_2$ and $\omega_1 + \omega_2$. Non-linear terms of higher than second order generate more intermodulation distortion terms. For example, a cubic term in Eq. (12.129) would cause intermodulation terms at $2f_1 + f_2$, $2f_1 - f_2$, $f_1 + 2f_2$, and $f_1 - 2f_2$.

A widely used standard for measuring intermodulation distortion is the SMPTE (Society of Motion Picture and Television Engineers) standard. It specifies that the amplifier input signal be the sum of two sine waves, one at 60 Hz and the other at 4 kHz. The amplitude of the 60 Hz term is specified to be greater than the amplitude of the 4 kHz term by a factor of four. Thus the input signal is of the form $v_I(t) = V_1 \left[\sin(2\pi 60 t) + 0.25 \sin(2\pi 4000 t)\right]$, where V_1 is a constant. Fig. 12.57 shows a simplified block diagram of a SMPTE intermodulation distortion analyzer. The amplifier output signal is first high-pass filtered to remove the 60 Hz term. The remaining 4 kHz term is envelope detected. This detects the amplitude modulation on the 4 kHz term caused by the 60 Hz term. The output of the envelope detector is read on a meter that is calibrated to read the percent intermodulation distortion.

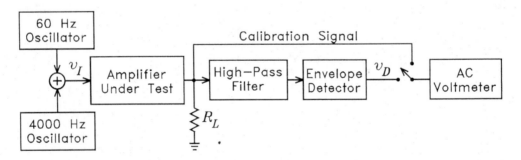

Figure 12.57: Diagram of intermodulation distortion analyzer.

To illustrate how the intermodulation distortion analyzer works, consider an amplifier with crossover distortion. Fig. 12.31(a) illustrates its v_O versus v_S characteristics. The IM test waveform is shown in Fig. 12.58(a). Fig. 12.58(b) shows the waveform of the amplifier output. Note that the amplitude of the high-frequency component is decreased when the signal goes through zero. Fig. 12.58(c) shows the signal after the low-frequency sine wave is filtered out. The amplitude modulation on the high-frequency sine wave is clearly visible. This amplitude modulation is detected by the envelope detector in Fig. 12.57 and is read on an ac voltmeter. The envelope detector consists of a full-wave rectifier and low-pass filter. The output of the rectifier is shown in Fig. 12.58(d). The output of the envelope detector is shown in Fig. 12.58(e) The amplifier output signal is used as a calibration signal for the voltmeter so that the distortion can be read as a percent of the output signal.

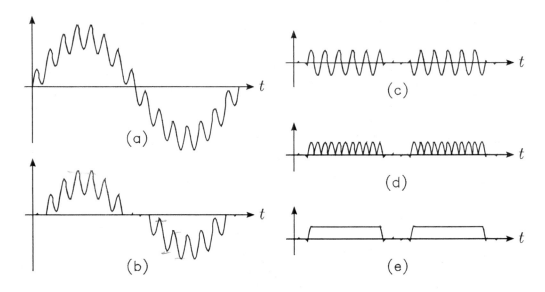

Figure 12.58: (a) IM test waveform. (b) Amplifier output voltage. (c) Output of high-pass filter. (d) Output of full-wave rectifier in envelope detector. (e) Output of envelope detector.

12.17   Problems

1. An amplifier is rated at an average sine-wave power $P_{ave} = 200\,\text{W}$ into an $8\,\Omega$ load. *(a)* Solve for the rms and peak output voltages. [40 V, 56.6 V] Solve for the peak output power. [400 W] *(b)* For a square wave output having the same peak voltage as the sine wave, solve for the average output power and peak output powers. [400 W for both] Solve for the rms and peak output voltages. [56.6 V for both]

2. An amplifier before feedback has the single-pole transfer function given by Eq. (12.16). *(a)* For the feedback factor $H(s) = b$, where b is a constant, solve for the closed-loop gain transfer function. Specify the dc gain constant A_f and the pole frequency ω_{1f}. $[A_f = A/(1 + bA),\ \omega_{1f} = (1 + bA)\,\omega_1]$ *(b)* Show that the product of the dc gain and the $-3\,\text{dB}$ bandwidth is independent of b. *(c)* For $A = 1000$ and $f_1 = 1000\,\text{Hz}$, sketch the Bode plot for $|V_o/V_i|$ for the values $b = 0.01$, 0.1, and 1.0. Label the gain of all zero slope asymptotes and the break frequencies.

3. An amplifier before feedback has the two pole transfer function given by Eq. (12.73). *(a)* For the feedback factor $H(s) = b$, where b is a constant, solve for the closed-loop transfer function. Specify the dc gain constant A_f, the resonance frequency ω_0, and the quality factor Q. $[A_f = A/(1 + bA),\ \omega_0 = \sqrt{(1 + bA)\,\omega_1\omega_2},\ Q = \omega_0/(\omega_1 + \omega_2)]$ *(b)* For A_f and ω_0 fixed, sketch the Bode plot for $|V_o/V_i|$ for $Q = 0.5$, 1.0, and 2.0.

4. For the circuit given in given in Example 21: *(a)* Derive the transfer functions $H_1(s)$ and $H_2(s)$. [Hint: Open C_2 to solve for $H_2(s)$ and short C_1 to solve for $H_1(s)$] *(b)* Show how $H_1(s)$ and $H_2(s)$ can be combined to form the transfer function for $H(s)$. *(c)* Under what conditions would this approximate technique for finding $H(s)$ not work? [when the poles are not well spaced]

5. For the amplifier of Example 21, let f_x be the frequency at which the Bode plots for $|G(j2\pi f)|$ and $|H(j2\pi f)|^{-1}$ intersect. Let A_x be the gain magnitude at f_x. *(a)* Show that A_x satisfies the equations $11/A_x = f_x/15.9k$ and $99.01/A_x = (f_x/10.1k)^2$. *(b)* Eliminate A_x between the equations and show that $f_x = 56.61\,\text{kHz}$. *(c)* Show that the phase margin is $\varphi_m = 66.6\,°$.

6. An amplifier before feedback has a dc gain $A = 20 \times 10^3$ and poles in its transfer function at $f_1 = 2\,\text{kHz}$ and $f_2 = 20\,\text{kHz}$. It is to be used with a resistive feedback network which sets its closed-loop gain at $26\,\text{dB}$. *(a)* Plot the asymptotic and the actual Bode magnitude plots for the closed-loop gain. What would you expect the high frequency square-wave response to look like? [$f_0 = 200\,\text{kHz}$, $Q = 9.1$, it would exhibit severe ringing] *(b)* Specify the new dc gain for $Q \simeq 1$. What is the new phase margin? Repeat the Bode plots of part (a). [$A' = 200$, $f_0 = 20\,\text{kHz}$, $\varphi_m \simeq 45°$] *(c)* Specify the frequency to which f_1 must be reduced for $Q \simeq 1$. What is the new phase margin? Repeat the Bode plots of part (a). [$f_1' = 20\,\text{Hz}$, $f_0 = 20\,\text{kHz}$, $\varphi_m \simeq 45°$] *(d)* Specify the frequency to which f_2 must be increased for $Q \simeq 1$. What is the new phase margin? Repeat the Bode plots of part (a). [$f_2' = 2\,\text{MHz}$, $f_0 = 2\,\text{MHz}$, $\varphi_m \simeq 45°$]

7. The circuit of an amplifier before feedback is given in Fig. 12.59. Q_5, Q_8, and Q_9 are connected as diodes. C_1 is a lead compensation capacitor in a dc level shift circuit, and C_2 sets the dominant pole. *(a)* Signal trace the circuit from each input to the output and identify which input is inverting and which is non-inverting. Treat Q_5 as a resistor and note that there are two forward paths from each input to the output. *(b)* Explain the purpose of R_1 and R_2. [They stabilize the circuit by reducing the gain of the input stage.] *(c)* Explain the purpose of C_1 and C_2. [C_1 is a lead capacitor. C_2 is a dominant pole lag capacitor.] *(d)* Design a feedback network which gives a midband gain of $32\,\text{dB}$ and a lower $-3\,\text{dB}$ cutoff frequency of $0.5\,\text{Hz}$. The input impedance of the feedback network at midband is to be $10\,\text{k}\Omega$. [$R_1 = 250\,\Omega$, $R_2 = 9.75\,\text{k}\Omega$, $C = 1273\,\mu\text{F}$]

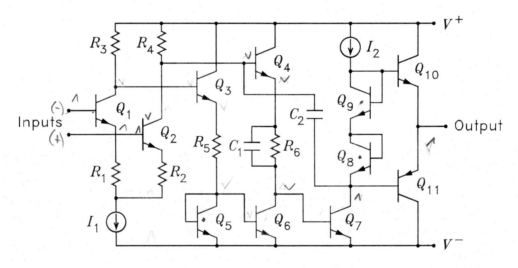

Figure 12.59: Circuit for problem 7.

8. The circuit of a feedback audio amplifier is shown in Fig. 12.60. The amplifier is to be designed for the following quiescent conditions: $V_O = 0$, $I_{C1} = I_{C2} = 2\,\text{mA}$, $I_{C4} = I_{C5} = I_{C8} = I_{C9} = 5\,\text{mA}$, $I_{C10} = I_{C11} = 12\,\text{mA}$, and $I_{C12} = I_{C13} = 50\,\text{mA}$. The base current in each transistor can be neglected. Also, it can be assumed that under quiescent conditions V_{BE} (or V_{EB}) is $0.6\,\text{V}$ for each transistor and $V_D = 0.6\,\text{V}$ for each diode. The following are given: $R_2 = 3\,\text{k}\Omega$, $R_3 = R_4 = 470\,\Omega$, $R_7 = 20\,\text{k}\Omega$, $R_9 = R_{10} = R_{11} = 180\,\Omega$, $R_{14} = 1\,\text{k}\Omega$, $R_{16} = 22\,\text{k}\Omega$, $R_{12} = R_{13}$, $R_{21} = R_{22} = 10\,\Omega$, $R_{23} = R_{24} = 0.33\,\Omega$, $R_{25} = R_{26} = 10\,\Omega$, $R_{27} = R_{28} = 100\,\Omega$, $C_4 = C_5 = 0.1\,\mu\text{F}$, $C_6 = C_7 = 100\,\mu\text{F}$, $C_8 = C_9 = 10\,\mu\text{F}$, $L_1 = 1\,\mu\text{H}$, and $V_Z = 4.3\,\text{V}$ for D_1. *(a)* Trace the circuit and verify that the feedback is negative. Note that there are two outputs from the diff amp. *(b)* Calculate R_8 for a gain of $26\,\text{dB}$ and C_2 for a lower half-power cutoff frequency of $0.5\,\text{Hz}$. [$R_8 = 1.05\,\text{k}\Omega$, $C_2 = 302\,\mu\text{F}$] *(c)* Calculate R_1 for minimum dc offset at the output. [$17\,\text{k}\Omega$] *(d)* Calculate C_1 for an upper $-3\,\text{dB}$ frequency of

180 kHz. [295 pF] *(e)* Calculate R_{17} for the specified currents in Q_1 and Q_2. [925 Ω] *(f)* Calculate R_{18} for the specified current in Q_5. [740 Ω] *(g)* Calculate the required value of R_5 and R_6. [1.65 kΩ for each] *(h)* Calculate R_{12}, R_{13}, and R_{15} such that the quiescent voltage across Q_7 can be set to any value between 2.8 V and 3.6 V by adjusting R_{14}. [500 Ω for each] *(i)* Calculate R_{19} for the specified currents in Q_8 and Q_9. [480 Ω] *(j)* Calculate R_{20} for the specified currents in Q_{10} and Q_{11}. [100 Ω] *(k)* If the power supply voltage drops by 8% under full load and the peak output voltage can swing to within 6 V of the rails, what is the maximum average sine-wave output power into an 8 Ω load? [66.6 W]

9. It is desired to design a feedback amplifier which has the gain bandwidth product $f_x = 8$ MHz and the large signal slewing rate $|dv_O/dt|_{max} = 50$ V/μS. The input stage is a differential amplifier with a resistively coupled single ended output. *(a)* If $R_E = 220$ Ω in the diff amp, specify the required values for the tail current I_Q and the compensation capacitor C_c. [4.29 mA, 42.9 pF] *(b)* If the amplifier is rated at $P_{ave} = 100$ W into 8 Ω for a sine wave input, what is the maximum frequency at which it can put out full rated power without slewing? [199 kHz]

10. Suppose $R_E = 0$ Ω in the amplifier of problem 9. *(a)* If I_Q is not changed, what is the new value of C_c for a gain-bandwidth product of 8 MHz? [821 pF] *(b)* What is the new slew rate? [2.61 V/μS] *(c)* What is the maximum frequency at which the amplifier could put out full rated power without slewing? [10.4 kHz]

11. Suppose $R_E = 0$ Ω in the amplifier of problem 9. *(a)* If C_c is not changed, what is the new value of I_Q for a gain-bandwidth product of 8 MHz? [224 μA] *(b)* What is the new slew rate? [2.61 V/μS] *(c)* What is the maximum frequency at which the amplifier could put out full rated power without slewing? [10.4 kHz]

12. Explain the purpose of capacitors C_1 through C_{10} in the amplifier of problem 8. [C_1 is part of an input low-pass filter to suppress rf pickup. C_2 is part of the feedback network which gives 100% dc feedback. C_3 sets the dominant pole. C_4 bypasses Q_7 at high frequencies. C_5 is part of a RC network that helps prevent parasitic oscillations by maintaining resistive loading at high frequencies. C_6 and C_7 are parts of low-pass filters on the rails which decouple the rail voltages to the input stages. C_8 and C_9 provide a low impedance high frequency ground reference on the rails at the point where the wires connect to the circuit board. C_3 sets the bandwidth from collector of Q_1 to the collector of Q_5. C_{10} sets the bandwidth from collector of Q_2 to collector of Q_5. These two latter bandwidths should be the same.]

13. Fig. 12.61(a) shows a feedback network which gives 100% feedback at dc. Assume that the input impedance to the inverting input of the amplifier is very large. *(a)* Explain how the network gives 100% feedback at dc. *(b)* Solve for the transfer function $H(s) = V_-/V_o$. [$H(s) = (1 + \tau_A s)/(1 + \tau_B s)$, $\tau_A = [R_3(R_1 + R_2)/(R_2 + R_3)]C$, $\tau_B = (R_1 + R_2\|R_3)C$] *(c)* It is desired to design the network so that its ac output impedance is less than 100 Ω. To achieve this, choose $R_3 = 100$ Ω and $R_1 = 10R_2$. Specify the values of R_1, R_2, and C for a midband amplifier gain of 20 (26 dB) and a lower -3 dB cutoff frequency of 0.3 Hz. [$R_2 = 2.09$ kΩ, $R_1 = 20.9$ kΩ, $C = 505.4$ μF] *(d)* Sketch the Bode magnitude plot for the mid-band and low-frequency gain of the amplifier. [midband gain of 20, zero at 0.015 Hz, pole at 0.3 Hz.]

14. Fig. 12.61(b) shows a frequency compensation technique that is called input compensation. *(a)* If $V_o = G(s)(V_+ - V_-)$, solve for V_o/V_i and show that the addition of Z effectively multiplies the loop-gain transfer function by $F(s) = Z/(Z + R_1 + R_2\|R_3)$. *(b)* If $Z = R$ and $G(s)$ has more than one pole, explain how adding R can be used to prevent oscillations. Illustrate this with a Bode plot of the loop gain before and after compensation. [R effectively decreases A so that the slope of the Bode plot at unity loop gain is -1 dec/dec] *(c)* If $Z = R + 1/Cs$, solve for $F(s)$ and show that it has a single pole and a single zero. Illustrate with a Bode plot of the loop gain before and after compensation how the addition of R and C can stabilize an amplifier without decreasing the dc loop gain. [the network adds a pole and a zero to the loop-gain transfer function]

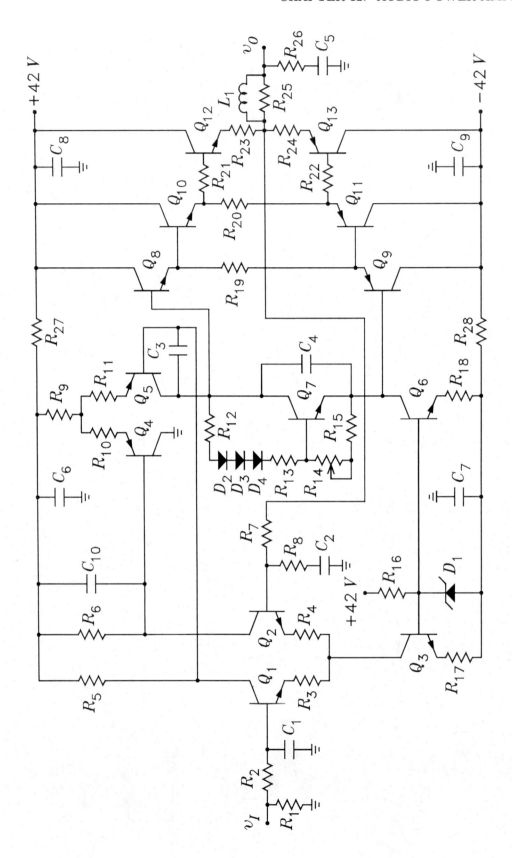

Figure 12.60: Circuit for problem 8.

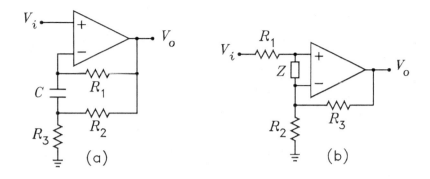

Figure 12.61: (a) Circuit for problem 13. (b) Circuit for problem 14.

15. It is desired to design an amplifier which has a gain-bandwidth product of 15 MHz and a large signal slew rate of 60 V/ μS. The input stage is a single differential amplifier with a resistively coupled single-ended output. For $R_E = 510\,\Omega$, specify the required value of the tail current I_Q and the total value of the compensation capacitor C_c. [$I_Q = 1.15\,\text{mA}$ and $C_c = 9.5\,\text{pF}$]

16. Sketch the waveforms of Fig. 12.58 for an amplifier that exhibits peak clipping.

Appendix A

References

J. R. Ashley and M. D. Swan, "Experimental Determination of Low-Frequency Loudspeaker Parameters," *J. Audio Eng. Soc.*, Oct. 1969.

J. R. Ashley and A. L. Kaminsky, "Active and Passive Filters as Loudspeaker Crossover Networks," *J. Audio Eng. Soc.*, vol. 19, p. 494, June 1971.

E. Bækgaard, "A Novel Approach to Linear Phase Loudspeakers using Passive Crossover Networks," *J. Audio Eng. Soc.*, vol. 25, p. 284-294, May 1977.

B. B. Bauer, "Notes on Radiation Impedance," *J. Acoust. Soc. Am.*, vol. 15, pp. 223–224, 1944.

B. B. Bauer, "On the Equivalent Circuit of a Plane Wave Confronting an Acoustical Device," *J. Acoust. Soc. Am.*, vol. 42, pp. 1095–1097, Nov. 1967.

J. E. Benson, "An Introduction to the Design of Filtered Loudspeaker Systems," *J. Audio Eng. Soc.*, Sept. 1975.

L. L. Beranek, *Acoustic Measurements*, New York: John Wiley, 1949.

L. L. Beranek, *Acoustics*, New York: McGraw-Hill, 1954.

L. J. S. Bradbury, "The Use of Fibrous Materials in Loudspeaker Enclosures," *J. Audio Eng. Soc.*, Apr. 1976.

C. A. Henricksen, "Ultimate Performance of Wide-Range High-Frequency Compression Drivers," *J. Audio Eng. Soc.*, vol. 24, pp. 639-642, Oct. 1976.

W. J. J. Hoge, "A New Set of Vented Loudspeaker Alignments," *J. Audio Eng. Soc.*, vol. 25, pp. 391-393, June 1977.

F. V. Hunt, *Electroacoustics*, Am. Inst. of Physics for the Acoust. Soc. Am., 1982.

J. M. Kates, "Radiation from a Dome," *J. Audio Eng. Soc.*, vol. 24, pp. 735-737, Nov. 1976.

J. M. Kates, "Analysis of Decoupled Cone Loudspeakers," *J. Audio Eng. Soc.*, vol. 25, pp. 15-23, Jan./Feb. 1977.

D. B. Keele, Jr., "Sensitivity of Thiele's Vented Loudspeaker Enclosure Alignments to Parameter Variations," *J. Audio Eng. Soc.*, vol. 21, pp. 246-255, May 1973.

D. B. Keele, Jr., "A Tabular Tuning Method for Vented Enclosures," *J. Audio Eng. Soc.*, vol. 22, pp. 97-99, March 1974.

D. B. Keele, Jr., "A New Set of Sixth-Order Vented-Box Loudspeaker System Alignments," *J. Audio Eng. Soc.*, vol. 23, pp. 354-360, June 1975.

L. E. Kinsler and A. R. Frey, *Fundamentals of Acoustics*, New York: John Wiley, 1962.

P. W. Klipsch, "A Low-Frequency Horn of Small Dimensions," *J. Acoust. Soc. Amer.*, vol. 13, pp. 137-144, 1941, and.*J. Audio Eng. Soc.*, vol. 27, pp. 141-148, Mar. 1979.

W. M. Leach, Jr., "On the Specification of Moving-Coil Drivers for Low-Frequency Horn-Loaded Loudspeakers," *J. Audio Eng. Soc.*, vol. 27, pp. 950-959, Dec. 1979.

W. M. Leach, Jr., "Loudspeaker Driver Phase Response: The Neglected Factor in Crossover Network Design," *J. Audio Eng. Soc.*, vol. 28, pp. 410-421, June 1980.

W. M. Leach, Jr., "Electroacoustic-Analogous Circuit Models for Filled Enclosures," *J. Audio Eng. Soc.*, vol. 37, pp. 586-592, July/August 1989.

W. M. Leach, Jr., "A Generalized Active Equalizer for Closed-Box Loudspeaker Systems," *J. Audio Eng. Soc.*, vol. 38, March 1990.

W. M. Leach, Jr., "On the Electroacoustic-Analogous Circuit for a Plane Wave Incident on the Diaphragm of a Free-Field Pressure Microphone," *J. Audio Eng. Soc.*, vol. 38, pp. 566–568, July/Aug. 1990.

W. M. Leach, Jr., "Computer-Aided Electroacoustic Design with SPICE," *J. Audio Eng. Soc.*, vol. 39, pp. 551–563, July/Aug. 1991.

W. M. Leach, Jr. "A two-port analogous circuit and SPICE model for Salmon's family of acoustic horns," *J. Acoust. Soc. Am.*, vol. 99, pp1459-1464, March 1996.

W. M. Leach, Jr., "Loudspeaker Voice-Coil Inductance Losses: Circuit Models, Parameter Estimation, and Effect on Frequency Response," *J. Audio Eng. Soc.*, vol. 50, no. 6, pp. 442-450, June 2002.

W. M. Leach, Jr., "Feedforward Compensation of the Amplifier Output Stage for Improved Stability with Capacitive Loads," *IEEE Trans. Consumer Electronics*, vol. 34, no. 2, pp. 334-338, May 1988.

H. Levine and J. Schwinger, "On the Radiation of Sound from an Unflanged Circular Pipe," *Phys. Rev.*, vol. 73, pp. 383-406, Feb. 1948.

S. H. Linkwitz, "Active Crossover Networks for Noncoincident Drivers," *J. Audio Eng. Soc.*, vol. 24, pp. 2-8, Jan./Feb. 1976.

S. H. Linkwitz, "Passive Crossover Networks for Noncoincident Drivers," *J. Audio Eng. Soc.*, Mar. 1977.

B. N. Locanthi, "Application of Electric Circuit Analogies to Loudspeaker Design Problems," *IRE Trans. Audio*, vol. PGA-6, March 1952, and *J. Audio Eng. Soc.*, vol. 9, pp. 778–785, Nov. 1971.

Microphone Handbook, Nærum, Denmark: Brüel & Kjær, 1996.

P. M. Morse, *Vibration and Sound*, New York: McGraw-Hill, 1948.

H. F. Olson, *Dynamical Analogies*, New York: D. Van Nostrand, 1943.

H. F. Olson, *Elements of Acoustical Engineering*, New York: D. Van Nostrand, 1947.

H. F. Olson, *Acoustical Engineering*, New York: D. Van Nostrand, 1957

D. J. Plach, "Design Factors in Horn-Type Speakers," *J. Audio Eng. Soc.*, vol. 1, Oct. 1953.

D. J. Plach and P. B. Williams, "Reactance Annulling for Horn-Type Loudspeakers," *Radio-Electron. Eng.*, pp. 15-18, Feb. 1955.

R. H. Small, "Constant Voltage Crossover Network Design," vol. 19, pp. 12-19, *J. Audio Eng. Soc.*, Jan. 1971.

R. H. Small, "Simplified Loudspeaker Measurements at Low Frequencies," *J. Audio Eng. Soc.*, vol. 20, pp. 28-33, Dec. 1972.

R. H. Small, "Direct-Radiator Loudspeaker System Analysis," *J. Audio Eng. Soc.*, vol. 20, pp. 383-395, June 1972.

R. H. Small, "Closed-Box Loudspeaker Systems, Parts I and II," *J. Audio Eng. Soc.*, vol. 20, pp. 798-808, Dec. 1972; vol. 21, pp. 11-18, Jan./Feb. 1973.

R. H. Small, "Vented-Box Loudspeaker Systems, Parts I-IV," J. Audio Eng. Soc., vol. 21, pp. 363-372, June 1973, pp. 438-444, July/Aug. 1973; pp. 549-554, Sept. 1973; pp. 635-639, Oct. 1973.

R. H. Small, "Passive Radiator Loudspeaker Systems, Parts I and II," J. Audio Eng. Soc., vol. 22, pp. 592-601, Oct. 1974, pp. 683-689, Nov. 1974.

A. N. Thiele, "Loudspeakers in Vented-Boxes, Parts I and II," *J. Audio Eng. Soc.*, vol. 19, pp. 382-392, May 1971; pp. 471-483, June 1971.

A. N. Thiele, "Load Circuit Stabilizing Networks for Audio Amplifiers," *J. Audio Eng. Soc.*, vol. 24, pp. 20-23, Jan./Feb. 1976.

J. E. Weaver & W. M. Leach, Jr., "Optical Measurement of Loudspeaker Driver Large-Signal Displacement," *J. Audio Eng. Soc.*, vol. 26, pp. 145-148, Mar. 1978.

J. R. Wright, "An Empirical Model for Loudspeaker Motor Impedance," *J. Audio Eng. Soc.*, vol. 38, pp. 749-754, Oct. 1990.

O. J. Zobel, "Theory and Design of Uniform and Composite Electric Wave Filters," *Bell Tel. Sys. Tech. J.*, vol. 2, no. 1, pp. 1-46, Jan. 1923.

Appendix B

Electroacoustic Glossary of Symbols

a	Radius (m), Equivalent piston radius of diaphragm (m)
B	Magnetic flux density (T), Parameter in QB3 vented-box alignments, Parameter in cardiod microphone pattern, Mass loading factor, Parameter in low-pass to band-pass frequency transformation
$B2$	$2nd$-order Butterworth infinite-baffle and closed-box alignment
$B4$	$4th$-order Butterworth vented-box alignment
c	Velocity of sound (345 m/s, 1131 feet/s)
C_A	Acoustic compliance (m^5/N)
C_{AB}	Acoustic compliance of volume V_{AB} (m^5/N)
C_{AP}	Acoustic compliance of passive radiator suspension (m^5/N)
C_{AS}	Acoustic compliance of diaphragm suspension (m^5/N)
C_{AT}	Total acoustic compliance of diaphragm suspension and enclosure (m^5/N)
C_{A1}	Acoustic compliance in circuit for piston air load impedance (m^5/N)
C_E	Electrical capacitance (F)
C_M	Mechanical compliance (m/N)
C_{MS}	Mechanical compliance of diaphragm suspension (m/N)
$C2$	$2nd$-order Chebyshev alignment
$C4$	$4th$-order Chebyshev vented-box alignment
D_{KE}	Kinetic energy density (J/m^3)
D_{PE}	Potential energy density (J/m^3)
e, E	Electrical voltage (V)
f	Force (N), Frequency (Hz)
f_B, ω_B	Helmholtz resonance frequency of vented box (Hz, rad/s)
f_C, ω_C	Closed-box system resonance frequency (Hz, rad/s)
f_ℓ, ω_ℓ	Lower -3 dB cutoff frequency (Hz, rad/s)
f_S, ω_S	Resonance frequency of driver in infinite baffle (Hz, rad/s)
f_u, ω_u	Upper -3 dB cutoff frequency (Hz, rad/s)
f_{u1}, ω_{u1}	Upper -3 dB cutoff frequency in pressure response of driver (Hz, rad/s)
f_{u2}, ω_{u2}	Upper -3 dB cutoff frequency in power response of driver (Hz, rad/s)
$G(s)$	Infinite-baffle low-frequency pressure transfer function
$G_{BP4}(s)$	Forth-order bandpass system low-frequency pressure transfer function
$G_C(s)$	Closed-box low-frequency pressure transfer function
$G_V(s)$	Vented-box low-frequency pressure transfer function
h	Vented-box system Helmholtz tuning ratio (f_B/f_S)
I	Acoustic intensity (W/m^2)
k	Wavenumber (m^{-1}), Parameter in C4 vented-box alignments, Mutual coupling coefficient

k_{pad}	L-pad voltage division ratio
ℓ	Length (m), Effective length of voice-coil wire that cuts air-gap flux (m)
ℓ_f	Flanged end correction (m)
ℓ_{uf}	Unflanged end correction (m)
L_P, L_V	Port or vent length (m)
L_e	Constant in equation for impedance of lossy voice-coil inductance
L_E	Electrical inductance (H)
m, M	Constants in equation for cross-sectional area of acoustic horn
M_A	Acoustic mass (kg/m^4)
M_{A1}	Acoustic mass in circuit for piston air load impedance (kg/m^4)
M_{AB}	Acoustic mass of air in box (kg/m^4)
M_{AC}	Acoustic mass of diaphragm and air load for driver on a box (kg/m^4)
M_{AD}	Acoustic mass of diaphragm (kg/m^4)
M_{AS}	Acoustic mass of diaphragm and air load for driver on infinite baffle (kg/m^4)
M_M	Mechanical mass (kg)
M_{MC}	Mechanical mass of diaphragm and air load for driver on a box (kg)
M_{MD}	Mechanical mass of diaphragm (kg)
M_{MS}	Mechanical mass of diaphragm and air load for driver on infinite baffle (kg)
n	Constant in equation impedance of lossy voice-coil inductance
p	Acoustic pressure (Pa)
p_D	Acoustic pressure difference (Pa)
p_{ref}	Reference pressure for SPL (2×10^{-5} Pa)
p_{sens}^{1V}	On-axis pressure sensitivity for $e_g = 1$ V and $r = 1$ m (Pa)
P	Total pressure (Pa), Power (W), Phons
P_A	Acoustic power (W)
P_{AR}	Acoustic power radiated (W)
P_E	Electrical power (W)
P_0	Static air pressure (1.013×10^5 Pa)
q	f_ℓ / f_S for vented-box system
Q	Quality factor
Q_{EC}	Closed-box system electrical quality factor
Q_{ES}	Infinite-baffle system electrical quality factor
Q_L	Vented-box enclosure quality factor
Q_{MC}	Closed-box system mecahnical quality factor
Q_{MS}	Infinite-baffle system mechanical quality factor
Q_{TC}	Closed-box system total quality factor
Q_{TS}	Infinite-baffle system total quality factor
$QB3$	Quasi-Butterworth 3*rd*-order vented-box alignment
R_A	Acoustic resistance (N·s/m^5)
R_{AB}	Acoustic resistance that models closed-box losses (N·s/m^5)
R_{AC}	$R_{AS} + R_{AB}$ (N·s/m^5) for closed-box system
R_{AE}	Acoustic resistance that models electrical losses (N·s/m^5)
R_{AL}	Acoustic resistance that models air leak (N·s/m^5)
R_{AS}	Acoustic resistance that models suspension losses (N·s/m^5)
R_{AT}	$R_{AE} + R_{AS}$ (N·s/m^5) for infinite-baffle system
R_{ATC}	$R_{AE} + R_{AC}$ (N·s/m^5) for closed-box system
R_{A1}, R_{A2}	Acoustic resistors in circuit for piston air load impedance (N·s/m^5)
R_E	Electrical resistance (Ω)
R_{ES}	Increase in voice-coil impedance at $\omega = \omega_S$ for infinite-baffle system (Ω)
R_M	Mechanical resistance (N·s/m)
R_{MS}	Mechanical resistance of diaphragm suspension (N·s/m)
S	Area (m^2), Sones

S_D	Area of diaphragm (m^2)
S_B	Inside area of box wall (m^2)
S_M	Mouth area of acoustic horn
S_T	Throat area of acoustic horn
SPL	Sound pressure level (dB)
SPL_{sens}^{1V}	On-axis SPL sensitivity for $e_g = 1$ V and $r = 1$ m (dB)
SPL_{sens}^{1W}	On-axis SPL sensitivity for $P_E = 1$ W and $r = 1$ m (dB)
S_D	Piston area of diaphragm (m^2)
S_P, S_V	Port or vent area (m^2)
$T_{u1}(s)$	Transfer function which models high frequency pressure response of driver
$T_{u2}(s)$	Transfer function which models high frequency power response of driver
u	Mechanical velocity, Particle velocity (m/s)
u_D	Mechanical velocity of diaphragm (m/s)
U	Volume velocity (m^3/s)
U_D	Volume velocity emitted by diaphragm (m^3/s)
U_L	Volume velocity emitted by air leak (m^3/s)
U_P, U_V	Volume velocity emitted by port or vent (m^3/s)
V	Volume (m^3)
V_{AS}	Volume compliance of driver suspension (m^3)
V_{AB}	Effective volume of air in box including filling effect (m^3)
V_{AT}	Net volume compliance of driver and enclosure (m^3)
V_B	Volume of air in unfilled enclosure (m^3)
W_{KE}	Kinetic energy (J)
W_{PE}	Potential energy (J)
x	Mechanical displacement (m), Distance (m)
x_D	Mechanical displacement of diaphragm (m)
$x_{\max}$	Maximum diaphragm displacement (m)
Y_E	Electrical admittance (Ω^{-1})
Y_M	Mechanical admittance (mech. Ω^{-1})
Y_A	Acoustic admittance (acoust. Ω^{-1})
Z_e	Impedance of lossy voice-coil inductance (Ω)
Z_E	Electrical impedance (Ω)
Z_M	Mechanical impedance (mech. Ω)
Z_s	Specific acoustic impedance (mks rayls)
Z_{VC}	Voice-coil impedance (Ω)
α	Compliance ratio C_{AS}/C_{AB} or V_{AS}/V_{AB}
δ	Passive radiator compliance ratio C_{AP}/C_{AB}
ϵ	dB ripple factor for Chebyshev alignments
η	Efficiency
η_0	Midband reference efficiency of driver
γ	Ratio of specific heat at constant pressure to specific heat at constant volume, Propagation constant for wave in acoustic horn
λ	Wavelength (m)
ρ_0	Density of air (1.18 kg/m^3)
τ	Time constant (s^{-1}), Crystal coupling coefficient (N/C)
ξ	Particle displacement (m)

Index